PROCUREMENT BY INTERNATIONAL ORGANIZATIONS

How do international organizations procure goods, services and works to carry out their institutional mission? How does this procurement activity affect individuals? Does the procurement relationship between international organizations and private subjects lead to an even distribution of rights and duties? Are international organizations accountable to private subjects and states when allocating their resources through procurement? This book explores the complex phenomenon of procurement by international organizations from the point of view of the relationship between international organizations and private subjects. It provides, for the first time, a systematization and conceptualization of the emerging rules and practices of procurement by international organizations. It also identifies the international political dynamics and interplay of interests underlying these rules and practices. In doing so, it shows how these dynamics shape the exercise of international public authority over private subjects, and the scope of private subjects' rights vis-à-vis international organizations.

Elisabetta Morlino is an assistant professor of administrative law at the University of Suor Orsola Benincasa of Naples. She holds a PhD in global administrative law from the Istituto Italiano di Scienze Umane (now part of the Scuola Normale Superiore di Pisa) and an LLM in International Legal Studies from the New York University (NYU) School of Law. She has been Hugo Grotius Scholar at NYU and visiting scholar at the Max Planck Institute for Comparative Public Law and International Law in Heidelberg. She has served as legal consultant for IFAD's Procurement Division in Rome and as an intern at the UN Office of Legal Affairs in New York. She is a member of ICON-S, the PCLG-Network, UACES and IRPA. She has previously published in the fields of global and European administrative law, international organizations and environmental protection.

PROCUREMENT BY INTERNATIONAL ORGANIZATIONS

A Global Administrative Law Perspective

ELISABETTA MORLINO

CAMBRIDGE
UNIVERSITY PRESS

CAMBRIDGE
UNIVERSITY PRESS

University Printing House, Cambridge CB2 8BS, United Kingdom

One Liberty Plaza, 20th Floor, New York, NY 10006, USA

477 Williamstown Road, Port Melbourne, VIC 3207, Australia

314–321, 3rd Floor, Plot 3, Splendor Forum, Jasola District Centre,
New Delhi – 110025, India

79 Anson Road, #06–04/06, Singapore 079906

Cambridge University Press is part of the University of Cambridge.

It furthers the University's mission by disseminating knowledge in the pursuit of
education, learning and research at the highest international levels of excellence.

www.cambridge.org
Information on this title: www.cambridge.org/9781108415750
DOI: 10.1017/9781108235112

© Elisabetta Morlino 2019

First published 2019

Printed and bound in Great Britain by Clays Ltd, Elcograf S.p.A.

A catalogue record for this publication is available from the British Library.

Library of Congress Cataloging-in-Publication Data
Names: Morlino, Elisabetta, author.
Title: Procurement by international organizations: a global administrative law
perspective / Elisabetta Morlino, University of Naples.
Description: New York: Cambridge University Press, 2018. | Includes bibliographical
references and index.
Identifiers: LCCN 2018015877 | ISBN 9781108415750 (alk. paper)
Subjects: LCSH: International organizations. | International agencies – Law and legislation. |
International agencies – Rules and practice. | Administrative law. | Public contracts.
Classification: LCC KZ4850 .M67 2018 | DDC 352.5/3211–dc23
LC record available at https://lccn.loc.gov/2018015877

ISBN 978-1-108-41575-0 Hardback

CONTENTS

FIGURES

viii

TABLES

ix

ACKNOWLEDGEMENTS

Writing a book is like a solo crossing of the Atlantic: long and, for the most part, solitary. Yet, you safely get to the destination with the help of those who provide you with navigation coordinates, who advise you of storms and droughts, who light beacons along your way and who give you fuel to speed you on. Many people have made such contributions to this adventure of mine.

Sabino Cassese, who was the first to give me travel maps, has my warmest gratitude for having always been an inexhaustible source of support and ideas.

Heartfelt thanks to Luisa Torchia, for showing me that Captain Courageous is really a woman and for spurring me on in my voyage, constantly expressing her trust, tenacious even when the destination seemed distant.

Very special thanks to Aldo Sandulli. I would never have had the serenity I needed to complete this work if he had not constantly counselled me along the way, as well as created the ideal conditions for study and research.

This book owes a lot to Stephan Schill and Joseph H.H. Weiler. I am deeply grateful to them for their support, advice and suggestions, which helped me to improve the manuscript.

For their detailed comments and observations on a preliminary version of this work, my thanks also go to Stefano Battini, Roberto Caranta, Lorenzo Casini, Giacinto Della Cananea, Claudio Franchini, Bernardo Giorgio Mattarella, Giulio Napolitano, Bernardo Sordi and Giulio Vesperini.

My research benefited from the generous sponsorship and hospitality of various universities and research centres in Europe and the United States. I am grateful to the Università Suor Orsola Benincasa in Naples, and in particular to Rector Lucio D'Alessandro, for believing in and sponsoring my research project; the New York University School of Law, and especially Richard B. Stewart and Catherine Kessedjian for agreeing to supervise my first attempts to frame the issue; the Max Planck Institute of International and Comparative Law of Heidelberg with special thanks to Anne Peters and Armin Von Bogdandy.

An analysis and understanding of the empirical aspects that were the basis for the book was made possible thanks to my work with organizations, first as an intern at the United Nations Office of Legal Affairs and then as a consultant for IFAD, and thanks to the many accounts from permanent employees of international organizations, collected over a period of about seven years. In particular, I wish to thank Sandro Luzzietti and Matthias Meyerhans for giving me the opportunity to experience the daily practice of an organization. Special thanks also to Enrico Labriola, who has been not only a steady contact with whom I could share opinions and reflections on the activity of organizations; to Nikiforos P. Diamandouros, who allowed me to deepen the empirical aspects of the research within European institutions; and to Paul Buades for his helpfulness and for the frankness with which we were able to discuss sensitive issues. And thanks to all officials of the organizations I included in the research, for granting me interviews and giving me their time and best explanations: in particular, Maria Vicien-Milburn, Jay Pozenel, Enzo de Laurentiis, Hunt Lacascia, Luigi Ferrara, George Jadoun, Maria Teresa Pisani, Sergio Benetti, Michael Dethlefsen, Gian Domenico Spota, Gian Luigi Albano, João Sant'Anna, Gian Luigi Faura, Durante Rapacciuolo, Pierpaolo Settembri and Panagiotis Stamatopoulos. Many others have requested and been promised anonymity and therefore cannot be named here, but I am indebted to them for their patience and interest.

Cambridge University Press was superb. Thanks to Kim Hughes, Finola O' Sullivan, Gemma Smith , Abigail Neale and Samantha Town for their interest in the work and their patience in bringing it to life.

Warm thanks to Sylvia Gilbertson for her meticulous work and her care and speed in assisting me in revising the text.

Finally, this journey was made possible above all thanks to the daily, loving support of various people who were able to calm the storms and securely set the course during the years this work took shape.

I am deeply grateful to Giulia Bertezzolo for her sincere and affectionate participation, and for teaching me that optimism is the first step towards the solution of any problem.

This book, as with every other enterprise I came across in my life, was made possible by the precious support of my sister Irene. To her goes my daily unspoken thanks for being an oasis of love, understanding and sharing.

To my parents, I dedicate this book with infinite love and inextinguishable gratitude for making this – and everything else – possible, since the beginning.

LIST OF CASES

International Court of Justice

'Certain Expenses of the United Nations. Advisory Opinion 20 July 1962', 20 July 1962 [1962] *ICJ Recueil des arrêts, avis consultatifs et ordonnances* 151
'Reparation for Injuries Suffered in the Service of the United Nations. Advisory Opinion' [1949] *ICJ Recueil des arrêts, avis consultatifs et ordonnances* 178

Court of Justice of the European Union

Case C-113/07 P, *SELEX Sistemi Integrati SpA v. Commission and European Organisation for the Safety of Air Navigation (Eurocontrol)*, 26 March 2009, not published in the ECR
Case C-182/91, *Forafrique Burkinabe SA v. Commission of European Communities* [1993] ECR I-2184
Case C-267/82, *Développement SA e Clemessy v. Commission* [1986] ECR I-1907
Case C-310/91, *Hugo Schmid v. Belgian State, represented by the Minister van Sociale Voorzorg* [1993] ECR I-3011
Case C-364/92, *SAT Fluggesellschaft mbH v. European Organisation for the Safety of Air Navigation (Eurocontrol)* [1994] ECR I-43
Case C-370/89, *SGEEM e Etroy v. BEI* [1992] ERC I-6211
Case C-411/98, *Angelo Ferlini v. Centre Hospitalier de Luxembourg* [2000] ECR I-8081
Case T-121/08, *PC-Ware Information Technologies v. Commission* [2010] ECR II-1541
Case T-155/04, *SELEX Sistemi Integrati SpA v. Commission*, 12 December 2006, not published in the ECR
Case T-160/03, *AFCon Management Consultants v. Commission of the European Communities* [2005] ECR II-981
Case T-199/14, *Vanbreda Risk & Benefits v. Commission*, 29 October 2015, not published in the ECR
Case T-211/07, *AWWW v. Eurofound*, 1 July 2008, not published in the ECR
Case T-216/09, *Astrim e Elyo Italia v. Commission*, 25 October 2012, not published in the ECR
Case T-299/11, *European Dynamics v. OHIM*, 7 October 2015, not published in the ECR

European Court of Human Rights

European Ombudsman

General Claims Commission (Mexico–United States)

National Courts

LIST OF INSTRUMENTS

Agreements and Constitutions

Agreement between the United Nations and the United States Regarding the Headquarters of the United Nations, 26 June 1947

Agreement Establishing the African Development Bank, 4 August 1963

Agreement Establishing the Asian Development Bank, 22 August 1966

Agreement Establishing the Inter-American Development Bank, 8 April 1959

Agreement Establishing the International Fund for Agricultural Development, 13 June 1976

Agreement on Government Procurement, 15 April 1994 [revised 6 April 2014]

Articles of Agreement of the International Monetary Fund, 22 July 1944

Busan Partnership for Effective Development Co-operation. Fourth High-Level Forum on Aid Effectiveness, Busan (Korea), 29 November–1 December 2011

Charter of Fundamental Rights of the European Union, 7 December 2000

Charter of the United Nations, 26 June 1945

Constitution of the Food and Agriculture Organization, 16 October 1945

Constitution of the United Nations Educational, Scientific and Cultural Organization, 16 November 1945

Constitution of the World Health Organization, 22 July 1946

Financial and Administrative Framework Agreement between the European Community, Represented by the Commission of the European Communities and the United Nations, 29 April 2003

General Agreement on Tariffs and Trade, 30 October 1947

International Bank for Reconstruction and Development (IBRD) Articles of Agreement, 27 December 1945

Treaties and Conventions

Convention Establishing the World Intellectual Property Organization, 14 July 1967

Convention for the Establishment of a European Space Agency, 30 May 1975

Convention on the Privileges and Immunities of the Specialized Agencies, 21 November 1947

Convention on the Privileges and Immunities of the United Nations, 13 February 1946

European Convention for the Protection of Human Rights and Fundamental
Freedoms, 4 November 1950
Treaty Establishing the European Atomic Energy Community, 25 March 1957
Treaty Establishing the European Coal and Steel Community, 18 April 1951
Treaty on European Union (Consolidated version 2016), OJ C 202 (2016)
Treaty on the Functioning of the European Union (Consolidated version 2016), OJ C
202 (2016)
Vienna Convention on the Law of Treaties, 23 May 1969

Statements and Declarations

Paris Declaration on Aid Effectiveness and the Accra Agenda for Action, Paris, 2 March
2005
Rome Declaration on Harmonization, Rome, Italy, 25 February 2003

Resolutions

ECOSOC, *Resolution 13 (III) on a Coordination Committee*, E/231, 21 September 1946
ECOSOC, *Resolution 288 (X) B*, 27 February 1950
FAO Conference Committee on Follow-up to the Independent External Evaluation of
FAO Immediate Plan of Action, *Resolution 1/2008. Adoption of the Immediate Plan
of Action (IPA) for FAO Renewal (2009–11)*, 19 November 2008
IBRD, *Resolution IBRD No. 93–10*, 22 September 1993
IDA, *Resolution IDA No. 93–6*, 22 September 1993
UN General Assembly, *2005 World Summit Outcome*, A/RES/60/1, 24 October 2005
UN General Assembly, *Amendments to the Staff Regulations and Staff Rules of the
United Nations*, A/RES/3353(XXIX), 18 December 1974
UN General Assembly, *Appointment of External Auditors*, A/RES/74(I), 7 December
1946
UN General Assembly, *Establishment of the Ad Hoc Committee of Experts to Examine
the Finances of the United Nations and the Specialized Agencies*, A/RES/2049(XX), 13
December 1965
UN General Assembly, *Further Measures for the Restructuring and Revitalization of the
United Nations in the Economic, Social and Related Fields*, A/RES/48/162, 20
December 1993
UN General Assembly, *Implementation of Section V of the Annex to General Assembly
Resolution 32/197 on the Restructuring of the Economic and Social Sectors of the
United Nations System*, A/RES/34/213, 19 December 1979
UN General Assembly, *Operational Activities for Development of the United Nations
System*, A/RES/37/226, 20 December 1982
UN General Assembly, *Organization and Management of Work of the Secretariat of the
United Nations*, A/RES/1446(XIV), 5 December 1959

WB, *Review of the Resolutions Establishing the Inspection Panel. 1996 Clarification of Certain Aspects of the Resolution*, 17 October 1996

Reports

AfDB, *Comprehensive Review of the AfDB's Procurement Policies and Procedures. Summary of Literature on Harmonization in Public Procurement*, March 2014

EBRD, *Annual Procurement Review 2006*, April 2007

EBRD, *Annual Procurement Review 2007*, May 2008

EBRD, *Annual Procurement Review 2008*, April 2009

EBRD, *Annual Procurement Review 2009*, April 2010

EBRD, *Annual Procurement Review 2010*, May 2011

EBRD, *Annual Procurement Review 2011*, March 2012

EBRD, *Annual Procurement Review 2012*, April 2013

EBRD, *Annual Procurement Review 2013*, April 2014

EBRD, *Annual Procurement Review 2014*, April 2015

EBRD, *Annual Procurement Review 2015*, February 2016

EBRD, *Annual Procurement Review 2016*, March 2017

ECOSOC, *Functioning of the Resident Coordinator System, Including Costs and Benefits. Report of the Secretary-General*, New York, E/2008/100, 10–14 July 2008

European Court of Auditors, *Efforts to Address Problems with Public Procurement in EU Cohesion Expenditure Should Be Intensified. Special Report no. 10*, 2015

European Court of Auditors, *The EU Institutions Can Do More to Facilitate Access to Their Public Procurement. Special Report no. 17/2016*, 24 May 2016

European Ombudsman, *1996 Annual Report*, OJ C 272, 8 September 1997

IEG, *The World Bank and Public Procurement. An Independent Evaluation, Volume II: Achieving Development Effectiveness through Procurement in Bank Financial Assistance* (Washington, DC: World Bank Group, 2014)

JIU, *Accountability and Oversight in the United Nations Secretariat*, JIU/93/5, September 1993

JIU, *Accountability Frameworks in the United Nations System*, JIU/REP/2011/5, 2011

JIU, *Delegation of Authority and Accountability. Part II. Series on Managing for Results in the United Nations System*, JIU/REP/2004/7, 2004

JIU, *Ethics in the United Nations System*, JIU/REP/2010/3, 2010

JIU, *More Coherence for Enhanced Oversight in the United Nations System*, JIU/REP/98/2, 1998

JIU, *National Execution of Projects*, JIU/REP/1994/9, 1994

JIU, *National Execution of Technical Cooperation Projects*, JIU/REP/2008/4, 2008

JIU, *Oversight Lacunae in the United Nations System*, JIU/REP/2006/2, 2006

JIU, *Procurement Reforms in the United Nations System*, JIU/NOTE/2011/1, 2011

JIU, *Report to the Twenty-Eighth Session of the General Assembly*, A/9112, July 1973

JIU, *Review of Long-Term Agreements in Procurement in the United Nations System*, JIU/REP/2013/1, 2013

JIU, *Review of the Administrative Committee on Coordination and Its Machinery*, JIU/
REP/99/1, 1999

JIU, *Review of United Nations Outsourcing Practices*, JIU/REP/2002/7, 2002

JIU, *State of the Internal Audit Function in the United Nations System*, 2016, JIU/REP/
2016/8

JIU, *The Audit Function in the United Nations System*, JIU/REP/2010/5, 2010

JIU, *Review of the Management of Implementing Partners*, JIU/REP/2013/4, 2013

OECD, *2008 Survey on Monitoring the Paris Declarations. Making Aid More Effective by
2010*, 2008

OECD, *Implementing the 2001 DAC Recommendations on Untying Aid*, DCD/DAC
(2011)4/REV1, 2011

OIOS, *Activities of the Office of Internal Oversight Services for the Period from 1 July 2010
to 30 June 2011. Report of the Office of Internal Oversight Services*, A/66/286 (Part I), 9
August 2011

OIOS, *Activities of the Office of Internal Oversight Services on Peace Operations for the
Period from 1 January to 31 December 2016*, A/71/227, 21 February 2017

OIOS, *Audit of Local Procurement in the United Nations Interim Security Force for
Abyei*, no. 2015/113, 30 September 2015

OIOS, *Audit of Local Procurement in the United Nations Mission in the Republic of
South Sudan*, no. 2015/133, 30 October 2015

OIOS, *Audit of Local Procurement in the United Nations Mission in Liberia*, no. 2014/
101, 30 September 2014

OIOS, *Audit of Local Procurement in the United Nations Mission in South Sudan*, no.
2013/126, 17 December 2013

OIOS, *Audit of Local Procurement in the United Nations Multidimensional Integrated
Stabilization Mission in Mali*, no. 2016/109, 30 September 2016

OIOS, *Audit of Local Procurement in the United Nations Multidimensional Stabilization
Mission in the Central African Republic*, no. 2016/050, 19 May 2016

OIOS, *Audit of Local Procurement in the United Nations Organization Stabilization
Mission in the Democratic Republic of the Congo*, no. 2016/065, 10 June 2016

OIOS, *Audit of Local Procurement in the United Nations Stabilization Mission in Haiti*,
no. 2016/179, 21 December 2016

OIOS, *Audit of Local Procurement in the United Nations Stabilization Mission in Haiti*,
no. 2013/081, 27 September 2013

OIOS, *Audit of Local Procurement in the United Nations Support Office for the African
Union Mission in Somalia*, no. 2014/141, 16 December 2014

OIOS, *Audit of Local Procurement of Goods and Services in the United Nations
Assistance Mission in Afghanistan*, no. 2013/132, 19 December 2013

OIOS, *Audit of Local Procurement of Goods and Services in the United Nations
Operation in Côte d'Ivoire*, no. 2013/099, 19 November 2013

OIOS, *Audit of Procurement Activities in the United Nations Assistance Mission for Iraq*,
no. 2016/153, 12 December 2016

OIOS, *Audit of Procurement Management in the Secretariat*, AH2008/513/01, 27 October 2009

OIOS, *Audit of Procurement Management in the Secretariat. Report of the Office of Internal Oversight Services*, A/64/369, 23 September 2009

OIOS, *Audit of Procurement Systems and Procedures in UNAMID*, Assignment no. AP2010/634/09, 9 February 2012

OIOS, *Audit of the Procurement Process in UNIFIL – UNIFIL Lacks Internal Control Mechanisms to Measure and Monitor the Efficiency and Effectiveness of Its Procurement Process*, UNIFIL AP2008/672/03, 21 July 2009

OIOS, *Horizontal Audit of the Procurement of Core Requirements in Peacekeeping Missions*, Assignment no. AP2007/600/07, 18 November 2008

OIOS, *Procurement of Local Contracts in UNMIL*, Assignment no. AP2010/626/01, 29 October 2010

OIOS, *Report of the Office of Internal Oversight Services on the Activities of the Procurement Task Force for the Period from 1 July 2007 to 31 July 2008*, A/63/329, 25 August 2008

OIOS, *Report of the Office of Internal Oversight Services on the Review of Procurement-Related Arbitration Cases*, A/53/843, 1 March 1999

OIOS, *UNHCR Local Procurement Activities in Kenya*, Assignment no. AR2010/112/01, 1 June 2011

United Nations, *Assessment of Member States' Contributions to the United Nations Regular Budget for the Year 2017*, ST/ADM/SER.B/955, 28 December 2016

United Nations, 'The Practice of the United Nations, the Specialized Agencies and the International Atomic Energy Agency Concerning Their Status, Privileges and Immunities: Study Prepared by the Secretariat' (A/CN.4/L.118 and Add. 1–2) in ILC, *Yearbook of the International Law Commission 1967* (New York: UN Publications, 1967), vol. II

UN ACABQ, *Financial Reports and Audited Financial Statements and Reports of the Board of Auditors for the Period Ended 31 December 2011. Report of the Advisory Committee on Administrative and Budgetary Questions*, A/67/381, 4 October 2012

UN ACABQ, *Financial Reports and Audited Financial Statements and Reports of the Board of Auditors for the Period Ended 31 December 2015. Report of the Advisory Committee on Administrative and Budgetary Questions*, A/71/669, 8 December 2016

UN ACABQ, *Financial Reports and Audited Financial Statements and Reports of the Board of Auditors (BOA) for the Period Ended 31 December 2012. Report of the Advisory Committee on Administrative and Budgetary Questions*, A/68/381, 4 October 2013

UN ACABQ, *Report of the Board of Auditors on the Accounts of the United Nations Peacekeeping Operations and Report of the Secretary-General on the Implementation of the Recommendations of the Board of Auditors Concerning United Nations Peacekeeping Operations for the Financial Period Ended 30 June 2013. Report of the Advisory Committee on Administrative and Budgetary Questions*, A/68/843, 24 April 2014

UN ACABQ, *Report of the Board of Auditors on the Accounts of the United Nations Peacekeeping Operations and Report of the Secretary-General on the Implementation of the Recommendations of the Board of Auditors Concerning United Nations Peacekeeping Operations for the Financial Period Ended 30 June 2015. Report of the Advisory Committee on Administrative and Budgetary Questions*, A/70/803, 2 May 2016

UN ACABQ, *Report of the Board of Auditors on the Accounts of the United Nations Peacekeeping Operations and Report of the Secretary-General on the Implementation of the Recommendations of the Board of Auditors Concerning United Nations Peacekeeping Operations for the Financial Period Ended 30 June 2014. Report of the Advisory Committee on Administrative and Budgetary Questions*, A/69/838, 10 April 2015

UN ACABQ, *Report of the Board of Auditors on the Accounts of the United Nations Peacekeeping Operations for the Financial Period Ended 30 June 2009. Report of the Advisory Committee on Administrative and Budgetary Questions*, A/64/708, 15 March 2010

UN ACABQ, *Report of the Board of Auditors on the Accounts of the United Nations Peacekeeping Operations and Report of the Secretary-General on the Implementation of the Recommendations of the Board of Auditors Concerning United Nations Peacekeeping Operations for the Financial Period Ended 30 June 2012. Report of the Advisory Committee on Administrative and Budgetary Questions*, A/67/782, 18 April 2013

UN ACABQ, *Report of the Board of Auditors on the Accounts of the United Nations Peacekeeping Operations and Report of the Secretary-General on the Implementation of the Recommendations of the Board of Auditors Concerning United Nations Peacekeeping Operations for the Financial Period Ended 30 June 2010. Report of the Advisory Committee on Administrative and Budgetary Questions*, A/65/782, 15 March 2011

UN ACABQ, *Report of the Board of Auditors on the Accounts of the United Nations Peacekeeping Operations and Report of the Secretary-General on the Implementation of the Recommendations of the Board of Auditors Concerning United Nations Peacekeeping Operations for the Financial Period Ended 30 June 2011. Report of the Advisory Committee on Administrative and Budgetary Questions*, A/66/719, 30 March 2012

UN ACABQ, *Towards an Accountability System in the United Nations Secretariat. Report of the Advisory Committee on Administrative and Budgetary Questions*, A/64/683, 26 February 2010

UN Administrative Coordination Committee, *Annual Report of ACC for 1975/1976*, E/5803, 1976

UN Board of Auditors, *Concise Summary of Principal Findings and Conclusions Contained in the Reports Prepared by the Board of Auditors for the General Assembly at Its Sixty-Third Session*, A/63/169, 24 July 2008

UN Board of Auditors, *Concise Summary of Principal Findings and Conclusions Contained in the Reports Prepared by the Board of Auditors for the General Assembly at Its Sixty-First Session*, A/61/182, 26 July 2006

UN Board of Auditors, *Concise Summary of Principal Findings and Conclusions Contained in the Reports of the Board of Auditors for the Biennium 2010–2011*, A/67/173, 24 July 2012

UN Board of Auditors, *Concise Summary of Principal Findings and Conclusions Contained in the Reports of the Board of Auditors for the Biennium 2012–2013 and Annual Financial Periods 2012 and 2013*, A/69/178, 23 July 2014

UN Board of Auditors, *Concise Summary of Principal Findings and Conclusions Contained in the Reports of the Board of Auditors for the Annual Financial Period 2014*, A/70/322, 14 August 2015

UN Board of Auditors, *Financial Report and Audited Financial Statements for the 12-Month Period from 1 July 2012 to 30 June 2013 and Report of the Board of Auditors. Volume II. United Nations Peacekeeping Operations*, A/68/5 (Vol. II), 17 January 2014

UN Board of Auditors, *Financial Report and Audited Financial Statements for the 12-Month Period from 1 July 2011 to 30 June 2012 and Report of the Board of Auditors. Volume II. United Nations Peacekeeping Operations*, A/67/5 (Vol. II), 18 January 2012

UN Board of Auditors, *Financial Report and Audited Financial Statements for the 12-Month Period from 1 July 2010 to 30 June 2011 and Report of the Board of Auditors. Volume II. United Nations Peacekeeping Operations*, A/66/5 (Vol. II), 17 January 2012

UN Board of Auditors, *Financial Report and Audited Financial Statements for the Biennium Ended 31 December 2011 and Report of the Board of Auditors. United Nations Office for Project Services*, A/67/5/Add. 10, 18 July 2012

UN Board of Auditors, *Financial Report and Audited Financial Statements for the Biennium Ended 31 December 2009 and Report of the Board of Auditors. United Nations Office for Project Services*, A/65/5/Add. 10, 27 April 2010

UN Board of Auditors, *Financial Report and Audited Financial Statements for the Biennium Ended 31 December 2007 and Report of the Board of Auditors. United Nations Development Programme*, A/63/5/Add. 1, 23 July 2008

UN Board of Auditors, *Financial Report and Audited Financial Statements for the Biennium Ended 31 December 2011 and Report of the Board of Auditors. United Nations Development Programme*, A/67/5/Add. 1, 30 April 2012

UN Board of Auditors, *Financial Report and Audited Financial Statements for Year Ended 31 December 2012 and Report of the Board of Auditors. United Nations Development Programme*, A/68/5/Add. 1, 30 June 2013

UN Board of Auditors, *Financial Report and Audited Financial Statements for the Year Ended 31 December 2015 and Report of the Board of Auditors. United Nations Relief and Works Agency for Palestine Refugees in the Near East*, A/71/5/Add. 4, 22 July 2015

UN Board of Auditors, *Financial Report and Audited Financial Statements for the 12-Month Period from 1 July 2010 to 30 June 2011 and Report of the Board of Auditors. Volume II. United Nations Peacekeeping Operations*, A/66/5 (Vol. II), 17 January 2012

UN Board of Auditors, *Financial Report and Audited Financial Statements for the Biennium Ended 31 December 2005 and Report of the Board of Auditors. United Nations Development Programme*, A/61/5/Add. 1, 18 August 2006

UN Board of Auditors, *Financial Report and Audited Financial Statements for the Biennium Ended 31 December 2007 and Report of the Board of Auditors. United Nations Development Programme*, A/63/5/Add. 1, 23 July 2008

UN Board of Auditors, *Financial Report and Audited Financial Statements for the 12-Month Period from 1 July 2014 to 30 June 2015 and Report of the Board of Auditors. Volume II. United Nations Peacekeeping Operations*, A/70/5 (Vol. II), 14 January 2016

UN Board of Auditors, *Financial Report and Audited Financial Statements for the 12-Month Period from 1 July 2013 to 30 June 2014 and Report of the Board of Auditors. Volume II. United Nations Peacekeeping Operations*, A/69/5 (Vol. II), 22 January 2015

UN Board of Auditors, *Financial Report and Audited Financial Statements for the Biennium Ended 31 December 2009 and Report of the Board of Auditors. United Nations Children's Fund*, A/65/5/Add. 2, 14 July 2010

UN Board of Auditors, *Financial Report and Audited Financial Statements for the Biennium Ended 31 December 2011 and Report of the Board of Auditors. United Nations Children's Fund*, A/67/5/Add. 2, 20 July 2012

UN Board of Auditors, *Financial Report and Audited Financial Statements for the Biennium Ended 31 December 2012 and Report of the Board of Auditors. United Nations Children's Fund*, A/68/5/Add. 2, 30 June 2013

UN Board of Auditors, *Financial Reports and Audited Financial Statements and Reports of the Board of Auditors for the Period Ended 31 December 2011. Report of the Board of Auditors. Volume I. United Nations*, A/67/5 (Vol. I), 26 July 2012

UN Board of Auditors, *Financial Reports and Audited Financial Statements and Reports of the Board of Auditors for the Period Ended 31 December 2015. Report of the Board of Auditors. Volume I. United Nations*, A/71/5 (Vol. I), 28 September 2016

UN Board of Auditors, *Financial Reports and Audited Financial Statements and Reports of the Board of Auditors for the Period Ended 31 December 2011. Report of the Board of Auditors. United Nations Relief and Works Agency for Palestine Refugees in the Near East*, A/67/5/Add. 3, 24 January 2012

UN Executive Committee of the High Commissioner's Programme, *Report of the Fifty-Ninth Session of the Executive Committee*, A/AC.96/1063, 22 October 2008

UN Fifth Committee (Administrative and Budgetary Committee), *Meetings 1635–1642 (minutes)*

UN Fifth Committee (Administrative and Budgetary Committee), *Plenary meeting 2325 (minutes)*

UN General Assembly, *Analytical Report of the Secretary-General on the Implementation of General Assembly Resolution 41/213*, A/45/226, 27 April 1990

UN General Assembly, *Analytical Report of the Secretary-General on the Implementation of General Assembly Resolution 41/213 (A/45/226). Report of the Advisory Committee on Administrative and Budgetary Questions*, A/45/617, 12 October 1990

UN General Assembly, *Comprehensive Review of the Whole Question of Peacekeeping Operations in All Their Aspects. Letter Dated 24 March 2005 from the Secretary General to the President of the General Assembly*, A/59/710, 24 March 2005

UN General Assembly, *Cooperation between the United Nations and the Organization of American States*, A/49/5, 1 November 1994

UN General Assembly, *Development and International Economic Cooperation: Trade and Development. Progress in the Implementation of Specific Action Related to the Particular Needs and Problems of Land-locked Developing Countries. Note by the Secretary-General*, A/48/487, 19 October 1993

UN General Assembly, *Measures to Strengthen Accountability at the United Nations. Report of the Secretary-General*, A/60/312, 30 August 2005

UN General Assembly, *Procurement Reform. Report of the Secretary-General*, A/53/271, 18 August 1998

UN General Assembly, *Procurement Reform. Report of the Secretary-General*, A/55/127, 10 July 2000

UN General Assembly, *Procurement Reform. Report of the Secretary-General*, A/57/187, 2 July 2002

UN General Assembly, *Procurement Reform: Definition of Exigency Needs. Report of the Secretary-General*, A/54/650, 15 February 2000

UN General Assembly, *Proposed Revisions to the Financial Regulations of the United Nations. Report of the Secretary-General*, A/57/396, 11 September 2001

UN General Assembly, *Report of Secretary-General*, A/C.5/1611, 1974

UN General Assembly, *Report of the Advisory Committee on Administrative and Budgetary Questions*, A/50/7/Add. 13, 8 March 1996

UN General Assembly, *Report of the Board of Auditors on Enhancing Accountability, Transparency and Cost-Effectiveness in the United Nations System: Proposal to Clarify and Enhance the Role of the Board of Auditors in the Conduct of Performance Audits*, A/66/747, 15 March 2012

UN General Assembly, *Report of the Group of High-Level Experts to Review the Efficiency of the Administrative and Financial Functioning of the United Nations*, A/41/49, Supplement no. 49, 15 August 1986

UN General Assembly, *Report of the Group of High-Level Experts to Review the Efficiency of the Administrative and Financial Functioning of the United Nations. Note by the Secretariat*, A/41/663, 1 October 1986

UN General Assembly, *Report of the Office of Internal Oversight Services on the Activities of the Procurement Task Force for the 18-Month Period Ended 30 June 2007*, A/62/272, 5 October 2007

UN General Assembly, *Review of the Efficiency of the Administrative and Financial Functioning of the United Nations. Procurement Reform. Fourth Report of the Advisory Committee on Administrative and Budgetary Questions*, A/51/7/Add. 3, 4 December 1996

UN General Assembly, *Review of the Efficiency of the Administrative and Financial Functioning of the United Nations. Procurement Reform. Report of the Secretary-General*, A/C.5/51/9, 29 November 1996

UN General Assembly, *Review of the Efficiency of the Administrative and Financial Functioning of the United Nations. Procurement Reform. Report of the Secretary-General*, A/52/534, 27 October 1997

UN General Assembly, *Towards an Accountability System in the United Nations Secretariat. Report of the Secretary-General*, A/64/640, 29 January 2010

UN Secretary-General, *United Nations System-Wide Application of Ethics: Separately Administered Organs and Programmes*, ST/SGB/2007/11, 30 November 2007

UN, *2014 Annual Statistical Report on United Nations Procurement*, 2015

UNDP-IAPSO, *Annual Statistical Report 2000*, July 2001

UNDP-IAPSO, *Annual Statistical Report 2001*, July 2002

UNDP-IAPSO, *Annual Statistical Report 2002*, July 2003

UNDP-IAPSO, *Annual Statistical Report 2003*, July 2004

UNDP-IAPSO, *Annual Statistical Report 2004*, July 2005

UNDP-IAPSO, *Annual Statistical Report 2005*, July 2006

UNDP-IAPSO, *Annual Statistical Report 2006*, July 2007

UNICEF, *Report on the Accountability System of UNICEF*, E/ICEF/2009/15, 23 April 2009

UNOPS, *2007 Annual Statistical Report on Procurement*, July 2008

UNOPS, *2008 Annual Statistical Report on United Nations Procurement*, July 2009

UNOPS, *2009 Annual Statistical Report on United Nations Procurement*, July 2010

UNOPS, *2010 Annual Statistical Report on United Nations Procurement*, July 2011

UNOPS, *2011 Annual Statistical Report on United Nations Procurement*, July 2012

UNOPS, *2012 Annual Statistical Report on United Nations Procurement*, July 2013

UNOPS, *2013 Annual Statistical Report on United Nations Procurement*, July 2014

UNOPS, *2014 Annual Statistical Report on United Nations Procurement*, July 2015

UNOPS, *2015 Annual Statistical Report on United Nations Procurement*, July 2016

US GAO, *International Food Assistance, Local and Regional Procurement Provides Opportunities to Enhance US Food Aid, But Challenges May Constrain Its Implementation*, GAO-09-757 T, 4 June 2009

US GAO, *Lessons Learned from Oil for Food Program Indicate the Need to Strengthen UN Internal Controls and Oversight Activities*, GAO-06-330, April 2006

US GAO, *Multilateral Development Banks. US Firms' Market Share and Federal Efforts to Help US Firms*, GAO/GGD-95-222, 28 September 1995

US GAO, *Observations on the Management and Oversight of the Oil for Food Program*, GAO-04-730 T, 28 April 2004

US GAO, *United Nations Peacekeeping. Lines of Authority for Field Procurement Remain Unclear, But Reforms Have Addressed Some Issues*, September 2008

US GAO, *United Nations: Progress of Procurement Reforms*, GAO/NSIAD-99-71, 15 April 1999

US White House, *Fact Sheet: Advancing US Interests at the United Nations*, 20 September 2011

WB Executive Board, *Decision Number 1: Inspection Panel's Mandate on Procurement Matters, The Inspection Panel. Report*, 1 August 1994 to 31 July 1996

WB, *OECD & Non-OECD Suppliers Totals 2000–2015*, available at http://web.world bank.org/WBSITE/EXTERNAL/PROJECTS/PROCUREMENT/0,, contentMDK:20251613~pagePK:84269~piPK:84286~theSitePK:84266,00.html (last access: January 2018)

WB, *Supplier Totals by Country 2000–2015*, available at http://web.worldbank.org/ WBSITE/EXTERNAL/PROJECTS/PROCUREMENT/0,, contentMDK:20251613~pagePK:84269~piPK:84286~theSitePK:84266,00.html (last access: January 2018)

Administrative Policies and Regulations

ADB, *Procurement Guidelines*, April 2015

ADB, *Promoting the Use of Country Systems in ADB's Operations. A Systematic Approach*, February 2015

Administrative Committee on Coordination (ACC), *National Execution and Implementation Arrangements*, New York, September 1998

AfDB, *Bank Group Approach towards Enhancing the Use of Country Systems*, May 2008

AfDB, *Comprehensive Review of the AFDB's Procurement Policies and Procedures*, March 2014

AfDB, *Review of AfDB's Procurement Policy, Procedures and Processes. Policy Framework Paper*, May 2014

AfDB, *Rules and Procedures for the Procurement of Goods and Works*, May 2008 (Revised July 2012)

EBRD, *Procurement Policies and Rules*, 1 November 2017

ESA, *Additional Arbitration Rules*, ESA/REG/006, 3 February 2014

ESA, *ESA Financial Regulations*, ESA/REG/005, rev. 1, 20 February 2015

ESA, *ESA Procurement Regulations and Related Implementing Instructions*, ESA/REG/ 001, rev. 4, 1 January 2016

ESA, *Industrial Policy Rules and Regulations. Regulation Concerning the Calculation of the Geographical Return Coefficients and on the Publication of Corresponding Statistics and Forecasts*, ESA/REG/009, 1 July 2015

ESA, *Security Regulations*, ESA/REG/004, rev.1, 22 October 2015

ESA, *Staff Regulations*, ESA/REG/007, 27 February 2014

EU, *General Regulations for Service, Supply and Works Contracts Financed by the EDF*, Annexed to Decision 2/2002 of the ACP-EC Council of Ministers of 7 October 2002

Regarding the Implementation of Articles 28, 29 and 30 of Annex IV to the Cotonou Agreement, OJ 2002 L 320, p. 1

EU, Practical Guide to Contract Procedures for EU External Actions, 15 January 2016

FAO, FAO Manual. Ch. 5 Property and Services, sec. 502 Procurement of Goods, Works and Services, January 2010

FAO, FAO Sanctions Procedures, 20 November 2014

FAO, Financial Regulations, 16 October 1945, and following amendments

IAEA, General Instructions for Bidders, August 2011

IAPWG, UN Procurement Practitioner's Handbook, November 2006 (amended in September 2012)

ICSC, Framework for Human Resource Management Glossary, August 2001

IDB, Guide for Acceptance of the Use of Country Procurement Systems, GN-2538-13, September 2013

IDB, Policies for the Procurement of Goods and Works Financed by the Inter-American Development Bank, GN-2349-9, March 2011

IDB, Strategy for Strengthening and Use of Country Systems, 2009

IFAD, Procurement Handbook, 2015

IFAD, Project Procurement Guidelines, September 2010

ILO, Financial Rules, 2009-12-0034-1.doc/v2, January 2010

ILO, Office Guideline on the ILO Accountability Framework: Key Standards and Mechanisms, IGDS no. 195, 2 October 2010

ILO, Statute of the Administrative Tribunal of the International Labour Organization, 9 October 1946 (and following amendments)

International Civil Service Commission, Standards of Conduct for the International Civil Service, July 2013

NATO, NATO International Staff Procurement Manual, EM(2010)0285-REV1, 14 June 2011

NATO, NSPA Procurement Operating Instruction, NSPA OI 4200–01, 9 September 2014

NATO, NSPO Procurement Regulations. NSPO Regulation No. 4200, 10 December 2013

OECD, Annex to the Recommendation of the Council on Guidelines for Managing Conflict of Interest in the Public Service, June 2003

OECD, Managing Conflict of Interest in the Public Service. OECD Guidelines and Country Experiences (Paris: OECD Publications, 2003)

OIOS, Audit Manual, March 2009

OIOS, Inspection and Evaluation Manual. Guidelines for the Conduct of Inspections and Evaluations in the United Nations Office of Internal Oversight Services, March 2004

OIOS, Investigations Manual, January 2015

UN, Debriefing and Procurement Challenges FAQ, available at www.un.org/Depts/ptd/complaints/debriefing-and-procurement-challenges-faq (last access: January 2018).

United Nations, Establishment of the Office of Internal Oversight Services, ST/SGB/273, 7 September 1994

United Nations, Financial Regulations and Rules of the United Nations, ST/SGB/2003/7, 9 May 2003

United Nations, *Financial Regulations and Rules of the United Nations*, ST/SGB/2013/4, 1 July 2013

United Nations, *General Business Guide for Potential Suppliers of Goods and Services with Common Guidelines for Procurement by Organizations in the UN System*, XX edn, June 2006

United Nations, *Guidelines to File a Procurement Challenge*, 2009, available at www.un .org/Depts/ptd/complaints/complaints-guideline (last access: January 2018)

United Nations, *Interpretation of United Nations Financial Rule 110.20. Meaning of the Term 'Publicly Opened' as Applied to Bids. General Procurement Practice*, 29 July 1994, para. 4, in United Nations, *United Nations Juridical Yearbook 1994* (New York: UN Publications, 1995)

United Nations, *Procurement Manual*, rev. 7, 1 July 2013

United Nations, *Staff Rules and Staff Regulations of the United Nations*, ST/SGB/2014/1, 1 January 2014

United Nations, *Standards and Guidelines of the Joint Inspection Unit*, A/51/34/Annex I

United Nations, *UN Supplier Code of Conduct*, September 2013

United Nations, *United Nations Guiding Principles on Business and Human Rights*, 2012

United Nations, *United Nations Procurement Practitioner's Handbook*, October 2017

United Nations, *United Nations Procurement Practitioner's Handbook*, November 2006 [revised in September 2012]

UNDP, *Financial Regulations and Rules*, 1 January 2012

UNDP, *Financial Rules and Regulations*, May 2005

UNDP, *Government Execution of Projects*, Decision 76/57, 2 July 1976

UNDP, *Guidelines for the Procurement of Equipment, Supplies and Services. Note by the Administrator*, DP/1982/56, 15 April 1982

UNDP, *Guidelines for the Procurement of Equipment, Supplies and Services. Note by the Administrator*, DP/1983/47, 25 March 1983

UNDP, *Guidelines for the Procurement of Equipment, Supplies and Services. Note by the Administrator*, DP/1984/59, 5 March 1984

UNDP, *Guidelines for the Procurement of Equipment, Supplies and Services. Note by the Administrator*, DP/1985/61, 6 March 1985

UNDP, *National Implementation by the Government of UNDP Supported Projects: Guidelines and Procedures*, 1 July 2011

UNDP, *Programme and Operations Policies and Procedures. Procurement*, 27 July 2016

UNDP, *The UNDP Accountability System. Accountability Framework and Oversight Policy*, DP/2008/16/rev. 1, 1 August 2008

UNDP/UNFPA/UNOPS Executive Board, *Internal Audit and Oversight (UNDP, UNFPA and UNOPS)*, EB decision 2007/37, 19 September 2008

UNESCO, *UNESCO Administrative Manual*, 2009 [updated 2014]

UNFPA, *Financial Regulations and Rules*, UNFPA/FIN/REG/Rev. 10, 1 July 2014

UNFPA, *Information Disclosure Policy*, 1 January 2009

UNFPA, *Policy and Procedures for Regular Procurement*, April 2015

UNFPA, *Policy for Vendor Review and Sanctions*, July 2015

UNFPA, *UNFPA Accountability Framework*, DP/FPA/2007/20, 25 July 2007

UNHCR, *Doing Business with UNHCR*, 2015

UNHCR, *Guidance Note No. 4 on Procurement with UNHCR Funds Undertaken by Partners*, 04/FP/S2-2, November 2014

UNHCR, *Policy and Procedures on Procurement by Partners with UNHCR Funds*, UNHCR/HCP/2014/11, 21 October 2014

UNHCR, *UNHCR Manual. Chapter 8: Supply Management*, December 2003 [latest version not published, nor available upon request addressed to the organization]

UNICEF Executive Board, *Decision No. 2/2008*, E/ICEF/2008/2, December 2007

UNICEF, *Book G: Supply Manual*, 1 January 2003 [latest version not published, nor available upon request addressed to the organization]

UNICEF, *Financial Rules and Regulations*, E/ICEF/2011/AB/L.8, 24 June 2011

UNICEF, *General Business Guide for Potential Suppliers of Goods and Services with Common Guidelines for Procurement by Organizations in the UN System*, June 2006

UNICEF, *Information Disclosure Policy of the United Nations Children's Fund*, 16 May 2011

UNICEF, *Policy Prohibiting and Combatting Fraud and Corruption*, CF/EXD/2013-008, 29 August 2013

UNICEF, *UNICEF Financial Regulations and Rules*, E/ICEF/2011/AB/L.8, 24 June 2011

UNIDO, *Procurement Manual*, July 2013

UNOPS, *Administrative Instruction. Prohibition of Accepting Gifts, Honours, Decorations, Favours or Non-UN Remuneration or Benefits from Governmental and Non-Governmental Sources*, AJJE0/20 12/01, 27 January 2012

UNOPS, *Administrative Instruction. Vendor Review Procedure*, AI/PG/2015/01, 8 December 2015

UNOPS, *Financial Regulations and Rules*, 13 February 2012

UNOPS, *Organizational Directive No. 10 (Revision 2)*, 26 August 2010

UNOPS, *Organizational Directive No. 16 (Revision 1), Procurement Framework*, 19 April 2010

UNOPS, *Organizational Directive No. 30 (Revision 1), Information Disclosure Policy*, 26 January 2012

UNOPS, *Organizational Directive No. 41 (Revision 1), Framework for Determining Vendor Ineligibility/Sanctions*, 8 December 2015

UNOPS, *Policy to Address Fraud*, 26 August 2010

UNOPS, *Procurement Manual*, 1 June 2017

UNOPS, *United Nations Office for Project Services Accountability Framework and Oversight Policies*, 24 September 2008

UNRWA, *Financial Regulations*, 8 May 1950 (and following amendments)

UNRWA, *Financial Regulations*, 8 May 1980

UNRWA, *Procurement Manual*, 1 August 2012

UN Secretary-General, *Ethics Office. Establishment and Terms of Reference*, ST/SGB/2005/22, 30 December 2005

UN Secretary-General, *Status, Basic Rights and Duties of United Nations Staff Members*, ST/SGB/2002/13, 1 November 2002

WB, *Use of Country Systems in Bank Supported Operations: Proposed Piloting Program*, R2008-0036, 3 March and 25 March 2008

WFP Executive Director, *Establishment of Ethics Office in WFP*, Executive Director's Circular no. ED2008/002, 31 January 2008

WFP, *Doing Business with the United Nations World Food Programme. International Food, Goods and Services Procurement*, July 2016

WFP, *Financial Rules*, January 2014

WFP, *Food Procurement Manual*, 2010

WFP, *General Regulations and General Rules*, January 2014 (latest version)

WFP, *Non-Food Procurement Manual*, 11 November 1999

WHO, *Good Procurement Practices for Artemisinin-based Antimalarial Medicines*, March 2010

WHO, *Manual for Procurement of Diagnostics and Related Laboratory Items and Equipment*, 2013

WHO, *WHO Procurement Strategy*, 27 April 2015

WIPO, *Financial Regulations and Rules of the World Intellectual Property Organization (WIPO)*, 11 October 2016 (last amendment)

General Terms and Conditions of Contract

Commission française d'études de l'union legislative entre les nations alliées et amies, *Project de Code des obligations et des contrats: texte dèfinitif approuvé à Paris en Octobre 1927*, Rome, 1928

ESA, *Regulations of the European Space Agency. General Clauses and Conditions for ESA Contracts*, ESA/REG/002, rev. 2, 29 June 2015

FAO, *FAO Revised General Terms and Conditions for Goods*, April 2015

FAO, *FAO Revised General Terms and Conditions for Services*, April 2015

FAO, *General Terms and Conditions Applicable to FAO Procurement Contracts*, March 2008

FAO, *General Terms and Conditions for Works and Services* [no date; applicable as per January 2018]

IFAD, *General Terms and Conditions for the Procurement of Goods* [no date; applicable as per January 2018]

IILO, *Terms and Conditions Applicable to ILO Contracts*, 1 December 2013

IFAD, *General Terms and Conditions for the Procurement of Services*, 2015

United Nations, 'Law Applicable to Contracts Concluded by the United Nations with Private Parties. Procedures for Settling Disputes Arising out of Such Contracts. Relevant Rules and Practices', 26 February 1976, in United Nations, *United Nations Juridical Yearbook 1976* (New York: UN Publications, 1976)

United Nations, *General Conditions for Aircraft Charter*, 2005

United Nations, *General Conditions of Contracts – De Minimis Field Contracts*, April 2012

United Nations, *General Conditions of Contracts for the Provision of Goods and Services*, April 2012

United Nations, *General Conditions of Contracts for the Provision of Goods*, April 2012
United Nations, *General Conditions of Contracts for the Provision of Services*, April 2012
UNDP, *General Conditions for Professional Services*, October 2000
UNDP, *General Conditions for Purchase Orders*, October 2000
UNDP, *General Conditions of Contracts for Civil Works*, October 2000
UNDP, *General Terms and Conditions for Contracts*, September 2017
UNDP, *General Terms and Conditions for Goods*, October 2000
UNHCR, *General Conditions of Contracts – De Minimis Field Contracts*, January 2010
UNHCR, General *Conditions of Contracts for the Provision of Goods*, January 2010
UNHCR, *General Conditions of Contracts for the Provision of Goods and Services*,
    January 2010
UNHCR, *General Conditions of Contracts for the Provision of Services*, January 2010
UNICEF, *Instructions to Bidders and General Terms and Conditions for Procurement of
    Services through ITB/RFQ* [no date; applicable as per January 2018]
UNIDO, *General Terms and Conditions* [no date; applicable as per January 2018]
UNIDROIT, *Principles of International Commercial Contracts*, Rome, 1994
UNIDROIT, *Principles of International Commercial Contracts*, Rome, 2004
UNIDROIT, *Principles of International Commercial Contracts*, Rome, 2010
UNIDROIT, *Principles of International Commercial Contracts*, Rome, 2016
UNOPS, *General Conditions of Contract for Construction Works*, April 1995
UNOPS, *General Conditions for Goods* [no date; applicable as per January 2018]
UNRWA, *General Conditions of Contract for Provision of Goods and Services*, 6 March 2009
UNRWA, *General Conditions of Contract for Provision of Goods Only*, 6 March 2009
UNRWA, *General Conditions of Contract for Provision of Services Only*, 6 March 2009

United Nations Collections of Documents

United Nations, *United Nations Juridical Yearbook 1994* (New York: UN Publications,
    1995)
United Nations, *Yearbook of the United Nations 1950* (New York: UN Publications,
    1950)
United Nations, *Yearbook of the United Nations 1974* (New York: UN Publications,
    1974)
United Nations, *Yearbook of the United Nations 1976* (New York: UN Publications,
    1976)
United Nations, *Yearbook of the United Nations 1978* (New York: UN Publications,
    1978)
United Nations, *Yearbook of the United Nations 1979* (New York: UN Publications,
    1979)
United Nations, *Yearbook of the United Nations 1980* (New York: UN Publications,
    1980)
United Nations, *Yearbook of the United Nations 1982* (New York: UN Publications,
    1982)

United Nations, *Yearbook of the United Nations 1983* (New York: UN Publications, 1983)

United Nations, *Yearbook of the United Nations 1984* (New York: UN Publications, 1984)

United Nations, *Yearbook of the United Nations 1985* (New York: UN Publications, 1985)

United Nations, *Yearbook of the United Nations 1994* (New York: UN Publications, 1994)

National and Regional Legislation Europe

Council of Europe, Council Directive 71/304/CE of 26 July 1971 Concerning the Abolition of Restrictions on the Freedom to Provide Services in Respect of Public Works Contracts and on the Award of Public Works Contracts through Contractors Acting through Agencies or Branches, 26 July 1971

Council of Europe, Council Directive 71/305/CEE of 26 July 1971, which Coordinates Procedures for Awarding Public Works Contracts, 26 July 1971

Council of Europe, *General Programme for the Abolition of Restrictions on the Freedom of Establishment*, 18 December 1961

EU Commission, *The WTO Agreement on Government Procurement*, MEMO/03/83, Brussels, 10 April 2003

EU Commission Delegated Regulation (EU) 2015/2462 of 30 October 2015 Amending Delegated Regulation (EU) No. 1268/2012 on the Rules of Application of Regulation (EU, Euratom) No. 966/2012 of the European Parliament and of the Council on the Financial Rules Applicable to the General Budget of the Union, OJ L 342, 29 December 2015, p. 7

EU Commission Delegated Regulation (EU) No. 1268/2012 of 29 October 2012 on the Rules of Application of Regulation (EU, Euratom) No. 966/2012 of the European Parliament and of the Council on the Financial Rules Applicable to the General Budget of the Union, OJ L 362, 31 December 2012, p. 1

European Union, Communication from the Commission to the Council and the European Parliament on European Contract Law, COM(2001) 398 Final, 11 July 2001, OJ No. C255, 13 September 2001

European Union, Communication from the Commission to the Council and the European Parliament. A More Coherent European Contract Law. An Action Plan, COM(2003) 68 Final, 12 February 2003, OJ No. C63, 15 March 2003

European Union, Council Regulation (EU) 2015/323 of 2 March 2015 on the Financial Regulation Applicable to the 11th European Development Fund, OJ No. L 58, 3 March 2015, p. 17

European Union, Decision (EU) 2016/245 of the European Central Bank of 9 February 2016 Laying Down the Rules on Procurement, OJ L 45, 20 February 2016, p. 15

National and Regional Legislation Germany

National and Regional Legislation United Kingdom

National and Regional Legislation United States of America

International Organizations Immunities Act, 29 December 1945
United States, Food for Peace Act [as amended through P.L. 113–79, enacted 7 February
  2014]

Note

Documents in the footnotes are all in the above *List of instruments*. To
facilitate reference to the full title of the document, the footnotes include
a short title of the document and the section within the *List of instruments*
where the document is listed. The sections are indicated as follows:

A&C   Agreements and constitutions
T&C   Treaties and conventions
S&D   Statements and declarations
RES   Resolutions
REP   Reports
AP&R   Administrative policies and regulations
GT&CC   General terms and conditions of contract
UNCDoc   United Nations Collections of Documents
N&RL   National and regional legislation (followed by the name of the
         country)

ABBREVIATIONS

ACABQ	Advisory Committee on Administrative and Budgetary Questions
ACC	Administrative Committee on Coordination
ADB	Asian Development Bank
AfDB	African Development Bank
AMISOM	African Union Mission to Somalia
APA	Alternative Procurement Arrangements
ARB	Award Review Board
ASG/OCSS	Assistant Secretary-General, Office of Central Support Services, Department of Management (UN)
BSTDB	Black Sea Trade and Development Bank
CDB	Caribbean Development Bank
CEB	Council of Europe Development Bank
CERN	European Organization for Nuclear Research
CPO	Chief Procurement Officer (Field Mission and/or OAH)
CPT	Common Procurement Team
DACON	Data on Consulting Firms
DEX	Direct Execution
DFS	Department of Field Support (HQ)
DIEC	Director General for Development and International Economic Co-operation
DOS	Division for Oversight Services
DPKO	Department of Peacekeeping Operations (HQ)
EBRD	European Bank for Reconstruction and Development
ECA	Economic Commission for Africa or United National Economic Commission for Africa
ECB	European Central Bank
ECE	Economic Commission for Europe
ECHR	European Court of Human Rights
ECJ	European Court of Justice
ECLAC	Economic Commission for Latin America and the Caribbean
ECOSOC	Economic and Social Council
ECSC	European Coal and Steel Community
EDF	European Development Fund

EEC	European Economic Community
EIB	European Investment Bank
EOI	Expression of Interest
ESA	European Space Agency
ESCAP	Economic and Social Commission for Asia and the Pacific
ESCWA	Economic and Social Commission for Western Asia
EU	European Union
FAO	Food and Agriculture Organization
GAL	Global Administrative Law
GATT	General Agreement on Tariffs and Trade
GC	General Conditions
GCC	General Conditions of Contract
GTC	General Terms and Conditions
GPA	Agreement on Government Procurement
HCC	Headquarters Committee on Contracts
HQ	Headquarters
IAEA	International Atomic Energy Agency
IAPSO	Inter-Agency Procurement Services Office
IAPSU	Inter-Agency Procurement Services Unit
IAPWG	Inter-Agency Procurement Working Group
IBRD	International Bank for Reconstruction and Development (World Bank Group)
ICAO	International Civil Aviation Organization
ICB	International Competitive Bidding
ICC	International Chamber of Commerce
ICSC	International Civil Service Commission
ICSU	International Council of Science
ICT	Information and Communications Technology
IDA	International Development Association (World Bank Group)
IDB	Inter-American Development Bank
IFAD	International Fund for Agricultural Development
IFC	International Finance Corporation (World Bank Group)
IFRC	International Federation of Red Cross and Red Crescent Societies
IGO	International Governmental Organization
ILO	International Labour Organisation
ILOAT	ILO Administrative Tribunal
IMF	International Monetary Fund
IMO	International Maritime Organization
INGO	International Non-Governmental Organization
INMARSAT	International Maritime Satellite Organization
INTOSAI	International Organization of Supreme Audit Institutions
IOS	Internal Oversight Service

IsDB	Islamic Development Bank
ITB	Invitation to Bid
ITU	International Telecommunications Union
JIU	Joint Inspection Unit
LOA	Letter of Assist
LTA	Long-Term Agreement
MAPS	Methodology for Assessing Procurement Systems
MDB	Multilateral Development Bank
MINUSMA	United Nations Multidimensional Integrated Stabilization Mission in Mali
MONUSCO	United Nations Organization Stabilization Mission in the Democratic Republic of the Congo
NATO	North Atlantic Treaty Organization
NCB	National Competitive Bidding
NEX	National Execution
OAH	Office away from Headquarters
OAI	Office of Audit and Investigation
OAS	Organization of American States
OAU	Organisation of African Unity
ODA	Official Development Assistance
OECD	Organisation for Economic Co-operation and Development
OHCHR	Office of the United Nations High Commissioner for Human Rights
OIG	Office of the Inspector General
OIOS	Office of Internal Oversight Services
OLA	Office of Legal Affairs
ONUC	Opération des Nations Unies au Congo
OSD	Oversight Services Division
PAM	Parliamentary Assembly of the Mediterranean
PO	Purchase Order
PRAG	Practical Guide to Contract Procedures for EU External Actions
PSO	Procurement Support Office
REOI	Request for Expression of Interest
RFI	Request for Information
RFP	Request for Proposal
RFQ	Request for Quotation
SAI	Supreme Audit Institutions
SMEs	Small and Medium-Size Enterprises
TEU	Treaty on European Union
TFEU	Treaty on the Functioning of the European Union
UN/PD	United Nations Secretariat Procurement Division (HQ)
UNAIDS	Joint United Nations Programme on HIV/AIDS
UNAMID	African Union – United Nations Hybrid Operation in Darfur

UNAVEM	United Nations Angola Verification Mission
UNCCD	United Nations Convention to Combat Desertification
UNCDF	United Nations Capital Development Fund
UNCITRAL	United Nations Commission on International Trade Law
UNCTAD	United Nations Conference on Trade and Development
UNDP	United Nations Development Programme
UNDT	United Nations Dispute Tribunal
UNEF	United Nations Emergency Force
UNEP	United Nations Environment Programme
UNESCO	United Nations Educational, Scientific and Cultural Organization
UNFCCC	United Nations Framework Convention on Climate Change
UNFPA	United Nations Population Fund
UNFSSTD	United Nations Financing System in Science and Technology Development
UNGCC	United Nations General Conditions of Contract
UNGM	United Nations Global Marketplace
UNHCR	Office of the United Nations High Commissioner for Refugees
UNICEF	United Nations Children's Fund
UNIDO	United Nations Industrial Development Organization
UNMIL	United Nations Mission in Liberia
UNOCI	United Nations Operation in Côte d'Ivoire
UNODC	United Nations Office on Drugs and Crime
UNOG	United Nations Office at Geneva
UNON	United Nations Office at Nairobi
UNOPS	United Nations Office for Project Services
UNOV	United Nations Office at Vienna
UNRWA	United Nations Relief and Works Agency for Palestine Refugees in the Near East
UNSO	United Nations Sudano-Sahelian Office
UNSOA	United Nations Support Office for AMISOM
UNSTAMIH	United Nations Stabilization Mission in Haiti
UNU	United Nations University
UPU	Universal Postal Union
USGAO	United States Government Accountability Office
USSR	Union of Soviet Socialist Republics
WB	World Bank
WFP	World Food Programme
WHO	World Health Organization
WIPO	World Intellectual Property Organization
WMO	World Meteorological Organization
WTO	World Trade Organization

1

Introduction

1.1 Setting the Questions

A book about public procurement by international organizations is likely to evoke the odor of a dusty technical treatise destined for equally dusty and esoteric lawyers. It is anything but – you are in for a surprise. Here are but three of many more considerations which will help dispel this first impression.

A huge number of international organizations are there to foster social and economic objectives, oftentimes social and economic justice. It might be as simple as ensuring that a letter is delivered, it may be as critical as supplying emergency food aid. Procurement, whether of goods, services and works, is a key instrument in the realization, or impediment, of these goals. To understand the deep structure, rather than the surface language, of this dimension of international organizations, one must abandon the lofty language of preambles and declarations and dive into the messy reality of money and its expenditure.

Consider further. There is not a single international organization, big or small, that can avoid some degree of procurement, thus a critical common thread of international organization practice regardless of their identity or function. If your interest is in the internal and external processes of governance of such organizations, (and who cannot be interested seeing how huge tranches of public administration have moved from the national to the transnational), public procurement offers a veritable and generalizable laboratory for analyzing such.

And finally there is theory. Theory is ultimately tested in its ability to provide understanding and insight into the empirical phenomena to which it is applied. Procurement by international organizations provides, as will be seen, a fertile ground with which to test extant theories conceptualizing and explaining transnational and international governance – not least the

1

théorie du jour, Global Administrative Law – and to generate new conceptualizations and theoretical insights into this phenomenon.

This book is both a law book and a book about the law. It is a law book in that it provides, for the first time I believe, a full account of both the positive law and the results of extensive empirical research of the actual practice of public procurement by international organizations. It is a book about the law in that it seeks to understand the significance, conceptual and theoretical of this law and practice well beyond the specific subject matter.

I will now explain in greater detail the premises, research questions, methodology and theoretical framework of the book.

In 2015, organizations belonging to the UN system spent more than $17.6 billion on the procurement of goods and services.[1] Since 2000, UN procurement volume has steadily increased, reaching $5 billion in 2003, $10 billion in 2007 and $15 billion in 2012. The overall increase from 2000 to 2015 is attributable to an overall increase in procurement activities of the UN system as a whole, but some organizations have increased more than others. For instance, the increase in volume since 2009 is mainly attributable to a rise in volume from three organizations: the United Nations Children's Fund (UNICEF) with $1,599 million, the United Nations Development Programme (UNDP) with $1,126 million and the World Health Organization (WHO) with $770 million. This significant growth trend has gone hand in hand with the growth of their functions and structure.

International organizations' procurement is made possible by member state contributions, which in many cases – like the United States, Japan, Germany, and Great Britain – amount to considerable sums. The United States, which in absolute terms is the largest funder of the UN system, contributed over $610 million (22 per cent of total contributions) to the regular budget of the United Nations in 2017.[2] By the end of 2016, the European Union Official Development Assistance (ODA) represented 0.51 per cent of EU gross national income (GNI), and development aid from European countries and contributions to development banks, which may or may not be managed by the European Commission, reached an average of 0.46 per cent of GDP per state. Thus, expenditure

---

[1] More precisely US$17,575,297.95. See UNOPS, *2015 Annual Statistical Report on United Nations Procurement* [ref. REP]. The report refers to UN organization(s) meaning by that the United Nations, its subsidiary bodies – including separately administered funds and programmes – specialized agencies, research and training institutes, and other subsidiary entities.

[2] More precisely US$610,836,578. See United Nations, *Assessment of Member States' Contributions to the United Nations Regular Budget* [ref. REP].

for international organizations has a significant impact on government budgets and contributors and, at the same time, is a business opportunity for individuals and enterprises.[3]

To manage these resources and balance the interests connected to them, a body of hard and soft rules has been gradually developed which regulates the relationships between international organizations and private parties. Whereas private subjects are free to choose their contractual counterparts, international organizations – similarly to national administrations – are bound to a set of administrative rules which govern primarily the vendor selection phase and, for certain aspects, also the contract. In 1962 Jenks envisaged the development of an international administrative law that would go beyond governing relationships between the organization and its officials to apply to relationships between international administrations and third parties as well:

> [a]s international organization develops certain matters cease to be governed by the conflict of laws and become subject to international administrative law. Within a generation this process has been virtually completed in respect of the legal relations of international organizations with their officials and employees ... At a later stage some of the legal relations and transactions of international organizations with third parties may become subject to international administrative law. At each successive stage of development difficulties may arise in determining whether the balance of advantage lies in applying the normal rules of conflict ...[4]

Rules governing international organizations' procurement are the latest steps of an evolutionary process from non-proceduralized modalities of administrative action to a more proceduralized and accountable exercise of functions by international organizations which affect private subjects not only – and not much – through a unilateral exercise of authority but mainly through their contractual activity. This regulatory phenomenon includes three apparently conflicting elements. First, for their functioning international organizations mainly rely on forms of cooperation with private subjects: the procurement procedure usually ends in a bilateral or multilateral public-private agreement (the contract).

---

[3] European Union, *EU Official Development Assistance Reaches Highest Level Ever*, Brussels, *press release*, 11 April 2017, also available at https://ec.europa.eu/europeaid/news-and-events/eu-official-development-assistance-reaches-highest-level-ever_en; and also OECD, *Development Aid Rises Again in 2016*, 11 April 2017, also available at http://www.oecd.org/dac/development-aid-rises-again-in-2016-but-flows-to-poorest-countries-dip.htm.

[4] Jenks, *The Proper Law*, pp. xxxvii–xxxix.

Second, in their contractual activity organizations become more and more bound by rules of action that confer administrative duties on the organizations and corresponding legal positions on private subjects. Third, despite the adoption of a cooperative paradigm, the proceduralization of contractual activity and the corresponding development of rights of private subjects, international organizations retain forms of administrative privilege over private subjects that the organizations claim to be justified by their international and public nature. Thus, this book aims to answer some questions arising from the observation of these trends. The first regards the features of the phenomenon: to what extent the procurement rules and practices of international organizations create rights for individuals[5] vis-à-vis international organizations? In carrying out procurement, do international organizations affect individuals through unilateral command mode patterns or, on the contrary, through a cooperative approach which provides for an even distribution of rights and duties among the parties of the process? More in general, in which direction the emergence of procurement rules of international organizations moves the balance point between international public authority and individual rights? Are these procurement procedures structured in such a way that they can function as legitimating devices for international organizations? These issues will be investigated in both direct and indirect procurement of international organizations. The former is the procurement directly carried out by international organizations. The latter is the procurement financed, regulated and supervised by international organizations, but implemented by recipient states. For this latter type of procurement, the questions set above have further implications. Regulation and supervision of international organizations over states, on one hand, entails the emergence, or strengthening, of private subjects' rights vis-à-vis states. On the other, it has a restrictive impact on the states' regulatory, administrative and contractual autonomy. Thus, the questions above also imply an analysis of the limits that international organizations put on such autonomy. The second set of questions relate to the causes of the phenomenon and draw a connection between the politics and the law of international organizations: how can the development of these rights, and the limits to it, be explained? Can they be understood in the light of the interplay of conflicting political and

---

[5] 'Contractual' is widely construed here to include the pre-contractual phase (selection of vendors), the contractual (negotiation and conclusion of the contract) and the post-contractual phase (contract execution).

economic interests underlying the international organizations' institutional dynamics? Avoiding too simplistic analogies to domestic law, this second set of questions is important to assess whether a further step towards a more transparent, accountable and cooperative exercise of international public authority is desirable and possible, and if possible, under what conditions. As will be shown, states play a crucial role in shaping the international organizations' institutional dynamics, and in extending or shrinking the scope of individual rights vis-à-vis international organizations. When it comes to exploring the reasons for the development of procurement rules and practices of international organizations, states are the active subjects which carry strong or weak political and economic interests, and concur to determine the emergence of private subjects' rights, but also their limits and the shortcomings in their effectiveness.

The answers to the questions set above require an analysis of several aspects. These include: the identification of the principles that guide the procurement activity of international organizations when carrying out procurement, both in regulatory terms and in practice; an understanding and assessment of the accountability mechanisms in place; an analysis of the contractual equilibria, to check whether contract negotiation and the clauses governing its execution fulfil the interests of both parties, or rather crystallize the primacy of international public interests over private ones; the identification of the dynamics of interests that shape the relationship between international organizations and private subjects.

This book is the first academic contribution on the topic. Despite the economic importance of the issue, the emergence of this regulatory framework and its significant implications for the debate on global governance, the procurement activity of international organizations has never been subjected to a comprehensive and in-depth legal analysis. With the exception of certain studies which appeared in the 1960s and 1970s on some aspects of international organizations' contractual activity,[6] and a few works dealing with a specific sector or a specific organization,[7] there is virtually no scholarship in

---

[6] For bibliographical references see footnotes in Chapter 4 and 5.

[7] The few works focusing on a specific sector are: with reference to defence procurement, Heuninckx, *The Law of Collaborative Defence Procurement through International Organisations in the EU*; id., 'Applicable Law to the Procurement of International Organisations in the European Union'; id., *The Law of Collaborative Defence Procurement in the European Union*; with reference to humanitarian food

this area. There are several reasons for this lack of attention to this emerging phenomenon. First, the phenomenon is relatively new. As the historical chapter of this volume shows, international organizations have undergone a lengthy process of reform that started to have concrete implementation only in the last decade through, for instance, the issuing of hard and soft rules and the pursuit of stricter observance of these rules. Second, the phenomenon is difficult to detect as it is not manifested at the macro level through traditional international public law tools such as international treaties or rulings by international courts. Instead, it emerges out of small incremental pieces of law, such as administrative regulations, circulars and procurement manuals, and is not shaped, with the exception of a few organizations, by judgments on this matter. Third, the practice of international organizations plays a fundamental role in the implementation of the rules, often *de facto* altering the letter of the norms. Moreover, on one hand it is extremely difficult, without working experience in international organizations, to acquire an in-depth knowledge of the implementing dynamics that follow the rules. On the other hand, although practitioners may have diverse and extensive work experience in the field, they have rarely chosen to investigate the implications that this body of rules and practices has on the paradigms that guide the exercise of public authority by international organizations and its possible reforms.

assistance, Sakane, 'Challenges for Humanitarian Food Assistance'; with reference to peacekeeping operations, *id.*, 'Public Procurement of UNPKO'. Works dealing with a specific organization or group of organizations are Reynaud, 'Le recours precontractuel au sein des marches publics des organisations internationales. Le cas de l'Agence Spatiale Europeenne'; and Neumann, *Procurement in the United Nations System* (mainly focused on UNIDO). Other works focus on procurement by financial institutions: Caroli Casavola, *La globalizzazione dei contratti delle pubbliche amministrazioni*, pp. 119–150; Williams-Elegbe, *Public Procurement and Multilateral Development Banks*; Lachimia, *Tied Aid and Development Aid Procurement in the Framework of EU and WTO Law*; de Castro Meireles, *The World Bank Procurement Regulations*; Verdeaux, 'The World Bank and Public Procurement'; and Morlino, 'Development Aid and the Europeanization of Public Procurement in Non-EU States'. Works taking a general approach are Killmann, 'Procurement Activities of International Organizations'; Renouf, 'When Legal Certainty Matters Less than a Deal' Carbonnier, 'Procurement of Goods and Services by International Organisations in Donor Countries'; and Morlino, 'Procurement Regimes of International Organizations'; *id.*, 'Cosmopolitan Democracy or Administrative Rights? International Organizations as Public Contractors'. More generally, on the relationships between international organizations and the private sector see Kell, 'Relations with the Private Sector'.

1.2   Research Design

Although the analysis concerns international organizations, it does not cover *all* international organizations. In this regard, I wish to clarify three points. The first is how the organizations have been identified, i.e. the methodology I have used to select the empirical referent. The second is why I have chosen certain organizations in my examples, that is the relevance of some organizations for my research purposes. The third is which organizations I have considered in my analysis, that is the actual object of analysis.

At the outset of my research – even before the identification of the research questions that then guided my analysis – the preliminary problem was to understand whether or not international organizations (all, some, or just a few) had rules that governed their procurement, just as states do. Thus, I conducted an empirical investigation following three stages of progressively increasing depth and focus. In the first stage, I carried out a preliminary study of about eighty intergovernmental organizations selected *prima facie* and on the basis of elements such as the organization's size, functions, activities and the possible presence or absence of internal rules regulating their institutional activities. This initial analysis allowed me to make a shortlist of approximately forty organizations relevant for my purposes. The shortlist included organizations of the UN family as well as other organizations. In a second stage, I compared the shortlisted organizations specifically with regard to their procurement, attempting in particular to identify the differences among the organizations in terms of procurement spending and development of specific regulatory architectures for procurement. In a third stage, from a slightly smaller empirical basis (approximately thirty-five organizations), I identified, on the one hand, the more common procurement organization and regulation patterns with their main characteristics and, on the other, the more notable exceptions to these patterns. In a fourth and final phase, corresponding to Chapter 2, I traced the connections between the types of organizations as identified by the relevant literature, and the characteristics of procurement as resulting from the conceptualization of the phenomenon. Thus, of these four stages, only the last is presented explicitly as such to the reader, while the others are implicit and preliminary.

With regard to relevance, the idea underlying the research has been not so much to take into account all international organizations regardless of size, functions and importance in the international context, but to consider all organizations that manifested, to a greater or lesser extent, the phenomenon of procurement and its legal implications, i.e. procurement regulation. The aim of the book is not neutral and all-encompassing. Rather, it is to answer some research questions and to identify the causes and consequences of a phenomenon from that point of view. Thus, I have assessed the relevance of the organizations on the basis of three criteria. The first is the presence of established rules and related practices of procurement within an organization. The second is the guiding role that the regulatory patterns of some organizations seem to have and their capacity to influence the rule making of other organizations (these driving patterns are often found in organizations with greater procurement volumes). The third, exactly opposite to the second, is the criterion of 'deviation'. In other words, I deemed interesting those regulatory solutions (and, by extension, the organizations that adopted them) that deviated, even if only in specific aspects, from the common patterns.

These three criteria led me to choose as examples – and here I come to the point of identifying the object of the analysis – a transversal variety of organizations mainly, but not only, belonging to the UN system. Certainly, the United Nations and its agencies are the most frequently mentioned examples as they are among the largest organizations, with greater procurement volumes and often with a developed apparatus of rules, but they are not the only organizations that I choose to explicitly mention in the work and, above all, are not the only organizations that constituted the empirical basis of my research. The European Union, the European Space Agency (ESA), the North Atlantic Treaty Organization (NATO) – to mention but a few – are some of the institutions that are relevant examples of 'deviations' from the most common regulatory patterns of procurement and are important for understanding in a comparative perspective the differences in the dynamics and interests underlying the different types of procurement.

1.3   Theoretical Framework

As noted, the relationship between international organizations and private subjects as well as the exercise of authority by international organizations affecting private subjects and states within the procurement process are the core issues explored in the book. The choice of this particular viewpoint on the activity of international organizations was determined by an empirical observation of the historical evolution and recent developments in international organizations. At the same time, this choice had an influence on the theoretical tools that have been chosen for the analysis. In this regard, some preliminary considerations are useful to clarify the theoretical background of the research and understand how this work relates to the existing literature on international organizations.

First, the approach on which the analysis has been built is inductive. The observance of the increasing magnitude and functions of international organizations has led me to explore what actually made possible the exercise of these functions, i.e. procurement, and, in turn, to investigate how this procurement activity was exercised, according to which rules and affecting which subjects. This preliminary empirical investigation showed that, although the phenomenon has never received attention from scholars, international organizations function thanks to procurement; over the years they have slowly developed rules governing procurement; and, most importantly, their procurement activity and the connected rules affect private as well as public subjects.

Second, these empirical findings needed some tools to be read, analyzed and interpreted. The most straightforward way to do this was to turn to the categories developed by the literature on international institutional law, as it has been the stream of literature that most comprehensively explored the internal functioning of the international organizations and the rules governing them.[8] Although being of crucial importance to understand the statics and dynamics of international organizations, this literature proves, however, to be tailored to an idea of international organizations that does not include an analysis of their procurement activity, of the rules governing it or of the legal problems arising from its implementation. The lack of analysis on this aspect of international organizations can be explained by two reciprocally related factors.

The first regards the actors that are deemed to be involved in and affected by the law of international organizations. International institutional law is mainly concerned with relations between international

---

[8] Seminal works in this regard are Sands and Klein, *Bowett's Law of International Institutions*; Schermers and Blokker, *International Institutional Law*; Amerasinghe, *Principles of the Institutional Law of International Organizations*. The traditional model of international institutional law, based on functionalism, however, has been questioned by Klabbers, see *inter alia* Klabbers, *An Introduction to International Organizations Law*; *id.* 'The Emergence of Functionalism in International Institutional Law'; *id.*, 'The Transformation of International Organizations Law'.

organizations and their member states. Thus, on one hand, it relates to intra-organizational relationships; while, on the other hand, as pointed out by some scholars, organizations' external relations are mainly conceptualized in terms of their treaty-making powers.[9]

The second factor is a consequence of the first. Based on the idea that there is a principal, i.e. the member states, assigning one or more functions to their agent, i.e. the international organizations,[10] international institutional law is built on the observation of a link between the functions exercised by the organizations and the rules governing them. The application of the principal–agent theory to organizations has been conceptualized in terms of functionalism.[11] International institutional law based on functionalism has had, on one side, the merit to describe and explain – when there were not yet descriptions and explanations – how international organizations are legally structured and carry out their activities. On the other side, the emphasis on functions, and their connection with the member states as subjects attributing them, implies also the tendency to view international organizations as subjects that are not accountable to any subjects other than states, but also that *should not* be accountable to any subjects other than states by virtue of the function exercised.[12] It is emblematic in this respect that, to the limited extent that relations with third parties are concerned, those are deemed to be governed by the doctrine of privileges and immunities of international organizations and responsibility comes into play, when it does, mainly as responsibility under international law. Moreover, emphasizing descriptive aspects without providing a critical analysis of these aspects gives the descriptive approach a normative value, because it is not questioned. But while this might have reflected and worked well with the traditional

---

[9] Klabbers, 'The Transformation of International Organizations Law', p. 22.

[10] On the control problems that the principal–agent relationship poses, see Vaubel, 'Principal-Agent Problems in International Organizations'.

[11] Klabbers has provided a seminal definition of 'functionalism': '[i]n a nutshell, as I shall reconstruct it, [functionalism] is essentially a principal–agent theory, with a collective principal (the member states) assigning one or more specific tasks – functions – to their agent', see Klabbers, 'The Transformation of International Organizations Law', p. 10.

[12] The normative component of international institutional law is explained by Klabbers in the following passage: '[a]dmittedly, functionalism in international organizations law has a descriptive component, but it is not a theory on how international organizations law works – in fact, it is far more normative than just this ... [F]unctionalism at the core of international organizations law aims to tell us how organizations should and may behave, not how they actually behave. It is in essence a theory not about law (not even institutional law) but, rather, about international organizations and their relationship to their member states', *ibid.*, p. 20.

concept of public power, it has become inadequate to explain the changes international public institutions are undergoing and, in particular, those regarding the relationship between these institutions and private subjects. Indeed, as a result of these most recent developments, the investigation must also include an assessment of how private parties are affected by the exercise of this power, as well as an investigation of the mechanisms of accountability, if any, and of the consequences these have on the legitimacy of international organizations.

Precisely for the purposes of considering these aspects, this work integrates the international institutional law perspective with that of global administrative law. It is then worth explaining for what reasons, in what ways, and within what limits my research takes a global administrative law approach and why I speak of integration with international institutional law and not substitution *tout court*. These reasons are in part implicit in what is discussed above regarding international institutional law, and in part autonomous and related to the particular activity being researched, i.e. procurement.

Breaking the expression 'global administrative law' (GAL)[13] into each of its component parts, i.e. global, administrative and law, and starting with the administrative component, there are two reasons for taking an administrative perspective. The first is to account for and highlight the growing, empirically observed, tendency of international organizations to affect and determine the legal positions of private parties. If administrative law is the law that typically governs the exercise of public powers and its relationships with private subjects, the administrative law perspective is particularly suitable for investigating, and questioning, public power and how it is exercised with regard to private subjects. This assessment is made in the light of the historic evolution of administrative law from the law *of* public administration to the law *on* public administrations, with its implications in terms of accountability and transparency. Of course, this approach requires as a prerequisite to

---

[13] Global administrative law literature is now rich and diversified. Without pretending to be exhaustive, see *ex multis* Kingsbury, Krisch and Stewart, 'The Emergence of Global Administrative Law'; Cassese (ed.), *Research Handbook on Global Administrative Law*; Cassese *et al.* (eds.), *Global Administrative Law: The Casebook*; and Casini and Kingsbury, 'Global Administrative Law Dimensions of International Organizations'. And from a normative perspective, see Savino, 'What If Global Administrative Law Is a Normative Project?'; and Stewart, 'The Normative Dimensions and Performance of Global Administrative Law'. Having a number of features that differ from the concepts developed in the GAL literature, but in many ways related to it, see von Bogdandy *et al.* (eds.), *The Exercise of Public Authority by International Institutions*.

interpret international organizations as administrations, in the sense of Dahl's proposed definition as bureaucratic bargaining systems[14] or, at least, to consider the administrative aspects of international organizations as constituent aspects.

This brings us to the second of the two reasons. Procurement by international organizations is intrinsically administrative and cannot be otherwise interpreted. Indeed, it not only involves the creation of procedural and contractual relationships between international organizations and private parties just in the same way as this happens in procurement by domestic public administrations, but also the procedures used to implement it and the rules governing it are based on those developed for domestic public administrations. This can be seen both by following the evolving process of how international organizations adopted these laws over time, and by analyzing the content of current procurement rules in relation to those applied to states. This connection must nevertheless also consider the political and institutional specifics of organizations and how international dynamics influence administrative regulations, resulting in a distortion of the regulatory model conceived for national administrations. In this regard, later in the book I refer to an anomalous type of legal transplant.[15]

Going on to the 'global' component and why this adjective is used to describe the administrative law perspective, we must once again begin by identifying the parties involved in procurement by international organizations and recognizing that neither the international dimension, nor the national administrative law dimension alone, offers a sufficient understanding of the phenomenon and its regulation. As will be explained in greater detail in Chapters 2 and 8, neither the emergence of procurement regulation, nor the functioning and application of the rules are based exclusively on either the binary relationship between international organizations and member states, or on the equally binary relationship between international organizations and private parties. On the contrary, the emergence of the rules and their implementation are based on a tripartite relationship among international organizations, states, and private subjects. The meaning of the adjective 'global' thus encompasses this particular relationship, which transcends the international and the national dimension.

---

[14] Dahl defines international organizations as *bureaucratic* bargaining systems, see Dahl, 'Can International Organisations Be Democratic?'

[15] See Chapter 8.

Finally, a last comment on the term 'law'. I use it broadly to include hard and soft law instruments because procurement regulations are mixed in this regard. However, my approach is not positivistic: an in-depth understanding of procurement by international organizations goes beyond an analysis of rules alone and is possible only by looking at rules and practice parallel to each other. Lack of oversight and accountability mechanisms in fact makes the discrepancy between rules and practice much more significant in international organizations than at the national level, essentially creating a difference between the normative dimension (that of rules), in the sense of what ought to be, and the actual dimension (that of practice), in the sense of what is.

In addition to these considerations, it should be nevertheless noted that the global administrative law approach alone does not allow for a full understanding of the phenomenon of procurement by international organizations, at least if we assume a strictly procedural approach of administrative law. Procurement by organizations and its regulation and implementation have an impact on private parties. They are largely determined by the interplay of political-economic interests, and by the interaction between international organizations and member states, and between the states themselves.[16] The dimension on which international institutional law is based is thus essential for a deeper understanding of the administrative procedural dimension and, in turn, the administrative procedural dimension is fundamental to develop a critical approach to the *status quo* that is reflected in the empirical findings. In this sense, I speak of integrating the two approaches rather than substituting one for the other. Put differently, one could also say that the categories of global administrative law must be interpreted using an interdisciplinary approach that makes it possible to investigate and understand the politics behind procedural phenomena.

1.4 Structure of the Book

The structure of the book reflects the combination of these approaches. It starts by providing a conceptual analysis of procurement by international organizations and is built around three objectives (Chapter 2). The first is to define the concept of procurement when referring to an international organization. Traditionally, 'public procurement' is the

---

[16] For example, the extent to which the decolonization process has affected the procurement rules is explained in Chapter 3.

term used by scholars and practitioners to indicate a certain empirical referent at the state level. However, when transposed to the realm of international organizations, the empirical referent of the term *procurement* changes, and it describes a partially different reality: international organizations' procurement has specific characteristics associated with the institutional structures and objectives of the organizations. The second objective is to build up a taxonomy of the various types of procurement carried out by international organizations. The third objective is devoted to tracing the links between the types of international organizations, classified according to some commonly agreed criteria, and the procurement they carry out. In other words, it explores how the nature of an international organization influences its procurement activity.

Chapter 3 traces the historical development of procurement regulation and practices within the major international organizations. The history of international organizations is often described by the relevant literature in terms of major policy changes and general administrative reforms. This approach, however, disregards the importance that these changes have had on the means and procedures adopted by international organizations to fulfil their functions and pursue their aims. This chapter traces the evolution of international organization procurement and its regulation, identifying the different stages of development, the main problems that have arisen at each stage and the solutions that have been devised. The analysis correlates the macro level, that is, the political and administrative transformation undergone by the international organizations, with the micro level, that is, the procurement management and its regulation. It argues that there has been a trend to gradually proceduralize and create a legal framework for procurement, which is due not only to an increase in the number and volume of organizational activities, but also to the pressures that financing states have exercised as a result of the shifting political balances within organizations.

Chapter 4 looks at the current discipline and practices of international organizations' procurement. It aims to provide an overview of the common features of vendor selection procedures, considering both direct and indirect procurement, and explaining the discrepancies between rules and practices. It does so also having as a parameter of comparison domestic public procurement law, when the comparative analysis proves to be useful for a better understanding of international organizations' procurement.

Once the vendor selection procedures have been examined, Chapter 5 moves on to analyze the contract eventually concluded. The parties to contracts differ depending on whether procurement is direct or indirect. In the former, contracts are signed between the international organization and a private subject. In the latter, contracts are usually (though not always) concluded between the state and a private subject under the auspices of the financing international organization. While the two situations pose different problems with regard to the contractual relationships, a common question emerges that the chapter seeks to address: do international organizations, by exercising their public authority within a contract, limit or influence the contractual autonomy of another party, be this an individual, an enterprise or a state? And if they do, to what extent do they do so?

Chapter 6 focuses on the law applicable to international organizations' contracts resulting from both direct and indirect procurement. The issue of which law is applicable to the contract is a crucial one in order to assess whether international organizations' contracts retain a private law or public law character. The outcome of such assessment is a further development of the question set forth in Chapter 5 on the exercise of public authority by international organizations with regard to the contract and it completes the view on the contractual balances between international organizations and private parties.

A crucial part of the investigation relates to accountability. A critical examination of accountability mechanisms and their limits and effectiveness with respect to the goals pursued by international organizations is central to assessing the effectiveness of the rules that regulate the vendors' selection phase and the clauses that govern the contractual relationship. It is also important to understand how the balance between the authority and liability of international organizations vis-à-vis private parties is shaped in procurement relations. Chapter 7 is, thus, devoted to an in-depth analysis of accountability mechanisms, including external and internal controls, as well as remedies of private subjects in the vendor selection phase and in contract execution.

Chapter 8 aims to provide an explanation of the rationale for current international organizations' procurement disciplines and practices. To do so it looks into the balance and interplay of economic and political interests that shape the content and development of procurement rules and practices and, hence, into the relationships between international organizations, states and individuals or enterprises that revolve around procurement. The last chapter concludes by summarizing the main findings of the analysis and answering the key questions posed in this introduction.

2

Procurement and International Organizations

A Conceptual Map

2.1 A Problem of Definition

The scarcity of studies on procurement by international organizations poses first of all a problem of definition and delimitation of this phenomenon. Procurement, in an absolute sense and without any specific reference to international organizations, means the process through which a public or private entity procures goods, services or work.[1] The qualification of 'public' or 'government' that sometimes precedes the term 'procurement' points to the nature of the subject that initiates and carries out the procurement process, usually a national administration.[2] Public procurement therefore consists of a proceduralized sequence of administrative acts implemented by a public body or a body governed by public law aimed at obtaining the supply of goods, services or works. This sequence is composed of three chronologically successive phases: the emergence of a procurement need; the selection through a tender of a vendor that can provide the required goods, services or works; and the contract conclusion and implementation. At the national level, these three phases are governed by administrative law (the first two) and by administrative law or common law (the third), depending on whether

---

[1] See *ex multis* Arrowsmith and Davies (eds.), *Public Procurement: Global Revolution*; Arrowsmith, Linarelli and Wallace, *Regulating Public Procurement: National and International Perspectives*; Dimitri, Piga and Spagnolo (eds.), *Handbook of Procurement*; Thai (ed.), *International Handbook of Public Procurement*.

[2] However, this remark only partially applies to legal traditions other than the English one, such as that of the French *contrat administratif,* where the identification of the subject as public is secondary. The public character is instead linked to the explicit and direct legislative or regulatory qualification. See Chabanol, Jouguelet and Bourrachot, *Le régime juridique des marchés publics*; Lichère, *Droit des contrats publics*; Richer, *Droit des contrats administratifs.*

the legal context is that of a civil law or a common law system.[3] The first phase is characterized by internal procedures, involving an exchange of information among national administrative offices. It is governed by rules specifically designed by the national administration for its internal activity. The second phase of the vendor selection regards procedures that have an impact on subjects external to the administration, i.e. the potential contractors. The procedures take place according to rules that are drafted by the administration and govern the relationship between the public procuring entity and private subjects. The third phase is substantive, as the parties agree on the contents of the contract and implement it. The contents of the contract may be the outcome of an agreement between the parties acting on an equal footing or may consist of clauses legitimately imposed by the administration on its private counterpart.

So far, studies on public procurement have focused primarily on national administrations. Also, when examining and theorizing on the 'internationalization' of public procurement, scholars have usually referred to national administrations and to the impact that principles and rules set forth in supranational fora[4] – such as European directives or the Agreement on Government Procurement (GPA) of the World Trade Organization (WTO) – have on the procurement processes of national administrations.

Procurement, however, despite having the descriptive significance mentioned above, acquires a different meaning according to its

---

[3] For a more extensive argumentation on this issue, see later in this chapter. On the general theory of the *contrats administratifs* developed by the French doctrine and jurisprudence, see *inter alia* Rivero, *Droit administrative*, p. 135 *et seq*. For an analysis of how public law elements interact with the private law regime within public procurement contracts in the English legal tradition, see Davies, *The Public Law of Government Contracts, passim*. For a comparative analysis among the various legal traditions, see Georgopulos, Hoekman and C. Mavroidis (eds.), *The Internationalization of Government Procurement Regulation*.

[4] On this, see more extensively Caroli Casavola, *La globalizzazione dei contratti*; Audit and Schill, *Transnational Law of Public Contracts*; Rege, 'Transparency in Government Procurement'; Arrowsmith and Davies, *Public Procurement: Global Revolution*; Arrowsmith, Linarelli and Wallace, *Regulating Public Procurement*; Auby, 'L'internationalisation du droit des contrats publics'; *id.*, *La globalisation, le droit et l'État*; Reich, *International Public Procurement Law*; Trionfetti, 'Home-based Government Procurement and International Trade'; Clerc, 'La mondialisation des marchés publics'. On the role of the WB on procurement, see *inter alia* Evenett and Hoekman, 'Government Procurement: Market Access, Transparency and Multilateral Trade Rules'; Hunja, 'Recent Revisions to the World Bank's Procurement'; Tucker, 'A Critical Analysis of the Procurement Procedures of the World Bank'; Arrowsmith, 'Transparency in Government Procurement'.

contextual anchoring. Its empirical referents change depending on whether it is procurement by states or by international organizations. Procurement by international organizations may not only, or not necessarily, include the empirical referents typical of national public procurement. Indeed, although taking national public procurement regulation as a model, procurement by international organizations has some distinctive features due to the different institutional structures and purposes of such organizations. Furthermore, it has followed an autonomous path of development, marked by the political and administrative changes that the organizations have undergone.[5]

Contextualization within international organizations and emancipation from the national dimension have led to a broadening of the denotation[6] of the term 'procurement' and to the integration of the definition of procurement at the national level with other features linked to the international context. When referring to international organizations, procurement not only indicates the sequence of the three phases process implemented by national procuring entities, but also is generally understood as the procedure set by international organizations for the procurement of goods, services and works instrumental to the pursuit of their institutional purposes, *whether or not* it is the international organization to materially implement the procurement process. Thus, procurement by international organizations has two distinctive fixed features: the nature of the subject that initiates procurement, directly or indirectly, is public and international (whereas the subject that actually carries out the procurement may not only be a public and international subject but also a national administration or a private subject); and the primary and ultimate purpose of procurement is the pursuit of the institutional mission of an international organization.

Besides these two fixed features, there are at least five variable features: the secondary or instrumental purposes of procurement; its modalities of execution; its regulation; the mechanisms of accountability in place; and the contract. The various features are shaped according to a mechanism of univocal dependence, by virtue of which the modalities of execution vary according to variations in the secondary purposes. Regulation, accountability mechanisms and the type of contract concluded change

---

[5] See Chapters 3 and 8.
[6] Denotation is here used as opposed to connotation, where the former is the precise literal meaning of a word, while the latter is the meaning that that word assumes consequent to a wide array of positive and negative associations and to the use of the word in a specific context. See Barthes, *Elements of Semiology*; Chandler, *Semiotics*.

according to the modality of execution. Regulation, accountability mechanisms and contracts are therefore direct functions of the modalities of execution and indirect functions of the secondary purposes. Being variable, these features reciprocally combine, giving rise to three main types of procurement by international organizations, which in turn constitute the empirical referents of the phenomenon.

2.1.1 Purposes

Secondary or instrumental purposes are the material needs which procurement promptly and actually serves. These may be internal or external. The former consist of the organization's everyday needs, which are instrumental to its good functioning. The procurement of office furniture, safety devices, computers and printers, consumer goods such as stationery, power, water and even procurement to build infrastructure for hosting the headquarters of the organizations serve internal purposes. This type of procurement is also often defined as corporate procurement. External purposes refer to the satisfaction of the needs of beneficiaries outside the organizations. Examples include procurement for the reconstruction of schools and hospitals in post-conflict territories, the supply of vaccines to fight epidemics, the monitoring and observation of internal elections and legal support for reforms of national legislation. This type of procurement is often indicated as project procurement, when it involves, for instance, a development project.

As we shall see, the different purposes do not affect regulation. To a limited extent, however, they have an impact on the interplay of interests underlying procurement. Procurement for internal purposes usually takes place in the countries where the organizations have their headquarters. Many of these are Western countries, which are also the stronger financiers of the organizations and whose undertakings are often awarded contracts in this type of procurement. In contrast, procurement for external purposes can also be, and often is, carried out in developing countries. Hence, the undertakings belonging to those countries have an increased chance of taking part in the procurement process and asserting their interests in the procedure. Chapter 8 will show, however, how these interests alter the general dynamics of procurement only to a very limited extent.

2.1.2 Modalities of Execution

The second variable feature is represented by modalities of execution, that is the modalities according to which procurement is carried out. These may be either direct, such as the Direct Execution (DEX) procedure, or indirect, such as the procedure to implement projects funded by financial institutions, the procedure using a letter of assist, or the National Execution (NEX) procedure used in non-financial organizations.

In direct execution, international organizations, through their competent offices, manage the typical three-phased procurement procedure (emergence of the need for procurement, tender procedure and contract implementation). The procedure for the selection of the contractor is, at least to a certain extent, similar to that followed by national public procurement entities.[7] The final contract may be concluded either with public or private subjects, such as private enterprises, international non-governmental organizations (INGOs), governments and other international agencies.

Conversely, in indirect modalities of execution, the international organization does not itself carry out the procurement procedure. This is performed by another public or private subject in agreement with the international organization. Indirect modalities of execution include a range of different variants. For example, in UN peacekeeping and peacebuilding missions, states may carry out the necessary procurement by virtue of an agreement, known as a 'letter of assist', between the organization and the states.

Another variant is that adopted by organizations with primary social and humanitarian purposes that operate through projects and programmes. International organizations, such as the UNDP, entrust the beneficiary state with the actual implementation of the single project or programme, including the related procurement.

A third variant is used by international financial institutions that grant loans to single states for the implementation of projects developed with, and approved by, the financing institutions. The project must fall within the institutional mission and purposes of these institutions. By virtue of an agreement with the financing institution, the beneficiary state carries out the procurement according to the rules and principles on procurement set forth in the agreement and in the texts to which the agreement refers. This is the case, for example, of the World Bank (WB), the Asian

---

[7] See Chapter 4.

Development Bank (ADB), the African Development Bank (AfDB), the Inter-American Development Bank (IDB), the European Bank for Reconstruction and Development (EBRD) and the International Fund for Agricultural Development (IFAD). EU institutions financing development projects through the European Development Fund (EDF) are in-between the second and the third variants.

In a fourth variant an international organization can allocate a task or a function belonging to the organization to another international organization which, in turn, will carry out this task or fulfil this function by procuring the goods, services and works needed for the purpose. For example, some organizations of the UN system, such as the United Nations, may allocate the implementation of a project to another UN agency, such as United Nations Office for Project Services (UNOPS).[8]

Finally, an international organization can outsource a task or an entire function belonging to the organization to a private subject that will in turn carry out this task or fulfil this function by procuring the goods, services and works needed for the purpose. Often this variant is used for internal purposes.[9]

Thus, two basic types of procurement may be identified in the practice of international organizations: direct procurement, which involves private parties as suppliers of goods, services or works; and indirect procurement, in its multiple variants (procedures by means of a letter of assist; NEX; procedures typical of financial institutions; procedures involving other international organizations; procedures involving private parties as the executors of a function or a task of the organization).

2.1.3 Regulation

The third variable feature concerns regulation and its three main elements: regulators, regulated subjects and the subject matter of regulation. This feature is shaped according to the purposes and the modalities of execution and changes depending on whether procurement is direct or indirect.

2.1.3.1 Direct Procurement

In direct procurement, the sources of regulation and its addressees coincide. Within organizations, the bodies in charge of drafting the

---

[8] On the reciprocal relations between international organizations, see Boisson de Chazournes, 'Relations with Other International Organizations'.
[9] See JIU, *Review of United Nations Outsourcing Practices*, para. 2 [ref. REP].

rules are usually not those bound to abide by them. The former are *ad hoc* commissions; the latter are requisitioners and procurement officers. At a macro level, however, they both belong to the organization and are internal to it. The rules regulate both the procedural and the contractual phases. Furthermore, in addition to the indirect references made in funding treaties, the procedural rules on procurement are generally included in the organization's financial regulations and administrative circulars,[10] which since the 1980s have been complemented or replaced by procurement manuals, mainly addressed to the staff of the organizations.[11] Unlike these, the clauses applicable to a contract and unilaterally imposed by organizations on private parties, which are included in the general terms and conditions, are drawn up by each organization and attached to the call for tenders. Therefore, procurement regulation relates both to the procedures to be followed for choosing a vendor and to some aspects of the contract.

2.1.3.2   Indirect Procurement through Letter of Assist

The more complex structure of indirect procurement, on the contrary, implies a thoroughly different regulatory framework. In procedures through a letter of assist, the political agreement between the international organization and the state generally leaves the latter much room for discretion. In this case, the subject matter of regulation is the procurement carried out by states. Regulators and the subjects regulated are both at the national level: the rules applied to procurement are drafted by the national legislator and the administrations subject to these rules are national. The subjects that perform procurement define their own rules.

2.1.3.3   Indirect Procurement through NEX and Loan Agreements

The NEX procedures[12] and the procedures of financial institutions are, in contrast, examples of hybrid regulation. In these cases, there is an

---

[10] This statement indicates a general trend. The development of procurement manuals is currently being carried out by most organizations, but not by all. For the main phases of the development process towards the codification of procurement rules by international organizations, see Chapter 3.

[11] On these, see more detail in Chapter 3.

[12] NEX has been defined as 'a method of carrying out programmes and projects where national entities retain the main responsibility for planning, formulating and managing the programme or project supported or funded by the United Nations system, for carrying out the activities and for the achievement of objectives and impact. The national authority becomes accountable for the formulation and management of

agreement between the organization and the state for the implementation of a project or a programme. The organization's choice of a subject to be entrusted with a function or a single operation is, of course, not the result of a quantitative and qualitative evaluation of the offers submitted (as, for instance, in direct procurement), but rather of complex economic, political and social assessments made within the framework of the institutional mission of each international organization.

The organization may develop some general strategies and, within them, draw up projects and programmes in collaboration with the representatives of the states concerned. Alternatively it is the state itself that submits to the organization a request for financial support or for a loan to implement a project that falls within some economic, social or political purposes of the organization. In agreement with the organization and with the support of *ad hoc* technical bodies identified by the latter , e.g. technical commissions or teams of experts, the state also drafts the project. The distinction between the two inputs is, however, often blurred due to the complexity of the organizations and the variety of their internal procedures, and the existence of a continuous exchange between the organizations' officers and the state representatives.

The state implements the project according to the agreement. A greater or lesser degree of autonomy of the state in the implementation stage is granted after an assessment by the international organization of the state's capability. This should also be understood in relation to the suitability of the national legislation to regulate the procurement procedures. In this regard, some organizations choose a minimalist option

programmes and projects by the programme country, in close cooperation with other national and United Nations entities' (Administrative Committee on Coordination (ACC), *National Execution and Implementation Arrangements* [ref. AP&R]; similarly see UNDP, *Financial Rules and Regulations,* 2005 [ref. AP&R]). Since the 1970s, the General Assembly has embarked on a process of restructuring the United Nations system (see Chapter 3). In 1976 the Governing Council of UNDP for the first time introduced national execution, originally designated as government execution (UNDP, *Government Execution of Projects* [ref. AP&R]). Subsequently, the General Assembly, in its resolution 47/199 of 22 December 1992 (UN General Assembly, *Triennial Policy Review of the Operational Activities* [ref. RES]), reiterated that national execution should be the norm for programmes and projects supported by the United Nations system. On NEX, also see Andic, Huntington and Maurer, *National Execution*; Galvani and Morse, 'Institutional Sustainability', p. 316; JIU, *National Execution of Projects* [ref. REP], which stresses the difficulties and problems encountered in the way in which NEX was put into practice and *inter alia* the lack of cooperation and coordination between partners and the low involvement of specialized agencies at all levels of the process; and JIU, *National Execution of Technical Cooperation Projects* [ref. REP].

requiring only a compatibility test on national legislation: when carrying out the procurement financed by the organization, the beneficiary state abides by its own legislation, but this has to be compatible with the principles on procurement set out by the organization. The assessments to be made by the organization are therefore twofold: one quantitative and the other qualitative. The organization ascertains the presence of a specific national set of rules regulating procurement and, in the case of a successful result, checks its compatibility with the international organization's rules on procurement. If, after the compatibility assessment, some rules turn out to be in conflict with the guidelines of the organization, they are disregarded and the relevant rules of the organization are applied. Other organizations, however, adopt a more maximalist option, according to which the main source of procurement regulation is the organization itself: the international organization provides the financial support and/or the loan for the implementation of the project conditional upon the adoption of the procurement rules drafted by the organization for states. This latter option, perhaps, is needed especially, but not only, in the case of states whose national procurement rules are scarce or non-existent.

The procurement rules set by the international organization may thus have different functions depending on their connection with, and impact on, national law: they may function as an external parameter to assess the national legislation on procurement; they may integrate national legislation (the integrative function); or they can substitute it (the substitutive function). In the first case, the rules of the international organization do not become part of the national law and the regulator and regulated subject coincide to the extent that they both belong to the national level. In the second scenario, the integration may be partial when some of the national rules conflict with the guiding principles set forth by the international organization, but it can also be total when there is a full regulatory gap in national legislation. In the third hypothesis, the rules of the international organization become temporarily an integral part of the law system of a state and replace all the existing national procurement rules for the implementation of that special project. The partially integrative function implies the presence of a hybrid regulator, the state and the international organization, and a single regulated subject, i.e. the national administration. When the international organization, instead, exercises a totally integrative function or a substitutive function, there is a single regulator, i.e. the international organization, and a single regulated subject, i.e. the state.

These dynamics are interesting from the point of view of administrative law and have also been observed in other types of administrative procedures. For instance, with regard to the citizens' right to participate in some national administrative procedures provided for by supranational rules, the rules imposed on national law systems 'from above' create a vertical opening, meaning that they force the authorities of a state to take private subjects into account.[13] In indirect procurement by international organizations, there is a similar phenomenon, but with a wider scope. The international organization does not only intervene in the relationship between the national administration and its citizens by creating for the latter new rights vis-à-vis their own administration. When performing a substitutive or a totally integrative function, the international organization might also provide for the adoption of an entire piece of legislation. In this way it informs the functioning of national administrations and guarantees that citizens may rely upon a whole range of procedural rights, rather than upon single rights, such as that of participation.[14]

Moreover, integration and substitution can have permanent effects on national legal systems. Especially in states with serious regulatory leaks, the permeability of the law system allows a transition from temporary integration and substitution to lasting legislative changes supported by the organization and consisting of the permanent inclusion in the national law system of the procurement rules drawn up at the supranational level.[15]

Constructivist scholars[16] have analysed the spread and the adoption within states of rules developed by international organizations or by other states in their international interactions. Finnemore and Sikkink identify a norm life cycle made up of three stages.[17] A first stage is norm emergence, in which individuals who are linked to an international

---

[13] Cassese, *Oltre lo Stato*, p. 137.

[14] The right to participation can be limited, however, by the regional character of the organization. On this point, see later in this chapter.

[15] On this, see Audit and Schill (eds.), *Transnational Law, passim*.

[16] More extensively on the constructivist theory, see Adler, 'Constructivism'; Barnett, 'Social Constructivism'; Fearon and Wendt, 'Rationalism vs. Constructivism'; Finnemore and Sikkink, 'International Norm Dynamics'; *id.*, 'Taking Stock'; Hay, 'Constructivist Institutionalism'; Hurd, 'Constructivism'.

[17] The definition of 'norm' provided by Finnemore and Sikkink is the following: 'a standard of appropriate behaviour for actors with a given identity' (Finnemore and Sikkink, 'International Norm Dynamics', p. 250). Similar definitions can be found in: Katzenstein, *The Culture of National Security*, p. 5; Finnemore, *National Interests in International Society*, p. 22.

organizational and operate as national representatives, and more rarely as officers, promote a specific rule or best practice within governmental or non-governmental international organizations or within networks of organizations.[18]

Once the promoters of a rule have managed to convince a certain number of states, whose acceptance of the rule is required to reach the so-called threshold or tipping point, the process turns to the second stage. The 'critical' states are those whose non-acceptance would jeopardize the essential purpose of the rule. For example, a rule prohibiting the use of anti-personnel mines would be useless without the acceptance of the states that manufacture or use such mines in their own military operations. The second stage is characterized by the successive adoption of the rule by an increasing number of states. This process is defined as 'international socialization' and scholars have proposed three reasons to explain the phenomenon: pressure for conformity and compliance; desire to enhance international legitimacy; and desire on the part of state leaders to enhance their public reputation. This means that states are led to accept a rule in their law system in order to show their alignment with the international community; to increase their legitimacy in the international arena; or even, through their leaders, to gain the esteem of their political counterparts in the international arena.

The third stage is that of internalization: the adopted rule becomes part of the national law system and, whenever required, is implemented by means of new organizational structures or by assigning new duties to existing bodies. The adoption of the procurement rules of international organizations by states may in part be interpreted in the light of constructivist theories, but also shows characteristics of its own which instead seem to refer to rational choices by international public actors. First of all, the rules at stake are not substantive, like most of the rules taken into account by constructivist theory, but rather have a procedural and administrative nature.

Second, if it is true that the adoption of an institutionalized administrative procedure by an international organization is the prerequisite for its later adoption by states, it is also true that, besides compliance, legitimation and reputation, there are at least two other reasons that guide states. The adoption of the procurement rules of an organization is

---

[18] The content of the norm is largely determined by the institutional mission of the organization and its administrative structure. On WB and UN norms, see Finnemore and Sikkink, 'International Norm Dynamics', p. 259.

often linked to internal expediency, rather than to the need for a good international reputation. Procurement procedures are, first of all, a tool for good management. Therefore, in the absence of political or material conditions that allow the adoption of a law reform and/or lacking a regulatory framework on the matter, some states deem it convenient to adopt the set of rules set forth in the guidelines on procurement of some international organizations, often, for instance, the WB. A lack of national rules and the need for them are aspects that some constructivist scholars have pointed out:

> [i]nternational organizations like the UN and the World Bank, though not tailored to norm promotion, may have the advantage of resources and leverage over weak or developing states they seek to convert to their normative convictions.[19]

The second factor that plays an important role in the choice by states to adopt rules set forth by organizations is what may be considered a variant of the third reason indicated by constructivists, i.e. the need to gain esteem and a good reputation. A state may be interested in attracting the most competitive offers and, therefore, in procuring from enterprises incorporated in other states. Within this different framework, esteem is a purpose not referring to an international relationship between two public subjects (a state that 'esteems' another state, i.e. a state's international reputation), but rather to a relationship between a public and a private subject. It is not a question of building a good reputation vis-à-vis other states, like being considered reliable by private enterprises willing to enter into a contract with a state. The adoption of procurement rules drafted at a supranational level, by an international organization, instead of national procurement rules with which the enterprises are unfamiliar, may contribute to this effect.

2.1.3.4 Indirect Procurement through Agreements between International Organizations

The fourth variant of indirect procurement is based on an agreement between international organizations. From a regulatory point of view, this hypothesis does not pose complex problems as usually the organizations agree to undertake the procurement, following the procurement rules of one or other of the organizations that are party to the agreement. For example, in the case of an agreement between the United Nations and

---

[19] Finnemore and Sikkink, 'International Norm Dynamics', p. 260.

UNDP by virtue of which the UNDP will implement a development project funded only or also by the United Nations, the legal sources regulating the procurement activities connected to the project implementation could either be the UN Procurement Manual or the UNDP Programme and Operations Policies and Procedures, depending on the will of the parties. Thus, the agreement may result in a horizontal transfer of regulatory powers from one organization to another. Reforms for the harmonization of procurement rules, especially in organizations of the UN system, are aimed precisely at smoothing this kind of transfer.

2.1.3.5   Indirect Procurement through Private Parties

The fifth variant of indirect procurement is based on a contract between the organization and a private party – which is entrusted with the exercise of a function. On the basis of this, the private party can in turn conclude contracts with other private subjects. The problem of which regulation to apply is therefore posed twice: first, in the selection of the subject to entrust with the function (first phase) and then in the selection of the contractual counterparts for procurement (second phase).

In the first phase, the international organization generally follows the rules for direct procurement that are included in the financial rules in procurement manuals and applies the general terms and conditions of the contract. In this case too, the regulators and the regulated subjects coincide – they are both part of the international organization – and, although the rules of direct procurement apply, the subject matter to be regulated is different. The subject of regulation is the procedure for the selection of an entity to be entrusted with a function, rather than the procedure for the selection of the contractor that provides goods, services and works.

In the second phase, the selection process is regulated and managed by public or private subjects who exercise the public function, but are external to the international organization. In national legal systems, the issue of whether these external private subjects should carry out procurement according to the same rules and principles guiding public administrations has been widely debated. In civil law systems, for example, the option of applying the same rules (in particular those on liability and judicial review) is usually preferred, while in common law systems private subjects can usually follow their own rules as long as these are compatible with the principles guiding national public procurement. Conversely, in the context of international organizations, private subjects are free to follow their own internal rules without specific procedural obligations on how to carry out procurement. However, they often have to adhere to some substantial minimum requirements included in the memorandum of understanding between them and the international organization, including for example, provisions prohibiting the use of child labour or the infringement of human rights.

2.1.4 Mechanisms of Accountability

The fourth variable feature concerns accountability, which encompasses both the control mechanisms on procurement management and the mechanisms through which private subjects may hold the administration accountable in the procedural phases of vendor selection and contract implementation. The issue of accountability will be analysed in detail in Chapter 7. Here, it is worth identifying and briefly sketching the mechanisms of accountability in place with regard to the various types of procurement.

In direct procurement, internal accountability is mainly ensured through controls on expenditure and on the management of resources. The subjects controlled are international bureaucracies, whereas the ultimate controllers are the financing states, which should act in the interest of their citizens and companies. Conversely, for most organizations – except the institutions of the European Union[20] – the mechanisms of accountability through which private subjects may challenge procurement decisions taken by international organizations are loose: the vendors claiming to have been unfairly excluded from a tender or an award may file a formal or informal complaint with the competent international administrative authorities. However, except for the possibility of addressing the Court of Justice of the European Union and the European Ombudsman for claims against European institutions, in none of the other organizations judicial review *stricto sensu* is assured.

In indirect procurement through NEX or loans and agreements, there are more stringent controls by the international organization on the recipient state, and stronger mechanisms to hold the national administration carrying out procurement accountable to private subjects. All organizations have mechanisms to monitor and control the results

---

[20] Here and elsewhere in this book, procurement carried out by European institutions is examined alongside procurement carried out by international organizations such as the United Nations, UNDP, UNICEF and others. It has been deemed useful for a better understanding of the phenomenon to consider both international organizations *stricto sensu* and supranational organizations.

achieved and the procedural modalities through which these results are achieved by states, including compliance with procurement procedures for the selection of the contracting parties. This is supervision accountability, rather than hierarchical accountability, as it is based on the delegation of executive authority by an independent sovereign public body, i.e. the international organization, to another independent sovereign body, i.e. the national administration, which are thus not linked through a hierarchical relationship. In addition, there are mechanisms set forth by international organizations to hold national administrations accountable vis-à-vis the potential contracting parties. By virtue of these mechanisms, the conduct of national administrations can be also subject to review by international organizations. In this type of procurement, accountability is mainly inter-administrative and involves public subjects belonging to two different levels of governance: national and international.

As for indirect procurement carried out by an international organization, accountability mechanisms are mainly inter-institutional as the organization carrying out the procurement will be accountable to the other, not so much for how the procurement was carried out, but as to whether the task or function outsourced has been effectively implemented. In addition, the organization carrying out procurement will be subject to the internal and external accountability mechanisms applicable to ordinary direct procurement.

Finally, in the case of indirect procurement carried out by private subjects, international organizations do not provide any specific rules regulating procurement carried out by the private parties to which a public function is outsourced. Therefore, the problem of the accountability of private parties to the vendors during the vendor selection phase is not even an issue regulated by the international organization. At most, during the phase of contract implementation, any possible infringement of the contractual obligations by either of the private parties may be challenged before a national court and according to national rules. When the nature of the relationship changes and it is no longer based on authority, the problem of accountability is posed in other terms, as it becomes reciprocal accountability among private parties set on an equal footing.

2.1.5   Contract

The fifth variable feature is contracts. One of the first issues that has emerged with regard to contracts with international organizations is that of the applicable law. As noted earlier, in direct procurement the contract is signed between an international organization and a private subject. Between the 1960s and the 1970s international law scholars long tried to identify the law applicable to contracts between international organizations and private subjects[21] and mostly argued in favour of the application of international private law.[22] As a matter of fact, the solution adopted by the United Nations and its agencies in many procurement contracts is more complex and merges elements arising from both the will of the parties, as well as from international public law and international private and commercial law.[23]

In indirect procurement through letter of assist, NEX and loan agreements, the presence of the state in the contractual relationship generally determines an 'attraction' of the private party under the umbrella of international commercial law or national law. The solution is less controversial for indirect procurement carried out by private subjects. While, for contracts between organizations and private subjects entrusted with a public function, the applicable law is identified in the same way as for direct procurement contracts, in a contractual relationship between two private subjects the applicable law is identified according to the will of the parties and this usually, but not always, depends on the country of citizenship in the case of natural persons, or of incorporation in the case of companies. Unless otherwise decided by the parties, either international commercial law in the case of subjects belonging to different national law systems or national private law if the parties belong to the same national law system applies.

2.1.6   A Taxonomy

By combining the non-variable features (i.e. public and international nature; primary purposes) with the five variable ones, a map of the two basic types of procurement by international organizations with their main characteristics may be drawn up: direct procurement and indirect procurement with several variations. Each of these modalities features elements that give more or less room to the presence and management of the international organization, the private subjects or states. Table 2.1

---

[21] Jenks, *The Proper Law*; Seyersted, 'Applicable Law'; Valticos, 'Les contrats conclus par les organisations internationales avec des personnes privées. Rapport provisoire'; *id.*, 'Les contrats conclus par les organisations internationales avec des personnes privées. Rapport définitif'. For further bibliographical references, see Chapter 6.

[22] On the meaning of international private law with reference to procurement by international organizations, see Chapter 6.

[23] See Chapter 6.

Table 2.1 *Procurement by international organizations (IOs): A taxonomy*

	Direct procurement	Indirect procurement				
		Letter of assist	NEX	Financial institutions	Other international organizations	Private parties
Nature of the subject initiating procurement	Public & international	Public & national			Public & international	Private
Primary purpose	Institutional objectives (e.g. peace and security, development, social justice, human rights promotion etc.)	Institutional objectives (e.g. peace and security, development, social justice, human rights promotion etc.)			Institutional objectives (e.g. peace and security, development, social justice, human rights promotion etc.)	Institutional objectives (e.g. peace and security, development, social justice, human rights promotion etc.)
Secondary purpose	Internal/external	External			Internal/external	Internal/external

Mode of execution		Direct	Indirect	Indirect	Indirect
Regulation	Regulators	IO	IOs/states	IOs	States
	Regulated	IO	States	IOs	Private subjects
Accountability mechanisms		Internal (to the IO)	External/internal	Internal/external (btw. IOs)	External (according to national law)
Procurement contract	Parties to the contract	IO & private party/NGO/IO	State-private party/NGO (on the grounds of an agreement between IO & state)	IO & private party (on the grounds of an agreement btw. IO & IO)	Private party & private party (on the grounds of a contract btw. IO & private party)
	Applicable law	International private and commercial law	National private law (or international private and commercial law)	International private and commercial law	National private law (or international private and commercial law)

shows how the combination of non-variable and variable features gives rise to the different types of international organizations' procurement.

Whereas national public procurement usually involves only two actors, i.e. the state and private subjects, the specificity of procurement by international organizations is that three actors are simultaneously involved in the process: the international organization, a state and a private subject. However, as shown by a combination of the variable features, the two main types of procurement differ according to the role played by each actor.

Direct procurement by an international organization is characterized by a pervasive presence of the organization, which drafts the rules governing the selection process, is a party to the contract, is subject to internal controls and, to a very limited extent, allows complaints from the private parties affected. Direct procurement is similar in many respects to indirect procurement carried out through an agreement with another international organization. Also in this hypothesis, the international organization's procurement rules are applicable and internal account-ability mechanisms are in place. There is, however, another layer of accountability represented by the inter-institutional control on the effective deployment of the function or task entrusted.

Indirect procurement by financial institutions has a national and an international component. The latter is stronger than the former both because of the pervasive nature of international regulations, such as those of the WB, and of the hybrid mechanisms of accountability. In indirect procurement procedures through NEX, the national component is usually stronger: the application of national rules is allowed as long as these are compatible with the procurement rules of the international organization. The mechanisms of accountability are then partly managed by the organization and partly by the state. Indirect procurement through letter of assist is the closest to domestic public procurement procedures: a state to which a mission is entrusted carries out the procurement in compliance with its own national rules on procurement and has in place domestic accountability mechanisms. Finally, indirect procurement carried out by private subjects has a prevailing private component. Although it exists by virtue of a public (international)–private contract, the rules governing the procurement procedures and setting forth the control and accountability mechanism are chosen by the private parties.

A triangle can be created where the various types of international organizations' procurement are located depending on their greater or lesser proximity to one of the aforementioned actors, where proximity indicates the prevalence of determination by a certain actor in the procurement process, i.e. drafting of the rules, management of the procedures, accountability mechanisms etc. (see Figure 2.1). The analysis that this book provides focuses on the main types of direct and indirect procurement, only partially covering the variants in which the national component prevails and procurement rules are mainly drawn from domestic law, i.e. indirect procurement through letter of assist and through private parties.

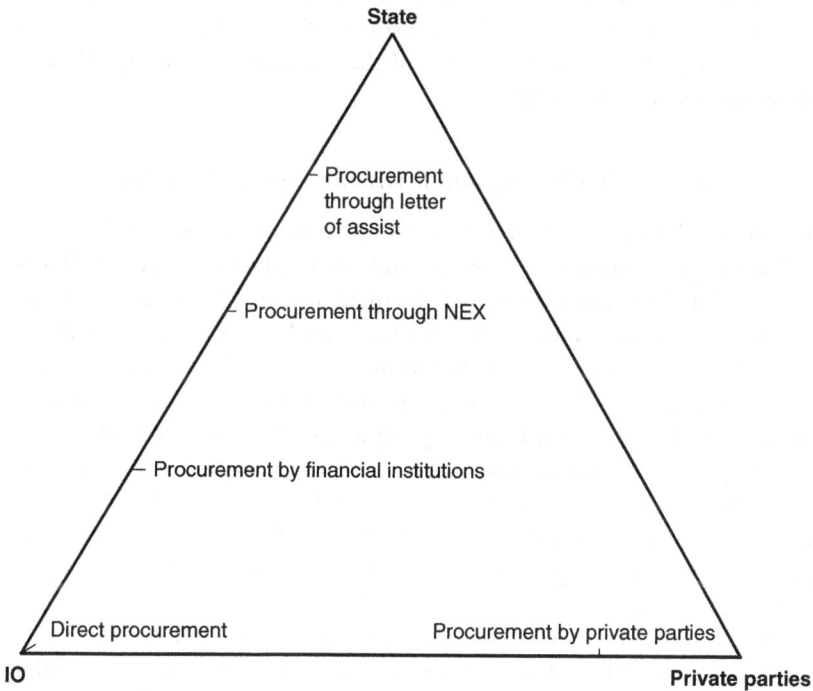

Figure 2.1   The triangle of proximity and institutional influence in international organizations' (IOs') procurement

2.2   Types of Organizations and Implications for Procurement

Various organizations carry out different types of procurement. It is possible to detect the existence of a link between procurement, its volume, the rules establishing its principles and governing its procedures, on the one hand, and the type of international organization on the other.

In fact, although classification of international organizations is difficult, if not impossible,[24] observation of the data relating to procurement by each organization, together with analysis of their procurement rules, allows us to make some hypotheses on the links existing among the above-mentioned elements. For instance, higher or lower volumes of procurement and the adoption of more or less competitive procedures vary according to the institutional mission of each organization.

The three traditional criteria for the classification of international organizations are membership,[25] function performed (and the purposes connected) and structure.[26] In the light of these criteria, the questions to be answered may be reformulated more precisely: whether and how do membership, functions/purposes and the structure of the organization influence its procurement?

2.2.1   Membership and Restrictions on Participation

Based on the criterion of membership, a distinction may be made between governmental (IGOs) and non-governmental (INGOs) international organizations and between universal and closed organizations. The distinction between IGOs and INGOs was introduced by a resolution of the UN Economic and Social Council of 1950, which stated that '[e]very organization which is not created by means of intergovernmental agreements shall be considered as a non-governmental organization'.[27] The two types differ due to the nature of their members: states in IGOs; private subjects, either individuals or associations, in INGOs. INGOs, nevertheless, are private subjects that perform functions of public utility by integrating and sometimes replacing the activity of the IGOs. Médecins sans frontières, for instance, provides assistance to refugee camps in collaboration with the Office of the United Nations High Commissioner for Refugees (UNHCR).

This distinction leads to a first important consequence with regard to procurement: it is the subjective nature of the organization, rather than the nature of the function performed, that determines the application of

---

[24] Smouts, *International Organizations*, p. 12.
[25] Specifically on membership, see Schermers and Blokker, 'International Organizations or Institutions, Membership'.
[26] Archer, *International Organisations*, p. 38 *et seq*.
[27] ECOSOC, *Resolution 288 (X) B* [ref. RES].

public or private rules to procurement. Because they perform a function of public utility, INGOs, like any other private subject, comply with the transparency rules required at the domestic level to ensure the proper management of private funds and with the rules on competition imposed by the law and generally applicable to private subjects. However, they are not bound to abide by the procurement procedures of a public subject, unless, as often happens, they turn out to be contractors to IGOs. In this case, the procurement rules of the international organization and the public interests pursued by such rules offset INGOs' contractual freedom. These rules require that the sub-contract is carried out in a way that is compatible with the principles governing procurement by IGOs and compliance may be subject to a check by the IGO. The criterion of membership and the public or private nature of the organization affect the scope of the procurement rules. These are applied to the procedures of IGOs rather than to those of INGOs. INGOs are conversely subject to their own rules and to the rules generally applicable to private subjects. However, when they contract with an IGO, their internal rules are subjected to a test of compatibility with the IGO's procurement principles.

Furthermore, the distinction between IGOs and INGOs sometimes becomes blurred with regard to membership. On the one hand, IGOs sometimes include among their members not only states but also groups, associations, organizations and individuals. On the other, hybrid INGOs may have some governmental representatives within them. In such cases, the qualification as IGO or INGO depends on the founding treaty of the organization itself: treaties or conventions among governments give rise to IGOs, whereas INGOs are the result of non-inter-governmental agreements.[28] The criterion for the adoption and application of procurement procedures, thus, shifts from mere membership of the organization, which is no longer sufficient to demarcate a line due to the mixed nature of the membership, to the founding act of the organization.

The distinction between universal and closed[29] organizations also has some repercussions on how procurement is carried out and on the

---

[28] The International Labour Organization (ILO), for example, despite having a mixed composition, as it includes trade unions of workers and employers, is to be considered an international organization because it is established by treaty among states. Conversely, the International Council of Science (ICSU), which includes academic unions as well as government representatives, is to be considered a hybrid body because it is established by an agreement between private entities. See Archer, *International Organisations*, p. 43.

[29] The distinction between universal and closed organizations is drawn by some scholars, such as Amerasinghe, *Principles of the Institutional Law*, p. 11; Schermers and Blokker, *International Institutional Law*, § 51.

content of the procurement rules. The distinction between universal or closed organizations is built on the possibility for any state, or for only some of them, to be admitted as members of the organization. In the case of universal organizations, such as the United Nations and its agencies, membership is open to all states with an international juridical status, following an actual assessment of the political compatibility of these subjects with the organization's purposes. In closed organizations, on the other hand, membership is conditional upon the presence of some specific characteristics, such as that they belong to the geographical area corresponding to the scope of the organization itself. A geographical criterion, in particular, may have different extensions and the organization may not only be regional, but also continental or sub-regional.

Whether an organization is universal or closed – and, in the latter case, whether it is continental, regional or sub-regional – has a significant impact on the contents of the procurement rules, affecting at least two aspects of procurement regulation: identification of the subjects that may submit bids and offers in the tender procedures and application of the principle of domestic preference.

Regarding the first aspect, closed membership basically implies that the subjects legitimated to submit offers and bids are only those belonging to the geographical area encompassing all the various member states that ratified the treaty or are third-party states that have signed special agreements with the organization. This is true for both direct and indirect procurement by IGOs. For example, Art. 119 Regulation (EU, Euratom) 2015/1929, amending Regulation (EU, Euratom) 2012/966 on the financial rules applicable to the general budget of the Union, provides, that

> [p]articipation in procurement procedures shall be open on equal terms to all natural and legal persons within the scope of the Treaties and to all natural and legal persons established in a third country which has a special agreement with the Union in the field of public procurement under the conditions laid down in that agreement.[30]

A mitigation of this rule is provided for by the following Art. 120 of the same text, which states

> [w]here the plurilateral Agreement on Government Procurement concluded within the World Trade Organisation applies, the procurement procedure shall also be open to economic operators established in the

---

[30] European Union, Regulation (EU, Euratom) 2015/1929

states which have ratified that agreement, under the conditions laid down therein.[31]

However, this exception seems to have limited scope if one considers that Art. 120 only applies in the presence of certain conditions and that the GPA has only been ratified by fifteen states, including the European Union, while South-American, Indian and African countries, and therefore most developing economies, are excluded.

Similar provisions are included by regional financial organizations in the guidelines on procurement for recipient states. For instance, the ADB's Procurement Guidelines restrict the range of potential bidders by establishing eligibility criteria linked to nationality:

> [t]o foster competition ADB permits bidders from all eligible member countries to offer goods, works, and services for ADB financed projects.[32]

The Rules and Procedures for Procurement of Goods and Works of AfDB establish the eligibility criteria for bidders, but also for goods and works that are the subject matter of procurement.[33]

As for the second aspect, i.e. domestic preference, regionalism may affect the scope of the preference allowed. In general, the procurement rules set forth by international financial organizations for beneficiary states allow such states a margin of preference for goods, services and works produced and provided by national or local enterprises. In some cases, nevertheless, this exception to the principle of competition is more strictly linked to the regional character of the organization and it extends to goods and contractors not only from the beneficiary state, but also from all the member states of the regional organization. Thus, for example, the Rules and Procedures for Procurement of Goods and Works of AfDB provide for a domestic and regional preference, and the latter is defined as follows:

> Similarly [i.e. as for domestic preference], a Borrower may, in agreement with the Bank, grant a margin of preference to goods produced in and services provided by contractors from other regional member countries which have joined the Borrowing country in a regional economic institutional arrangement when evaluating bids and comparing those bids with other bids, subject to the conditions specified in these Rules.[34]

As a margin of preference is a mitigation of the pure principle of international competition, enlargement of the scope of applicability of this margin has at least two results, which are apparently conflicting.

---

[31] *Ibid.*   [32] ADB, *Procurement Guidelines*, para. 1.6 [ref. AP&R].
[33] AfDB, *Rules and Procedures*, App. 4, para. 1 [ref. AP&R].   [34] *Ibid.*, App. 2, para. 2.

On the one hand, it extends the exception to the detriment of subjects outside the regional area that intend to participate in the tender procedure. On the other, it mitigates the anti-competitive effect that the application of the mere domestic preference would have by enlarging, although in a limited way, the number of subjects included in the margin of preference. The prevailing result is, in all events, the first one, whereas the second is a mitigation of the first: the regionalism of the organization has implications for the procurement procedures and alters the pure principle of competition.[35]

2.2.2   The Functions of Organizations and the Expenditure Volumes for Procurement

The functions performed by each organization, even more than its membership, have implications for procurement and in fact determine the very emergence of the need for procurement. The notion of function, charged with meaning in the literature on national administrations, has a relatively simpler and more limited meaning when referring to international organizations. Virally explains that the theory of international organizations may be thought of as characterized by two main features: the sovereignty of states and the notion of function.[36] The latter includes a basic element for the study of international organizations, i.e. that of the purposes of function or else of the purposes of the organizations. As Schermers and Blokker point out, the creation of an international organization is the result of a will of states to cooperate within an institutional framework that makes this cooperation possible or easier. This motivation arises as an attempt to solve problems that go beyond the reach of each single state.[37] In this sense, the existence of international organizations is instrumental and directly linked to the performance of some specific functions, or to the achievement of the well-defined purposes (peacekeeping, development, environment protection and so on) for which each organization has been created. The state, on the contrary, exercises its functions with regard to any aspects of individual life which have implications for a certain (national) community and therefore has an intrinsic and general justification for its existence. In the light of this difference, Charles Rousseau talks of *finalité functionnelle* with reference

---

[35] See Chapter 4.   [36] Virally, 'La notion de fonction'.
[37] Schermers and Blokker, *International Institutional Law*, § 15.

to international organizations and of *finalité intégrée* with reference to states.[38]

The function, mainly understood as the purposes of organizations and the activity instrumental to the achievement of these purposes, is the characterizing feature and the main criterion according to which a distinction may be made between organizations. According to this criterion, the literature has suggested different classifications.[39]

Procurement and the rules governing it are strictly linked to the purposes pursued by the organization. Keohane and Nye, and similarly Padelford, suggest a tripartite division between organizations with military or defence purposes, organizations with political and social purposes, and organizations with economic or technical purposes.[40] Aggregate data on procurement, when available, show that, while the first two types of organizations carry out procurement for internal and external purposes, i.e. respectively, corporate procurement and project procurement, international financial organizations, with some exceptions, mostly carry out corporate procurement. The exceptions are represented by those organizations that, despite having an economic character, also have social purposes. This is the case for the WB, ADB, AfDB, IDB, EBRD and IFAD.

This tripartition intertwines with the distinction among the purposes of procurement. As already mentioned, procurement by international organizations may be driven by internal purposes, i.e. procurement of goods, services and works for the daily functioning of the organization, or by external purposes, i.e. procurement that responds to the needs of a community of individuals belonging to the member or non-member states. While tender procedures aimed at the performance of internal activity are typical of all international organizations, tender procedures as a means to pursue external purposes are typical of only some organizations and, in particular, are a constant feature of organizations with social and political purposes, such as the World Food Programme (WFP), the

---

[38] Rousseau, 'L'indépendance de l'État dans l'ordre international'.

[39] See Padelford, 'Regional Organizations and the United Nations'; Keohane and Nye (eds.), *Transnational Relations*, p. 430 *et seq.*; Haas and Rowe, 'Regional Organizations in the United Nations'; Virally, 'Définition et classification'; LeRoy Bennet and Oliver, *International Organizations, passim.* Others, however, point to the difficulty of exactly identifying the function of international organizations. Often constituent documents refer to a variety of purposes, sometimes even reciprocally conflicting, and there can be a discrepancy between the formal goals of an organization and the reasons for its creation. See Klabbers, 'The Transformation of International Organizations Law'.

[40] Keohane and Nye (eds.), *Transnational Relations*; Padelford, 'Regional Organizations and the United Nations'.

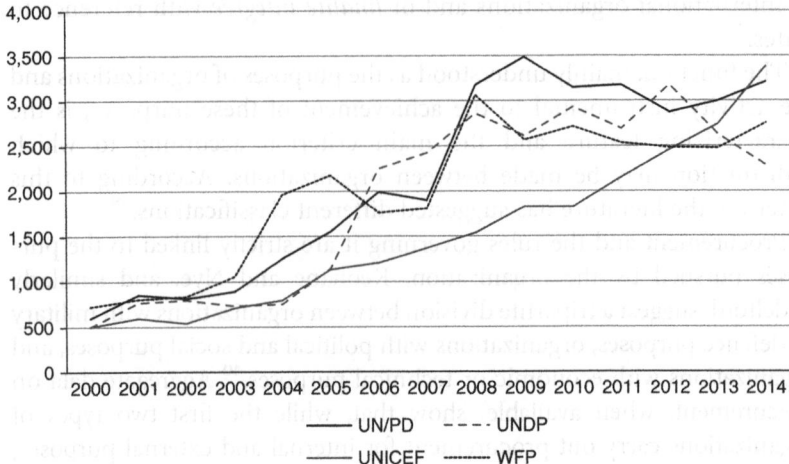

Figure 2.2 Organizations of the UN system with highest procurement volumes (in millions of US dollars)[41]

United Nations, and the UNDP, and UNICEF; but also the WB, ADB, AfDB and IDB. In the light of the above, data on the high volumes of procurement are understandable as being an essential component of the performance of political and social external functions, rather than being for mere corporate procurement. By way of example, between 2000 and 2014 the four organizations of the UN system with the highest and steadily increasing procurement volumes were the United Nations Procurement Division (UNPD), UNDP, WFP and UNICEF (see Figure 2.2).[42] Statistics for the same years also show that procurement by these organizations usually regarded – in descending order – health, transport, construction and engineering, food and farming, management and administrative services.

2.2.3   The Administration Structure and Procurement Management

When classifying international organizations according to their structure, international law scholars often identify a recurring organizational pattern.

---

[41] See UNOPS annual statistical reports on procurement from 2007 to 2015 and UNDP-IAPSO annual statistical reports on procurement from 2000 to 2006 (reference to the single reports can be found at the beginning of this book in the List of Instruments, ref. REP).

[42] The graph is based on data collected in the statistical reports on UN procurement issued between 2000 and 2015, which cover about thirty-five organizations of the UN family.

This usually includes an assembly or an equivalent body, open to participation by all member states, which sets the political priorities; a more restricted body, made up of only some members, with power to decide; a secretariat in charge of the management of the organization; and, in some cases, a supervisory or judicial body or bodies. For the present analysis, what makes the difference in the institutional structure is the presence of a secretariat.[43] All the organizations whose internal or external activity requires procurement are generally characterized by the presence of an administrative organ and, within it, by offices in charge of the direct or indirect management of procurement (procurement divisions).

It is interesting to analyse the internal structure of the administration that deals with procurement and to see how the organization's purpose influences the way it is shaped. Organizations having mainly political and social functions with a focus on external activity to be performed on their territory have mostly adopted a decentralized administrative structure, characterized by the presence of minor procurement divisions, so-called field procurement offices, temporarily or permanently operating in the areas of intervention, which are subject to monitoring by the offices at the headquarters. However, decentralization for some organizations, especially those belonging to the United Nations system, has been an achievement rather than a starting point. There are at least two reasons for evolution towards decentralization. The first is increasing external administrative activity of these organizations. The rise in the number of peacekeeping and peacebuilding operations, as well as the creation of a third generation of interim administrations characterized by a stronger presence of international organizations in territories where they operate, are among the reasons for this increased administrative activity.[44] The second are economic and efficiency reasons that lead to a shortening of the distance between the administrative offices entrusted with procurement and the offices to which procurement is destined, thereby saving on control and transportation costs.

Conversely, for financial and technical organizations, for which procurement is mostly a means of survival and operation of the organization itself, the administrative structure in charge of procurement is almost exclusively centralized and located at the premises of the organization.

When identifying a link between structure and procurement, the logical relationship is inverted if compared to that of the other criteria, so that it is not the structure which affects procurement, but rather the

---

[43] On secretariats, see Piiparinen, 'Secretariats'.   [44] See Chapter 3.

other way round: where there has been a need for procurement, the organization has also provided for the presence of administrative bodies in charge of carrying it out, for example, a secretariat, and within it the competent offices. On the other hand, analysis of structure accompanies that of purposes. Therefore, there are usually decentralized administrative structures in organizations with political and social purposes, as well as defence and safety purposes, whereas there are centralized structures in financial or technical organizations that specifically carry out procurement for internal purposes.

2.2.4 Relationships

To answer the question posed at the beginning of this section, it is, therefore, possible to trace some links between the membership, purposes and structure of international organizations and the procurement they perform.

Regarding whether membership and purposes influence procurement, the answer is positive: although in different ways, the public, private or mixed composition of organizations, their universal or closed nature and their purposes, i.e. defence purposes, political and social purposes, technical and financial purposes, are significant both with regard to the existence and volume of procurement, as well as to the rules governing it.

As for whether the administrative structure influences procurement, the question is badly posed. It is not the administrative structure that influences procurement, but rather it is the need for procurement that affects the existence of a certain structure and its articulation. The need for procurement arises in turn from the purposes of the international organization. Consequently, it is primarily the purposes that inform the administrative structure in charge of the procurement management.

With regard to how membership and purposes influence procurement and the administrative structure in charge of procurement, two remarks can be made. The first concerns membership. Membership is extremely relevant to the nature of the rules applicable and to their contents. Whether organizations are entirely made up of public or private subjects or they are hybrid determines the nature of the rules regulating the vendor selection phase. In the case of organizations made up of states, or in general of public subjects, the vendor selection will be carried out according to a specific procedure drafted by the organization (although Chapter 3 will show that this has not always been the case in the history of international organizations). On the contrary, in the case of organizations made up of private subjects, the selection of contractors is not necessarily proceduralized, is made according to the free will of the organization, and is performed in compliance with the common rules of negotiation between private subjects. The membership criterion therefore determines the nature of the law governing the pre-contractual relationships between the organization and the potential contractors. In the case of IGOs, the administrative rules drafted by the same organization govern the vendor selection process, whereas in the case of INGOs the relationships will be governed instead by international private law.

Moreover, membership is important with regard to single aspects of the contents of rules. As noted above, regionalism of an organization implies some restrictions on membership and a deviation from the principles of competition in procurement procedures. In the evaluation of offers and bids, the procuring administration may guarantee some margins of preference to bids submitted by natural or legal persons that have the nationality of (or are incorporated in) the recipient state, or the nationality of a member state of the regional area that has economic agreements with the recipient states, by extending the exception to the principle of competition.[45]

The second remark concerns function and purposes. These affect the very existence of procurement, its volume and the nature and structure of the administration in charge of its management. With regard to the first three aspects (existence, volume and nature), the relationship is not only intuitive but also supported by empirical evidence: organizations with peacekeeping and defence purposes and organizations with political and social objectives (in which development banks may also be included) invest remarkable portions of their budget in functional procurement, i.e. procurement aimed at the performance of external administrative activities, much more than on corporate procurement, which is for the performance of their administrations' internal activity. On the contrary, financial and technical organizations have lower volumes of expenditure on procurement.

Purposes inform the type of procurement and, through the latter, the structure of the administration that deals with its management. Differences in structure are mainly expressed in terms of administrative centralization and decentralization: networks of decentralized offices are found in organizations mostly dealing with functional procurement

---

[45] See Chapter 4.

(organizations that have political and social purposes or peacekeeping and defence tasks); centralized organization models are more widespread among international organizations mainly performing procurement with internal purposes (technical or financial organizations). The membership of organizations and their purposes are therefore fundamental in explaining the nature of the rules governing tenders, their contents and the structure of the competent administration.

3

The Institutional Roots of Change

From Private Negotiations to Public Tenders

3.1 Introduction

The history of international organizations, which the literature recounts in terms of major political shifts and general organizational reforms, fails to reveal the impact these changes have had on the methods organizations use to perform their functions and pursue their goals, and in particular on their procurement activity. Conversely, it is possible to trace the evolution of these methods and of the rules and regulations governing them and relate them to political changes that have caused important shifts in the life of international organizations. This connection between political history and administrative procedures can be found in both direct and indirect procurement, and although there are different repercussions due to the specific aspects of the two types of procurement, for both it is possible to identify common international political macro causes and rules that have developed along similar lines. The following sections break down the history of procurement by international organizations into four phases, with common causes indicated for both direct and indirect procurement and specific changes noted for each type of procurement.

3.2 The Institutionalization Phase: Contracts

Direct procurement emerged together with the founding of organizations: the need to procure goods and services and works was tied to the very existence of organizations and the performance of their external functions.[1] Nevertheless, compared to the beginning, the methods the organizations now use to procure goods, services and works have

---

[1] For a general overview of the history of international organizations see *inter alia* Chimni, 'International Organizations, 1945-Present'; Herren, 'International Organizations, 1865–1945'.

changed significantly. In this regard some quantitative data are important to mention: in the annals of the UN organizations, which include the most important documents from the birth of the first organizations to the present day, the word 'procurement' only began to appear with a degree of frequency around the mid-1970s. There are later peaks in the 1990s, when the UN reform was underway, and most recently in the first decade of the twenty-first century during some major corruption scandals around the Oil for Food programme in Iraq.[2] Before then, in the 1950s and 1960s, reference was made primarily to 'contracts', meaning the employment contracts of officials, but also contracts that international organizations concluded with external parties for the supply of goods, services and works. The international law studies of those years[3] were consistent in this approach and were primarily concerned with trying to address the problem of the law applicable to contracts.

The reasons for this special interest in contracts, rather than in the public law-type procedures that precede them – i.e. tenders – lay in the absence of procedural rules regulating the selection of contractors. Early international organizations performed limited market research, identified contractors, contacted them and concluded contracts with them without following a pre-determined public procedure. Essentially, they acted more like private enterprises than contracting administrations in the modern sense of the term. They often preferred long-term contracts over short-term contracts, which would require them to seek out new contractors. The explanation given by the Secretary-General in 1950, during the fourth session of the General Assembly, illustrating the steps being taken in preparation for the construction and outfitting of the UN building, is paradigmatic of this approach:

> [r]epresentatives visited many countries to investigate possible sources of supply and to discuss with manufacturers and suppliers both the immediate and long-range needs of the Organization.[4]

---

[2] The elementary application of content analysis methodologies proposed takes into consideration the doubts that many have expressed regarding these methodologies, and in any case has no 'probative' effect. Nevertheless, this is a significant means of evaluation concomitant with other factors illustrated later in the text. On content analysis methodologies, see Berelson, *Content Analysis*; Holsti, *Content Analysis*; Krippendorff, *Content Analysis*; Neuendorf, *The Content Analysis Guidebook*; Roberts (ed.), *Text Analysis*; Weber, *Basic Content Analysis*.

[3] *Inter alia* Jenks, *The Proper Law*; Seyersted, 'Applicable Law'. More generally on internationalist legal theory regarding the contracts of international organizations see Chapter 5.

[4] United Nations, *Yearbook of the United Nations 1950*, p. 177 [ref. UNCDoc].

This *modus operandi* was in part due to the limited activities of organizations during their very first years and the resulting insufficient organization of their operations, and also in part due to political reasons: the newly created system had the full support and trust of the United States, which was also its most important financier.[5]

The nearly unanimous vote of the United States Senate on the Charter of the United Nations and the provisions of the United Nations Participation Act of 1945 are testimony to a political approach that saw the UN system as an effective instrument to help promote US interests in the international scenario. In the United Nations's first ten years of operation, due to the Security Council's intervention, Soviet troops were pushed out of Iraq, France pulled its troops out of Syria and Lebanon, and multilateral diplomatic efforts under the auspices of the United States prevented North Korea from invading South Korea. In general, the United States acted as a promoter or ally in a series of initiatives that enjoyed varying degrees of success: the adoption of the Universal Declaration of Human Rights and the Uniting for Peace resolution;[6] the launch of economic development and technical assistance programmes; the creation of various commissions within the Economic and Social Council; the Baruch Plan's proposal for control of nuclear weapons; the General Assembly's adoption of Eisenhower's Open Skies programme; and the start of the decolonization process. During the first years of operation of the United Nations and its agencies, the United States was the country that made the largest financial contributions, covering up to 40 per cent of the UN budget and had no particular interest in pushing for the development of procurement procedures that could favour the participation of non-US firms.[7]

Indirect procurement and its regulation were also at an early stage of development. The only organization that engaged in something similar to today's indirect procurement was the WB.[8] Nevertheless, the characteristics of this phenomenon were very different from what later developed, for several reasons. First, the WB was established[9] mainly with the initial objective of financing post-war reconstruction in Europe and

---

[5] See Rivlin, 'UN Reform'; Meisler, *United Nations*; Moore and Pubantz, *To Create a New World?*; Turner, *La frontiera nella storia americana.*
[6] UN General Assembly, *Uniting for Peace* [ref. RES].   [7] Rivlin, 'UN Reform'.
[8] For an overview on the history of the WB see Kapur, Lewis and Webb, *The World Bank: History.* Specifically on the history of WB procurement see Williams-Elegbe, *Public Procurement and Multilateral Development Banks*, pp. 9–29.
[9] In 1944, through the Bretton Woods Agreements.

Japan. It, thus, handled large infrastructural projects, which were aimed at a rapid restoration of the *status quo ante*. The issue regarding the development of the rules on procurement was a secondary concern.

The second reason was that the new international economic order produced by Bretton Woods clearly sanctioned the supremacy of the United States, which was further reinforced by the adoption of the Marshall Plan (the European Recovery Program, 1948–1952). Thus, one of the collateral objectives of financing the WB was not to ensure global competition, but to encourage the penetration of foreign markets by US enterprises.

Moreover, this was also compatible with market conditions – which leads to the third reason: the market was characterized by a significantly uneven development between Western and non-Western economies. The firms able to provide goods, services and works for these big infrastructure projects were mainly Western, and in particular American, given that many European countries were recovering from the war. The result was that the US pressure to enter European markets was not counterbalanced by strong economic capacities of European or non-Western economies, some of which were still colonies.

The fourth reason related to the legal context within which these activities were carried out: in the absence of a globalized market, the culture of public procurement that developed over more recent years and that entails proceduralization, transparency, and publicity, had not yet spread either nationally or internationally.

The fifth reason was that the WB's action still involved only a limited number of countries, and thus the procedures these countries were required to follow could easily be regulated on an individual basis by single loan agreements. In addition, in the aftermath of World War II, other development banks such as the IDB, ADB and AfDB had not yet been established, and so the WB was the only organization that could abstractly have the problem of how to regulate financed procurement.

Based on these considerations, from its inception the WB decided to adopt vendor selection methods based on international competitive bidding (ICB). This was because ICB was deemed as the best procurement method that allowed foreign firms, and in particular American firms, to take part in the tender procedures launched by European public entities. It is no coincidence that, according to various historic reconstructions provided by the WB itself, the prime driver behind the Bank's adoption of ICB was its first Engineering Advisor, retired US General R.A. Wheeler, on the grounds that 'ICB was viewed as the counterpart to foreign exchange financing provided by the Bank'.[10] Consistent with these objectives, starting in 1951 the Bank adopted ICB as a preferential method for indirect procurement. Moreover, in 1956 it established that only firms from member states (plus Switzerland) would be eligible to submit bids, and, in 1958, that if local enterprises were able to win ICB contracts, 'the Bank would limit its financing to the foreign exchange component only'.[11] So, from the start, the WB's approach to procurement was characterized by different and only seemingly conflicting trends: on one hand, the early adoption of ICB; on the other, the close and often explicit tie between financing and contracts awarded, and thus between financing states and successful bidders. The former – ICB – was instrumental to the latter – the tie between financing and awards.

3.3 The Emergence of Procurement Procedure and Its Problems (the 1960s and 1970s)

The situation began to change by the end of the 1950s[12] and during the 1960s, when the political bipolarism between the United States and the Soviet Union, which had emerged immediately after World War II – Baruch used the term 'Cold War' during a speech in South Carolina on 16 April 1946 – intertwined with the decolonization process and, consequently, with the strategic position assumed by the non-aligned countries. Two factors in particular had direct and indirect repercussions on procurement activity: the increased numbers and functions of organizations and a shift in the equilibrium within their decision-making organs.

With regard to the first factor, the organizations, and in particular the United Nations and the agencies that were part of the UN system, gradually expanded their membership[13] and shifted their attention to the political, economic and social problems of the new states that had just emerged from colonial domination and were seeking support for their political independence and economic growth, through international fora.[14] As emerges from a study commissioned by the General

---

[10] WB, *The World Bank's Procurement Policies and Procedures: Policy Review*, p. 2 [ref. AP&R].

[11] *Ibid.*, p. 2.

[12] In general, 1955 is designated as the first year in which the United States could no longer count on an automatic two-thirds majority in the General Assembly, see Caffarena, *Le organizzazioni internazionali*, p. 89.

[13] For a graphic idea of the increase in membership, see *ibid.*, p. 93.

[14] Müller (ed.), *The Reform of the United Nations*; Caffarena, *Le organizzazioni internazionali*, pp. 93–94.

Assembly,[15] from 1956 to 1965 the expenses of the United Nations and its specialized agencies more than doubled: there was a growth in the number of organs, a considerable increase in the size of the secretariat, major expenses for the maintenance of personnel, and multiple development initiatives aimed at bridging the gap between the Global North and South. New organizations were also established. In 1965 the UNDP was founded (and is now one of the agencies with the highest volume of procurement) with the goal of achieving technical cooperation in developing countries. In 1963, the Food and Agriculture Organization (FAO) and UN General Assembly instituted the WFP (currently the largest humanitarian organization in the world and one of the top organizations for procurement volume) for the purposes of providing direct aid, such as the supply of foodstuffs, and indirect aid, such as support in the production, sale and distribution of food. Development banks were also established around this time: the IDB in 1959, the AfDB in 1964 and the ADB in 1966. These banks were created using the WB as a model and with the aim of financing development projects in countries emerging from decolonization. The decolonization process thus led to an increased volume of direct procurement, and, most importantly, the increase also in indirect procurement became an essential tool to support development in more disadvantaged geographical areas.

Nevertheless, and this is the second factor, the entry of new members in organizations also altered the decision-making balance. Around the mid-1970s, there was a reversal in the decision-making influence that the United States and the Soviet Union had once had within the General Assembly: while in the early years of the organizations the USSR voted against a majority of countries led by the United States, in the international situation transformed by decolonization the USSR was supported by the votes of many developing countries and had a majority of about two-thirds in the General Assembly.

The concomitance of these two factors – the exponential growth in the costs of activities of the organizations and a shift in the balance of decision-making power – brought mainly the United States, but also other Western countries, to take a stricter approach to both disbursing contributions and controlling them, especially in peacekeeping operations.[16] In some cases this even led to conditioning financing on

---

[15] UN General Assembly, *Establishment of the Ad Hoc Committee of Experts* [ref. RES].

[16] On this shift see also Nelson, 'International Law and US Withholding of Payments to International Organizations'. On the crisis of legitimation undergone by international

a general administrative reform of the organizations and on revising the non-transparent methods that the organizations used when procuring goods, services and works.[17]

As for direct procurement, during these years, there was a series of rather unsuccessful initiatives aimed at improving the efficiency and economy of administrative action. In 1959, following the United Nations's first financial crisis due to the failure of the Security Council to reach an agreement on financing peacekeeping missions in Congo (ONUC) and the Middle East (UNEF), the General Assembly was asked to appoint a Commission of experts to review the activities and organization of the UN Secretariat 'with a view to effecting or proposing further measures designed to ensure maximum economy and efficiency in the secretariat'.[18] In 1961, as a result of the refusal of certain member states to contribute to peacekeeping operations, a working group of fifteen member states, known as the 'Group of Fifteen', was established to review the methods for covering the costs of peacekeeping operations, as well as the organization's administrative and management procedures.[19] In 1965, a General Assembly resolution established the aforementioned commission to analyze in detail the financial system of the United Nations and all its agencies, with two specific objectives in mind:

> on the one hand, to secure better utilization of the funds available through rationalization and more thorough co-ordination of the activities of the organizations and, on the other hand, to ensure that any expansion of those activities takes into account both the needs they are intended to meet and the costs member states will have to bear as a result.[20]

A few years later, in 1968, the Secretary-General appointed a seven-member commission to review the organization of the secretariats of the United Nations, United Nations Conference on Trade and Development (UNCTAD), United Nations Industrial Development Organization (UNIDO) and the regional economic commissions 'with a view to

organizations in this period see Schachter, 'Alf Ross Memorial Lecture'. As for peace-keeping operations undertaken after the Cold War see Ratner, *The New UN Peacekeeping*.

[17] In this regard, Babb has traced a link between reform of multilateral development banks and the American influence on them. She argues that the reluctance of US Congress to fund the banks has enhanced the influence of the United States on them by making credible America's threat to abandon the banks if its policy preferences were not followed, see Babb, *Behind the Development Banks*. On these points, see also Taylor, 'The United Nations System Under Stress'.

[18] UN General Assembly, *Organization and Management of Work* [ref. RES].

[19] Müller (ed.), *The Reform of the United Nations*, p. 18.

[20] UN General Assembly, *Establishment of the Ad Hoc Committee of Experts* [ref. RES].

ensuring the most efficient functioning of the secretariat and the optimum use of available resources'.[21]

The results of these initiatives were modest, and the various study commissions and working groups often did not achieve the results for which they had been established. With regard to procurement in particular, the changes brought by the reforms were insignificant.

Nevertheless, apart from the specific objectives of the reform initiatives, the changed political reality produced three new trends. First, the greater volume of transactions and the insistent demand for more transparent operations contributed to the first development of rules and regulations for procurement. Second, the appearance of new organizations within the system and the ever-increasing interconnection among the various agencies, due in part to their escalating activities, created the need for coordination and, instrumental to this, for the harmonization of procedures. Third, spurred by the political imperatives of developing countries, but also based on considerations of cost-effectiveness and efficiency, economic and social appeals suggested for the first time that procurement by international organizations should be seen as an instrument to promote local institutions and guarantee cost savings, given the proximity of the sources of production to those benefiting from the organizations' activities.

As for indirect procurement, the attention paid to procurement arrangements in these decades was cursory[22] and, at the outset, the newly established development banks did not provide a comprehensive regulatory framework for governing financed procurement.[23] Procurement regulation was introduced only several years later. During the 1960s, however, the WB adopted its first formal procurement directive, which has been the precursor to further regulatory developments and a model for all the other development banks.[24] Notwithstanding the lack of a legal framework on procurement, the agreements that established the banks were not silent on issues related to loan implementation, and thus contained provisions relevant also to procurement. On one side, the WB's Articles of Agreement, and later the Agreements establishing

---

[21] Müller (ed.), *The Reform of the United Nations*, p. 21.
[22] The statement is in WB, *The World Bank's Procurement Policies and Procedures: Policy Review*, p. 2 [ref. AP&R] but it is even more true for the other development banks.
[23] Williams-Elegbe, *Public Procurement and Multilateral Development Banks*, p. 18 *et seq.*
[24] Hunja, 'Recent Revision to the World Bank's Procurement', p. 218.

the IDB, the AfDB and the ADB,[25] required loans to be implemented according to the purposes for which they were established and with due consideration to economy and efficiency.[26] On the other side, these constraints could never result in interference by the banks in the political affairs of the member states.[27]

3.3.1   Codification Proposals in Direct and Indirect Procurement

In the 1960s, the term 'procurement' first appeared in regulatory texts, in the sense of a procedure to follow in order to procure goods, services and works. A minimum core of rules was also included in the financial regulations and rules of many organizations. This was accompanied by patchwork non-uniform administrative implementation memoranda from various agencies, directed exclusively at the personnel of the organizations.

For direct procurement, the first demands to codify these operating rules were not made until the mid-1970s, and came as a response to pressure from certain member states – the United States in particular – for greater clarity and transparency in procedures. In 1974, for example, the General Assembly voted to approve, without passing a formal resolution, a decision of the Fifth (Administrative and Budgetary) Committee on the procurement of experts and consultants for the UN Secretariat, stating:

> the Committee . . . decided to request the Secretary-General to take them [i.e. certain recommendations from the Joint Inspection Unit] fully into account in the preparation and implementation of the comprehensive system of policies/procedures and practices he had undertaken to issue soon in the form of *codified administrative instructions* applicable to all departments and offices of the Secretariat.[28]

---

[25] IBRD Articles of Agreement, Art. III (5) 2 [ref. A&C]; Agreement Establishing the Inter-American Development Bank, Art. III (1) [ref. A&C]; Agreement Establishing the African Development Bank, Art. 12 [ref. A&C]; Agreement Establishing the Asian Development Bank, Art. 8 [ref. A&C].

[26] Williams-Elegbe, *Public Procurement and Multilateral Development Banks*, p. 18 *et seq.*

[27] IBRD Articles of Agreement, Art. IV (10) [ref. A&C]; Agreement Establishing the Inter-American Development Bank, Art. VIII (5)(f) [ref. A&C]; Agreement Establishing the African Development Bank, Art. 38 [ref. A&C]; Agreement Establishing the Asian Development Bank, Art. 36 (2) [ref. A&C].

[28] United Nations, *Yearbook of the United Nations 1974*, p. 933 [ref. UNCDoc]; UN General Assembly, *Amendments to the Staff Regulations* [ref. RES]; UN Fifth Committee (Administrative and Budgetary Committee), *Meetings 1635–1642* (minutes) [Ref. REP]; UN Fifth Committee (Administrative and Budgetary Committee), *Plenary Meeting 2325* (minutes) [Ref. REP]; JIU, *Report to the Twenty-Eighth Session of the General Assembly*

Nevertheless, most of the organizations would not codify these administrative instructions into true procurement manuals on contracts for goods, services and works until a few years later.

The codification of indirect procurement rules came at an earlier stage, compared to direct procurement, especially due to the initiative of the WB, which acted as a driving force for other organizations. Twenty years after its establishment in 1961, the Bank recognized the need to provide specific guidelines on procurement procedures and approved the first written procurement rules to provide guidance to staff.[29] Subsequently, in 1964 the Bank's Board of Executive Directors adopted the first formal instructions on ICB[30] and then, in 1966, the Guidelines on Selection and Employment of Consultants.[31] To guarantee that these rules were followed and to fulfil its fiduciary obligations to ensure that the financing was used for the intended purposes, the Bank was responsible for reviewing and explicitly approving all contracts. By the 1960s, however, explicit approval was replaced by a no objection procedure, thus 'acknowledging the Bank's role as financier and not a party to the contracting process'.[32]

3.3.2 First Attempts at Coordinating Procurement Activities and Harmonizing Direct Procurement Rules

In conjunction with the first codification proposals and guidelines, the coordination of the organizations and harmonization of their procedures began to be discussed. The Administrative Committee on Coordination (ACC) had been established in 1946 by a resolution of the Economic and Social Council (ECOSOC).[33,34]

[ref. REP]; UN General Assembly, *Report of Secretary-General*, A/C.5/1611 [ref. REP]; UN General Assembly, *Report on Use of Experts and Consultants* [ref. REP].

[29] WB, *The World Bank's Procurement Policies and Procedures: Policy Review*, p. 2 [ref. AP&R].

[30] *Ibid.*, p. 2. They are also known as the 'red book'. See also Gorski, 'The Reform of World Bank's Procurement Rules', pp. 6–7. Williams-Elegbe, *Public Procurement and Multilateral Development Banks*, p. 16 *et seq.*

[31] WB, *The World Bank's Procurement Policies and Procedures: Policy Review*, p. 2 [ref. AP&R]. They are also known as the 'green book'. See also Gorski, 'The Reform of World Bank's Procurement Rules', pp. 6–7. Williams-Elegbe, *Public Procurement and Multilateral Development Banks*, p. 16 *et seq.*

[32] WB, *The World Bank's Procurement Policies and Procedures: Policy Review*, p. 2, footnote 4 [ref. AP&R].

[33] ECOSOC, *Resolution 13 (III)* [ref. RES].

[34] *Ibid.* Also see Hill, 'The Administrative Committee on Coordination', p. 129.

It was composed of the executive heads of the most important agencies of the United Nations, including financial institutions, like the WB and the International Monetary Fund (IMF), and organizations responsible for managing funds and programmes, such as UNDP, UNICEF, the WFP and others.[35]

In the following years, the Commission's mandate was extended to include coordinating the programmes of the various agencies of the United Nations and the general promotion of cooperation within the UN system.[36] In 1977[37] the Commission included the following passage among its conclusions and recommendations for restructuring the economic and social sectors of the UN system:

> [m]easures should be taken to achieve maximum uniformity of administrative, financial, budgetary, personnel and planning procedures, including the establishment of a *common procurement system*.[38]

These recommendations would be adopted by the General Assembly in a resolution during that same year.[39] A year before these declarations, the UNDP's Office of Project Execution (OPE) was assigned the task of acting as a focal point for the coordinated management of procurement services for the various agencies,[40] and two years later, in 1978, the Inter-Agency Procurement Services Unit (IAPSU) was established at UNDP. It was given both regulatory duties, which included developing common guidelines on procurement by the organizations within the United Nations system, and operational duties, principally managing requests from various UN agencies for the supply of goods, services and works.

A connection was thus made between the objectives of the 1977 resolution and the agreements between the United Nations and its

---

[35] It has now been replaced by the United Nations System Chief Executives Board for Coordination.

[36] JIU, *Review of the Administrative Committee* [ref. REP], para. 2.

[37] But it had already begun to address the issue in previous years. See UN Administrative Coordination Committee, *Annual Report of ACC* [ref. REP]. With regard to the ACC's activity in 1976, it says: '[o]ther administrative and financial subjects discussed by ACC during the year included the coordination of rules and procedures for procurement and contracts and the possibility of developing a common methodology for estimating the cost of inflation', also in United Nations, *Yearbook of the United Nations 1976*, p. 643 [ref. UNCDoc].

[38] Emphasis added.

[39] UN General Assembly, *Restructuring of the Economic and Social Sectors of the United Nations System*, Annex, para. 32 [ref. RES].

[40] United Nations, *Yearbook of the United Nations 1976*, p. 370 [ref. UNCDoc].

agencies, including the International Atomic Energy Agency (IAEA). The Economic and Social Council was given the task of overseeing the execution of these agreements 'with a special view to determining how the application of those agreements could best contribute to the achievement of the aims set forth in the 1977 resolution' and, in particular, to the development of a common procurement system.[41]

Implementation of the objective of harmonization was specifically assigned to the resident coordinators[42] of all the organizations that engaged in development support activities. In a 1979 resolution, the General Assembly

> requests the Secretary-General to ensure, in consultation with the Governments and the executive heads of the organizations concerned, that in the exercise of his functions the resident coordinator shall be enabled ... [t]o help in the implementation at the country level of the objective stated in paragraph 32 of the annex to resolution 32/197, namely the achievement of maximum uniformity in administrative, financial, procurement and other procedures.[43]

The objectives of coordinating agencies and harmonizing rules and regulations nevertheless encountered obstacles that slowed their realization. The procedures adopted by the organizations still showed significant differences. An example of this was the direct procurement of consulting services. The working group established in 1974, following the decision of the General Assembly,[44] with the task of performing a comparative investigation of the procedures of the various agencies regarding consulting services and developing a common text, had still not reached any conclusions four years later, due to the extreme diversity of procurement methods:

> [the] working group had studied the practices in various departments and services, but had discovered that the subject was a difficult one and that departmental requirements and procurement methods varied widely.[45]

---

[41] United Nations, *Yearbook of the United Nations 1979*, p. 962 [ref. UNCDoc].

[42] On the current function of resident coordinators, see the recent ECOSOC, *Functioning of the Resident Coordinator System, Including Costs and Benefits* [ref. REP].

[43] UN General Assembly, *Implementation of Section V of the Annex to General Assembly Resolution 32/197*, para. 6, lett. e) [ref. RES].

[44] Earlier in this chapter.

[45] United Nations, *Yearbook of the United Nations 1980*, p. 1245 [ref. UNCDoc].

3.3.3 Declarations on Principles and Actual Practices in Direct and Indirect Procurement

During the 1960s and 1970s several principles were identified and spelt out in formal declarations to guide international organizations in their procurement activities. The declarations of the General Assembly regarding procurement mentioned, on one hand, the principles of competition, efficiency and cost-effectiveness, and, on the other, the need for equitable geographical distribution, so that in evaluating offers preference could be given to local contractors or to contractors in developing countries (in development and humanitarian aid programmes, the two categories coincided). These values, which actually conflicted, were well expressed in a passage of a General Assembly resolution of 1970 regarding development programmes in the UN system:

> [w]hen necessary to ensure the maximum effectiveness of Programme assistance or to increase its capacity, and with due regard to the cost factor, increased use may appropriately be made of suitable services obtained from governmental and non-governmental institutions and firms, in agreement with the recipient Government concerned and in accordance with the *principles of international competitive bidding*. Maximum use should be made of national institutions and firms, if available, *within the recipient countries.*[46]

And also:

> [i]n the selection of individual experts, institutions or firms, in the procurement of equipment and supplies and in the provision of training facilities, the principle of equitable geographical distribution consistent with maximum effectiveness will be observed.[47]

There were essentially two reasons for preferring local contractors, and these related to the advantages offered to both international administrations and countries with developing economies. First, there was an attempt to achieve greater efficiency and effectiveness in procurement: if suppliers were close to the beneficiaries of the activity, costs could be reduced while also reducing the time required to complete procurement. In addition, there were reasons involving economic and social promotion – and in this case the principle partially overlapped with that of the

---

[46] Emphasis added. UN General Assembly, *The Capacity of the United Nations Development System*, Annex, para. 41 [ref. RES].
[47] *Ibid.*, para. 44.

equitable geographical distribution of suppliers: procurement made in situations of emergency, hunger, famine, or more generally when development aid was needed became a means that could be used, when possible, to favour disadvantaged business enterprises. The social and political goals of the organizations were thus supposed to inform the tender procedures, in theory also altering the principle of selecting the most advantageous offer. The General Assembly clearly expressed itself in a 1982 resolution:

> [t]he General Assembly ... [i]nvites all organs, organizations and bodies of the United Nations system engaged in operational activities for development to adopt appropriate measures leading to a greater use of the capacities of developing countries in local or regional procurement of material and equipment, in training and in services, in facilitating the increased use of local contractors, and in the recruitment of training, technical and managerial personnel ...[48]

Nevertheless, as would become clear in the decades to follow, the principles set out in the resolutions would long remain a dead letter. International competitive bidding, which represented a shift in the private negotiating methods prevalent in the organizations, as well as the principle of domestic preference, remained a little-observed principle in direct procurement. While the General Assembly's statements were a step forward in the traditional approach to procurement, they had more value as an appeal to best practice than as a reflection of actual practice. In undertaking direct procurement, the organizations continued to seek out their contractors rather than announce tenders open to all possible bidders.

However, even preference for local procurement had different or unexpected consequences than what was declared and hoped for. Indeed, as the headquarters of most international organizations were in European countries or the United States, in the case of direct procurement for internal purposes a preference for local contractors meant primarily commercial opportunities for American and European firms. This is in fact what occurred, so that for a long time the implementation of a preferential approach to local enterprises made the principle of equitable geographical distribution little more than an appeal to good intentions. In direct procurement for external purposes, the principle of preference to some extent coincided with that of geographical distribution. However, along with the international administration's insufficient control and accountability mechanisms, the emergency nature of the

---

[48] UN General Assembly, *Operational Activities for Development*, para. 12 [ref. RES].

operations, and the absence of local rule of law traditions, in practice it often translated into corruption and collusion. One of the many examples occurred in 1979 when the Board of Auditors, with regard to procurement of the United Nations Relief and Works Agency for Palestine Refugees in the Near East (UNRWA)

> cited instances of unusual contract-awarding practices, non-conformance with prescribed procedures, and liberal interpretation and use of emergency powers.[49]

Similarly, in indirect procurement, the primary effect of explicit adoption of ICB as the preferred method for vendor selection was to give Western firms a better chance to obtain the award. In this sense, ICB has been interpreted as 'a means for selling the institution[s] to important developed-country constituencies'.[50] This goal also appeared to shape the actual decisions of procurement officials. As reported by Devesh, Lewis and Webb with regard to the WB, '[m]any prominent executive director offices in developed countries kept a close tab on Bank projects and contracts therein, to help domestic firms in their constituencies'.[51] The consequences of the link between the broad use of ICB and the increased economic opportunities for Western firms are clear from the data on WB indirect procurement: between 1966 and 1970, suppliers from Western Europe, the United States, Canada, and Japan accounted for 62 per cent of the International Bank for Reconstruction and Development's (IBRD's) disbursement, and the percentage was even higher in 1971 when it reached the peak of 80 per cent of the International Development Association's (IDA's) disbursement.[52] This trend was slightly counterbalanced by two factors. The first related to low-value contracts: as reported by the WB itself, 'contracts considered too small or too scattered to be let economically under ICB were not financed by the Bank and were awarded using local procurement procedures that were uniformly accepted as satisfactory to the Bank'.[53] In order to understand the impact of this provision, one must, however, consider that during this phase projects related mainly to large infrastructure, such as ports, highways, telecommunications, power, and school construction.[54] Small contracts were thus a minority. The second is that since

[49] United Nations, *Yearbook of the United Nations 1979*, p. 1231 [ref. UNCDoc].
[50] Devesh, Lewis and Webb, *The World Bank*, p. 37.   [51] *Ibid.*   [52] *Ibid.*
[53] WB, *The World Bank's Procurement Policies and Procedures: Policy Review*, p. 2 [ref. AP&R].
[54] *Ibid.*, p. 2.

1966 the World Bank has permitted some forms of preference for domestic suppliers and contractors.[55]

3.4   A System in Transition (the 1980s)

At the end of the 1970s, the financial reports of the Board of Auditors repeatedly denounced the weaknesses of the organizations belonging to the UN system in (direct) procurement matters. Although action to reform the system had begun, it still required improvements:

> [a]lthough encouraged by the action taken to improve procurement systems and accounting procedures for expendable and non-expendable property, the Board indicated that more improvements needed to be made.[56]

Regarding UNICEF, for example, 'the Board ... indicated weaknesses in the procurement system', while for the UNHCR the Board identified at least two deficient areas: coordination among the various offices responsible for procurement[57] and lack of accountability and control of the agencies that implemented projects.[58]

In 1981, the UNDP's Governing Council authorized an internal organ (Administrator) to establish, in collaboration with the Inter-Agency Procurement Working Group (IAPWG) and IAPSU, procurement guidelines for the organizations within the United Nations system, with priority given to identifying their common features and differences. After almost three years of consulting with the organizations and reported difficulties in making comparisons given the variety of practices and rules,[59] in 1984 the Governing Council was presented with a final recognitive report of the

---

[55] Devesh, Lewis and Webb, *The World Bank*, p. 37.

[56] United Nations, *Yearbook of the United Nations 1978*, p. 1242 [ref. UNCDoc].

[57] 'The Board drew attention to shortcomings with respect to the administration of contracts to provide supplies for refugees and a lack of coordination in the procurement function and in the evaluation of business ventures', see United Nations, *Yearbook of the United Nations 1980*, p. 1242 [ref. UNCDoc].

[58] 'Commenting on project accountability of implementing agencies, the Board expressed concern over inadequate financial records and delays in submission of financial and narrative reports ... The Board commented that the internal audit be strengthened', *ibid.*

[59] See UNDP, *Guidelines for the Procurement of Equipment, Supplies and Services. Note by the Administrator*, 1982 [ref. AP&R]; *id.*, *Guidelines for the Procurement of Equipment, Supplies and Services*, 1983 [ref. AP&R]; *id.*, *Guidelines for the Procurement of Equipment, Supplies and Services*, 1984 [ref. AP&R]; United Nations, *Yearbook of the United Nations 1982*, pp. 658–659 [ref. UNCDoc].

research conducted[60] and, based on this, the following year the IAPSU prepared guidelines for all the agencies (which, however, were merely internal and not accessible by the businesses interested in submitting bids) entitled *Common Principles and Practices,* which included and compared the procurement procedures of all the organizations.[61]

The study provided a critical framework that reported elements characteristic of a system in transition: no longer semi-private contracting methods, but not yet a concrete realization of the public law principles of procurement. The critical aspects related to substantive and procedural problems: difficulty in achieving complete harmonization, hesitance of administrations to ensure procedural guarantees to tender participants, such as publicity, transparency and reason giving and, finally, difficulty in balancing the principle of competition with that of equitable geographical distribution. Attempts were made to respond to these three basic problems.

3.4.1 Codification and Harmonization in Direct Procurement

During the early 1980s the first manuals regulating direct procurement appeared, as supplements to the financial regulations and rules of each organization. They collected and organized in a single document the administrative circulars that had offered a fragmentary and uneven regulation of the tender procedure during previous years. Available exclusively to the competent administrations and not to the public, these documents established the principles of activity and more or less precisely described the functions of the competent administrative authorities and the various steps in the procedures. However, they did not provide for external impartial organs that would systematically monitor their compliance.

Although the content of the procurement manuals was uniform in many ways, complete harmonization did not seem possible for reasons related to the functions of the various organizations:

> [although] the agencies reached a consensus that unification of procurement procedures was welcome, desirable and necessary in the long-term interest of facilitating increased transparency ... some differences in individual agency rules and practices would continue to exist in light of

---

[60] UNDP, *Guidelines for the Procurement of Equipment, Supplies and Services,* 1985 [ref. AP&R].
[61] United Nations, *Yearbook of the United Nations 1985,* p. 475 [ref. UNCDoc].

the varying degrees of specialization and of the procurement volume as
well as operational requirements.[62]

The argument over the diversity of functions thus justified the maintenance of a certain degree of differentiation.[63]

Nevertheless, even considering this factor, there were areas where the rules and regulations were not influenced by the exercise of functions, and where, despite that, there was little harmonization.[64] In general, the administrative structure and the relationships within the administration, and in particular those between the requisitioners and the procurement officers, were regulated in similar ways in the various organizations. On the contrary, there was greater fragmentation and diversification in the external procedural phase when contractors were selected and the contract awarded, which involved the possible contractors and bid winners. For instance, there began to be a certain degree of uniformity in solutions to issues related to the nature and formulation of internal requests for goods, services or works,[65] the role of officials responsible for formulating specifications, the procedures to follow in the case of inadequate specifications, the time frames for responding to procurement requests, the division of responsibilities between headquarters and local offices based on the size of the tender, and the thresholds below which non-competitive procedures could be followed. With regard to these aspects, the 1985 report noted as follows:

> analysis ... has revealed a marked uniformity of approach among the
> agencies and where there are minor deviations (usually among larger

---

[62] UNDP, *Guidelines for the Procurement of Equipment, Supplies and Services,* 1985, p. 2 [ref. AP&R].

[63] On how the functions performed by the organizations still influence the procurement carried out by each of them, see Chapter 2.

[64] The internal/external dichotomy in this transition has a different significance from that used in the past. We are not talking about internal administrative activity related to the life of the organization or external administrative activity aimed at providing a service to outside parties. As explained more fully later in this work, internal/external refers to the two segments of tender procedures. The first corresponds to a request from the operating unit, the so-called requisitioner, to the procurement officer for a certain volume of goods, services, and work. It is internal in the sense that it involves exclusively the organization's administrative organs. The second segment corresponds to the tender procedure itself, which involves the individuals or firms who could become contractors. In this sense, it is thus external.

[65] This refers to requests from the unit that performs the function and, on a time by time basis, indicates its needs for goods, services and work, the so-called requisitioner. These requests are directed to the procurement officer, who is responsible for carrying out the tender procedures.

agencies) these appear to be due to the varying nature of the concerned agency's field establishment.[66]

On the contrary, there were diverse solutions in the pre-registration procedures for potential contractors and in the policies on transparency, publicity and reason giving applied during the tender procedures. Thus, on balance, during these years the situation still showed some diversity in some of its most important aspects.

3.4.2 Publicity, Transparency, Reason Giving in Direct Procurement: The Long Road towards Open Procedures

While the provisions on publicity, transparency and reason giving for tender award decisions differed in certain important ways, a general trend could nevertheless be traced – Schermers and Blokker's expression 'unity within diversity' is a good way to describe this situation.[67] The process of opening up procurement procedures had begun and was underway, but during this stage procedures were still far from being open and truly competitive.

In direct procurement, instead of open calls for tenders, two-thirds of the organizations sent letters of invitation to the firms they considered to be suitable bidders. Often, firms were asked to present bids on recommendation by the governments which benefited from the organization's activity. Only three agencies had a system for pre-qualifying firms, and consequently a list of pre-qualified firms. Two-thirds of the agencies gave no information on the names or nationalities of the firms invited to submit bids, or the names of the firms that submitted the bids. Many did not provide for the public opening of bids. There was no common established policy on notifying bidders who were not awarded the contract. Most agencies provided notification upon express request only, and provided only general comments on the weakness of the bid. Moreover, this reason giving was always oral, never in writing. In the declared intentions of the organizations, lack of reason giving was explained by the need to protect the interests of firms 'to prevent a given firm from possibly obtaining proprietary or confidential information on bids from

---

[66] UNDP, *Guidelines for the Procurement of Equipment, Supplies and Services*, 1985, p. 7 [ref. AP&R].

[67] Schermers and Blokker express it this way: 'although each organization has its own legal order, they often benefit from each other's rules and practical experience, and they do have common rules or principles', see Schermers and Blokker, *International Institutional Law*, § 23.

other participating firms'[68] and by it being objectively impossible to provide details on the decision 'due to a lack of available manpower to provide more elaborate details'.[69] Finally, tender documents were accessible to neither winning nor losing firms.

On these crucial points, the applicable rules still seemed quite similar to the practices that the organizations used immediately after their foundation, but with an important difference that marked a transition. Perception of their legitimacy and justifiability changed – including because these were no longer simple practices, but practices that had crystallized into the guidelines that most organizations were drawing up during this period. Thus, in 1985, under political pressure from decolonized countries and in conjunction with a new financial crisis in international organizations provoked by the United States, what had once been the normal *modus operandi* of organizations became an area that needed reform.

The absence of an adequate degree of transparency, publicity and reason giving began to be treated as a problem that jeopardized two procurement objectives in particular – namely, efficiency and equitable geographical redistribution of commercial opportunities – and, through these, ended up threatening the effectiveness of the organizations' action.

The link between inadequate publicity and transparency on the one hand and equitable geographical distribution on the other translated into a much-deplored inequality in the accessibility of tenders to firms in developing countries. In this regard, a 1985 report identified five critical points where reform was desirable:

> (a) The difficulties experienced by the United Nations procurement system in communicating available opportunities to the manufacturers/suppliers in the underutilized major donors and developing countries; (b) The lack of sufficient awareness in these countries of how the United Nations procurement system functions, in spite of the information disseminated through seminars, printed materials, etc.; (c) The traditional, pre-independence, procurement practices which the United Nations system tends to follow; (d) The location of the headquarters of the agencies which tends to favour procurement from the host or immediately adjacent countries; (e) The traditional reliance on experience and known sources of supply by field staff of the agencies.[70]

---

[68] UNDP, *Guidelines for the Procurement of Equipment, Supplies and Services*, 1985, para. 9 [ref. AP&R].
[69] *Ibid.*   [70] *Ibid.*, para. 13.

Operators in developing countries were not the only ones damaged. Among the factors that influenced the willingness of states to give a greater or lesser financial contribution to international organizations there was that of using these contributions to indirectly increase business opportunities for their firms. In this way, taxes paid by citizens and companies went through the international organization and returned to taxpayers in the form of contracts awarded. The lack of publicity, transparency and reason giving contributed to muting this indirect effect and neutralizing the objectives of major financing states. Without adequate guarantees, firms were discouraged from participating or, if they were not the usual business partners of the organizations or if governments had not recommended them to the organization, they might remain unaware of an organization's procurement need.

3.4.3 The Difficult Balance of Interests in Direct Procurement

Furthermore, lack of transparency and publicity, and the absence of the right to know the reason for a decision or gain access to documents, compounded the problem of how the principle of competition could co-exist with the preference accorded to firms in developing countries. As had already emerged in previous years, one of the effects that decolonization had on the procurement methods of international organizations was a push to adopt the principle of equitable geographical distribution when evaluating bids. Unlike the principle of cost effectiveness and efficiency, application of the principle of equitable geographical distribution was supposed to translate into preferential treatment that was justified by considerations other than solely economy and cost saving by the administration. Nevertheless, during these years counter-interests were balanced in a way that primarily guaranteed the administration's interest and that of the financing states, and only secondarily guaranteed the value of economic and social promotion:

> [w]hile recognizing the desirability of increasing procurement from developing countries and from underutilized major donor countries, it was emphasized that no country had the right to, nor would expect, preferential treatment, apart from the Governing Council decision.[71]

---

[71] Ibid., para. 5.

In addition, there was a widespread belief that a more equitable geographical distribution could be achieved not necessarily by permitting preferential treatment, but by opening the market and guaranteeing greater opportunities to firms in developing countries. In this sense, the principle of competition was proposed as instrumental to that of equitable geographical distribution:

> [a] more equitable geographical distribution of procurement would be achieved, *inter alia*, by providing better opportunities for these countries to provide bids. In this context, the importance of retaining the overall principle of international competitive bidding was generally agreed upon.[72]

During these years, the actual functioning of competition mechanisms was still limited, due to the aforementioned issues regarding publicity, transparency and reason giving, and to the broad exceptions to competition that most organizations permitted in their rules and regulations, and especially their practices. There were many situations where competition could be abandoned in favour of private contracting mechanisms: whenever an organization felt that the size of the contract made a tender procedure uneconomical; when the prices of goods or payment for services were set by national legislation; when required standards made competition impossible; when particular needs did not permit the delays that the bidding process involved; when the contract involved exclusive articles or perishable goods; when the agency felt that a competitive procedure might not produce satisfactory results; and finally, when a high administrative official so determined.[73] If one considers that most goods, services and works for international organizations are for emergency situations, that in particular for agencies like the FAO, WFP and UNHCR the goods involved are often perishable, and that there was also wide discretion for organizations not to carry out competitive procedures, one can understand why, despite codification of the first rules and frequent references to transparency and competition, most procurement by organizations during these years still took place through non-competitive processes. In addition, although it was supposed to promote development, the principle of competition, even when applied, translated into opportunities for Western firms more often than for firms from developing countries.

---

[72] *Ibid.*, para. 5.   [73] *Ibid.*, para. 9.

3.4.4 Indirect Procurement: Codification, Standardization and the Emergence of National Procurement Procedures

In the 1980s also indirect procurement regulation underwent a period of transition and adjustment. As noted above, unlike direct procurement, the rules on indirect procurement were codified in the form of guidelines at an early stage: the WB acted as a driving force, and other development banks followed its lead. So by the 1980s, all major banks had a set of rules that, while much briefer than they would later become, governed the implementation of procurement by borrowing states. These rules pointed to ICB as the preferred vendor selection method. Nevertheless, there were changes during these years, in particular within the WB. These related to the codification and standardization of rules; the vendor selection procedures and the adoption of domestic preference criteria; and the banks' role in controlling the projects' implementation and assessing the procurement systems of the borrowing states.[74]

In terms of codification and standardization, beginning in the early 1980s the WB, followed by other development banks, expanded its policies and procedures and made them more detailed.[75] In the case of the WB, these changes were codified into a formal bank policy.[76] In addition, in the late 1980s, there was a progressive standardization of documents related to projects and in particular to procurement. Banks prepared standard bidding documents for ICB that became obligatory for borrowing states in the early 1990s.[77] But standardization went beyond the vendor selection phase and also affected contracts: banks began to provide model contracts to national contracting authorities.[78] Nevertheless, the emergence of this process of standardization not only took place within each bank, but also triggered a process of harmonization among the banks themselves, which would culminate in the 1990s.[79]

The 1980s also marked a significant change in terms of the approach to vendor selection methods. Along with ICB, which was accused of favouring Western firms, other methods of selecting vendors were added. The decolonization process strengthened the economic capacities and

---

[74] See WB, *The World Bank's Procurement Policies and Procedures: Policy Review*, p. 3 [ref. AP&R]. And also Williams-Elegbe, *Public Procurement and Multilateral Development Banks*, pp. 19–20.

[75] WB, *The World Bank's Procurement Policies and Procedures: Policy Review*, p. 3 [ref. AP&R].

[76] WB, *Operational Manual* [ref. AP&R].   [77] *Ibid.*, p. 3.   [78] *Ibid.*, p. 3.

[79] AfDB, *Comprehensive Review of the AFDB's Procurement Policies and Procedures* [ref. AP&R].

interests of post-colonial countries within the organizations and this played a role in diversifying procurement methods: the WB, for instance, 'set predefined cut-offs in terms of contract size above which ICB was required and below which national competitive bidding (NCB) or local shopping was allowed'.[80] Furthermore, it became more common to authorize international or local shopping for minor, off-the-shelf items.[81]

Finally, there were significant changes in how banks controlled procurement activities. Until the 1980s, control took the form of approval, at first explicit, and then only implicit (through a no-objection procedure), of award decisions made by national administrations. This approval was prior to conclusion of the contract and aimed at verifying that national administrations had followed the bank's guidelines. In the 1980s, the exponential increase in the number of contracts, accompanied by a desire to give more autonomy to borrowing countries, led banks to introduce *ex post* reviews, when contracts had already been concluded, especially for low value or less complex contracts.[82] At the same time, again with an eye to economy of resources and also given the increased impact of local procurement, banks developed and gradually introduced systems for preliminary assessment of national procurement systems. With regard to the WB, this transition is explained as follows:

> [u]p to that point, the Bank seemed sanguine about local procurement processes and capacities, especially in the early years when the Bank did not finance much in the way of locally-procured items. That changed in the mid-1980s with the introduction of Country Procurement Assessment Reviews (CPARs).[83]

The assessment had the objective of evaluating the adequacy of the borrower procurement capacity, rules and procedures, and eventually preparing a plan to improve them.[84] While to begin with this type of assessment applied only to countries with weak procurement systems, it later became one of the prerequisites for the loans.

3.5   Administrative Reforms and Procurement Regulation (the 1990s)

Procurement methods and procurement rules went through a period of reform between 1985 and 2000. There were two main reasons for the change, one internal and one external.

---

[80] WB, *The World Bank's Procurement Policies and Procedures: Policy Review*, p. 3 [ref. AP&R].
[81] *Ibid.*   [82] *Ibid.*   [83] *Ibid.*, p. 4.   [84] *Ibid.*

The first was that between 1984 and 1985 the United Nations and its agencies experienced a serious financial and political crisis that would last for a number of years, which worsened when the Soviet bloc collapsed. The major financing states expressed their dissatisfaction with the management of the organizations' activities, use of resources, decision-making processes on budgetary matters, and allocation of costs among the various states. The United States in particular, following the oil crisis of 1977–1978 and the rapid growth of the domestic budget deficit, started drastically to reduce its contributions to the United Nations and UN agencies and to adopt a campaign against the organizations and their aid and development programmes. In December 1984, it left UNESCO[85] and in the same year Congress approved the first Kassebaum provision, which reduced US contributions to all the organizations within the UN system by $500 million for the period 1984–1987. In 1985, a second Kassebaum amendment proposed reducing the contribution ceiling from 25 per cent to 20 per cent if the United Nations failed to approve a new system of voting on budgetary matters.

In reality, apart from the economic-financial motives and the declared goals of administrative reform, the primary reasons for the American decisions seem to have been related to political balance within the organizations. In 1988, Bertrand, a UN management expert, wrote:

> [a]bove all it was not a question of improving the functioning of the World Organization through a process of management or to increase its efficiency, but solely a matter of regaining control over the United Nations and thereby preventing them from being able to continue serving as a propaganda forum against the United States and against Reagan.[86]

While it is true that the political element was decisive, it is also true that the political motives were shielded behind requests for administrative, personnel and procedural reorganization, and, due to the lack of resources caused by the crisis, translated into an attempt at administrative rationalization, in particular a revision of the rules on procurement.

The second cause was external: the disintegration of the Soviet bloc brought about changes in the organizations' operations. For example, in the United Nations overcoming the institutional impasse within the Security Council led to an increase in peacekeeping operations and international 'interim' administrations. From 1986 to 1995, the total expenditure by the United Nations system (United Nations and its

---

[85] Armstrong, Lloyd and Redmond, *From Versailles to Maastricht*, p. 116.

[86] Bertrand, 'The Process of Reform in the United Nations', p. 3 *et seq.*

agencies) more than doubled, going from $6,137 million to $13,164 million. The proportions of these total figures also changed: while in 1986 a twenty-fifth ($242 million) of the $6,137 million was for peacekeeping operations, in 1995 expenditure on peacekeeping operations accounted for more than a quarter ($3,364 million) of total expenditure, accompanied by exponential growth in the expenditure of individual agencies, many of which were also active in peacekeeping to provide support and guarantee its instrumental aspects.[87] Between 1990 and 2000, thirty-five new peacekeeping operations began – almost double the number of all the peacekeeping operations during the previous thirty years.[88]

The change was not only quantitative, but also qualitative: the international *interim* administrations established to steer populations emerging from war to peaceful institutional structures were different from those of the previous decades.[89] In the new wave of interim administrations, international organizations replaced the territorial state, and consequently concentrating all three powers of the state – legislative, administrative, and judicial – into temporary organs established by the organization.[90]

A similar trend can be detected, for other reasons, in development banks, which experienced an increase in their workload. For example, between 1988 and 1996 the contracts subject to WB prior review had grown from 3,100 to 11,300.[91] At the same time, the size of contracts significantly decreased, going from an average of $2.4 million per contract in 1988 to $1.1 million per contract in 1996.[92] This was the result of a shift in the kind of activity financed by the WB: 'the share of contracts in the social sectors, typically involving smaller contracts than those in

---

[87] On this point, see the table reconstructed by Hüfner, 'Financing the United Nations', p. 33.

[88] Caffarena provides a good graphic representation of these differences (see Caffarena, *Le organizzazioni internazionali*, p. 114). These numbers include not only peacekeeping operations in the narrow sense, but also operations that would be more appropriate to the operations of interim administrations.

[89] Some have spoken of a third phase of international interim administration. See Abraham, 'The Sins of the Savior'; Morlino, 'UN Interim Administrations'.

[90] In the words of Abraham: '[all the] substantial civil administration, including the administration of justice and the rule of law' (Abraham, 'The Sins of the Savior', p. 1301).

[91] WB, *The World Bank's Procurement Policies and Procedures: Policy Review*, p. 5 [ref. AP&R].

[92] *Ibid.*, p. 5.

infrastructure, had increased from 7 percent to 40 percent of the number of contracts reviewed'.[93] The interaction of internal and external causes and their consequences on the activity of the organizations was the basis for administrative reform. This reform was undertaken to resolve the conflict between two contradictory realities: on the one hand, the financial crisis of the organizations; and on the other, a rise in international intervention, made possible but also rendered increasingly necessary by the disruption of the world's macro-equilibrium. The process of rethinking the system of administrative management of resources, and in particular procurement, involved the still incomplete implementation of the principles of competition, transparency and accountability.

3.5.1 Phases of the Reform in Direct Procurement

Two phases of reform can be identified with reference to direct procurement: from 1985 for a period of five years, and from 1993 for about eight years. During the first phase, the changes mainly regarded the organizations' general budgets and accounting aspects. The second phase involved administrative activities with a direct impact on external public or private subjects, and so primarily procurement.

In 1985, a group of eighteen experts (the so-called 'Group of Eighteen') was established with a mandate to review the administrative organization and financial functioning of the UN system. Based on the group's recommendations,[94] the Assembly approved a general reform programme.[95] Some of the most significant measures planned and then implemented by the individual agencies included the approval of new planning and budgetary procedures, reductions in personnel, reorganization of the Secretariat, streamlining of the inter-governmental machine, improved management of information activities and control instruments, and evaluation and inspection of the administrative activities of personnel.[96]

---

[93] *Ibid.*, p. 5.

[94] UN General Assembly, *Report of the Group of High-Level Experts*, A/41/49, Supplement no. 49 [ref. REP]; *id.*, *Report of the Group of High-Level Experts*, A/41/663 [ref. REP]. See also Müller (ed.), *The Reform of the United Nations*, Vol. I, pp. 50–93 and pp. 94–97.

[95] UN General Assembly, *Review of the Efficiency of the Administrative and Financial Functioning*, A/41/213 [ref. REP].

[96] UN General Assembly, *Analytical Report of the Secretary-General on the Implementation of General Assembly Resolution 41/213*, April 1990 [ref. REP]; *id.*, *Analytical Report of the Secretary-General on the Implementation of General Assembly Resolution 41/213*,

The second phase of reform took place from 1993 to 1995, with the emergence of cases of poor administration and fraud in procurement for new peacekeeping operations. In 1993, the Assembly appointed a group of experts (known as the Ad Hoc Intergovernmental Working Group of Experts) to identify areas where more urgent reform was necessary.[97] The final report from the experts noted the presence of 'financially significant instances of fraud or presumptive fraud in United Nations peace-keeping operations'[98] and concluded: 'procurement constituted a major risk area for possible fraud or abuse'.[99]

Based on these recommendations and within the sphere of a more general plan for increased impartial controls of administration activities,[100] the General Assembly appointed the UN Board of Auditors to conduct a specific investigation on procurement in peacekeeping operations.[101] The investigation[102] showed frequent and arbitrary recourse to emergency procedures, unfairness in the process of selecting contractors, irregularities in agreements for the supply and transport of goods, and inadequate compliance with the Financial Regulations and Rules. Consequently, the recommendations were first of all to reduce flexibility in using exceptions to normal tender and award procedures: emergency needs had to be set out in advance in a special list, to be updated and reviewed regularly; the nature of the emergency had to be documented; bids had to be adequately evaluated; and open (not restricted) competition had to be guaranteed, at least for larger tenders. In addition, to promote efficient procurement, rosters of suppliers had to be kept and regularly updated and reviewed in order to reflect the

---

October 1990 [ref. REP]; *id.*, *Review of the Efficiency of the Administrative and Financial Functioning*, A/45/16 (Part I) [ref. REP]. See also Müller (ed.), *The Reform of the United Nations*, Vol. II, pp. 514–582 and pp. 583–586.

[97] UN General Assembly, *Review of the Efficiency of the Administrative and Financial Functioning*, A/RES/48/218B [ref. RES]; *Id.*, *Review of the Administrative and Financial Functioning of the United Nations*, A/RES/49/418 [ref. RES].

[98] United Nations, *Yearbook of the United Nations 1994*, p. 1359 [ref. UNCDoc].

[99] *Ibid.* The group of experts also hoped for a strengthening of instruments of accountability, and also proposed expanding the jurisdiction of the UN Administrative Tribunal over cases of this type: 'To promote transparency, the Assembly should study further the usefulness and scope of establishing a new intergovernmental body or bodies of experts to . . . monitor the contracting process. The Statute of the United Nations Administrative Tribunal should be amended to give it jurisdiction to adjudicate financial claims against staff members', *ibid.*

[100] *Ibid.*, p. 1365.

[101] UN General Assembly, *Development and International Economic Cooperation* [ref. REP].

[102] UN General Assembly, *Cooperation between the United Nations and the Organization of American States* [ref. REP].

outcomes of previous contracts; information had to be provided on the technical skills and financial stability of the parties; and activities involved in procurement had to be monitored according to previously established parameters.

3.5.2 Problems and Partial Reforms in Direct Procurement

The analysis performed by these organs concentrated primarily on UN procurement, but it highlighted problems common to the various UN agencies. Three principles in particular were key to the focus of criticism: competition, transparency (and publicity) and accountability.

3.5.2.1 Competition

In 1994, the value of tenders authorized by the UN Headquarters Committee on Contracts (i.e. larger tenders that required central authorization) was $1,378,861,841. Of this, $395,591,849 was for procurement activities assigned to governments through letters of assist, $513,623,701 was awarded through competitive procedures, and $469,646,291 was the total value of contracts concluded using exceptional procedures (primarily letters of invitation). Thus, at the central level and for larger contracts, about 60 per cent of the total volume of expenditure (contracts concluded with letters of assist and contracts that fell within the exception) was disbursed without applying the principle of competition. Along with this, a whole series of contracts did not have to be awarded competitively, nor did they pass through the Headquarters Committee on Contracts as they were below the thresholds set out in the Procurement Manual.

Furthermore, even when considering the overall procurement activity of the United Nations, including the headquarters in New York, but also the offices in Geneva, Nairobi and Vienna, the other regional commissions and the peacekeeping operations, as well as UNHCR, multiple failings were reported in the organization of the procurement function and in all phases of the procurement process. Between 1994 and 1995, for instance, the Office of Internal Oversight Services (OIOS) conducted 224 audits in the area of procurement[103] and found problems relating to the organization of the procurement function, such as outdated rules and lack of budgetary mechanisms to ensure controls, as well as irregularities in the planning and initiation of contracts, which included 'abuse of

---

[103] UN General Assembly, *Report of the Secretary-General on the activities of the Office of Internal Oversight Services*, A/50/459 [ref. REP].

emergency purchases and the use of immediate operational requirements in the field missions resulting from poor or inadequate planning',[104] '[l]ack of fair and competitive bidding',[105] followed by '[i]mproper evaluation of vendors' proposals resulting in the wrong choice of contractor'.[106]

In addition, implementation of the principle of competition was threatened not only during the phase of vendor selection, but even before that, when the specifications were drawn up. According to the United Nations's Policies and Procedures Handbook,[107] these had to be sufficiently general and neutral to avoid creating an implicit method of discrimination. Nevertheless, contract practice showed a different picture. In the 1995 report on procurement activities of the Department for Development Support and Management Services, the OIOS noted that in 46 per cent of the contracts awarded the technical specifications were either very restrictive or actually designed for a single source in a manner that precluded competitive bidding or made it very difficult.[108]

There was little compliance with the principle of competition also in decentralized procurement procedures. As noted, for example, in a series of audits that the OIOS conducted between 1996 and 1997 for the UN Angola Verification Mission (UNAVEM),[109] contracts were often awarded through restrictive and non-transparent procedures:

> [s]ome goods were procured from a restricted group of middlemen, at higher prices, under doubtful circumstances. Goods and services were procured, and payments made, without following the established procedures for procurement and without issuing purchase orders.[110]

In addition, procurement requests were split in order to bypass open tender procedures (as they would be below the minimum threshold for their application) and avoid controls by the Local Committee on Contracts, and urgent situations were artificially created that justified exceptions to the principle of competition:

> [i]n several instances, the Mission's Procurement Section interfered in the requisitioning process, resulting in splitting of requisitions and lengthy

---

[104] Ibid., para. 51.   [105] Ibid., para. 51.   [106] Ibid., para. 51.
[107] Now replaced by the United Nations, Procurement Manual, 2013 [ref. AP&R].
[108] UN General Assembly, Report of the Secretary-General on the Activities of the Office of Internal Oversight Services, Annex, A/50/945 [ref. REP]; id., Report of the Secretary-General on the Activities of the Office of Internal Oversight Services, A/51/432, para. 68–69 [ref. REP].
[109] UN General Assembly, Review of the Efficiency of the Administrative and Financial Functioning, Annex, A/52/881 [ref. REP].
[110] Ibid.

delays in processing. The splitting of requisitions allowed bypassing of the normal procurement procedures and of scrutiny by the Local and Headquarters Committees on Contracts. The delays in processing of requisitions resulted in rush purchases without providing adequate opportunity for competition among a wide range of suppliers.[111]

In line with these trends, an examination conducted by the OIOS on the activities of regional commissions[112] for the period 1996–1997[113] showed, for one of these in particular, an absence of market investigations to verify the real competitiveness of the contractor selected.

Following repeated pressure from the General Assembly and criticisms from control and auditing organs, between 1994 and 2000 some substantive and procedural reforms were implemented that aimed to expand the sphere of application of the principle of competition, restrict exceptions, and ensure a more rigorous application of the principle when implementing procedures.

a Substantive Reforms In 1998 the requirement of open competitive procedures was extended to categories of goods that formerly had been obtained primarily through private-like negotiations. For instance, the original version of Financial Rule 110.19 (f), which excluded the application of competitive procedures for professional services, no longer appeared justifiable in the light of the new market conditions.[114] Similarly, Financial Rule 110.19 (g) made it possible to not apply the principle of competition to procedures for the acquisition of medicines, medical equipment, and hospital and surgical supplies. While previously this exemption could be explained by the existence of fixed prices in many states for that type of goods, this was no longer true in a free market economy. As the OIOS explains in its report:

> in today's international commodity markets where generic products can be obtained at competitive prices, exemption of these goods is no longer justified and may limit the Organization's ability to obtain the best value.[115]

---

[111] *Ibid.*
[112] Economic Commission for Africa (ECA), Economic Commission for Latin America and the Caribbean (ECLAC), Economic and Social Commission for Asia and the Pacific (ESCAP), Economic and Social Commission for Western Asia (ESCWA).
[113] UN General Assembly, *Review of the Efficiency of the Administrative and Financial Functioning*, Annex, A/52/776 [ref. REP].
[114] 'It no longer appears to be justified in view of the competitive market for such services' (UN General Assembly, *Review of the Efficiency of the Administrative and Financial Functioning*, A/52/813, para. 15 [ref. REP]).
[115] *Ibid.*

Parallel with an expansion of the category of goods and services, the scope of exceptional situations where private-like negotiations were possible was reduced. As noted above, the rules on procurement by international organizations permitted private negotiations when there were particular needs, that is when longer and more complex procedures would have prevented an effective intervention. In this regard, the United Nations's Financial Rule 110.19 established the following:

> [c]ontracts may be awarded without calling for proposals, advertising or formal invitations to bid when: . . . d) The exigency of the service does not permit the delay attendant upon the issue of invitations to bid or the calling for proposals.[116]

In this case, reforms were made on a number of fronts. First of all, prerequisites and requirements were redefined. The broad interpretation of the term 'exigency', which was often adopted in practice, was criticized and a more restrictive interpretation was suggested. After repeated calls to define and limit the concept,[117] in 2000 the General Assembly, based on instructions from the Secretary-General,[118] adopted a new definition of 'exigency',[119] which was then incorporated into the Procurement Manual[120] of the United Nations and other agencies, and proposed a non-exhaustive list of situations where an exception could be made.

Second, *a priori* control mechanisms were set up to avoid an arbitrary and unjustified recourse to this practice. The Assistant Secretary-General for Central Support Services had to approve the decision and verify whether it was based on considerations of effective action, or if the extended time required by normal tender procedures could undermine or seriously impede the mission from achieving its objectives or

---

[116] These are circumstances that arise primarily during various phases of peacekeeping operations: during the initial phase, when execution of the Security Council's mandate requires the rapid deployment of troops or civil personnel; and during the central phase of expanding the mission, when a sudden change in the mission's mandate requires it.

[117] UN General Assembly, *Resolutions Adopted by the General Assembly [on the report of the Fifth Committee] (A/52/746/Add. 1)*, para. 8 [ref. RES]; Id., *Procurement Reform. Report of the Secretary-General*, A/53/271, para. 10 [ref. REP]; Id., *Procurement Reform*, A/RES/ 54/14, para. 18 [ref. RES].

[118] A first operating definition of 'exigency' had been given in April 1998 (UN General Assembly, *Review of the Efficiency of the Administrative and Financial Functioning*, A/ C.5/52/46, sec. 1 [ref. REP]) and was then replaced by a new one in August of that same year (UN General Assembly, *Procurement Reform*, A/53/271, para. 10 [ref. REP]).

[119] UN General Assembly, *Procurement Reform*, A/54/650 [ref. REP]; Id., *Procurement Reform*, A/55/127, para. 18 [ref. REP]; Id., *Review of the Efficiency of the Administrative and Financial Functioning*, A/55/532/Add. 2, para. 19 [ref. REP].

[120] UN General Assembly, *Procurement Reform*, A/57/187, para. 19 [ref. REP].

otherwise jeopardize the life or property of individuals.[121] In addition, the requisitioner had to provide a detailed justification of the reasons and circumstances that caused it to choose this exceptional option.

The reform also affected the relationship between requisitioners and procurement officers, that is between the units that presented requests for procurement and the administrative authorities responsible for managing the tender procedure. Due to greater administrative decentralization and the establishment of field offices, the practice of explicitly expressing a preference for one or more suppliers was widely adopted by requisitioners, especially in the field. Although repeatedly criticized by the Secretary-General, the Advisory Committee on Administrative and Budgetary Questions (ACABQ)[122] and the Board of Auditors, as it undermined the principle of segregating responsibilities between requisitioners and procurement officers, the practice was first tolerated with a few precautions[123] and then explicitly forbidden:

> [a]s a rule, the use of suppliers recommended by requisitioners or substantive offices is not permitted.[124]

It was, however, still allowed in specific situations, such as for the supply of legal, research, training or medical services, or the supply of goods patented solely by specific companies. In these cases the requisitioner had to provide a written justification.[125]

Moreover, this was complemented by the updating and expansion of the lists of qualified suppliers. If the legitimate purpose of requisitioners expressing preferences was to facilitate the selection of suppliers in a broad and geographically varied market, this purpose could be achieved by using a list of pre-qualified suppliers. These lists had also the advantage of more effectively preventing episodes of collusion (between

---

[121] UN General Assembly, *Procurement Reform*. A/53/271, para. 10 [ref. REP].

[122] UN General Assembly, *Report of the Advisory Committee*, A/50/7/Add. 13, para. 22 [ref. REP]; Id., *Review of the Efficiency of the Administrative and Financial Functioning*, A/51/7/Add. 3, para. 15 [ref. REP].

[123] In 1996 the Secretary-General established that '[a]ny supplier recommended by a requisitioner, if it is registered on the Supplier Roster, is subjected to the same selection process applied to other suppliers. Under the revised procedures, when a supplier has been suggested by a requisitioner, the Division uses extreme caution to ensure that the supplier will not receive any preferential treatment by any department, office or individual' (UN General Assembly, *Review of the Efficiency of the Administrative and Financial Functioning*, A/C.5/51/9, para. 25 [ref. REP]).

[124] UN General Assembly, *Review of the Efficiency of the Administrative and Financial Functioning*, A/52/534, para. 26 [ref. REP].

[125] Also see UN General Assembly, *Procurement Reform*, A/57/187, para. 19 [ref. REP].

requisitioners and suppliers) and unfair preference.[126] Based on these considerations, for instance, the list of pre-qualified suppliers for the UN was revised and expanded: from 1996 to 1997 it went from 1,550 registered suppliers to about 3,000.[127] In addition, as instructed by the General Assembly,[128] a systematic attempt was made to include suppliers from developing countries through the mediation of permanent and temporary missions from these countries.[129] The result, at least on paper, was a larger number of suppliers registered and less room for anti-competitive practices.

b Procedural Reforms Substantive changes were accompanied by procedural innovations introduced to administrative rules, but administrations often also made independent *de facto* changes in their daily management of procurements.

A significant change was introduced in the process of selecting contractors. The basic method adopted by international organizations to select suppliers had been – and continued to be[130] – the restricted procedure: only suppliers to whom the organization had sent bidding documents could submit bids or offers.[131] UN procurement officers had long abused this process by sending bidding documents only to some of the many suppliers who had indicated an interest – i.e. shortlisting – and did not justify their decision either internally, to their supervisors, or externally, to the suppliers not included on the shortlist. This was

---

[126] The Advisory Committee on Administrative and Budgetary Questions emphasizes this link: 'The Advisory Committee believes that if the supplier roster were a complete and comprehensive one, there would be no need for requisitioners to recommend suppliers' (UN General Assembly, *Review of the Efficiency of the Administrative and Financial Functioning*, A/51/7/Add. 3, para. 15 [ref. REP]).

[127] UN General Assembly, *Review of the Efficiency of the Administrative and Financial Functioning*, A/52/534, para. 16 [ref. REP].

[128] UN General Assembly, *Procurement Reform*, A/RES/51/231, para. 26 [ref. RES], which states: '[the General Assembly] 26. [e]mphasizes that concerted efforts should be made to identify potential vendors in the developing countries and countries with economies in transition and to increase the representation from those countries in the bidding for and award of contracts, so as to develop a supplier base that is more representative of the membership of the Organization'.

[129] UN General Assembly, *Review of the Efficiency of the Administrative and Financial Functioning*, A/52/534, paras. 18–23 [ref. REP].

[130] See Chapter 3.

[131] On the contrary, the basic procedure, for example, provided by European directives on tender contracts is an open procedure where anyone interested in participating in the tender can respond by submitting bids with no necessity for the intermediate step in which the competent administrative authorities send bidding documents.

a widespread practice linked to the semi-private approach of international administrations to procurement, as discussed above, but became the subject of repeated criticism by the General Assembly, which insisted on the need for reforms.[132]

Thus, starting in 1999, the application of restricted selection procedures was balanced with the provision of a general obligation to send bidding documents to all suppliers registered for a specific sector. On this point the Secretary-General offered an assurance:

> ... the previous practice of short-listing candidates from the vendor roster to be invited to participate in the bidding process has been curtailed. Since April 1999, all registered vendors for the required product or service are given the opportunity to participate in the tender exercise.[133]

The new rules thus tended to make the pool of registered suppliers (registration was by sector of interest) the same as the pool of those who could submit bids. In this way, the regulator intended to reduce the anti-competitive effect of restricted procedures and at the same time maintain a good level of efficiency.

However, there was an exception to the rule[134] that significantly reduced its impact: if there were so many suppliers that a 'reasonable' procurement process was impossible, the competent administrative authority could send bidding documents to a smaller number of suppliers. The assessment of reasonableness was presumably based on a predicted estimate of the expenditure necessary to manage a large selection process and the time required for this process. The competent authority then had to combine this assessment with information on the resources available and the time beyond which the contractual objective could no longer be achieved. Administrative circulars from this period did not, however, offer guidelines on the concept of reasonableness and its application, and instead only provided an obligation to keep records of the procedure for a minimum period of time, so to make it possible to identify ex post facto the factors that were taken into account in the selection process.

---

[132] '[The General Assembly] ... 15. Also requests the Secretary-General to send invitations to tender, to the fullest extent possible, to all vendors registered under specific categories and services on the supplier roster' (UN General Assembly, *Procurement Reform*, A/RES/54/14, para. 15 [ref. RES]).

[133] UN General Assembly, *Procurement Reform*, A/55/127, para. 15 [ref. REP].

[134] Others would later be added to the procurement manuals.

Finally, in many cases, emergency circumstances made the period of time between announcing the tender and expiry of the invitation to bid too short to guarantee an adequate distribution of information and thus effective competition. In a situation where online tenders were still not common (they began to be in the late 1990s) and where the principal source of advertising invitations to tender was printed periodicals, a suitable time frame for advertising became an essential requirement for receiving bids from more competitors. Thus, one of the seemingly minor procedural reforms, but which was actually important for competition, was to limit in situations where advertising time frames were short and to establish minimal time limits to keep the tender open.[135]

3.5.2.2 Transparency and Publicity

The principles of transparency and publicity, instrumental to allowing competition, began to guide the activity of the organizations, albeit with many limits and enormous differences compared to the state systems of the time. The instrumental role of transparency and publicity changed the content of the principles. Traditionally, in the life of organizations, the accounting and financial concerns of states – especially the United States – as representatives of taxpaying citizens, were what informed the rules on transparency. Thus, the measures adopted were aimed principally at improving the internal transparency of administrative action.

Within this framework, the innovations of the Kofi Annan years were qualitative as well as quantitative. On the one hand, internal transparency improved, primarily due to changes in hierarchical accountability mechanisms. On the other hand, new forms of advertising and external transparency of administrative activity were introduced, making the administrative authorities more accountable to suppliers and potential suppliers.

What made reform possible, or at least facilitated it, was the availability of a rapid easily accessible system for disseminating information: the internet. The first experiments with computerization began in the late 1990s, and this factor was also taken into account in the new rules on procurement.

In procedures for advertising invitations to bid, publication in the media, daily newspapers and trade journals was, until then,

---

[135] UN General Assembly, *Procurement Reform*, A/55/127, para. 8 [ref. REP].

required only 'where feasible'.[136] In June 1997, a website for the United Nations's Procurement Division was started where tenders for contracts worth more than $200,000 were announced, albeit only experimentally and with no permanent obligation required.[137] In 2000, it became obligatory to publish tender invitations on the UN Procurement Division's website for all contracts that required competitive procedures. This was accompanied by an obligation to email the tender announcement to the missions of all member states, to the peripheral offices, and to the data centres of all UN organizations.[138]

The intermediate phase of opening bids and awarding the contract went from completely opaque methods to practices that were in certain respects more protective of suppliers. In 1994, a request sent to the United Nations's Office of Legal Affairs (OLA) on the authentic interpretation of the term 'publicly opened' included in Financial Rule 110.20 extended the possibility of attending the bid opening to the general public, including the media and anyone else interested. The request to the Office of Legal Affairs originated from the United Nations' Procurement Division, which admitted only selected suppliers to the opening of bids, and not, for example, all suppliers who had expressed an interest in the tender by submitting a bid or representatives of national missions, or journalists. The 1982 version of Financial Rule 110.20 (and similarly the accounting rules of other organizations) provided:

> [a]ll bids shall be publicly opened at the time and place specified in the invitation to bid and an immediate record made thereof.[139]

The OLA set out two possible interpretations of the rule. The first was a literal interpretation of the text: access to opening procedures should not be limited to a particular group or category of persons. The second was a context-based interpretation according to which a restrictive application of the rule might be permitted. The OLA referred in particular to Art. 31(2) of the United Nations Commission on International Trade Law (UNCITRAL) Model Law on Procurement of Goods, Construction, and Services, which provided that

---

[136] 'Open advertising of requirements through the media, newspapers and trade journals is utilized where feasible' (UN General Assembly, *Review of the Efficiency of the Administrative and Financial Functioning*, A/C.5/51/9, para. 26 [ref. REP]).

[137] UN General Assembly, *Review of the Efficiency of the Administrative and Financial Functioning*, A/52/534, para. 21 [ref. REP].

[138] UN General Assembly, *Procurement Reform*, A/55/127, para. 21, lett. a)–b) [ref. REP].

[139] United Nations.

[a]ll suppliers or contractors *that have submitted tenders*, or their representatives, shall be permitted by the procuring entity to be present at the opening of tenders.[140]

Notwithstanding the fact that the UNCITRAL Model Law was only applicable to states and not to international organizations, when the problem arose of which standard of publicity to apply, the OLA referred to the UNCITRAL Model Law and its narrower standard to justify the past practices of the Procurement Division. However, this did not prevent the Office of Legal Affairs from requiring more transparency in future procedures:

> [n]evertheless, we are *constrained* to give some effect to the word 'publicly', and therefore in our view there would be no basis under rule 110.20 for not allowing persons lawfully present on United Nations premises, including representatives of the media, to attend a bid opening, if they so requested.[141]

The opinion appears to be contradictory and not impartial: the Office of Legal Affairs said it was 'constrained' to draw its legal conclusions according to the letter of the rule, and thus to recognize the rights of private parties to participate in the procedure; but because the UNCITRAL Model Law was non-binding and moreover not intended for international organizations, the Office of Legal Affairs recognized as legitimate a practice that was, as the Office of Legal Affairs itself recognized, contrary to the rule that directly governed it.

The assessment was innovative and relevant for future procurements, yet preserved the *status quo*. It was innovative because it formally recognized that private parties had the right to transparency in procurement procedures. In a situation where neither the substance of the action, nor the rule governing the action, could be taken for granted, this recognition represented a break with the past and laid the foundations for future change. On the other hand, it was conservative because the formal recognition of rights had no consequences. There was no sanction for an administration that did not comply (with the letter of the rule), or compensation for any damages incurred by other parties (suppliers who did not participate in the tender because they were not invited to submit bids). And while the decision certainly had no retroactive effect, neither was it pro-active: the restrictive practice continued to be tolerated. In this sense, the contradictory nature of the solution to the question of publicly

---

[140] Emphasis added.
[141] United Nations, *Interpretation of United Nations Financial Rule 110.20*, pp. 497–498.

opening bids marked a not insignificant transition from non-recognition to recognition, i.e. from the absence of a formal and substantive right to its recognition as a formal right, albeit with no substantive content.

Moreover, this decision marked the beginning of years of critical comments on this single aspect of procedural transparency, although it remained essentially unchanged in practice. In 1996 the Secretary-General presented the Assembly with the results of the OIOS's examination of the tender activities of the organizations in the UN system: in thirteen of the twenty-six sample cases examined, the requirements of sealed bids and publicly opening them were not communicated to suppliers, and the respective obligations were not respected.[142]

Access to documents was another issue that, during this period, was subject to reform. The justifications that had until then protected the administration from the obligation to disclose tender-related documents began to be questioned. The traditional shield of official secrecy, used by the organizations to deny access to information on the procurement procedure, began to be challenged, especially given that there was not even a duty to give reason for the award. In 1994, the UN OLA issued a draft administrative memorandum – which was then approved – on the right of access to documents. For the most part based on and replicating the UNCITRAL Model Law on Procurement of Goods, Construction, and Services, it listed the information to be made available not only to tender participants but also to anyone interested in the tender procedures and outcome. Understandably, the amount of information was more restricted for parties who were simply interested than for 'qualified' interested parties, but for the first time everyone was guaranteed, at least in theory, a minimum level of information: a brief description of the goods, services or works required and the reason for the tender; and the names and addresses of the firms that submitted bids and of the contract winner.[143]

3.5.2.3 Accountability

The debate on the accountability of administrative authorities responsible for tenders during this phase in the history of procurement went in two directions. The first related to internal and hierarchical accountability, understood as the responsibility of subordinates to their superiors.

---

[142] UN General Assembly, *Report of the Secretary-General on the Activities of the Office of Internal Oversight Services*, A/50/945, Annex, II (3) [ref. REP].

[143] United Nations, *Interpretation of United Nations Financial Rule 110.20*, pp. 498 [ref. AP&R].

The second related to accountability to suppliers who participated (or intended to participate) in the tenders, and to third parties.[144]

a Internal Controls The 1994 Ad hoc Intergovernmental Working Group of Experts, mentioned above, as well as the Board of Auditors in the 1994–1995 report, dedicated much of their analysis to the problem of internal accountability. Internal accountability, at the level of the micro management of resources, was both a basis for internal controls, and for external control, such as the financial control exercised by member states through the Board of Auditors.

The system of internal controls that emerged in UN organizations was deficient in terms of structure and rules: there were no clear lines of authority, responsibility or supervision; and there were no guidelines for the composition and functioning of the headquarters committees on contracts, when in place. In addition, administrative practice highlighted frequent recourse to *ex post facto* controls that should have been exceptional: the rule was that for contracts that exceeded a certain threshold, the Headquarters Committees on Contracts would make a legitimacy check to verify compliance with the internal rules on tenders and consistency between evaluation and final award. But empirical findings on this period show a different reality. For example, in 1995, within the United Nations, 500 of the 1,058 cases subject to the Commission's precautionary control, i.e. 50.7 per cent, were presented *ex post facto* or partially *ex post facto*.[145] And the percentage increased for peacekeeping operations: in the two years between 1994 and 1995, 57 per cent of the contracts of the Department for Peacekeeping Operations (DPKO) were submitted for the Commission's approval only after they were already concluded.[146]

Administrative reform sought to remedy this failure of the system, intervening at both the organizational level and at the procedural level. Decolonization and the growth in the volume of activity of organizations had led to decentralization of the administrative structure of organizations: new peripheral procurement offices were

---

[144] The distinction is not complete and requires additional elucidation, but it sufficiently makes the point at this juncture. The issue of accountability will be discussed in greater detail, including in terms of theory, in Chapter 7.

[145] UN General Assembly, *Review of the Efficiency of the Administrative and Financial Functioning of the United Nations. Procurement Reform*, A/C.5/51/9, Annex VIII [ref. REP]. And also *id.*, *Procurement Reform*, A/53/271, para. 7 [ref. REP].

[146] US GAO, *United Nations: Progress of Procurement Reforms*, p. 7 [ref. REP].

established, and significant delegations of authority were granted. Nevertheless, for a long time decentralization was not accompanied by corresponding control mechanisms and audits of procurement activities. The Ad hoc Intergovernmental Working Group of Experts, the Board of Auditors, and the United States Government Accountability Office (US GAO) especially denounced the results of this 'lame' decentralization process, where delegations of authority flowed from the top down without a corresponding return of accountability in the other direction. The reform sought to remedy this omission by maintaining the decentralized structure but multiplying and strengthening the supervisory powers of higher level organs. For instance, with reference to the UN:[147]

> prior to the reorganization, authority for procurement was not centralized within the Secretariat, but after reorganizing, all procurement has to be conducted under the Authority of the Procurement Division.[148]

In particular, at headquarters procurement had to be carried out under the direction of the Assistant Secretary-General for Central Support Services,[149] or his counterparts in other international organizations, who had the last word on procurement initiatives and awards through the commissions he designated.[150] In peripheral offices, the Assistant Secretary-General appointed general managers who had, at the peripheral level, powers similar to his at the central level and were required to periodically report information on the procurement activities carried out.

The organizational reform was accompanied by a revision of control procedures. This was accomplished principally by adjusting administrative practices rather than legislation. For example, in the UN supervisory powers were centralized in the hands of the Assistant Secretary-General. In an April 1996 memorandum to the Assistant Secretary-General for Planning and Support and in a subsequent memorandum of July 1996,

---

[147] This, moreover, began around the mid-1990s with precise initiatives, and culminated in 2003 with an extensive amendment of the Financial Regulations and Rules (United Nations, *Financial Regulations*, ST/SGB/2003/7 [ref. AP&R]). For a precise and critical comparison between the old and new regulations and rules, see UN General Assembly, *Proposed Revisions to the Financial Regulations*, pp. 16, 47, 49–58 [ref. REP].

[148] US GAO, *United Nations: Progress of Procurement Reforms*, p. 10 [ref. REP].

[149] The Assistant Secretary-General is responsible to the Under Secretary-General, who is responsible to the Secretary-General.

[150] For a more in-depth analysis of the powers of the Assistant Secretary-General and his relationships with subordinate officials, see Chapter 6.

addressed to all officials at headquarters, and to the administrative heads of peripheral offices and international criminal courts, stricter procedures were established for the admissibility of *ex post facto* or partially *ex post facto* approvals. In particular, the officials who authorized these cases would be considered personally responsible for the decision and would have to justify it[151] (in the past there had been no requirement to provide reasons) by showing a serious threat to the achievement of the mission's objectives and/or a real danger to the lives of troops or remaining personnel.[152]

The consequence of the reform was a drastic reduction in awards that had not first been controlled by the Headquarters Committees on Contracts or the equivalent at the local level. In the UN, from 1995 to 1998 the percentage of *ex post facto* approvals dropped from 18.81 per cent to 4.96 per cent, and partially *ex post facto* approvals from 31.87 per cent to 9.58 per cent, for a total of 50.68 per cent in 1995 to 14.54 per cent three years later.[153]

Greater control by the headquarters committees on contracts and the effective reduction of *ex post facto* approval practices, at least within the UN, along with closer supervision by the Assistant Secretary-General, had an impact on competition, or rather on situations in which the responsible officials decided to award a contract competitively (which increased during these years compared to the previous decade) rather than through private negotiations. Proving the fact that accountability and controls play an important role in implementing rules on competition, the Secretary-General noted that '[a]s a result of the above directive [i.e. the 1996 memoranda], procurement through competitive bidding has increased'.[154] In his analysis, the Secretary-General thus found that the reforms of internal accountability mechanisms encouraged a more competitive system.

---

[151] In this regard, the Secretary-General noted: 'all officials concerned have been directed to explain fully, and to justify each case in writing, bearing in mind their respective full accountability for their actions. The new procedures will be strictly monitored and enforced' (UN General Assembly, *Review of the Efficiency of the Administrative and Financial Functioning*, A/C.5/51/9, para. 40 [ref. REP]).

[152] *Ibid.*, para. 37.

[153] Percentages for the intermediate years are: in 1996, *ex post facto* 14.32 per cent, partially *ex post facto* 18.28 per cent, for a total of 32.6 per cent; in 1997, *ex post facto* 5.28 per cent and partially *ex post facto* 7.70 per cent, for a total of 12.98 per cent. The percentages are reported in UN General Assembly, *Procurement Reform*, A/53/271, paras. 7–8 [ref. REP].

[154] *Ibid.*

b External Controls External controls, that is controls by independent bodies, which were also not involved in the procurement process, had been set up for international organizations in the UN system since their establishment and their first years of activity. The Board of Auditors was established in 1946[155] with the task of performing periodic audits of the United Nations and connected agencies. A portion of its responsibilities thus extended to controlling expenditure for procurement activities. In 1966 an experimental Joint Inspection (JIU) Unit[156] was established and was made permanently operational in 1976,[157] with the power to investigate any matter related to the efficiency of the organizations' activities and appropriate use of funds. In this role, over the years it directly and indirectly handled issues related to procurement, investigating specific problems such as accountability and decentralization.

Since 1994, in addition to these organs with a general scope of action, other bodies were established in each organization, such as the OIOS for the United Nations and bodies corresponding to the OIOS in other organizations. These bodies did not have sector-specific responsibilities – even though they referred to the activity of only one organization – and were also external to the procurement process. In particular, the role and functions of the OIOS will be examined in detail later in this work. The purpose here is primarily to show two innovative aspects of these bodies: independence and openness to private parties.

With regard to the former, until 1993 internal control functions (on the conduct of personnel) were, for all organizations, handled by department units responsible for administration and management. In the case of the UN, for example, it was the Department of Administration and Management. But demands for greater transparency and accountability[158] gradually led the controllers to separate and distance themselves from the controlled: in August 1993, the UN Secretary-General established a special Office for Inspections and Investigations, under the direction of the Assistant Secretary-General. During subsequent years, similar bodies were established in the other organizations belonging to the UN system.

As for openness to private parties, a document drafted in 1994 by the Secretary-General for UN administrative personnel explained the

---

[155] UN General Assembly, *Appointment of External Auditors* [ref. RES].
[156] UN General Assembly, *Report of the Ad Hoc Committee of Experts to Examine the Finances of the United Nations* [ref. RES].
[157] UN General Assembly, *Statute of the Joint Inspection Unit* [ref. RES].
[158] In particular, for a criticism of the Secretariat's system of accountability and supervision, see JIU, *Accountability and Oversight in the United Nations* [ref. REP].

functions of the OIOS and offered the following clarification of the investigative function:

> [t]he Office may receive and investigate reports from staff and *other persons* engaged in activities under the authority of the Organization suggesting improvements in programme delivery and reporting perceived cases of possible violations of rules or regulations, mismanagement, misconduct, waste of resources or abuse of authority.[159]

This passage was interpreted narrowly: the parties with standing to present complaints to the OIOS were administrative personnel and anyone whose activities were under its supervision, thus, for example, private parties having an outsourcing contract with the international administration. Based on this reading, suppliers who had not been awarded a tender were excluded. Nevertheless, subsequently, and in an informal manner to make up for the absence of an impartial body to determine the propriety of procurement procedures, the practice was established, not only for the UN but also in other organizations within the UN system, of allowing private parties who were more generally involved in the activity of international organizations (and not necessarily connected to them through a contract of outsourcing) to confidentially report any dubious conduct by awarding administrations to these organs. Thus, tenderers were included among these.

3.5.3   Harmonization, Country Ownership and Accountability in Indirect Procurement

For indirect procurement as well, the 1990s and early 2000s were a phase of significant reform as it became clear that the development policies financed by the WB and other banks were substantially ineffective.[160] For the WB, for example, the rate of satisfactory outcomes for bank-financed investment operations was only 66 per cent at the beginning of the 1990s.[161] The ineffectiveness of aid was due

---

[159] Emphasis added. United Nations, *Establishment of the Office of Internal Oversight Services*, para. 18 [ref. AP&R].

[160] WB, *The World Bank's Procurement Policies and Procedures: Policy Review*, p. 5 [ref. AP&R]; AfDB, *Comprehensive Review of the AfDB's Procurement Policies and Procedures*, p. 1 [ref. REP].

[161] WB, *The World Bank's Procurement Policies and Procedures: Policy Review*, p. 5 [ref. AP&R].

to various factors, some of which were related to procurement. On one hand, according to the countries receiving the financing, the causes were ascribable to donor country policies. Donors often linked financing to certain specific conditions, such as awarding a percentage of contracts to their own firms. In this way, development aid was an alibi to promote a protectionist approach.[162] Moreover, beneficiary countries complained that the coexistence of different rules and conditions based on the origin of the financing, often adopted in addition to or in lieu of national rules, created a fragmentary situation and regulatory misalignment, leading to inefficiency especially in the African region. In this regard, the following passage from the AfDB is significant:

> each donor [whether bilateral or multilateral] brought in a different set of Rules, Guidelines and bidding documents. This constituted a nightmare scenario for borrower executing agencies. Under the circumstances, the large number of donor interventions, coupled with the various policy orientations, turned the development scene into a battle ground.[163]

On the other hand, donor states, in particular the United States, were highly critical of how borrowing states managed the financing, and how the banks supervised this management. The idea behind such criticism was not only that resources were being wasted, but also that the emergence of new markets, including local ones, was jeopardizing the economic returns to financing states in terms of contracts awarded to their companies. Moreover, as noted at the beginning of this section, this widespread criticism emerged within the context of significant growth and change in the banks' functions.

All this spurred the organizations on in a process of reforming indirect procurement. The process was driven by the WB, followed by other development banks, with the United States as the primary promoter of

---

[162] AfDB, *Comprehensive Review of the AfDB's Procurement Policies and Procedures*, p. 1 [ref. AP&R].

[163] *Ibid.*, p. 2. Similar words are used by Foster: '[p]roblems have arisen where Governments with weak management capacity have been overwhelmed by the sheer numbers of donors and of donor projects, with the result that public expenditure has become an unplanned aggregation of donor projects lacking a coherent framework of policies, priorities and service standards … Donor technical capacity frequently overwhelms Government, who are unable to respond to the barrage of technical and policy advice they receive', from Foster, *New Approaches to Development Co-operation*, pp. 18 and 20. And in the same direction WB, *The World Bank's Procurement Policies and Procedures: Policy Review*, pp. 6–7 [ref. AP&R].

it.[164] It consisted of an organizational restructuring within the various banks; of a regulatory reform, in particular related to the procurement rules applicable to borrowing states; and of a revision of control and accountability mechanisms.

Internal organizational reforms entailed an increase of procurement personnel, accompanied by a decentralization of management. For example, from 1998 to 2003, the WB nearly doubled the number of personnel working in procurement, from 81 to 156 units.[165] At the same time, it implemented the decentralization of country programme management, giving more responsibilities and decision-making power to the Bank's offices in borrowing states.[166] The objective was to shorten the distance between the bank and borrowing states, giving the latter direct assistance in the event of management problems. From the bank's perspective, this new structure was supposed to guarantee more uniform management and effective control.

Along with a general internal reorganization, regulatory reforms were undertaken that were primarily aimed at harmonizing procurement rules among the various banks and adopting a common regulatory framework within the same bank, in order to prevent borrowing states from falling into the misalignment and fragmenting described above. This process also took place within the sphere of a more general codification of international rules on domestic public procurement. While the *Tokyo Round* Code on Government Procurement in fact dates to 1981, a critical turning point in the regulation of procurement was the adoption, in 1994, of the GPA as part of the WTO. In addition, the Model Law on Procurement of Goods, Construction, and Services was issued by UNCITRAL in 1993.

In this context of general standardization of procurement rules, development banks also promoted the harmonization of such rules. The harmonization process formally began with the establishment, in 1999, of a forum for procurement harmonization 'aiming to provide a coherent mechanism for procurement cooperation between MDBs, IFIs and key development partners'.[167] Also around the end of the

---

[164] For an analysis of the dominant role of the Unites States in the various development banks especially with regard to the creation of accountability mechanisms, see Park, 'Accountability as Justice for Mutilateral Development Banks?'.

[165] WB, *The World Bank's Procurement Policies and Procedures: Policy Review*, p. 5 [ref. AP&R].

[166] *Ibid.*

[167] AfDB, *Comprehensive Review of the AfDB's Procurement Policies and Procedures*, p. 2 [ref. AP&R]. Among the financial institutions involved were: the ADB, the AfDB, the Black Sea Trade and Development Bank (BSTDB), the Caribbean Development Bank

1990s, development banks began to work jointly to prepare Country Procurement Assessment Reports. This process continued with the *Monterrey Consensus on Financing for Development* in 2002, which included the harmonization of procurement policies among its goals. Then, starting in the early 2000s, policies for harmonizing indirect procurement rules were incorporated in the broader commitment to harmonization sponsored by the Organisation for Economic Co-operation and Development/Development Assistance Committee (OECD/DAC) Working Party on Aid Effectiveness and Donor Practices. The Working Party acted through round tables on specific topics and technical working groups, both sponsored by the multinational development banks.[168] The harmonization efforts of the 1990s and 2000s produced a body of rules that, while formally separate from organization to organization and with a few differences specific to individual banks, is essentially homogeneous: rules are not only inspired by the same principles, but also adopt similar solutions, and even often use the same wording.

At the same time, the reform introduced more flexible regulatory systems that allowed the application of national rules. This entailed the development and strengthening of country procurement capacities. Decentralization and harmonization were in fact accompanied by increasingly incisive attempts to develop the autonomous capacities of national procurement systems and improve domestic procurement practices. In this sense, reforms attempted to lighten the bank's managerial burden by encouraging ownership of the relative procedures by borrowing states. This process was formalized under the Rome Declaration on Harmonization in 2003 in which both donors and partner countries recognized that

> [t]he key element that will guide this work is a country-based approach that emphasizes country ownership and government leadership, includes capacity building, recognizes diverse aid modalities (projects, sector approaches, and budget or balance of payments support).[169]

With specific reference to procurement, the objective of strengthening country procurement capacities translated into the Johannesburg

---

(CDB), the Council of Europe Development Bank (CEB), the EBRD, the European Investment Bank (EIB), the IDB, the WB and the Islamic Development Bank (IsDB).
[168] WB, *The World Bank's Procurement Policies and Procedures: Policy Review*, p. 7 [ref. AP&R].
[169] Rome Declaration on Harmonization, para. 5 [ref. S&D].

Declaration in 2003. The declaration followed the activity of earlier round tables held in 2002 and organized by the WB and the OECD/DAC, as a sub-group of the Working Party on Aid Effectiveness. It was then endorsed at the high level forum on Aid Effectiveness in Paris in 2005 which included the use of country systems among its main goals.

The third area of reform in indirect procurement affected control and accountability mechanisms. As for controls, the increase in functions of organizations and the change in the type of operations carried out shifted the subject of the review: while review and clearance procedures were originally designed to apply primarily to a few large contracts, they later applied to a small number of very large and complex contracts, but also to an increasing the number of low-value contracts.[170] This led to a need to revise review and clearance procedures: in the 1990s, on one hand, the thresholds for prior reviews were raised and, on the other hand, post reviews and audits were reinforced.[171]

At the same time, mechanisms to combat fraud and corruption began to be included in the reform priorities. For example, in 1996 the procurement policies of the WB defined for the first time the concept of corruption in procurement and linked it to the bank's ability to declare misprocurement, withdraw the funds intended to finance that contract, and possibly cancel the loan. This provision, which was then further developed by the subsequent reform of guidelines, was also accompanied by the establishment of the Integrity Department specifically competent to investigate instances of fraud and corruption in transactions financed by the bank.

Finally, during this period new accountability mechanisms were developed to hold development banks and borrowing states accountable to private parties negatively affected by the projects. Some commentators have marked this innovation as a shift from 'accountability as control' to 'accountability as justice'.[172] In 1993 the WB first introduced a formal accountability mechanism through which private parties negatively affected by a bank financed project could petition an impartial outside body, the Inspection Panel. Within ten years, the other development banks moved in the same direction and adopted

---

[170] WB, *The World Bank's Procurement Policies and Procedures: Policy Review*, pp. X–XI [ref. AP&R].

[171] *Ibid.*, p. 5.

[172] Park, 'Accountability as Justice for Mutilateral Development Banks?', *passim*.

similar mechanisms. However, while these mechanisms have been a significant development towards accountability of financial institutions and borrowing states, they did not regard an essential aspect of the implementation process, that is procurement. Accountability tools specifically related to procurement began to be developed during these years but would consolidate only in the late 2000s, and would be shaped mainly as reason-giving duties, rather than as proper complaint mechanisms.[173]

3.6 Codification, Proceduralization and Publicization: Scope and Limits

The above analysis shows the direction of a trend: international organizations went from a procurement method that consisted primarily of forms of direct contracting, where administrations operated in a fully autonomous manner like any private party, seeking possible contractors in the market without procedural constraints, to methods marked by a procedure and characterized by some degree of competition and transparency, both intra-administrative and between the administration and private parties. The history of organizations, thus, shows a gradual codification, proceduralization and publicization of procurement activity: procedures were developed to guide international as well as national administrations in selecting a contractor and preventing the risk of arbitrary decisions. Administrations began to be subjected, at least formally, to duties of transparency to possible suppliers. All this took place through the codification of rules that had an early development in multilateral development banks and a more gradual evolution in other organizations.

The decisive factors in this evolution were to some extent different from those that led to similar developments in national contexts. Indeed, in addition to the natural growth of apparatuses and their functions, reasons of international policy emerged after decolonization and the end of the Cold War, along with the related reasons of cost-effectiveness and economy of administrative activity. These induced certain states, and namely the United States, to individually promote administrative reforms, but also to define the contours and the limits of these reforms and their effective implementation, making them instrumental to their policies and economic interests.

[173] See Chapters 4 and 7.

4

The Regulatory Architecture

Principles and Practices

4.1 Introduction

International organizations procure goods, services and works following administrative procedures regulated by detailed rules. In this way, the award decision should be the result of an ordered sequence of acts and intra-procedural decisions, rather than of a random assessment process. This chapter aims to provide an overview of vendor selection procedures, considering both direct and indirect procurement. In doing so, it investigates, first, the main features of procurement regulation applicable to procurement. Second, it assesses the degree of compliance with the rules by focusing on the discrepancies between the rules and the procurement practices of organizations. Third, it explores to what extent and in which respects the rules regulating procurement by international organizations differ from those regulating domestic public procurement. It, thus, combines a purely positivistic approach with an empirical one.

The chapter is divided into three parts. The first part identifies the sources of regulation, their scope of application, and the relationships among the different sources.

The second part provides a description of the various phases of the procurement process. The procedures follow a scheme that is basically similar to that followed by states for their own procurement (as laid down, for instance, in the European public procurement directives and in the GPA): tender launching, evaluation of offers and award.

The third part is devoted to identifying the principles guiding international organizations' procurement, not only as evinced from legal texts but also from the everyday practices of international organizations. The chapter shows how each of the main principles is shaped and implemented in direct and indirect procurement and in what respects each differs from the same principle in national procurement, taking as a parameter of comparison the European public procurement directives and the GPA. It considers the principle of competition and its limitations. It illustrates how the adoption of restricted procedures is the most common option for selecting vendors in direct procurement. With reference to this type of procurement, an account of anti-competitive practices is provided as they emerge from the relevant documentation and interviews with officials and vendors. Consideration is also given to the adoption of open procedures as basic procedures in indirect procurement, and how they interact with the principle of domestic preference, which is established in the procurement guidelines applicable to that kind of procurement. Furthermore, it explores the principle of transparency and its functioning, analyzing the concrete modes through which this is implemented and to what extent.[1] In this respect the duties of tender advertisement, notification of award, and reason giving are scrutinized in the various organizations and the different types of procurement are compared to analogous duties in domestic public procurement. Finally, the chapter deals with the principle of integrity, mentioned in most procurement manuals, looking in particular at the rules of conduct governing the action of procurement officials and the enforcement practices.

4.2 The Law Applicable to Procurement

The issue of which law is applicable to international organizations and, in particular, whether and to what extent national law is applicable to international organizations, has been widely debated in the literature with different, and sometimes opposing, views on the point.[2] It is beyond the scope of this chapter to dissect that debate. It is, however, important to our ends to make two macro distinctions with regard to the applicable law. The first is that between the various legal capacities in which international organizations act: an organization can act as a public international subject in its relationships with other organizations or states. It can act as an administrative public authority in its relationships with the staff or with third parties involved in an administrative procedure carried out by the organization, e.g. procurement. It can act as an international

---

[1] In general on the principle of transparency in international law and international organizations see Peters and Bianchi (eds.), *Transparency in International Law*; Tallberg, 'Transparency'.

[2] The debate is particularly relevant for accountability reasons and for the limits imposed by privileges to the application of domestic law. See, for instance, Reinisch, 'Accountability of International Organizations According to National Law'.

public entity in its relationship with individuals affected by its activity outside an administrative or contractual link. It can act as a private party when entering into a contract. International organizations, thus, have a multi-faceted legal capacity that is regulated by the coexistence of different sets of rules, even with reference to the same activity. As for the source of regulation, these rules include but are not limited to national rules. As for the content of regulation, the applicable rules pertain to different areas of law: public international law, global and national administrative law (or, according to some scholars, international institutional law), international and national criminal law, international and national commercial law, as well as international and national private law. Given these, there is, however, a set of rules that falls under the umbrella of public international law, but is specific to the organizations, transects the various areas of their activity, and is capable of limiting the applicability of all the other rules: the founding treaties of the organizations and the treaties on privileges and immunities, as well as customary international law, exempt organizations from the application and implementation of rules external to the organizations, e.g. national rules, when this can jeopardize the functioning of the organizations and the fulfilment of their institutional mission. International organizations are, for example, exempted from the rules imposing direct taxation, customs duties, and search and seizure of their property.

The other macro distinction pertains to the ways in which organizations affect natural and legal persons. A relationship between an international organization and a private subject can be extra-contractual or contractual and, within extra-contractual activities, a further distinction can be drawn between relationships created outside a procedure or inside a procedure. As for extra-contractual activities, the relationship between an organization and a private party can be created *ipso facto* due to the simple circumstance that the organization's activity has an impact on the legal position of a party (non-procedural). It does so, for instance, when the organization causes harm to third parties in deploying its institutional functions, and it is consequently held liable for the acts committed. However, a relationship can also be procedural and be created due to the involvement of private subjects in an administrative procedure that may lead to a unilateral decision of the organization or to the conclusion of a contract with that party. For example, procurement procedures create a link between an organization and the vendors taking part in the tender launched by the organization. On one hand, the sequence of intermediate decisions adopted by organizations within the procedure directly affect vendors, even those who are not awarded the contract. On the other hand, the link also results from the intention of private subjects to enter into the procedure, expressed through the submission of an expression of interest or a bid/proposal. Similarly, an administrative link is created in the procedure to select officials, which may or may not end up with a contract. Another example pertains to the administrative procedures necessary to obtain a certification from international organizations. As for contractual activities, the relationship is based on a contract, and thus on a voluntary agreement between the parties. It is so for procurement contracts, but also for labour contracts between an organization and its officials.

Leaving aside the complex analysis of the law applicable to the extra-contractual non-procedural relationships and postponing a discussion of the law applicable to procurement contracts,[3] the relationship resulting from an extra-contractual procedural activity is, from the point of view of the applicable law, less controversial. The administrative procedural link is usually governed by the internal rules of the organizations. However, while these rules traditionally regulated the procedures for hiring officials, and thus related to individuals who could become part of the organization, the history of the organizations shows the progressive development of internal administrative rules which affect third parties[4] who may or may not become contractors of the organization and will at any rate never become part of the organization itself.

Thus, unlike other areas of activity, the problem of which law is applicable to international organizations when undertaking procurement has a more straightforward solution. In direct procurement, the activity of the organizations and the procedures through which the organizations select vendors are governed by the rules set forth in the founding treaties, in the financial rules and regulations, in the policy documents on procurement, in the administrative and procurement manuals, and in additional administrative circulars.[5] Indirect procurement is mainly

---

[3] See Chapter 6.   [4] See Chapter 3.

[5] Reference to all relevant administrative and procurement manuals, as well as to the applicable circulars, is to be found, for each organization, at the beginning of this book in the *List of Instruments*, under 'APR'.

regulated by the procurement guidelines[6] of the organizations, but also by national rules on public procurement. However, given this basic answer, some further issues that relate to direct and indirect procurement are worth examining.

4.2.1   Direct Procurement

One of the issues relating to direct procurement regards the relationships between the procurement rules of organizations and the international, supranational and national laws on public procurement. More precisely, there are two questions to be addressed. The first is to what extent international, supranational and national procurement laws have served as a model upon which the rules of organizations have been shaped. The second question is whether or not the rules of international organizations for the award of contracts have to comply with some or all international or supranational procurement laws, and namely the GPA and the European public procurement directives.

The first question concerns the impact that supranational and international sources regulating domestic public procurement have on the procurement rule making of international organizations. A comparison between domestic public procurement regulation set by supranational and international legal sources and procurement regulation by international organizations for their own purposes shows that, in drafting the latter, international organizations have taken the former into consideration, while twisting and significantly adapting them to their necessities and their institutional objectives. These aspects will be analyzed in terms of the content of the rules in the next sections of this chapter and in terms of the mechanisms used for legal transplant in Chapter 8.

The second question relates mainly to those organizations, namely the European Union, that are multiple rule makers, meaning that in relation to the same subject matter they produce different sets of rules depending on the recipients of the rules. With regard to procurement regulation, for example, the European Union produces its own internal rules that govern direct and indirect procurement. But it establishes also rules for public procurement of member states through *ad hoc* directives. Furthermore, as a signatory of international agreements, such as the GPA, it

---

[6] Reference to all relevant administrative and procurement manuals, as well as to the applicable circulars, is to be found, for each organization, at the beginning of this book in the *List of Instruments*, under 'APR'.

contributes to the making of the international rules and is also subject to them. Thus, within the same organization, there are different coexisting sets of rules for the organization, for the beneficiary states and for the member states. To a certain extent, this regulatory conundrum encourages a form of blending, but it also poses problems of cohabitation. At least three of them are worth mention and relate to the applicability of the GPA to procurement by EU institutions, the applicability of EU procurement directives to EU institutions, and the applicability of EU procurement directives to international organizations having their headquarters or operating in EU member states.

With regard to the GPA, the Agreement is fully applicable to EU institutions. EU adhesion to the GPA agreement includes both EU institutions and EU member states, and its applicability does not create regulatory conflicts. The level of detail provided by the GPA and the financial rules applicable to EU institutions' procurement is different. The GPA gives some basic procurement rules, while EU financial rules and regulations set up an all-encompassing regulation of procurement), and the content of the rules is harmonized. Also, the cohabitation of the legal texts, however, is also made possible by specific provisions that manage and solve conflict where this can arise. In this regard, the main issue concerns the eligibility of vendors. Article 119 of the Financial Rules applicable to the EU general budget states that

> [p]articipation in procurement procedures shall be open on equal terms to all natural and legal persons within the scope of the Treaties and to all natural and legal persons established in a third country which has a special agreement with the Union in the field of public procurement.[7]

This provision implies that not only vendors from EU member states can take part in procurement procedures, but also those established in other countries, provided that there is an agreement in this regard.

Furthermore, where the GPA applies, i.e. in procurement above specified threshold values, the procurement procedure shall also be open to economic operators established in the states that have ratified that agreement.[8] Thus, the GPA integrates the set of rules applicable to procurement by EU institutions and allows an extension of the scope of competition. Of course, the commitments made by the parties to the GPA may contain exceptions. The EU commitments, for example,

---

[7] European Union, Regulation (EU, Euratom) No. 966/2012 (and following amendments), Art. 119 [ref. N&RL-EU].
[8] *Ibid.*, Art. 120.

exclude Canadian suppliers from procurement by EU sub-central entities as a result of reciprocity: Canada does not include its sub-central entities under the GPA umbrella. Moreover, the GPA does not apply to procurement made in furtherance of tied aid to developing countries; nor does it apply to contracts awarded under an international agreement intended for the joint implementation or exploitation of projects, such as for humanitarian aid, assistance and international cooperation; nor does it apply to contracts awarded under an international agreement relating to the stationing of troops.[9]

The relationship between EU procurement directives and the financial rules applicable to procurement by EU institutions is, instead, marked by the separation between the scope of application of the former and the scope of application of the latter. European public procurement directives govern the procurement of member states, and are not legally binding upon EU institutions.[10] EU institutions financed from the general budget abide by the rules laid down in the EU Financial Regulation[11] and the Rules of Application.[12] The European Central Bank (ECB) is instead subject to *ad hoc* rules set out in a decision adopted by its Executive Board.[13] This legal framework is illustrated in Figure 4.1.

The separate scope of application does not, however, preclude harmonization among the rules. The rules EU institutions have drafted for themselves are broadly in line with procurement directives, with some differences. One relates to the approach to small and medium-size businesses whose participation is not encouraged by EU institutions' procurement rules as it is by public procurement directives.[14] The other concerns preliminary market consultations, which, according to public procurement directives, have the twofold objective of facilitating planning and carrying out the procurement procedure (internal objective) and informing economic operators (external objective). EU Financial Regulations instead provide for market consultations only with the internal objective.[15]

---

[9] See EU Commission, *The WTO Agreement on Government Procurement* [ref. N&RL-EU].
[10] See European Court of Auditors, *The EU Institutions Can Do More to Facilitate Access to Their Public Procurement*, para. 5 [ref. REP].
[11] European Union, Regulation (EU, Euratom) No. 966/2012 (and following amendments) [ref. N&RL-EU].
[12] EU Commission Delegated Regulation (EU) No. 1268/2012 (and following amendments) [ref. N&RL-EU].
[13] European Union, Decision (EU) No. 2016/245 [ref. N&RL-EU].
[14] On this issue see European Court of Auditors, *The EU Institutions Can Do More to Facilitate Access to Their Public Procurement*, para. 30 [ref. REP], and later in this chapter.
[15] *Ibid.*, para. 31.

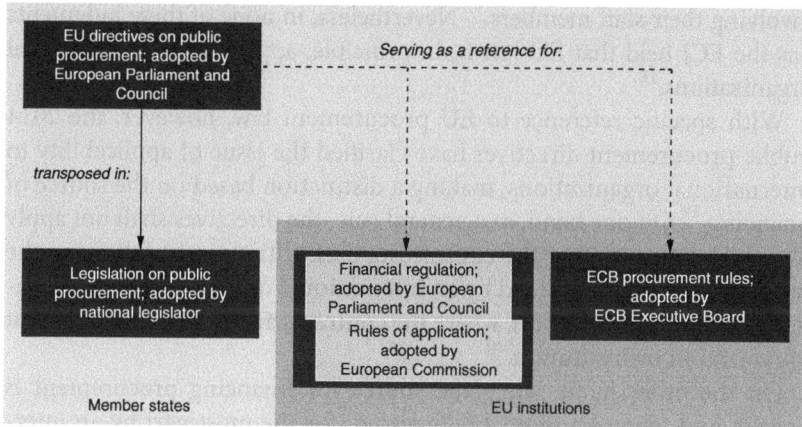

Figure 4.1 The European legal framework for public procurement
(Source: European Court of Auditors, *The EU Institutions Can Do More to Facilitate Access to Their Public Procurement. Special Report No. 17/2016*, 24 May 2016, Figure 2)

The third problem arising from the cohabitation of different sets of rules within the European Union relates to the applicability of EU procurement directives to international organizations. More precisely, the question is whether the EU law on public procurement applicable to member states is also applicable to international organizations, and in particular to those having their premises or operating in EU member states. The issue arises because, in principle, EU law applies to any natural and legal person belonging to or operating in the territory of the member states. In this respect, it could be argued that an international organization having its premises and/or operating in the member states should be subject to EU law, except for application of the privileges and immunities regime. International organizations have in fact legal personality and could be entitled to rights and duties according to EU law like other private or public parties operating within the EU jurisdiction. The European Court of Justice (ECJ) has, for example, deemed EU law to be applicable to international organizations in some competition cases[16] and in cases

---

[16] See Case C-364/92, *SAT Fluggesellschaft mbH* v. *European Organisation for the Safety of Air Navigation (Eurocontrol)* [1994] ECR I-43; Case T-155/04, *SELEX Sistemi Integrati SpA* v. *Commission*, 12 December 2006, not published in the ECR; Case C-113/07 P, *SELEX Sistemi Integrati SpA* v. *Commission and European Organisation for the Safety of Air Navigation (Eurocontrol)*, 26 March 2009, not published in the ECR.

involving their staff members.[17] Nevertheless, in none of these judgments has the ECJ held that EU law is, in principle, applicable to international organizations.[18]

With specific reference to EU procurement law, however, the 2014 public procurement directives have clarified the issue of applicability to international organizations, making a distinction based on the source of financing.[19] On one hand, as a general rule, the directives shall not apply to public contracts that the contracting authorities award following the procurement rules provided by an international organization or international financing institution, where the contracts are fully financed by that organization or institution.[20]

On the other hand, when the source for financing procurement is hybrid, and the procurement is financed 'for the most part by an international organization or international financing institution', but for the rest by the European Union, then the parties must agree on applicable procurement rules.[21] The applicability of EU procurement law thus follows a substantive criterion and the concrete application of such law is the result of an inter-institutional agreement.

4.2.2   Indirect Procurement

The issue of which law is applicable to indirect procurement is briefly analyzed in Chapter 2, where a distinction is made between organizations that operate by means of a loose-knit regulatory system and leave some

---

[17] See Joint Cases 389/87 and 390/87, *GBC Echternach and A. Moritz* v. *Minister van Onderwijs en Wetenschappen* [1989] ECR 723; Case C-310/91, *Hugo Schmid* v. *Belgian State, represented by the Minister van Sociale Voorzorg* [1993] ECR I-3011; Case C-411/98, *Angelo Ferlini* v. *Centre hospitalier de Luxembourg* [2000] ECR I-8081.

[18] For an analysis of this case law see Heuninckx, 'Applicable Law to the Procurement of International Organisations in the European Union'.

[19] Before the 2014 directives, the issue was not clearly defined. An interesting proposal to tackle the issue was put forward by Heuninckx in 2011. He suggested that a distinction had to be made between international organizations 'controlled' by EU member states and those not controlled by EU member states. In the former, since EU member states held a controlling majority in the decision-making process, 'the principles of EU law flowing from the EC Treaty that are applicable to public procurement would still apply to the procurement activities'. In the latter, there would be no applicability of EU law. See Heuninckx, 'Applicable Law to the Procurement of International Organisations in the European Union', *passim*.

[20] European Union, Directive 2014/24/EU, Art. 9(2) [ref. N&RL-EU]. And similarly, European Union, Directive 2014/25/EU, Art. 20(2) [ref. N&RL-EU].

[21] European Union, Directive 2014/24/EU, Art. 9(2) [ref. N&RL-EU]; European Union, Directive 2014/25/EU, Art. 20(2) [ref. N&RL-EU].

autonomy to states, those that adopt a maximalist option according to which the main source of procurement regulation is the organization itself, and those that 'lend' their procurement rules to states with few or no national procurement rules.

The preference for one approach over the other has changed over the years within each organization. There is a growing shift towards looser regulatory approaches that favour regulatory ownership by the borrowing states. This can be explained, on one hand, by an evolution in development policies, which, including those based on considerations of effectiveness, increasingly tend to prefer approaches that safeguard and strengthen the institutional and regulatory framework of the states. The WB has been explicit in this regard when stating that

> [i]n recent years, it has been increasingly recognized that strengthening and using national procurement arrangements is a key factor in achieving more effective development outcomes.[22]

Several international treaties have contributed to promoting this vision. On one hand, in 2005 the Paris Declaration on Aid Effectiveness and the Accra Agenda for Action[23] reaffirmed commitments to develop sustainable reforms and monitor their implementation. Within these objectives, it was agreed to commit sufficient resources to support and sustain medium and long-term procurement reforms and promote capacity development. In 2011 the Busan Partnership for Effective Development Co-operation[24] called on donors to initiate a process that would eventually lead to the full use of a national procurement system.[25] On the other hand, this approach is made possible by the progressive development of domestic procurement rules, also in states which did not have their own procurement regulations.

To counterbalance the loosening of regulatory requirements, however, organizations have also established a stricter inter-institutional accountability system.[26] Some organizations have witnessed a shift from

---

[22] WB, *Draft Guide to the APA Assessment Methodology*, sec. II [ref. AP&R].

[23] The Paris Declaration on Aid Effectiveness and the Accra Agenda for Action, Paris, 2 March 2005 [ref. S&D].

[24] Busan Partnership for Effective Development Co-operation. Fourth High-Level Forum on Aid Effectiveness, Busan (Korea), 29 November–1 December 2011 [ref. A&C].

[25] See WB, *Draft Guide to the APA Assessment Methodology*, sec. II [ref. AP&R]. The Paris Declaration on Aid Effectiveness [ref. S&D], as well as the Busan Partnership, are explicitly recalled by the WB as the legal background of the reform undertaken by the Bank and an introduction to the use of alternative procurement arrangements (APA).

[26] See Chapter 7.

a regulatory-based approach to an administrative-based approach where the administrative checks and controls by the financing organization offset a lighter regulatory net.

The main example of this evolution is the WB. In 2008 the Bank launched a pilot project for the use of country systems. According to this project, national procurement procedures and methods could be deemed consistent with the Bank's procurement guidelines and, thus, applicable to procurement financed by the Bank. The assessment was to be conducted by the Bank.[27] A few years later, in 2011, the Use of the Country System was included in the WB procurement guidelines.[28] The 2016 Procurement Regulations for borrowers have brought the use of the country system a step forward and introduced a binary system.[29] As a general rule, a legal agreement governs the relationship between the Bank and the borrowing state, and

> [t]he Procurement Regulations are applicable to the procurement of Goods, Works, Non-consulting Services and Consulting Services in IPF operations, as provided for in the Legal Agreement.[30]

There can, however, be 'alternative procurement arrangements' (APA).[31] The borrower can request the Bank to apply different rules, namely the procurement rules and procedures of another multilateral or bilateral agency or organization,[32] or the procurement rules and

---

[27] The Pilot Program was described in WB, *Use of Country Systems in Bank Supported Operations: Proposed Piloting Program* [ref. AP&R]. Even before the piloting programme the Bank had adopted policies permitting the use of country systems in financial management and in national competitive bidding procurement, and discussed how to expand its use, on this see WB, *Expanding the Use of Country Systems in Bank-Supported Operations* [ref. AP&R]; and WB, *Frequently Asked Questions on the Use of Country Systems in Bank-Supported Operations* [ref. AP&R].

[28] WB, *Guidelines. Procurement of Goods, Works, and Non-Consulting Services*, para. 3.20 [ref. AP&R]. The assessment of the country procurement systems, of course, had to include different layers of regulations and could be complex when regarding federal states. See, for instance, WB, *Assessment of the Procurement Systems of the Brazilian Federal Government* [ref. AP&R].

[29] On the WB procurement reform see *inter alia* Trepte, 'All Change at the World Bank? The New Procurement Framework'; and on the reforms of the multilateral development banks see Williams-Elegbe, *Public Procurement and Multilateral Development Banks*, p. 243 *et seq.*

[30] WB, *The World Bank Procurement Regulations for IPF Borrowers*, para. 2.1 [ref. AP&R].

[31] The expression is used in WB, *The World Bank Procurement Regulations for IPF Borrowers*, para. 2.4 [ref. AP&R].

[32] In such a case, with the agreement of the Bank the other organization can take a leading role in providing the implementation support and monitoring of procurement activities (WB, *The World Bank Procurement Regulations for IPF Borrowers*, para. 2.4 [ref. AP&R]).

procedures of an agency or entity of the borrower. These arrangements require an assessment by the Bank and are compounded by the detailed provision of oversight mechanisms.

With regard to the assessment, the Bank has developed an all-encompassing methodology aimed at assessing the legal and regulatory framework and the capacity and capability of a borrower implementing agency.[33] The assessment must evaluate not only compliance with the requirements set by the Bank for the legal and regulatory framework, but it must also use an evidence-based approach, analyzing procurement data and gathering the views of the private sector 'to determine the performance of the arrangement'.[34] In drafting the methodology, the Bank has used as its model the OECD Methodology for Assessing Procurement Systems (MAPS), adding however to the OECD methodology another pillar on procurement operations and the use of minimum standards.

The successful first case of an APA has been implemented in Bhutan. A small landlocked nation located in the eastern Himalayas, Bhutan was assessed as having a robust regulatory framework with an independent Anti-Corruption Commission and independent external and internal audit mechanisms. The government was deemed to have a system-wide capacity-building programme for procurement officers. Finally, and most importantly, Thimphu Thromde, an agency under the country's Ministry of Works and Human Settlement and responsible for municipal services and their governance in the capital city, was approved for the use of national procurement arrangements on a case-by-case basis for Bank-financed investment projects. No wonder the assessment has been fully positive, as Thimphu Thromde

> has been one of the major implementing agencies for Bank-funded operations since 1999. It is considered one of the highest performing agencies from a procurement perspective in Bhutan. It's not only one of the best in Bhutan, but as the first APA, it will be among the best on a global scale.[35]

---

[33] See WB, *Draft Guide to the APA Assessment Methodology* [ref. AP&R].

[34] *Ibid.*, sec. II. As explained by the Bank, '[t]his assessment framework is made up of five pillars ... The five pillars cover all elements of robust procurement arrangements from the regulatory framework, complaints handling, dispute resolution, anti-corruption measures through to the procurement processes and procedures, and subsequent contract administration/management', *ibid.*, sec. III.

[35] Schafer, 'Strengthening the Rules of the Game: Bhutan's Alternative Procurement Experience'.

The agency was deemed to have a well-established complaints management system and regularly publicizes information on rules and procedures, bidding opportunities, contract awards and data on resolution of procurement complaints.[36] Every few years, Thimphu Thromde undergoes a review performed by the Bank to ensure the agency continues to meet the standards for alternative procurement arrangements.

India was the second case of APA implementation. PowerGrid Corporation of India Limited is an Indian state-owned electric utilities company that transmits about 50 per cent of the total power generated in India on its transmission network. The WB has partnered with PowerGrid since its inception in 1989. Since 2005, PowerGrid has concluded about 150 contracts under Bank financing for around $2.7 billion.[37] Following an assessment by the Bank, the company was deemed to have the laws, regulations, capacity and performance record to meet the Bank's fiduciary requirements, and to work as implementing agency for Bank financed projects.

The WB is, however, a pioneer in the adoption of the APA approach and there are few projects where this has been tried as an experiment. Many other financial institutions, such as the ADB, the AfDB and the IDB, still use a traditional approach, according to which the procurement guidelines drawn up by institutions apply to all contracts for goods and works financed in whole or in part by banks. The guidelines usually allow for the use of country systems in national competitive bidding procedures for public procurement in developing member countries, specifying that country procedures may be used if they ensure economy, efficiency and transparency; and if they are broadly consistent with the bank's procurement rules, following an assessment by the bank. The AfDB, for instance,

> commenced assessment of the National Competitive Bidding (NCB) procedures and documents of [Regional Member Countries] in 2009. By December 2013, the Bank had completed assessments on 48 countries representing 89% of the RMCs and found that 77% had national procedures and documents acceptable for use under Bank-financed projects, subject to a few amendments required by the action plan identified by the review.[38]

---

[36] WB, 'Bhutan Agency Approved for Alternative Procurement Arrangements by the World Bank'.

[37] WB, 'India's PowerGrid Endorsed for Alternative Procurement Arrangements by the World Bank'.

[38] AfDB, *Review of ADB's Procurement Policy, Procedures and Processes*, para. 6.3 (and more generally on the use of country systems, paras. 6.1–6.4) [ref. AP&R].

However, strict adherence to the Bank's guidelines is required for international competitive bidding.[39] Moreover, for procurement not financed by institutions, the borrowing state is allowed to adopt other procedures. In these cases as well, however, the financial institution undertakes an assessment of the procurement rules to be applied.[40] The traditional approach seems, however, to be more and more put into question by an ongoing debate within organizations on the possibility of using country systems, at least in middle-income countries.[41]

4.3 The Phases of the Procurement Procedure

Within direct and indirect procurement of international organizations at least three macro phases can be distinguished: the emergence and formalization of the procurement need, the vendor selection and the contract award. Each phase encompasses a sequence of acts and decisions whose basic features are common to procurement of various organizations.

This is the basic scheme for any type of procurement undertaken by organizations, but some further clarifications are needed. In direct procurement,[42] organizations govern all phases of this process primarily through their policies, financial rules, procurement manuals and guidelines.[43] In indirect procurement, instead, the rules established by the organization relate directly to the vendor selection and contract award phases. The phase involving the emergence and formalization of the procurement need, on the contrary, includes two sub-phases,

[39] ADB, *Promoting the Use of Country Systems*, p. 7 [ref. AP&R].

[40] ADB, *Procurement Guidelines*, para. 1.5 [ref. AP&R]; AfDB, *Rules and Procedures for the Procurement of Goods and Works*, para. 1.5 [ref. AP&R]; ADB, *Procurement Guidelines*, para. 1.5 [ref. AP&R].

[41] See, for instance, ADB, *Promoting the Use of Country Systems, passim* [ref. AP&R]; AfDB, *Review of ADB's Procurement Policy, Procedures and Processes*, para. 6 [ref. AP&R]; AfDB, *Bank Group Approach towards Enhancing the Use of Country Systems* [ref. AP&R]. For a comprehensive overview on the topic see Williams-Elegbe, *Public Procurement and Multilateral Development Banks*, p. 251 *et seq.*; and for the single banks, Sharma, 'An Update on Procurement Reforms at the African Development Bank'; Salazar and Lopez, 'The Inter-American Development Bank'; Jackholt, 'The Procurement Policies and Rules and the Procurement Activities of the European Bank for Reconstruction and Development (EBRD)'.

[42] As well as indirect procurement for internal purposes.

[43] In outsourcing, in fact, contractor selection follows the five classical steps, as governed in procurement manuals. The private contractor is then in turn responsible for procuring the goods and services necessary by contract, according to the methods and rules it establishes.

governed by rules whose sources are mixed. The first sub-phase consists of planning procurement needs. These are usually set in a project or plan and, thus, are identified jointly by the organization and the state according to a procedure set by the organization. The second sub-phase, related to the concrete emergence of the single procurement need, takes place within the states and is regulated by domestic administrative rules.

The following analysis takes these differences into account. The various phases are examined with reference to the rules and practices of direct procurement and indirect procurement by identifying the recurring patterns in both, the differences between the two types of procurement, and when significant, the deviations from those patterns that some organizations have introduced.

4.3.1   The Emergence and Formalization of Procurement Needs

The phase of emergence and formalization of procurement needs includes two stages: one that involves procurement planning and the other that involves requisitioning, i.e. the concrete emergence of the procurement need and the relevant request submitted by the administrative units to the procurement officers.

4.3.1.1   Procurement Planning

The purpose of procurement planning is to clarify in advance which goods, services and works are necessary to achieve the institutional objectives, within what time frames and with what financial outlay. Also for emergency situations, where precise estimates are not possible, advance planning is necessary and useful to better and more quickly meet the supply needs submitted to the competent authorities during the course of operations.

Many international organizations undertaking direct procurement use at least two types of planning: consolidated procurement plans, which are usually developed for the entire organization, and individual procurement plans, which refer to the single procurement process.[44] The goals, time frames and responsible bodies change in the two types of planning. On the contrary, the preparatory activities that must be performed and the contents of the plans are similar, with details that vary solely due to the complexity of the operation.

---

[44] For the characteristics of each see United Nations, *United Nations Procurement Practitioner's Handbook*, 2017, para. 5.1 [ref. AP&R].

Plans of any type usually include a preliminary analysis of the needs related to the operation and the selection of appropriate management strategies to limit waste and ensure the efficiency of the administrative action; an indication of estimated costs; an examination of sources, such as their existence and availability; delivery time, or completion time and place; vendor selection method to be adopted; reasons for adopting non-competitive procedures; adequate description of purchases to be made; criteria to be used for the evaluation; and application of long-term contracts. As noted, the plans are necessary to anticipate procurement needs, but are not binding on the purchasing administrations. They are useful to procurement officers in order to comply with all necessary formalities in advance and to have a general idea of future procurement operations, while making it possible to diverge from these estimates for proven contingent needs. They are, in fact, relevant primarily for internal purposes. And, although the UN Procurement Practitioner's Handbook indicates that it is good practice to publish general procurement plans in order to provide 'information to the outside world of upcoming procurement activities',[45] it is not common practice to do so[46] and, moreover, this instruction does not extend to individual plans.

Furthermore, whilst planning is crucial to subsequent procurement, control bodies have often reported inadequate procurement planning by several organizations, especially in emergency situations, and have shown the existence of a close link between poor planning and procurement practices eluding internal controls and violating the principle of competition. A recurring case is, for example, that of unnecessary *ex post facto* contracts, i.e. contracts resulting from procurement undertaken without prior presentation to the competent review body for approval. This kind of option is often presented by procurement officers as being due to exigencies, while instead it could have been foreseen with adequate planning.

In indirect procurement, planning is also preliminary to any procurement activity, but it is done jointly by the organizations and the borrowing state. The borrowing state is responsible for preparing a draft of the project procurement strategy and a procurement plan. The plan includes *inter alia* a description of the contracts, the selection methods

---

[45] *Ibid.* [ref. AP&R].

[46] With some exceptions: general procurement plans of peacekeeping operations are, for example, published, also if often subject to changes due to the high level of uncertainty of the operations.

to be applied, the cost estimates and the time schedules.[47] The organization reviews the project procurement strategy and approves the plan during the loan negotiations. Once approved, the plan is legally binding for the borrowing state. Updates or deviations from the procurement plan must be submitted by the borrowing state to the organization for approval.

Thus, whereas in direct procurement planning has mainly internal relevance, planning in indirect procurement is a parameter for inter-institutional accountability. At an initial stage, the organization controls the compatibility and adequacy of the implementation proposal drafted by the state with the objectives of the organization and of the single project. Later, the procurement plan allows the organization to have a parameter for checking the compliance of the project implementation carried out by the borrowing states to the objectives of the organization and those stated in the lending agreement.

4.3.1.2 Requisitioning

After planning, but in emergency cases even during such, comes the phase of formulating procurement requisitions and submitting them to the competent procurement officer. The manuals governing direct procurement of each organization identify in similar ways the objectives, parties responsible, sub-phases of the process and the contents of requisitions and controls. Requisitioning is, instead, usually not regulated by guidelines governing indirect procurement and, thus, its management is mainly left to the autonomy of states.

In direct procurement, during this phase administrative units – the requisitioners – formulate the requests for the goods, services and works actually necessary for the fulfilment of their tasks and transmit them to the competent procurement officers. Based on these requests and within the limits of these requisitions, procurement officers may legitimately initiate the vendor selection procedure.

Responsibility in this preliminary phase lies with the requisitioners, who are, at the same time, the administrative units responsible for

---

[47] See WB, *The World Bank Procurement Regulations for IPF Borrowers*, paras. 4.1–4.5 and Annex V [ref. AP&R]; ADB, *Procurement Guidelines*, para. 1.16 [ref. AP&R]; AfDB, *Rules and Procedures for the Procurement of Goods and Works*, para. 1.16 [ref. AP&R]; IDB, *Policies for the Procurement of Goods and Works Financed by the Inter-American Development Bank*, para. 1.16 [ref. AP&R]; EBRD, *Procurement Policies and Rules*, para. 3.5 [ref. AP&R].

drafting the procurement request and the final recipient of the procurement. In addition, in the case of direct procurement, although the requisitioner is primarily responsible, the procurement officer also intervenes with consulting and control functions.

Once the requisitioners have identified the purposes that the goods, services and works must fullfil and the concrete performances they must guarantee, they prepare the specifications for goods, the terms of reference for services and the statement of works. Each of these documents usually contains a description of the functions the item must perform, the purposes for which it is to be used, its expected performance (which may require a reference to international standards) and, finally, its technical characteristics.

In general, a reference to brands or specific companies is not recommended, but is also not prohibited. Such reference can be made, but only as 'a guide' to procurement. In addition, in certain particular purchases of goods, restrictive specifications or particular brands may be necessary to guarantee compatibility with goods already purchased.

The requisition package usually consists of three elements: in addition to the specifications/terms of reference/statement of works, also financial documents and proof of compliance with administrative obligations are to be included in the package. In this form, it is sent to the competent authorities for a preliminary control. The review should ensure that the technical specifications are generic enough not to favour any specific vendor over another and that funds are available for the procurement. At the same time, the controller will check that the requisition is clear enough to allow procurement needs to be identified. A lack of clarity in fact prevents the procurement officer from preparing the call for tender. Often bodies performing overall controls on the procurement activity of organizations have pointed to the links between misprocurement and poor acquisition descriptions, including insufficient detail to be able to identify actual procurement needs, or, on the contrary, excessively detailed description, which appears to be tailored to a single vendor.

4.3.2 Vendor Selection

The vendor selection phase contains a number of steps which are regulated by the organizations, both in direct and indirect procurement:[48]

---

[48] This is true for indirect procurement unless the organization has allowed the use of APA or national procurement rules (see above in this chapter).

conducting market analysis, choosing the procurement strategy, preparing and transmitting the relevant documents to the vendors, evaluating the offers and, finally, awarding the tender. Selecting the procurement strategy entails, in particular, both the adoption of a vendor selection method, that is competitive or non-competitive procedures (open procedure, restricted procedure or negotiated procedure), and the choice of one solicitation method over another (request for proposals, invitation to bid or request for quotations).

Procurement officers are responsible for this phase. Indeed, to avoid collusive relationships between requisitioners and vendors whenever possible, a system of segregation of duties has been established by most organizations between requisitioning operating units and procurement officials responsible for selecting the vendor. By virtue of this system, as we have seen, the former are responsible for preparing the actual requisition – which is also based on general market research aimed at identifying the characteristics of goods, services and works on the market – while the latter are responsible for implementing all the procedures needed to procure the goods, services and works, and thus selecting contractors, concluding the contract and monitoring contract execution.

4.3.2.1   Market Analysis

Both in direct and indirect procurement, officers are firstly required to conduct market analysis.[49] They do this often by referring to internal information already acquired by international organizations and national administrations, and information provided by vendors following formal requests. Procurement officers may in fact access central or local rosters of suppliers previously selected and registered for the procurement of similar goods, services and works, or rosters of suppliers related to the organization through past contracts. They may consult informally with their counterparts in the same organization or in other organizations. Reference can be made also to company rosters outside the organization, for example Data on Consulting Firms (DACON) prepared by the WB and IDB. Names of recommended companies may be requested from national chambers of commerce, permanent missions to the organizations and national bodies that manage and coordinate domestic public contracts.

---

[49] In indirect procurement, however, the provisions regarding market analysis are extremely concise and limited to the few indications provided by the international organizations to borrowing states.

In addition, procurement officers can send companies formal requests for information or publish requests for expression of interest. The two options are not mutually exclusive and publishing requests for expressions of interest is a duty only in some organizations. The request for information (RFI) is specific and relates to technical characteristics, availability and prices for individual categories of goods and services. The request for expression of interests (REOI) is comprehensive and aimed at examining subjective and objective elements. It includes both the characteristics of the company (in particular its financial stability, experience in the sector and reliability in executing past contracts) and the characteristics of the goods, services and works it intends to provide for a determined contract.

In international organizations with greater volumes of purchases, the information and expressions of interest are considered only if they come from pre-qualified companies. In organizations where pre-qualification is not required, the competent authorities also perform an eligibility review at the time the information is requested.

In addition to formal requests, the daily practice of procurement shows that there are many cases of direct contact between procurement officers and possible suppliers. Especially for more complex operations, surveys and interviews may be conducted with suppliers identified at the discretion of the procurement officer. In the organizations of the UN system, this practice must be compatible with obligations of impartiality: 'surveys of and interviews with key people can be conducted, as long as they are comprehensive enough to not create any perceived favouritism'.[50] The obligation has, however, a significant limitation that jeopardizes its full effectiveness: the rule that prescribes such obligation is a rule of conduct and it is not complemented by a system of sanctions. Thus, even during this first phase of information gathering, organizations may, if desired, contact a pool of vendors and the identification of these can be made with a high degree of discretion.

4.3.2.2   Choosing the Methods of Solicitation

While seeking out information, the procurement officer faces two other issues: selecting the most appropriate procurement method and choosing the best way to solicit offers. The first type of choice consists of selecting

---

[50] United Nations, *United Nations Procurement Practitioner's Handbook*, 2017, para. 6.1 [ref. AP&R].

the desired level of competition and evaluating the merits and feasibility of alternatives to direct procurement.

The alternatives to direct procurement are represented by two categories of options: the so-called non-buy options and indirect buy options.[51] The former includes recourse to resources that are already within the organization (e.g. in the case of translation services, the procurement officer may tend to use internal services rather than contract the service to private firms); or recourse to a national administrative bodies, which can avoid having to purchase from third parties. Among the guiding criteria in a comparative evaluation, there are the respective overall costs (including administrative costs), the time required for completion, the actual availability of a certain good, service or work and the impact a potential delay in supply would have on the organization's action.

The procurement officer must also consider indirect buy options, such as adding the requisition to other requisitions for the supply of similar goods, services and works, or to long-term agreements[52] already concluded by the organization or by other organizations in the UN system; purchasing from other international organizations; or else outsourcing the entire procurement function to leading agencies for procurement (e.g. within the UN system, the Inter-Agency Procurement Services Office (IAPSO), United Nations Population Fund (UNFPA) and UNOPS, which are responsible for managing procurements common to various organizations. Depending on the organizations, this last method is governed by either preliminary inter-agency agreements or by actual competitive processes, with a call for tenders and the adoption of standard vendor selection criteria.

Thus, where the type of procurement has not already been selected at the beginning of the project or mission, the procurement officer is responsible for making this choice prior to the vendor selection. It is also important to emphasize that the procurement officer, at least in

---

[51] The alternative to direct procurement is not indirect procurement are as direct and indirect procurement are instrumental to different institutional functions.

[52] Long-term contracts have been defined as 'a written agreement between a[n] ... organization and a supplier setting out all the commercial terms applicable to the orders that may be issued against the LTA for pre-selected goods or services i.e., pricing, discounts, payment, delivery and packaging and any other relevant special terms as well as the general terms and conditions', in United Nations, *United Nations Procurement Practitioner's Handbook*, 2017, para. 6.6 [ref. AP&R]. The objectives of long-term contracts are principally to stabilize costs, create economies of scale and eliminate the duplication of procedures for purchasing goods, services and works.

theory, shall turn to direct procurement only after evaluating and discarding all alternative options for procuring goods, services and works that avoid contracts with third parties. The procurement rules of most organizations set a hierarchy of preferences among the various types of procurement, where procurement should constitute a last resort. Indeed it carries a greater risk of undermining the principle of best value for money. However, in practice the choice of procurement is usually straightforward and it is not the result of a considered assessment of the various alternative options.

Once it is determined that direct procurement – as opposed to non-buy options and indirect buy options – should be carried out, the procurement officers must choose the vendor selection method in accordance with the international organization's procurement rules and based on their own discretionary evaluations. Opting for a certain method determines the degree of competition that the procedure will have. A more detailed analysis of the rules and practices on competition and of the exceptions to them and how they have been applied is provided in a special section below. Here, it is sufficient to emphasize that the decision is based on at least four factors: the value of the contract, with thresholds set in procurement manuals; the market conditions, which are evaluated by the procurement officer; the underlying policy objective of procurement, whether for instance this is a contribution to the development of local firms or to firms incorporated in the financing states or whether the main objective is the economy of the international organization's resources; and the urgency of the procurement (in emergency situations). In general, competition is guaranteed (or should be) as the value of the contract increases and buying options are available on the market. Nevertheless, as we shall see, in most international organizations, with the exception of the European Union and the international financial institutions, for example, the WB, the EBRD, the IDB etc., the basic level of competition is in the form of restricted procedures, while open procedures are not contemplated. Thus, the procurement officer does not choose between open competition, restricted competition and private negotiations, but only between restricted competition and private negotiations.

4.3.2.3 Invitation to Bid, Request for Quotations, Request for Proposals

Once all other internal or indirect procurement options are discarded and the recourse to private negotiations is ruled out, the procurement officer can initiate the vendor selection procedure by publishing the call for tender.[53] In both direct and indirect procurement, organizations usually envisage three basic types of call for tender: a request for quotation (RFQ), an invitation to bid (ITB), and a request for proposal (RFP), which type of call for tenders is selected depends on various factors.

A RFQ is a simple request for a price. It is sent whenever the purchase value is low and for products, services and works that are well defined and have standard characteristics. Procurement manuals of the organizations usually identify a threshold beyond which other solicitation methods shall be applied. The overall process of evaluating quotations is not marked by other clear procedural provisions. The evaluation is based mainly on a quantitative criterion: the lowest offer that also meets the basic content requirements is the one that is awarded the contract. Finally, the contractual instrument is a simple purchase order and not a contractual agreement with detailed provisions.

The ITB and RFP are instead utilized in the alternative, if the contract exceeds the above-mentioned thresholds. Recourse to one or the other method depends on the content of the procurement. Due to the nature of the goods or works requested, the ITB can state the technical requirements completely and in detail during this phase. Thus, it is not necessary to specify performance through subsequent negotiation with the private subject. The submission procedure has a firm cut-off deadline and formal obligations are usually provided to guarantee publicity.

The procurement officer will send out a RFP, instead, whenever the requisition requirements cannot be sufficiently detailed due to the complex nature of the procurement and when suppliers must offer innovation and expertise in order to complete the requisition. A RFP is mostly used to procure services. However, it is also adopted for the procurement of complex goods and works, in particular when the requisition is mixed and includes both. With a RFP, the organization or the borrowing state provides only a preliminary project and the companies are responsible not only for determining the price, but also for defining the technical project in detail in order to complete and supplement the general operating scheme.

In general, both an ITB and a RFP include the invitation documents and a draft of a possible contract.[54] In fact, unlike a RFQ, both procedures

[53] As will be seen later in this chapter, the publication of the call for tenders is usually a duty of the procuring entity. In practice, the observance of publication duties is, however, often jeopardized by several factors.

[54] See Chapter 5 for a detailed discussion on the contents of the draft contracts.

conclude with a written, fully detailed contract. During the period between publication of the call for tenders and expiration of the period for submitting bids, the procuring entities and candidates may exchange information, within certain limits.

4.3.2.4   Evaluation of Offers

In direct procurement, bids and proposals are evaluated under the supervision of the procurement officer, who, depending on the value and complexity of the operation, acts alone or as the head of an evaluation committee. A committee is usually established when the value of the procurement exceeds a certain threshold, which varies from organization to organization. It has a mixed composition, as it can include other procurement officers, outside experts and, in the case of a RFP, representatives of the requisitioning administrative unit. It has a dual responsibility: before RFPs are sent, it prepares a plan for selecting suppliers (in many organizations, the so-called Source Selection Plan), which indicates technical evaluation criteria, the percentage ratio between technical factors and price, and a numerical or verbal evaluation scale. The committee then has the task of evaluating offers based on these predetermined criteria. Nevertheless, the contents of the evaluation plan are not public and are not revealed to the vendors.

In indirect procurement, the evaluation may be carried out only by the national procuring entity or jointly by the national administration and the international organization. In procurement financed by the WB, ADB or AfDB, for example, evaluation is entrusted to the national procuring entity. This responsibility is, however, complemented by control mechanisms for purposes of validity and by the possible revision of the final award decision by the international organization.

Award criteria vary depending on whether the call for tenders was issued in the form of an RFQ, ITB or RFP. In particular, the criteria can be formal, technical and financial. Formal criteria are basic requirements set for all types of tender notices. Offers that do not meet the formal criteria set out by the relevant rules and by the call for tenders do not go on to the next phase of substantive evaluation. Formal criteria include eligibility, pre-registration if necessary, providing guarantees if required, attachment of the necessary documents and all other formalities required for the proposal to be valid. Substantive criteria, such as technical and financial ones, are instead applied differently depending on the solicitation method. For an RFQ or an ITB, the award is usually based on the criterion of lowest price among the offers that are in technical compliance with the request. The proposal is, thus, evaluated as a whole, without providing separate evaluations on the technical-qualitative elements and the price. Moreover, the term 'price' is often given a broad interpretation. It must in fact include both the amount of money necessary to procure certain goods, services or works and the 'cost', that is the expense necessary to 'operationalize' those goods, services or works for the entire period of the contract or project. The contractor is identified through a semi-automatic evaluation, which, after verifying the formal admissibility of the offers according to the parameters set in the call for tenders, is aimed at ascertaining what is defined as the 'best' offer based on a purely quantitative criterion.

The award criterion for an RFP is instead compound. The commercial evaluation of the price must in fact be combined with an evaluation of technical elements of an even broader nature, such as the characteristics of the project, as well as with the guarantees of financial stability and trustworthiness offered by the candidate for the award. The procurement officer or the specially appointed committee first evaluates the technical proposals, giving each one a score; they subsequently assess the financial proposals, which are given a separate score. The technical proposal usually has a greater percentage weight than the financial proposal: typically 40–60 per cent or 30–70 per cent. The sum of the two components produces the final score and the identification of the successful vendor. This kind of evaluation is not automatic, as the counterparty is identified based on the administration's complex choice. The procuring entity bases its final decision mainly on a comparison of dissimilar technical elements, as each proposal is the vendor's autonomous and original fulfilment of the administration's request. Compared to other types of evaluation, this mechanism ensures a wide margin of discretion to the administration, especially considering that in direct procurement the procuring entity is only partially accountable for this decision.

4.3.3   Award

The award and the contracts become valid and effective for both parties once they receive authorization and approval from the competent authorities. In organizations with the highest volumes of procurement and undertaking direct procurement, the authorities responsible for drafting recommendations on the award are the permanent committees on contracts. These are bodies usually established by the financial rules of each organization, while their functions are set out in administrative regulations, such as procurement manuals or administrative circulars. In complex organizations, a binary system is provided, consisting of a central committee established at the headquarters of the organizations and local committees established in the field offices. The competence of central and local committees is based on the criterion of threshold amounts. In particular, proposals for the award of contracts that exceed certain thresholds, whether they originate at the central or peripheral level, must always be submitted for control by the headquarters committees. Proposals that originate at the peripheral level and exceed the threshold for which authority was delegated to the individual procurement officer, but not the threshold for requesting approval from the headquarters committees, are subject to control by the local committees on contracts.[55]

It should be added that in emergency situations some organizations allow submissions that are completely or partially *post facto*. Recourse to subsequent approval is permitted under circumstances that are formally defined by regulations, but which give the procurement officer flexibility to act, as well as discretion in managing resources.

In indirect procurement, there are administrative mechanisms that ensure that award decisions conform to the objective of the financing organization. This decision is in fact subject to the *ex ante* or *ex post* approval of the organization. Through approval of award decisions, organizations can closely control the evaluations performed by national administrations. In this way, the organizations not only ensure that national administrations follow the procedural rules set by the organizations themselves but also, when this is not required, that the evaluations and decisions are compatible with the principles and objectives set by the organizations.

4.4 Principles in Practice: Competition Through Indicators and Ladders of Transparency

Economy, impartiality and competition are principles that traditionally govern national public procurement. The last forty years, however, have witnessed a change in the hierarchy among these principles. Globalization and the overarching objectives of free trade and open markets have had an impact on public procurement, triggering a transition from the traditional principle of economy (*internal* to public

---

[55] For a more extensive analysis of the type of internal control performed, see Chapter 7.

administrations) to the objective of competition (*external* to public administrations). So while economy has been traditionally the guiding principle of national public procurement, nowadays it is pursued as long as it is instrumental to ensure competition and global access to the market of national public procurement.

The financial rules and procurement manuals of most international organizations similarly contain principles that govern vendor selection procedures in direct procurement: '[f]airness, integrity and transparency; [e]ffective competition; [b]est value for money; [b]est interest of the organization'.[56] With some substantial variations and additions, these same principles are also stated in the rules and regulations governing indirect procurement. For instance, the procurement guidelines of the ADB, the AfDB and the IDB identify at least four considerations that shall guide a bank's financed procurement:

> the need for economy and efficiency in the implementation of the project, including the procurement of the goods, works and non-consulting services involved; ... the [Bank's] interest in giving all eligible bidders from developed and developing countries the same information and equal opportunity to compete in providing goods, works and non-consulting services financed by the Bank; ... the [Bank's] interest in encouraging the development of domestic contracting and manufacturing industries in the Borrowing country; and ... the importance of transparency in the procurement process ... Open competition is the basis for efficient public procurement.[57]

The extent to which these principles are implemented in the procurement procedure and the hierarchy among them changes, however, depending on the institutional context (a state or an international organization) and on the type of procurement (direct or indirect). The objective of the following sections is to understand to what extent these principles are developed and implemented with the objective of

---

[56] They are listed in this order by, *inter alia*, the JIU in JIU, *Procurement Reforms in the United Nations Systems*, para. 57 [ref. REP]. Although sometimes changing the order of the list, these objectives are mentioned in the procurement manuals of organizations such as the United Nations, UNDP, UNOPS, UNHCR, WFP, UNRWA etc.

[57] This wording is used in ADB, *Procurement Guidelines*, paras. 1.2–1.3 [ref. AP&R]; AfDB, *Rules and Procedures for the Procurement of Goods and Works*, paras. 1.2–1.3 [ref. AP&R]; IDB, *Policies for the Procurement of Goods and Works Financed by the Inter-American Development Bank*, paras. 1.2–1.3 [ref. AP&R]; IFAD, *Project Procurement Guidelines*, sec. II [ref. AP&R]. Similarly WB, *The World Bank Procurement Regulations for IPF Borrowers*, paras. 1.2.–1.3 [ref. AP&R].

ensuring the interests of the international organization (in direct and indirect procurement), those of domestic administrations (in indirect procurement), or those of economic operators (in direct and indirect procurement). To this end, whereas the main focus of the analysis will be on the rules and practices of international organizations, the principles and rules guiding national public procurement, especially those provided for by European public procurement directives and the GPA, will be often presented as a useful term for comparison.[58]

4.4.1   Competition and Its Limits

European public procurement directives and the GPA are grounded on the idea that competition is the guiding principle of public procurement, as it ensures that commercial opportunities deriving from public procurement are widely accessible to companies regardless of their nationality. Competition is ensured first and foremost in the vendor selection phase and in the related procedures.

The same cannot be said for the procurement of international organizations, where both rules and practices show that, while competition is formally included among the principles guiding procurement, it is not a political priority, as it is outweighed by other interests ascribable to international organizations and to the states funding the organizations.

If this is true for procurement of international organizations in general, a major difference can, however, be found between direct and indirect procurement in terms of the extent to which competition is pursued in each of them. Indeed, while in direct procurement competition requirements must be met by the organization, in indirect procurement, procedures ensuring competition are undertaken by national procuring entities. This structural difference explains the partially dissimilar objectives underlying the application of the principle of competition in the two situations and in turn determines the degree and scope of the principle.

4.4.1.1   Competition Indicators in Direct Procurement: Regulatory Restrictions and Anti-Competitive Practices

A comparative analysis of the rules and practices of organizations leads to the identification of at least six main indicators that are useful to anchor and measure the degree and scope of competition in direct procurement.

---

[58] Chapter 8 analyzes, instead, the interplay of interests that explains the differences.

First is the basic type of procurement procedure adopted and, more in particular, whether it is an open or restricted procedure or another type of procedure. Second is the geographical scope of competition. This indicator refers to limits on the geographical area where prospective vendors must be incorporated or to the link between the nationality of the companies and the possibility of submitting an offer. Third is the existence and recurrence of competition waivers. Fourth is the time frames within which vendors must submit their offers. The shortening of time frames can in fact hinder competition, resulting in the formal implementation of competitive procedures that in reality do not give vendors the chance to participate. Fifth is the practice of artificially splitting the value of the contracts, in this way bypassing competition requirements. Sixth is the use of extensions to existing contracts and of long-term agreements in lieu of initiating competitive procedures to award new contracts.[59] The analysis provided in the following sections is built around these indicators.

Along with these primary indicators, there are also micro-practices that independent control bodies have criticized, in particular with regard to field procurement: invitation of vendors who are not pre-qualified, based on the independent evaluations of the procurement officer;[60] unjustified acceptance of late offers;[61] and inadequate internal control of compliance with the principle of competition, due to the absence of data collection practices, are some of the critical points that have been raised by control bodies.[62]

a   **The Type of Procedure: Open and Restricted Competition**   One of the main differences in the approach to competition between domestic public procurement and procurement of international organizations lies in the basic type of vendor selection procedures provided in the relevant rules. Three types of procurement procedures are set out by the EU public procurement directives and the GPA: open, restricted and negotiated procedures.[63] Open procedures are tenders open to any operator

---

[59] A general, albeit brief assessment on competition in international organizations within the UN system can be found in JIU, *Procurement Reforms in the United Nations System*, paras. 58–59 [ref. REP].

[60] OIOS, *Procurement of Local Contracts in UNMIL*, para. 15 [ref. REP].   [61] *Ibid.*

[62] JIU, *Procurement Reforms in the United Nations System*, paras. 204–205 [ref. REP].

[63] EU procurement directives also include competitive dialogue among the basic procurement procedures.

who is interested.[64] Restricted procedures are those in which any economic operator may request to participate but whereby only those economic operators invited by the procuring entity may submit an offer.[65] Negotiated procedures are procedures in which the contracting authorities consult companies of their choice and negotiate the terms of contract with one or more of them.[66]

The option to use one or another type of procedure depends in part on the administration's discretionary decision and in part on meeting predetermined conditions. While, in fact, open and restricted procedures are considered basic methods for selecting contractors and can be used in the alternative at the discretion of the procuring entity, negotiated procedures can be carried out only when the conditions prescribed by the relevant rules are met.

Traditionally, when carrying out direct procurement, the vast majority of international organizations adopt only two types of vendor selection procedures, rather than three as for domestic public procurement: restricted procedures and direct contracting (the equivalent of the negotiated procedure). In indirect procurement, on the contrary, three procedures have always been provided by the relevant rules: open procedures, restricted procedures, and direct contracting. The 2006 version of the UN Procurement Practitioner's Handbook, revised in 2012, described the difference in these terms: 'while some organizations (e.g. WB) require open competition for all solicitations over specified thresholds, most UN organizations often apply a process of limited/restricted competition'.[67]

Currently, a majority of organizations still have a dual approach (restricted procedure and direct contracting) when undertaking direct procurement. Examples include the United Nations, WFP, WHO, FAO and UNRWA.[68] In these organizations, usually the approach to

---

[64] European Union, Directive 2014/24/EU, Art. 27; European Union, Directive 2014/25/EU, Art. 45 [ref. N&RL-EU]. GPA, Art. I(m).

[65] European Union, Directive 2014/24/EU, Art. 28; European Union, Directive 2014/25/EU, Art. 46 [ref. N&RL-EU]. GPA, Art. I(q), Art. IX, para. 4–6.

[66] European Union, Directive 2014/24/EU, Art. 29, Art. 32; European Union, Directive 2014/25/EU, Art. 47, Art. 50 [ref. N&RL-EU]. GPA, Art. I(h), Art. XIII.

[67] United Nations, *United Nations Procurement Practitioner's Handbook*, 2006, pp. 3–38 [ref. AP&R].

[68] United Nations, *Procurement Manual*, paras. 6.1 and 9.3; UNDP, *Programme and Operations Policies and Procedures. Procurement*, sec. 'Procurement Methods', paras. 8–9; WFP, *Non-Food Procurement Manual*, para. 2.2; *Id.*, *Food Procurement Manual*, para. 4.1.1; WHO, *Manual for Procurement of Diagnostics and Related Laboratory Items and Equipment*, para. 3.2; *Id.*, *Good Procurement Practices for Artemisinin-Based*

competition results from the procedural requirements that the procurement officer must meet. Sometimes, however, the exclusion of open competition procedures is explicit and is justified by reasons connected with the highly specialized nature of the goods or services to be procured. The WHO rules for the procurement of diagnostics, for instance, although recognizing that international competitive bidding is a standard procurement method according to the Model Law on Public Procurement developed by UNCITRAL, provide that 'due to the highly-specialized nature of some laboratory products, bidding should be restricted to suppliers who can provide specific equipment models, reagents, consumables and durables'.[69] In the case of WHO, however, restricted competition has to 'be fully justified with written evidence for selection'.[70] The same justification requirement does not apply to other organizations, where open competition is not even acknowledged as the standard procurement method.

Procurement rules of the organizations with the highest volume of procurement prescribe the restricted procedure as the basic procedure for vendor selection, not including an open procedure among the options, and then identify specific circumstances and thresholds that allow for direct contracting. Thus, by choosing how many and which vendors to invite, it is always the contracting authority that filters and scales the degree of competition to be applied to a single procurement.

A minority of organizations instead adopts open competition as the default procedure, together with restricted procedures, at the discretion of the procurement officer. Examples in this regard include EU institutions, ESA, NATO and a few UN agencies such as UNOPS, UNFPA, UNDP and UNIDO.[71]

Antimalarial Medicines, para. 5.1; FAO, *FAO Manual*, sec. 502.8–502.9; UNRWA, *Procurement Manual*, paras. 2.2.3(1), 5.3.1, 5.3.2 [for all manuals ref. AP&R].

[69] WHO, *Manual for Procurement of Diagnostics and Related Laboratory Items and Equipment*, para. 3.2 [ref. AP&R].

[70] *Ibid.*

[71] UNDP, *Programme and Operations Policies and Procedures. Procurement*, sec. 'Procurement Methods', para. 8; UNOPS, *Procurement Manual*, paras. 6.2.1–6.2.2; UNFPA, *Policy and Procedures for Regular Procurement*, paras. 6.2.1–6.2.2; UNRWA, *Procurement Manual*, para. 2.2.3 (1) and paras. 5.3.1–5.3.2; UNESCO, *UNESCO Administrative Manual*, sec. 10.2 (para. 5.2), sec. 10.2A (para. 4.8), sec. 10.2A (paras. 5.2, 5.3, 5.4); UNIDO, *Procurement Manual*, para. 10.2.1; NATO, *NSPO Procurement Regulations*, para. 3.5.10; ESA, *ESA Procurement Regulations and Related Implementing Instructions*, art. 13 [for all documents ref. AP&R]; European Union, Regulation (EU, Euratom) No. 966/2012 (and following amendments) [ref. N&RL-EU].

As said, when carrying out a restricted procedure, organizations have wide discretion in identifying the shortlist of vendors which are allowed to submit an offer. The only constraint to exercising discretion is represented by the minimum number of vendors to be invited. The pool of vendors to whom the invitations are sent in some organizations (see the United Nations)[72] corresponds to the number of enterprises that have been pre-qualified for a certain sector of activity. Nevertheless, in most other organizations (e.g. FAO, WFP, UNDP, WHO, UNOPS and UNFPA)[73] not all vendors pre-qualified by sector are also the vendors to be invited. This is either because there are no pre-qualification mechanisms in place, or because nothing is provided in this regard by the relevant rules, or because the rules explicitly state that there is no obligation of this type. The WFP Food Procurement Manual is, for instance, an example of this last hypothesis where it states that

> [t]he selection of vendors for invitation to bid in a particular RFQ will not always include the entire list of registered vendors for a particular commodity, as not all of these vendors will be suitable for inclusion in every tender.[74]

In addition, where, as in the United Nations, there is a provision that registered vendors and invited vendors must coincide, it is still possible to invite fewer vendors than those registered (and this actually occurs quite frequently). The UN Procurement Manual contains a non-mandatory list ('examples of circumstances') of formal and substantive reasons that can justify this deviation from the general rule:[75] an excessively long list of vendors (but without defining what length would become excessive); the presence of a single vendor on the market (a 'sole source') that in the procurement officer's opinion is capable of supplying those particular goods, services or works; security reasons; low value procurements; and finally, '[w]here, in the opinion of the Chief of Section, UN/PD, or the CPO [Chief Procurement Officer], other exceptional circumstances warrant such limitation'.[76] The system, thus, gives the procuring entity very

---

[72] United Nations, *Procurement Manual*, para. 9.5, no. 2 [ref. AP&R].

[73] UNDP, *Programme and Operations Policies and Procedures. Procurement*, sec. 'Procurement Methods', paras. 9–13; WFP, *Non-Food Procurement Manual*, para. 2.12.1; *id.*, *Food Procurement Manual*, para. 11.3.1; UNOPS, *Procurement Manual*, para. 3.1; WHO, *Manual for Procurement of Diagnostics and Related Laboratory Items and Equipment*, paras. 3.2.1, 3.2.2; FAO, *FAO Manual*, sec. 502.9.4; UNFPA, *Policy and Procedures for Regular Procurement*, para. 3.1 [for all documents ref. AP&R].

[74] WFP, *Food Procurement Manual*, para. 11.3.1 [ref. AP&R].

[75] United Nations, *Procurement Manual*, para. 9.5, no. 2 [ref. AP&R].   [76] *Ibid.*

broad discretion. For some categories of goods, this discretion can translate into a semi-permanent restriction of competition. In particular, the first of the circumstances listed, that is an excessively long list of vendors registered for a determined category of goods, services or works, actually produces the result that some of these categories, in which many vendors are registered, can, at the administration's discretion, continuously be excluded from the business opportunities offered by the organization, even though the decision must be reiterated case by case.

Furthermore, even if pre-qualified vendors and the vendors to be invited are not the same, rules on the minimum number of vendors to be invited vary from organization to organization. In most organizations, such as FAO, UNDP, WFP, UNOPS, NATO and ESA,[77] the minimum is three vendors (or at least three offers shall be received and evaluated). In others, such as the UN and EU institutions, the minimum is five or more vendors, depending on the value of the contract.[78] Nevertheless, the requirement is often not stated as an obligation, but rather as a guideline. This is exemplified by the passage in the UN manual: '[t]he Procurement Officer should endeavour to invite the following minimum number of Vendors ... to ensure an appropriate level of competition'.[79] The optional nature of this requirement has in practice led to overly restricting the number of parties invited. For example, between 2006 and 2008, of the 1,972 bidding procedures announced by the United Nations (which is one of the most compliant within the UN system in terms of adhering to the principle of competition), 15 per cent (297 tenders) were called with an invitation to two to four vendors, 10 per cent (197 tenders) solicited offers from a single vendor, and about 28 per cent (539 tenders) invited twenty-five or more vendors.[80] This means that, considering the prescriptive value that the Procurement Manual is supposed to have,

---

[77] FAO, *FAO Manual*, sec. 502.3.4; UNDP, *Programme and Operations Policies and Procedures. Procurement*, sec. 'Procurement Methods', para. 12; WFP, *Food Procurement Manual*, para. 4.1.3; *Id., Non-Food Procurement Manual*, para. 2.2; UNOPS, *Procurement Manual*, para. 5.7.1(f); NATO, *NSPO Procurement Regulations*, para. 8.2.; ESA, *ESA Procurement Regulations and Related Implementing Instructions*, Art. 13, para. 3 [for all documents ref. AP&R].

[78] United Nations, *Procurement Manual*, para. 9.6 [ref. AP&R]; European Union, Regulation (EU, Euratom) No. 966/2012 (and following amendments), Art. 104, para. 4 [ref. N&RL-EU].

[79] *Ibid.*, The 'recommended' number of vendors to be invited grows, nevertheless, as the value of the procurement operation grows.

[80] The data are reported in OIOS, *Audit of Procurement Management*, A/64/369, para. 38 [ref. REP].

there is a high percentage of non-compliance with the guidelines on the minimum number of vendors to invite. In addition, if we compare the two extremes, that is the number of cases below the recommended threshold (fewer than five) and the number of cases well above this threshold (twenty-five and beyond), we see that the percentage of the former (35 per cent) is several points higher than the latter (28 per cent) and that, compared to the total, more than a third of bidding procedures do not meet minimum competition requirements. On this point, the European public procurement directives differ both in the larger number of vendors that the authority must involve compared to the majority of international organizations, and in the obligatory nature of the requirement, which does not permit diverging practices without sanctions.[81]

b   Competition and Nationality   Although the international nature of the organizations would seem to make nationality in the procurement procedure irrelevant, the nationality of vendors plays a significant role in shaping the award decisions of organizations. This can occur in various ways and to different degrees, depending on the organization. Explicit formulations of this criterion range from a generic reference to equitable geographical distribution to specific provisions on regional or local competition procedures, to ties imposed by financing states. Indeed, five main formulas can be identified that increasingly tie nationality to the contract award decision.

The first is the previously mentioned generic reference to equitable geographical distribution of vendors. The UN Manual is an example of this approach where it states that

> [t]he Procurement Officer shall always strive to ensure equitable geographical representation of invited Vendors ... All efforts must be engaged by the procurement staff to raise business opportunities for Vendors from Developing Countries and Countries with Economies in Transition.[82]

The provision appears to set a general policy objective to which procurement officers should aim, rather than a specific prescription of conduct complemented by sanctions in case of violation. Whereas

---

[81] European Union, Directive 2014/24/EU, Art. 65(2) [ref. N&RL-EU]. On this point, the 1994 version of the GPA contained a loose-knit group of rules and regulations that nevertheless referred to principles of non-discrimination and protection of competition as the fundamental criteria when making the selection and required the number to be as high as possible compatibly with the efficiency of the system. This reference nevertheless no longer appears in the current version of the GPA.

[82] United Nations, *Procurement Manual*, para. 9.7.1 [ref. AP&R].

pro-development policies, as part of the organization's institutional mission, guide the administrative activity, they do so in a non-binding fashion, at least in procurement, and leave room for the inclusion of other considerations and criteria in the award decision. This also explains why, as will be discussed later,[83] the share of procurement contracts that have been awarded to developing countries has increased over the years, but in 2014, seven of the top ten countries supplying the organizations of the UN system were still developed economies.[84]

The second modality through which the procurement award decision is linked to nationality is to restrict competition, from the outset, to a certain country or region. UNDP, UNOPS and UNRWA are some of the organizations in which this procedure is allowed. In these organizations international competition is usually the preferred mode of procurement. However, national or regional competition is also allowed when one or a combination of circumstances exists. UNDP, for example, combines quantitative criteria, such as a procurement value that is less than $150,000, with qualitative ones.[85] The latter includes situations in which

> [t]he required goods/services/works are available locally at about the same or lower prices compared to those of comparable quality from the global market ... [T]he requirement is for construction works that are expected to be geographically scattered in various parts of a country and intensive in the use of local labour, and the country has a sufficient base of contractors with the qualifications and competence needed to complete the works ... Services needed require a substantive depth of knowledge and understanding of the local environment, culture, language, sociopolitical dynamics or national systems that an international entity will probably not possess ... There is a very low probability that an international entity will be interested in submitting an offer or partnering with national entities.[86]

Similar qualitative criteria – compounded or not by quantitative criteria – are also applied by UNESCO[87] and UNRWA.[88] Thus, the reasons for choosing national competition do not lie in the objective of providing commercial opportunities for local suppliers, but primarily in the

---

[83] See Chapter 8.
[84] See *inter alia* UNOPS, *2014 Annual Statistical Report*, p. 8 [ref. REP].
[85] UNDP, *Programme and Operations Policies and Procedures*, sec. 'Procurement Methods', para. 1 [ref. AP&R].
[86] *Ibid.*, sec. 'Procurement Methods', para. 1(a), (b), (c), (d).
[87] UNESCO, *UNESCO Administrative Manual*, sec. 10.2, para. 5.4 [ref. AP&R].
[88] UNRWA, *Procurement Manual*, para. 5.3.2 (2) [ref. AP&R].

interests of the international organization, which can find it more convenient to procure locally rather than internationally.

The third limit to competition comes from the application of international policy considerations. International resolutions adopted by the principal organs of the organizations set the political priorities of the organizations and, thus, have an impact on their administrative activity. The UN Procurement Manual is clear, albeit generic, in this regard:

> [t]he procurement of goods and/or services by the United Nations shall be in compliance with Security Council resolutions, and the rules, regulations and policies promulgated by the United Nations' principal organs.[89]

UNDP procurement rules are more specific, making reference to the identification of mandatory criteria by these organs and providing a hierarchy of considerations that shall guide the organization:

> [f]our considerations consistently guide consideration of UNDP's interest: ... [a]ccess to procurement opportunities for all interested and qualified offerors worldwide, except where other criteria are mandated by the UN Security Council or UN General Assembly.[90]

The international resolutions to which the texts refer usually entail restrictions to trade and, as a consequence, the exclusion of certain vendors incorporated in the state subject to sanctions. Explicit reference to trade sanctions can be found, for example, in the procurement rules applicable to WFP: '[o]ther vendors could be excluded because of sanctions imposed by the UN General Assembly or Security Council, preventing or restricting trade in certain areas or circumstances'.[91] Thus, as all UN agencies are subject to resolutions adopted by overarching international bodies where all or some states' members are represented, joint political considerations play an essential role in guiding the administrative activity of these organizations and have a direct impact on private subjects.

The fourth deviation from international competition comes from the application of the donor funding criterion. Contrary to international policy criteria, which are the result of a joint agreement between states, the donor funding criterion is specifically linked to a state: a single state

---

[89] United Nations, *Procurement Manual*, para. 1.1.1(c) [ref. AP&R].

[90] UNDP, *Programme and Operations Policies and Procedures*, sec. 'Procurement Overview and Principles', para. 9(b) [ref. AP&R].

[91] WFP, *Non-Food Procurement Manual*, para. 11.3.1 [ref. AP&R].

shapes competition by imposing the procedural requirements with which the organization must comply. This also implies that the same organization can adopt different degrees of competition for the same type of procurement, depending on the origin of the financing. When coming from a single state, the donor funding criterion is the expression of formal or informal tied aid.[92] The criterion is explicit in some organizations, such as WFP, but present, even if not explicit or only briefly mentioned, in other organizations. According to the donor funding criterion

> [t]here may be donor preferences as to the vendors to be included, or the countries or areas where a particular procurement should take place and these should be respected provided they are not contrary to WFP's interests or procurement policy.[93]

The states financing a certain procurement action or, more generally, a project or programme, can define not only the scope of competition, but also the degree of competition, even expunging it from the procedure when a single vendor is already identified (usually a vendor from the financing state). In such cases, the possibility of determining the outcome of the administrative decision can go further to exclude vendors on the grounds of political hostility between the financing state and the state where the vendor is incorporated, or because of different standards adopted by those states. Both a political and a technical factor, which can however conceal political reasons, may play a role in restricting competition. WFP procurement rules are explicative in this respect:

> some vendors may not be suitable for certain contracts because of, for example, the situation between the country of origin and the recipient country, which has caused the recipient country to ban imports from the country of origin. This could be because of phytosanitary reasons, such as the prevention of the spread of agricultural diseases, or because of friction between the countries.[94]

Similarly, in the UNDP and UNRWA the basic rule of international competition has exceptions linked to specific donor requests, even if these are not supported by political hostility or incompatibility of standards, and subject to approval by competent authorities: 'UNDP does not

---

[92] In general, on tied aid procurement see Lachimia, *Tied Aid and Development Aid Procurement, passim.*
[93] WFP, *Food Procurement Manual*, para. 11.3.1 [ref. AP&R].   [94] *Ibid.*, para. 11.3.1.

accept the restriction of awards to exclusive contractors or countries, unless explicitly mentioned in a donor agreement approved by the Chief Procurement Officer'.[95] Or, also: '[n]ational or regional tenders are typically conducted . . . [i]f a donor agreement provides for procurement from a limited geographical area'.[96]

Thus, the procedure is based on a hierarchy of interests ascribable to different international public actors. The principle of competition, primarily conceived to ensure the best value for money to the international organization rather than to give opportunity to vendors, is in any event recessive when it conflicts with the international political and economic interests of the financing state.[97]

The fifth modality through which international competition is distorted by preference based on nationality is the geographical return criterion, to be interpreted as a further development of the donor funding criterion. As will also be discussed later,[98] the practice by member states of linking funding to a certain return in terms of awarding procurement to domestic companies exists in all organizations. However, it is usually not codified by the relevant rules. The underlying idea is that an international organization must be equidistant from member states and, if preferential treatment is to be given, it must favour the development of emerging economies. However, even if most organizations embody this approach in their procurement rules, thus avoiding reference to any connection between financing and returns, the explicit recognition of this link can sometimes explain an organization's whole procurement regulatory framework. The best example in this regard is ESA. As made clear in the ESA implementing instructions:

> [o]ne of the main orientations governing the ESA industrial policy is the geo-return principle which enables the Executive to conduct and implement an effective European Space programme.[99]

---

[95] UNDP, *Programme and Operations Policies and Procedures*, sec. 'Procurement Overview and Principles', para. 8 and with a different wording, but providing for the same limitations, also *ibid.*, sec. 'Procurement Methods', para. 2(d)(ii) ('[w]here a donor agreement requires a UNDP business unit to agree on any limitations or conditions that may compromise, or are in conflict with, any of the above principles to any extent, the business unit must obtain prior approval from the UNDP Chief Procurement Officer before the agreement is finalized') [ref. AP&R].

[96] UNRWA, *Procurement Manual*, para. 5.3.2(2)(d) [ref. AP&R].

[97] See Chapter 8 for further discussion on this point.   [98] See Chapter 8.

[99] ESA, *ESA Procurement Regulations*, Annex II, Art. 1 [ref. AP&R].

The prior objective of having secure and sufficient funds to support costly space missions has led the organization to build a detailed system to measure and control the financing-return ratio. The core element of such a system is nationality. To ensure that the nationality of companies is correctly taken into account in the procurement decision, the organization has set up a two-step process that includes an *ex ante* registration process and an *ex post* check on the nationality requirement. During the registration, the company has to declare its nationality. Then, following the award, the contract is accounted against the nationality declared by the company.[100] During both phases, audits can be initiated if doubts arise as to the nationality declared by the company in relation to the criteria laid down in the ESA Convention.[101] The objective of these audits

> is to be assured or alternatively obtain evidence that an enterprise can effectively be considered to belong to specific ESA Member States, allowing as such the ... contracts awarded to this company to be counted as realised industrial return for those specific Member States.[102]

Audits can be initiated not only by ESA and at the request of the member states, but also following the initiative of '[t]he company, in whose opinion ESA is not considering its nationality correctly and which therefore considers that such might have effects on its ability to bid for certain procurements'.[103] Thus, although a procurement system strictly based on nationality does not guarantee *ipso facto* the right of any company to participate in the procurement procedure, it strengthens procedural rights (compared to organizations adopting different systems) for those private subjects who belong to the states financing the organizations. Indeed, in pursuing their own interests, vendors become the tool to ensure the functioning of the financing-return mechanism. In organizations where the financing-return mechanism is not codified, i.e. all UN agencies, the financing-return link also functions as a strong driver in guiding award decisions of the organization. However, chances for companies to be awarded a contract are supported mainly by informal political pressure of the states within the organizations by virtue of the connection of nationality between certain states and the vendors. At the same time, private subjects' procedural rights are developed to the extent to which member states have an interest in open competition and are willing to grant it.[104]

---

[100] *Ibid.*, Annex II, Preface.   [101] *Ibid.*, Annex II, Preface.   [102] *Ibid.*, Annex II, Art. 1.
[103] *Ibid.*, Annex II, Art. 2.1.   [104] For further discussion on these points see Chapter 7.

c **Waivers of Competition**   Just as in national public procurement, procurement rules of international organizations also provide for procedures, called negotiated procedures, in which competition is excluded from the outset and the organization directly negotiates with the vendor. In direct procurement, the manuals of the organizations almost uniformly indicate certain exceptional circumstances and when these may occur: if the market of reference is not competitive, for example, in the case of a monopoly; if the prices are fixed by government regulations; if the procurement is managed jointly with other international organizations; if offers for identical products and services have already been received in the past; if the formal tender procedure has not produced results; if the contract relates to the acquisition of real property ownership and market conditions are not competitive; if services are involved that cannot be evaluated based on objective parameters; if the value is below the threshold established for the application of tender procedures; above all, if the administrative official feels there is a 'genuine exigency' (and not an 'extreme urgency' as the GPA instead provides); and in all cases where the administrative head of the department foresees that a tender could not produce any results.

These last two circumstances have allowed many organizations to tender contracts using non-competitive procedures (waivers), while the other exceptional requirements have often been interpreted broadly. Although in the last two decades there have been more controls over the use of waivers and exceptions, such practices have been and are still widespread among various organizations, especially within the UN system. Since 2005, in several cases across different UN entities, high levels of sole-source contracts and the invocation of operational exigencies for exceptional procurement actions have been detected.[105] In the biennium 2010–2011, for example, 55 per cent of all contracts over $300,000 (contracts over $300,000 represented 99.7 per cent of all UN contracts) concluded at the UN headquarters were processed without competitive

---

[105] See UN Board of Auditors, *Financial Report and Audited Financial Statements*, A/67/5 (Vol. I), paras. 110–117; UN ACABQ, *Financial Reports and Audited Financial Statements and Reports*, A/67/381, para. 60. And also, UN Board of Auditors, *Concise Summary of the Principal Findings and Conclusions*, A/69/178, para. 82; *ibid.*, *Concise Summary of the Principal Findings and Conclusions*, A/67/173, para. 49 [for all documents ref. REP].

tendering.[106] The trend still appeared to be in place in 2015 when the UN Board of Auditors found that there were unjustified waivers for a high number of cases, especially related to proprietary software, maintenance support and implementation services.[107] But also procurement in UN missions, in particular in peacekeeping, assistance and stabilization missions, is problematic from the point of view of competition. With regard to such activities, the UN Board of Auditors[108] and OIOS[109] have indeed repeatedly detected irregularities and deficiencies jeopardizing competition, including lack of full transparency in the process of inviting vendors and lack of competitive bidding justified by exigency reasons, or not justified at all.

Several international organizations within the UN system have shown similar problems. Over the biennium 2010–2011, for example, UNOPS was reported to have an elevated number of procurement cases that were not solicited through formal competitive bidding processes: the list of approvals by the competent authorities at UNOPS indicated that a total of 248 cases over the biennium, valued at $305.9 million, had not been solicited through formal means.[110]

The data on UNDP's procurement activity are also illustrative: from 2005 to 2008, the organization exempted from competitive procedures contracts for the supply of goods and services worth $879,000,000, that is about 58 per cent of total resources spent on procurement. In particular, value fluctuated from $259,000,000 in 2005 (about 50 per cent of total purchases), to $409,000,000 in the following year (about two-thirds of the total), dropping to $210,000,000 (about 54 per cent of the total) in

---

[106] UN Board of Auditors, *Financial Reports and Audited Financial Statements*, A/67/5 (Vol. I), para. 111 [ref. REP].

[107] UN Board of Auditors, *Financial Reports and Audited Financial Statements*, A/71/5 (Vol. I), paras. 220–235; UN ACABQ, *Financial Reports and Audited Financial Statements*, A/71/669, para. 36 [all documents in ref. REP].

[108] Reference to these problems can be found in many of the UN Board of Auditors reports on peacekeeping operations, as well as in the UN ACABQ reports. Reference to the relevant reports of the UN Board of Auditors and the UN ACABQ regarding peacekeeping can be found at the beginning of this book in the *List of Instruments*, under 'Reports' [ref. REP].

[109] Reference to the relevant reports of the OIOS regarding peacekeeping in Haiti, Mali, Congo, Central African Republic, South Sudan, Abyei, Somalia, Liberia, Afghanistan and Côte d'Ivoire can be found at the beginning of this book in the *List of Instruments*, under 'Reports' [ref. REP].

[110] UN Board of Auditors, *Financial Report and Audited Financial Statements*, A/67/5/Add. 10, para. 98(b). High rates of waivers were also detected by the Board of Auditors in previous years, see, *inter alia*, UN Board of Auditors, *Financial Report and Audited Financial Statements*, A/65/5/Add. 10, para. 397 [both documents in ref. REP].

2006.[111] Moreover, many cases have been reported where UNDP country offices, e.g. in Venezuela, Chad, Indonesia and Myanmar, procured goods and services through direct contracting without proper justification.[112]

In the biennium 2010–2011, UNRWA granted 445 waivers with a combined value of $90.8 million. While the total value was low, the number of waivers was considered high by the UN Board of Auditors and the waivers were not linked to genuine exigencies.[113] The problem did not seem to be overcome five years later, when the Board underlined that not only were waivers still frequent, but they were also inadequately justified: for example, at the Gaza Office, only 20 per cent of the sample waivers scrutinized were supported by acceptable reasons.[114]

UNICEF presents similar issues: although '[e]ffective procurement is vital for UNICEF operations and requires that the Fund implement effective procedures to ensure sufficient competition'[115] and '[t]he UNICEF Supply Manual specifies that with certain exceptions, all purchases must be the result of competitive bidding',[116] over the years many cases of non-compliance with the requirement of competitive bidding have been reported.[117]

However, while several organizations bypass the established rules through anti-competitive practices, there are also cases where the relationship between rules and practices is inverted and the rules that provide

[111] The data are reported in Russel, 'UNDP Procurement: Exceptions Are the Rule'. Similar data for the biennium 2006–2007 are also in UN Board of Auditors, *Financial Report and Audited Financial Statements*, A/63/5/Add. 1, paras. 246–250, where it is stated that '[t]he percentage of waivers of competitive process reported was 63 per cent in 2007 and 64 per cent in 2006' (para. 248). These data are also recalled in UN Board of Auditors, *Concise Summary of Principal Findings and Conclusions*, A/63/169, para. 79 [ref. REP].

[112] UN Board of Auditors, *Financial Report and Audited Financial Statements*, A/67/5/Add. 1, para. 106. UN Board of Auditors, *Financial Report and Audited Financial Statements*, A/68/5/Add. 1, para. 57 [all documents in ref. REP].

[113] UN Board of Auditors, *Financial Reports and Audited Financial Statements*, A/67/5/Add. 3, paras. 84–94 [ref. REP].

[114] UN Board of Auditors, *Financial Report and Audited Financial Statements*, A/71/5/Add. 4, para. 45 [ref. REP].

[115] UN Board of Auditors, *Financial Report and Audited Financial Statements*, A/67/5/Add. 2, para. 129 [ref. REP].

[116] *Ibid.*, para. 130.

[117] See, for instance, UN Board of Auditors, *Financial Report and Audited Financial Statements* (UNICEF), A/68/5/Add. 2, paras. 8–9; *ibid.*, *Financial Report and Audited Financial Statements* (UNICEF), A/67/5/Add. 2, paras. 130–131; *ibid.*, *Financial Report and Audited Financial Statements* (UNICEF), A/65/5/Add. 2, paras. 155, 158 [all documents ref. REP].

for exceptions to competition are considered to be insufficiently developed to reflect practices. In at least one instance, with reference to UNFPA, the UN Advisory Committee on Administrative and Budgetary Questions noted that, although UNFPA had launched new procurement procedures to provide guidance on instances of exceptions, 'established procurement practices at UNFPA show that the reasons given for using exceptions to the established procurement practices did not constitute an exhaustive list and that other reasons ... may apply'.[118]

d   Competition and Time Frames for Bid Submission   Apart from the distortions created by interpreting exceptional cases, poor implementation of the principle of competition also takes the form of imposing short timelines to submit bids, even though the procedure is formally competitive.

Appropriate timelines to submit bids are an essential condition to ensure competition, as they allow vendors to be notified of the business opportunity and to submit their expression of interest or offer. Organizations' procurement manuals usually establish a minimum time frame for vendors to submit their expression of interest or their offers. However, organizations present a variety of solutions in this regard, which range from mandatory (very few organizations) to only regulatory provisions on time frames (most organizations); and in this latter case, which allow more or less room for the procurement officer to define the appropriate time frame for the specific procurement activity.

Strictly binding prescriptions on time frames, for example, apply to procurement by EU institutions. The time frames vary depending on the type of procedure adopted, but in any case they are in line with those prescribed by the public procurement directives regulating procurement by EU member states.[119] Within the UN system, UNFPA procurement rules set time limits, although these tend to be shorter.[120] The binding character of these time frames is strengthened by the requirement to provide justification when the procurement officer seeks to shorten the timelines. In addition, shorter time frames can be possible only for low-value procurement, non-complex processes, or on an exceptional basis.[121]

---

[118] UN ACABQ, *Financial Reports and Audited Financial Statements and Reports of the Board of Auditors*, A/68/381, para. 31 [ref. REP].

[119] EU Commission Delegated Regulation (EU) 2015/2462, art. 152(2)–(3) [ref. N&RL-EU].

[120] UNFPA, *Policy and Procedures for Regular Procurement*, paras. 5.3.2 (for expressions of interest), 6.3.1.2 (for request for quotations), 6.3.2.1(b) (for invitations to bid), 6.3.2.2(b) (for request for proposals) [ref. AP&R].

[121] *Ibid.*, paras. 6.3.2.1(b) and 6.3.2.2(b).

An example of a more flexible approach to time frames is provided by UNOPS. The procurement rules prescribe that '[d]epending on the complexity and nature of the goods/services/works being procured, a *recommended* minimum of ten days should be granted for responses [to requests for expression of interest]'.[122] Exceptions to these time frames can be authorized, '[i]f due cause exists'[123] and if the procurement official justifies the decision for waiving the minimum day requirement, describing the reasons and explaining how the requirement for competition has been met notwithstanding the shortened solicitation period.[124] However, for procurement of works in particular, 'a shortened bid period is usually not recommended'.[125]

In other UN organizations, the time frames prescribed by the rules appear to be regulatory rather than mandatory, and procurement officials have room for discretionary decisions. In the United Nations, for instance, the procurement officer must post a notice of request for expression of interest on the United Nations Secretariat Procurement Division (UN/PD) website and advertise in the international print and internet media for a period ranging from two to four weeks 'depending on the circumstances of the case'.[126] The non-binding character of the time frames has been repeatedly pointed out by the competent authorities. In 2013, the UN Secretary-General emphasized that 'solicitation timelines in the Procurement Manual are only a recommendation'.[127] UNDP sets a stricter time frame which, however, also gives the procurement officer room for discretion: when engaging in open competitive bidding, '[a]dvertisements *should* remain online for a minimum of two weeks' to allow the submission of a bid or a proposal.[128]

Other organizations either do not identify a specific minimum period to submit expressions of interest or offers, or else provide purely indicative timelines. The NATO Procurement Manual, for example, identifies typical (but not mandatory) timelines for bid submissions, depending on the procurement method adopted.[129] Similarly, the UNIDO

---

[122] Emphasis added. UNOPS, *Procurement Manual*, para. 5.5 (with reference to requests for expression of interest) [ref. AP&R].

[123] *Ibid.*, para. 6.5.1(b)(ii). [124] *Ibid.*, para. 6.5.1(b)(ii). [125] *Ibid.*, para. 6.5.1(b)(ii).

[126] United Nations, *Procurement Manual*, para. 9.8.1 [ref. AP&R].

[127] The statement is reported in UN ACABQ, *Report of the Board of Auditors on the Accounts of the United Nations Peacekeeping Operations*, A/67/782, para. 16 [ref. REP].

[128] Emphasis added. UNDP, *Programme and Operations Policies and Procedures*, sec. 'Procurement Methods', para. 6(c) and similarly paras. 42 (for invitations to bid), 54 (for requests for proposals) [ref. AP&R].

[129] NATO, *NSPO Procurement Regulations*, para. 7.3 [ref. AP&R].

Procurement Manual provides procurement timelines that should be considered appropriate by the competent officer.[130] Thus, such timelines appear to be benchmarks *for* the administration to avoid unduly long procedures and waste of resources, rather than procedural safeguards to allow vendors sufficient time for submitting their expressions of interest or offers.

In general and with the exception of a few organizations, a common feature among most organizations appears to be the non-binding character of the prescriptions on time frames for submissions of expressions of interest or offers. Procurement officers are often given recommendations to advertise the commercial opportunity for a certain period of time, but the exact determination of the deadline is then left to their discretion to be exercised on a case-by-case basis depending on the circumstances. Furthermore, even when the time frames are mandatory, organizations within the UN system link the necessity of time frames to the objective of competition as the best way to obtain best value for money. Thus, the observance of time frames is required mainly in the interest of the organizations, rather than of the vendors. In this regard, the following passage from the summary of the principal findings and conclusions contained in the report of the UN Board of Auditors for the year 2012 is emblematic:

> [s]hort tender submission time frames lead to low vendor response rates due to there being insufficient time for bidders to prepare properly for the tender process and meet the delivery schedule. This limits the scope of competition among vendors, potentially reducing value for money and increasing the risk of fraud and corruption.[131]

Conversely, in procurement by EU institutions, time frames appear to be conceived as safeguards for competition, primarily in the interest of vendors, i.e. to allow them enough time to submit their offers. This is clear from the instructions provided to contracting authorities:

> [t]he contracting authority shall lay down time limits for the receipt of tenders and requests to participate. When fixing time limits, the contracting authority shall take account of the complexity of the contract and the time required for drawing up tenders.[132]

---

[130] UNIDO, *Procurement Manual*, para. 11.1 [ref. AP&R].

[131] UN Board of Auditors, *Concise Summary of the Principal Findings and Conclusions*, A/69/178, para. 82 [ref. REP].

[132] EU Commission Delegated Regulation (EU) 2015/2462, Art. 152(1) [ref. N&RL-EU].

Given the non-binding nature of the prescriptions on time frames and the discretion entrusted to procurement officers in many organizations, it is not rare that especially field offices and peacekeeping missions tend to shorten the recommended time frames, thus reducing the room for competition. The UN Board of Auditors, the UN ACABQ, as well as OIOS have reported that the shortening of the tender period is one of the recurring obstacles to competition.[133] For example, between 2006 and 2008, in the three sectors in which the United Nations made the greatest volume of procurements (airline management and operations, freight forwarding and shipping), the rates of response to invitations varied from 2 per cent to 7 per cent.[134] In this regard, OIOS noted that 'sometimes the time allowed for vendors to submit proposals or bids was extremely short'.[135] OIOS has found that the United Nations Multidimensional Integrated Stabilization Mission in Mali (MINUSMA), the United Nations Stabilization Mission in Haiti (UNSTAMIH), the United Nations Organization Stabilization Mission in the Democratic Republic of the Congo (MONUSCO) and the United Nations Operation in Côte d'Ivoire (UNOCI) did not provide vendors with sufficient time to respond to solicitations.[136] UNSTAMIH, in particular, has been paradigmatic in this respect. With reference to this mission, in 2013 the OIOS has conducted a review of a sample of thirty-eight invitations to bid. These were found to allow vendors to submit a bid within a period of time shorter than that prescribed by the UN Procurement Manual. The result was that only 27 per cent of invitees responded to solicitation and that in many cases only one or two responses were received.[137] Due to exigency reasons but also to poor planning, the practice of shortening time periods is particularly widespread in peacekeeping missions.

---

[133] See, inter alia, UN ACABQ, Report of the Board of Auditors on the Accounts of the United Nations Peacekeeping Operations, A/67/782, para. 16; ibid., Report of the Board of Auditors on the Accounts of the United Nations Peacekeeping Operations, A/65/782, para. 16; ibid., Report of the Board of Auditors on the Accounts of the United Nations Peacekeeping Operations, A/64/708, para. 18 [all documents in ref. REP].

[134] OIOS, Audit of Procurement Management in the Secretariat, A/64/369, para. 38 [ref. REP].

[135] Ibid., para. 37.

[136] OIOS, Activities of the Office of Internal Oversight Services on Peace Operations, A/71/227, para. 33 [ref. REP].

[137] OIOS, Audit of Local Procurement in the United Nations Stabilization Mission in Haiti, Audit report no. 2013/081, 27 September 2013 [ref. REP].

In addition to missions, however, these practices have also been detected in the ordinary procurement of other organizations.[138]

e **Splitting of Awards and Avoidance of Competition** While shortened time frames can result from poor planning or true exigency and, thus, be an unintentional side effect of procurement management, splitting contracts and their value is, on the contrary, usually a voluntary practice that, on one hand, makes it possible formally to comply with the procurement rules in place, diversify suppliers and obtain the best value for money. On the other hand, when used improperly, the practice makes it possible to avoid controls by the competent authorities, such as the headquarters committees on contracts, and control over compliance with competition requirements.[139]

In most organizations, the practice of splitting is allowed. The United Nations,[140] as well as UNESCO,[141] UNRWA,[142] UNOPS[143] and UNFPA,[144] for example, all provide for the possibility of fragmenting procurements. At the same time, however, the rules of all these organizations prohibit splitting when its aim is to avoid competition and controls over procurement activity. The UN Procurement Manual, for instance, while not excluding the possibility of splitting awards, recommends that '[s]plitting of awards should only be done in accordance with the BVM [i.e. Best Value for Money] principle. Under no circumstances should it be done in order to favour a particular Vendor'.[145] Thus, the Manual seems to consider the detrimental effects of contract splitting on competition among vendors, but allows the splitting practice as long as it is in the interest of the organization. Some organizations go even further, and make explicit reference to the risk of using such practice to bypass accountability mechanisms. The UNESCO Administrative Manual, for example, states that '[s]ingle contracts may not be broken up or split into

---

[138] UN Board of Auditors, *Concise Summary of the Principal Findings and Conclusions*, A/69/178, para. 82; UN ACABQ, *Financial Reports and Audited Financial Statements*, A/71/669, para. 34 [all documents in ref. REP].

[139] OIOS, *Audit of Procurement Management in the Secretariat*, AH2008/513/01; JIU, *Procurement Reforms in the United Nations System*, para. 206 [all documents in ref. REP].

[140] United Nations, *Procurement Manual*, para. 11.26(5) [ref. AP&R].

[141] UNESCO, *UNESCO Administrative Manual*, sec. 7.2, para. 3.1(d)(vi) [ref. AP&R].

[142] UNRWA, *Procurement Manual*, para. 8.2 (3–4) [ref. AP&R].

[143] UNOPS, *Procurement Manual*, para. 6.5.2 (f) [ref. AP&R].

[144] UNFPA, *Policy and Procedures for Regular Procurement*, para. 8.4.1 [ref. AP&R].

[145] United Nations, *Procurement Manual*, para. 11.26 (5) [ref. AP&R].

several contracts for the purpose of sidestepping Contracts Committee oversight . . . to avoid formal competitive bidding procedures'.[146]

There is an even more extensive list of the internal and external side effects of the splitting of requirements in the NATO Procurement Manual. These include, in addition to restrictions to competition and avoidance of accountability mechanisms, the fact that it does not allow the organization to benefit from economies of scale and is therefore not cost effective; and it increases the administrative workload, and monitoring problems.[147]

Given that splitting of procurements is or is not allowed depending on the specific goal pursued by the procurement officer, the subjective element, i.e. the intent of the procurement officer, becomes the basic criterion for making the distinction. Since, however, it seems difficult, if not impossible, to prove the psychological element of an administrative apparatus, the line that divides the practice of splitting a procurement into lots to achieve best value for money and diversify vendors from the anti-competitive practice of artificially fragmenting tenders to bypass controls, can often be blurred.

Few organizations have singled out objective indicators to detect practices mainly aimed at bypassing controls and avoiding competitive requirements. The European Court of Auditors has identified specific criteria, such as the subject matter of procurement, the value of the contracts and the time range within which the tenders were launched. So, for example, in 2014 the European Parliament procured office furniture 'from one supplier through four different negotiated procedures with a single tenderer in a period covering less than 2 months'.[148] The European Court of Auditors found that the subject matter of procurement was very similar in the four contracts. Furthermore, the value of each of the four contracts was slightly below the threshold beyond which publicity requirements would apply, but the total value was well above that threshold.[149] On these grounds, the European Court of Auditors concluded that it was an instance of anti-competitive conduct contrary to the rules applicable to EU institutions.

UNDP is even more precise in this regard, identifying a quantitative criteria:

---

[146] UNESCO, *Administrative Manual*, sec. 7.2, para. 3.1 (d)(vi) [ref. AP&R].
[147] UNFPA, *Policies and Procedures for Regular Procurement*, para. 7.1.2 [ref. AP&R].
[148] *Ibid.*, para. 43.   [149] *Ibid.*, para. 43.

> [s]plitting high-value requirements into parts valued at less than US $5,000 solely to apply micro-purchasing is a serious deviation from standard UNDP procurement policies and procedures, and must be avoided at all times.[150]

The majority of other organizations, however, do not provide guidance on the criteria to be applied. As a consequence, although not as widespread as the practice of waivers, splitting the value of contracts has been reported in several instances, especially in peacekeeping missions where the need for expedited procedures makes it more convenient for procurement officers to bypass long and cumbersome competitive procedures. With regard to peacekeeping missions, for example, the splitting of awards was reported as a common practice in MONUSCO, United Nations Support Office for AMISOM (UNSOA), United Nations Mission in Liberia (UNMIL),[151] MINUSMA and UNSTAMIH.[152] Moreover, sometimes the strategic nature of this practice (i.e. to avoid controls by the relevant authorities) can easily be inferred from the way it is implemented. A case at UNSOA was emblematic:

> a short-term contract for shipment services was deliberately valued at $999,999, one dollar under the threshold requiring approval by the Headquarters Committee on Contracts. The contract was subsequently extended six times on an ex post facto basis with the total value rising to $9.04 million before a long-term contract was approved by Headquarters.[153]

Instances of splitting awards, however, have been reported not only for UN peacekeeping missions, but also for other UN agencies. For instance, UNDP has been criticized several times for splitting purchase orders and for the lack of oversight over such practices.[154] With regard to UNDP, in 2006 the UN Board of Auditors 'analysed procurement statistics detailing

[150] UNDP, *Programme and Operations Policies and Procedures. Procurement*, sec. 'Procurement Method', para. 27 [ref. AP&R].
[151] For MONUSCO, UNSOA and UNMIL see UN Board of Auditors, *Financial Report and Audited Financial Statements*, A/66/5 (Vol. II), paras. 111–116 [ref. REP].
[152] For MINUSMA, UNSTAMIH and MONUSCO see OIOS, *Activities of the Office of Internal Oversight Services on Peace Operations*, A/71/227, para. 34 [ref. REP].
[153] UN ACABQ, *Report of the Board of Auditors on the Accounts of the United Nations Peacekeeping Operations*, A/66/719, para. 22 [ref. REP].
[154] UN Board of Auditors, *Financial Report and Audited Financial Statements* (UNDP), A/61/5/Add. 1, paras. 364–365; UN Board of Auditors, *Financial Report and Audited Financial Statements* (UNDP), A/63/5/Add. 1, paras. 225–229 [all documents in ref. REP].

more than one purchase order issued to the same vendor on the same day from the same country office with an accumulated value of more than $30,000'.[155] The analysis showed that 3,274 purchase orders with a value of $160,830,000 were the result of the fragmentation of bigger procurement contracts.[156]

Based on opposite considerations, splitting a procurement contract into more than one lot has been regarded as instrumental to competition when related to procurement by EU institutions. The idea behind this approach is that splitting into lots increases the number of companies that can benefit from the commercial opportunity provided by public administrations through procurement, encourages participation of small and medium-size enterprises (SMEs) in the tender process and, eventually, fosters competition.

The extent to which this is achieved by the rules and practices of EU institutions' procurement is, however, limited. On one hand, Art. 168 of the Rules of Application of EU Regulation No. 966/2012 provides that 'whenever appropriate, technically feasible, and cost efficient contracts are to be awarded in the form of separate lots within the same procedure'.[157] As noted by the European Court of Auditors, this wording gives procurement officers broad discretion over whether or not to use lots.[158] On the other hand, the reason for splitting contracts into lots, i.e. to favour SMEs, does not appear to be a priority in the procurement rules applicable to EU institutions. Although the procurement rules of EU institutions broadly follow the EU public procurement directives for member states, a significant deviation relates precisely to SMEs. Whereas one of the main objectives of the 2014 EU public procurement directives is to facilitate in particular the participation of SMEs in public procurement,[159] the rules regulating procurement by EU institutions do not support a similar goal.[160] Reference to SMEs is briefly made in the 2015 amendment to the Rules of Application of the EU Financial Rules, which states that '[i]n the interests of administrative

---

[155] UN Board of Auditors, *Financial Report and Audited Financial Statements* (UNDP), A/61/5/Add. 1, para. 364 [ref. REP].

[156] *Ibid.*

[157] EU Commission Delegated Regulation (EU) No. 1268/2012 (and following amendments), p. 7 [ref. N&RL-EU].

[158] European Court of Auditors, *The EU Institutions Can Do More to Facilitate Access to Their Public Procurement*, para. 42 [ref. REP].

[159] European Union, Directive 2014/24/EU, recital 2 [ref. N&RL-EU].

[160] European Court of Auditors, *The EU Institutions Can Do More to Facilitate Access to Their Public Procurement*, para. 30 [ref. REP].

simplification and in order to encourage participation of small and medium-sized enterprises, it is appropriate to provide for negotiated procedures for middle-value contracts'.[161] However, neither the EU financial rules nor the ECB rules on procurement provide legal tools to promote the participation of SMEs. This approach also resulted in a few hypotheses of lots splitting.[162]

Apart from the exceptional situations of procurement split into lots to increase accessibility to business opportunities for SMEs, the strategic fragmentation of contracts to avoid publicity requirements and oversight by control authorities has been identified and criticized as an anti-competitive practice in EU institutions as well. Yet strategic splitting of the value of contracts appears to be much less widespread among EU institutions than among other international organizations.

f   Extension of Existing Contracts and Use of Long-Term Agreements (LTAs)

In addition to anti-competitive practices affecting the tendering phase, restrictions to full competition can also come from the renewal and extension of existing contractual arrangements. A common practice within international organizations is to renew contractual ties with the same private contractor by extending the contractual term of validity and not announcing a tender. This has been reported in direct procurement for internal as well as for external purposes, in particular at the local level and in individual missions. With reference to the UN, for example, multiple extensions of contracts were found with regard to technology equipment, such as information and communication equipment.[163] Contracts for technology equipment are particularly subject to renewal not only for reasons internal to the administration and related to procurement, i.e. to avoid competition and speed up the procurement procedure, but also because of the specific nature of the procured goods: existing contractors often adopt technologies that can be updated or integrated only by themselves, thus tying the organizations to their products. More often, however, the extension of an existing contract is due to poor procurement planning and delays in procurement, which are in

---

[161] EU Commission Delegated Regulation (EU) 2015/2462, recital 15 [ref. N&RL-EU].

[162] See European Court of Auditors, *The EU Institutions Can Do More to Facilitate Access to Their Public Procurement*, Box 2 [ref. REP].

[163] UN ACABQ, *Financial Reports and Audited Financial Statements*, A/71/669, para. 36 [ref. REP].

turn overcome by avoiding the competitive procedure, but which, at the same time, generate increased cost due to the lack of competitiveness. The link between poor planning and extension of contracts has been emphasized especially in relation to peacekeeping missions. Several cases of this kind have been reported by the UN Board of Auditors and OIOS, especially in UN peacekeeping operations.[164]

Similar links are also found in other organizations. With regard to UNHCR's activity in Kenya, for example, OIOS has detected systemic problems: '[d]ue to a lack of planning, LCC was requested and granted extensions for the majority of the contracts that had expired, often retroactively, two months after the expiration of the contract'.[165] Furthermore, contract extensions can be combined with other types of anti-competitive practices, such as the splitting of contract value. As mentioned earlier, an emblematic case was reported at UNSOA in 2012. Here not only a short-term contract for shipment services was valued at $999,999, i.e. one dollar under the threshold requiring approval by the Headquarters Committee on Contracts, but the contract was subsequently extended six times, with the total value rising to $9.04 million.[166]

Competition is also limited through the use of LTAs (also referred to as system contracts, framework contracts or framework agreements). This kind of legal tool does not completely eliminate competition: in order to award an LTA, the procurement officer must, as for other types of contracts, issue a call for tenders and undertake a competitive procedure. However, the frequency with which competition is sought is what varies compared to other legal instruments: once the LTA is concluded, the same vendor can provide repeated goods or services over an agreed period of time, with no need for the administration to initiate a competitive procedure when the procurement need arises.

Although organizations within the UN system use different terminology and a slightly different definition for LTAs, the JIU has identified some common elements among the organizations.[167] LTAs are '[f]or the

---

[164] UN Board of Auditors, *Concise Summary of the Principal Findings and Conclusions*, A/70/322, para. 67 [ref. REP].

[165] In OIOS, *UNHCR Local Procurement Activities in Kenya*, para. 34 [ref. REP].

[166] See earlier in this section. UN ACABQ, *Report of the Board of Auditors on the Accounts of the United Nations Peacekeeping Operations*, A/66/719, para. 22 [ref. REP].

[167] A definition of LTA is provided in JIU, *Review of Long-Term Agreements*, para. 10 [ref. REP].

repeated purchase of particular goods or services';[168] they are '[v]alid for a specific period of time (usually more than one year) and extendable';[169] they 'secure the supply of goods or services over a fixed period under certain terms and conditions (for example, lower price and technical specifications)';[170] and, finally, they are 'non-binding and non-exclusive, placing the organization under no obligation to use the LTA or purchase a certain amount (unless the contract guaranteed a minimum order)'.[171] Furthermore, LTAs concluded by the UN or one of its agencies can also be used by other organizations within the UN system.[172] Joint procurement through LTAs has often been encouraged among UN agencies, as it combines the advantages of LTAs with those of joint procurement, i.e. mainly reducing administrative costs and avoiding the duplication of procedures. Notwithstanding that, system-wide collaboration through the use of LTAs is still limited.[173]

When not misused, LTAs are legal tools that can help strike a balance between, on one hand, the companies' interests in participating in competitive procedures and, on the other hand, the international organization's need to speed up procurement (particularly in emergencies), reduce administrative costs, obtain best value for money and take advantage of economies of scale.[174] The rules and practices on LTAs show, however, that this balance is often in favour of international organizations. First, as mentioned above, in the organizations of the UN system, concluding an LTA does not necessarily entail an obligation to procure. For instance, the FAO procurement manual defines the framework agreement as 'a type of contract which sets forth the terms and conditions under which procurement of goods, works or services can be effected over a specified period, but which places no obligation on the Organization to procure'.[175] Similarly, in the UNRWA 'LTAs are entered

---

[168] *Ibid.*, para. 9.   [169] *Ibid.*, para. 9.   [170] *Ibid.*, para. 9.   [171] *Ibid.*, para. 9.

[172] See, *inter alia*, UN Board of Auditors, *Concise Summary of Principal Findings and Conclusions*, A/61/182, para. 118 [ref. REP].

[173] JIU, *Review of Long-Term Agreements*, para. 94 [ref. REP]. One of the more significant experiences in this regard has been the Common Procurement Team (CPT), established between FAO, WFP and IFAD. The CPT took advantage of the circumstance that all the organizations involved were based in Rome. The LTAs entered into by the CPT, however, mainly regarded items that could be procured through the local market and which did not require complex technical specifications, such as office supplies, travel management services, furniture, electricity, cleaning services and building maintenance services. Other items, for example, those that required consolidation and standardization of complex technical specifications, were instead excluded.

[174] For a brief analysis of the advantages for the organizations, see *ibid.*, para. 11.

[175] FAO, *FAO Manual*, sec. 502.1.1 [ref. AP&R].

into on a non-exclusive basis and are not a mandatory source of purchase'[176] and the same wording is used in UNFPA rules on procurement.[177] In some other organizations, the quantities to be ordered under the system contract cannot be specified or, if specified, the quantities are not binding.[178]

Second, in order to avoid anti-competitive effects, LTAs usually have a maximum duration of three to five years depending on the organization.[179] Nevertheless, procurement rules of all organizations provide for the possibility of extending the agreements, sometimes making renewal subject to explicit justification by the procurement officer.[180] Indeed, the rule of maximum duration has often exceptions. For example, in UNDP, LTAs can last longer than the maximum five years allowed 'where the nature of the market or the requirement justifies a longer duration'.[181] The UNDP Procurement Programme and Operations Policies and Procedures list some of the possible causes for extension. These include but are not limited to instances in which the selected vendors need 'to develop costly technologies or infrastructure that require longer engagement to recover investment costs';[182] where the costs resulting from changing vendor is demonstrated to be more expensive and the duration is too short;[183] when '[t]here are no changes in requirements, but the retendering period is expected to exceed nine months, or a large amount of effort is required to complete the process';[184] and when '[g] oods or services [are] being sourced from a monopolistic market' and the situation is not expected to remain so.[185] Thus, reasons usually for the most part refer to the convenience of the international organization.

Other formulations of circumstances justifying extensions are defined even more vaguely, and the rules leave it up to the procurement officer to identify the specific reasons. For example, the ESA procurement regula-

---

[176] UNRWA, *Procurement Manual*, para. 5.2(3) [ref. AP&R].

[177] UNFPA, *Policy and Procedures for Regular Procurement*, para. 11.4 [ref. AP&R].

[178] United Nations, *Procurement Manual*, para. 13.9.6 [ref. AP&R].

[179] Ibid., *Procurement Manual*, para. 13.9(4); UNDP, *Programme and Operations Policies and Procedures*, sec. 'Long Term Agreements', para. 10; ESA, *ESA Procurement Regulations*, Art. 15, para. 6 [all documents in ref. AP&R].

[180] See, for instance, WFP, *Non-Food Procurement Manual*, para. 2.17 [ref. AP&R].

[181] UNDP, *Programme and Operations Policies and Procedures*, sec. 'Long Term Agreements', para. 10 [ref. AP&R].

[182] *Ibid.*, para. 10(a).   [183] *Ibid.*, para. 10(a).   [184] *Ibid.*, para. 10(b).

[185] *Ibid.*, para. 10(c).

tions allow for extensions of framework agreements for unspecified 'operational reasons'.[186]

The rules governing procurement by EU institutions are stricter in relation to exceptions. Here the maximum duration of framework contracts is four years, and only in exceptional cases, duly justified by the subject of the contract, may the contract duration exceed this time period.[187] However, 'reducing administrative costs for the contracting authority should not be considered a valid reason' for justifying an extension.[188] The mere convenience of the public administration cannot be called upon to restrict competition. Apart from these situations, the procurement officer is free to assess whether a framework contract should be renewed or not.

This loose approach to LTAs adopted by the majority of international organizations has often generated an overuse of LTAs, with consequent restrictive effects on competition. The combination of these elements has resulted in quite extensive usage of LTAs in organizations within the UN system and, to a lesser extent, in EU institutions. Although statistics on the point are incomplete, a survey of twelve organizations[189] conducted by the JIU in 2013 revealed that 'the use of LTAs in the system reaches significant or high levels' and that there was a growing trend from 2008 onwards.[190] UNICEF, United Nations and UNFPA have been the leading organizations in the use of LTAs: in 2011, the percentage of procurement done through LTAs amounted to 73 per cent in the UN Secretariat and 93 per cent in UNICEF; UNFPA did not provide data for that year, but for 2010 the procurement done through LTAs reached 45 per cent.[191]

Even EU institutions that, according to the relevant rules, 'shall not use framework contracts improperly or in such a way that their purpose or effect is to prevent, restrict or distort competition',[192] have been reported to excessively extend framework contracts. For instance, between 2013

---

[186] ESA, *ESA Procurement Regulations*, Art. 15, para. 7 [ref. AP&R].

[187] European Union, Regulation (EU, Euratom) No. 966/2012, Art. 101 (2); EU Commission Delegated Regulation (EU) No. 1268/2012 (and following amendments), Art. 122 [ref. N&RL-EU].

[188] European Court of Auditors, *The EU Institutions Can Do More to Facilitate Access to Their Public Procurement*, para. 54 [ref. REP].

[189] The organizations included in the JIU report are the UN Secretariat, UNDP, UNHCR, UNRWA, UNFPA, UNICEF, WFP, FAO, UNESCO, International Civil Aviation Organization (ICAO), International Maritime Organization (IMO) and UNAIDS.

[190] JIU, *Review of Long-Term Agreements*, para. 17 [ref. REP].   [191] *Ibid.*, para. 17.

[192] European Union, Regulation (EU, Euratom) No. 966/2012, Art. 102, para. 2 [ref. N&RL-EU].

and 2015 the European Court of Auditors found that 'the Council has frequently used the exception clause to extend considerably the duration of framework contracts awarded in connection with its buildings'.[193] By 2016 at least six framework contracts stipulated by the Council had a duration of seven to sixteen years.[194]

4.4.1.2 Competition Indicators in Indirect Procurement: Open Procedures and Domestic Preference

In indirect procurement, also, the degree of competition ensured in the procedure can be assessed based on the type of basic procedure prescribed, the waivers of competition, the time frames prescribed to allow the submission of bids, the possibility of splitting the awards, the allowed restrictions linked to nationality, and finally, the use of existing contracts. In general, although single procurement provisions vary from organization to organization, there are two recurring and distinctive features in indirect procurement compared to direct procurement: the explicit or implicit provision of open tender as the basic procedure to select vendors, and the possibility of favouring local suppliers through the so-called domestic preference criteria.

a Open Competition and Waivers With regard to procurement methods, the rules on indirect procurement by the European Commission and the EDF, for example, identify three basic types of procedures: open tenders, at the international or local level; restricted procedures; and competitive negotiated procedures.[195] The choice of one or the other is made by the national procuring entity but is tied to a combination of two criteria set by EU rules: the subject of the procurement (whether goods, services or works) and the threshold value set by the relevant rules. In addition to these three basic procedures, there are three other procedures that a beneficiary state can choose to undertake, namely the dynamic purchase system, competitive dialogue and the negotiated procedure/single tender procedure, which can be used in particularly complex contracts (competitive dialogue) or only in exceptional and duly justified cases, provided the factual or legal circumstances described by the relevant rules are met (negotiated procedures). Thus, this detailed procedural design is grounded on the idea that open

---

[193] European Court of Auditors, *The EU Institutions Can Do More to Facilitate Access to Their Public Procurement*, para. 55 [ref. REP].
[194] *Ibid.*, Box 6.   [195] EU, *PRAG*, paras. 2.4.1–2.4.8 [ref. AP&R].

competitive procedure, at the international or local level, is the basic procedure (whereas, as shown earlier, in direct procurement the basic procedure is the restricted one) and that, in any event, '[w]hatever the procedure used, the contracting authority must ensure that the conditions allow fair competition'.[196]

The rules and regulations of development banks such as the WB, EBRD, ADB, AfDB and IFAD provide for a less detailed panoply of procurement methods. Nevertheless, they generally favour the adoption of open and competitive procedures by states. The EBRD Procurement Policies and Rules, for example, state that

> [c]ompetition is the foundation for good procurement practice. In addition to economy and efficiency, the public sector requires transparency and accountability for the use of public funds, and this affects the choice of the procurement method and the documentation and procedures that are used.[197]

Competition is, thus, necessary to pursue not only the organization's interest in economy and efficiency, but also to ensure that the funds are spent according to the objectives they are designated to achieve. Similarly, the WB, ADB, AfDB and IFAD indicate competition as the basis for efficient procurement.[198]

Consistent with this statement of principle, the rules and guidelines of development banks distinguish between three levels of competition: open competition procedures, which give all eligible bidders the opportunity to submit an offer and are opened by a public call for tenders;[199] limited competition procedures, where only invited vendors can submit an offer and the call for tenders is not advertised;[200] and direct contracting, which

---

[196] *Ibid.*, para. 2.4.9.   [197] EBRD, *Procurement Policies and Rules*, para. 3.1 [ref. AP&R].

[198] WB, *The World Bank Procurement Regulations for IPF Borrowers*, para. 6.11. And a different wording but same content is expressed in the rules of ADB and AfDB: '[i]n most cases, therefore, the Bank requires its Borrowers to obtain goods, works and non-consulting services through ICB open to eligible suppliers, service providers and contractors' (ADB, *Procurement Guidelines*, para. 1.3; AfDB, *Rules and Procedures for the Procurement of Goods and Works*, para. 1.3); IFAD, *Project Procurement Guidelines*, para. 23 [all documents in ref. AP&R].

[199] WB, *The World Bank Procurement Regulations for IPF Borrowers*, paras. 6.11; ADB, *Procurement Guidelines*, paras. 2.1.–2.10; AfDB, *Rules and Procedures for the Procurement of Goods and Works*, paras. 2.1.–2.9; IFAD, *Project Procurement Guidelines*, Annex, paras. 3–4; EBRD, *Procurement Policies and Rules*, para. 3.8 [all documents in ref. AP&R].

[200] WB, *The World Bank Procurement Regulations for IPF Borrowers*, para. 6.12; ADB, *Procurement Guidelines*, para. 3.2; AfDB, *Rules and Procedures for the Procurement of Goods and Works*, para. 3.2; IFAD, *Project Procurement Guidelines*, Annex, paras. 5–6; EBRD, *Procurement Policies and Rules*, para. 3.8 [all documents in ref. AP&R].

is allowed in specific cases and circumstances defined by the rules of the organizations.[201] As an alternative to these procedures set by the bank, the beneficiary state may also be allowed to use national procurement procedures, given an *ex ante* positive assessment by the organization on the compatibility of these procedures with the core principles set in the regulations and guidelines of the organization.

The provision of open tender as the basic procedure is also reflected in the practice of indirect procurement, as shown by the data made available by some organizations. The annual procurement reviews of EBRD, for example, report that from 2006 to 2016 the majority of contracts were consistently awarded through open tendering: in 2006 'the public sector contracts awarded through open tendering actually represent[ed] 82.4% of the number of eligible contracts or 94.4% of the total eligible contract value when consultancy services contracts are excluded'.[202] Ten years later, in 2016, 'the majority ... of the public sector contracts were awarded through open tender. This represents 82 percent of the total number of contracts awarded and 59 percent of the total contract value'.[203]

It must be highlighted, however, that the definition of open and restricted procedures set by the rules of organizations does not exactly correspond to that adopted by international rules governing domestic public procurement, such as the GPA and European public procurement directives. As will be seen later in this chapter, the fundamental difference concerns the advertisement of the call for tender and, thus, the level of publicity required. International rules for national public procurement impose the same level of publicity on open and restricted procedures, as the call for tender must be duly advertised in both procedures. On the contrary, in indirect procurement of international organizations, open

---

[201] WB, *The World Bank Procurement Regulations for IPF Borrowers*, paras. 6.8–6.10; ADB, *Procurement Guidelines*, para. 3.6; AfDB, *Rules and Procedures for the Procurement of Goods and Works*, para. 3.6; IFAD, *Project Procurement Guidelines*, para. 27 and Annex, paras. 13–14; EBRD, *Procurement Policies and Rules*, para. 3.9 [all documents in ref. AP&R].

[202] EBRD, *Annual Procurement Review 2006*, para. 2.2 [ref. REP].

[203] EBRD, *Annual Procurement Review 2016*, March 2017, para. 2.5. The data are consistent in all Annual Procurement Reviews from 2006 to 2016. See EBRD, *Annual Procurement Review 2007*, para. 2.2; *id.*, *Annual Procurement Review 2008*, para. 2.6; *id.*, *Annual Procurement Review 2009*, para. 2.6; *id.*, *Annual Procurement Review 2010*, para. 2.6; *id.*, *Annual Procurement Review 2011*, para. 2.7; *id.*, *Annual Procurement Review 2012*, para. 2.7; *id.*, *Annual Procurement Review 2013*, para. 2.7; *id.*, *Annual Procurement Review 2014*, para. 2.7; *id.*, *Annual Procurement Review 2015*, para. 2.7 [all documents in ref. REP].

procedures require advertisement of the call for tender, while restricted procedures do not. As publicity of the call for tender is the essential pre-condition for competition, the difference is relevant precisely due to its implications for competition. In indirect procurement of international organizations, open procedures are the only procedures, which grant a level of competition equivalent to that provided by international rules on national public procurement. All other procedures, including restricted ones, offer a diminished level of competition.

Although restrictions to competition are allowed through the use of restricted competition procedures and direct contracting, the rules of international organizations provide special obligations for national administrations to safeguard competition in these procedures as well. For instance, when choosing to undertake restricted procedures, national administrations must invite all vendors that went through a process of pre-qualification: '[a]ll Applicants that substantially meet the minimum qualification requirements are invited to submit a Bid'.[204] Thus, there is a mechanism that makes the pool of pre-qualified vendors fully correspond to those to be invited. In this way, the discretion of the national administration is limited, at least for those procurements where pre-qualification is necessary due to the complexity of the supply.

Moreover, in organizations such as WB and EBRD, departure from open competitive procurement and the use of waivers of competition must be justified by the national authorities vis-à-vis the organization.[205] As open competitive procurement is deemed to be the rule, other non-competitive procedures are the exceptions that the beneficiary state should duly explain to the organization. In particular with regard to direct contracting, justification must include the existence of specific circumstances, and these are usually previously identified by the rules of the organization. Even when the list of circumstances connected to the possibility of undertaking direct contracting is not exhaustive[206] and the

---

[204] Emphasis added. WB, *The World Bank Procurement Regulations for IPF Borrowers*, para. 6.23. Or, at least, the list of invited suppliers should include all suppliers when there are only a limited number (ADB, *Procurement Guidelines*, para. 3.2; AfDB, *Rules and Procedures for the Procurement of Goods and Works*, para. 3.2; IFAD, *Project Procurement Guidelines*, Annex, para. 6; EBRD, *Procurement Policies and Rules*, para. 3.8) [all documents in ref. AP&R].

[205] WB, *The World Bank Procurement Regulations for IPF Borrowers*, para. 6.12; EBRD, *Procurement Policies and Rules*, para. 2.2 [ref. AP&R].

[206] WB, *The World Bank Procurement Regulations for IPF Borrowers*, paras. 6.8–6.10; ADB, *Procurement Guidelines*, para. 3.6; AfDB, *Rules and Procedures for the Procurement of Goods and Works*, para. 3.6; IFAD, *Project Procurement Guidelines*,

concrete circumstances are subject to assessment by the procurement officer, the recognition of this discretion is counterbalanced by the provision of *ex ante* or *ex post* controls of the procurement activity by the international organization, and of the type of procedures chosen.[207]

b Nationality and Domestic Preference Although indirect procurement is more oriented towards competition than direct procurement, the rules ensuring competition are complemented by provisions allowing deviations from the principle. The deviations are mainly linked to nationality and relate to evaluation criteria, without affecting the type or structure of the procedure. Indeed, although best value for money is one of the main criteria that shall guide the selection of vendors, and competition is indicated as the best way to ensure it, both may become secondary when weighed against socioeconomic objectives inherent in the institutional mission of certain organizations.[208] The adoption of competitive procedures does not preclude beneficiary states from giving preference to domestically manufactured goods and local contractors in case of works. The WB, for instance, allows that

> [t]he Borrower may, with the agreement of the Bank, grant a margin of preference in the evaluation of Bids/Proposals in open international competitive procurement to Bids/Proposals offering certain Goods manufactured in the country of the Borrower, when compared to Bids/Proposals offering such Goods manufactured elsewhere.[209]

Similarly, local suppliers of works can be preferred over foreign ones.[210] ADB, AfDB and IFAD procurement guidelines contain analogous provisions.[211] In this respect, it is useful to draw a comparison with European and global rules on national public procurement, which include solutions that ensure pure competition, precisely in order to avoid creating preferences for domestic contractors. Directive 2014/24/EU states:

---

para. 27 and Annex, paras. 13–14; EBRD, *Procurement Policies and Rules*, para. 3.9 [all documents in ref. AP&R].

[207] See Chapter 7 of this book.

[208] See Chapter 2, and for a development of this point, see Chapter 8.

[209] WB, *The World Bank Procurement Regulations for IPF Borrowers*, Annex VI, para. 2.1 [ref. AP&R].

[210] The same is stated for domestic Bidders/Proposers providing works in WB, *The World Bank Procurement Regulations for IPF Borrowers*, Annex VI, para. 2.6 [ref. AP&R].

[211] ADB, *Procurement Guidelines*, App. 2; AfDB, *Rules and Procedures for the Procurement of Goods and Works*, App. 2; IFAD, *Project Procurement Guidelines*, paras. 65–66 [all documents in ref. AP&R].

[t]he award of public contracts by or on behalf of Member States' authorities has to comply with the principles of the Treaty on the Functioning of
the European Union (TFEU), and in particular the free movement of
goods, freedom of establishment and the freedom to provide services, as
well as the principles deriving therefrom, such as equal treatment, non-
discrimination, mutual recognition, proportionality and transparency.[212]

The GPA, referring to a more heterogeneous market space that
includes both industrialized countries and emerging economies, on one
hand, recognizes the principles of equality of treatment and non-
discrimination and, on the other, is open to the possibility of special
and different treatment for developing countries.[213] Art. IV, para. 1 in
fact states that each party to the agreement shall accord to the suppliers of
any other party offering goods or services, treatment no less favourable
than the treatment the party adopts for its own suppliers.[214] But Art.
V also encourages member states to give special consideration to the
development, financial and trade needs and circumstances of developing
countries and least developed countries.[215]

Thus, while the option set out in European public procurement directives is mainly instrumental to the principle of competition, the GPA's
approach also includes considerations of a political and social nature.
This latter approach differs, however, from that adopted in indirect
procurement of international organizations in at least two respects.

First of all, the GPA only generally refers to policies and does not go into
detail on preferential rules for evaluating offers, which are left to the states
to draw up: states are free to decide on whether to adopt preferential rules
and how to shape them. Secondly, the empirical referents and the final
objectives of the rules are different. GPA provisions refer to international
relations, and in particular those between a member state, presumably with
a developed economy, and states with developing economies. They encourage the diversification of procurement sources and promote policies that
globally should favour economic growth. Rules on domestic preferences in
indirect procurement of international organizations, instead, refer to public-private relationships within the state itself. As the states that receive
funding are often developing countries, these provisions make it possible
to 'internalize' and nationalize the business opportunity offered by procurement. They allow the state to give preference to its own enterprises and
support its own economic growth.

---

[212] European Union, Directive 2014/24/EU, recital 1 [ref. N&RL-EU].
[213] On this point, also see McCrudden, *Buying Social Justice*, p. 273 *et seq.* and 470 *et seq.*
[214] GPA, Art. IV(1).   [215] *Ibid.*, Art. V(1).

c **Time Frames for Bid Submission** Application of the principle of competition is also supported by provisions on the time frames to submit bids and on the splitting of awards. As seen in the previous section, short time frames are also an issue in direct procurement, as they can jeopardize effective competition even if all the other procedural requirements are formally met. However, while the prescriptions on time frames in direct procurement are often only regulatory rather than mandatory, and usually identify short periods of time (from a few days to a couple of weeks), in indirect procurement the prescriptions on time frames are always stricter and the minimum period prescribed to allow the submission of offers is on average twice as long as that allowed in direct procurement. The WB, for example, identifies both qualitative and quantitative criteria that the national authority must apply in determining the time frames. As regards qualitative criteria, the time allowed for the preparation and submission of bids and proposals must be determined with due consideration for the particular circumstances of the project, as well as the magnitude, risk and complexity of the procurement.[216] As for the quantitative criteria, the WB rules prescribe a minimum period of thirty business days for open international competitive procurement, unless otherwise agreed with the Bank.[217] Similar provisions are included in the procurement rules set by the ADB[218] and EBRD.[219] In some organizations, such as ADB, obligations to set minimum time frames are also extended to the invitation to prequalify for bidding on specific contracts.[220] Exceptions, i.e. shortening the time frames, are instead usually allowed in case of emergency situations. The ADB procurement rules, for example, ensure greater flexibility under disaster and emergency assistance conditions.[221]

d **Splitting of Awards** Other provisions supporting competition are those that prohibit the splitting of awards. Most international organizations undertaking indirect procurement explicitly mention the decision to fragment the contract value as anti-competitive conduct, and

---

[216] WB, *The World Bank Procurement Regulations for IPF Borrowers*, para. 5.36 [ref. AP&R].

[217] *Ibid.*

[218] In ADB the minimum time frame is six weeks, see ADB, *Procurement Guidelines*, para. 2.44 [ref. AP&R].

[219] In EBRD the minimum time frame is forty days but can be extended for large or complex works or items of equipment, see EBRD, *Procurement Policies and Rules*, para. 3.20 [ref. AP&R].

[220] In these cases 'a minimum period of six weeks shall be allowed for the submission of prequalification applications', see ADB, *Procurement Guidelines*, para. 2.10 [ref. AP&R].

[221] In those cases, restricted procedures are the norm to procure goods and minimum bidding periods will range from one to two weeks, *ibid.*, para. 3.18.

condemn the intent of reducing the value of the resulting contracts below these thresholds to circumvent the rules and controls of the financing organization. The practice is, thus, often forbidden.[222] In some organizations the prohibition can be overcome if the organization gives prior approval to the practice and ascertains the need for it and the lack of anticompetitive objectives.[223]

e   Extending Existing Contracts and the Use of LTAs   Finally, development banks generally provide for the possibility of extending existing contracts or concluding LTAs. However, these non-competitive options are usually allowed for specific types of contracts, under circumstances listed by the relevant rules and only with the bank's approval. For example, the WB can agree to an extension of an existing contract for consulting services if it is properly justified, no advantage may be obtained by competition, and prices are reasonable; or for tasks that represent a natural continuation of previous work carried out by a consultant; or if the procurement is of both very low value and low risk; or in exceptional cases, as in response to emergency situations.[224] Thus, the possibility of avoiding competition and relying on existing contractual arrangements tends to be thought of in terms of exception to the rule and, thus, closely monitored by the organizations. An assessment of the level of competition in direct and indirect procurement, built around the indicators mentioned above, is provided in Table 4.1.

4.4.2   Ladders of Transparency

The rules governing national public procurement include transparency among the guiding principles.[225] Four main components of transparency can be identified in relation to national public procurement: publicness of procurement rules, publicity of administrative decisions, reason giving and access to documents. Each component, added to the previous one,

---

[222] WB, *The World Bank Procurement Regulations for IPF Borrowers*, paras. 6.10(b) and 7.15 (b); ADB, *Procurement Guidelines*, footnote 40; EBRD, *Procurement Policies and Rules*, para. 3.8 [all documents in ref. AP&R].

[223] ADB, *Procurement Guidelines*, footnote 40 [ref. AP&R].

[224] Other circumstances are listed in WB, *The World Bank Procurement Regulations for IPF Borrowers*, para. 7.14 [ref. AP&R].

[225] For an in-depth and cross-sectoral analysis of transparency in international organizations, see Peters and Bianchi (eds.), *Transparency in International Law*.

Table 4.1 *Competition by indicators*

Indicators of competition	Direct procurement	Indirect procurement
Procurement methods	• Restricted procedures • Negotiated procedures • Sole source	• Open procedures • Restricted procedures • Negotiated procedures • Sole source
Nationality	• Equitable geographical distribution (policy objective) • International policy considerations, e.g. trade sanctions • Donor funding criterion • Geographical return criterion	• Domestic preference (subject to IOs' control and approval) • Membership requirements in regional IOs
Waivers	Recurring pattern	• Possible, but subject to IOs' control and approval • Not recurring
Time frames	• Regulatory • Short • Non-compliance recurring	• Mandatory • Medium/long • *Ex ante* and *ex post* controls on compliance
Splitting contracts	Recurring pattern	• Possible, but subject to IOs' control and approval • Not recurring pattern • Policies for SMEs
Extensions of previous contracts/use of LTAs	Recurring pattern	• Not recurring pattern • Subject to IOs' control and approval

provides a progressively higher level of transparency. At the same time, each component alone shows an increased degree of openness of the administration towards private subjects. Considering these aspects, the four components can be arranged in a ladder pattern[226] in which higher rungs, together with the rungs preceding them, correspond to a more transparent and participatory form of managing public resources and, thus, to a more egalitarian relationship between the public bodies who make administrative decisions and the individuals affected by such decisions.

At the bottom of the ladder there is the publicness of the rules, through their publication. In order to enforce accountability mechanisms, it is essential for private subjects affected by the administrative decision to be able to know what procedural rules the public administration should follow when making decisions. The private subject can claim a violation of a rule only if it knows what rule ought to be applied. Also, the rules are the essential parameter against which an independent body can assess the legality of the administrative decision. In national public procurement of Western legal systems, the publication of procedural rules and their availability to the public at large is mandatory and obvious. The rule of law requires that public procurement regulations are enacted through laws. Thus, they are approved by the legislative branch or by the government, and are public, the public administrations are under an obligation to follow these rules and the courts ensure their observance.

An advanced component of transparency pertains to publicity of procurement decisions. In public procurement, decisions affecting private subjects are made at various stages of the procedure and include the call for tenders and the award decision. As will be seen below, rules regulating national procurement generally ensure a high level of publicity for these decisions.

---

[226] In social sciences literature, the metaphor of the ladder is used to define a variety of concepts. Arnstein, for example, uses the ladder pattern to iconographically illustrate the different types of participation, organized according to the extent of citizens' power in determining administrative decisions, see Arnstein, 'A Ladder of Citizen Participation'; Damgaard and Lewis, 'Accountability and Citizen Participation'. In the ladder conceived by Arnstein, however, each rung indicates a different level of participation and the levels are mutually exclusive. In the ladder proposed here, instead, each rung is a component of transparency that individually reflects a different degree of openness of the administration, but at the same time is usually added to the other components to create an upgraded level of transparency.

Further transparency is achieved when the public administration has the duty to disclose and notify the affected subject of the reasons for its decision. In most Western countries, rules regulating national procurement impose this obligation on public administrations in order to foster the accountability and legitimacy of public bodies. Indeed, reason giving should increase awareness and favour acceptance of the administrative decision by those affected by it. But it also provides private subjects with the necessary elements to bring a claim against the public administration if they deem the decision to be illegal or unjust.

At the end of the spectrum of transparency in public procurement there is the fourth component, namely access to documents. The right to access administrative documents has different characteristics in the various legal systems. For instance, in some legal systems, any citizen can request and obtain access to documents, while in other systems, only the subject affected by the administrative decision has this right, or limits to the right of accessing documents may vary or be applied in different ways. Notwithstanding these dissimilarities, the right to access administrative documents, including those regarding public procurement, is a recurring feature in most Western legal systems.

International organizations also include transparency among the principles guiding their direct procurement. However, whereas the history of organizations shows an increase in the level of transparency applied to procurement, its limits are still significant when compared to the standards that apply to domestic public procurement. Transparency of an international procuring entity vis-à-vis private subjects has at least three concrete manifestations: publication of the rules according to which the procuring entity must undertake procurement; publicity of the administration's intent to contract; and reason giving. It does not include other more pervasive instruments that are usually found at the domestic level, such as the right of individuals to access administrative documents. Thus, in the ladder of transparency for direct procurement by international organizations, the higher rung, that is the right to access documents, is always lacking. The other rungs, including the basic one, i.e. publication of the rules, are implemented to a greater or lesser extent. Furthermore, all are forms of transparency whose activation depends solely on the administration and cannot result from a private subject's request.

Transparency in indirect procurement entails other types of considerations. Although the transparency obligations of national procuring entities shape their relationship with private subjects, they are conceived primarily to allow the international organization to hold beneficiary states accountable to the organization itself and to control, albeit indirectly, the proper management of resources by the beneficiary states.[227] The ladder of transparency includes the same rungs mentioned for direct procurement: publication of the rules, obligations to publicize the call for tenders and a duty to give reasons for decisions. However, the way transparency is achieved differs from direct procurement in two important respects. The first relates to the degree of transparency. In indirect procurement, each component of transparency is drawn by the rules, and has a stricter implementation and fewer exceptions than direct procurement. The second significant difference relates to the institutional architecture on which indirect procurement is built and the possibility of complementing transparency vis-à-vis private subjects with inter-institutional transparency. Indeed, whereas a right to access documents is not usually established by the procurement guidelines, national public administrations have a duty to disclose procurement documents to the international organization. This duty must be fulfilled not only during ordinary oversight by international organizations of the national administration's procurement activity, but also when, as analyzed later in this book, a private subject appeals to the international organization against a decision of the national procuring entity.[228]

For illustrative purposes, the ladders of transparency and the degree of transparency achieved respectively in national public procurement, direct procurement of international organizations, and indirect procurement of international organizations are compared in Table 4.2. The following sections will analytically break down the concrete manifestations of transparency.

4.4.2.1   Publicness of the Rules

While publicness of the rules is necessary and obvious in national public procurement, the same cannot be said for procurement by international organizations. The degree of transparency in this regard varies greatly between indirect and direct procurement. All organizations which engage in indirect procurement, including the WB, ADB, AfDB, IFAD, EBRD and the EU Commission (when engaging in indirect procurement), publish the rules that beneficiary states should follow. Often, together with the regulations or guidelines, these organizations also

---

[227] On this point, see also Chapters 7 and 8.   [228] See Chapter 7.

Table 4.2 *Ladders of transparency (transparency degrees: H=High; M=Medium; L=Low; A=Absent)*

Ladder of transparency for procurement	National public procurement (i.e. GPA, European public procurement directives)	Direct procurement by IOs	Indirect procurement by IOs
Publicness of procurement rules	H	M/L	H
Publicity of administrative decisions	H	M	H
Reason giving	H	L	M/H
Access to documents	H	A	A

release and publish the related policy documents and texts guiding the interpretation of the rules, as well as reports or other documents attesting to the implementation of such rules.

The approach is significantly different in direct procurement, where the organizations are less inclined to publish and share the rules governing their activity. In fact, although since the late 1990s there has been a trend towards greater transparency in this respect, many organizations still refrain from publishing these texts, and refuse to provide them upon the request of a citizen. So, while for instance the United Nations, UNDP, UNOPS, UNFPA, NATO, ESA and EU institutions have updated procurement rules and regulations available online, organizations such as UNICEF, UNHCR, WFP and FAO have a strict non-disclosure policy that preserves the opaqueness of the institutions and their daily activity.

While further discussion on the reasons explaining this mixed picture can be found in Chapter 8, some of the possible explanations are worth mentioning here. This coexistence of different approaches can be explained by the existence of opposite and conflicting trends. On one hand, international organizations have inherited from national public administrations the opaqueness that has historically characterized administrative activity, which was based on an unequal relationship between the state and its citizens. Furthermore, in international organizations this lack of transparency has played an important role in preserving the interplay of interests underlying the functioning of the organizations themselves, and continues to do so.

On the other hand, however, international organizations are subject to external and internal drivers of change. With regard to the former, international organizations have been subject to the influence of an evolving institutional context. Technology, together with specific institutional, political and economic factors, has brought about a gradual shift in the administrative culture of most Western countries and in the relationship between public authorities and private subjects. One of the most prominent manifestations of this change has been the enactment of policies for greater transparency in public administration. In turn, this has had an impact on organizations that, at the initiative of some member states, have undergone a process of modernization and emancipation from the traditional concept of public administration, especially vis-à-vis the increasing impact organizations have on individuals.

The internal driver has to do more specifically with political changes and shifting international equilibria within organizations. As already discussed in Chapter 3, the decolonization process, together with the end of the Cold War and the increasing activities of organizations, has brought some states, especially those that provided the largest financial contributions, to require more competitive and transparent procurement procedures in order to ensure, at least partially, an economic return in terms of contracts awarded to their companies.[229]

On the contrary, the magnitude of organizations' activities and procurement volumes does not seem to play a role in the decision to publish the procurement rules. While one might expect that the more an organization enters into contractual relations with private subjects, the greater the need to define the rules governing the procurement relationship established, reality shows that some of the organizations with greater procurement volumes, such as UNICEF, UNHCR, WFP and FAO, are precisely the ones that do not publish the legal texts regulating their procurement, nor share them upon request. At the same time, other organizations with a similar volume of procurement and contracts do instead publish and share those rules. This reluctance to make the rules public is even more striking if one considers that procurement regulations are

---

[229] See also Chapter 8 for further discussion on this point.

published in all Western countries – the same countries that are members of the international organizations.

In direct procurement, the different approaches to the publication of procurement rules have a consequence in terms of organizations' accountability to private subjects. As the availability of the rules to the affected parties is an essential precondition for bringing a claim against the decisions of a procuring entity, in organizations where procurement rules are not disclosed, the accountability mechanisms provided to private subjects are usually weak, if not completely lacking. At the same time, those organizations whose rules are more transparent also tend to complement this with the provision of more detailed and effective mechanisms of accountability, for example, by establishing formal procedures to bid protest and/or *ad hoc* bodies with the task of reviewing contested decisions.[230]

4.4.2.2   Publicity of Decisions

Publicity obligations come into play during at least three different stages of the procurement procedure: when the administration decides to announce a call for tenders, when the tender commences and when the contract is awarded.

a   Duties of Prior Information   EU public procurement directives establish stringent publication rules in all three stages just mentioned. Through prior information notices, contracting authorities make known their intentions of planned procurement. These notices are provided for the procurement of goods, services and works that exceed the threshold amounts indicated in the directives.[231] They are not, however, mandatory, unless the procuring entities decide to reduce the time limits for receiving bids.[232] The content of the obligation is very detailed and the notice must include various types of information, such as information on the contracting authority and a brief description of the procurement, i.e. the nature and extent of the works, the nature and quantity or value of the supplies, and the nature and extent of the services.[233] The goal of publication is to provide notice of anticipated procurement operations to the public. The GPA also makes it possible, although not obligatory, to publish the notice of planned procurement.[234]

---

[230] For further discussion on the accountability mechanisms in place, see Chapter 7.
[231] European Union, Directive 2014/24/EU, Art. 48 [ref. N&RL-EU].
[232] *Ibid.*, Art. 27(2).   [233] *Ibid.*, Annex V(B).
[234] The contents that the notice shall have are listed in GPA, Art. VII, para. 4–5.

With regard to direct procurement of international organizations, a non-compulsory obligation of prior information is provided, for example, by Art. 123 of the Rules of Application regulating the direct procurement of European institutions: 'the European contracting authority may make known its intentions of planned procurement for the financial year through the publication of a prior information notice'.[235]

For procurement financed by the EU Commission and the EDF, there are also prior information obligations that consist of 'individual contract forecasts'. The obligation applies to contracts that exceed the thresholds set out in the Practical Guide to Contract Procedures for EU External Actions (PRAG). The notice must contain general information such as a brief description of the procedure adopted, the contracting authority,[236] the nature of the contract, the content of the contract and the intended timing of publication of the following contract notice.[237] The beneficiary state must send it to the European Commission and it will then be published in the Official Journal of the European Union. Thus, unlike the information notices provided for in the European public procurement directives for states and in the regulations for direct procurement of EU institutions, these notices are first of all obligatory. This can be explained by the dual function they serve: not only, as in the case of national public procurement, to ensure respect for the principle of competition and transparency, but also to allow the Commission to control the contractual determinations of the beneficiary state. This meets both external transparency needs, i.e. those vis-à-vis private subjects, and inter-institutional transparency needs, i.e. those between the international organization and the national administration.

On the contrary, this obligation has no equivalent in the rules on either direct or indirect procurement by organizations within the UN system or by other international organizations. In direct procurement, information regarding planned procurement operations in fact flows completely within the organization (between the various administrative levels, in particular, the central and peripheral levels), while in indirect

---

[235] EU Commission Delegated Regulation (EU) No. 1268/2012 (and following amendments), Art. 123, para. 2 [ref. N&RL-EU].

[236] In direct management, the contracting authority is the European Union, represented by the European Commission on behalf of and for the account of the partner country/ countries; in indirect management, the contracting authority is the partner country.

[237] EU, *PRAG*, Annex A5(d), Annex B1, Annex C1, Annex D1 [ref. AP&R]. And for the EDF, see Art. 36(7) of the European Union, Council Regulation (EU) 2015/323, p. 17 [ref. N&RL-EU].

procurement, the exchange of information is between the international organization and the national administration. Notwithstanding this, the practice has revealed some cases where procurement plans have been publicized on the websites of the organizations. The UN headquarters' acquisition plans and the UN peacekeeping missions' acquisition plans, for example, are usually made available through online publication. Nevertheless, for the other organizations, publication of this type of information is sporadic and never mandatory.

b Call for Tenders The publication of the call for tenders is a common feature of national public procurement. To a certain extent, this is also true for international organizations.

In national public procurement, publication of the call for tenders has the objective of ensuring competition by informing all economic operators of the business opportunities provided by public procurement and, in the case of restricted procedures, by allowing these businesses to express their interest. The tight link between competition and publication of the call for tenders is highlighted, for example, by Directive 2004/24/EU, applicable to EU member states, which states that '[c]ontract notices shall be used as a means of calling for competition in respect of all procedures'.[238] Thus, due to this tight link and to the centrality of competition in the European regulation of public procurement, duties to publish the call for tenders are particularly pervasive. The obligation to advertise is extended to all public procurements or framework agreements above certain thresholds to be awarded through open, restricted and negotiated procedures, as well as through competitive dialogue and partnership for innovation. The only exception is negotiated procedures, which expressly provide for the absence of preliminary advertisement under specific conditions enumerated by the directives.[239] The published documents must contain all information needed to provide sufficient knowledge of the tender and its conditions. The GPA sets out a similar publicity obligation, although in less detail.[240]

In procurement by international organizations, provisions requiring publication of tender documents vary depending on whether direct or indirect procurement is involved, and their details differ from organization to organization. In direct procurement, at least four levels of publicity can be identified: the procurement rules may

---

[238] European Union, Directive 2014/24/EU, Art. 49 [N&RL-EU].   [239] *Ibid.*, Art. 32.
[240] GPA, Art. VII(1).

lack any reference to the obligation of publishing the tender, such as for FAO, WFP or UNICEF; publicity obligations can be attached to certain solicitation methods, i.e. restricted procedures, but exceptions to these obligations can be applied at the organization's discretion, such as in the United Nations; publicity obligations can refer to open procedures (for those organizations that allow open procedures) and be linked to fixed parameters set out in the rules, but without effective controls and sanctions on compliance with the obligation (such as for UNDP and UNOPS); and advertising the tender notice can be always mandatory, as in the case of procurement by EU institutions, which follows the model of the European public procurement directives and the GPA.

The first level of publicity is the one most commonly adopted by international organizations in the U N system. Nevertheless, despite the fact that procurement rules do not provide for such obligations, in practice some organizations, on a case-by-case basis and when necessary for purposes of market research, publish calls for tenders on a website common to all organizations within the UN system, namely the United Nations Global Marketplace (UNGM).

An intermediate form of publicity is provided by the procurement rules set by the UN, which is one of the organizations in the UN system that has more precise requirements in this regard. Financial rules provide that tenders must be published: 'tenders for equipment, supplies and other requirements shall be invited by advertisement'.[241] However, the object of the advertisement, the degree of stability/changeability of the content of the notice, the ability to make exceptions to the rule, the controls of compliance with the obligation and time frames greatly differ from those set in public procurement rules, such as the European public procurement directives and the GPA.

With regard to content, the tender documents are usually not published from the outset. The organization sends out a request for information or a request for expression of interest, following which vendors express their interest, and only then does the administration select those to whom the tender documents are sent. The degree of publicity is tied to the vendor selection method. As seen earlier in this chapter, in the UN, as well as in many other organizations, the basic procedure is the restricted procedure rather than the open one. Advertisement of the request for information or the request for expression of interest has a more limited purpose than that of an actual call for tenders, as this

---

[241] Regulation 5.13 of United Nations, *Financial Regulations*, ST/SGB/2013/4 [ref. AP&R].

allows the vendors to express their interest while not yet submitting an offer. Accordingly, a request for expression of interest usually provides a brief description of the requirements and may include mention of selection criteria. However, no other details are provided in relation to the mandatory content of the advertisement, such as those set out in the European public procurement directives.

Furthermore, one of the main characteristics of a request for information or a request for expression of interest is the flexibility of its contents. Neither of the two binds the administration like a call for tenders, and the procurement officer may at any time amend it or eliminate some of the requirements included in it:

> [t]he REOI [i.e. request for expression of interest] does not constitute a solicitation; responding to the REOI does not guarantee that the Vendor will be invited to participate in the Solicitation when issued; and the UN reserves the right to change or cancel the procurement at any time during the REOI process or the formal Solicitation process.[242]

In addition, advertisement is an obligation that is subject to important exceptions. According to the financial rules and regulations of the United Nations, for example, deviations from the general rule of advertisement are permitted when a formal and a substantive condition are jointly met. The former is the express authorization of the organization's administrative head, the latter is the organization's interest (to be defined on a case-by-case basis). Rule 5.13 of the Financial Regulations and Rules of the United Nations does indeed set an obligation to advertise, but also states: 'except where Secretary-General deems that, in the interests of the Organization, a departure from this regulation is desirable'.[243] The UN Procurement Manual goes further, where it establishes that '[i]f the Procurement Officer decides not to post a REOI, he/she shall document the reasons in a written note to the procurement case file'.[244] This latter provision seems to broaden the exception provided for in the financial rules both in terms of the institutional parties who may decide it (the procurement officer and not only the Secretary-General) and in terms of the situations in which this can be done, i.e. not the 'interests of the organization', but under the even more general circumstances that lead to such a decision. Furthermore, the text does not specify these circumstances, and this remains at the discretion of the individual procurement

---

[242] United Nations, *Procurement Manual*, para. 9.8.5 [ref. AP&R].

[243] Regulation 5.13 of United Nations, *Financial Regulations*, ST/SGB/2013/4 [ref. AP&R].

[244] United Nations, *Procurement Manual*, para. 9.8.1 [ref. AP&R].

officer, whether operating at the central level or in the field offices. Compliance with the obligation of advertisement is subject to controls only through a note to be attached to the documents regarding the procedure carried out.

Finally, the methods of advertisement consist of placing the request of expression of interest on the UN website and on UNGM. UNGM, developed by the IAPWG, is the electronic portal of reference for both the contracting authorities of the UN system and the vendors. On one hand, it provides a list of pre-qualified vendors, and on the other it ideally collects the business opportunities and the requests of expression of interest of all organizations in the UN system. In reality, the advertised requests of expression of interest cover only a small percentage of the procurements that UN organizations undertake.

A third and higher level of publicity is ensured by other organizations, such as the UNDP, UNOPS and NATO, which have set up a more extensive publicity system. This is linked to the type of tender procedure the organizations undertake. Indeed, as recalled earlier, these organizations have established three procedures for selecting contractors, in which the basic procedure is the open one. In an open procedure the call for tenders must make it possible for the candidate to directly submit his offer without the organization sending a preliminary invitation. To this end, the procurement manuals of these organizations often introduce two variations to the solutions set out in the approach to publicity previously described. First, they link the advertisement requirements to the various types of solicitation methods and procedures, as well as to procurement thresholds. Second, they provide additional details on how publication should be undertaken. A combination of both can be found, for example, in UNDP. Here, advertisement in international media is required for any invitation to bid or request for proposals related to contracts valued at $150,000 and above. Thus, for this type of contract, open international competition is ensured. On the contrary, in cases of direct contracting for any amount, micro purchasing for low-value contracts and requests for quotations for procurements between $5,000 and $149,999, open advertisement is not required. Indeed, there is no competition in direct contracting, or there is limited (international or national) competition in the other cases.[245] When required, advertisement must consist of publication of the invitation to bid or the request for

---

[245] UNDP, *Programme and Operations Policies and Procedures. Procurement*, sec. 'Procurement Methods', para. 3 [ref. AP&R].

proposals through international media, including print and electronic media. In any event, the procurement opportunity must be advertised or published on the procurement advertisement pages of both UNDP's corporate website and the UN Global Marketplace for a minimum of two weeks.[246] Although the advertisement obligation is broader, in these organizations as well, the bodies conducting the controls and monitoring, such as the UN Board of Auditors, have sometimes detected non-compliance with publicity obligations.[247]

At the end of the transparency spectrum, there are EU institutions. The standards of publicity that apply to EU institutions are essentially the same as those set out by the European public procurement directives addressed to states. In addition to the pre-information notice previously discussed, European institutions are in fact required to publish calls for tenders with an estimated value equal to or greater than the thresholds laid down in the Financial Regulation.[248] Furthermore, even procurements below those thresholds 'shall be advertised by appropriate means'.[249] The only exception is linked to negotiated procedures. Pursuant to Art. 134 of the Rules of Application, the institutions may use the negotiated procedure without prior publication of a contract notice 'for building contracts, after prospecting the local market'.[250] As explained by the European Court of Auditors, building contracts, such as purchase, long lease, usufruct, leasing, rental or hire purchase, of land, existing buildings or other real estate, can be concluded by negotiated procedure without publication of a contract notice, after the local market has been prospected.[251] These exceptions, however, seem to have limited applicability in practice. For example, as reported by the Commission, from 2009 to 2014 only three procedures were launched in which the exception was applied and the building prospection notices were not published in the Official Journal.[252]

---

[246] Ibid., sec. 'Procurement Methods', paras. 6, 9, 42, 54.

[247] See, inter alia, UN Board of Auditors, Financial Report and Audited Financial Statements, A/67/5/Add. 1, para. 108 [ref. REP], where it states that 'the Board reviewed the procurement process at country offices and noted the following weaknesses and non-compliance with the UNDP procurement principles, policies and procedures: ... Required advertisement methods were not always followed to solicit potential vendors, reducing the pool of interested suppliers'.

[248] European Union, Regulation (EU, Euratom) No. 966/2012, Art. 103, para. 1 [ref. N&RL-EU].

[249] Ibid., Art. 103, para. 2.

[250] EU Commission Delegated Regulation (EU) No. 1268/2012, Art. 134 [ref. N&RL-EU].

[251] European Court of Auditors, The EU Institutions Can Do More To Facilitate Access to Their Public Procurement, Box 1 [ref. REP].

[252] Ibid., sec. 'Replies of the European Commission', para. 34.

In indirect procurement, in particular that of international financial institutions, the level of publicity applicable to the call for tenders is similar to what is required by national public procurement rules, such as by the GPA or European public procurement directives. There is, however, one specific feature. Publicity falls under the control of the financial institution, which materially provides for it. WB regulations (and, with the exception of IFAD, the guidelines of the other development banks, namely AfDB and ADB, have the exact same provisions) provide that '[t]imely notification of bidding opportunities is essential in competitive bidding'.[253] Thus, for projects that entail international competitive bidding procedures, the beneficiary state must prepare a draft General Procurement Notice and submit it to the bank. The bank will then arrange for publication of the notice.[254] The draft notice must contain the information prescribed by the bank's regulations, i.e. the name of the borrower (or prospective borrower), the purpose and amount of the financing, the scope of procurement reflecting the procurement plan, the borrower's contact point, if available, the address of a free-access website on which the subsequent Specific Procurement Notice will be posted, and if known, an indication of the scheduled dates for the specific procurement opportunities.[255] In restricted procedures, the call for tenders and bidding documents cannot be issued by the procuring entity, and thus the companies cannot be invited to submit the offer before publication of the General Procurement Notice.

European rules on indirect procurement financed by the EU budget and the EDF contain a variation of this model, as they set up a complex system of publicity depending on the subject of procurement (supply, services and works), the threshold amounts and the tender procedures adopted (international open procedure, local open procedure, restricted procedure, negotiated procedure etc).

All supply contracts which meet or exceed a certain threshold amount[256] must be launched through an international open tender and

---

[253] WB, *The World Bank Procurement Regulations for IPF Borrowers*, para. 5.22. And with the same wording AfDB, *Rules and Procedures for the Procurement of Goods and Works*, para. 2.7; ADB, *Procurement Guidelines*, para. 2.7 [all documents in ref. AP&R].

[254] WB, *The World Bank Procurement Regulations for IPF Borrowers*, para. 5.22; AfDB, *Rules and Procedures for the Procurement of Goods and Works*, para. 2.7; ADB, *Procurement Guidelines*, para. 2.7 [all documents in ref. AP&R].

[255] WB, *The World Bank Procurement Regulations for IPF Borrowers*, para. 5.22; AfDB, *Rules and Procedures for the Procurement of Goods and Works*, para. 2.7; ADB, *Procurement Guidelines*, para. 2.7 [all documents in ref. AP&R].

[256] In 2017 the threshold was €300,000. Publicity requirements for supply contracts are in European Union, *PRAG*, para. 4.3.1.2 [ref. AP&R].

published in the Official Journal of the European Union, on the EuropeAid website, and in all other media considered appropriate. The contracting authority drafts the contract notice and sends it to the Commission, which in turn handles publication in the Official Journal and on the website. The beneficiary state must instead directly provide for publication in the local media, when necessary. The procurement notice must provide vendors with all information necessary to submit a bid. In particular, selection criteria must be clearly and unambiguously indicated, according to a template provided by the PRAG. Furthermore, the deadlines set for presenting bids must be designed to permit effective competition.[257] Below the aforementioned threshold (but above a lower threshold indicated by the relevant rules),[258] the procedure can be a local open tender, and the publicity requirements that apply to the contract notice are less stringent.[259] Finally, when the procurement value is under the lowest thresholds, competitive negotiated procedures can be adopted and, contrary to the same procedures set by the European public procurement directives, do not entail publication.

Service contracts, on the contrary, apply either a restricted procedure if the amount of the contract is equal to or greater than the above-mentioned thresholds[260] or a negotiated procedure if the amount is lower.[261] Publicity requirements regarding contract notices in restricted procedures are the same as those applicable to supply contracts in international open tenders. Below the thresholds, however, there are no specific duties to advertise the contract notice.

Finally, for procurement of works,[262] the threshold amounts are increased and the applicable procedures include all those noted above, i.e. international open tenders or restricted procedures (for procurement equal to or greater than the highest threshold),[263] local open tenders (for procurement between the highest and the medium threshold)[264] and

---

[257] The time frame shall be no less than thirty days after publication. *Ibid.*, Annex A11e.

[258] The gap is €100,000 to €300,000.

[259] The notice is not published in the Official Journal of the European Union but only in the Official Journal of the partner country and on the EuropeAid website. Publication is the responsibility of the partner country, and the notice can be very brief, providing only minimal information.

[260] The threshold is €300,000.

[261] Publicity requirements for service contracts are provided in EU, *PRAG*, paras. 3.3.1.2 and 3.4 [ref. AP&R].

[262] Publicity requirements for service contracts are provided in *ibid.*, paras. 5.3–5.6.

[263] The highest threshold is €5,000,000.

[264] Local open tenders are applicable to contracts of at least €300,000 and under €5,000,000.

competitive negotiated procedures (under the medium threshold, which is nevertheless quite high).[265] The publicity requirements that apply are those already mentioned above for each of these procedures.

Thus, with regard to the contract notice, two features seem to recur in indirect procurement. The first concerns the balance between publicity requirements imposed by the organization and the autonomy of the national contracting authority in implementing those requirements. Organizations undertaking indirect procurement require a much higher level of transparency and publicity from states than what the organizations themselves adopt in direct procurement. This is particularly true for publication of contract notices, which is crucial to ensure participation and competition among companies. However, as competition is not an institutional objective of the organizations, publicity requirements are not as far-reaching as those required by the GPA or by the European public procurement directives, where, for instance, publication of contract notice is mandatory in every procedure, including negotiated ones. On the contrary, requirements set by organizations for beneficiary states that relate to the advertisement of contract notices gradually lose their importance and binding nature as the contract value decreases. As a result, this gives beneficiary states room to exercise their autonomy by defining their own degree of transparency on a case-by-case basis, also given that the thresholds below which the states have discretion are quite high.

The second feature is complementary to the first one and relates to the control the international organization exercises over the beneficiary state's fulfilment of publicity requirements. The balance between publicity requirements and autonomy is possible as long as this is monitored, and sometimes managed, by the organizations. As mentioned earlier, for contracts above a certain threshold, monitoring may include the organization's assessment of the content of the contract notice and direct publication by the organization of such notice; but even for contracts under a certain threshold, the organization has general powers of *ex ante* or *ex post* review of the procedure, which also includes contract notice.[266]

Thus, the system of publicity applicable to the call for tenders is based on a form of controlled autonomy of states, where the control takes the shape of requirements and procedural monitoring, and autonomy is

---

[265] Competitive negotiated procedures can be undertaken for procurement contracts under €300,000.
[266] See Chapter 7.

ensured as long as this does not conflict with the organization's interests. The final result is a level of transparency and publicity that is higher than that applied to direct procurement, but lower than that usually imposed on states by international and supranational rules on procurement, namely the GPA and European public procurement directives.

c **Award Notice** Publication of the award decision is the last step in the vendor selection procedure. According to European public procurement directives, national administrations that have awarded a procurement contract or concluded a framework agreement must send a contract award notice of the results of the award procedure within thirty days after the award.[267] The Publications Office of the European Union that receives the notice must then publish it no more than five days after it was sent. The procuring entity may avoid publication formalities only under specific circumstances enumerated by the directives, i.e. when the disclosure of information could impede law enforcement or is otherwise contrary to the public interest, negatively affects the legitimate business interests of public or private economic operators, or may prejudice fair competition among them.[268]

The GPA contains very similar provisions. Art. XVI provides that no later than seventy-two days after the award, procuring entities must publish results where indicated by the agreement itself (for European countries this is the Official Journal), and also describes the required contents of this publication.[269] In addition to the information released to the public, each unsuccessful candidate may request additional information.

In direct procurement, there are different degrees of publicity applicable to the award decision: high, when the relevant rules make publication mandatory; medium, in organizations where the rules do provide for possible publication, but this is at the discretion of the procurement officer; low, when the rules do not contain any reference to a duty of publication or refer to publication as an option. A number of

---

[267] European Union, Directive 2014/24/EU, Arts. 50–51; European Union, Directive 2014/25/EU, Arts. 70–71 [directives in ref. N&RL-EU].

[268] *Ibid.*

[269] In particular, the nature and quantity of goods and services subject to the award; the name and address of the procuring entity; the name and address of the successful bidder; the value of the winning bid or the maximum and minimum value of the offers taken into consideration in the evaluation; the date of the award; the type of procedure used to select the contractor; and, in the case of a negotiated procedure, a description of the circumstances that justified it. GPA, Art. XVI, para. 2.

organizations fall within the first category. UNOPS procurement rules, for example, set extensive publication requirements on the assumption that '[o]mitting to disclose contract award information undermines the procurement principle of transparency and is detrimental to the reputation of UNOPS'.[270] Thus, regardless of the value of the contract, UNOPS is under a duty to post information on its website about all awarded contracts, with the exception of so-called Individual Contractor Agreements, which are issued to individuals.[271]

EU institutions also provide an example of strict publication requirements that are, however, linked to the value of contracts. EU contracting authorities are subject to the same publicity standards that are set by the public procurement directives for states. They are under a duty to publish award decisions for contracts that exceed the threshold identified in the relevant regulation.[272] Also, exceptions to this duty are taken from those applicable to the public procurement rules for states:

> [p]ublication of certain information on a contract award may be withheld where its release would impede law enforcement, or otherwise be contrary to the public interest, would harm the legitimate commercial interests of economic operators or might prejudice fair competition between them.[273]

Similarly, within the UN system, UNDP[274] and UNFPA[275] are under a duty to post all contract awards valued above a certain threshold[276] on UNGM (for UNFPA) or on the websites of the country office and the corporate UNDP website (for UNDP). However, the notice of award needs to contain only basic information, i.e. the name of the contractor, its country of origin, the contract amount and a description of the contract.

A variation of this type of publicity is provided by NATO rules. In this organization, contract awards exceeding a certain financial value must be published periodically on the pertinent electronic information system. However, significant exceptions are also allowed that are not linked to an objective need, such as law enforcement or commercial interests, but rather 'when the customer has stipulated that publication is not wanted'

---

[270] UNOPS, Procurement Manual, para. 10.2.1 [ref. AP&R].   [271] *Ibid.*
[272] European Union, Regulation (EU, Euratom) No. 966/2012, Art. 103.
[273] *Ibid.*, Art. 103(3).
[274] UNDP, *Programme and Operations Policies and Procedures. Procurement*, sec. 'Award and Management of Contract. General Considerations of Contracting', para. 17 [ref. AP&R].
[275] UNFPA, *Policy and Procedures for Regular Procurement*, para. 10.2.2 [ref. AP&R].
[276] For UNFPA $50,000 or more.

or for classified contracts.[277] Thus, exceptions to the rules can be also the result of an agreement between the parties to the contractual relationship, regardless of the interests of other companies that took part in the procedure and of the public at large.

Few organizations fall within the second category. ESA is an example: '[a]ward notices on procurement actions may be published at the Agency's discretion'.[278] In any event, when published, only basic information is provided through award notices, including the title of the procurement action and the invitation to tender reference, the name of the company that was awarded the contract and the price of the contract but only if 'such publication does not affect the economic interest of the successful Tenderer'.[279] To this end, the successful company may be consulted prior to publication of said award notice. Thus, the arrangements for publication appear to be based on two elements: one is the discretion of the organization, and the other is the company's interest in protecting its privacy and the confidentiality of the operations. The rules recognize the potential of the latter to prevail over other interests, such as those of competing undertakings and the public at large. Actual prevailing interests are, however, decided on a case-by-case basis by the organization, which balances the various interests at stake.

Within the UN system, WFP and FAO rules also give the procuring entity significant room for discretion. WFP procurement rules provide, for example, that requests for tender proposals should include a clause stating that the organization reserves the right to post details of the award on its website, or make it public by other means.[280] The publication of award decisions is not a duty of the organization, with the corresponding right of competing companies or the public at large to be informed. Rather, it is a right of the organization, which may or may not exercise it. With a slightly different approach but identical practical results, procurement rules applicable to FAO provide that 'for public solicitations, the Buyer [i.e. the organization] will determine the appropriate means for publication of the solicitation results'.[281] From the wording of the provision, there does not seem to be discretion as to whether or not to publish the award decision, which should be published, but rather on the modalities of publication. Organizations' practice, however, shows a loose interpretation of the rule, with discretion extended to the *an*

---

[277] NATO, *NSPO Procurement Regulations*, para. 10 [ref. AP&R].
[278] ESA, *ESA Procurement Regulations*, Art. 45(2) [ref. AP&R].   [279] *Ibid.*
[280] WFP, *Food Procurement Manual*, para. 13.2 [ref. AP&R].
[281] FAO, *FAO Manual*, sec. 502.16.17 [ref. AP&R].

rather than related only to the *quomodo*. The rate of publication of award decisions is in fact very low compared to the large number of contracts concluded by organizations for internal and external purposes.[282]

Finally, the third category includes those organizations whose procurement rules do not require publication of the award decision. The UN is the most emblematic case in this regard. While the procurement manual sets a procedure for ensuring that unsuccessful vendors are informed of the result of the procurement, it does not provide for specific procedural duties resulting in publication of the award decision. Avoiding doing so does not imply, however, that UN contracts are never published. On the contrary, the contracts concluded and the purchase orders issued by UN headquarters for internal purposes and for peacekeeping missions are regularly published on the UN/PD website and on UNGM.

Overall, even in those organizations where the rules clearly set out obligations to publish award decisions, there is a widespread failure to comply with those prescriptions – with the exception of EU institutions. Even more so, when procurement rules and regulations give the procuring entity the option to choose whether to publish or not, economy and time saving reasons, together with a general tendency to keep procurement activities secret and confidential, often cause procuring entities not to publish their award decisions.

In indirect procurement, on the other hand, the publicity standards applied to beneficiary states are essentially equivalent to those set by the international and supranational rules for domestic public procurement. The guidelines of WB, ADB and AfDB provide that, after submitting the award decision to the bank and following the no-objection period, the award notice must be published by the beneficiary country or by the bank.[283] The content of the information is indicated in the procurement manuals of the organizations and must include a broad spectrum of information, especially when compared with the meagre list of information that organizations sporadically provide on their own contracts. Moreover, there are no exceptions to the obligation: the relevant rules

---

[282] Since 2010, statistics on some of the awarded contracts have been collected and are published online once a year.

[283] WB, *The World Bank Procurement Regulations for IPF Borrowers*, paras. 5.73, 5.76, 5. 93–5.95; AfDB, *Rules and Procedures for the Procurement of Goods and Works*, para. 2.60; ADB, *Procurement Guidelines*, para. 2.60; IFAD, *Project Procurement Guidelines*, App. I, para. 2, VIII [all documents in ref. AP&R].

do not list circumstances that can justify the failure to publish, and furthermore, publishing is not related to threshold amounts.

With regard to exceptional circumstances and thresholds, rules on indirect procurement by the Commission and the EDF once again offer an alternative solution that is closer to what is stated in European public procurement directives. On one hand, regardless of the type of vendor selection procedure, the national procuring entity must send a notice of award to the European Commission. The Commission will then publish it in the Official Journal and other places it deems appropriate. On the other hand, the obligation of publicity is tied to certain threshold amounts and does not arise under certain conditions. In particular, there is no obligation in specific cases, i.e. when the contract was declared secret (and the secrecy is still relevant at the time of the award); when performance of the contract must be accompanied by special security measures; and when protection of the essential interests of the European Union or the partner country so requires, and publication of the award notice is not considered appropriate.[284] Thus, compared to the indirect procurement rules and regulations of financial institutions, those of the Commission and the EDF make room for broader, more undefined, exceptional situations, which guarantee greater flexibility for the system but that the Commission still assesses at the central level.

4.4.2.3 Patterns of Reason Giving

National and international rules on domestic public procurement recognize that the obligation to give reasons is one of the key requirements for guaranteeing the transparency of the administrative action. The obligation to give reasons, intended as the duty to indicate the factual premises and legal reasons for the administrative decision, has a dual function. It ensures that parties affected by the administrative decision are informed of the reasons that led the administration to make the decision. Furthermore, it enables private subjects to challenge administrative decisions before a higher administrative authority, an independent administrative body, or a judicial body if they consider it illegitimate and in violation of their rights.

Overturning the traditional approach of an opaque public administration, the European public procurement directives have introduced the obligation to reason-giving at various stages of public procurement

---

[284] EU, *PRAG*, para. 2.9.3.1 [ref. AP&R].

procedures. Currently, Directive 2014/24/EU provides that contracting authorities have an obligation to inform candidates of award decisions and, at the request of the interested party, to give unsuccessful candidates the reasons for rejecting their offer, and finally, to inform each vendor of the characteristics and advantages of the tender selected and the name of the party who was awarded the contract.[285] Moreover, this information must be provided within a short deadline: as soon as possible and in any event no more than fifteen days after receipt of the request.[286] Reason giving may be omitted in specific cases: if the release of information would impede law enforcement, is contrary to the public interest, would prejudice the legitimate commercial interests of public or private economic operators, or might prejudice fair competition between them.[287] The GPA essentially replicates European rules, and also provides similar reasons for exceptions to the obligation.[288]

a Direct Procurement   Reason giving has also been gradually introduced for international organizations that engage in direct procurement. The new generation of procurement manuals of many organizations provide that contracting authorities have a duty to spell out the grounds for their award decisions, either automatically or upon the request of interested parties. However, the ways in which this duty is shaped by the rules and the level of implementation vary greatly among organizations. While there are no data available on implementation, except for EU institutions, based on the rules it is possible to identify at least four patterns of reason giving, each corresponding to a reduced level of transparency: compulsory reason giving, optional reason giving, exceptional reason giving and no duty to give reason.

The compulsory reason-giving pattern usually has the following characteristics: the duty to give reasons comes with the award decision; it can include not only a brief statement of the reasons that led to the award, but also, once the brief statement is provided, further explanations if so requested by the interested party; it must be fulfilled in writing; and the fulfilment of such duty should be scrutinized by an impartial body, external to the procuring entity. Thus, reason giving is automatic, takes place through a two-step process, must be in written form and the public administration is accountable for it. It takes the shape of a duty of public administrations, with a corresponding right of private subjects. The only

---

[285] European Union, Directive 2014/24/EU, Art. 55 (2) [ref. N&RL-EU].
[286] *Ibid.*, Art. 55(2).   [287] *Ibid.*, Art. 55(3).   [288] GPA, Art. XVII.

organizations to adopt this specific pattern are EU institutions. According to the EU financial rules the contracting authority shall notify all candidates or tenderers of the grounds of the decision.[289] In addition, the contracting authority shall provide each tenderer with information regarding the name of the winning tenderer, the characteristics and relative advantages of the successful tender, and the price paid or contract value.[290]

As in national public procurement, exceptions are allowed but are specifically identified: the request can be rejected and information withheld if its disclosure impedes law enforcement, is contrary to the public interest, prejudices the legitimate commercial interests of public or private enterprises, or could endanger fair competition between them.[291]

According to the interpretation given by the General Court and the Ombudsman, this duty to give reason and the corresponding rights of private subjects are grounded on the fundamental principles of the Treaty, and namely on Art. 253 of the Treaty establishing the European Community, according to which regulations, directives and decisions shall state the reasons on which they are based. The article does not explicitly mention administrative decisions, but both the General Court and the Ombudsman have interpreted it extensively. In this regard, the European Ombudsman has emphasized that in the contract-awarding procedures there is an obligation of transparency deriving from Art. 253 of the EC Treaty as this obligation enables the European courts and the Ombudsman to verify that the principle of equal treatment of tenderers has been complied with.[292]

Notwithstanding these connections with the core principles of the European Union, there are some limits to implementation of the duty to give reasons. The first concerns the discretion of EU institutions and the scope of the review by the Court of Justice. EU institutions have broad discretion with regard to the factors to be taken into account when evaluating offers and awarding contracts. Thus, review by the Court of Justice must be limited to 'checking that the rules governing the procedure and statement of reasons are complied with, the facts are correct and there is no manifest error of assessment or misuse of powers'.[293]

---

[289] European Union, Regulation (EU, Euratom) No. 966/2012, Art. 113(2) [ref. N&RL-EU].
[290] *Ibid.*, Art. 113(3). [291] *Ibid.*
[292] European Ombudsman, *Decision of the European Ombudsman on Complaint 1859/2005/ BB and 1858/2005/BB Against the European Monitoring Centre for Racism and Xenophobia*, 16 July 2007.
[293] European Court of Auditors, *The EU Institutions Can Do More to Facilitate Access to Their Public Procurement*, footnote 38 [ref. REP].

The second limit regards the standard of review that has been applied to implementation of the duty to give reasons or, in other words, what the Court and the Ombudsman have deemed sufficient to fulfil this duty. In several judgments related to procurement by EU institutions, the Court has held that the contracting authority fulfils its obligation to state reasons if it merely communicates to the unsuccessful tenderer the reasons for the rejection of its tender and indicates to tenderers who have submitted an admissible tender, and who expressly request it, the characteristics and relative advantages of the successful tender and the name of the successful tenderer. EU institutions are not bound to provide further explanations.[294] For example, the contracting authority is not bound, by reason of its obligation to state reasons, to debate the merits of an unsuccessful tenderer's offer in relation to those of the successful tender. Furthermore, the requirement to state reasons must be assessed on a case-by-case basis, based on the circumstances of the case, and in particular the content of the measure, the nature of the reasons relied on, and the interest of the private subject. According to the Court, this is consistent with the purposes of the obligation to state reasons laid down in Art. 253 of the Treaty establishing the European Community: on one hand, to enable the private subjects concerned to know the justification for the measure taken, so that they can assert their rights, and on the other hand, to enable the court to exercise its power of review. On these same grounds, if the reasons justifying the award do not allow the court to exercise its review, the duty to give reasons shall be deemed as not met and the procedure subject to annulment.[295]

Consistently with the Court's judgments, the Ombudsman has considered that the obligation to give reasons was also met when the grounds for the decision were only generally enunciated, as long as this was accompanied by adequate prior information on the criteria for the decision. For example, in a case filed against the European Commission for insufficient reason giving, the European Ombudsman stated that

---

[294] This approach is clear from several judgments. See, *inter alia*, Case T-211/07, *A W W W* v. *Eurofound*, 1 July 2008, not published in the ECR, para. 43; Case T-50/05, *Evropaïki Dynamiki* v. *Commission* [2010] ECR II-313, paras. 132–134 (for a comment on the case see Saurer, 'Transition to a New Regime of Judicial Review of EU Agencies'); Case T-554/08, Evropaïki Dynamiki v. Commission [2012] 24 April 2012, not published in the ECR, paras. 136–139; Case T-121/08, *PC-Ware Information Technologies* v. *Commission* [2010] ECR II-1541, paras. 92–94; Case T-216/09, Astrim e Elyo Italia v. Commission, [2012] 24 April 2012, not published in the ECR, paras. 136–139.

[295] Case T-556/11, *European Dynamics Luxembourg and Others* v. *EUIPO*, 7 October 2015, not published in the ECR, para. 145.

uncertainty on the grounds of the decision would have been avoided if the criteria and percentage weightings applied to the evaluation had been made clear *ex ante*.[296] Based on these considerations, the Ombudsman, on one hand, opted for a minimalist interpretation of the requirement of reason giving. It found that the obligation to provide reasons was fulfilled even if only summary information was provided. Thus, there was no instance of maladministration by the Commission. On the other hand, in order to increase the level of transparency, the Ombudsman stated that the summary nature of the *ex post* reason must be offset by a clear *ex ante* determination of all evaluation criteria:

> [t]he transparency of the selection procedure could be improved by making clear that the Commission's decision may include factors other than the criteria and percentage weightings. It would be further improved if the Commission were to specify what those factors are.[297]

Even within this loose net of standards for review, implementation by EU institutions of the duty to give reasons appears to be fairly effective. The European Court of Auditors, for example, found that between 2009 and 2014 the General Court completed 3,419 cases, of which 106 dealt with public procurement by EU institutions, with an average of 17.6 cases per year. The 106 cases relating to public procurement produced a total of 123 decisions (sixty-six judgments and fifty-seven orders). However, actions for annulment were successful only in thirteen cases, and in ten out of the thirteen cases the reason for annulment of the decision was the contracting authority's failure to comply with its duty to state reasons. These data raise several interesting issues. First, litigation connected to procurement by EU institutions seems to have a small but not negligible impact on the overall litigation rate. Second, the possibility of obtaining an annulment of the decision is very low. Third, violation of the duty to state reasons is almost the only reason for granting an annulment. This could be a consequence of the fact that violations of the duty to state reasons are more manifest than other types of violations, but may also be due to the fact that the duty to state reasons appears to be safeguarded by the courts, notwithstanding the narrow interpretation explained above.

---

[296] European Ombudsman, *Decision of the European Ombudsman on Compliant 52/1995/ JL/B Against the European Commission*, 27 July 1995; European Ombudsman, *1996 Annual Report* [ref. REP]; for a comment, see Kalogeras, 'Remedies in the Field of Public Procurement'.

[297] European Ombudsman, *1996 Annual Report*, p. 27 [ref. REP].

The second pattern is that of optional reason giving. It shows a much lower level of transparency compared to that adopted at the EU level and usually has the following characteristics: it is optional; it consists of a brief statement regarding the characteristics of the offer that led to excluding it from the award; it is given only orally; and there is no impartial body scrutinizing its implementation. Most organizations adopt this pattern: ESA, NATO, United Nations, UNFPA, UNESCO, UNDP and UNICEF are examples in this regard.[298]

Reason giving is optional to the extent that the contracting authority is not compelled to state its reasons when making the award decision. However, the unsuccessful vendor is notified of the decision and can make a formal request to receive a debrief. The contracting authority may respond to this request, providing a debriefing. Thus, the optional nature of this pattern of reason-giving has some salient features. First, the legal status that provides grounds for the notification often does not take the form of a right of the private subject. Some organizations make this explicit by using expressions underlying how notification is a concession made by the organization to the private subject. This implies that the private subject has a legitimate interest in the notification, rather than a proper right vis-à-vis the administration. UNESCO and UNFPA are explicit in this regard stating that

> [s]uppliers that submitted a bid but were not awarded a contract should be, either verbally or in writing, notified by the office having issued the contract as a *matter of courtesy* given the effort bid preparation takes.[299]

Second, the procuring entity *may* respond to the unsuccessful vendor, but does not have a duty to do so. The use of the modal verb 'may' is found in the procurement rules of organizations such as NATO, United Nations, UNDP, UNESCO and UNFPA.

As for the content of the reasons provided, this pattern consists of a one-step process, rather than a two-step process as for EU institutions, and reason giving amounts to only a debriefing that meets specific objectives and has several limitations as to what can and cannot be

---

[298] For example, ESA, *ESA Procurement Regulations*, Arts. 34(8), 46; NATO, *NSPO Procurement Regulations*, para. 15.6; United Nations, *Procurement Manual*, para. 6.1(5); UNFPA, *Policy and Procedures for Regular Procurement*, para. 10.2.1; UNESCO, *UNESCO Administrative Manual*, para. 9.4; UNDP, *Programme and Operations Policies and Procedures. Procurement*, sec. 'Handling of Procurement Complaints', paras. 3–5 [all documents ref. AP&R].

[299] Emphasis added. UNESCO, *Administrative Manual*, para. 9.4; UNFPA, *Policy and Procedures for Regular Procurement*, para. 10.2.1 [all documents ref. AP&R].

included. NATO, for example, is particularly explicit in pointing to the objectives of the debriefing, making clear to whom these objectives pertain and what should be the content of the debriefing:

> a debriefing may take place as to the basis for the selection decision, mentioning strong and weak points of their proposals. This should be a 'lessons learned' experience for the unsuccessful bidder, enabling the bidder to respond better to future solicitations.[300]

Similar wording, with some variations, is used by other organizations.[301] UNDP's debriefing objectives, for instance, include not only instructing the vendors and allowing them to make better offers in future solicitations, but also the opportunity for the organization to enhance its legitimation and avoid litigation:

> the debriefing contributes to building the trust of the business community in UNDP; and ... it is an opportunity for UNDP to clarify its decision in a cordial manner, thus avoiding potential escalation of bidder concerns into formal complaints.[302]

Thus, the objectives of debriefing mainly support the interests of organizations (justification and avoidance of litigation) and only to a lesser extent those of the private subject. Furthermore, these rules do not usually have the interest of vendors in mind, i.e. the interest in having enough information to bring a claim against the administration in relation to a specific procedure, but rather are aimed to help them 'learn a lesson' for future procurements and be more successful. Besides the rather patronizing approach expressed by this wording, it is clear that debriefing of international organizations does not aim to enable the private subject to challenge the organization's award decision, which, on the contrary, is assumed to be stable and incontrovertible.

These objectives also shape the content of debriefing and its limits. Again, the wording of the rules of most organizations is emblematic in this regard: the expression often used to describe the content of the debriefing is 'shall be limited to'. In particular, as also mentioned

---

[300] NATO, *NSPO Procurement Regulations*, para. 15.6 [ref. AP&R].

[301] ESA, *ESA Procurement Regulations*, Art. 46(4); United Nations, *Procurement Manual*, paras. 9.16, 11.40; UNDP, *Programme and Operations Policies and Procedures. Procurement*, sec. 'Handling Complaints', paras. 3–5; UNESCO, *Administrative Manual*, para. 9.4; UNFPA, *Policy and Procedures for Regular Procurement*, para. 10.2.1 [all documents ref. AP&R].

[302] UNDP, *Programme and Operations Policies and Procedures. Procurement*, sec. 'Handling Complaints', para. 3 [ref. AP&R].

above, the information provided only relates to the strengths and weaknesses of the proposal submitted by the bidder who requested the debriefing, and does not include either the vendors' comparative ratings or other information related to proposals of other vendors. It is important to emphasize how the debriefing from these organizations focuses on the vendor's offer, and not the reasons that led the administration to award a contract, as seen for EU institutions. By giving reasons, EU institutions must disclose the contracting authority's line of reasoning in a clear and unequivocal fashion.[303] Reason giving relates to something internal to the administration and external to the private subject. Moreover, it is the process for reaching the decision that must be shared. On the contrary, other organizations provide information external to the contracting authority and internal to the private subject, i.e. regarding its offer, which the private subject is supposedly already aware of. Furthermore, debriefing regards single aspects of the offer, rather than the entire process that led to the decision.

The limits of debriefing, however, also relate to its modalities, timing, thresholds, costs and accountability mechanisms. As for the modalities, debriefing by these organizations is usually provided verbally rather than in writing, takes place at the organization's premises and is given by the procurement officer involved. This does not imply an exchange or a debate between the procurement officer and the vendor. As made clear by the UN, 'the debrief is not an adversarial proceeding; rather, it is a collaborative learning opportunity'.[304] In some organizations a written answer may also be allowed, but only when the oral feedback is deemed insufficient. UNFPA is an example in this regard:

> [n]ormally only verbal feedback in response to the bidder's request is given. If the supplier has questions after receiving the verbal feedback, they can make a written request for clarification on specific issues and UNFPA may respond in writing.[305]

As for the timing, in some organizations the request for a debriefing is subject to a very short deadline. Examples include NATO, where the deadline is five days following receipt of the notification, and ESA and the United Nations.[306] However, except for some organizations, again such

---

[303] Case T-70/05, *Evropaïki Dynamiki* v. *EMSA* [2010] ECR II-313, para. 169.
[304] United Nations, *Debriefing and Procurement Challenges FAQ* [ref. AP&R].
[305] UNFPA, *Policy and Procedures for Regular Procurement*, para. 10.2.1 [ref. AP&R].
[306] The deadline is ten days.

as ESA,[307] NATO[308] and the United Nations,[309] most of the others do not have a time limit to respond to a request for debriefing.

Furthermore, some organizations, such as the UN, limit the possibility of providing a debriefing to procurement above certain thresholds, which are quite high. By way of example, the UN offers vendors an opportunity to obtain additional information on their unsuccessful proposals or bids through the debrief process only if they participated in high-value solicitations, i.e. resulting in awards above $200,000.

From the standpoint of the economic sustainability of debriefing, some organizations make it clear that the costs related to the debriefing must be borne by the vendor who requested it. UN and UNHCR procurement rules, for example, state that the debrief will be conducted in English, but translators and other special arrangements will be considered, if deemed necessary by the UN, as long as the vendor pays for any associated costs and arrangements. This, however, creates an asymmetry, as it is the organization that makes the decision that results in the costs, but the vendor then has to pay for the decision. Finally, given the above-mentioned characteristics of optional reason giving, it is not usually linked to any accountability mechanism involving impartial outside bodies, nor internal review bodies.

The third pattern of reason giving is the exceptional one. The organizations adopting this approach do not normally provide a debriefing. However, in exceptional circumstances they can do so, according to rules similar to those regulating optional reason giving. It is not a widespread pattern, and the most emblematic case in this regard is UNOPS. The organization's procurement rules state that

> UNOPS does not routinely debrief unsuccessful bidders. However, in the case of technical or complex awards, a debriefing may be conducted upon written request from an unsuccessful bidder.[310]

Thus, although there has to be an exceptional factual precondition, i.e. a complex procurement, the assessment of this precondition and the following decision on whether or not to hold the debriefing is left completely to the discretion of the contracting authority.

The fourth pattern is the least transparent, as reason giving is not provided by the applicable rules. The organization may, at its sole discretion and on a case-by-case basis, provide reasons for its award

---

[307] The deadline is twenty days.   [308] The deadline is thirty days.
[309] The deadline is thirty days.
[310] UNOPS, *Procurement Manual*, para. 10.2.3 [ref. AP&R].

decision. The practice shows that in these organizations the vast majority of award decisions are not followed by explanations. Among organizations with a greater volume of procurement, neither the WFP nor the FAO include provisions on reason giving in their procurement rules. Similarly, smaller organizations do not usually regulate this aspect of the procedure.

b   Indirect Procurement   The standard of reason giving is, instead, on average higher in indirect procurement. At least two different patterns can be identified here. The first resembles the compulsory reason giving mentioned above. Notice must be given of the national authority's award decision, and it must be followed by a statement of the reasons for the decision. In addition, an unsuccessful vendor may request further information on the tender, which will be provided by the contracting authority. The limits that apply and that relate to the confidentiality of third parties are the same as those seen in compulsory reason-giving for direct procurement. This is the pattern, for example, adopted in the procurement procedures financed by the EU budget and the EDF, where the wording replicates that of the EU financial regulations.[311]

The almost perfect correspondence between this pattern and the pattern laid down for direct procurement by EU institutions can be explained by the fact that indirect procurement financed by the European Union can also be implemented by EU institutions themselves, and not only by national entities.[312] Thus, those institutions are subject to the same duties, even if generated by different legal sources, e.g. the EU Financial Rules and Regulations and the PRAG. The contrary would

---

[311] EU, *PRAG*, para. 2.9.3.1 [ref. AP&R].

[312] Procurement financed by the European Union can be carried out through three management modes: direct, indirect and shared. As explained by the PRAG, in direct management the European Commission is in charge of all EU budget implementation tasks, which are performed directly by its departments either at headquarters or in the EU delegations or through European executive agencies. In this way, the European Commission or the European executive agency is the contracting authority and makes decisions on behalf and for the account of the partner countries. In indirect management, the European Commission entrusts budget implementation tasks to partner countries (or to bodies designated by them); international organizations; development agencies of EU member states; and other bodies. In shared management, the European Commission delegates implementation tasks to the EU member states. See EU, *PRAG*, para. 2.2 [ref. AP&R].

generate an uneven situation where EU institutions would be bound to different duties in similar situations.

In this pattern, however, accountability mechanisms differ from the compulsory reason-giving model described for direct procurement. Whereas, in the case of direct management, the EU Commission is subject to the scrutiny of the General Court and the Ombudsman, in the case of indirect management, the EU Commission exercises an *ex post* or *ex ante* review of the correctness of the procedure undertaken by the national authority and, thus, also of fulfilment of the duty to give reasons.

The second pattern is that adopted by financial institutions, and provides for a stronger mechanism of reason giving. Procurement rules of the WB, but also of the ADB,[313] AfDB,[314] EBRD[315] and IDB[316] establish a three-step procedure. The first and second steps take place before national authorities, the third before the international organization.

The first step includes the notification of intention to award together with the statement of the reasons why the offer was deemed unsuccessful.[317] The WB is even more specific with regard to the information that can and cannot be disclosed during this first phase: the procuring entity may not divulge any confidential or proprietary information regarding other vendors.[318]

The second step consists of debriefing at the request of the unsuccessful vendor. The debriefing procedure is similar to that found in direct procurement of other organizations. The debriefing may be done in writing or verbally. The vendor who requested the debriefing must also bear the costs of attending a debriefing meeting. However, in this regard, the WB further specifies that

---

[313] ADB, *Procurement Guidelines*, para. 2.65 and App. 3, para. 15 [ref. AP&R].

[314] AfDB, *Rules and Procedures for the Procurement of Goods and Works*, para. 2.65 and App. 3, para. 15 [ref. AP&R].

[315] EBRD, *Procurement Policies and Rules*, para. 2.10 [ref. AP&R].

[316] IDB, *Policies for the Procurement of Goods and Works*, para. 2.65 and App. 3, para. 15 [ref. AP&R].

[317] WB, *The World Bank Procurement Regulations for IPF Borrowers*, para. 5.74; ADB; *Procurement Guidelines*, para. 2.60; AfDB, *Rules and Procedures for the Procurement of Goods and Works*, para. 2.60 [all documents in ref. AP&R].

[318] WB, *The World Bank Procurement Regulations for IPF Borrowers*, para. 5.74(d) [ref. AP&R].

> [t]he Borrower shall not impose undue formal requirements that would restrict the Bidder's/Proposer's/Consultant's ability to receive a timely and meaningful debriefing.[319]

As for the content of the debriefing, while the rules of the ADB and the AfDB are not specific, WB provisions require a dynamic exchange between the national procuring entities and the vendors. According to these provisions, at a minimum the debriefing must re-state the information contained in the notification of intention of award, but the procurement official must also be ready to respond to any related questions from the unsuccessful vendor. However, just as for direct procurement, there is no detailed comparison with other vendors' offers, and information that is confidential or commercially sensitive to other vendors may not be disclosed.[320]

Furthermore, the rules provide for the financial institution's control over the debriefing process. Banks have the power to control and approve (or reject) the entire procurement procedure prior to its conclusion and also assess compliance of the debriefing with the standards set by the institutions. This is particularly explicit in the WB rules, which state that

> [a] written summary of each debriefing shall be included in the official procurement records, and copied to the Bank for contracts subject to prior review.[321]

Although the above-mentioned financial institutions basically follow a common pattern in relation to debriefing, the WB provisions set up a mechanism that goes even further in ensuring the transparency of administrative activity vis-à-vis private subjects. It does so by adding two variations to the common pattern. The first, and most relevant, concerns the phase of the procedure during which the procuring entities must provide the debriefing. In direct procurement, as well as in indirect procurement by financial institutions such as the ADB, AfDB and IDB, debriefing can be requested and provided only once the decision of award has been made and, hence, when the decision reaches an advanced level of stability. In indirect procurement by the WB, on the contrary, the debriefing process takes place after notification of the intention to award, but before the decision of award is formally adopted. Moreover, a standstill period is required from the national entity after notification of the intention to award. Thus, when the debriefing is given, the award

---

[319] WB, *The World Bank Procurement Regulations for IPF Borrowers*, para. 5.85 [ref. AP&R].
[320] *Ibid.*, paras. 5.81–5.87.   [321] *Ibid.*, para. 5.87.

decision is not stable and final; rather, the outcomes of the procedure can be influenced by the bank's assessment of the debriefing process. The second difference relates to time frames. In direct procurement the time frames for submitting a debriefing request are very short, while those for the procuring entity to provide the debriefing either are not indicated, or are much longer. In indirect procurement by financial institutions such as the ADB, the AfDB, the IDB and the EBRD, time frames are not indicated. The WB provisions, instead, not only prescribe specific time frames but also align the very short time frames that apply to the vendors to those that apply to the national procuring entity: the request must be submitted by the vendor within three business days; in turn, the national procuring entity must give the debriefing within five days, unless the borrowing state decides, for justifiable reasons, to provide the debriefing outside this time frame.

The third step of the process, after reasoned notification and debriefing, is triggered by the vendor and takes place before the international organizations. Financial institutions, such as the WB, the ADB, the AfDB, the IDB and the EBRD, allow the vendor to seek a debriefing directly by the bank, when the explanations provided by the national authority are unsatisfactory. This will serve to further clarify the grounds of the decision by the national authority. On the contrary, the debriefing may not discuss the bids or proposals of other vendors, nor may it investigate the bank's position that has been conveyed to the borrower (in the case of prior review contracts).[322]

Thus, the institutional triangle typical of indirect procurement,[323] which includes the international organization, the state and the private subjects, allows a higher level of transparency and, with regard to reason giving in particular, extends the private subject's sphere of rights by multiplying the opportunities to obtain an explanation and diversifying the institutional sources bound to give reasons. It is, thus, a strengthened form of compulsory reason-giving, if one compares it to compulsory reason-giving in direct procurement. A comparative analysis of the patterns of reason giving in direct and indirect procurement is shown in Table 4.3. Each pattern (compulsory-strengthen, compulsory, optional, exceptional and none) is the result of a combination of elements relating to whether reasons are provided (or, to put it another way,

[322] WB, *The World Bank Procurement Regulations for IPF Borrowers*, para. 5.96; AfDB, *Rules and Procedures for the Procurement of Goods and Works*, App. 3, para. 15; ADB, *Procurement Guidelines*, App. 3, para. 15 [all documents in ref. AP&R].
[323] See Chapter 2.

Table 4.3 *Patterns of reason giving (Y stands for Yes, N stands for No)*

		Compulsory-strengthen	Compulsory	Optional	Exceptional	None
If	Automatic (together with notification of award/intention to award)	Y	Y	N	N	N
	Upon request	Y	Y	Y	N	N
	Exceptional circumstances	Y	Y	Y	Y	N
How	Brief/simple motivation (First stage)	Y	Y	N	N	N
	Debriefing (Second stage)	Y	Y	Y	Y	N
	Debriefing by an external entity (Third stage)	Y	N	N	N	N
	Accountability mechanisms	Y (inter-institutional)	Y (legal)	N	N	N
Who		E.g.: WB, ADB, AfDB, IDB, EBRD (indirect procurement)	E.g.: EU institutions (direct procurement); EU institutions and EDF (indirect procurement)	E.g.: United Nations, UNDP, UNFPA, UNHCR, UNICEF etc. (direct procurement)	E.g.: UNOPS	E.g.: WFP, FAO, other small organizations

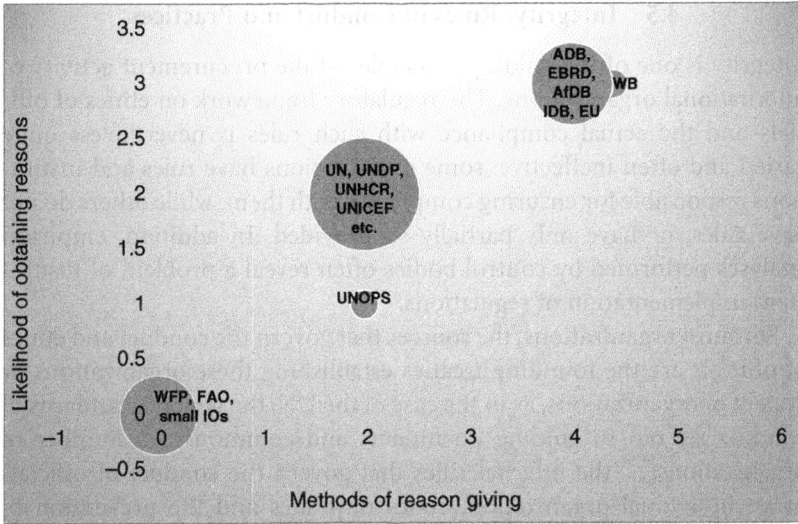

Figure 4.2   Organizations and reason giving
[Methods of reason giving include: Brief/simple reason (1); Debriefing by procuring entity (2); Debriefing by external entity (3); Accountability mechanisms (4). Likelihood of obtaining reasons includes: Exceptional circumstances (1); Upon request (2); Automatic (with notification) (3)]

whether it is likely to obtain reasons), how reason giving is provided and by which organizations.

The link between the different patterns of reason giving and some of the organizations with greater volumes of procurement is shown in Figure 4.2. The graph takes into account both qualitative elements (the methods of reason giving and the likelihood to obtain reasons) and quantitative elements (the number of organizations that adopt a certain pattern). One dimension of the graph (x axis) provides a measurement of the methods of reason giving, going from no reason giving to brief/simple motivation, to debriefing by the procuring entity, to debriefing by an external entity (which also includes simple motivation and debriefing by the procuring entity), to accountability mechanisms. Thus, this dimension follows a trend towards increasing transparency. The second dimension (y axis) reflects the spectrum that goes from no opportunity to obtain reasons to automatic reason giving. It measures how likely and easy it is for a vendor to obtain reasons. A third dimension, expressed by the size of the circles, takes into account how frequently a certain pattern recurs among organizations with a greater procurement volume.

4.5   Integrity: Rules of Conduct and Practices

Integrity is one of the guiding principles of the procurement activity of international organizations. The regulatory framework on ethics of officials and the actual compliance with such rules is nevertheless quite varied and often ineffective: some organizations have rules and institutions responsible for ensuring compliance with them, while others do not have rules, or have only partially so provided. In addition, empirical analyses performed by control bodies often reveal a problem of insufficient implementation of regulations.

For most organizations, the sources that govern the conduct and ethics of officials are the founding treaties establishing these organizations or system of organizations, as in the case of the UN; the general standards of conduct set out in guiding documents and common to a number of organizations;[324] the internal rules that govern the conduct of officials of an individual organization; codes on ethics and the prevention of corruption, if they exist; and finally, for procurement activity, procurement manuals or procurement guidelines, depending on whether direct or indirect procurement is involved. In terms of content, the rules generally aim at regulating three basic aspects of an official's conduct, as they could potentially be in conflict: the relationship between the official and the organization; the relationship between the official and the state of citizenship; and the relationships between the official and the private subjects with whom he must interact when performing his functions.

For organizations within the UN system, the regulatory reference is in the Charter of the United Nations. Art. 101 establishes that '[the] paramount consideration in the employment of the staff and in the determination of the conditions of the service shall be the necessity of securing the highest standards of efficiency, competence and integrity'.[325]

The *Standards of Conduct for the International Civil Service*, originally conceived in 1954 and revised in 2013 by the International Civil Service Commission,[326] are standards of conduct to guide all organizations

---

[324] The standards are not binding. As clarified by the United Nations Secretary-General: '[t]he standards of conduct do not have the force of law as they provide a discussion of expected standards to help staff understand their role as international civil servants rather than a set of binding rules', in UN Secretary-General, *Status, Basic Rights and Duties of United Nations Staff Members* [ref. AP&R].

[325] UN, Charter of the United Nations, Art. 101 [ref. A&C].

[326] International Civil Service Commission, *Standards of Conduct for the International Civil Service* [ref. AP&R].

within the UN system in defining their own internal regulations. Most organizations refer to these standards in their procurement manuals. Some organizations have gone further, developing sections in their procurement manuals that are specifically dedicated to ethics and conduct, though still based on these standards.[327] In addition to defining the general principles of conduct for officials, such as honesty, truthfulness, impartiality and incorruptibility, the standards include concise rules on aspects that could compromise observance of these principles, such as the relationship with the state of citizenship, acceptance of gifts and favours from governmental entities or private subjects and conflict of interest.

As to the relationship with the states, the Standards of Conduct create a loose-knit system where there is room for the influence of nation states to the extent these benefit the organization's interest. While the relationship between officials and nation states is in fact traditionally and formally based on the Drummond model and the service relationship is disassociated from the citizenship relationship,[328] the rules on conduct demonstrate how this original model can suffer from distortions when applied based on broad interpretations of the same standards. Art. 100 of the Charter of the United Nations states: 'in the performance of their duties, the Secretary-General and the staff shall not seek or receive instructions from any Government or from any other authority external to the Organization'.[329] Nevertheless, the impartiality and independence of the official do not imply neutrality with regard to the interests of states. As clarified by the International Civil Service Commission:

> [t]he independence of the international civil service does not conflict with, or obscure, the fact that it is the member States that collectively make up ... the organization. Conduct that furthers good relations with

[327] JIU, *Procurement Reforms in the United Nations System*, para. 163 [ref. REP].

[328] On this point, see Langrod, *La fonction publique internationale*; Bastid-Basdevant, *Les fonctionnaires internationaux*; Plantey, *Droit et pratique de la function publique international*; Amerasinghe, *Law of the International Civil Service*; Burns, 'International Administration'. In particular on the Drummond model and the influence of the English civil service system on international administrations, see Walters, *A History of the League of Nations*; Jordan, 'The Influence of the British Secretariat Tradition on the Formation of the League of Nations'.

[329] Similarly, the rules for the staff of European institutions provide that '[a]n official shall carry out his duties and conduct himself solely with the interests of the Union in mind. He shall neither seek nor take instructions from any government, authority, organization or person outside his institution. He shall carry out the duties assigned to him objectively, impartially and in keeping with his duty of loyalty to the Union' (Art. 11 of the European Union, Regulation No. 31 (EEC), 11 (EAEC), and following amendments [ref. N&RL-EU]).

individual member States and that contributes to their trust and confidence in the organizations' secretariat strengthens the organizations and promotes their interest.[330]

In other words, impartiality and independence do not prevent the possibility of taking decisions that tend to favour a state if this also benefits the interest of the organization and falls within one of its institutional policies. Thus, the states fund the organization, it is in the organization's interest for them to maintain a sufficient level of 'trust' in the organization so that they consider it beneficial to be members of it and continue to make financial contributions. Conversely, conduct that results in arbitrarily preferential treatment, even if only perceived to be so, is not prohibited but is not recommended: '[i]nternational civil servants *should* avoid assisting third parties in their dealings with their organization where this might lead to actual or perceived preferential treatment'.[331] This flexible interpretation of the concepts of impartiality and autonomy is particularly important in the dynamics of procurement, because apart from codified preference percentages (when they exist), it allows individual officials and in general evaluation committees to consider the interests of nation states, on a *de facto* basis and through informal channels, when awarding the contract.

This interpretation, however, does not extend to a situation where the goal of the official's conduct is no longer that of the organization, but is exclusively individual and in potential conflict with that of the organization. Standards, internal regulations and procurement manuals all contain rules that, in greater or lesser detail, limit the acceptance of honours, decorations, gifts, remuneration, favours or benefits from either governments or private subjects, as they are liable to compromise autonomy and impartiality. Solutions range from a policy of zero tolerance to compromise solutions.[332] For example, the UNDP procurement rules establish

---

[330] In International Civil Service Commission, *Standards of Conduct for the International Civil Service*, para. 11 [ref. AP&R].

[331] Emphasis added. *Ibid.*, para. 24.

[332] On this point, the JIU compared the rules and regulations of twenty-five organizations within the UN system, identifying those that have a zero tolerance policy (among others, the United Nations, UNDP, UNICEF, UNIDO, UNOPS, UNHCR, FAO, World Intellectual Property Organization (WIPO) and IMO) and others that instead permit gifts of nominal value (among others, WFP, UNESCO, UNFPA, UNRWA, IAEA, ICAO, ILO, International Telecommunications Union (ITU), Universal Postal Union (UPU) and WHO), JIU, *Procurement Reforms in the United Nations System* [ref. REP]. The survey performed by the JIU is nevertheless based on the different ways organizations interpreted the questionnaire submitted by the JIU. For example, the United

a prohibition without exceptions.[333] And outside the UN system, the Procurement Manual of NATO provides: '[t]he Procurement Service of NATO's International Staff maintains a policy of zero tolerance in respect of receiving any favour, gift or hospitality from any individual or organization currently having or seeking to establish a commercial relationship with NATO's International Staff'.[334] The regulation applicable to European officials adopts a compromise solution that permits the acceptance of honours, recognitions, favours and gifts only after approval by the competent authority.[335] The UN Staff Rules have set up a similar arrangement, providing a centralized system of prior approval by the Secretary-General. Officials shall not accept any honours, favours, gifts or remuneration from government bodies, while they can accept them from non-governmental bodies only after approval by the Secretary-General.[336] Nevertheless, even within this solution there are numerous variations that leave more or less room for the discretion of the Secretary-General and the official. The UN Procurement Manual notes that the Secretary-General may give his approval in exceptional cases, taking the organization's interest into account. Also, officials may occasionally accept gifts of nominal value without prior approval, notifying it to their immediate supervisor.[337] Thus, there is no general prohibition, but rather a prohibition with possible exceptions that can be permitted at the discretion of the Secretary-General or the official himself. This arrangement is shared by many organizations (such as the FAO, for

Nations declares that it has a zero-tolerance policy. In reality, although officials are subject to a general prohibition on accepting gifts, favours, etc., significant exceptions are permitted. This is unlike UNDP, which also states that it has a zero-tolerance policy and actually does not allow exceptions.

[333] UNDP, *Programme and Operations Policies and Procedures. Procurement*, sec. 'Procurement Ethics, Fraud and Corrupted Practices' [ref. AP&R].

[334] NATO, *NSPO Procurement Regulations*, para. 3.6.3 [ref. AP&R]. There are no exceptions to the prohibition: '[i]t is inconsistent that a Procurement staff member involved in any aspect of procurement accepts any gift from an outside source regardless of the value and regardless of whether the outside source is or not soliciting business with NATO. All staff members involved in procurement shall decline offers of gifts, including drinks, meals, tickets, hospitality, transportation, or any other form of benefits, even if it is in association with an official working visit', *ibid*.

[335] European Union, Regulation No. 31 (EEC), 11 (EAEC), Art. 11 [ref. N&RL-EU].

[336] United Nations, *Staff Rules and Staff Regulations of the United Nations*, Regulation 1.2(l) [ref. AP&R]. Similarly, for the other organizations see International Civil Service Commission, *Standards of Conduct for the International Civil Service*, para. 50 [ref. AP&R].

[337] United Nations, *Staff Rules and Staff Regulations of the United Nations*, Rule 1.2(m) [ref. AP&R].

example), but contrary to the UN, some of them set a figure for 'nominal value'. Thus, in the case of UN agencies, the various officials may set the threshold at different and sometimes arbitrary levels.[338]

Due to the decentralization of procurement activity, with field offices located in countries with very different economic situations, along with lack of supervision at the central level,[339] in practice officials responsible for procurement can give an elastic interpretation to these requirements. In organizations that, on the contrary, establish the 'nominal value' in advance, discretion is limited, but sometimes the threshold is so high that it neutralizes the prohibition.[340]

Conflict of interests is the other situation where the goals of the organization are not in alignment with the objectives of the procurement official. On one hand, the Standards of Conduct of the International Civil Service define this as a circumstance in which international civil servants, directly or indirectly, may benefit improperly, or allow a third party to benefit improperly, from their association with their organization.[341] This is the definition generally used in internal regulations and in the procurement manuals of international organizations within the UN system, but similar wording is also used by organizations that are not part of the UN system. On the other hand, however, the conflict of interest is not simply prohibited. In this regard, the Standards offer a general indication of conduct to authorities responsible for managing the conflict: 'such questions [i.e. questions entailing a conflict of interest] can be very sensitive and need to be *treated with care*'.[342]

In addition, some organizations supplement these rules with duties of communication for the party experiencing a conflict of interest. UNOPS, UNRWA, UNFPA, FAO and ILO all have rules which state that officials 'should' report their conflict of interest as soon as it emerges. Thus, it is a voluntary declaration. Nevertheless, other organizations (including the United Nations, UNIDO and WHO) have gone further, making it

---

[338] UN Secretary-General, *Status, Basic Rights and Duties of United Nations Staff Members*, Commentary to Rule 101.2(j) [ref. AP&R].

[339] See Chapter 7.

[340] JIU, *Accountability Frameworks in the United Nations System*, para. 68. The minimum threshold values vary greatly from organization to organization: from 300 Swiss francs for the UPU (with no limits in the number of gifts) to €50 for the IAEA, to $20 for UNHCR, in JIU, *Procurement Reforms in the United Nations System*, para. 173 [all documents in ref. REP].

[341] International Civil Service Commission, *Standards of Conduct of the International Civil Service*, para. 23 [ref. AP&R].

[342] Emphasis added. *Ibid.*

mandatory for officials to provide an annual declaration of no conflict of interest or a declaration for every significant contractual activity.[343] In general, a precautionary approach to conflicts of interest is taken that also covers potential situations of apparent conflict,[344] but in some organizations the consequences of the conflict of interest are not specified and the decision to report the conflict is left to the person who is in conflict and may have an opposite interest in not reporting it.

Thus, the obligations to report cases of corruption and conflicts of interest fall in part (for the conflict of interest) on the parties involved and in part on third parties who are aware of the conflict. Since there are often no sufficient guarantees of compliance for those who are directly involved in the situation, the effectiveness of the rules depends largely on third parties and, if these are officials within the same organization, on the protection guaranteed to them against possible internal retaliation – i.e. whistle-blower policies. Many organizations in the UN system (including the United Nations, UNDP, WFP, UNESCO, UNFPA, UNICEF and UNIDO)[345] have started developing policies along these lines, in addition to the rules of conduct and regulations on ethics and preventing fraud. Still in 2010, however, the JIU reported that '[a]t the specialized agencies and IAEA, whistleblower protection policies are largely absent, or only just being developed'.[346]

Furthermore, empirical investigations by control bodies have revealed poor implementation of these policies: while most managing executives state that the number of reports received is an indicator that the protection mechanisms are functioning well, responses from lower level

---

[343] JIU, *Procurement Reforms in the United Nations System*, para. 166 [ref. REP].

[344] The potential that is supposed to be inherent in the definition of conflict of interest is not so self-evident. In legal and economic literature and in international regulatory provisions, a conflict of interest in the public sector is defined as a group of circumstances that creates a risk or increases an already existing risk that primary public interests could be compromised by the pursuit of secondary private interests, see among others, OECD, *Annex to the Recommendation of the Council on Guidelines for Managing Conflict of Interest in the Public Service* [ref. AP&R]; *id.*, *Managing Conflict of Interest in the Public Service* [ref. AP&R]. The distinctive element is the risk, or in other words the potential that a particular set of circumstances could result in disruption of guaranteed interests. The conflict is thus different from the corruption, which is the event in which the risk becomes manifest, and is also different from any action actually taken that would constitute an offence.

[345] On the other hand, FAO, UNESCO, WHO, IAEA, ICAO, IMO, ITU, WIPO and World Meteorological Organization (WMO) do not have policies for the protection of those who report misconduct.

[346] JIU, *Ethics in the United Nations*, para. 68 [ref. REP].

officials shed light on a different situation. Many officials are not aware of the existence of these policies, although they are formally in effect, and most important, they are still reluctant to file reports due to the lack of confidentiality of reports and the risk of internal retaliation from which whistle-blowers are not sufficiently protected. In particular, there have been cases within organizations in the UN system where individuals who have reported misconduct have been *de facto* sanctioned with dismissal, failure to renew their contract or lack of promotion. The United Nations Administrative Tribunal, which hears the relevant disputes, has awarded compensation for damages, but in no case has an official been reinstated to his position.[347] On one hand, these episodes have significantly discouraged whistle-blowing and on the other they have also weakened any incentives to follow rules of conduct. The first aspect has been highlighted by the JIU, which has stated: 'these high profile cases are well known by the staff members and seen to be serving as a bad example and implicit warning of what will happen if a staff member does report misconduct'.[348]

Thus, as a whole, the rules of conduct for international officials that are relevant for purposes of procurement are characterized, first of all, by an integration of ethics principles with needs of a political and administrative nature: autonomy and impartiality become a function of the interest of the organization and the states, in fact permitting preferential evaluations, provided they are instrumental to this interest and are not arbitrary.

Secondly, they show a lack of imperativeness and leeway for discretion given not only to the official's supervisors, but also to the official. The decision on whether to accept gifts and favours is often not completely prohibited but rather depends on the approval of a higher administrative authority or, if the value is nominal, is deferred to the official himself; the conflict of interest is to be 'managed with caution' and does not necessarily involve the official's abstention or disciplinary measures.

Finally, there is a significant contrast between declared objectives to provide incentives to comply with and implement the rules of conduct on one side, and the ineffectiveness of some of the mechanisms proposed to ensure the achievement of these objectives, on the other. Although

---

[347] JIU, *Accountability Frameworks in the United Nations System*, para. 22–23 [ref. REP].
[348] *Ibid.*, para. 70.

whistle-blower policies are formally in effect in most organizations, they do not guarantee sufficient protection from retaliation to the persons within those organizations who are responsible for reporting.

As for indirect procurement, the rules of organizations such as the WB, the ADB and the AfDB impose over the borrowing states high standards of ethics and set up mechanisms to ensure observance of such standards by the states. States borrowing from the WB, for example, are subject to the Anti-Corruption Guidelines and to the Procurement Regulations which have an Annex entirely devoted to fraud and corruption. The Procurement Regulations, first of all, provide clear definitions of what is meant by corrupt practice, fraudulent practice, collusive practice, coercive practice, obstructive practice and conflict of interest, and prohibit the national contracting authorities to enter in any of these situations. Then, they build an articulated mechanism through which the bank controls the observance of its ethics rules and sanctions their violation. Indeed, the bank controls the procurement undertaken by the state as it reviews it and eventually approves the procurement award.

Furthermore, the bank has several tools to ensure that the procedure undertaken by the national contracting authority is in line with the standards and objectives set by the bank. First, it has powers over the final award, such as to reject a proposal for award if it determines that the firm, as well as its personnel, agents, sub-consultants, sub-contractors, service providers, suppliers and/or employees, has, either directly or indirectly, engaged in corrupt, fraudulent, collusive, coercive or obstructive practices in taking part in the procurement procedure.[349] Second, it can activate the legal remedies set out in the relevant Legal Agreement signed jointly by the bank and the borrowing states. Third, and in addition to the previous measures, the bank may take other appropriate actions, including declaring misprocurement.[350]

The array of tools that can be activated by the bank is, thus, particularly effective as it goes beyond the options explicitly provided by the rules, and is open to be defined at the discretion of the bank and according to what the bank deem more appropriate and effective. Other international

---

[349] WB, *The World Bank Procurement Regulations for IPF Borrowers*, Annex IV, para. 2.2(b) [ref. AP&R].
[350] *Ibid.*, Annex IV, para. 2.2(c).

financial institutions replicate this model of control, although in less detail.

4.6 Conclusions

The analysis has shown that the procurement of international organizations follows a clear procedural path, which is designed along the same lines as the procedures for national public procurement. Proceduralization must be read as the result of a historic process that, in the case of direct procurement, began with non-proceduralized processes for choosing contractors equivalent to those of private enterprises and, in the case of indirect procurement, with procurement requirements included in the individual loan agreements.

Just as with domestic public procurement, the various phases of the procedure are, at least formally, guided by principles of efficiency, competition, transparency and integrity. However, despite a similar procedural scheme and an analogous set of principles, the rules of the organizations result in a significantly different picture of rights to which private subjects are entitled. Furthermore, the analysis of applied practice reveals significant discrepancies between regulatory provisions and implementation.

Competition appears to be one of the principles guiding international organizations' procurement, but not the primary one. Especially in direct procurement, and to a lesser extent in indirect procurement, it encounters limitations taking the shape of restricted procedures, national preferences, waivers of competition, purely regulatory procedural time frames, splitting of awards to avoid controls and extensions of existing contracts to avoid competitive procedures. At the same time, principles instrumental to competition, such as transparency in the form of publicness of the rules, publicity of the decisions, reason giving and access to documents, are developed to the extent required by this specific order of priority. Thus, although with a significant difference between direct and indirect procurement, the spectrum and the quality of rights that private subjects enjoy vis-à-vis international organizations are somewhat diminished compared to those ensured at the national level and vis-à-vis national administrations.

As will be discussed more in depth in Chapter 8, this order of priority is linked to the specific institutional context within which procurement is carried out. The EU public procurement directives and the GPA clearly set competition as the principle guiding domestic public procurement: the institutional objective of both the European Union and the WTO is primarily, even if not solely, the integration of markets and the free circulation of goods and persons. International organizations have rather different institutional objectives, such as humanitarian aid, development and world peace, to mention but a few, but also their own institutional interest, such as economy of administrative action. Furthermore, and above all, the derivative nature of the organizations binds them to the financing states and their agenda for procurement.

Procurement Contracts and Limits to the Contractual Freedom of Private Parties and States

5.1   Introduction

The last step in the vendor selection phase, both in direct and indirect procurement, is the conclusion of a contractual arrangement. However, while in direct procurement the contractual relation is between the international organization and the private party,[1] in indirect procurement it is between the national administration and the private party. Thus, the two situations pose different problems. The direct or indirect presence of an international organization in the contractual relationship as a contracting party or financier creates a common problem: to what extent can an international organization limit the freedom of contract of another subject, be it a private party or a state?[2] And what are these limits? The following analysis provides an answer to these questions and inquires whether and to what extent the public international interests of international organizations shape not only the vendor selection phase – as shown in the previous chapters – but also the formation and execution of the contract.

To this end, contracts resulting from direct and indirect procurement are analyzed separately. In direct procurement contracts, the relevant contractual balance is that between the international organization and private parties. Its main features can be deduced from a whole set of contractual clauses that are common to the majority of these contracts and relate to all the most salient aspects of the contractual relationship. In indirect procurement, the contractual balance between the national administration and the private parties is shaped – at least to a certain

---

[1] In some cases it can also be another public entity.

[2] Conversely, most contributions to the theory of global administrative law and a portion of this work too have addressed the global limits to national *administrative* activity. See, *inter alia* Cassese, 'Global Standards for National Administrative Procedure'; Kingsbury, 'Global Administrative Law: Implications for National Courts'.

extent – by the international organization. In fact, some provisions of organizations' guidelines (or other sources) impose restrictions on the contractual freedom of national administrations and limit their contractual relationships with private parties. The structure of this chapter mirrors this twofold viewpoint on the issue of procurement contracts as it is divided into two parts, devoted respectively to direct and indirect procurement contracts.

5.2   Contracts and Limits to the Contractual Freedom of Private Parties in Direct Procurement

By way of premise, it should be noted that not all types of contract that international organizations conclude are preceded by a proceduralized phase of vendor selection that involves some degree of publicity. There are cases where, due to the subject matter of the contract, the vendor selection process does not involve particular procedures and need not meet publicity requirements. For instance, contracts for the purchase, sale and management of real estate are of this type, as well as contracts of financial institutions which are strictly related to their institutional mission, such as loan, mortgage or guarantee contracts.

The objective here is not to examine the entire range of contracts that international organizations may conclude,[3] or to analyze the entire spectrum of features common to one type of contract. Rather, the goal is to selectively assess the clauses that recur in contracts concluded following procurement procedures, keeping certain basic questions in mind: is the relationship between the international organization and the private party shaped in terms of rights and duties evenly distributed between the two parties? Or, on the contrary, does the administration dominate   the   contractual   relationship,   unilaterally   imposing

---

[3] Studies and research by international law scholars during the 1960s and 1970s offer a general analysis of the contracts of organizations. See: Salmon, 'Les contrats de la Banque internationale'; Groshens, 'Les Marchés passés par les organisations internationales'; Monaco, 'Osservazioni sui contratti conclusi da enti internazionali'; Valticos, 'Les contrats conclus par les organisations internationales avec des personnes privées. Rapport provisoire'; id., 'Les contrats conclus par les organisations internationales avec des personnes privées. Rapport définitif'. For more recent works on the issue, also see: Colin and Sinkondo, 'Les relations contractuelles des organisations internationales'; van Hecke, 'Contracts between International Organizations and Private Law Persons'; Reinisch, 'Contracts between International Organizations and Private Law Persons'; Audit, 'Les marchés de travaux, de fournitures et de services passés par les organisations internationales'. On the specific issue of applicable law, see Chapter 6.

burdensome conditions on the private party, thus using the contract not as a fully consensual instrument but as a *de facto* administrative decision? Answers to these questions are important in order to understand whether and to what extent the presence of a public party to the contract not only shapes the pre-contractual relationship, i.e. the process of vendor selection, but also intrudes into the contractual phase and affects the formation and execution of the contract itself.

In domestic legal systems, legislators, courts and legal scholars have provided answers to these questions by adopting a variety of different approaches. The predominance of public law also in the contractual relationship to which the public administration is a party has been widely recognized in some legal systems. These contracts are usually subject to special public law rules, and disputes arising from them fall under the jurisdiction of administrative courts. In others countries, contracts concluded by public administrations have been interpreted mainly as private law contracts, which, however, may include single and exceptional provisions necessary to ensure the performance of the public function. Paradigmatic of these two approaches are, on the one hand, the *contrats administratifs* developed by the French administrative law tradition, and on the other hand, public contracts as regulated in the English and German legal systems. Analysis of the main features associated with each of these approaches helps to identify the elements within the contracts of international organizations that are relevant to the question of the balance between the contracting parties.

The French concept of *contrats administratif* encompasses all the contracts concluded between a public entity and a private party that are expressly assigned by statutory provisions to the jurisdiction of administrative courts, or else in which the subject matter involves the performance of a public service, or finally, in which the relationship is regulated by some *clauses exorbitantes*. Clauses are *exorbitantes* when they invest the parties with rights and obligations not usually assumed by private individuals or firms in their contracts;[4] or when they are an expression of

---

[4] The definition is taken from Cappelletti (ed.), *International Encyclopedia of Comparative Law*, Vol. VII, ch. 4, p. 28. Subject matter and extraordinary clauses are moreover alternatives to each other, although they are not incompatible. On the one hand, the presence of just one of these two criteria suffices to classify a contract as administrative. On the other hand, relying on a private party to provide a public service is in itself an 'exorbitant' circumstance in that it goes beyond any performance that could form the subject matter of a contract between private parties. The criteria of subject matter and extraordinary clauses do not apply to contracts between public parties for which the administrative nature is presumed. In general, on *contrats administratifs* see De

the prerogatives characteristic of public powers; or when their content goes beyond a private party's freedom of contract; or, generally, when as a whole they create a system that diverges from that created by a private law contract. For instance, during contract formation, the general and special terms and conditions of contract, the so-called *cahiers des changes*, which the administration sets out unilaterally and that are not negotiable by the private party, are a means of defining contractual provisions that generate disparity between the parties. During contract execution, the powers to manage and control, to unilaterally change the contractual contents, to revoke or rescind for reasons related to exercising the public function and to impose penalties in the case of breach are some of the clauses that have been considered an expression of the administration's prerogatives and justified by the contract's function of meeting public needs. The qualification of a contract as a *contrat administratif* implies that its execution is governed by special public law rules and the disputes arising from it are subject to the jurisdiction of administrative courts.

In the German system, *Verwaltungsverträge* (administrative contracts) are identified by the law and are intended to establish, modify or extinguish a public law relationship.[5] A relationship of this type is created whenever certain legislatively established conditions are cumulatively met: the party to the relationship is a public authority; the subject of the contract is engaging in an administrative activity; and the phase that precedes the contract and is preparatory to it is an administrative procedure. When these requirements are met, the contract is regulated by the law on administrative procedure, i.e. the Administrative Procedure Act

---

Laubadere, *Traité théorique et pratique des contrats administratifs*; Vedel, *Droit administratif*; De Laubadere, Moderne and Delvolvé, *Traité des contrats administratifs*; Drago, 'Le contrat administratif aujourd'hui'; Sinkondo, 'La notion de contrat administratif'; Flogaïtis, *Les contrats administratifs*; Rivero and Waline, *Droit administratif*; Waline, *Droit administratif*; Richer, *Droit des contrats administratifs*.

5   On *öffentlicher Verträge*, see Mayer, 'Zur Lehre vom öffentlich-rechtlichen Vertrage'; Achterberg, 'Der öffentlich-rechtliche Vertrag'; Correll, 'Problembereiche und Möglichkeiten des öffentlich-rechtlichen Vertrags'; Fluck, 'Grundprobleme des öffentlich-rechtlichen Vertragsrechts'; Henke, 'Allgemeine Fragen des öffentlichen Vertragsrechts'; Maurer, 'Der Verwaltungsvertrag'; Püttner, 'Wieder den öffentlich-rechtlichen Vertrag zwischen Staat und Bürger'; Scherzberg, 'Grundfragen des verwaltungsrechtlichen Vertrages'; Stelkens, Bonk and Sachs, *Verwaltungsverfahrensgesetz – Kommentar*; Masucci, *Trasformazione dell'amministrazione e moduli convenzionali*, p. 131 *et seq.*; Erichsen and Martens, 'Il contratto di diritto amministrativo', p. 63 *et seq.*

(*Verwaltungsverfahrensgesetz*)[6] and for all the aspects not covered by this law by the civil code; the administrative courts have jurisdiction over any disputes that may arise.

This hybrid regulation was conceived to prevent the administration from using the contractual tool to force the private party to make an unanticipated and disproportionate sacrifice. According to the Administrative Procedure Act, in a public law contract '[t]he consideration must be in proportion to the overall circumstances and be materially connected with the contractual performance of the authority'.[7] Performance and consideration are linked by equality considerations. Thus, if the original circumstances that determined the content of the contract have changed 'so substantially that one party to the agreement cannot reasonably be expected to adhere to the original provisions of the agreement',[8] both the parties may demand a change in the content of the contract or terminate it. However, pursuant to the established case law, the administration may amend the terms of the contract only when public interest requires it. Thus, this is not in the administration's discretion and is applicable only under specific conditions. The administration may also terminate the contract 'to avoid or eliminate grave harm to the common good'[9] (and only in these cases), but the reasons for the termination must be stated and termination must be accompanied by indemnification of the private party. Overall, this appears to be a legal regime[10] that shows primarily civil law features, with the exception of the jurisdiction of administrative courts and certain changes to normal contractual practice, which, however, are aimed at balancing the administration's public-law-type needs with the rights of the private contractor.

The assimilation of contracts concluded by a public body to private law contracts is even more evident in the English system. Here, public contracts are those entered into by a public body and are not subject to a particular legal system, except for the statutory laws that indicate their objectives and purposes and, at least until Brexit, for the EU public procurement directives and the internal statutory sources regulating the vendor selection procedures.[11] The problem of reconciling the

---

[6] Verwaltungsverfahrensgesetz, 25 May 1976 [ref. N&RL-Germany].   [7] *Ibid.*, para. 56.
[8] *Ibid.*, para. 60.   [9] *Ibid.*
[10] For the purposes of this work, it was not considered useful to go into particular detail on the regime of contract invalidity, which, however, has certain peculiarities compared to private law contracts.
[11] Regarding the English experience, see *inter alia* D'Alberti, *I 'public contracts' nell'esperienza britannica*; Turpin, *Government Procurement and Contracts*; Emery, *Administrative*

performance of a public function with obligations typical of a private law contract has been closely scrutinized in case law, leading to application of the *ultra vires* doctrine in the contractual sphere as well. According to this, administrations must only perform the duties assigned by the law. On the one hand they may not use contracts to engage in activities that go beyond their legally assigned functions, and on the other, contracts may not require the assumption by the public body of obligations that would compromise its institutional purposes set out by the law. Thus, the *ultra vires* doctrine functions at the same time both as a limit to the administrative activity and as a guarantee that it will be performed.

This brief overview of national approaches to administrative contracts makes it possible to select and assess the elements in the contract that help to determine whether and to what extent the contracts of international organizations show deviations from private law contracts due to the public and international nature of the contracting party, or, to put it differently, whether and to what extent these contracts are *administrativized*. In the contract formation phase, one of the useful indicators for this assessment is whether or not the contractual conditions are set unilaterally. During contractual performance, it will be important to check whether the clauses are 'exorbitant' in the French meaning or, on the contrary, similar to those normally set by private individuals or firms in their mutual contracts (exorbitant clauses will include provisions on the power to make unilateral changes, uneven conditions for contract termination, and the related duties of justification and indemnification); the applicable law, be it public or private law; and the submission of disputes to an administrative court or an ordinary court. The following analysis will focus on several of these elements, in particular on the unilateral setting of contractual provisions and on the most common contractual clauses, while the question of applicable law and the competent contract dispute settlement bodies will be addressed in subsequent chapters.

5.2.1 Legal Personality and the Capacity to Enter into a Contract

The assumption implied in analyzing the contracts of international organizations is that international organizations have the capacity to

Law: *Legal Challenges to Official Action*, p. 241 *et seq.*; Leyland and Woods, *Administrative Law*; Craig, *Administrative Law*; Davies, *The Public Law of Government Contracts*; Trybus, 'An Overview of the United Kingdom Public Procurement Review and Remedies System'; Trybus and Craig, 'Public Contracts'.

enter into contracts. However, far from being straightforward, this assumption has been the object of analysis and codification since the foundation of these organizations.

The power of international organizations to enter into contracts is acknowledged in several legal texts – both international treaties and internal statutory provisions – and is widely recognized in the relevant case law and literature. This power is a specific manifestation of the broader concept of *domestic* legal personality, i.e. the right to exercise all those legal powers that allow an international organization to engage in its institutional activity and to have rights and duties within the territory where this activity actually takes place. This does not mean that organizations become a legal person in the sense of national law, but that '[i]t is merely recognized on the international plane that they can function as a national legal person insofar as required for the effective fulfilment of their purposes'.[12]

Conversely, the concept of *international* legal personality has been more controversial[13] and refers to the organization's capacity to have independent rights and obligations in the international area, and thus vis-à-vis states and other international bodies. For our purposes, what is important is the domestic legal personality of organizations, and in particular the nature of this personality and how its content is formulated, by whom it is attributed and who recognizes it.

Domestic legal personality may be original or derivative, depending on the institutional relationships between the organizations that have it. For example, according to Art. 104 of the UN Charter, the United Nations

---

[12] Muller, *International Organizations and Their Host States*, p. 92.

[13] Recognition of international legal personality has been the subject of debate among international law scholars. On the basis of legal personality see Tunkin, 'The Legal Nature of the United Nations', p. 20 *et seq.*; Seyersted, 'Objective International Personality of Intergovernmental Organizations'; ICJ, 'Reparation for injuries suffered in the service of the United Nations. Advisory Opinion' (1949) *ICJ Recueil des arrêts, avis consultatifs et ordonnances* 178. On legal personality in general, see Mosler, 'Réflexions sur la personnalité juridique en droit international public'; Rama-Montaldo, 'International Legal Personality and Implied Powers of International Organizations'; Barberis, 'Nouvelles questions concernant la personnalité juridique internationale'; Dominicé, 'La personnalité juridique dans le système du droit des gens'; Conforti, *Scritti di diritto internazionale*, p. 3 *et seq.* On the domestic legal personality of international organizations in general, see Muller, *International Organizations and Their Host States*, p. 72 *et seq.*; Schermers and Blokker, *International Institutional Law*, p. 987 *et seq.*; Amerasinghe, *Principles of the Institutional Law*, p. 77 *et seq.*; and for individual organizations see Kasme, *La capacité l'ONU de conclure des traités*; Manin, 'La Convention de Vienne sur les accords entre Etats'; Puissochet, 'L'affirmation de la personnalité internationale des Communautées Européennes', p. 437 *et seq.*

'enjoy[s] in the territory of each of its Members such legal capacity as may be necessary for the exercise of its functions and the fulfilment of its purposes'.[14] This capacity can be exercised both through its officials and through subsidiary bodies or agencies, such as UNICEF, UNRWA or others. Thus, by virtue of the delegation of functions entrusted to them and within the limits of that delegation, these bodies or agencies have a *derivative* legal capacity in the domestic legal systems in which they operate, and they can enter into contracts in their own name.[15] Conversely, the institutions of the European Union have no derivative legal personality among themselves and legal personality is attributed to the European Union as a whole pursuant to Art. 47 Treaty on the European Union (TUE).[16]

Domestic legal personality is in many cases affirmed generally in the treaties founding organizations, in their statutes or internal regulations, or in bilateral treaties between the organization and the individual state. In addition, through national regulatory and administrative acts states themselves may recognize the organization's personality. In the first case, there is an actual attribution of personality, while in the second one there is a unilateral recognition of it.

The attribution of personality by the treaties establishing organizations or in bilateral agreements between the organization and the state has at least three different formulations: a functional formulation that links personality to the exercise of a function, an analytical-descriptive formulation that indicates the individual capacities of the organization, and a formulation that consists of making reference to an external legal source. An example of a functional formulation can be found in the previously mentioned Art. 104 of the UN Charter: '[t]he Organization shall enjoy in the territory of each of its Members such legal capacity as may be necessary *for the exercise of its functions and the fulfilment of its purposes'*.[17] Similar formulations are also found in the founding treaties of organizations such as the FAO, WIPO and WHO.[18] At the same time, reference to function also serves as an element that justifies and places

---

[14] Charter of the United Nations, Art. 104 [ref. A&C].

[15] United Nations, 'Law Applicable to Contracts Concluded by the United Nations with Private Parties', p. 159 *et seq.* [ref. GT&CC].

[16] With the exception of the ECB, which as an independent body has a separate legal personality pursuant to Art. 282, para. 3 Treaty on the Functioning of the European Union (TFUE), and the European Investment Bank (EIB), pursuant to Art. 308 TFEU.

[17] Emphasis added. Charter of the United Nations, Art. 104 [ref. A&C].

[18] *Constitution of the Food and Agriculture Organization*, Art. XVI, para. 1 [ref. A&C]: '[t]he Organization shall have the capacity of a legal person to perform any legal act appropriate

a limit on the exercise of this capacity. In this second respect, it also operates as a mechanism that should ensure the proportionality of international organizations' actions and decisions: the functional attribution of personality gives the organization standing to exercise the powers strictly necessary to guarantee that its institutional purposes will be achieved.

An analytical-descriptive formula, which is rare, is found, for example, in the agreement establishing the IMF:

> [t]he Fund shall possess full juridical personality, and in particular, the capacity: (i) to contract; (ii) to acquire and dispose of immovable and movable property; and (iii) to institute legal proceedings.[19]

Similar formulations can also be found in the TFUE[20] and in the agreement establishing the ESA.[21]

Of the third type are those formulations consisting of a reference to treaty law sources that are indirectly at the origin of the organization. For instance, Art. XII of UNESCO's Constitution regarding the organization's legal status states:

> [t]he provisions of Articles 104 and 105 of the Charter of the United Nations Organization concerning the legal status of that Organization, its privileges and immunities, shall apply in the same way to this Organization.[22]

Finally, there are also cases of founding treaties that do not contain specific provisions on personality. In such cases, legal personality has been deduced by way of interpretation.

---

to its purpose which is not beyond the powers granted to it by this Constitution'. *Convention Establishing the World Intellectual Property Organization*, Art. 12, para. 1 [ref. T&C]; '[t]he Organization shall enjoy on the territory of each Member State, in conformity with the laws of that State, such legal capacity as may be necessary for the fulfilment of the Organization's objectives and for the exercise of its functions'. *Constitution of the World Health Organization*, Art. 66 [ref. A&C]: '[t]he Organization shall enjoy in the territory of each Member such legal capacity as may be necessary for the fulfilment of its objective and for the exercise of its functions'.

[19] *Articles of Agreement of the International Monetary Fund*, Art. IX, sec. 2 [ref. A&C].

[20] TFUE, Art. 335 [ref. T&C]. Article 335 of the TFEU, transposing the old article from the Treaty establishing the European Community, states: '[i]n each of the Member States, the Union shall enjoy the most extensive legal capacity accorded to legal persons under their laws; it may, in particular, acquire or dispose of movable and immovable property and may be a party to legal proceedings', TFUE, Art. 335 [ref. T&C]. *Convention for the Establishment of a European Space Agency*, Annex I, Privileges and Immunities, Art. 1: '[t]he Agency shall have legal personality. It shall in particular have the capacity to contract, to acquire and dispose of movable and immovable property, and to be a party to legal proceedings', [ref. T&C].

[21] TFEU, Art. 335 (former Art. 281 TEC) [ref. T&C].

[22] *Constitution of the United Nations Educational, Scientific and Cultural Organization*, Art. XII [ref. A&C].

However, for the attribution of legal personality to be effective within national legal systems, states must recognize the effectiveness of the treaty law sources that provide for them. While this occurs automatically in certain national legal systems due to the state's membership of the organization or by virtue of national laws that *a priori* guarantee recognition of the international organizations of which the state is a member, others require the adoption of case-by-case legal provisions that recognize the individual organization. In the United States, the International Organizations Immunities Act requires Congress and the President to recognize an intergovernmental institution of which the United States is a member and to formally designate it as an international organization, attaching to this qualification the national legal capacity of the organization itself.[23] In the United Kingdom, the International Organizations Act 1968, subsequently amended in 2005, provides that, with regard to the organizations of which Great Britain is a member:

> Her Majesty may by Order in Council ... make any one or more of the following provisions in respect of the organization so specified ... (a) confer on the organization the legal capacities of a body corporate.[24]

There is thus a two-step process: a decision to designate as an international organization an organization of which Great Britain is a member and a decision recognizing the national legal personality. Indirect recognition mechanisms, i.e. through a law or an *ad hoc* judicial decision, are also adopted by states to recognize the legal personality of an organization of which they are not a member.[25]

5.2.2 Types of Contracts, Competition and the Contractual Freedom of Private Parties

Upon conclusion of the public procurement procedure, international organizations have two basic contractual instruments through which they define the relationships with private parties: purchase orders and

---

[23] See International Organizations Immunities Act, sec. 2, title 1 [ref. N&RL-USA].
[24] International Organizations Act, para. 48(2) [ref. N&RL-UK].
[25] The decision may be made not only by an administrative authority, but also, in the context of a dispute, by a judge who recognizes personality through interpretation, deducing it from domestic or international laws. For an analysis of individual cases, see Schermers and Blokker, *International Institutional Law*, p. 1013 and Amerasinghe, *Principles of the Institutional Law*, p. 70 *et seq.*

contracts. These are both contracts, but the use of different terminology serves to distinguish negotiated instruments that differ in the value of the performance, in certain characteristics of the public procurement procedure that precedes them, in the contractual content and in the private party's room for negotiation.

Purchase orders are usually used for services below a certain value, following informal contractor selection procedures.[26] Conversely, contracts are generally the result of formal contractor selection procedures and relate to complex services and/or services that require a significant financial outlay by the organization. The UN Procurement Manual, for example, distinguishes various threshold values and connects them to different contractor selection procedures and contractual instruments.[27] Below the lowest threshold, informal procedures are used to select contractors, and either a simple purchase order or a contract can be concluded. Nevertheless, in practice the first alternative is much more common than the second. For goods and services of intermediate threshold values, informal selection procedures may still be used (but, as we have seen, the procedure must commence with a request for a bid) and the contractual instruments may be purchase orders or contracts). Although the two instruments are formally on the same level, in practice there is a tendency to opt for actual contracts as the value of the requested good or service increases. For values that exceed the maximum threshold, the contractor selection procedure must open with an invitation to bid, and the contractual instrument used must be the contract, unless the procurement officer, consulting with the section chief, the director of the procurement division or the chief procurement officer, decides to use a simple purchase order. Likewise, in all cases where a request for proposal procedure must be used because the object of the performance cannot be sufficiently defined *ex ante* and

---

[26] On contractor selection procedures see Chapter 4. The criterion for the value threshold to distinguish between purchase orders and contracts is the one the United Nations formally selected in its Procurement Manual, and it is in common use among the organizations in the UN system. Nevertheless, there are organizations, such as UNHCR and FAO, which, at least in their procurement manuals, adopt a qualitative criterion according to which purchase orders are utilized to procure goods, and contracts are used for the procurement of services. See UNHCR, *UNHCR Manual. Chapter 8: Supply Management*, December 2003, para. 2.5.5; FAO, *FAO Manual. Ch. 5 Property and Services*, sec. 502 *Procurement of Goods, Works and Services*, January 2010, para. 502.1.14 [all documents in ref. AP&R].

[27] United Nations, *Procurement Manual*, rev. 7, 1 July 2013, para. 9.9 (2) [ref. AP&R].

unilaterally by the administration, the form of the contractual instrument must be an actual contract.

In addition to these two basic types, there are a number of variations, the most significant of which are systems contracts, framework contracts and long-term agreements. These are utilized by many UN organizations in cases where the procurement officer, generally in consultation with the requisitioning administrative unit and based on past experience and current project needs, establishes that the same deliverables should be procured on a recurring basis over an extended period of time.[28] The organizations' intent is that this type of contract should facilitate prompt processing of the administrative unit's procurement requirements, minimize the number of repeated solicitations for the same supply and benefit from the unit price advantages created by an economy of scale.[29] Then, within a systems contract, the individual deliverables are provided based on purchase orders whose terms and conditions must be compatible with those of the systems contract.[30]

As for the content of the contracts, general terms and conditions are normally included both in purchase orders and in contracts. Nevertheless, while for purchase orders certain organizations use simplified versions of the terms and conditions rather than standard ones, in contracts, general terms and conditions are usually included in their entirety, with individual aspects subject to negotiation.[31] This circumstance leads administrations to *de facto* unilaterally define the general terms and conditions attached to purchase orders and to be particularly rigid about the possibility of changing them at the private party's request. The lower value of purchase orders, the fungibility of the goods or services involved and thus, ultimately, considerations of administrative efficiency, make administrations less inclined to negotiate changes to the provisions of these contractual instruments. On the contrary, in contracts

[28] On this point see also Chapter 4.

[29] These objectives are set out in United Nations, *Procurement Manual*, para. 13.9 [ref. AP&R].

[30] As in United Nations, *Procurement Manual*, para. 13.9 (8) [ref. AP&R], but other organizations in the UN family also follow a similar scheme. On the other hand, so-called blanket purchase orders are a simplified form of system contract. They are utilized, particularly by the United Nations, for repeated supplies with an overall value that does not exceed a certain threshold and for low-value goods that are not held in stock by organizations, or for services required at short notice, or, more generally, for goods and services with a unit price that tends to be the same throughout the market (*ibid.*, para. 13.4).

[31] This nevertheless varies depending on the international organizations considered. On this point, see later in this chapter.

that are more complex, more valuable, or in which the goods or services can be provided by only one or a few private parties, there is more leeway for negotiation, even though, as we shall see, certain essential clauses are still not negotiable.[32]

Finally, as a result of the value of their subject matter, different contractual forms require final approval from different levels of authority. Thus, the decision to use a purchase order or contract is important in at least two respects. First, it has implications on competition in the procurement procedures and on the relative internal control mechanisms. Second, it affects the freedom of contract guaranteed to the private party.

In the first respect, purchase orders result from procedures that consider the objective of competition to be secondary to that of efficiency. They are issued with no need for particular internal authorizations from hierarchically higher competent authorities. Similar effects can be found in systems contracts, which cover all possible orders of a certain deliverable for a prolonged period and thus eliminate new opportunities for competition among undertakings, at least with regard to that deliverable.

In the second respect, purchase orders have stricter contractual provisions, which are determined by the administration and are difficult to change at the request of the private contractor. These considerations underlie both the broad leeway many procurement manuals ensure in terms of the ability to use purchase orders, and the excessive use of purchase orders. With regard to the latter, there is a widespread practice across organizations and especially in field offices – in the past also criticized by the United Nations General Assembly and recently by the JIU and the OIOS – of fragmenting procurement requests so that individually they do not reach thresholds that would require competitive procedures and the conclusion of contracts rather than simple purchase orders. In this same way, control bodies have frequently detected and criticized the improper use of systems contracts when they are not strictly justified by ongoing supply needs.[33] Practices for selecting the contractual instruments, thus, demonstrate a tendency to prefer contractual forms that involve less burdensome, more streamlined administrative obligations during the pre-contractual phase and more rigid solutions during the contractual phase, to the detriment of more competition

---

[32] Later in this chapter.
[33] See UN General Assembly, *Review of the Efficiency*, A/52/881; JIU, *Procurement Reforms in the United Nations System*, pp. 47–48; OIOS, *Audit of Procurement Management in the Secretariat* [all documents in ref. REP]. Also see Chapters 3 and 4.

among undertakings on the one hand and the private party's freedom of contract on the other.

5.2.3   General Terms and Conditions

All organizations with large procurement volumes have set bodies of clauses that provide the standard regulation of their contractual relationships.[34] These are usually indicated as 'general terms and conditions'. Nevertheless, the methods organizations use to select clauses to apply in a specific contract are subject to varying practices. The organization can decide to insert in the call for tenders the entire body of general terms and conditions, or else formally include all the conditions but with amendments to some of them tailored to the specific subject matter of the contract or purchase order (PO). In addition, it can decide whether or not to make the bid and the award subject to the *ex ante* and express acceptance of these conditions, and thus to leave more or less leeway for negotiation of some of these clauses during the contractual phase.

5.2.3.1   Strict and Flexible Approaches

According to the option selected, the private party's margin for negotiating the content of the contractual clauses varies, being almost completely absent in situations of mandatory and conditional general conditions (inflexible approach), and increasing in cases where the express acceptance of general conditions, even if attached to the call for tenders, is not a prerequisite for the validity of the bid and the award (flexible approach). In the practice of some organizations and for some types of contract, acceptance of the general terms and conditions included in the call for tenders is essential for the bid to be considered and the award to be valid. At the same time, all the conditions are included without any advance selection of some clauses or changes in standard individual clauses. For example, the UNDP *Programme and Operations Policies and Procedures* establishes the following:

---

[34] Not all general terms and conditions bear a date, but since early 2000 their basic aspects have essentially remained unchanged. Reference to all the relevant general terms and conditions can be found at the beginning of this book in the List of instruments, under 'General terms and conditions of contract'. Comments on the general terms and conditions of contract may be found in Seyersted, *Common Law of International Organizations*, p. 76 and pp. 474–479.

[a] substantially responsive offer is one that conforms to ALL the requirements, terms, conditions and specifications indicated in the solicitation
documents, without material deviations, modifications or reservations.[35]

Similarly, UNICEF's *Instructions to Bidders & General Terms and
Conditions for Procurement of Services through ITB/RFQ* provide as
follows:

[t]he contract will be awarded to the Bidder . . . whose Bid is in compliance with all Instructions and General Terms and Conditions contained
in the Bid.[36]

Thus, the strict approach implies that the determination of the content of all the main contractual clauses is deferred to the organization,
and participation in the bidding requires express or *de facto* acceptance of the contractual conditions set out in the call for tenders. This
approach is used mainly in simplified contracts, such as the purchase
orders that organizations use for routine purchases with values below
the indicated thresholds, but also, regardless of the value of the contract, in contracts used by organizations such as the ESA where the
complexity and high sensitiveness of the goods, services and works to
be procured requires the private party to simply accept certain
conditions.

Conversely, in other organizations and/or in other types of contract,
the approach can be more flexible and open. At least two variations of
the flexible approach can be observed. There are cases, where the call for
tenders is accompanied by general contractual clauses to which the
private party may express reservations when presenting the bid.
Failure to simply accept these conditions will not eliminate the private
party from the bidding, but it becomes important when comparing bids:
if the technical and commercial evaluations of two bids are equal, the
bid that does not contain objections to the general conditions will most
likely be given preference. Then, during the contractual phase, if reservations have been expressed, the private party can negotiate a series of
special clauses to be added to the general terms and conditions. Thus,
the contract is composed of two parts containing both general and
special terms and conditions, in a hierarchical relationship of rules

---

[35] The capitalization appears in the original citation. In UNDP, *Programme and Operations Policies and Procedures*, sec. 'Evaluation of Offers', para. 21(d) [ref. AP&R].

[36] UNICEF, *Instructions to Bidders and General Terms and Conditions*, para. 3.9 [ref. GT&CC].

and exceptions by virtue of which the special clauses will prevail in a case of conflict.

An alternative model is that in which the entire contract is attached to the call for tenders right at the outset. This is the result of *ad hoc* unilateral preparation by the organization based on procurement needs: the competent officials write the contract, selecting clauses from a body of terms and conditions prepared by the organization for internal use. This practice is much adopted for instance by the FAO.[37] At the time the bid is presented, a private party who participates in the bidding may express certain reservations about the contract attached to the call for tenders and subsequently negotiate if successful. The difference from the previous flexible approach, thus, lies in the fact that, while in the first case the contract is standardized with exceptions possible at the private party's request, in the second case there are as many different types of contract as the organization deems appropriate, and the private party has a margin to propose changes and deviations to the one chosen by the organization. From the perspective of the private party's leeway for negotiation, the two situations are equivalent, as the distinction is whether the acceptance of the general terms and conditions is conditional or unconditional. The different approaches of preparing one standard contract or using many different contracts reflect, if anything, the greater or lesser variety and total volume of the goods, services or works to be purchased and the greater or lesser development of a certain organization's procurement approaches.

The distinction between strict and flexible approaches affects the contractor selection process, the freedom of contract and the formation of the private party's consent. With regard to the first, in some organizations strictness and flexibility have an effect on the impartiality with which bids are assessed and contractors are selected. In the daily practice of organizations it is indeed not unusual for the contractor to accept the conditions or the contract attached to the solicitation for bids in order to present the most competitive bid and then later, after being awarded the contract, to ask to negotiate certain clauses. In these situations, while the conditional nature of the acceptance (strict approach) does not result in annulment of the entire selection procedure,[38] it is

---

[37] For goods, see FAO, *GTC Procurement Contracts*. For services and works, see FAO, *GTC Works and Services* [both ref. GT&CC]. More precisely, the procurement officers of the FAO may choose from about twenty different contract templates, which act as a basis for preparing the contract to be attached to the offer. These models are in fact adapted according to contingent needs.

[38] The final ranking of the best bids is not changed.

likely to have the effect of shifting the award to another vendor or of re-announcing the call for tenders. On the other hand, in the case of flexible approaches, even if the acceptance of conditions or of the contract is supposed to make the commitment binding, sometimes organizations hold to the decision to award to that contractor and thus agree to negotiate. The reasons for the decision vary: a large gap in the technical and/or commercial score between the first- and second-ranked contractors, urgent needs, trust in the performance capacity of a contractor who has been used before, or also political reasons, such as to give preference to a contractor incorporated in a certain state. Thus, in practice, the obligation created by acceptance may be tempered by considerations of convenience and efficiency of the administrative action, which, however, also have a retroactive effect on the impartiality of the contractor selection process (another vendor may not have been selected because it expressed reservations over the general conditions).

5.2.3.2   Freedom of Contract

The distinction between strict and flexible approaches is relevant as, to a greater or lesser extent, it affects the private party's freedom to contract, especially if compared with normal contractual practices among private subjects.[39] Analyzing the contractual terms and conditions of the International Maritime Satellite Organization (INMARSAT) as an example,[40] Seyersted illustrates the controversial nature of the issue in these terms:

---

[39] Here we are assuming the 'perfect' definition of a contract between private parties as a tool through which both parties satisfy their own interests in a completely free and autonomous way. Thus understood, the contract has in principle a preliminary negotiation phase that permits the interests of both parties to be weighed and balanced and a mutually agreed determination of the contractual provisions used to govern the relationship. On the other hand, the increased economic power of certain undertakings has resulted in the emergence of so-called adhesion contracts, in which one of the two parties sets the contractual conditions while the other party can only accept them, with no possibility of negotiating any possible changes. Such a dynamic raises doubts regarding the real existence of freedom of contract. According to some, it is a formal freedom that refers solely to the decision on whether or not to enter into the contract: 'est à prendre ou à laisser, il n'est pas à discuter', in Hariou, *Principes de droit public*, p. 211. See Galgano, 'Squilibrio contrattuale e mala fede del contraente forte'.

[40] INMARSAT is a mobile satellite telecommunications services provider. Originally an intergovernmental organization, it was privatized in 1999. In 2003 it was acquired by a consortium of banks, and it has been listed on the stock market since 2005.

[s]ome considered these [i.e. the Terms and Conditions for the Utilization by Coast Earth Stations of the INMARSAT Space Segment] as purely contractual terms, which could be modified only by agreement between INMARSAT and each national or private telecommunications entity which INMARSAT authorized to use the INMARSAT telecommunications system. Others considered these as expressing an administrative power of the organization, which may withdraw and/or decide new conditions for the use of the space system.[41]

Indeed, the use of terms and conditions by organizations may lead to acknowledging the difference between these contracts and those among private parties, and to framing the issue of the private party's freedom to contract as a problem of how and to what extent an administrative power in the contract is exercised.

While there is no question that the contractual relationship between an organization and a private party is consensual, as terms and conditions become applicable only if they are accepted by the private party when presenting the bid, it is also true that the private party's freedom of consent is limited and subject to external influence, for general reasons that are also common to contracts of national administrations, and for reasons that are specific to international organizations.[42] Among the general reasons, the position held by the administration in the selection process plays an important role. This can be interpreted as a position of advantage that is intrinsic to the process: it does not arise from the special nature of the public body, but from the very fact that the administration finds itself actively playing the role of an economic operator who can choose from different bids. That is, because it is the administration that selects the private party through a bidding procedure in which various competitors participate, the administration and the private party each have different options that increase or reduce their freedom of choice and impact on their negotiating power. While the fact that the tender procedure places different participants in competition with each other always theoretically gives the organization more alternatives from which to choose (so that, if the exceptions one supplier requests are not deemed acceptable, it can go to another supplier[43]), the private party has only one

---

[41] Seyersted, *Common Law of International Organizations*, p. 76.

[42] In general, due to increasingly frequent situations of heteronomy in determining contractual provisions, the crisis in the principle of contractual autonomy and freedom of contract has been the subject of numerous studies. See, *ex multis,* Atiyah, *Rise and Fall of Freedom of Contract.*

[43] An exception is the situation in which the goods or services are only provided in the market by a single private party.

alternative: to participate, with or without reservations, or not to participate at all, in which case it loses its chance and any possible profit.

Among the specific reasons, there is first of all the conditional nature of strict approaches and their prevalence in various organizations and many contracts, especially those of lower value (whose total value is nevertheless considerable). As we have seen, strict approaches subject the award to the acceptance of the contract terms and conditions in their entirety and, thus, negatively affect the freedom of contract of the private party.

Second, even in flexible approaches, acceptance with reservations is not entirely without consequences, because together with the technical and commercial bid, a request to negotiate the content of the contract is, expressly or tacitly, one of the elements that the administration uses in its overall assessment of the bid. In this sense, it is also one of the factors that guides the private party in deciding whether or not to accept the provisions proposed by the organization. For example, the UN Procurement Manual allows for this possibility when it states that

> Solicitation Documents shall also indicate that reservations to or non-acceptance of any of the terms of the UNGCC may lead to a rejection of, or to higher risk rating of the Vendor's Submission.[44]

Third, both flexible approaches and, to an even greater extent, strict approaches are based on contractual provisions that are prepared first and foremost by the organization – except for the final details regarding performance when the private party's participation, from the technical and commercial standpoints, is required to determine them. In this latter case, leeway for determining the contents of the contract is granted to the private party at a later time and as an exception accorded by the organization based on considerations of internal convenience.

Fourth, in the case of flexible approaches, the administration's openness to negotiation depends on factors ascribable to the private party and the type of performance governed by the contract. While there is no express formally recognized correlation, large undertakings with monopolies in the market and those incorporated in states that provide major funding for the organization are often granted more leeway to negotiate, both because their home states may be willing to intervene informally in negotiations in order to support the undertaking's rights, and because the

---

[44] United Nations, *Procurement Manual*, para. 9.17 (3) [ref. AP&R].

organization has no valid alternatives available on the market. Thus, the private party's freedom of contract and the administration's ability to unilaterally define the contractual provisions become variables dependent upon the economic and political weight of a particular undertaking. This also has consequences in terms of the impartiality of the administrative action, as freedom of contract and the consent of smaller undertakings that provide fungible goods, services or works and whose home countries are non-members or are under-represented within the organization or have less political weight in the organization are much more limited and subject to the unilateral determinations of the administrations, with opposite effects to those the organizations formally state in the regulations governing their procurement processes.

Fifth, both in strict and flexible approaches, the contracts concluded by international organizations always include some clauses that are never or only rarely modified, as they are connected to the special status the organizations enjoy in the international arena and to their exercise of a public function. These include clauses on privileges and immunity from jurisdiction and execution, which result from the relative international treaties, and also clauses on the unilateral rescission and termination of the contract, compensation for damages, indemnification, exemption from national taxation and, more generally, prohibitions connected to the protection of fundamental human rights.[45] As we shall see later in this chapter, any rare modifications of certain aspects of these clauses are due to factors such as the economic weight of the contractual partner, the willingness of its home state to represent its interests during negotiations, the impossibility of finding an alternative on the market, and loyalty to certain specific undertakings due to the need for procurement continuity or to individual interests that are not truly based on administrative efficiency.

Finally, these 'fixed' clauses, in addition to being not subject to negotiation, also usually contain asymmetrical provisions for the two parties to the contract, with the administration's needs prevailing over those of the private party due to the protection of international public interests. In this case, asymmetrical content means both the absence of reciprocity, i.e. the private party has duties that do not apply to the administration, and the presence of reciprocal duties, which, while related to the same

---

[45] Neither the supplier nor any of the entities connected to him may be involved in the production and sale of anti-personnel mines, permit sexual exploitation or violate the fundamental rights of workers.

aspect of contractual regulation, are different in terms of the degrees of onerousness and the effects they produce.

Thus, the terms and conditions that international organizations impose on private parties, using both strict and flexible approaches, significantly limit the private party's freedom of consent and its ability to negotiate contractual provisions. In similar contracts between private parties, such as adhesion contracts, the practice of unilaterally setting the conditions of contract is justified by needs related to industrialization and mass production, for reasons of efficiency and practicality of transactions. At the same time, this is brought to extremes by a globalized, competitive economic system that creates market players capable of creating monopolies[46] and imposing their contractual conditions on an unlimited number of users and consumers.

Only a few of these motivations are valid for international organizations. Expanding functions and growth in the size of organizations have certainly been among the factors that have driven organizations to develop general conditions applicable to all parties who express interest in entering into a contractual relationship with them. But these reasons of efficiency are based on numbers much lower than those that drive large multinationals to do the same thing: suffice it to note the thousands of contracts that giants like Google or Microsoft enter into every day with users of the services and products they offer. Moreover, while a private undertaking has freedom of self-determination and can choose the contractual methods it considers most beneficial in compliance with the law, the international organization's activity is constrained from the start in terms of its assigned function, and is then limited in terms of the principles that govern its activity. Thus, efficiency alone is not enough to explain this common approach among international organizations.

Certain circumstances facilitate this approach. The first is a widespread lack of opposition by member states. Private parties who enter into a contract with an international organization have an interest in being able to negotiate the provisions of the contract, rather than have them imposed with little room for modification. Yet the states that are members of such organizations, including the home states of the contracting undertakings, have in general never opposed this approach.

---

[46] 'Their [i.e. of the general conditions of contract] origin is connected to the transition from a system of more or less free competition to a system of monopolies that suppress the market', in Hart, 'Un caso esemplare: la giurisprudenza sulle condizioni generali di contract', p. 143.

The reasons for this – which as we shall soon see are consistent with condoning 'extraordinary' contractual provisions – will be analyzed in depth in the chapter on the interplay of interests.[47] Suffice it to note here that, on one hand, during the vendor selection phase member states have an interest in seeing that the contract is awarded to an undertaking from their own country, and they safeguard principles such as competition, transparency and publicity (thus protecting the entitlements of the private parties participating in the bidding) only as long as this serves their objectives. On the other hand, once the contract has been awarded as a matter of principle, states no longer have an incentive to induce the organization to negotiate contracts with private parties and grant them particular rights. This would not only create the risk of a loss of efficiency, but it would also not create any particular advantage for the national economy.

In confirmation of this, as already noted, the sole exceptions to states' practice of abstention from influencing the contractual phase are cases where they intervene, at the private party's informal request, to strengthen that party's position during negotiations. However, this is always intervention related to single contracts and in support of certain undertakings, not a systematic intervention aimed at inducing a change in an administration's contractual policies and approaches. There follows an analysis of various fixed or semi-fixed clauses that characterize the contracts of organizations, with an examination of their contents, variations among different organizations, and the principal consequences from the perspective of the relationship between the organizations and private parties.

5.2.4 Privileges and Immunities

The issue of the privileges and immunities of international organizations will be addressed in detail later in the chapter on the accountability mechanisms of procuring entities vis-à-vis private parties. Here, it can be briefly pointed out that nearly all international organizations, with the exception of certain financial institutions and European institutions, add a reference to international treaties in their contracts that guarantee them immunity from jurisdiction and execution of judgment. For example, the United Nations's general terms and conditions provide:

---

[47] Chapter 8.

> [n]othing in or relating to the Contract shall be deemed a waiver, express
> or implied, of any privileges and immunities of the United Nations,
> including its subsidiary organs.[48]

From the perspective of contractual balance between parties, this is an 'exorbitant' clause that has no equivalent in either national procurement contracts or in contracts between private parties, and it should serve the organization's institutional mission: it allows or makes it easier for a public body that does not have territorial sovereignty – the international organization – to engage in activity within the territory.[49] This recognition is the result of a determination by the individual states who are parties to conventions on the privileges and immunities of international organizations, and is thus based on an international agreement that nevertheless has a direct impact on contractual or non-contractual relationships between international organizations and private subjects.[50]

Precisely for this reason, some organizations limit or waive immunity, thereby also avoiding reference in their contracts to conventions that establish it. The objective is to facilitate relationships with private parties by ensuring that one of the essential elements of the contractual relationship, i.e. reciprocal accountability of the parties, is comparable to a business contract between private parties. In the case of EU institutions, there is also the goal of competition: making it possible to invoke immunity would have the effect of limiting competition, and discouraging small and medium-size undertakings from participating in calls for tenders because they would not be financially capable of bearing possible losses arising from failure to enforce a judgment.

Finally, it should be noted that, while the absence of an explicit reference to immunity is rare (as noted, the option is only selected by certain financial organizations and European institutions), reference to conventions on privileges and immunities does not automatically imply that the organization will plead immunity in any case of dispute in order to protect against possible liability. It implies, instead, that the option is available to the organization, and it may use it at its discretion as it deems appropriate and in some cases it can also waive it. This has also the side-effect of generating a high degree of uncertainty for the private party who *ex ante* can only make a vague projection of the consequences of bringing

---

[48] United Nations, *GCC Goods and Services*, para. 18. In agreement: United Nations, *GCC Goods*, para. 17; *id.*, *GCC Services*, para. 17; UNHCR, *GCC Goods*, para. 19; Id., *GCC Services*, para. 19; Id., *GCC Goods and Services*, para. 20 [all documents in ref. GT&CC].

[49] In agreement, Glavinis, *Les litiges relative aux contrats*, p. 123.

[50] As in Duffar, *Contribution à l'étude des privilèges et immunités*, p. 248.

a claim against the organization. Thus, there is a dual anomaly that changes the balance in relationships between organizations and private parties, both with respect to business contracts between private parties and with respect to those between national administrations and private parties: the applicability of a system of immunity that discharges the administration from paying the consequences of a contractual violation and the discretion that the administration gives itself in applying this system.

5.2.5   Termination of Contract

Regulation of the termination of the contractual relationship is where the asymmetry between international organizations and private parties is most evident, both because it appears in clauses that can only rarely be negotiated and modified, and because it gives organizations rights that private parties do not enjoy, with private parties responsible for a number of duties that do not correspond to similar duties for organizations.[51] The general terms and conditions of the organizations that have the highest volumes of procurement (the United Nations, UNDP, UNHCR, UNICEF and FAO) establish five situations in which the contractual relationship may be terminated: termination for cause (available to the international organization and to the private party), termination for convenience (available only to the international organization), termination for non-performance (regulated only with regard to private party performance), termination due to *force majeure* (available to the international organization and to the private party with uneven rights and duties) and termination due to a change in the private party's situation (available only to the international organization).

---

[51] It should be added that, while the general terms and conditions of contracts address situations of unilateral rescission and termination of contract, giving the administration true powers of self-protection, no specific rules are provided, either in procurement manuals or in other relevant regulations, regarding another possible manifestation of the power of self-protection, this time related to the phase prior to conclusion of the contract, i.e. revocation of the call for tenders and subsequent actions for reasons of public interest. In reality, the international administration can either refuse to award the contract based on issues of legality or, for substantive reasons, or, once the award has been made, can revoke the call for tenders and the subsequent actions, but this occurs unofficially, with no particular laws that impose duties to provide justification or other duties aimed at minimizing the possible harm caused to private parties.

While the contractual terms and conditions of certain organizations – the United Nations, UNHR, UNDP – allow either the organization or the private party to terminate the contract for cause, in addition, most organizations provide for and regulate the different hypothesis of the unilateral rescission of contract, activated by the international organization and due to reasons of convenience.

The asymmetry becomes even clearer in clauses related to termination for default by the private party, *force majeure*, or change in conditions. In all the general terms and conditions of UN organizations and other organizations such as NATO (European institutions are an exception), the default provided for and regulated is only that of the private party; *force majeure*, when it jeopardizes the private party's performance or that of the international organization, produces duties on the private party and rights of the international organization; a change in conditions refers exclusively to the private party's legal or financial status to the extent that this may jeopardize fulfilment of its contractual obligations.

5.2.5.1   Unilateral Rescission for Public Convenience and Duties of the Parties

With regard to unilateral rescission by the organization, the concept of 'convenience' of the international organizations is not usually specified or explained in the general terms and conditions. For instance, the UNOPS *General Conditions for Goods* contain no definition and leave determination to the organization:

> UNOPS may, upon notice to the Vendor, terminate this Contract, in whole or in part, at any time for its convenience.[52]

The *General Terms and Conditions Applicable to FAO Procurement Contracts* are even more vague:

> FAO may, in its sole discretion, terminate this contract, in whole or in part, for any reason upon written notice to Contractor without liability other than that set forth herein.[53]

Other organizations, such as the United Nations UNHCR, make a distinction between 'qualified' convenience and simple convenience. The former includes cases connected to the exercise of the international organization's public functions, for example, a change of a single

---

[52] UNOPS, *GC Goods*, para. 19.1 [ref. GT&CC].
[53] FAO, *GTC Procurement Contracts*, para. 22. In agreement, IFAD, *GTC Goods* [both ref. GT&CC].

mandate or mission at the base of the contract or a cut in financing. The latter includes all the rest, i.e. all the circumstances in which the cause for rescission is not linked to the exercise of the public function. The distinction is relevant as it implies different duties on the part of the international organization.

When unilateral rescission is based on reasons related to exercise of the public function, there is no obligation to justify the decision of rescission, nor any obligation regarding the term for notice, which in limited situations may even be the date on which the contract becomes ineffective between the parties. In this regard the United Nations's General Conditions of Contract provide:

> UN may terminate the Contract *at any time* by providing written notice to the Contractor in any case in which the mandate of UN applicable to the performance of the Contract or the funding of UN applicable to the Contract is curtailed or terminated, whether in whole or in part.[54]

In all other situations, which do not relate to the exercise of a function, the organization can terminate the contract at its own discretion and without providing the other party with a reason. The absence of justification, however, is usually compensated by a longer term for written notice.[55]

The different provisions are based on a balance of interests, which is specific to the contracts of international organizations. There is a tension underlying this kind of contract between the interest of the organizations, which is linked to its public nature, and the private party's interest, i.e. the private party's reliance on a continued contractual relationship. Since, however, the organization enters into the contract precisely in order to eventually perform its public functions and fulfil its institutional objectives, the organization is on an equal footing with the private party in terms of duties and rights related to termination of the contract only as long as there is no change in the exercise of that function.

The 'dormancy' of the public nature and, thus, a slightly stronger protection of the private party's reliance on a continued contractual relationship can instead be found in all situations where the cause of the rescission is not strictly related to the exercise of the public function.

---

[54] Emphasis added. United Nations, *GCC Goods*, para. 13.2; *id.*, *GCC Services*, para. 13.2; *id.*, *GCC Goods and Services*, para. 14.2; UNHCR, *GCC Goods*, para. 14.2; Id., *GCC Services*, para. 14.2; Id., *GCC Goods and Services*, para. 15.2 [all documents in ref. GT&CC].

[55] United Nations, *GCC Goods*, para. 13.2; *id.*, *GCC Services*, para. 13.2; *id.*, *GCC Goods and Services*, para. 14.2; UNHCR, *GCC Goods*, para. 15.2; *id.*, *GCC Services*, para. 15.2; *id.*, *GCC Goods and Services*, para. 16.2 [all documents in ref. GT&CC].

This explains the longer term of notice for rescission required for simple convenience, and, conversely, immediate rescission in the event of particular conditions related to the mandate of the organization.

The possibility of terminating the contract at any time for reasons related to public interest, with no notice and no costs to the administration, compromises the stability of the contract and reliance on the contract by the private party. In national legal systems, cases of unilateral termination by an administration are often provided for by law or, if not, the courts have restrictively interpreted the power of public administration to unilaterally terminate contracts. On the contrary, in international organizations, the source of regulation in this respect is mainly the contract and there are no substantial limits to the exercise of this power.

Furthermore, the clauses that, in addition to the termination for qualified convenience, provide also for termination for simple convenience, with no compensation or indemnity for the private party, also appear to be 'exorbitant'. Unless we apply subjective criteria and consider an interest to be public solely because it comes from a public administration, the balancing in this case is not between a public interest and a private party's interest, but rather between the discretionary intent of a public body whose reasons are unknown and a private party's interest. The distinction between qualified and simple convenience does not, however, exist for all organizations. The general terms and conditions of most organizations, instead, provide for unilateral rescission by the international organization due to an undefined 'convenience'.

Within simplified solutions that refer to the organization's 'convenience' without defining it, there are, nevertheless, provisions where the discretionary and autocratic element is stronger, and others where this element is softened by guarantees tied to minimum notice periods for informing the private party. The first type includes, for example, the UNOPS *General Conditions for Goods*, which give the administration – and not the private party – the ability to terminate and do not prescribe a minimum term for giving notice:

> [t]he notice of termination shall state that termination is for UNOPS's convenience, the extent to which performance of the Vendor under the Contract is terminated and the date upon which such termination becomes effective.[56]

---

[56] UNOPS, *GC Goods*, para. 19.1. Similar provisions, i.e. the absence of reciprocity and a minimum notice period, also appear in the clauses in the general terms and conditions of the FAO (FAO, *GTC Procurement Contracts*, para. 22) [all documents in ref. GT&CC].

Of the second type are, for example, the general terms and conditions of UNIDO, which include thirty days' notice that the organization must respect, and which may be reduced to seven days if the private party's performance has become impossible due to *force majeure*.[57]

Concomitant with the organization's right to terminate the contract for convenience, duties of the private party arise that are connected to performance. The general terms and conditions of the United Nations, UNHCR and UNOPS, for example, establish that, after termination by the organization, the private contractual party must take all steps necessary to immediately bring all of its services to a close, reducing expenses to a minimum. It must also refrain from assuming additional commitments, entering into subcontracts, and ordering new materials, services or structures. It must terminate all existing contracts or subcontracting orders; deliver to the organization fabricated and not yet fabricated parts, work in progress and completed work, supplies and other material produced or acquired for the portion of the contract terminated; deliver all plans, drawings, information and other completed or partially completed property, which, if the contract had been completed, would have had to be furnished to the organization; and complete any work not yet terminated. Finally, it must take any other action necessary, or which the organization requires, to minimize losses and ensure the protection and preservation of any property, connected to the contract that is in the possession of the contractor and in which the organization has or can reasonably expect to acquire an interest.[58] In the contracts of other organizations – FAO, for example – the list of duties for the private party is not so clear, but nevertheless requires that activities are brought to an immediate close, the reduction of expenses to a minimum and that the private party abstains from entering into new subcontracting relationships.[59]

---

[57] UNIDO, *GTC*, para. 12: 'UNIDO may terminate this Contract in whole or in part and at any time, upon thirty (30) days' notice of termination to the Contractor' and para. 11(d): '[i]f the Contractor is rendered permanently unable, wholly or in part, by reason of Force Majeure, to perform its obligations and meet its responsibilities under this Contract, UNIDO shall have the right to terminate this Contract on the same terms and conditions as provided for in paragraph 12, 'Termination' except that the period of notice may be seven (7) days instead of thirty (30) days' [ref. GT&CC].

[58] This list of duties appears in United Nations, *GCC Goods*, para. 13.3; *id.*, *GCC Services*, para. 13.3; *id.*, *GCC Goods and Services*, para. 14.3; Also in UNHCR, *GCC Goods*, para. 15.3; *id.*, *GCC Services*, para. 15.3; *id.*, *GCC Goods and Services*, para. 16.3. Along similar lines, UNOPS, *GC Goods*, para. 22.1 [all documents in ref. GT&CC].

[59] FAO, *GTC Procurement Contracts*, para. 22 [ref. GT&CC].

Based on these duties of the private party, the general terms and conditions usually establish limitations on the administration's liability. The United Nations and UNHCR

> shall not be liable to pay the Contractor except for those goods delivered and services provided to [the organization] in accordance with the requirements of the Contract, but only if such goods and services were ordered, requested or otherwise provided prior to the Contractor's receipt of notice of termination from [the organization] or prior to the Contractor's tendering of notice of termination to [the organization].[60]

Similar provisions can be found in the contracts of the FAO, UNOPS and UNICEF,[61] with certain variations in terms of the date following which the organization is no longer responsible for payment.

In any case, no indemnification is provided for unilateral termination by the organization, not even when this happens without the minimum notice for reasons related to exercise of the public function. A reimbursement clause in the case of unilateral termination for convenience appears only in UNICEF's terms and conditions, which provide that, in addition to payment for the goods and services provided, the organization shall reimburse the contractor for any reasonable costs incurred by the contractor prior to the notice of termination.[62] Nevertheless, this clause is an exception to the general terms and conditions of most organizations, which usually make the private party responsible for any expenses connected to unilateral termination.

Thus, in general, with the exception of European institutions, the power to unilaterally terminate the contract by the organization is not subject to limits or restrictions, either in terms of the prerequisites for exercising it, or in terms of its financial consequences. Clauses of this type, which require the private party to bear the costs of the organization interrupting the contractual relationship, and provide for no reciprocity, not only diverge from private contractual practices, but are also anomalous when compared to the rules and practice of contracts concluded in national public procurement.

In many national legal systems, such provisions are considered illegal and not binding. As seen above, German law always requires

---

[60] See United Nations, *GCC Goods*, para. 13.4; *id.*, *GCC Services*, para. 13.4; *id.*, *GCC Goods and Services*, para. 14.4; Also in UNHCR, *GCC Goods*, para. 15.4; *id.*, *GCC Services*, para. 15.4; *id.*, *GCC Goods and Services*, para. 16.4 [all documents in ref. GT&CC].

[61] FAO, *GTC Procurement Contracts*, para. 22 [ref. GT&CC].

[62] UNICEF, *GTC*, sec. 'Termination' [ref. GT&CC].

a justification and indemnification.[63] In Italy, although the power of unilateral rescission is considered to be inherent to the power of the administration to enter into a public law contract,[64] Italian courts has set limits to both the prerequisites for and the effects of exercising this power: the administration may terminate the contract not for just any public law need, but only for those considered to be 'sufficiently serious'. Unilateral termination must be considered an *extrema ratio*, used only when alternatives less burdensome to the private party are not possible. Moreover, the action must be justified and the justification must indicate that public and private interests have been weighed against each other. At the financial level, the administration must pay the private party an indemnification commensurate with any harm done. Violation of these parameters is subject to judicial review.

5.2.5.2 Termination Due to Non-Performance of the Private Party

As in most domestic legal systems, the contracts of international organizations give the administration the power to unilaterally terminate the contract when the private party has breached contractual obligations. This is a power that, as national legal scholars have also noted, appears to be in line with the reasons behind the contract, as it is aimed not at allowing the administration to nullify what it agreed to with the private party, but rather to more effectively safeguard its interest in full implementation of the agreement.[65] Nevertheless, while national legislators and courts in the various domestic legal systems have stepped in to explain the nature of this power, identifying its legal foundation and above all setting out its premises and delimiting its effects, the same has not been done for international organizations. Thus, international organizations' contracts, substantially formulated by the organizations and the sole regulatory sources of this power, often permit great leeway for exercising such power.

---

[63] On this specific aspect, see Stelkens, Bonk and Sachs, *Verwaltungsverfahrensgesetz – Kommentar*; Masucci, *Trasformazione dell'amministrazione e moduli convenzionali*, p. 104 *et seq.*

[64] In agreement, Bruti Liberati, *Consenso e funzione*, p. 211, which continues: 'as this power, like any other administrative power, is inexhaustible and indispensable, the administration may, when serious public interests which can otherwise not be met so require, exercise it again and dissolve the contractual relationship'.

[65] *Ibid.*, 203–204.

Termination due to the private party's breach of contract is provided for in most of the general terms and conditions of the various organizations as a generic and non-justified 'default' by the private party. On the contrary, no provision regulating the potential breach by the organization is included. In some general terms and conditions, the 'default' that legitimizes the exercise of the power to terminate the contract is a failure to meet any of the obligations arising from the contract. Other terms and conditions, instead, make it possible to terminate the contract only if essential requirements for the performance are not met. An example of the first type is UNOPS's *General Conditions for Goods*:

> UNOPS, without prejudice to any other remedy for breach of Contract, by written notice of default sent to the Vendor, may terminate the Contract, in whole or in part if: 20.1.1 the Vendor fails to deliver any or all of the Goods within the period specified in the Contract; 20.1.2 the Vendor fails to perform *any other obligation* under the Contract.[66]

Examples of the second type are the terms and conditions of contract of the United Nations, UNHCR and FAO. Violations that result in default are connected to performance: non-performance, delivery later than the scheduled dates and performance that does not conform with the agreed procedures. Alternatively, there are violations of obligations connected to fundamental rights, such as a prohibition on producing anti-personnel mines, the use of child labour or sexual exploitation. Nevertheless, some room for discretion is usually granted to the organization in identifying further causes for termination, even in those contracts where there is express mention of the various categories of causes. For example, the FAO's terms and conditions state:

> [i]n case of failure by Contractor to perform under the terms and conditions of this Contract, *including but not limited* to failure to make delivery of all or part of the Goods by the scheduled date(s), or to complete the Services required within the scheduled date(s), FAO may . . . (4) terminate this Contract without liability for FAO.[67]

In addition, in no case does violation of a certain contractual duty *ipso iure* result in termination of the relationship. It is the organization that must always determine whether, despite the non-performance, it is appropriate to continue the relationship or to terminate it for this reason.

---

[66] Emphasis added. UNOPS, *GC Goods*, para. 20. The other situations provided for by para. 20 are bankruptcy and insolvency [ref. GT&CC]. See later in this chapter.

[67] Emphasis added. FAO, *GTC Procurement Contracts*, para. 18, sec. 'Remedies for Default' [ref. GT&CC].

It is, thus, a discretionary power that the contract provides for in order to meet the public interest.[68]

The advent of these circumstances creates a duty for the private party to provide notice and information,[69] and in contracts with certain organizations, such as UNOPS, UNICEF or FAO, there is also a duty to compensate any damages and costs the organization has incurred as a result of non-performance or violations of the terms and conditions of contract.[70] So, on one side, as in the case of the organization's unilateral termination for convenience, even without notice or justification, damage to the private party (consequential damages and lost earnings) creates no duty to compensate or indemnify as the contract allows the organization's public interest to prevail. On the other side, the private party's non-performance, even where notice has been given, creates a duty in the private party to compensate the international organization. In addition, as already noted, the effects of the organization's potential non-performance are not regulated, as the contract does not contemplate such a circumstance.

5.2.5.3   Termination Due to Force Majeure

Termination due to *force majeure* is provided for in the general terms and conditions of most organizations, such as UNDP, UNICEF, UNHCR, FAO, WFP, UNOPS and UNIDO. The organization is allowed to terminate the contract on the occurrence of certain events that jeopardize certainty of performance by the private party or violate one of the terms in the contract with regard to modes of performance. Exceptions are the United Nations and UNHCR, whose contracts permit termination of the contract due to *force majeure* not only when the *force majeure* could jeopardize the private party's ability to perform, but also in the different

---

[68] Similarly, in some national legal systems, determinations based on a declaratory judgment of annulment should be considered discretionary and aimed at achieving the public interest. In other words, a declaratory judgment of annulment is interpreted as an administrative provision with a broader function, in that it is also aimed at protecting the public interests involved in the administration's conditions arising from the granting provision.

[69] See UNOPS, *GC Goods*, para. 20.1; United Nations, *GCC Goods*, para. 13.6; *id.*, *GCC Services*, para. 13.6; *id.*, *GCC Goods and Services*, para. 14.6. And in UNHCR, *GCC Goods*, para. 15.6; *id.*, *GCC Services*, para. 15.6; *id.*, *GCC Goods and Services*, para. 16.6 [all documents in ref. GT&CC].

[70] UNOPS, *GC Goods*, para. 20.2; UNICEF, *GTC*, sec. 'Termination' [all documents in ref. GT&CC].

and specular situation when the organization's ability to perform is for some reason put at risk.

The definition of *force majeure* is particularly important for organizations whose institutional mission includes promoting development in disadvantaged areas, distributing humanitarian aid, or providing military intervention in war zones or areas of political unrest, which mean that they operate in exceptional, unpredictable situations. The general terms and conditions of contract of the United Nations, UNHCR and UNOPS define *force majeure* as

> any unforeseeable and irresistible act of nature, any act of war (whether declared or not), invasion, revolution, insurrection, terrorism, or any other acts of a similar nature or force, *provided that* such acts arise from causes beyond the control and without the fault or negligence of the Contractor.[71]

The definition does not include events that are an inherent part of the exceptional situations in which contract execution may occur:

> the Contractor must perform in areas in which UN is engaged in, preparing to engage in, or disengaging from any humanitarian or similar operations, any delays or failure to perform such obligations arising from or relating to harsh conditions within such areas, or to any incidents of civil unrest occurring in such areas, shall not, in and of itself, constitute *force majeure* under the Contract.[72]

The risk arising from this type of situation is, thus, borne solely by the private party whose partial or total failure to perform in these cases would not be justified by *force majeure*.

The emergence of *force majeure* creates duties of notice for the party whose performance could be difficult or impossible. As noted at the start of this section, in most organizations the general terms and conditions consider only situations in which *force majeure* affects or could affect the

---

[71] United Nations, GCC Goods, para. 12.3; *id.*, GCC Services, para. 12.3; *id.*, GCC Goods and Services, para. 13.3. And in UNHCR, GCC Goods, para. 14.3; *id.*, GCC Services, para. 14.3; *id.*, GCC Goods and Services, para. 15.3; UNOPS, GC Goods, para. 24.1. The general terms and conditions of FAO and UNICEF contain a similar definition: 'acts of God, war (whether declared or not), invasion, revolution, insurrection or other acts of similar nature or force', in FAO, *GTC Procurement Contracts*, para. 20 and UNICEF, *GTC*, sec. 'Force Majeure. Other Changes in Conditions', lett. c). Similarly UNIDO, *GTC*, para. 11 [all documents in ref. GT&CC].

[72] United Nations, GCC Goods, para. 12.3; *id.*, GCC Services, para. 12.3; *id.*, GCC Goods and Services, para. 13.3. And in UNHCR, GCC Goods, para. 14.3; *id.*, GCC Services, para. 14.3; *id.*, GCC Goods and Services, para. 15.3. Similarly UNOPS, GC Goods, para. 24.1 [all documents in ref. GT&CC].

private party's performance, and thus the duties of notice refer to the private party. For example, UNOPS's general conditions of contract for the procurement of goods establish duties of notice regarding the emergence of *force majeure* as well as any consequences that it could have on contract performance.[73] In addition, the private party must prepare a statement of the expenses it expects to incur as a result of *force majeure*.[74] The duties of the private party also refer to performance, and in this regard are the same as those that arise upon the organization's unilateral termination of contract: in summary, immediate cessation of activities, reduction of expenses and abstention from entering into new sub-contractual relationships.

Following the notice, the organization usually has the right to take any action it deems appropriate or necessary under the circumstances. Options range from a simple extension of the contract in order to permit performance to termination of the contract if the private party is wholly or in part unable to execute it. The administration may evaluate the circumstance of *force majeure* and the private party's ability to perform, as well as decide whether to amend the contractual provisions or instead to terminate the contract. Thus, it has complete discretion to determine the fate of the contract and to make any changes to it. This is particularly clear, for example, in para. 20 of the *General Terms and Conditions Applicable to FAO Procurement Contracts,* which states that the contract will be terminated '[i]f *FAO determines* that the Contractor is rendered unable, wholly or in part, by reasons of *force majeure* to perform any of its obligations'.[75] Similarly, UNOPS's *General Conditions for Goods* highlight that, upon the occurrence of *force majeure,* 'UNOPS shall take such action as it considers *in its sole discretion,* to be appropriate or necessary in the circumstances'.[76]

---

[73] UNOPS, *GC Goods*, para. 24.2 [ref. GT&CC].

[74] *Ibid.* The general terms and conditions of other organizations contain similar expressions. See, for example, UNICEF, *GTC*, sec. 'Force Majeure. Other Changes in Conditions', lett. a); FAO, *GTC Procurement Contracts*, para. 20; UNIDO, *GTC*, para. 11(b); IFAD, *GTC Goods*, para. 10(d). The general terms and conditions of the United Nations and UNHCR also contain these same provisions, but they do not refer to private parties in particular, but to one of the two contractual parties whose performance may change or be rendered impossible due to the emergence of *force majeure,* also in United Nations, *GCC Goods*, para. 12.1; *id., GCC Services,* para. 12.1; *id., GCC Goods and Services,* para. 13.1. And in UNHCR, *GCC Goods,* para. 14.1; *id., GCC Services,* para. 14.1; *id., GCC Goods and Services,* para. 15.1 [all documents in ref. GT&CC].

[75] Emphasis added. Also in FAO, *GTC Procurement Contracts*, para. 20 [ref. GT&CC].

[76] Emphasis added. UNOPS, *GC Goods*, para. 24.2 [ref. GT&CC].

When *force majeure* affects, instead, the performance of the international organization, termination of the contract gives the organization rights and duties similar to those for unilateral termination,[77] such as notice of termination by the organization (which, however, for the United Nations, UNHCR, UNOPS, UNICEF and UNIDO is only seven days as in unilateral termination), and payment to the private party is limited solely to goods and services that were provided before the notice of termination.[78]

5.2.5.4 Termination Due to Changes in the Status of the Private Party

Another reason justifying contract termination by organizations is a real or potential change in the private party's situation, both formal, if related to legal status, and substantive, if related to a change in its financial situation. The general terms and conditions of contract adopted by the United Nations and UNHCR, for example, include various situations, most of which also recur in simplified form in the contractual formulas of other organizations.[79] The organizations have the right to terminate the contract if the private party goes bankrupt, is liquidated or becomes insolvent; if it requests a moratorium on any of its obligations or asks to be declared insolvent; if it is granted a moratorium or is declared insolvent; if it assigns its assets to one or more creditors as payment for its obligations; if a liquidator is appointed to manage its insolvent status; if it proposes a settlement in lieu of bankruptcy; and finally, if the organization reasonably determines that the contractor's financial condition has undergone a materially adverse change that would have substantial repercussions on its ability to meet any of its contractual obligations.[80]

---

[77] On this point, all general terms and conditions contain a reference to the rules and regulations on unilateral rescission.

[78] The references are the same as for unilateral rescission.

[79] See FAO, *GTC Procurement Contracts*, para. 8; UNOPS, *GC Goods*, para. 20.1 (no. 20.1. 8–20.1.13); UNICEF, *GTC*, sec. 'Termination'; UNDP, *GCC Special Services Agreement*, para. 13; UNIDO, *GTC*, para. 13 [all documents in ref. GT&CC].

[80] The following formula is used: 'the United Nations reasonably determines that the Contractor has become subject to a materially adverse change in its financial condition that threatens to substantially affect the ability of the Contractor to perform any of its obligations under the Contract', in United Nations, *GCC Goods*, para. 13.5.6; *id.*, *GCC Services*, para. 13.5.6; *id.*, *GCC Goods and Services*, para. 14.5.6; UNHCR, *GCC Goods*, para. 15.5.6; *id.*, *GCC Services*, para. 15.5.6; *Id.*, *GCC Goods and Services*, para. 16.5.6. The text of the general terms and conditions of the FAO is less detailed: '[i]n the event that Contractor becomes insolvent or bankrupt or the control or legal status of Contractor changes for any other reason, FAO may terminate the Contract, without prejudice to any

This last situation is not cited in the general terms and conditions of all organizations, but the formula is used in contracts with the United Nations and UNHCR, as well as with UNDP and UNOPS. In particular, UNOPS's *General Conditions for Goods* give the administration the right to terminate the contract even if a change in financial conditions could only potentially threaten proper performance:

> a materially adverse change in its financial condition that *threatens to endanger* or otherwise substantially affect the ability of the vendor to perform any of its obligations under the Contract.[81]

In cases of bankruptcy and insolvency, termination follows the emergence of a legal circumstance that is not subject to different interpretations. On the contrary, the organization's ability to assess the private party's financial solidity and possibly terminate the contract acts as a catch-all clause for all situations where the undertaking's difficulties are not formalized and proceedings have not been initiated with a view to doing so. The formalization of these situations is replaced by the organization's discretionary assessment, which may also consist of a prognostic judgment of a merely potential risk. Moreover, the margin for discretion is broad as there is a dual potential: the organization will pre-emptively assess whether or not potential negative financial situations will eventually occur and also whether or not they have repercussions that can affect performance.

The occurrence of one of the above-mentioned conditions justifies not only the organization's right to terminate a contract but also the private party's duties to provide notice of the emergence of these circumstances, to provide information on its financial situation, and above all to compensate for damages and costs that the organization incurs for these reasons.[82]

In the general terms and conditions of certain organizations a change in the legal status or corporate control of the private party is also included among the hypotheses that legitimize termination of the contract by the organization.[83] Terminating the contract due to a change in corporate

---

other rights and remedies, by giving Contractor written notice of termination', FAO, *GTC Procurement Contracts*, para. 8 [all documents in ref. GT&CC].

[81] Italics added. UNOPS, *GC Goods*, para. 20.1.13 [ref. GT&CC].

[82] For United Nations, for example, see United Nations, *GCC Goods*, para. 15.6; *id., GCC Services*, para. 15.6 [all documents in ref. GT&CC].

[83] The general terms and conditions of the FAO establish that '[i]n the event that ... the control or legal status of Contractor changes for any other reason [previous reasons are insolvency and bankruptcy], FAO may terminate the Contract, without prejudice to any other rights and remedies, by giving Contractor written notice of termination', also in FAO, *GTC Procurement Contracts*, para. 8 [ref. GT&CC].

control is moreover in line with the overall caution that the general terms and conditions of organizations show when addressing subcontracting.[84] Indeed, these forms of substantive assignment of contractual duties and rights are deemed risky by organizations as they bring into the contract parties who have not passed the initial preliminary qualification screening required and carried out by the organizations themselves.[85]

5.2.6   Subcontracting

Generally speaking, the contracts of international organizations allow the private party to subcontract all or part of the performance. Nevertheless, this possibility is subject to conditions and procedures that ensure that the organizations can achieve their internal organizational objectives and their external policy goals. The former include guaranteeing the efficiency of procedures and ensuring contract execution, while the latter are aimed at avoiding any jeopardy to implementing procurement policies, especially when based on criteria other than strict competition.

5.2.6.1   Risks

From the international organization's perspective, subcontracting involves risks that the main contract seeks to prevent. As seen in Chapter 4, organizations follow certain procedures when selecting a contractor. The selection is made from a supplier roster set up by the organization itself after verifying the existence of subjective and objective elements: the undertaking's characteristics, i.e. its financial stability, experience in the sector and reliability in executing past contracts; the characteristics of the goods, services and works that the undertaking intends to provide for a particular tender; and its willingness to conclude the contract. This initial selection process is performed by specialized staff who collect and screen relevant documents and information. Thus, if it were not subject to equivalent conditions, subcontracting would compromise the objectives of this preliminary phase, with possible negative effects in terms of administrative efficiency and contract execution. In this first respect, the results achieved with human and financial resources specially intended to further the smooth performance of the contract would be nullified.

In a second respect, subcontracting can have negative repercussions on the stability of the contractual relationship and on the regularity of

---

[84] See later in this chapter.   [85] See Chapter 4.

performance resulting from the use of partners who are unreliable or have not been screened, or have not been tried and tested by the organization. Moreover, compared to national public procurement, these risks are boosted by two factors: the international nature of the market in which the contractors operate and the context in which the procurement is requested. On the one hand, the fact that undertakings come from all over the world results in less extensive control of the subcontracting company, with extensive control meaning the administration having the ability to easily gather information on the undertaking and the outcome of its previous commissions. On the other hand, in the case of local subcontracting companies, especially in certain economically disadvantaged areas or areas with unstable political conditions, the risk of corruption, fraud or criminal infiltration increases.

In a third respect, even if it is not bound by a direct contractual relationship with the subcontractor, the organization may find itself associated with undertakings that do not respect its principles and values, such as those related to the protection of human rights. Besides being a violation of the founding treaties, this would also be to the detriment of the international organization's image and legitimacy.

Finally, in certain situations organizations award contracts that make exceptions to the principle of strict competition and impartiality, based on a criterion of preference to promote local firms or ensure an economic return to funding states. Subcontracting creates the risk of a nullification of these objectives. It makes it possible to assign execution of the contract to undertakings that are not part of the economic area that the organization intends to promote and can thus result in diverting a portion of the organization's resources to parties other than those for whom they are intended.

5.2.6.2   Regulating the Subcontract

To prevent these risks, general terms and conditions provide a series of clauses that can be grouped into three fundamental categories common to the various organizations. The first defines the role that the organization may play in selecting the subcontractor. The second governs liability for any breach by the subcontracting company. The third relates, more generally, to the applicability to the subcontract of the provisions included in the principal contract.

With regard to the first category, general terms and conditions usually establish that the undertaking may subcontract the performance only with the organization's consent, which must be in writing. Consent is given after the organization performs a discretionary evaluation of the subcontractors' qualifications. A negative evaluation will act to limit the contractual capacity of the successful bidder, which, for purposes of the specific performance, may not enter into any contractual relationship with the undertaking that the organization has determined to be unsuitable. Thus, the administration has the power to determine whether or not a contractual relationship can be established between two private parties. Moreover, it may also indirectly affect the fate of the subcontract, once signed. Indeed, the organization has the right to remove any subcontracting company from its premises and offices with no justification, even if this in fact jeopardizes contractual performance, and the continued existence of the subcontract relationship. Nevertheless, neither the organization's refusal to approve the subcontract, nor the removal of the subcontractor by the organization may be considered justification for delaying contractual performance or for non-performance by the principal private contractor.

The relative rules on liability are consistent with organizations' objectives of efficiency and financial protection. The principal contractor remains the sole party liable to the organization for contractual performance and fulfilment of the obligations assumed, and the existence of internal contractual relationships between the principal contractor and the subcontractor has no external relevance during the execution phase.

The third aspect relates to the regulations set out in the subcontract. These are tied to the terms and conditions of the original procurement contract with the organization in two ways. First, some provisions of the original procurement contract are directly applicable to the subcontractor. Second, with regard to any aspects of the subcontract that are not directly covered by the original contract or are subject to interpretation, the subcontract must be consistent with the provisions of the original contract. A recurring formula used in the main contract is:

> [t]he terms of any subcontract shall be *subject to*, and shall be construed in a manner that is *fully in accordance with*, all the terms and conditions of the Contract.[86]

The principal contract establishes the rights of the organization and the duties of the winning bidder that intends to avail itself of the

---

[86] Emphasis added. Also in United Nations, GCC Goods, para. 3; *id.*, GCC Services, para. 3; *id.*, GCC Goods and Services, para. 4; UNHCR, GCC Goods, para. 5; *id.*, GCC Services, para. 5; *id.*, GCC Goods and Services, para. 6 [all documents in ref. GT&CC].

subcontract. Nevertheless, in one case, that of the FAO, the general terms and conditions also govern the opposite case where the organization subcontracts or assigns the contract to third parties. In these situations, the objective of contractual regulation is different: to permit full exercise of the organization's discretionary power and its freedom of contract. The organization does in fact have discretion to assign, transfer, grant, subcontract or in any other way manage the contract or portions of it or any of its rights and duties arising from it. In this regard, there are two significant differences from the regulation of the winning bidder's subcontracting.

First of all, protection of the private party to the principal contract is based exclusively on notice duties that the organization can fulfil before as well as after conclusion of the subcontract agreement. Their function is to inform the private party, but they do not enable it to perform any control or to veto the conclusion of the subcontract agreement or other types of transfer or assignment.

Second, the organization's range of possibilities is not limited to subcontracting, but also includes other situations, such as assigning the contract (or single rights and duties deriving from it) to another party. However, there is a major difference between subcontracting and assigning the contract to another party. A subcontract signed by the international organization does not involve the establishment of a direct relationship between the party that entered into the original procurement contract and the subcontractor chosen by the organization. Conversely, assignment of the contract by the organization to another private or public party means that a new contracting party steps in and, thus, a direct relationship is established between that party – in lieu of the organization – and the vendor who was originally awarded the contract. At the domestic level, when there is an assignment within a contract between private parties, national private law usually provides that assignment by one party requires the other party's consent. Unlike what occurs in relationships between private parties at the domestic level, in the assignment governed by the international organizations' general terms and conditions the winning bidder may find itself bound to a contractual relationship with a private or public body without having specifically consented to it, with its freedom of contract curtailed not so much in terms of how the contract is executed (the *quomodo*) but in terms of whether to enter into a contract with a certain party (the *an*).

5.2.6.3   Limits to the Contractual Freedom of Private Parties: A Comparative Perspective

The objectives of efficiency and effectiveness of administrative action, along with the organization's international nature, result in subcontract regulation that is different from that of national administrations. The GPA does not specifically regulate subcontracting. European public procurement directives require states to establish provisions on subcontracting and set rules for the principal economic operator's liability, but do not give the contracting administrations the right to authorize the subcontract. Neither do they impose qualitative or quantitative limits on it, nor set conditions on the relationship between the contractor and the subcontractor. The principal goal of directives in guiding national authorities is, in this case, 'facilitating in particular the participation of small and medium-sized enterprises (SMEs) in public procurement'[87] without discrimination based on nationality. Priority is given to the goals of transnational competition and non-discrimination.

Thus, EU procurement directives require national systems to provide a subcontracting option, but they defer to national legislators the task of defining the concrete limits within which this option can be exercised. National legislation must regulate those aspects of the system that do not have significant repercussions beyond national borders, but which, if not safeguarded, could jeopardize the efficiency and effectiveness of the administrative action and erode the administration's resources. Often, at the national level, subcontracting is permitted on the condition that the contractor sends the awarding entity certification attesting that the subcontractor meets the general qualification requirements provided by the law and that she is not subject to any definitive judicial measures. National administrations will, then, consent to the subcontract based on an examination of the subcontractor's requirements and through an authorization procedure.

The authorization by the administration or the approval by an international organization does not create a direct contractual relationship between the administration (or the organization) and the subcontractor. The result is that in national regulations, as well as those of international organizations, the main contractor remains liable to the administration, or the organization, even if it is the subcontractor who is in breach.

---

[87] European Union, Directive 2014/24/EU, Recital 2 and European Union, Directive 2014/25/EU, Recital 4 [all documents in ref. N&RL-EU].

Nevertheless, in terms of the limits that shape the content of the subcontract, there is a substantial difference between subcontracting a contract with an international organization and subcontracting one with a national administration. In the case of international organizations, the absence of framework legislation means that the subcontract must absorb the provisions of the main procurement contract in essential aspects that do not specifically relate to the relationship between the administration and the contractor, such as laws on human rights, the protection of workers etc. Moreover, the absence of such legislation means that the main contract must act as a parameter for interpreting the subcontract. The provisions of the main contract, thus, indirectly govern the parties to the subcontract agreement.

Conversely, in national regulations, the procurement contract and subcontract are, in terms of content (and excluding the specifics of performance), independent, as both are subject to national law for everything that is not expressly regulated by the main contract. In the first case, the source of regulation is the organization itself, and its determinations have an impact on the content of not only the contractual relationship between it and the private party, but also on the relationship between two private parties. In the second case, national legislation, and not the administration, sets the basic terms of both the contract between the administration and the private parties and the contract between the private parties.

In summary, there are similarities and certain substantial differences between subcontracting objectives and regulations in the contracts of national administrations and those of international organizations. The comparison gives an idea of how and to what extent international organizations affect the freedom of contract of private parties in some specific respects. Common objectives, such as efficiency (avoiding the circumvention of vendor selection procedures) and effectiveness (avoiding contractual performance risks that could be created by contracting parties who are for various reasons unreliable), are accompanied by specific institutional policy objectives of international organizations that have no equivalent in the contracts of national administrations. In fact, in contracts with international organizations, contractual regulation of subcontracting also serves to prevent the diversion of resources from the private parties who are supposed to receive them in accordance with institutional policies. On the contrary, in the contracts of national administrations, regulation is often designed to promote small and medium-sized undertakings.

In international organizations, there is a need that favours more restrictive contractual regulation of subcontracting and of the freedom of contract of the main contractor and of the subcontractor. In domestic public procurement, objectives of competition and non-discrimination set at the supranational level (e.g. in EU public procurement directives and the GPA) weigh against the objectives of efficiency and effectiveness pursued by national administrations and, thus, soften national subcontracting regulation. The differences are reflected in the rules and regulations that govern not so much the creation of the subcontracting relationship as the definition of its contents and the survival of that relationship. Both in national public procurement and in international organizations' procurement, in fact, the authorization from the public entity results in the creation of a contract between private parties and acts as a filter to screen out undertakings that are considered insufficiently reliable. However, unlike national administrations, international organizations give themselves the power to dictate rules also on subcontracting relationships, as well as a power to influence the fate of that obligation.

Both at the national and the international level, authorization should meet the objective of efficiency and effectiveness of administrative action and, in the case of international organizations, also meet the need to control the actual allocation of resources of international organizations. The extension of the organization's regulatory power beyond the procurement contract and the ability to affect the fate of the subcontract are, however, a peculiarity of international organizations.

5.2.7   Liability of Private Parties

In addition to duties to perform according to the modalities set out in the contract, a private party that contracts with international organizations has at least two other categories of duties, which are not reflected in similar duties for the organization and serve to discharge the organization from non-contractual responsibilities to third parties. These are 'internal' duties relating to the private contractor's employees who execute the contract, and 'external' duties that relate to third parties potentially affected by the contractual performance.

5.2.7.1   Liability towards Employees

In the first regard, as it is responsible for final contractual performance, the private contracting party is responsible for the technical and professional expertise of the personnel employed through the contract or subcontract, their moral and ethical standards of conduct, and their compliance with laws and respect for local customs. Despite this, the contracts of some organizations give the organization itself the discretion to review the personnel employed by the private party after the contract is awarded, and the unilateral power to decide whether or not to employ these personnel.[88]

Furthermore, the organization may intervene in the relationship between the private contractor and its employees, at least with regard to individual performance, even later on when contractual performance has already begun. While, on one hand, the qualifications required of personnel may be changed during the course of contractual performance with the agreement of both parties, on the other hand, if this should occur the organization may at any time and at its own discretion request the removal or replacement of personnel. This possibility takes on the substance of a right in that it is specified that the request not only does not need to be justified but above all that it may not be unreasonably refused.[89] Moreover, an evaluation of the reasonableness of a refusal is deferred to the organization, creating a circular mechanism that guarantees the organization the power to unilaterally impact a relationship between private parties (the undertaking and its employee) by virtue of the fact that the ultimate goal of this relationship is the performance required by a contract between the organization and the private party (the undertaking).

Nevertheless, as for subcontracting, recognition of this power does not imply the establishment of a relationship between the organization and the personnel hired by the private party: the organization can decide which personnel are selected at the outset, and it can request and obtain removal or replacement without justification and without meeting

---

[88] Also in United Nations, *GCC Services*, para. 2.3; *id.*, *GCC Goods and Services*, para. 3.3; UNHCR, *GCC Services*, para. 3.3; *id.*, *GCC Goods and Services*, para. 4.3 [all documents in ref. GT&CC].

[89] '2.4.1 The United Nations may, at any time, request, in writing, the withdrawal or replacement of any of the Contractor's personnel, and such request shall not be unreasonably refused by the Contractor. 2.4.2 Any of the Contractor's personnel assigned to perform obligations under the Contract shall not be withdrawn or replaced without the prior written consent of the United Nations, which shall not be unreasonably withheld', also in United Nations, *GCC Services*, para. 2.2. And also in *id.*, *GCC Goods and Services*, para. 3.3; UNHCR, *GCC Services*, para. 3.3; *id.*, *GCC Goods and Services*, para. 5.3 [all documents in ref. GT&CC].

particular conditions, but these powers in no way create any liability on the part of the organization to the personnel.[90]

More specifically, contracts generally provide that the organization is not liable for losses, damage or injury suffered by the contractor or those who work on behalf of the contractor to execute the contract. To deal with this eventuality, the contractor has a duty to maintain insurance coverage for the relative damages and must present proof of such at the time the contract is concluded. Moreover, the contractor must compensate for damages caused to the organization. For instance, in contracts signed by the UN and many of its agencies the contractor must pay all expenses resulting from loss, destruction or damage to the property of the organizations caused by personnel employed by the contractor or a subcontractor, or anyone directly or indirectly employed by the contractor or one of its subcontractors.

The contracts of European institutions contain provisions that are analogous only in part. The private contractor must guarantee that the personnel it uses have the professional skills and experience needed to perform the duties assigned. Moreover, the private party is solely responsible for its employees: personnel have no contractual relationship with the European institution and, thus, cannot assert any rights against it arising from the contract.

Consistently with the concentration of liability in the private party, however, the powers that an EU institution may exercise over the private contractor's employees are limited. First, no power to review and select individual employees in advance is provided for. Second, the possibility of replacing employees once performance has begun is based on the occurrence of two situations set out in the general terms and conditions of the contract: performance is interrupted due to the action of an employee, or a staff member's expertise does not match the profile established in the contract. Only in these cases does the EU administration have the right to replace the employee and the contractor has the corresponding duty to so provide. In any event, the administration's request must be justified and the reasons must fulfil one of the concrete cases established. The broad discretion guaranteed in the contracts of

---

[90] '2.5 Nothing in Articles 2.2, 2.3 and 2.4, above, shall be construed to create any obligations on the part of the United Nations with respect to the Contractor's personnel assigned to perform work under the Contract, and such personnel shall remain the sole responsibility of the Contractor', also in United Nations, *GCC Services*, para. 2.5. And also in *id.*, *GCC Goods and Services*, para. 3.5; UNHCR, *GCC Services*, para. 3.5; *id.*, *GCC Goods and Services*, para. 4.4.

organizations in the UN system (as well as organizations like NATO), which are characterized principally by the greater number of powers the organization may exercise by the vague nature of the situations where these powers may be exercised and by the absence of a duty to provide justification, is much more circumscribed in the contracts of European institutions.

5.2.7.2   Liability towards Third Parties

In terms of 'external' duties, i.e. duties related to third parties whose legal position may be jeopardized by contractual performance, the contracts of most organizations[91] shelter the organization from the possible legal consequences of violations of third-party rights during contractual performance. The private contractor is generally required to indemnify, discharge from all liability and defend, at its own expense, the organization and its officials, representatives and employees in the case of disputes, proceedings, complaints or direct claims against it, arising from the acts or omissions of the contractor, its employees, officials, representatives or subcontractors.[92] Moreover, these duties arise with the contract but are not extinguished when it expires, as they are related to the consequences, including long-term consequences, of the performance.

More generally, in addition to incurring the costs of a possible legal action, contracts require the private contracting party to bear any expenses arising from damages caused to third parties due to the actions or omissions of personnel employed by the contractor. For the contractor, this results in the duty to maintain insurance that covers any eventuality, from damage to another party's property to personal injury and death. The amount of costs the private party must bear is moreover unlimited as there is no cap on liability.

Also with regard to third-party liability clauses, the contracts of EU institutions are different from those of other organizations. In third-party legal actions against the EU administration for damage caused during execution of the contract, the expenses incurred by the private party can be paid by the European Union, while in other organizations they are entirely the responsibility of the private party. In addition, while it is usually established that the administration is not liable for damages caused by the contractor during execution of the contract, there are also

---

[91] All those within the UN system, but also, for example, NATO.
[92] This formula is found without significant variation in the contracts of the United Nations, UNDP, UNHCR, FAO, UNICEF and other organizations.

exceptions to this clause that consider the Commission's causal contribution to the damage: in the case of wilful misconduct or gross negligence by the institutions, they must bear the costs of liability. Furthermore, apart from exceptional situations, the contractor's liability is not unlimited, but rather proportional to the value of the contract. The contractor is liable for any loss or damage in an amount that is not to exceed three times the value of the contract. Only in cases of wilful misconduct or gross negligence by the contractor will it bear unlimited liability. Thus, the possibility that the administration may bear legal expenses, the quantitative limits to the private party's duty to compensate, and the exceptions to the duty to compensate that contemplate a joint liability with the administration distinguish the contracts of European institutions from most of the other international organizations, mitigating the effects of an asymmetrical contractual structure.

5.2.7.3   Clauses Exorbitantes and Implications for Competition

The duties of insurance and unlimited compensation for damages to the organization and third parties can be considered a divergence from the provisions that national legal systems consider lawful in contracts between private parties. The 'exorbitant' nature of these provisions has at least three effects in the contractual practices of organizations. The first is the *de facto* selection of certain large suppliers and discouragement of bids from smaller suppliers from the outset. Indeed, companies of modest size that provide goods, services or works of limited value are often reluctant to expose themselves to possible obligations to pay compensation for damages that could be well beyond their financial means and capabilities. The second effect is that these liability clauses are what private parties most frequently seek to negotiate with the organization, even after the contract has been awarded, by asking for a provision that caps the private party's liability. The third effect, which is connected to the first two, is that the greater or lesser inflexibility that organizations show in negotiating this clause is closely connected to both subjective factors, which concern the private contractor, and objective factors, which are related to performance.

As already noted, the contractor's economic weight and power play an important role in making the organization flexible in negotiations and achieving a result based on an agreement between the parties and not just a unilateral imposition by the organization. It is the undertaking's economic weight in a national or global market that often convinces representatives of the undertaking's home state to exert pressure, most often informally, on the international organization to relax liability clauses. However, for these purposes, the type of performance the organization requires is also important. If the performance requires technical expertise that is difficult to find on the market, something that only one or a few suppliers possess, or which consists of supplying goods, services or works that are otherwise unavailable on the market, international organizations in fact become more inclined to negotiate and to grant requests to limit liability. The same holds when the performance involves problems of compatibility with goods, services or works previously provided by a certain undertaking, and thus issues of procurement continuity. For example, this is the case with procurement contracts for software utilized to manage an organization's entire IT system.

Nevertheless, the convergence of all these aspects, or the presence of a single one of them, is not a frequent eventuality. It is instead more common, namely in the practice of UN organizations, to include clauses on unlimited liability and insurance even though they are particularly burdensome for the private party, and to include these clauses unilaterally, without negotiation. From the perspective of competition, burdensome and rigid clauses create de facto restrictions for small and medium-sized firms desiring to take advantage of the commercial opportunities created by organizations, especially if these firms are local and from undeveloped areas. On the other hand, as the different approach of European institutions shows, limiting liability proportionately to performance and apportioning the costs of any disputes favours the ability of small and medium-sized undertakings to participate in their tenders and promotes competition.

A comparison of organizations in terms of liability clauses leads to more general considerations on the reasons for the differences, which will be examined later.[93] Here, suffice it to say that the different approach to liability is one of the many manifestations of the different objectives and priorities of European institutions compared to other international organizations and, moreover, that from this one may deduce a close link between competition as a primary objective of EU institutions and the non-autocratic nature of the administrative action of these institutions within the contract.

[93] See Chapter 8.

5.3   Contracts in Indirect Procurement and Limits to the Contractual Freedom of States

Some international organizations make funding conditional not only on the compliance of national administrations with requirements or regulations related to the vendor selection process, but also on the inclusion of certain specific provisions in contracts subsequently concluded by the national administration. Thus, the international organization impacts not only on the public procedure carried out by the national administration to select a vendor, but also on the exercise of powers that most national legal systems subject to private law. The goal is, first, to ensure that even after the award, when executing the contract, the funding disbursed is used for the purposes established by the organization for the individual development project and is managed in accordance with its institutional policies. Another purpose is to ensure that the international organization does not incur liabilities arising from contractual execution.

Conditions and limits to the power to contract apply to any contract financed by the international organization, even in part, and are established using the same guidelines that govern the contracting party's selection procedures. For instance, the ADB, AfDB, IDB and EBRD guidelines state that the procedures outlined in the guidelines apply to all contracts for goods and works financed in whole or in part by the bank.[94] The provisions included in the guidelines can either be limited to indicating the elements the contract must contain or extend to governing the content of certain aspects of the contract. In this second case, the provision can be general, indicating the guiding objectives on which the regulations must be based, or specific, such as establishing quantitative limits.

5.3.1   Types of Contract

As seen above, on one hand, direct procurement contracts, organizations use different types of contractual arrangement (purchase orders or contracts) and this distinction is connected to the greater or lesser degree of

---

[94] AfDB, *Rules and Procedures for the Procurement of Goods and Works*, para. 1.5; ADB, *Procurement Guidelines*, para. 1.5; EBRD, *Procurement Policies and Rules*, para. 3.3; IDB, *Policies for the Procurement of Goods and Works*, para. 1.5. And similarly: WB, *The World Bank Procurement Regulations for IPF Borrowers*, Annex IX, paras. 2.2–2.3 [all documents in ref. AP&R].

competition in the contractor selection procedures and to the freedom of contract left to the private party. In indirect procurement, on the other hand, there is no provision for different types of contractual arrangement. The types of contract financed by organizations are not restricted by specific indications in the guidelines, although states must include in the contracts certain provisions and adopt standard documents, if required by the organization. Furthermore, if no relevant standard bidding documents have been issued, the borrowing state must use contract forms acceptable to the organizations.[95] In the case of the EBRD, the organization's scrutiny of the contract form is based on whether it adequately achieves the project's objectives: '[t]he form of contract to be used must be appropriate to the objectives and circumstances of the project'.[96]

The different priorities in the objectives that distinguish direct procurement contracts from indirect procurement ones are thus also reflected in the form of the contractual arrangement and the relative requirements. While in the former the objective is primarily to guarantee the efficiency and promptness of administrative action, in the latter the contractual form is important only to the extent that it may act to elude the organization's controls or may not adequately ensure the pursuit of its stated objectives.

5.3.2   Conditions of Contract

The provisions on the conditions of contract included in most guidelines and regulations are an example of how these two modalities are interconnected and how objectives are pursued. The guidelines of the WB, ADB and AfDB require the contract to clearly define the object of the performance (and, thus, the sphere of the works that must be performed, the goods that must be supplied and the services that must be rendered), the rights and obligations of both parties, and the duties and responsibilities of the personnel employed by the beneficiary state to supervise and administer the contract. In addition, the general conditions of contract must be supplemented by the *ad hoc* conditions of contract required by the specific type of goods, services or works, indicating the place where

---

[95] AfDB, *Rules and Procedures for the Procurement of Goods and Works*, para. 2.12; ADB, *Procurement Guidelines*, para. 2.12(a); IDB, *Policies for the Procurement of Goods and Works*, para. 2.12 [all documents in ref. AP&R].

[96] EBRD, *Procurement Policies and Rules*, para. 3.24 [ref. AP&R].

performance is to be rendered.[97] Thus, the requirements leave a degree of discretion to national administrations.

Added to this, however, is an indication of the criteria for structuring the relationship between the parties: the conditions of contract must guarantee a balanced allocation of risks and responsibilities between the two contracting parties.[98] The objective, explicitly mentioned, for example, in the guidelines of the EBRD, is to obtain the most economical price and efficient execution of the contract.[99]

Thus, on the one hand, organizations impose an interpretation of the contract between the state and the private party as a tool that two parties on equal footing can use to reach an agreement, overcoming any different approach expressed in the national legal systems under which the contract is executed. On the other hand, they justify this obligation – in some cases explicitly – based on their interest in ensuring that the resources provided are used effectively and not wasted. The nexus between an equal footing concept of a contract concluded between the state and private parties and the interests of the organization can be explained through the tripartite relationship established in indirect procurement contracts: establishing that the contract between the national administration and the private party must provide a balanced allocation of rights and duties helps to minimize the risk of a contract in which the public power gives itself prerogatives that place it in a position of superiority over the private contractor, with the management of resources dictated by the interests of the national administration (or the interests of the national administration's officials) that are not consistent with the objectives of the international organization or actually in conflict with them. In this sense, the rights that must be granted to private contractors within the sphere of the contract have a function in part analogous to that granted to participants in the bidding process during the phase of contractor selection: the organization makes sure that, as private parties pursue their own interests, they also safeguard the proper execution of the contract and, thus, supplement the control that the organization has over the borrowing state.[100]

A *contrario*, this also explains why regulation within contracts between international organizations and private parties continues to give important prerogatives to the former to the detriment of the latter's freedom of contract. In these contracts the interest that private parties act as 'guardians' of the proper execution of the

---

[97] *Ibid.*   [98] *Ibid.*   [99] *Ibid.*, para. 3.24.   [100] See Chapter 7.

contract is nullified, and the need to balance the rights and duties of the contracting parties is also weakened, making it more advantageous for the organization to have a contractual structure that gives the organization the flexibility to make decisions it considers to be more in line with its own interests.

5.3.3   Performance Warranties and Compensation for Damages

The concern that the resources provided may be lost during execution of the contract is also the basis for certain provisions on warranties and compensation for damages. Various financing organizations require contracts to provide that the private party must pay a security guaranteeing contractual execution. In particular, in works contracts, national administrations must demand payment of a security that sufficiently protects them in the case that the private party breaches the contract. The amount may vary based on the type of security provided and on the nature and extent of the works, but a portion of it must also extend beyond the date on which performance is expected to be completed in order to cover liability for any defects or maintenance costs until the national administration's final acceptance. Moreover, in the case of periodic payments, contracts may provide that a percentage of the payment is withheld each time as a warranty until final acceptance.[101]

In the case of contracts for the provision of goods, national administrations may or may not require a warranty, based on their discretionary assessment of market conditions and commercial practices for that particular type of goods. If a warranty is required, it must be reasonable and adequately protect the administration from breach of contract.[102] In addition, the regulations of most organizations establish that contracts must give the national administration the right to compensation for damages when delays in the delivery of goods or the completion of works or failure of the goods, works or services to meet performance

---

[101] WB, *The World Bank Procurement Regulations for IPF Borrowers*, Annex IX, para. 2.4. And also AfDB, *Rules and Procedures for the Procurement of Goods and Works*, para. 2.39; ADB, *Procurement Guidelines*, para. 2.39; IDB, *Policies for the Procurement of Goods and Works*, para. 2.39 [all documents in ref. AP&R].

[102] WB, *The World Bank Procurement Regulations for IPF Borrowers*, Annex IX, para. 2.4. And also in AfDB, *Rules and Procedures for Procurement of Goods and Works*, para. 2.40; ADB, *Procurement Guidelines*, para. 2.40; IDB, *Policies for the Procurement of Goods and Works*, para. 2.40 [all documents in ref. AP&R].

requirements would generate additional costs, or lost earnings, or loss of other benefits for the administration.[103]

In all these cases, the restriction on the contractual provisions imposed by the organization is designed to ensure that the resources provided are not lost as a result of a private party's breach of contract. However, the regulations give the national administration some leeway for discretion to make a case-by-case assessment: the requirement to provide warranties is mandatory for more costly and complex contracts, but it is optional for contracts for the supply of goods. In this second case, the insertion of the relevant clause, the amount of the warranty and the procedures for providing it must be assessed according to the basic parameters indicated by the organization (market conditions and commercial practice).

The decision to limit the contractual power of national administrations and to demand a corresponding warranty from the private party meets a need that cannot be satisfied solely by the international organization's monitoring of the proper use of resources. And in fact, as we shall see, monitoring ensures that the national administration implements the funded project properly, including and above all in terms of expenses, but it does not cover situations where the private party fails to meet its contractual duties during contractual performance.[104]

5.3.4   Arbitration

Finally, the guidelines contain provisions on the law applicable to contracts and jurisdiction over disputes that may arise from them. The conditions of contract set by the national administration must indicate both which law is applicable and which body is competent for settling disputes arising from the contract. Nevertheless, the organizations offer precise directions with regard to the second aspect: the most suitable method for settling contractual disputes is international commercial arbitration, and thus all disputes arising from contracts for the procurement of goods, services and works funded by the organization and concluded by national administrations must be settled using this procedure.

---

[103] WB, *The World Bank Procurement Regulations for IPF Borrowers*, Annex IX, para. 2.9. And also in AfDB, *Rules and Procedures for Procurement of Goods and Works*, para. 2.41; ADB, *Procurement Guidelines*, para. 2.41; IDB, *Policies for the Procurement of Goods and Works*, para. 2.41 [all documents in ref. AP&R].

[104] See Chapter 7.

Exceptions to this rule may be made in two cases. The first exception is when the organization has exempted the borrowing state from this requirement because there are national rules and regulations and equivalent arbitration procedures (the state's request must nevertheless be justified and shall be approved by the bank). The second exception is when the contracts at issue were awarded to a private party of the same nationality as the borrowing state.[105] In general, the funding organization may not be appointed as an arbitrator in the dispute and may not itself identify and appoint an arbitrator.

Such conditions are an implementation of the reasoning found in the requirements regarding the contract in general: responsibilities and duties that must be distributed in a 'balanced manner' are rendered effective when it becomes possible to claim any violations of them before a neutral third party. This offers an important additional confirmation of the idea that the equal footing of the parties in the distribution of rights and duties is instrumental to the proper management of resources. Except in specifically identified cases, international organizations require the decision to be made by a body that provides guarantees of impartiality due to the fact that it is identified on a case-by-case basis with the consent of both parties, and that it acts as an arbitrator.

Even in the first of the two exceptions provided, admissibility depends on a judgment of equivalence that the organization reserves the right to make. And in fact, even assuming that it is possible to use procedures other than international commercial arbitration, there must be an equivalence between the rules and procedures of national arbitration and those of international commercial arbitration. In substance, it must always be arbitration and not, for example, a decision by an administrative court. Once more, the funding organization must perform an assessment that allows it to avoid the risk of partisan decisions.

The second exception gives the state greater autonomy. The reasons lie in a balancing of the values and needs emerging in this situation. The organization's interest in the proper management of resources weighs against other motives that are not decisive when considered individually but become so when considered together: recognition of the state's sovereignty over its citizens; considerations of convenience by virtue of which if, in a dispute between a state and a party with that state's

---

[105] WB, *The World Bank Procurement Regulations for IPF Borrowers*, Annex IX, para. 2.25. And also in AfDB, *Rules and Procedures for Procurement of Goods and Works*, para. 2.43; ADB, *Procurement Guidelines*, para. 2.43; IDB, *Policies for the Procurement of Goods and Works*, para. 2.43 [all documents in ref. AP&R].

nationality, the law applicable to the contract is national law (as it is in the vast majority of contracts of this type), then national courts should apply national law; and finally, motives linked to economy of resources and to competition, which change in the contractual phase compared to the vendor-selection phase. Indeed, during this phase, organizations have an interest in ensuring international competition so that resources are employed according to the relevant international organization's objectives and, thus, not wasted. However, once the contract is awarded to a private party with the nationality of the funded state following competitive procedures that involve a pool of bidders of various nationalities, the problem of discrimination based on nationality is no longer an issue and appointing a body of that nationality to judge a particular dispute becomes the most simple solution and has no particular counterindications, at least in terms of non-discrimination and assuming the borrowing state has a reliable judicial system. The fact that international arbitration is required in all other cases, i.e. when the contract is concluded between a state and an undertaking of a different nationality, confirms this last consideration.

5.4 Conclusions

The questions posed at the beginning of this chapter were whether and to what extent do international organizations impose limits on the freedom of contracts of private parties and states. In direct procurement contracts, this question is designed to determine whether there are clauses that can be considered 'exorbitant' – i.e. that diverge from and go beyond the normal contractual practices between private parties. Indeed, this is one of the aspects that, along with the law applicable to the contract[106] and the protection of private parties in disputes arising from its execution,[107] make it possible more generally to assess the nature of an organization's contract, determining whether the contract is shaped and dominated by the presence of an international and public party.

In direct procurement contracts, various elements appear to diverge not only from normal practices of contracts between private parties but also from those typical of public procurement contracts at the national level: the adoption of general terms and conditions of contract formulated unilaterally by the organization with little room for change at the private party's request, even in the case of flexible approaches; the

---

[106] See Chapter 6.   [107] See Chapter 7.

applicability of immunity from jurisdiction and execution; clauses relating to contract termination that are characterized by a significant lack of reciprocity and guarantee the organization the ability unilaterally to rescind the contract if a public interest arises, with no notice, no justification and no indemnification, or to unilaterally rescind the contract at its discretion without justification and little notice; the discretion to decide the fate of the contract due to *force majeure* or a change in the private party's situation, even if these events do not result in an actual breach by the other party; the imposition of subcontract conditions and procedures that ensure that the organization's objectives are achieved to the detriment of the private party's autonomy in establishing its own contractual relationships with other private parties (the organization determines whether or not the subcontracting relationship may be established, may influence its outcome and may define its content); and regulation of the private party's liability, which in relationships between the private party and its employees gives the organization the power to intervene in the employment relationship and in relationships between the private party and third parties, and which burdens the private party with unlimited liability to indemnify and defend the organization at its own expense.

To this should be added one system consideration. As also occurs for national administrations, the basis for recognizing these powers is the idea that they should always be aimed at meeting the public interest, and therefore the decisions that manifest them can and must be modified when the public interest so requires. However, in national legal systems these powers are always subject to and limited by the relevant national law: the law sanctions the balance of interests, for example, by giving the administration a power of revocation, but at the same time establishes an obligation to indemnify the private party. The same cannot be said of the contracts of international organizations. In the absence of legislation that *a priori* delimits the powers of the organizations in their contractual activity, the organizations themselves determine the balance of interests in a unilaterally established contract and give themselves the powers to re-establish this balance when it is altered. Even afterwards and in the event of a dispute, the arbitrator in fact plays a secondary role in this regard, because, as we shall see,[108] there is little litigation involving the contractual activity of organizations.

---

[108] See Chapter 7.

The direct procurement contracts of international organizations appear to be primarily instruments for ensuring the interest of the organizations, which is linked to the international nature of these bodies and the regulatory context in which they operate. Thus, the contractual relationship is based on a significant imbalance between the two parties and a substantial limitation of the private party's autonomy.

In indirect procurement contracts, international organizations establish limits that, to a certain extent, bridle states' contractual autonomy. Organizations require that the contractual rights and duties must be equitably distributed between the national administration and the private contracting party; that the private party must provide adequate performance warranties and be liable for compensation if there are changes in the contractual performance; and, finally, that an arbitrator must be identified to impartially settle disputes between the national administration and the private party. The international public interest, or more properly that of the international organization, is to protect itself against improper management by the national administration. Thus, on one hand, the organization tends to expand the private party's legal sphere – in particular compared to what it is granted in direct procurement contracts, acting to contain and control the national administration's contracting power. On the other hand, it requires the national administration to ensure that the funds provided are not wasted. The national administration's autonomy in determining contractual provisions is limited to the extent that it must support the international organization's institutional objectives, with the result that the rights and duties of the national administration and the private party become more balanced in the contractual relationship that binds them.

6

Contracts and Applicable Law

Blurring the Lines between Public and Private Law

6.1 Introduction

The issue of which law is applicable to contracts concluded by an international organization[1] is, as seen in the previous chapter, one of the elements to be examined to assess the public or private nature of these contracts. In the past, the issue of applicable law has been the subject of analysis by international law scholars and empirical studies on the functioning of organizations.[2] These analyses, however, have usually covered the entire spectrum of contracts concluded by these organizations, including, for example, rental or loan agreements and employment contracts. A critical reconstruction of past studies on this issue will be instrumental to analyzing the current trends. This reconstruction will, however, refer only to certain types of contracts, specifically those which comprise the following features: the contract enables the

---

[1] The question does not arise for contracts resulting from indirect procurement. The law applicable to these contracts is the national law of the recipient state, which has, however, to be compatible with the principles set forth in the guidelines of the organization (see Chapter 4) and the national law of the administration that it is disbursed to.

[2] The study that most analytically investigates the problem of the applicable law with regard to the various types of contracts concluded by international organizations is Jenks, *The Proper Law*. The issue, however, has been the subject of several studies since the 1960s. See Mann, 'The Proper Law of Contracts'; Batifol, *Problèmes des contrats privés internationaux*; Delaume, 'The Proper Law of Loans'; *id.*, 'Issues of Applicable Law in the Context of the World Bank Operations'; Glavinis, *Les litiges relatifs aux contrats passés entre organisations internationales et personnes privées*; Valticos, 'Les contrats conclus par les organisations internationales avec des personnes privées. Rapport provisoire'; *id.*, 'Les contrats conclus par les organisations internationales avec des personnes privées. Rapport définitif'; van Hecke, 'Contracts between International Organizations and Private Law Persons'; Schneider, 'International Organizations and Private Persons'; Sinkondo, 'Le rôle de la volonté de l'organisation internationale dans la détermination du droit applicable'; Seyersted, *Common Law of International Organizations*; Audit, 'Les marchés de travaux, de fournitures et de services passés par les organisations internationales'; Rigo Sureda, 'The Law Applicable to the Activities of International Development Banks'.

261

organization to fulfil its institutional mission; the contract is the result of a tender procedure that has been carried out in accordance with the principles and rules established in the organization's procurement manuals or other internal regulations; and the contract has a commercial nature and not organizational, as in the case of employment contracts. Therefore, the scope of this analysis does not include employment contracts, rent or loan agreements, or any other type of contract that does not meet these criteria. These contracts will be referred to only as occasional comparative benchmarks.

6.2 Theories and Practices in the History of International Organizations

In the past, the issue of the applicable law has been addressed by looking at the actual practices of organizations and also from a normative perspective, examining which law ought to be applicable in the event of a dispute between parties. Numerous solutions have been proposed.

In 1959, Mann observed that contracts between private and international persons – including in the category states and international organizations – were governed by the 'municipal law' chosen by the parties. Nevertheless, Mann called for an internationalization of these contracts, arguing that the applicable law should not be the national law but public international law, defined as a set of 'those principles of law accepted sempre ubique et ab omnibus, which govern the treaties, particularly the "commercial treaties", between international persons'.[3] Mann, therefore, by analogy proposed applying the system of rules governing agreements between states – i.e. treaties – to contracts between international and private subjects, and argued for this proposal on the basis of two considerations.

The first consideration was that these two types of contractual relationship do not differ much in their content: 'the nature and subject-matter ... are not substantially different'.[4] The second was pragmatic: just as one state in negotiating an obligation with another state does not want to agree to submit to the law of the other state, similarly a private subject entering into a contract with an international body may not want to be bound by the law of the contractual counterpart, be it a state or an

---

[3] Mann, 'The Proper Law of Contracts', p. 43.   [4] *Ibid.*, p. 44.

international organization.[5] According to Mann, the references to these general principles of law contained in some of the contracts concluded between international parties and individuals must be interpreted in the light of these considerations. These principles cannot constitute an independent source of regulation of the contractual relationship: 'unless they are equiparated to public international law, the general principles are not a legal system at all'.[6] Given the lack of development of these principles, if a different role is attributed to the general principles of law, adequate sufficient level of regulatory coverage would not be ensured for the entire range of situations and disputes that could arise from a contractual obligation.[7]

A partially different thesis was held by Jenks. In 1962, Jenks noted that, while relationships between international organizations and other international persons were regulated according to international law, relationships and transactions between international organizations and private subjects and corporate bodies were governed by the administrative law of the organization – this is the case, for example, with employment relations with officials – and by the applicable national law identified in the event of a conflict of laws.[8] In predicting future developments, Jenks also observed a tendency among international organizations to move away from national legal systems to develop their own system of administrative law rules to be applied, not only to the internal relations with their officials, but also to their relationships with private subjects that are not part of the organization.[9] In particular, Jenks foresaw an evolution from a binary system, based on the administrative law of the organization that governs its relations with officials and on the national law governing transactions with private subjects that are not a part of the organization, to a system where the rules of administrative law produced by the organization govern both the internal relations between the institution and its officials and its external relations, between the institution and third parties, individuals or private legal entities.

In an intermediate stage, however, such as when Jenks was writing, the practice of defining the general principles of law as the law applicable to contracts, as opposed to public international law, which could also be an option given the principle of autonomy of the parties, was quite

---

[5] *Ibid.*, p. 46.   [6] *Ibid.*, p. 46.   [7] *Ibid.*, p. 44 and pp. 51–52.
[8] See Jenks, *The Proper Law*, p. xxxv.   [9] *Ibid.*, p. xxxviii.

widespread.[10] The doubt as to whether these choices could guarantee the same level of certainty and precision as that of a national law could only be overcome through a case-by-case approach. The parties would have to evaluate, in practice and depending on the nature of the transaction, how opportune it was to opt for the general principles of law (or for public international law), by making a prediction of the contractual obligations that would require more clearly defined rules to deal with any disputes that could possibly arise from the contract.[11] If the contract was silent as to which law was applicable, this assessment was carried out by the arbitrator called upon to settle the dispute: in the absence of specific references to applicable law, the arbitrator would refer to the general principles of law or apply a subjective test, interpreting the underlying intention of the parties, or even carry out an objective test, evaluating if these principles were adequate and exhaustive to regulate all the aspects of that specific transaction. But also in this case, as for the administrative law regarding third parties external to the organization, Jenks warned: '[w]e are not dealing with the clearly settled principles of an established legal system but with experimental developments which have not passed beyond their infancy'.[12]

On the other hand, Batifol proposed a system to identify which law was applicable depending on the type of contract concluded. In this interpretation the criterion to determine the applicable law is objective, as it is connected to the particular function that the contract fulfils. This differs from the subjective criteria suggested by other scholars and is based solely on the will of the parties. Batifol identified three types of contract that an international organization may conclude: ordinary or auxiliary contracts, such as those for the provision of stationery, in which the parties may agree to consider the national law applicable; contracts with officials, to be covered by 'public international law' – this is interpreted as being international administrative law or the internal law of the organization – and, finally, contracts relating to the functions of the

---

[10] '[T]he possibility of adopting the general principles of law recognized by civilised nations as the proper law of a contract must . . . be regarded as established by current international practice', *ibid.*, p. 153. In support of the possibility of choosing as applicable law the 'general principles of law', Jenks recalls the theses developed by both McNair and Jessup in McNair, 'The General Principles of Law Recognized by Civilised Nations'; Jessup, *Transitional Law*.
[11] Jenks, *The Proper Law*, pp. 150–154.   [12] *Ibid.*

organization that are governed, in theory, by public international law although the organization itself may be subject to national law.[13]

With regard to this last type of contract, Batifol suggested an analogy with the administrative law contracts (*contrat administratif*) of the French legal tradition, and based on this analogy interpreted public international law as a body of rules produced by the international organization itself. In particular, he recalled a judgment of the French Conseil d'État of 11 January 1951 on a dispute concerning a contract between the French state and a Lebanese supplier that required the supplier to perform a public function. The ruling stated that such a contract should be considered subject to the rules of public law and classified under the category of administrative law contracts. Similarly, the intention of an international organization to enter into a contract with a private subject to perform one of the organization's public functions must be considered a crucial element in determining the applicable law and in the identification of the nature of the contract. The exercise of a public function justifies the application to the contract and to the disputes arising from it of public international law, to be interpreted as a body of rules produced by the organization and functional to the performance of its mission. The private subject subscribes to the contract knowingly accepting this.[14] If, on the contrary, the organization chooses to submit the contract to national law, it would be conducting itself as if it were a private subject and the contract would assume all the characteristics of an agreement between private subjects.[15]

About twenty years after these theories, in 1977 the Institut de Droit International issued a report on the contracts of international organizations with private subjects.[16] The study was the result of empirical research conducted through questionnaires and interviews with twenty-seven major international organizations, including the United Nations and all its agencies (UNICEF, UNESCO, FAO, ILO, UNDP etc.), the

---

[13] Batifol, *Problèmes des contrats privés internationaux*. For a critical analysis of the arguments set out by Batifol, see Seyersted, *Common Law of International Organizations*, pp. 453–455 and Glavinis, *Les litiges relatifs aux contrats passés entre organisations internationales et personnes privées*, pp. 189–194.

[14] 'Le contractant a accepté que la loi de l'organisme régisse une opération propre à cet organisme', in Batifol, *Problèmes des contrats privés internationaux*, p. 95.

[15] See Glavinis, *Les litiges relatifs aux contrats passés entre organisations internationales et personnes privées*, pp. 190–191.

[16] Valticos, 'Les contrats conclus par les organisations internationales avec des personnes privées. Rapport définitif'.

IMF, the WHO, and the member states of the European Community.[17] The result was a composite and diversified picture that shows the main factors that influence the choice of law are the nature and functions of the international organization and the type of contract concerned.[18] For instance, the fact that the organization is global or, conversely, regional, and therefore is composed of numerous and diverse member states or of a smaller and more homogeneous set of states, has a significant weight in determining the adoption of 'general principles of law' or, rather, the application of a national law. A lesser or greater level of legislative homogeneity among the member states respectively requires the organization to be equidistant from the various legal systems of the member states or, conversely, allows the organization to adopt the law of one member state that does not differ from or is essentially equivalent to the laws of other member states. Furthermore, implications on the applicable law vary depending on whether the organization performs an institutional public interest function, such as the provision of humanitarian aid, education support services, reconstruction of health systems in countries emerging from armed conflicts, or technical activities, such as that of the ESA, or financial or commercial services, such as those carried out by the IMF or the IBRD. Financial organizations, for instance, operate in the market and carry out transactions that are similar in nature and quality to those of private entities, such as banks and businesses. In order to perform these activities they often renounce their immunity and accept that the national law applies to the contracts they enter into, and, moreover, accept the jurisdiction of national courts that this choice entails.

Nevertheless, even within the same organization there are different types of contract. Contracts with a connection to the territory, such as leases, rent agreements or contracts for the supply of gas, electricity, water or cleaning services, and contracts with technical or financial contents, such as mortgages, loans and performance guarantees, are more frequently subject to national law, at least in some respects. In contrast, contracts related to the mission of an organization, in which the territorial component is heterogeneous, are not usually subject to national law. Examples of these include contracts for the provision of humanitarian aid concluded between an international organization that

---

[17] For a complete list of the organizations surveyed, see Valticos, 'Les contrats conclus par les organisations internationales avec des personnes privées. Rapport provisoire', p. 5 (fn. 12).

[18] *Ibid.*, pp. 9–19. See Chapter 2.

is headquartered in a state and a private subject who is incorporated in another state to perform a service in a third other state.

A more homogeneous picture, however, is provided by two reports, specifically on the subject of the applicable law, prepared by the UN Secretariat and issued respectively in 1967[19] and 1976.[20] Homogeneity is explained by the fact that the organizations analyzed all belong to the United Nations system (the United Nations, its agencies and the IAEA) and, therefore, have common recurring traits. In particular, two features emerge from the research: one is regulatory and the other is practical.

On the first point, the general legislation, such as the Charter of the United Nations, the Convention on the Privileges and Immunities of the United Nations and the regulations that give contractual capacity to individual agencies,[21] do not provide any indication as to which law to apply to contracts. The capacity of the United Nations to contract can be assumed by Art. 104 of the UN Charter. Moreover, it is reiterated in Art. I Section 1(a) of the Convention on Privileges and Immunities and extends to all UN agencies.[22] These general regulatory provisions, however, do not presume in favour of a particular applicable law for contracts. The absence of an explicit reference to the applicable law is interpreted by the Secretariat as an indication of the international character contracts should have, even when there seems to be an opening for a national legal system. The Headquarters Agreement between the United Nations and the United States, for example, provides that '[e]xcept otherwise as provided in this agreement or in the General Convention, the federal, state and local law of the United States shall apply within the district headquarters'.[23] However, first, federal, state and local law are applied as long as this does not conflict with the rules and regulations issued by the organization: '[n]o federal, state or local law or regulation of the United States which is inconsistent with a regulation of

---

[19] United Nations, 'The Practice of the United Nations, the Specialized Agencies and the International Atomic Energy Agency Concerning Their Status, Privileges and Immunities' [ref. REP].

[20] United Nations, 'Law Applicable to Contracts Concluded by the United Nations with Private Parties', p. 159 *et seq.* [ref. GT&CC]. In 1976 the United Nations Secretariat drafted a document in response to the questionnaire submitted by the Institut de Droit International to the United Nations and its agencies, such as UNICEF, UNRWA etc. for the preparation of the report.

[21] *Ibid.*, p. 160.   [22] See Chapter 5 and Chapter 7.

[23] Agreement between the United Nations and the United States, Art. III (7)(b) [ref. A&C].

the United Nations authorized by this section shall, to the extent of such inconsistency, be applicable within the district headquarters'.[24]

Moreover, even in the absence of an apparent conflict with the rules of the organization, the interpretation of the Secretariat is restrictive and is strictly functional to the performance of the mission of the organization: the provision concerning the application of American law in the district headquarters of the organization does not imply that all contracts concluded by the organization should be subject to this law. This restrictive interpretation is justified by reasons of administrative efficiency. Some contracts are, in fact, concluded and executed at the headquarters of the organization, but many others, involving both the United Nations and its agencies, are concluded in and by field offices or offices of other agencies, and of these most are performed in countries other than the United States and the District of New York. Interpretation of the provision on the application of American law as covering all contracts concluded in the headquarters of the organization would create a dichotomy: on the one hand, US law (federal, state and local) should be applicable to a number of contracts concluded in the headquarters and executed at the headquarters or in the field; on the other, the general principles of law or the law specified in the contract should apply to a whole range of other contracts concluded in locations other than at the headquarters. The main consequence of this approach would be to undermine the effective functioning of these organizations: '[t]his could result in confusion and in difficulties not consonant with the proper and efficient performance of the functions of the Organization'.[25] In contrast, reasons related to impartiality are not mentioned and this confirms an orientation that is still focused on the organization's internal rationale, something that is further confirmed by the still under-developed vendor selection procedures in 1976.

The second feature concerns the contract methodology. At the time of drafting a contract, be it of an employment or commercial nature, the applicable law is usually not specified.[26] The internal regulations of the organization apply for employment contracts, and are part of a system of international administrative law that is developing independently of any

---

[24] *Ibid.*, Art. III (7).
[25] United Nations, 'Law Applicable to Contracts Concluded by the United Nations with Private Parties. Procedures for Settling Disputes Arising out of Such Contracts', p. 161 [ref. GT&CC].
[26] With regard to contracts it is stated that '[g]enerally speaking, the United Nations contracts (both those of a commercial nature and employment contracts) have not specified the law considered to be applicable to such agreements', *ibid.*, p. 162.

national legal system.[27] References to national law that some of these contracts contain only relate to certain specific areas, such as work safety legislation or the rules on social security, or are inserted to provide a benchmark for the quantification of remuneration or allowances. Already when the Secretariat conducted its first survey – in 1967 – references to national laws on wages and allowances had almost disappeared and, in general, 'at no time did they amount to a choice of an actual system of municipal law to govern the entire terms of an employment contract'.[28] Any reference to national law, therefore, if there is one, is sector-based and specific and, even when in arbitration the issue of which law to apply has been raised, the United Nations Administrative Tribunal has referred to not only the internal regulations but also the general principles of law, thereby avoiding the application of national rules.

In the same way, any reference to state law in commercial contracts is avoided, as choice of law clauses is absent. However, even though this is generally true, the two reports of the Secretariat highlight two further aspects that relate to the stages following the signing of a contract. The first concerns procedural law. The opinion published in 1967 pointed out that contracts, while not containing any clause referring to the applicable law, provide a way of resolving disputes that has implications for the applicable law: if an amicable settlement is not reached, the parties can resort to arbitration. Consequently, most contracts concluded with companies incorporated in the United States or Latin America state that the arbitration is to take place in accordance with the procedures developed respectively by the American Arbitration Association and the Inter-American Arbitration Association. In all other cases, the reference is to the procedures of the International Chamber of Commerce. Therefore, the opening is not for the law of the state but for regulations produced by private institutions, which are in turn established and governed by national law. However, this opening refers primarily to procedural aspects and does not imply the application of national law to matters of substance of a dispute.

The second aspect specifically concerns the substantive law to be applied to resolve the dispute. As highlighted by the report issued in 1976, provided that there is no indication in the contract on the applicable law,

> it has been the practice of the United Nations to interpret the contracts concluded by it on the basis of general principles of law, including

[27] *Ibid.*, p. 208.   [28] *Ibid.*, p. 208.

international law, and upon the standards and practices established by its
internal law, including its financial regulations, principles of delegation of
authority under the charter and the internal rules and procedures pro-
mulgated thereunder.[29]

Therefore, this combination of the general principles of law and the
regulations of the organization form the legal reference system of the
contract, while there is no express reference to national law. However, it
also adds that it is common practice to draw up contracts, as far as
possible, 'in general conformity' with the law of the place where the
contract is concluded and must be performed, and the national law of
the private subjects with whom the contract is concluded. Given its
general character, the parameter of conformity should be interpreted
loosely: unless there is a clear conflict, the national law is not binding
on the international organization. This orientation implies, in practice,
that special attention is sometimes given to the national law through
consultations, mostly fact-finding in nature, with local authorities on the
content of regulations and their possible effects. The Secretariat refers to
these practices as 'a matter of comity', with an emphasis on a purely
voluntary and not mandatory consultation.

6.3   The Current Approaches

Some of the guidelines on the applicable law that were developed between
the 1960s and 1980s were then consolidated in conjunction with the
increase in the number of contracts concluded by international organizations and the enlargement of the membership of some of the organizations.
In contrast, some other trends that had been advocated by scholars of
international law have never taken shape or have only partially materialized.

6.3.1   Reasons for the Choice of Law

Albeit with a degree of approximation, due to the variety of organizations
considered and the number and diversity of contracts that are concluded,
there are at least three considerations that currently guide organizations
in their choice of law. Some of these have been in place since the
foundation of the organizations and have either remained constant or

---

[29] United Nations, 'Law Applicable to Contracts Concluded by the United Nations with
Private Parties. Procedures for Settling Disputes Arising out of Such Contracts', p. 164
[ref. GT&CC].

have been strengthened over the years; others have been taken into account by the organizations more recently.

The first is related to the position that international organizations have in comparison to nation states. During the nineteenth and early twentieth century, the dominant view was that in the international order the only entities with legal capacity were states, as they had sovereignty and independence. Since the 1940s, however, this view was gradually abandoned and replaced by the idea that, in order to carry out their functions, the newly founded international organizations should have legal capacity and be considered in all respects subjects of international law separately and independently from their member states.[30] From this perspective, therefore, to systematically apply national law to the transactions concluded by an international organization would limit its functional independence: it forces the organization, usually sovereign in its own self-determination, to comply with a national legislation the formation of which it was not involved, but to which it would only consent *ex post* in the negotiation of the contract. One of the main objectives of an organization in the choice of applicable law is, therefore, to maintain as much as possible its functional autonomy.

A second consideration is political. The international nature of organizations requires them to maintain, at least formally, an equal distance from all the member states. Consequently, choosing *a priori* the laws of one state to be applicable to all contracts can be interpreted as a sign of political preference in favour of a state. This would go against the very nature of the organization and its constitution. The only case in which this would not be interpreted as preferential treatment is if there was an explicit agreement among all member states to adopt a specific national legislation.

A third consideration concerns convenience and efficiency. In this respect, a choice in favour of a national law has, in fact, at least three negative effects. First, the details of the laws and their implications might not be fully understood or known to the officials of the organization. Second, the implementation of the contract would be subject to changes in national legislation that the organization would not be able to predict or control. Third, the organization would be subject to a multitude of national legal systems and this would lead to an unjustified coexistence of a variety of regulatory regimes to be applied to different contracts, so that even for contracts that have a similar object there might be different laws

---

[30] See Chapter 5.

governing them. These three effects mutually interact and thereby reinforce each other: the coexistence of a plurality of legal systems for individual contracts accentuates the problem of knowledge regarding the various
national laws and their implications, as well as that of the ongoing changes
in national rules. These dynamics have an impact on efficiency: to have
knowledge of the various national laws requires the use of personnel
delegated to studying them, and any diversification of the legislation
requires the same diversification of legal knowledge and expertise. This
also runs contrary to the many ongoing attempts at harmonization
between the various international organizations. In addition, there are
repercussions on the certainty of the legal position held by the international administration: the administration would be subject to changes in
the national law and could not foresee the implications that the choice in
favour of a particular national law would have on a contract.[31]

The independence and sovereignty of the organizations, the political
equidistance from the various member states, efficiency and certainty are
all internal reasons related to the expediency of the international organization rather than to rights of the vendors taking part in the selection
procedure. This political equidistance is, moreover, a concept that must
be understood in a different way to that of impartiality towards vendors.

Impartiality, in general, refers to the selection of the contractor by the
organization: it is the condition upon which a vendor can build its
expectation to be awarded a contract, and thus its expectation of an
economic return in the form of contracts awarded to national businesses.
In national public procurement governed by European law, impartiality
has been essential for the achievement of the objectives of European
integration and the creation and maintenance of a single market. Also
in national contracts governed by the GPA, it is instrumental to the free
movement of goods and services. As seen in previous chapters, international organizations are bound to the principle of impartiality in the
vendor-selection phase, but only within the limits of pursuit of their
institutional objectives and the economic benefits that can be derived to
the states that fund the organizations.

Equidistance from the legal systems of the member states is, however,
a requirement that is especially important in the contract implementation

---

[31] The problem of changes in national law had been resolved in the past, and still is for some
of those contracts that keep the reference to national law, with the inclusion in the
agreement of stabilization clauses. On this point, see Valticos, 'Les contrats conclus par
les organisations internationales avec des personnes privées. Rapport provisoire',
pp. 10–11.

phase. The reasons for this do not have much to do with the benefit of the vendor who has already been awarded the contract – which would actually be facilitated if the applicable law were that of the state where it is incorporated – or with external reasons connected to the fulfilment of institutional objectives, such as a single market. Equidistance in the contract execution phase is important for reasons of internal policy of the organization and is linked to its founding principles, according to which all member states are part of the organization on an equal footing. Moreover, in connection with these reasons, there are considerations of economic opportunity: for their functioning, organizations must ensure that ordinary and extraordinary financial contributions come from all member states. Finally, there are considerations of internal political balance among member states: the systematic adoption of a national law in the contracts of the organization could trigger internal *retaliation* measures in areas other than those of procurement by states whose law has not been preferred.

Furthermore, the choice of law could also be a relevant issue in the pre-contractual stage, during the selection of contractors. Indication in the tender of the use of national law could encourage businesses of a certain state at the expense of another and act as a discriminating factor. In this case the issue of the applicable law would be relevant as a condition to ensure impartiality.

These three considerations, however, have developed in a context that, with respect to the beginning, has seen progressive change in some of the constitutive elements of organizations due to internal and external reasons. The aspect regarding their independence has become increasingly relevant in the development of these organizations. On the one hand, the enlargement of the *membership* of the organizations in favour of developing countries, consequent to decolonization, has opened an internal political debate on the role that new members should be granted in the decision-making process, especially in response to the dominant role played by the few economically strong states. On the other, the supply of goods, services and works has followed a trend of steady growth since the foundation of the organizations, with a significant increase in quantity from the 1990s onwards. At the same time, this has been accompanied by an increasing percentage of contracts awarded to suppliers from countries in the developing world.[32] Equidistance, even if only in appearance, from the legal systems of the various states has therefore become one of several signs of a broader change in international politics and internal management policy.

Moreover, since the start of the twenty-first century, in conjunction with an increase in functions and in the procurement volume, a trend towards the decentralization of procurement has begun to take root in many organizations: no longer do headquarters of organizations provide for the procurement of goods, services and works for their field offices, but it is the latter that are delegated a number of functions to manage the procurement and contracting procedure below a certain value threshold, under the supervision and control of the headquarters. These decentralization policies have had an impact in terms of the applicable law, as they have reinforced the belief that it is more efficient to avoid a difficult coexistence within the same organization of contracts subject to different systems of law, and therefore specific references to national laws are omitted.

The growth in the volume of acquisitions along with decentralization has also had another effect. It has favoured the process of standardization of contracts within a single organization, and the harmonization of contract terms and conditions between the organizations belonging to the same system, such as the United Nations and all its agencies. This standardization is necessary to guide and check the contracts concluded by field offices, and therefore also to facilitate the supervisory task of central offices. Harmonization is a requirement that is still far from being fully achieved. It is a result of the increasingly frequent interactions between organizations, both in the conduct of individual missions and, in some cases, in the joint performance of the specific function of procurement through the creation of networks between administrations, the goal of which is to combine requests and obtain cost savings (e.g. the *Common Procurement Team* of the FAO, IFAD and WFP). It must be added that the content of the terms and general conditions of contracts has been developed and consolidated. Standardization, harmonization and consolidation of contractual terms have led operators to opt for formulae that do not attribute the applicable law to a state in particular, but rather provide solutions that are general enough to not compromise

---

[32] As seen in Chapter 3, among other effects this has also resulted in some states, such as particularly the United States, having strongly supported policies to reform the process of vendor selection and to grant greater transparency and competition during these processes.

these objectives and that at the same time comply with the other requirements of efficiency and equidistance from the various member states.

Finally, the legal framework within which organizations operate has gradually changed. Since the 1920s there have been experiments to unify the laws of the different national legal systems – *The Draft Code of Obligations and Contracts*, adopted in Paris in 1927,[33] can be considered the first of these. However, most of these early attempts only referred to certain activity sectors and in any case were not followed up by practical application.[34]

Between the 1990s and 2000, to complete a trend that had been maturing for a while, efforts to build a single body of principles and cross-sector regulations common to the national legal systems of the same regional area, such as Europe, have multiplied. For example, the principles developed by UNIDROIT for international commercial contracts, the first version of which dates back to 1994 and which was followed by three others, in 2004, 2010 and 2016,[35] belong to this second type. The same international organizations have been able to take advantage, then, of the tools developed for contracts between private subjects, integrating the terms developed for such contracts with the contractual provisions likely to respond to the needs of the organization as a public entity.[36]

6.3.2 The Hybrid Solution: Between Contracts, Private Law and Public Law

The analysis of the current available approaches to applicable law requires some preliminary aspects to be clarified. The first concerns identification and distinction of the various stages of the contract management process in which the issue of applicable law arises. These are both the contract negotiation phase, when the parties have to

---

[33] Commission française d'études de l'union legislative entre les nations alliées et amies, *Project de Code des obligations et des contrats* [ref. GT&CC].

[34] For a description of the past attempts at unification of private law with reference to specific sectors, see David, *The International Unification of Private Law*; Bonell, 'The UNIDROIT Initiative'.

[35] UNIDROIT, *Principles of International Commercial Contracts*, Rome, 1994; *id.*, *Principles of International Commercial Contracts*, Rome, 2004; *id.*, *Principles of International Commercial Contracts*, Rome, 2010; *id.*, *Principles of International Commercial Contracts*, Rome, 2016 [all documents ref. GT&CC].

[36] On this point, see later in this chapter and Böckstiegel, 'The Application of the UNIDROIT'.

indicate the legal context in which the contract is to be performed, and the possible successive phase of a dispute between the parties, when an arbitrator has to identify the appropriate law to govern and resolve the controversy. The two phases are closely linked to each other and the second largely depends on the decisions taken in the first. However, contracts drafted by international organizations often lack explicit reference to the applicable law and arbitrators have a degree of autonomy in determining the issue. It is therefore necessary to keep a distinction between the applicable law chosen by the parties in drafting the contract and the applicable law identified by the arbitrator to resolve the dispute.

The second aspect concerns the nature of the applicable law. The relevant literature usually includes in the generic term 'applicable law' the rules regulating different aspects of the contract management process. In contrast, for contracts of international organizations a distinction also has to be drawn between a substantive applicable law regulating contract performance and any dispute that may arise from this, and a procedural law that deals with the procedures through which the resolution of contractual dispute may be brought about.

The issue of applicable law can therefore be analyzed from at least three points of view: the organization's influence in the choice of law applicable to the contract, in other words if the organization and the private subject have the same decision-making power in its determination; the identification of the law within the contract, i.e. if the contract contains information about the substantive law and the applicable procedures and, if so, what these indications are; and finally, the choice and application of the law by an arbitrator called to resolve a dispute. The second and third aspects are dealt with together as they are closely related.

6.3.2.1   The Decision-Making Power of the Organization in Determining the Applicable Law

With reference to the influence of the organization in the choice of law, some elements play an important role and interact with each other: the inclusion or omission within the terms and conditions attached to the tender notice of any reference to the applicable law; the economic strength of the contractual counterpart and/or its indispensability as a provider of certain goods, services or works; and the type of performance requested.

With regard to the first element, if the general terms and conditions drawn up by the organization, acceptance of which is binding to bid for a tender, already indicate the applicable substantive and procedural law, the private subject basically does not have any margin of choice. The European institutions' general terms and conditions of contract, for example, indicate the applicable substantive and procedural law so that normally there is no margin of influence by the private subject as regards this aspect. However, as will be seen below, the general terms and conditions lack information as to the substantive law to be applied, while they usually contain provisions on the sources of procedural rules. In this sense, the organization unilaterally provides a solution by delegating the power to identify the applicable substantive law to the arbitrator if there is a dispute.

Moreover, even in the absence of an indication as to the applicable substantive law, companies with strong bargaining power because of the economic importance they have in the market, or that provide unique goods, services or works, while not expecting to include in the contract any generic reference to a certain national legal system, may insist during negotiations that some sensitive aspects of the contract, such as copyright for companies providing computer products, are subject to a certain national legal system or are regulated by a body of clauses that the companies themselves have drafted. This, for example, is the case for large multinational computer product companies that supply technically complex goods, the characteristics of which have been specifically developed to suit the needs of the organization. This possibility is institutionalized and expanded in international organizations for whom the supply of technical goods is of crucial importance and is extremely complex, and thus requires the *a priori* identification of a specific legal system, even if a dispute does not occur. The general terms and conditions of the ESA, for example, on the one hand, impose a body of detailed provisions relating to copyright, and on the other, point to the special conditions for identifying the applicable law. The special conditions result from a joint determination by the parties, and in ESA contracts usually the applicable law is that of the country in which the supplier is established. Consequently, unlike in other organizations, the final determination of the applicable substantive law is *de facto* made by the supplier, to the extent that it is linked to the country in which the company is incorporated.

6.3.2.2 The Applicable Law for Substantive Issues

The second and third aspects – the substantive and procedural law to which the contract explicitly refers and its application by an arbitrator – allow for numerous distinctions that are mainly dependent on the type of organization and contract, and on the different role that the considerations and conditions mentioned above play with regard to these aspects. The need for equidistance from the member states in the choice of applicable law has a decisive role in the organizations of the UN family, as these organizations are characterized by universal membership and a high degree of heterogeneity of the legal systems of the states that are part of them. For these organizations, the phenomenon of the growth of their functions and the choice in favour of decentralization has excluded solutions regarding the applicable law that could give rise to a fragmented and overly diversified legal framework with every contract being traced to a different national legal system. To these considerations it must be added that international organizations show a low rate of litigation, at least when compared to national administrations. In fact, while there is no known data on complaints relating to tender procedures as they are usually filed in informal ways – at least for organizations belonging to the UN system – the available data show that the number of arbitrations for the resolution of contractual disputes is quite low when compared to the total volume of expenditure on contracts.[37]

This lack of litigation, combined with the other considerations mentioned above (the need for equidistance from the member states etc.), leads organizations, and especially those of the UN family, to adopt essentially two alternative options as to the applicable substantive law (to which can be added a third that mostly concerns regional organizations or some specific contracts). The first and most common is exclusion of any reference to the applicability of a specific substantive law. This is, for instance, the case in the terms and general conditions of contracts drafted by the United Nations, UNDP, UNOPS, UNICEF and UNHCR. When, however, a clause of the applicable law is omitted, there are other useful references in the contract that indicate the primary source that governs the relationships is the contract itself. Emphasis on the provisions of the contract as the only law governing the relationship has led some scholars to argue that the contracts of international organizations fall within the scope of the notion of

---

[37] See Chapter 7.

a *contract without a governing law*[38] – the expression used in French jurisprudence is *contrat sans loi.*[39] In this type of contract, the set of rules governing the relationship between the parties comprise the terms of the contract itself to the exclusion of any national legal system. The theory of *contrat sans loi* is based on the concept that the will of the parties replaces the collective will, as expressed by state law. Thus, according to some scholars, it may well apply to contracts in which one party is a public entity that sets the rules. Such a view, however, equates to the exclusion of any reference to a national legal system and the absence of a legal context *tout court*, denying the inclusion of the contract in a context of law that is different from that produced by the parties.

In international organization contracts, on the contrary, the contract terms are not the only source of regulation. To the extent to which they are expressly referred to in the contract, the international conventions and all the other legal texts that the contract assumes, including the internal law of the organization, become applicable to the relationship between the parties. As regards this, the general terms and conditions of UN contracts, and using them as a model, also the terms and conditions of other organizations, provide that '[t]he contractor shall comply with all laws, ordinances, rules, and regulations bearing upon the performance of its obligations under the terms of this Contract. In addition, the Contractor shall maintain compliance with all obligations relating to its registration as a qualified vendor of goods and services to the United Nations, as such obligations are set forth in the United Nations vendor registration procedures'.[40] Moreover, '[n]othing in or relating to the

---

[38] This is argued by Verdross. See Verdross, 'Die Sicherung von auslandischen Privatrechten aus Abkommen zur wirtschaftlichen Entwicklung'; *id.*, 'Protection of Private Property under Quasi-International Agreements'. For a critique, based on arguments other than those developed in this chapter, see Mann, 'The Proper Law', p. 48 *et seq.*; Fatouros, *Government Guarantees to Foreign Investors*, pp. 193 *et seq.*; Level, 'Le contrat dit sans loi'; Weil, 'Problèmes relatifs aux contrats passés entre un Etat et un particulier', pp. 177–184. Mann, in particular, is strongly critical of the idea of a contract without law, see Mann, 'The Proper Law', pp. 49–50.

[39] The notion of *contrat sans loi* has been summarized as follows: 'l'hypothèse où le contrat constitue un ordre juridique autosuffisant et où la volonté s'inscrit dans le cadre du monisme subjectiviste', from Pommier, *Principe d'autonomie et loi du contrat*, p. 273. For more, in general, on the notion of *contrat sans loi*, see Peyrefitte, *Le problème du contrat dit sans loi*, p. 113 *et seq.*; Level, 'Le contrat dit sans loi', p. 209 *et seq.*; Beraudo, 'Faut-il avoir peur du contrat sans loi?'; Gannagé, 'Le contrat sans loi en droit international privé'; Arfaoui Ben Mouldi, 'L'interprétation arbitrale du contrat de commerce international'.

[40] The general terms and conditions of contracts are usually available on the website of each organization and on the website of the United Nations Global Marketplace (UNGM) where the tender notices are published. They are part of the tender notice (see Chapter 5).

Contract shall be deemed a waiver, express or implied, of any of the privileges and immunities of the United Nations, including its subsidiary organs'.[41] By signing the contract, the private party gives its consent to the application of all the provisions contained in the organization's founding treaties and in the other treaties the organization has concluded, such as protocols on privileges and immunities, as well as to the application of all the rules produced by the organization.

The substantive law to which contracts refer, therefore, is a composite regulatory framework that includes: the contract clauses, the unalterable core of which is defined by the international organization in the general terms and conditions of the contract;[42] the rules connected to the international and public nature of the organization and to its relationships with other international entities, mainly states (international treaties); and the rules governing the exercise of public functions by the international administration (internal regulations). It is not, therefore, a unified system of law but a web of rules with a different origin and nature, but with a common element: autonomy from the state dimension.

The contract clauses are for the most part set by the organization and to a lesser extent are the result of a negotiation with the private party,[43] at least when the latter has, for reasons related to its market position, strong bargaining power, or when it comes to complex contracts that require the participation of the private party in the definition of some aspects of the contract. They show similarities to the provisions laid down in contracts between private parties, but compared to these also have some unique features determined by the public nature of the objectives pursued by the contract. Pursuit of these objectives affects the interests of the private counterpart, which turn out to be recessive vis-à-vis public interests, as they allow the adoption of a series of 'unilateral' clauses such as those on the unilateral withdrawal by the administration without notice and without compensation, limited subcontracting, indemnity and liability.

Those adopted by the United Nations and its agencies have common features or are in many cases identical. See United Nations, *GCC Goods and Services*, para. 26. And likewise *inter alia* United Nations, *GCC Goods*, para. 25; *id.*, *GCC Services*, para. 25; UNHCR, *GCC Goods*, para. 23; *id.*, *GCC Services*, para. 23; *id.*, *GCC Goods and Services*, para. 24; UNDP, *GTC Contracts*, para. 32 [all documents in ref. GT&CC].

[41] See United Nations, *GCC Goods and Services*, para. 18. And likewise *inter alia* United Nations, *GCC Goods*, para. 17; *id.*, *GCC Services*, para. 17; UNHCR, *GCC Goods*, para. 21; *id.*, *GCC Services*, para. 21; *id.*, *GCC Goods and Services*, para. 22; UNDP, *GCC Contracts*, para. 24; *id.*, *GC Professional Services*, para. 17; *id.*, *GCC Civil Works*, para. 72 [all documents in ref. GT&CC].

[42] See Chapter 5.   [43] See Chapter 5.

At the same time, the contract is in part regulated by public international law, given that includes references to international treaties and agreements. Yet again, it is the public and international character of the organization and the implications that this entails in terms of the need to perform its function in the interest of the international community that justifies, for example, its immunity from jurisdiction and execution. This, however, does not imply that rules governing agreements between states are also to be applied to contracts between an international and a private entity – as suggested by Mann – but that public international law has a direct effect on the private subject when this subject is a party to a contract with an international organization. These effects are, of course, limited to those connected with the object of the contract and affect the private subject by virtue of the consent that this subject has given when entering into the contract.

Finally, apart from the general terms and conditions of contracts, which can be more or less rigid, the rules produced by organizations are those governing the vendor-selection phase, the violation of which may have implications and consequences for any subsequent contract. This first composite solution is very common in many of the organizations of the UN family. Contracts of these organizations usually lack any indication of what should be the applicable law for issues that do not directly entail a public international interest. The arbitrator will therefore combine and integrate different sources: the contract clauses, international public law, the internal law of the organization and any other provisions of a legislative nature, which, while not defined in any of these sources, may be necessary to settle the dispute.

This first solution does not, therefore, allow for explicit reference to the general principles of private law. The reason, according to some, pertains to practicality and negotiating strategies:

> the major reason why general principles of law, or the general principles of the law of the member States, are not referred to more frequently, is probably that they are not defined anywhere, and that express reference to them in contracts therefore might provoke the other party to press for an explanation of what they would involve with regard to any specific issue that might arise.[44]

There is also a favourable condition that allows this omission: the unwillingness of both the organization and the private entity to enter into conflict with one another, so that, given the low number of disputes,

[44] Seyersted, *Common Law of International Organizations*, p. 510.

it is realistic that, even from a practical and negotiating strategy perspective, parties prefer to include no more explicit references to a specific applicable law than is strictly necessary. Nevertheless, the practice shows that, also when there is no explicit guidance, when deciding disputes arbitrators often resort to the general principles of law.[45] This circumstance leads also to an impairment of the reasons of practicality mentioned above, especially in the light of the recent advancements towards the elaboration of common principles.[46]

The second solution adopted by some organizations of the UN system differs from the first in terms of the explicit inclusion in the text of the contract references to the general principles of commercial law. The general terms and conditions of the FAO, for example, provide that '[n]otwithstanding any specific provision herein, this Contract and any disputes arising therefrom shall be governed by *general principles of law*, to the exclusion of any single national system of law'.[47] More specifically, the general terms and conditions of IFAD provide that '[t]he Contract will be governed by (a) the Headquarters Agreement; (b) the UNCITRAL Model Law on Procurement of Goods and Construction; and (c) rules and regulations bearing upon the performance of its obligations under the terms of this Contract'.[48] The broad formulation employed by an organization such as the FAO has to be interpreted as including rules of public international law, administrative law (of the organization) and private international law.[49] With regard to

---

[45] Seyersted refers to several arbitral awards that support this point, which, however, relate to disputes between a state and foreign private companies, *ibid.*, pp. 510–511, fn. 9. According to him, however, this should demonstrate that, even more so, reference to the general principles of law should be possible for international organizations, which do not have a unified system of rules of public and private law.

[46] See, for instance, Böckstiegel, 'The Application of the UNIDROIT', pp. 53–54.

[47] Emphasis added. FAO, *FAO Revised GTC Goods*, para. 17.2 and *ibid.*, *FAO Revised GTC Services*, para. 21.2 [all documents in ref. GT&CC].

[48] Emphasis added. IFAD, *GTC Goods*, para. 32; *id.*, *GTC Services*, para. 30 [all documents in ref. GT&CC].

[49] Seyersted recalls that '[g]eneral principles of law comprise, in principle, the general principles of all legal systems: national law, international law of IGOs and international law. The actual choice depends upon the purpose. For the purposes of commercial and other relationships of a private law nature, as primarily considered in the present context, general principles of law means largely general principles of national law, since IGO law and international law do not as yet have many applicable rules' (Seyersted, *Common Law of International Organizations*, p. 512). In fact, the absence in the general terms and conditions of FAO of any specific indications on the applicable law – except for the international treaties on privileges and immunities entered into by the organization – might suggest a literal interpretation of the expression as to include various branches of law.

arbitration, the general terms and conditions of UNRWA provide that '[t] he decisions of the arbitral tribunal shall be based on *general principles of international commercial law*'.[50] In the same way, even when more specific expressions are used that refer to the applicability of private law and international trade, such as those found in the terms and conditions of UNRWA or IFAD, other clauses allow for the applicability to the contract of treaties and international agreements, especially those on privileges and immunities, and of the administrative rules of the organization.[51]

The third solution, typical of regional organizations and European institutions, is to declare a particular national or supranational law applicable. Therefore, for example, contracts of the European institutions mostly use a standard formula: '[t]he Contract shall be governed by Union law, complemented, where necessary, by the national substantive law of Belgium'.[52] The regulatory context is again composite and includes legal sources of European origin, such as treaties, directives, regulations and principles developed by the Court of Justice of the European Union, which directly or indirectly define the legal positions of private subjects in relation to institutions and national legislation, applied by analogy to relationships between European institutions and private entities. Therefore, also in this case the applicable rules have mixed characteristics, as they derive from European public law, the administrative law of the EU institutions, European private law and national private law.[53] The choice in favour of this solution is made possible, first, by

---

[50] UNRWA, *GCC Goods Only*, para. 17.2; *id.*, *GCC Services Only*, para. 17.2; *id.*, *GCC Goods and Services*, para. 18.2 [all documents in ref. GT&CC].

[51] See UNRWA, *GCC Goods Only*, para. 20: '[t]he Contractor shall comply with all laws, ordinances, rules, and regulations bearing upon the performance of its obligations under the Contract. In addition, the Contractor shall maintain compliance with all obligations relating to its registration as a qualified vendor of goods or services to UNRWA, as such obligations are set forth in UNRWA vendor registration procedures'. And similarly, *id.*, *GCC Services Only*, para. 20; *id.*, *GCC Goods and Services*, para. 21 [all documents in ref. GT&CC].

[52] This formula is used with minor variations in all draft contracts that are attached to the tender notice and are binding for the private party. Also see Chapter 5.

[53] The notion of a 'European private law' has had, however, multiple interpretations. On the historical origins of the concept, which, according to some scholars, date back to the Roman legal tradition, see Monateri, 'Black Gaius'; Hesselink, *The New European Legal Culture*; Poillot-Peruzzetto (ed.), *Vers une culture juridique européenne?* The literature has dealt with European private law, focusing on the theory of the contract and on civil liability. Among the most significant contributions, see Zimmermann and Whittaker (eds.), *Good Faith in European Contract Law*; Gordley (ed.), *The Enforceability of Promises*; von Bar, *The Common European Law of Torts*; Kötz and Flessner, *Europaeisches Vertragsrecht*; Ranieri, *Europaeisches Obligationenrecht*.

a sufficiently developed body of common principles among EU states and, second, by the high degree of political and legislative integration between the various legal systems of EU states. It is this latter aspect that allows it to make the law of only one European country, Belgium, applicable without having to consider issues, such as political equidistance and legislative diversity, which motivate the choice of the applicable law in the United Nations and its agencies.

As for regional organizations that do not, however, have an equal level of political integration, the law of a single state, i.e. the state of the private party or where the contract is implemented, is usually preferred so that different contracts of the same organization may refer to different legal systems. This is, for example, the case of the ESA, which, as already mentioned, generally includes in its contracts a clause that makes the law of the state of the private contractor applicable. State law has, however, only a residual role for those aspects not covered in the contract, or to interpret ambiguous contractual clauses. Furthermore, it is always subject to the laws that protect the prerogatives of the international organization. The general terms and conditions of the ESA, for example, state that:

> [w]ithout prejudice to ESA's special status as an Intergovernmental Organization with respect to its Privileges and Immunities ... reference shall be made to a substantive law to be identified in the contract: a) when a matter is not specifically covered by the Contract or the ESA General Clauses and Conditions; or b) for the interpretation of a contract provision when such is ambiguous or unclear and not specifically covered by these General Conditions.[54]

In addition to regional organizations, it is mainly technical or financial organizations that include a reference to a state law in contracts related to the performance of their functions (loan agreements, insurance contracts etc.).

Finally, even in organizations of a universal character, the object of the contract may be decisive as to whether to refer to national law in a contract. This includes cases where performance is not directly related to the mission of the organization, but is instrumental to its functioning and the performance of which is, at the same time, closely linked to the country where the organization is based. Rental contracts, property purchase or management, utilities (gas, electricity and water), cleaning of premises and construction of infrastructure are contracts of this kind. However, also in these contracts the reference to state law often only

---

[54] ESA, *Regulations of the European Space Agency*, Clause 34 [ref. GT&CC].

covers certain aspects of the relationship between the parties, for example, in cleaning contracts or infrastructure construction only the national rules on safety at work are applicable and not all the relevant national legislation for other aspects of the contractual relationship. Moreover, also in contracts in which the national law applies to the entire relationship or only to certain aspects of it, there are references to the conventions on privileges and immunities, with the exception of EU contracts and those of some financial institutions.

6.3.2.3 The Law Applicable to the Procedures for Dispute Resolution

The picture is simpler and the solutions less problematic for the applicable procedural law. As will be seen in more detail in the chapter on accountability,[55] most organizations do not have permanent jurisdictional bodies competent to settle contractual disputes between the organizations themselves and private parties, and contracts. Therefore, they provide for the possibility of referring the resolution of disputes to arbitrators identified by the parties when required, by mutual agreement and in accordance with procedures established in the contract and/or external sources of international or national law as identified in the contract. The practice again shows three main variants: the use of the procedural rules established by international organizations; the provision of procedural rules in the contract and, subordinate to these, reference to the regulations issued by an international organization or national legislation; and finally, reference to national procedural law.

Nearly all the organizations of the UN family (the United Nations, UNDP, UNOPS, UNICEF, UNIDO, UNHCR, FAO etc.)[56] and some other organizations, including regional ones, make reference in their contracts to the regulations established by the UNCITRAL on the procedures of conciliation and arbitration.[57] These are rules of law formulated by an international body and designed to regulate disputes that arise from transactions between private entities, between states or between states and private entities. However, in this context they apply, through

---

[55] See Chapter 7.

[56] A partial exception is IFAD, whose general terms and conditions already dictate the basic procedures for the selection of the arbitrator and recall the UNCITRAL Arbitration Rules as a residual source in cases of disagreement on the identification in practice of the arbitration panel (IFAD, *GTC Goods*, para. 33 [ref. GT&CC]).

[57] The UNCITRAL Arbitration Rules, formulated for the first time in 1976, were subsequently amended in 1982, in 2010 and most recently in 2013.

an explicit reference in the contract, to a relationship between an international organization and private parties.

A slightly different solution is adopted by other organizations, which are mostly regional, in whose contracts the procedural aspects of the arbitration proceeding are distinguished from the execution of the arbitration award. The former are governed by the contract and subordinately by the procedural rules formulated by another international organization, and the latter by state law. The general terms and conditions of the ESA, for example, show the coexistence of rules from different levels of government:

> [i]f no other arbitration is foreseen in the Contract, any disputes arising out of the Contract shall be finally settled in accordance with the *Rules of Arbitration of the International Chamber of Commerce* (ICC) by one or more arbitrators appointed in conformity with those rules. Conduct of such proceedings shall be in accordance with the ICC rules in force at the time arbitration is requested by either of the Parties ... The enforcement of the award shall be governed by the rules of procedures in force in the state/country in which it is to be executed.[58]

The third solution is mainly adopted in contracts of the European institutions. In line with the option adopted with regard to the applicable substantive law, in fact, contracts devolve the power to settle disputes arising from a contract to the courts of Brussels. The applicable procedural law, regarding the identification of the competent organ, area of competence and the measures that it may adopt is therefore accorded to a specific state: Belgium.

6.4   Conclusions

The above analysis identifies the current and most frequently adopted solutions with regard to the choice of law in international organizations' contracts, considering three different aspects: the role played by the international organization in determining which law is applicable, or, to put it in other terms, whether the organization and the private party have the same weight and influence in this determination; the content of the contract and, in particular, whether contracts contain specific clauses on the procedural and substantial law to be applied, and, if so, what the most common prescriptions are in this regard; finally, the role of arbitrators and what law arbitrators choose and apply to solve a controversy

---

[58]   ESA, *Regulations of the European Space Agency*, para. 35.2 [ref. GT&CC].

arising from the contract. The second and third aspects have been treated together, as they are closely related.

Ultimately, there is no straightforward answer to the question of which law is applicable to substantive and procedural issues arising from contracts with international organizations. However, it is clear that, as for several other contract clauses,[59] it is the international organization that defines the issue of the applicable law in accordance with its institutional nature and needs. In this regard at least three patterns of choice can be identified. First, the contracts of international organizations do not spell out which law ought to be applied. In such cases, the applicable law will be made up by the arbitrator itself and will be a mix of contract clauses and their interpretation, international treaty law, and the institutional rules and regulations of the international organization. Second, the contract includes explicit reference to the general principles of law or to the principles of international trade law, which have to be complemented by contract clauses, including those concerning the immunity of international organizations, the legal grounding of which is in treaty law. Third, the contract explicitly points to a specific national legal order. Although this last option is quite uncommon, it is sometimes chosen in contracts concluded by regional organizations or when the contract needs to be executed in exceptional circumstances.

Thus, due to the public and international legal nature of international organizations, the applicable law does not result from reference to a single legal system but from a combination of legal sources at both the national and supranational level, which in turn leads to the application by the arbitrator of selected rules of public law and private law. Both the national and supranational divide and the public and private divide appear to be blurred in the light of a specific interaction of interests and objectives that underlie these types of contracts.

---

[59] See Chapter 5.

7

Accountability in Procurement

7.1 Introduction

The expansion of the functions and funding of international organizations have increasingly brought to the attention of member states the problem of the accountability of organizations. This growing complexity has, indeed, led first to a decentralization of the functions connected to direct procurement. The United Nations, UNDP, WFP, UNHCR, FAO and UNICEF have increasingly delegated the duties of selecting the vendor and managing contractual relationships with private parties to field offices.[1] This tendency has created a need for effective mechanisms to ensure the internal accountability of field offices to administrative authorities at the headquarters, and of administrative authorities to member states. In addition, cases of serious mismanagement and misappropriation of resources – such as the oil-for-food scandal – have been attributed to inadequate internal controls[2] and have resulted in urgent public calls for reform in this area.[3] Second, the increasing number of missions and projects funded by organizations, together with the fact that their implementation has been entrusted to beneficiary states, has made it necessary to adopt forms of accountability that ensure that the goals of the missions and projects are achieved while minimizing any misappropriation or waste of funds.

[1] On the tendency towards decentralization and the problems it poses, see in particular JIU, *Procurement Reforms in the United Nations System*, p. 7 [ref. REP]. The connection between decentralization and the development of functions is highlighted in Beigbeder, *The Internal Management of the United Nations Organisations*; and Conyers, 'Decentralization: The Latest Fashion in Development Administration?' In general, for a review of the literature on decentralization and the development policies of organizations up to the 1980s, see Conyers, 'Decentralization and Development'.

[2] Along these lines, see in particular the observations of the United States in US GAO, *Observations on the Management and Oversight of the Oil for Food Program* [ref. REP]; *id.*, *Lessons Learned from Oil for Food Program* [ref. REP].

[3] See Chapter 3.

In response to these needs, starting in the mid-1990s, a process of administrative reform was initiated within many organizations,[4] and the question of accountability was added to the agenda of the organizations as a matter of priority. For instance, in 1993 the JIU issued its first exhaustive report on accountability and oversight in the UN Secretariat.[5] This focused on mechanisms of internal control, in particular control of financial management, evaluation and monitoring. It noted functional weaknesses, fragmentation and excessive distribution of responsibilities. It called for a reorganization and strengthening of these mechanisms. Eventually, it proposed the establishment of a United Nations Office of Accountability and Oversight. It did not, however, touch on the possibility of an appeal mechanism being made available to private parties.

The various institutional and functional components of accountability within the organizations of the UN system were gradually developed on the basis of this first report and as a result of the inter-institutional dialogue[6] that it triggered between the General Assembly and consulting and control bodies, in particular the ACABQ, the JIU[7] and the Boards of Auditors. Some organizations also adopted specific policies or framework documents on accountability (known as accountability frameworks). Between 2000 and 2010, the ILO,[8] UNDP,[9] UNFPA,[10] UNICEF[11] and UNOPS drafted a number of general documents with the goal of re-examining the operation of existing accountability mechanisms and establishing new ones.[12] The first accountability

---

[4] See Chapter 3.   [5] JIU, *Accountability and Oversight in the United Nations* [ref. REP].

[6] The reform process is evidenced by various resolutions of the General Assembly and reports from independent bodies, which, during the mid-1990s and the first decade of the twenty-first century, generally related to administrative reform of these organizations, in particular aspects of accountability. Certain member states, in particular the United States, played a fundamental role in pushing for reform (see Chapter 3; and US White House, *Fact Sheet: Advancing US Interests at the United Nations*, 20 September 2011 [ref. REP]), while the JIU, the ACABQ, and the Secretary-General had an important operating function in terms of proposals for and oversight of the implementation of reforms approved by the General Assembly.

[7] Reports on the issue prepared by the JIU from 1993 onwards addressed various aspects of accountability, from the ethics of administrative officials to investigative and control functions to the recruitment and appointment of senior managers.

[8] ILO, *Office Guideline on the ILO Accountability Framework* [ref. AP&R].

[9] UNDP, *The UNDP Accountability System* [ref. AP&R].

[10] UNFPA, *UNFPA Accountability Framework* [ref. AP&R].

[11] UNICEF, *Report on the Accountability System of UNICEF* [ref. REP].

[12] On the other hand, it should be emphasized that many organizations still do not have an accountability framework, only individual components of one: these include WFP, FAO and UNIDO.

framework regarding the activities of the UN Secretariat dates from 2010.[13]

An analysis of accountability in procurement, and more specifically of the mechanisms that currently guarantee it, the limits it encounters and its efficacy in achieving the objectives pursued is central to assessing the effectiveness of the administrative rules set out in the vendor selection phase and the clauses that govern the contractual relationship. It is also important to understand where the balance between authority and responsibility lies in the (pre-contractual and contractual) relationship between international organizations and private parties.

This chapter explores oversight mechanisms, both in direct and indirect procurement. It also includes an analysis of the instruments for safeguarding private parties' rights vis-à-vis international organizations in direct procurement and vis-à-vis national administrations in indirect procurement.

As we shall see, the accountability mechanisms connected to procurement by international organizations to some extent follow the schemes used in the forms of control and protection found at the state level, but have many specificities that can be explained by the international nature of the organizations, their different institutional structure and the distinctive interplay of interests underlying international organizations' procurement.

7.2 Operational Definitions and Components of International Organizations' Accountability

Accountability[14] is a relational concept[15] that implies the existence of two players, the accountee and the accountor, with the former having the

---

[13] UN General Assembly, *Towards an Accountability System in the United Nations Secretariat*, A/64/640 [ref. REP].

[14] For the purposes of this work, some useful conceptualizations of the concept of accountability can be found in: Behn, *Rethinking Democratic Accountability*; Bovens, *The Quest for Responsibility*; id., 'Analysing and Assessing Accountability: A Conceptual Framework'; Keohane, 'Global Governance and Democratic Accountability'; Grant and Keohane, 'Accountability and Abuses of World Power'; Mulgan, '"Accountability": An Ever-Expanding Concept?'; id., *Holding Power to Account*; Mashaw, 'Structuring a "Dense Complexity"'; Stewart, 'Accountability and the Discontents of Globalization'; id., 'Accountability, Participation, and the Problem of Disregard in Global Regulatory Governance'; Ferejohn, 'Accountability in a Global Context'; von Bogdandy, 'Demokratie, Globalisierung, Zukunft des Völkerrechts'; Aman Jr., 'Globalization, Democracy and the Need for a New Administrative Law'; Reinisch, 'Securing the Accountability of International Organizations'; Koppell, 'Accountable Global Governance Organizations'; Peters, 'Accountability in Public Administration'; Papadopoulos, 'Accountability and Multi-Level Governance'; Goodhart, 'Accountable International Relations'; Koenig-Archibugi, 'Accountability'; de Cooker, *Accountability, Investigation and Due Process in International Organizations*.

[15] Stewart, 'Accountability and the Discontents of Globalization', p. 10.

right to demand and receive an account of the latter's conduct, to evaluate its performance, to impose sanctions and obtain compensation in the case of violation of the substantive rules underlying the relationship or the procedural rules that govern it. This may also imply that the accountable party is required to provide reasons and justifications for its conduct.

The accountee and the accountor may be both public bodies, such as states and international organizations; or, within an organization, independent bodies with oversight functions and administrative divisions; or, within the same administrative division, central and field offices. But an accountability relationship may be established also between private and public parties.

The source of the relationship may be an act delegating authority and/ or resources or a rule that requires a certain form of conduct. In the first case, the accountable party is required to act in accordance with the terms of the delegation, and in the interest of the delegating party or a third party. If this does not occur, the delegation may be revoked or the funding granted may be withdrawn or cut. This type of accountability can be found, for example, in decentralized direct procurement or in indirect procurement.

In the case of a rule prescribing a certain conduct, the obligation can have various sources. For example, there may be legislative or regulatory provisions, or a contract, violation of which may be alleged before a neutral and impartial body. The accountability mechanisms regulated by the procedural rules that govern the vendor selection process are of this kind as they give private parties recourse against any improper actions taken by an awarding administration. Similarly, mechanisms aimed at ensuring contract performance are provided in contracts between organizations and private parties. However, unlike the mechanisms available during the tender procedures, these are characterized by reciprocity, as they are actionable both by the administration against a non-performing private party and vice versa.

The operational definitions of accountability that are found in the framework documents of many international organizations refer mostly to accountability between member states and the organizations or between bodies within the same organization, or even between offices, while the component of accountability to private parties is often left aside. After various criticisms and ongoing changes, in 2010 the General Assembly approved a definition of accountability for the UN Secretariat that served as a model also for other UN agencies:

[a]ccountability is the obligation ... to be answerable for all decisions made and actions taken ... and to be responsible for honouring ... commitments, without qualification or exception. Accountability includes achieving objectives and high-quality results in a timely and cost-effective manner, in fully implementing and delivering on all mandates to the Secretariat approved by the United Nations intergovernmental bodies and other subsidiary organs established by them in compliance with all resolutions, regulations, rules and ethical standards; truthful, objective, accurate and timely reporting on performance results; responsible stewardship of funds and resources; all aspects of performance, including a clearly defined system of rewards and sanctions; and with due recognition to the important role of the oversight bodies and in full compliance with accepted recommendations.[16]

This definition establishes the five aspects of the Secretariat's accountability: the object of accountability, that is the decisions and actions necessary to economically and efficiently carry out the institutional mandate; the parties to whom the international administration is accountable i.e. political bodies, composed of member states; the sources of accountability i.e. regulation through general resolutions, implementing regulations and standards; the oversight bodies; and finally, the consequences in the case of failure to comply with the duties of responsibility i.e. the imposition of sanctions.[17] Thus, this definition does not include

---

[16] In UN General Assembly, *Towards an Accountability System in the United Nations Secretariat*, A/RES/64/259 [ref. RES].

[17] The definition is broader than the one originally conceived, which limited accountability according to the availability of resources and the constraints posed by external factors. An early formulation, approved in 2006 by the General Assembly, in fact, provided that '[a]ccountability represents the obligation of the Organization and its staff members to be answerable for delivering specific results that have been determined through a clear and transparent assignment of responsibility, *subject to the availability of resources and the constraints posed by external factors*. Accountability includes achievement of objectives and results in response to mandates, fair and accurate reporting on performance results, stewardship of funds, and all aspects of performance in accordance with regulations, rules and standards, including a clearly defined system of rewards and sanctions' (emphasis added), in UN General Assembly, *Towards an Accountability System in the United Nations Secretariat*, A/64/640 [ref. REP]. Nevertheless, this first proposal formulated by the Secretary-General did not meet the approval of the other institutions: the General Assembly criticized it as being insufficient; the ACABQ felt it was limited (in particular where it linked accountability to the availability of adequate resources), that it lacked clarity, and that in any event a definition was needed that was applicable to all entities under the responsibility of the Secretary-General (on this point see UN ACABQ, *Towards an Accountability System in the United Nations Secretariat* [ref. REP]); the Board of Auditors emphasized that references were lacking for the concepts of efficiency,

accountability to private parties with whom the administration establishes a direct relationship.

The elements that constitute this definition are also set out in earlier formulations by other bodies and organizations within the UN system. The Framework for Human Resource Management Glossary of the International Civil Service Commission (ICSC), for example, defines accountability as

> [a] [c]oncept which implies taking ownership of all responsibilities and honouring commitments; delivering outputs for which the staff member has responsibility within prescribed time, cost and quality standards; operating in compliance with organizational regulations and rules; supporting subordinates, providing oversight and taking responsibility for delegated assignments; taking personal responsibility for personal shortcomings and, where applicable, those of the work unit.[18]

While, the accountability framework of UNDP states that

> [a]ccountability is the obligation to (i) demonstrate that work has been conducted in accordance with agreed rules and standards and (ii) report fairly and accurately on performance results vis-à-vis mandated roles and/or plans.[19]

Within the sphere of a broader plan to harmonize accountability policies, this definition was intended to be adopted by UNOPS and UNFPA as well.[20] However, while UNOPS actually added it to its accountability framework,[21] UNFPA retained a more detailed and specific definition:

> [a]ccountability is the process whereby public service organizations and individuals within them are held responsible for their decisions and actions including their stewardship of public funds, fairness, and all aspects of performance, in accordance with agreed rules and standards,

---

effectiveness and timeliness of the administrative action, and on the role of control institutions; finally, OIOS noted the absence of references to the personal responsibility of officials for results achieved. In JIU, *Accountability Frameworks in the United Nations System*, para. 6 [ref. REP].

[18] In ICSC, *Framework for Human Resource Management Glossary*, para. 20 [ref. AP&R].

[19] In UNDP, *The UNDP Accountability System*, part I(a), no. 3 [ref. AP&R].

[20] 'UNDP, UNFPA and UNOPS have agreed that the harmonization of the definitions should be based on authoritative sources and that the key definitions, including that of accountability, are harmonized with UNFPA and UNOPS at the request of the Executive Board', *ibid.*, paras. 2–3.

[21] See UNOPS, *United Nations Office for Project Services Accountability Framework*, part. II (a), para. 16(b) [ref. AP&R].

and fair and accurate reporting on performance results vis-à-vis mandated roles and/or plans.[22]

While the guidelines for the ILO accountability framework identify the principles that must inform accountability policies:

> clarity of responsibility; alignment of accountability with organizational-wide goals; delegation of authority; cost-benefit considerations; performance monitoring and reporting, and the highest standards of integrity and ethical conduct.[23]

Overall, the operational definitions of accountability of each organization are based on several common features. First, reference is made to decisions, actions and commitments adopted in compliance with the institutional objectives jointly agreed by the member states, or in accordance with internal rules, regulations and ethical standards, or based on a delegation of authority. This type of accountability finds its source in the agreements establishing the organizations and in rules that the administration sets out for itself. It does not, however, explicitly include a possible public–private contractual origin of accountability requirements.

Second, the mechanisms to which the most detailed definitions refer are those that provide for oversight by bodies outside the administrative structure, which are composed of experts designated by states to check the administrative activity. Also, they refer to mechanisms established among the various levels of the same administration. The difference between external oversight[24] and internal oversight has been clearly underscored by the JIU:

> [i]nternal oversight mechanisms are primarily tools to assist Executive Heads in fulfilling their management responsibilities. They are accountable to Executive Heads for providing advice on internal controls and management practices based on a systematic and independent review of an organization's entire operations . . . internal oversight mechanisms are a tool of the Executive Heads.[25]

---

[22] In UNFPA, *UNFPA Accountability Framework*, para. 3 [ref. AP&R]. The *Report on the Accountability System of UNICEF* includes substantially similar wording. It states that '[a]ccountability is the obligation to demonstrate that work has been conducted in accordance with agreed rules and standards, and that performance results have been reported fairly and accurately', in UNICEF, *Report on the Accountability System of UNICEF*, para. 2 [ref. REP].

[23] In ILO, *Office Guideline on the ILO Accountability Framework*, para. 9 [ref. AP&R].

[24] External vis-à-vis the administration, not the organization.

[25] JIU, *More Coherence for Enhanced Oversight*, paras. 29–30 [ref. REP].

On the other hand, external oversight mechanisms have been defined as "a tool of member states in the legislative organs. They are accountable to member states for providing objective information and advice directly to them regarding the management of organizations".[26] However, the definitions again do not contemplate accountability mechanisms vis-à-vis private parties.

Third, accountability objectives are primarily internal. Performance and conduct are subject to oversight based on objectives of cost effectiveness and efficiency.

It was the very absence of explicit references to accountability to private subjects and, at the same time, the finding that the activities of organizations affect an increasingly large pool of individuals and companies that led the JIU to indicate that the essential components of the organizations' accountability should also include mechanisms to make international organizations accountable to private parties. According to the JIU, accountability should be ensured not only through external oversight and internal oversight by higher administrative levels or by internal independent bodies, but also through the provision of complaints by private parties against international organizations, in particular against decisions made while engaging in their procurement activity.[27]

The provision and implementation of the three components of accountability (external, internal and vis-à-vis private subjects) change depending on the organization. For example, while in organizations within the UN system accountability to private subjects is present in some instances but weak and ineffective – with several variations among the organizations – this component is, instead, strengthened in European institutions, which are called to respond to judicial or quasi-judicial bodies.

7.3 External Controls

Member states determine organizations' mandates. They collectively establish the policy objectives and priorities for action. They orient international organizations' activities. They provide funding. Precisely

---

[26] *Ibid.*, para. 30.
[27] The 2011 report from the JIU is built on these three components. See JIU, *Accountability Frameworks in the United Nations System* [ref. REP].

to ensure that the use of resources is in harmony with the mandate, objectives, priorities and guidelines, mechanisms are provided that enable the actions of organizations to be checked. These types of control are also referred to as external controls, both because they are exercised by external bodies which are independent of the administrative structure and because they are instrumental to state oversight of the administrative activity of organizations. While these mechanisms are an important part of the architecture of accountability, there are a few organizations (e.g. the United Nations, UNDP and UNICEF) whose accountability frameworks explicitly include reference to state oversight and the bodies through which this is achieved.[28]

The Executive Board, the Board of Auditors and the JIU are the bodies that are entrusted with the external oversight of the international administrations of the UN system. Executive Boards are responsible for individual organizations or groups of organizations – in particular those whose institutional activity is carried out primarily through funds and programmes.[29] The other bodies have transversal responsibility, overseeing the activity of nearly all the organizations in the system and creating a common system of controls. Executive Boards are composed of delegates from the states. In the cases of the Executive Board of the UNDP, UNOPS and UNFPA, and that of the United Nations, FAO and WFP,[30] for example, all the member states of the organizations have rotating representation within the body.

According to the 1993 mandate from the General Assembly, the function of the Executive Boards is

> [to] provid[e] inter-governmental support to and supervision of the activities of each fund and programme in accordance with the overall policy guidance of the General Assembly and the Economic and Social Council, in accordance with their respective responsibility as set out in the Charter, and for ensuring that they are responsive to the needs and priorities of recipient countries.[31]

---

[28] See JIU, *Accountability Frameworks in the United Nations System*, para. 47 [ref. REP].

[29] On the nature, type and functions of Executive Boards see Wessel, 'Executive Boards and Councils'.

[30] In both cases there is a single Executive Board for all three organizations.

[31] In UN General Assembly, *Further Measures for the Restructuring and Revitalization of the United Nations*, Annex I, para. 21 [ref. RES]. The formula is also repeated in UNDP, *The UNDP Accountability System*, para. 40 *et seq.* [ref. AP&R]; UNOPS, *United Nations Office for Project Services Accountability Framework and Oversight Policies*, para. 32 *et seq.* [ref. AP&R]; UNICEF, *Report on the Accountability System of UNICEF*, para. 44 *et seq.* [ref. REP].

The Executive Boards have decision-making functions instrumental to the implementation of policies formulated by the General Assembly and guidelines established by the ECOSOC, such as the approval of new programmes, the budget and plans for administrative activity. They have the task of monitoring the performance of organizations. Based on monitoring results, they can develop recommendations for new initiatives to the Council, and through it, to the General Assembly. They submit annual reports to the Council that include recommendations to improve coordination at the peripheral level.[32] Thus, a two-way relationship is established between the General Assembly and the ECOSOC on one side and the Executive Boards on the other: General Assembly and the ECOSOC indicate their policies to the latter, but also, working in the opposite direction, the Executive Boards make recommendations to the Assembly and the Council. Central to this relationship is the fact that member states can obtain information on the administrative activity of organizations, both directly through their delegates who serve on the Board, and indirectly through the annual reports prepared by the Board.

The Board of Auditors is an external body, which, unlike the Executive Boards, is the same for twenty-four of the organizations within the UN system. This body is intended to guarantee transparency and accountability towards states and eventually to increase the legitimacy of international institutions in the eyes of citizens. These goals are highlighted in the following passage by the Secretary-General:

> [a]ccountability and transparency presuppose public insight into the activities of public organizations; and performance auditing is a way for legislatures and citizens to obtain such insight into the management and outcomes of administrative and operational activities. Performance audit therefore helps to build legitimacy and trust of the public organizations concerned.[33]

---

[32] These functions are described in UNDP, *The UNDP Accountability System*, para. 40 [ref. AP&R]; UNOPS, *United Nations Office for Project Services Accountability Framework and Oversight Policies*, para. 32 [ref. AP&R]; UNICEF, *Report on the Accountability System of UNICEF*, para. 45 [ref. REP].

[33] UN General Assembly, *Report of the Board of Auditors on Enhancing Accountability, Transparency and Cost-Effectiveness*, para. 10 [ref. REP].

In this regard, there are also more openly utilitarian considerations that link the accountability to funding states to the interest of the organizations:

> [i]ndeed, it is in the interest of the United Nations system, which is reliant on donations from Member States, that it continue to mandate its external auditors to conduct independent performance audit, especially in a rapidly changing, uncertain and complex world with limited resources.[34]

These objectives also explain the procedures for setting up the Board of Auditors and its *modus operandi*. It is a body composed of three members (auditors), each of whom is selected and appointed by the General Assembly[35] in rotation with candidates proposed by the states.[36] The selection of auditors is not so much determined by individual personal evaluations as it is by their identification with national bodies responsible for financial control, such as the Court of Audit in France or other bodies that perform a similar function in the various countries. The auditors appointed to the Board must in fact be the 'Auditor-General (or officer holding the equivalent title) of a Member State'.[37] Confirmation that the two offices, auditor and head of a national control body, are linked, is set out in the rules on removal from office: if a person ceases to hold the office of Auditor-General or the equivalent position in her country, she ceases to hold the office of auditor on the Board.[38] Thus, the composition of the Board is decided on the basis of policy evaluations that take into account primarily the

---

[34] *Ibid.*

[35] See UN General Assembly, *Appointment of External Auditors*, (c) [ref. RES]. General Assembly Resolution 74(I) of 1946 is the one that establishes the Board of Auditors.

[36] There are, however, exceptions to this system: four cases in which auditors are in fact permanent even if they are replaced when their term of office has expired: the French *Cours des comptes* for UNESCO, the United Kingdom National Audit Office for WFP, the Comptroller and Auditor General of India (which replaced Great Britain) for WHO and the *Bundesrechnungshof* (the German Court of Auditors) for the IAEA. In addition, two organizations that are part of the UN system, WB and IFAD, and two that are not part of the system, Global Fund and International Federation of Red Cross and Red Crescent Societies (IFRC), have appointed private companies as external auditors. The so-called big four are: PricewaterhouseCoopers, Deloitte and Touche, KPMG and Ernst and Young.

[37] UN General Assembly, *Appointment of External Auditors* [ref. RES].

[38] *Ibid.*, (f) states: 'if any member of the Board ceases to hold the national office ... he shall cease to be a member of the Board, on which he shall be succeeded by his successor in the national office'. In this regard, Battini emphasizes the intertwining of national administrative law and supranational administrative law, see Battini, *Amministrazioni senza Stato*, p. 181.

national component. In the past this has meant that the procedure for selecting auditors has not guaranteed equal opportunities for all states.[39]

Organic identification should not, however, mean partiality in the evaluation: in their evaluations, the Auditors shall remain independent from their states of origin.[40] In general, they must not only follow the provisions of the Financial Regulations and Rules of the United Nations,[41] but also the principles of independence established in the 1977 Lima Declaration of Guidelines on Auditing Precepts, which were subsequently reiterated in the 2007 Mexico Declaration on SAI Independence.

The audit function of the Board is twofold: it is financial, as the Board certifies financial statements, but it also consists of controlling the administration's performance. In this latter regard, the Board makes observations on the efficiency of financial procedures, accounting systems, internal financial controls, and the administration and management of the organization.[42] Control of these last two aspects does not extend to the merits of administrative decisions, but rather to the effects that these decisions have on the organization's finances:

> [t]he Auditors should not criticize purely administrative matters, but it is within their discretion to comment upon the financial consequences of administrative action.[43]

The effects of administrative management – and, thus, also procurement activity – which are relevant to the organization's finances also include actual or suspected fraud, waste or improper use of resources,

---

[39] This aspect is evidenced in JIU, *The Audit Function in the United Nations System*, para. 129 [ref. REP], which states: '[o]ne external auditor reported that the selection process did not provide equal opportunities for all'.

[40] 'External auditors should also be fully independent from their own Governments, and represent a truly independent source of information to the legislative/governing body on the accuracy and reliability of financial statements and internal control of the organization', *ibid.*, para. 120. On the audit function in the UN system see also JIU, *State of the Internal Audit Function in the United Nations System* [ref. REP].

[41] In fact, Regulation 7.6 of United Nations, *Financial Regulations*, ST/SGB/2013/4 [ref. AP&R] states: '[t]he Board of Auditors shall be completely independent and solely responsible for the conduct of the audit'.

[42] Regulation 7.5 of United Nations, *Financial Regulations and Rules of the United Nations* ST/SGB/2013/4 [ref. AP&R].

[43] In UN General Assembly, *Appointment of External Auditors*, (h), para. v [ref. RES].

and control of the use of resources for the purposes provided by the General Assembly.[44]

The Board is required to communicate the results of its audit in a report that is submitted to the legislative and governing bodies of the organizations, and thus to the states,[45] and to make them available to the general public. Reports are issued annually or biannually, depending on how often the budgets for the individual organization are approved. A section in the reports is specifically devoted to procurement.

The need for efficiency and cost-effectiveness results in the general principle of *single audit*, i.e. the Board must perform a single audit for each organization according to the established frequency. However, states can also request independent audits and *ad hoc* reviews of management when these controls are connected to funds that they have specifically disbursed. From 2005 to 2010, in organizations such as the United Nations, UNDP, UNICEF, UNOPS, UNFPA, FAO, UNESCO, UNIDO and others, 55 per cent of requests received from donor states were to conduct special audits, 40 per cent to access and directly verify accounting records, and 5 per cent to perform a unilateral audit.[46] For example, an agreement between the United Nations and the European Union regarding operations managed by the United Nations and financed by the EU Commission[47] allows the Commission to perform on-site controls:

> the European Communities may undertake, including on the spot, checks related to the operations financed by the European Communities.[48]

---

[44] *Ibid.*, (h), para. viii, no. 3.

[45] Moreover, before presenting reports to these bodies, the Board submits a draft to the directors of the organization and to the internal audit committees in order to elicit their comments.

[46] The data are reported in JIU, *The Audit Function in the United Nations System*, para. 171 [ref. REP].

[47] Financial and Administrative Framework Agreement between the European Community, Represented by the Commission of the European Communities and the United Nations [ref. A&C].

[48] In particular, on the one hand, the European Commission 'will be given access to the site of the project and/or the headquarters of the United Nations Secretariat or relevant organizations and programmes', *ibid.*, p. 15. On the other hand, the United Nations 'will supply all relevant financial information and will explain to the European Commission representatives, with appropriate concrete examples, how the accounts are managed and the procedures observed to ensure transparency and accuracy in the accounts and to guard against the misuse of funds and fraud', *ibid.*, p. 15.

Thus, in addition to scheduled checks, there are also situations of targeted checks, the end purpose of which is to allow states to monitor the use of their resources and ensure that these resources will continue to be provided to the organization.

The JIU is the other body responsible for monitoring twenty-six of the organizations in the UN system. Initially established experimentally in 1966, and then confirmed as a permanent body in 1976, it is composed of eleven members who are selected regardless of whether they belong to a national body, as instead happens with Board members. Inspectors are selected by the General Assembly based on their administrative and financial experience and in accordance with the principle of equitable geographical distribution and rotation needs. As such, they may come from national bodies with supervisory and inspection functions similar to those of the JIU, or have suitable qualifications without belonging to any national administrative body. In addition, the selection process includes more formalization and proceduralization than that for Board of Auditors members: in consultation with the member states, the President of the General Assembly prepares a list of countries to be asked for a candidate. The states identified propose their candidates. In consultation with the President of the ECOSOC, the Chairman of the Administrative Committee on Coordination and the states themselves, the President prepares a list of suitable candidates and submits it to the General Assembly for the appointment.[49]

Unlike the Board of Auditors, which specializes in monitoring finance and resource management, the JIU has transversal competences that consist of the power to investigate the efficiency of the services provided by the UN organizations, and inspection and evaluation powers aimed at improving administrative management and methods of activity.[50] In reality, over time the JIU has shown preferences for some of these duties over others. During the 1970s, its activity concentrated primarily on preparing reports containing evaluations and evaluation methodologies, which were designed to guide evaluation groups within the various

---

[49] UN General Assembly, *Statute of the Joint Inspection Unit*, Annex, Art. 3 [ref. RES].

[50] The Statute states: '1. The Inspectors shall have the broadest powers of investigation in all matters having a bearing on the efficiency of the services and the proper use of funds. 2. They shall provide an independent view through inspection and evaluation aimed at improving management and methods and at achieving greater co-ordination between organizations', *ibid.*, Art. 5. The definition of the functions of investigation, inspection and evaluation is contained in UN General Assembly, *Standards and Guidelines of the Joint Inspection Unit*, para. 4–5 [ref. AP&R].

organizations. From the 1980s onwards, the increasing preoccupation of the member states with administrative management[51] shifted the attention to reviewing the efficiency of services and verifying the proper use of funds for this purpose.[52]

The result of this approach was that procurement by the organizations and aspects connected to it were the subject of several recommendations by the JIU and this body not only had a role in oversight, but also an important function of driving the relative reforms. The JIU operates by preparing reports, notes or confidential letters. The three methods differ in the degree of proceduralization in the preparation phase, in the recipients to whom they are directed and in how binding they are. Reports must contain both an analytical section and recommendations for action. Once prepared, they are submitted to the executive heads of the organizations involved, who may make comments and must immediately distribute them, with or without comments, to the member states of the respective organizations. In addition, within six months of receiving the report, the executive heads must submit them with their comments and those of the executive heads of all other organizations affected by the report to the competent bodies within each organization, which may or may not approve them.[53] The reports and recommendations contained in them are not binding. Nevertheless, the decision of the organization's competent bodies to approve the report is binding.[54] Once there has been formal approval, the reports must be implemented and the executive heads become responsible for ensuring implementation. This implementation may then be subject to verification by the bodies that approved the reports and by the JIU, which can prepare a second report on the implementation at the request of these bodies or on its own initiative.[55] The reports are then made available to the public.

On the contrary, confidential notes and letters are sent to the executive heads without any specific procedure for preparation and approval. Moreover, as there are no approval decisions, they are not binding and are utilized by the executive heads 'for use ... as they may decide'.[56] Finally, while notes are available to the public, letters are not.

---

[51] See Chapter 3.
[52] In UN General Assembly, *Statute of the Joint Inspection Unit*, para. 5 [ref. RES].
[53] In general on the appointment methods, functions and independence of Executive Heads see Chesterman, 'Executive Heads'.
[54] UN General Assembly, *Statute of the Joint Inspection Unit*, Art. 11, para. 3 [ref. RES].
[55] *Ibid.*, Art. 12.   [56] *Ibid.*, Art. 11, para. 5.

7.3.1 The Effectiveness of Controls and the Role of States

The various methods that states use to monitor the administrative activity of organizations in general, and procurement in particular, are thus characterized by elements in common. First, states are part of the process of forming the bodies responsible for oversight and are part of the bodies themselves (even though the members of the body must be independent). Indeed, they are both beneficiaries of the results of oversight activity and parties to whom the administrative structure is accountable. In particular, state presence in the composition of oversight bodies takes different forms: it may consist of a relationship of representation, as in the case of members of Executive Boards; it may be a case of institutional identification i.e. identification with certain institutions, as in the Board of Auditors; or it can be a bond of nationality without delegation, as in the JIU. States are also the accountees in various institutional settings. The Executive Board makes the administrative structure of an individual organization accountable to all states represented in the General Assembly and in the ECOSOC. The Board of Auditors and the JIU make the administrative structure of an organization accountable to the legislative and governing bodies of that organization, and, by publicizing the reports, accountable to the general public as well.

In addition, in all three cases, the subject of oversight includes various aspects of administrative activity: oversight by the Executive Board is aimed at determining whether administrative management is compatible with policy objectives; oversight of the Board of Auditors is intended to ascertain the propriety of administrative management from the financial perspective; and oversight of the JIU is designed to draw the attention of states to possible problems in the efficiency of services and proper management of resources, including in terms of malfunctions of the administrative activity. Moreover, all three bodies not only monitor, but also give recommendations. Recommendations are not binding except in the case of the Board of Auditors, where there is prior (but optional) approval by the competent bodies of the organization involved. Thus, it is still always legislative and governing bodies who can regulate the impact and consequences of oversight.

In the opinion of the JIU, the overall system of external controls is effective: 'organizations possess strong reporting mechanisms for reporting to their legislative bodies and . . . there are no identifiable gaps in this area'.[57] Thus, on one hand, these controls provide states with a detailed knowledge of the overall administrative activity and of any specific problems in procurement activity. On the other hand, decisions that direct and reform administrative activity are still the responsibility of governing bodies, which on the basis of various interests can decide whether or not to follow up on the recommendation of oversight bodies.[58]

7.4 Internal Controls on Direct Procurement

The International Organization of Supreme Audit Institutions (INTOSAI) defines internal control as

> an integral process that is effected by an entity's management and personnel and is designed to address risks and to provide reasonable assurance that in pursuit of the entity's mission, the following general objectives are being achieved: executing orderly, ethical, economical, efficient and effective operations; fulfilling accountability obligations; complying with applicable laws and regulations; safeguarding resources against loss, misuse and damage.[59]

This definition was taken up by the JIU. For both international organizations and national administrations, internal controls consist of activities carried out by offices within the same administration, which are aimed at making the responsibility of officials effective, ensuring the economic rationality of the organization and improving correlation between objectives and disbursements of resources.

For direct procurement, two types of internal controls are of particular importance: checks on the conduct of the individual officials who manage procurement, and checks on the actual procurement activity itself, in particular on the legitimacy[60] of procedures. In organizations within the UN system, the former are performed by the ethics offices and

---

[57] In JIU, *Accountability Frameworks in the United Nations System*, para. 62 [ref. REP].
[58] See Chapter 8.
[59] INTOSAI, *Guidelines for Internal Control Standards for the Public Sector*, para. 1.1 [ref. AP&R].
[60] Legitimacy is here, and elsewhere in this chapter, intended as the quality of being in compliance with the relevant rules. In other chapters of this book it has a different meaning, i.e. as the quality of a public authority, for example, an international organization, of being recognized, accepted and, as relevant, supported by the people. The distinction derives from Weber. See especially Bendix, *Max Weber*, pp. 290–297. For the empirical adaptation of this distinction see Lipset, *The Political Man*, pp. 64 *et seq.*

internal offices with investigative[61] and auditing[62] functions. The latter are carried out by internal offices with monitoring,[63] evaluation[64] and inspection[65] functions and by commissions or individual officials within the vendor selection procedure who are responsible for checking the individual decisions within the procedure.

7.4.1   Controls on the Conduct of Officials

The conduct of officials is governed in part by the binding framework found in the founding treaties, regulations, administrative circulars and procurement manuals, and in part by soft law instruments such as standards of conduct set in *ad hoc* texts.[66] The ethics offices and internal organs with investigative powers are those that monitor compliance with these rules.

7.4.1.1   Ethics Offices

The bodies in charge of monitoring compliance with ethics rules have been established at a later stage in the life of the organizations. It was only in 2005 that the executive heads of the various organizations in the UN system began to submit proposals to the respective legislative bodies for the establishment of *ad hoc* bodies responsible for monitoring the conduct and ethics of officials. In 2005, the United Nations Secretary-

---

[61] Investigations are control activities aimed at detecting the existence of abuses or conduct in violation of the organization's rules.

[62] Audits are controls aimed at verifying the cost-effectiveness, efficiency and legitimacy of financial and administrative management, see OIOS, *Audit Manual*, para. A.2 [ref. AP&R].

[63] Monitoring is a control activity aimed at verifying the results of programmes and activities while they are being executed.

[64] Evaluation consists of the assessment of programmes and activities in terms of their objectives. A definition is provided in the OIOS guidelines on inspection and evaluation functions: evaluation is 'a systematic and discrete process, as objective as possible, to determine relevance, efficiency, effectiveness, impact, and/or sustainability of any element of a programme's performance relative to its mandate or goals', in OIOS, *Inspection and Evaluation Manual*, para. 1.2 [ref. AP&R].

[65] Inspection is the activity of checking specific activities or organizational units in response to reports of management inefficiency. See Battini, *Amministrazioni senza Stato*, p. 177. According to OIOS guidelines regarding inspections and evaluations, an inspection may be defined as 'a review of an organizational unit, issue or practice perceived to be of potential risk in order to determine the extent to which it adheres to normative standards, good practices or other pre-determined criteria and to identify corrective action as needed', in OIOS, *Inspection and Evaluation Manual*, para. 1.2 [ref. AP&R].

[66] See Chapter 4.

General first proposed to the General Assembly the establishment of an independent office responsible for monitoring the ethics of Secretariat officials.[67] The office was established in that same year.[68] At the request of the General Assembly,[69] this was followed by a series of concrete guidelines set out by the Secretary-General to assist the other organizations of the UN system in establishing similar internal offices.[70] However, while almost all the funds and programmes approved the creation of ethics offices (e.g. UNDP[71] and UNICEF[72] in 2007, WFP,[73] UNFPA[74] and UNHCR[75] in 2008), only some specialized agencies did create such offices (e.g. FAO,[76] UNESCO[77] and ITU).[78] The difference is explained by the extent and volume of activity of these organizations.[79] In fact, it was primarily the smaller agencies that did not assign the function of monitoring the conduct of officials to a special body. Nevertheless, there are also cases, like that of the ILO, where despite the significant size of the administrative structure and a large volume of activity, control functions were entrusted to the Legal Advisor (the so-called dual-function post),[80] with a risk of creating conflicts of interest.

Recruitment for the position of head of ethics offices is usually made through non-public notices, so candidates are usually internal to the

[67] The proposal is in UN General Assembly, *Measures to Strengthen Accountability*, para. 40 [ref. REP].

[68] UN Secretary-General, *Ethics Office* [ref. AP&R].

[69] UN General Assembly, *2005 World Summit Outcome*, para. 161(d) [ref. RES] states: '[w]e request the Secretary-General to submit details on an ethics office with independent status, which he intends to create, to the General Assembly at its sixtieth session'.

[70] UN Secretary-General, *United Nations System-Wide Application of Ethics* [ref. REP].

[71] UNDP/UNFPA/UNOPS Executive Board, *Internal Audit and Oversight* [ref. AP&R].

[72] UNICEF Executive Board, *Decision No. 2/2008* [ref. AP&R].

[73] WFP Executive Director, *Establishment of Ethics Office in WFP* [ref. AP&R].

[74] UNDP/UNFPA/UNOPS Executive Board, *Internal Audit and Oversight* [ref. AP&R].

[75] UN Executive Committee of the High Commissioner's Programme, *Report of the Fifty-Ninth Session of the Executive Committee*, sec. III(c) [ref. REP].

[76] FAO Conference Committee on Follow-up to the Independent External Evaluation of FAO Immediate Plan of Action, *Resolution 1/2008* [ref. RES].

[77] UNESCO General Conference, *Resolution 34C/2.2*; *id.*, *Resolution 34C/66.3*; *id.*, *Resolution 34C/57* [all documents in ref. RES].

[78] For a general overview, see JIU, *Ethics in the United Nations System*, Annex I [ref. REP].

[79] See *ibid.*, para. 24.

[80] The proposal that the executive head should at the same time be the administrative head and controller of last resort of the conduct and ethics of officials (dual-function post) was advanced by the JIU in 2006, but only for small organizations. See JIU, *Oversight Lacunae in the United Nations System*, para. 49. This practice was thus criticized when it was adopted in larger organizations, see JIU, *Ethics in the United Nations System*, para. 37 [all documents in ref. REP].

organization. Only certain organizations (the United Nations and UNESCO) formally publicize the call and make it possible for outside candidates to participate, while a common practice for these positions is to recruit high-level officials from the organization itself who are close to retirement.[81] In addition, in most organizations there is no set term of office, or, if there is, differing practices in fact create exceptions to this. For example, in UNICEF and UNESCO, the maximum terms of office are five years and four years respectively, but in fact their ethics officers are appointed for two years and one year respectively and the appointment can be renewed at the discretion of the executive head.[82] In this regard, it has been emphasized that neither the absence of a minimum term of office, nor practices that create exceptions to rules on re-appointment, provide sufficient guarantees of independence: in both cases, officials must rely on the decision of the executive head for the continuity of their position.

At the same time, ethics offices have regulatory, consulting and oversight functions and are responsible for training officials and reporting to administrative heads. They are in fact responsible for preparing standards and developing policies regarding ethics and conduct;[83] training officials and making them aware of their rights and duties;[84] providing confidential advice and guidance to officials regarding issues related to ethics and conduct;[85] implementing whistle-blower policies;[86] managing the programme to disclose the financial situation of officials;[87] and, finally, providing the executive heads with an annual report on the activities of the ethics office and the results of these activities.[88]

Their duties do not explicitly include the handling of complaints from officials or third parties that are intended to draw the office's attention to conduct in violation of the rules. Nevertheless, with regard to the function of consulting and protection from retaliation following complaints, the Secretary-General has mentioned the possibility of officials filing complaints with the office.[89] In these situations, complaints take the form of a request for confidential advice or, in the sphere of whistle-blower protection policies, of 'level two' complaints,

---

[81] JIU, *Ethics in the United Nations System*, paras. 39–40 [ref. REP].

[82] *Ibid.*, para. 47 and Annex IV.

[83] UN Secretary-General, *United Nations System-Wide Application of Ethics*, sec. 3(a) [ref. REP].

[84] *Ibid.*, sec. 3(b).   [85] *Ibid.*, sec. 3(c).   [86] *Ibid.*, sec. 3(e).   [87] *Ibid.*, (g).   [88] *Ibid.*, (h).

[89] *Ibid.*, sec. 4, para. 4.3.

as they are a consequence of a previous complaint to other bodies, for example, the OIOS, regarding conduct in violation of the rules of conduct. Thus, ethics offices cannot receive complaints from third parties (i.e. from individuals or companies outside the organization). Exceptions to this basic system can be found in a few organizations, such as UNESCO, which, while following the Secretary-General's indications, also gives external stakeholders the possibility of filing complaints with its ethic office.[90]

Furthermore, the offices do not have investigative powers, or the power to impose penalties. Instead, once a complaint has been received the office must evaluate its *prima facie* grounds within a certain period of time (often forty-five days). If it determines that there are proper grounds for the complaint, it refers the case to an internal control office with investigative powers. In the case of the UN, the office in question is the OIOS.[91] These offices must generally conclude the investigation within a given period of time and send the results to it. Based on these results, the ethics office will prepare its recommendations to the head of the office involved and to the Under Secretary-General for management in the United Nations, to the Executive Director in UNICEF, UNFPA and WFP, or to parties with equivalent administrative positions in other organizations of the UN system. These parties may then take the steps they consider to be appropriate.

Finally, the various duties attributed to the ethics offices also include reporting the results of their control activity to executive heads. In UNDP, for example, the ethics office directly presents its annual report to the organization's Executive Board. In the UN, the Secretary-General presents the General Assembly with an annual report of activities carried out by the ethics office. In some organizations such as WFP, UNICEF and UNFPA, when the Executive Directors present their annual report to the Executive Board they also include a special section on the activities of the ethics office.[92] Nevertheless, most agencies in the UN system do not

---

[90] The Mission Statement of UNESCO's Ethics Office states that '[the Office] [r]eceives concerns from UNESCO personnel and external stakeholders on possible unethical behaviour via the reporting system', in UNESCO, *Ethics Guidance*, which can be consulted at www.unesco.org/new/en/ethics-office/ethics-guidance/ (last access: January 2018).

[91] With regard to offices with investigative responsibilities within other organizations, see *ibid.*, para. 5.1.2.

[92] For a comparison of various organizations on this point, see JIU, *Ethics in the United Nations System*, Annex IV [ref. REP].

provide direct accountability procedures between the ethics offices and their legislative bodies.

7.4.1.2 Bodies with Investigative Powers over the Conduct of Officials

As we have seen, the ethics offices procedure is as follows: it initiates in these offices, then responsibility shifts to other internal bodies with the investigative powers that the ethics offices lack. In almost all organizations the offices consist of administrative units with audit, evaluation, inspection, monitoring and investigative functions, according to the different organizational models. In organizations such as the United Nations, and also UNRWA, WIPO and WMO, all the functions are concentrated in a single internal control body. In others, such as UNESCO, UNFPA and WHO,[93] a single body performs only the audit, evaluation and investigative functions. In still others, a single body carries out a combination of the audit, investigation and inspection functions, e.g.: FAO, ILO, UNIDO and WFP.[94]

Thus, there is no single organizational model but nevertheless there are certain elements in common: member state participation in the process of selecting the heads of the office, although they are formally appointed by the Secretary-General in the case of the United Nations, or by an equivalent body in other organizations; operating independence in performing functions; and a direct relationship between these oversight offices and administrative heads and also an indirect or direct relationship with legislative bodies.

Within the UN system, the OIOS has competence over the UN Secretariat and a large number of related programmes and missions,[95] but it has served also as an example followed by other organizations with

---

[93] And some less important from the standpoint of procurement activity, such as IAEA, ICAO and IMO.

[94] JIU, *The Audit Function in the United Nations System*, Annex I [ref. REP].

[95] OIOS has competence not only over the activities of the UN Secretariat in New York, Geneva, Nairobi and Vienna, but also over five regional commissions, peacekeeping missions and humanitarian operations. It also provides assistance to funds and programmes administered separately under the authority of the Secretary-General, such as UNHCR, the United Nations Environment Programme (UNEP) and the Office of the United Nations High Commissioner for Human Rights (OHCHR), and entities that have requested its service, such as the United Nations Convention to Combat Desertification (UNCCD) and the United Nations Framework Convention on Climate Change (UNFCCC).

their own internal offices.[96] In operation since 1994,[97] it has the principal duty of assisting the Secretary-General in meeting her responsibility to monitor proper management of resources and the conduct of officials. Although it is an internal oversight body, member states still play an important role in the procedure for appointing the office head: the Secretary-General identifies and appoints a suitable candidate, but only after consulting with member states and formal approval from the General Assembly. In addition, professional profiles must be evaluated giving consideration to the geographical component, so that certain states do not create a monopoly over the position to the detriment of other states.[98]

From the functional perspective, it operates under the authority of the Secretary-General,[99] but it has operational independence: it may initiate any action it considers necessary to perform its assigned function, carrying out investigations, holding hearings and performing inspections and evaluations,[100] either *ex officio* or at the request of a party. The duration of the OIOS head's term of office is also a factor that should contribute to independence from the head of the administrative structure and from the offices subject to its control: contrary to the above comments regarding the uncertainty of the term of office of the heads of ethics offices, in this case it is five years, non-renewable, and the holder cannot be removed from office without the approval of the General Assembly.

Deferring to the next section an analysis of OIOS's contribution to the legitimacy and correctness of procurement activity as a whole, suffice it to say here that OIOS's duties include investigation of the conduct of individual officials and that this aspect of its activities has been quantitatively

---

[96] In this regard, the Under Secretary-General for Internal Oversight Services has affirmed: 'OIOS as an independent and comprehensive internal oversight mechanism has become a catalyst for increased attention to and strengthening of similar functions throughout the UN system. A number of the specialized agencies, as well as separately administered funds and programmes, have enhanced their own oversight units along the lines of the OIOS concept, and continue to seek our advice. At the meeting of the representatives of internal audit services of the United Nations organizations and multilateral institutions in Paris this year, the system-wide impact of OIOS as a trend-setting model was explicitly recognized', in UN General Assembly, *Report of the Secretary-General on the Activities of the Office of Internal Oversight Services*, A/54/393, Preface [ref. REP].

[97] UN General Assembly, *Review of the Efficiency of the Administrative and Financial Functioning of the United Nations*, A/RES/48/218B [ref. RES].

[98] *Ibid.*, para. 5(b), ii.   [99] *Ibid.*, para. 5(a).

[100] Before 1994, these functions were performed separately by a number of distinct bodies.

one of the most significant.[101] Nevertheless, it should be added that investigations into the conduct of individual officials are closely related to and sometimes not clearly distinguishable from those into other activities, in particular procurement as a whole. By way of example, OIOS has handled cases of officials accused of favouritism towards suppliers,[102] as well as of officials responsible for serious irregularities in managing resources in procurement and in recruitment.[103] The principal distinction is in the consequences arising from the investigation: when an investigation into the conduct of officials reveals violation of the relative rules of conduct, it leads to the formulation of recommendations to the Secretary-General, who may impose disciplinary sanctions. As we have seen, an investigation may also be part of a compound proceeding initiated by the ethics office,[104] with similar results at the disciplinary level. The results of controls on procurement as a whole instead appear in reports to be submitted to the attention of the Secretary-General, who has the obligation to transmit them to the General Assembly with her comments.[105]

In other organizations of the UN system, offices responsible for investigating the conduct of officials[106] have similar basic characteristics (the role of the states in identifying heads of offices, operational independence and at the same time the duty to report to the administrative head), with minor variations in terms of the general monitoring by states of the activity of these offices. For example, in the case of UNDP the OAI not only presents all its reports to the administrative head, but also directly to the Executive Board. Unlike the United Nations, where the link between internal oversight bodies and states is mediated by the Secretary-General, in other organizations this link is direct. In reality, the actual difference is not extremely important, as in both cases member states can obtain

---

[101] For example, between 2010 and 2011, twenty-nine new cases regarding personnel were opened and thirteen reports were closed, compared to thirteen new cases and six reports closed regarding irregularities related to procurement and eighteen new cases and six reports on financial irregularities. Other items regard inventory/assets (four new cases, two reports), management (six new cases, nine reports), sexual exploitation (two new cases, two reports), sexual harassment (two new cases, one report) and irregularities involving UN programmes (two reports). In OIOS, *Activities of the Office of Internal Oversight Services for the Period from 1 July 2010 to 30 June 2011* [ref. REP].

[102] *Ibid.*, para. 47, ID Case 0121/10.   [103] *Ibid.*, para. 53, ID Case 0456/10.

[104] See earlier in this chapter.   [105] See later in this chapter.

[106] For example, for UNDP it is the Office of Audit and Investigation (OAI), for WFP it is the Oversight Services Division (OSD), for FAO the Office of the Inspector General (OIG), for UNESCO the Internal Oversight Service (IOS) and for UNFPA the Division for Oversight Services (DOS).

information on the results of the oversight activities of investigative bodies.[107]

7.4.1.3   Shortcomings of Internal Controls over the Conduct of Officials

Thus designed, this system of controls over the conduct of officials, despite being highly proceduralized, has various shortcomings. The first is the discretionary power of the body that performs the investigations. Although the internal oversight offices have operational independence, they have no duty to act and may, at their own discretion and with no justification, decide not to initiate investigations into the cases submitted for their attention by the ethics offices or by parties reporting violations. Empirical evidence shows that such situations have in fact occurred.[108]

Another critical issue relates to disciplinary decisions that follow a finding that rules of conduct have been violated. Empirical investigations show that, in certain organizations, even though the procedure is set up under the terms described above, in practice it never or only rarely results in disciplinary sanctions. The ineffectiveness of the system is due, as noted above, in part to the competent bodies' discretionary power to take action. But it can be also explained by the high burden of proof required to be imposed on the interested party when filing an administrative appeal against the decision of the oversight bodies, or when bringing an action in the administrative tribunals within organizations, when they exist:

> [t]he United Nations Dispute Tribunal (UNDT) and the ILO Administrative Tribunal (ILOAT) required a high burden of proof on par with criminal cases.[109]

Finally, sometimes there is a form of internal corporate protection through which 'the higher the position held, the more staff [are] protected and able to avoid formal disciplinary measures'.[110] This last element is consistent with a more general difference in perception between high-level and lower-level officials regarding the effectiveness of policies

---

[107] This possibility has, moreover, been criticized by the JIU because it would compromise the accountability of internal oversight bodies to administrative heads and of administrative heads to member states. That is, it would create a mix of external and internal controls (JIU, *More Coherence for Enhanced Oversight*, p. 17 [ref. REP]).

[108] JIU, *Accountability Frameworks in the United Nations System*, para. 70 [ref. REP].

[109] *Ibid.*, para. 75.   [110] *Ibid.*, para. 75.

on corruption and fraud. While, in fact, managers, who are also responsible for imposing disciplinary sanctions, tend to minimize the incidence of cases of corruption, fraud or conflict of interest or to demonstrate that the relative investigations were conducted according to the required standards, staff council representatives report a significant number of cases that executive heads have shelved despite the fact that the evidence pointed against such a decision, and cases in which the report of misconduct led to failure to renew the contract of the whistle-blower or other forms of soft retaliation.[111]

7.4.2   Internal Controls on Direct Procurement

Internal controls on procurement as a whole are of two types: hierarchical, by higher level offices than those making the procurement decisions; and independent, such as the committees on contracts and OIOS (or equivalent bodies). Both types of controls can be specific and refer to individual decisions made during the various phases of procurement, or general and refer to all procurement activity within a certain period of time.

7.4.2.1   Hierarchical Controls

Fundamental aspects of hierarchical controls are the source of the power to control and the manner in which they are performed. In the first regard, the organizational prerequisite for controls is the delegation of authority among offices at different hierarchical levels. A clear description of responsibilities and the establishment of required value thresholds for making the decisions are fundamental conditions for a satisfactory degree of accountability.[112] This in fact makes it possible to identify the party with the authority to make a decision and then to make that party responsible to hierarchical superiors. Delegation on procurement matters is defined at the regulatory level principally in financial rules, and in procurement manuals.

From the regulatory standpoint, the lines of authority and the respective delegation have not always been clearly defined, especially with reference to procurement by field offices and peacekeeping missions.

---

[111] *Ibid.*, para. 108.

[112] *Ibid.*, para. 93 *et seq.*; JIU, *Delegation of Authority and Accountability*. This latter report notes that '[t]o be accountable for results, managers have to be duly empowered through the clear delegation of authority in all areas, including, and in particular, human resources management', *ibid.*, para. 6 [ref. REP].

In particular, empirical investigations conducted by the JIU have revealed misalignments between authority and responsibility. A transition to a more decentralized structure and an increase in procurement activities managed in cooperation with various agencies within the sphere of UN programmes or projects have resulted in more cases in which officials are in fact assigned duties and responsibilities, but without a formal delegation of authority. The consequence of this is that, to perform their duties, officials' formal decisions on procurement must move up through the hierarchy, which increases process times and makes the action less effective.[113] In addition, with specific reference to peacekeeping missions, in the past the United States has highlighted how difficult it is to identify the limits of the authority and responsibility of individual offices and officials responsible for procurement in a system where the management of operations and resources has been traditionally assigned to two different bodies, i.e. the Department of Management and the Department of Field Support (DFS).[114]

Once again, even when the delegation of authority and value thresholds are formally defined, they are often not taken into account at the local level, especially when they involve a request for authorization to use non-competitive selection methods.[115] Such irregularities have been revealed by controls on particularly delicate operations in political and humanitarian terms, as for example the UN operation in Darfur (African Union – United Nations Hybrid Operation in Darfur – UNAMID).[116]

With regard to the manner in which the controls are conducted, effective internal monitoring, evaluation and reporting mechanisms are lacking for the overall procurements of each organization, or, when these mechanisms are present, the data provided are vague. Frequently, small organizations still do not have an effective system that guarantees accountability among different levels of the administrative hierarchy. But even in larger organizations such as the United Nations, UNOPS, UNICEF, UNRWA and UNIDO, which on the contrary require procurement data to be submitted to top administrative managers or governance bodies, these requirements are not regularly met or are only met on

---

[113] See JIU, *Accountability Frameworks in the United Nations*, para. 46 [ref. REP].

[114] US GAO, *United Nations Peacekeeping* [ref. REP]. For a historical overview, see Chapter 3.

[115] For example, see OIOS, *UNHCR Local Procurement Activities in Kenya*, para. 30 [ref. REP].

[116] *Id.*, *Audit of Procurement Systems and Procedures in UNAMID*, Assignment No. AP2010/634/09, 9 February 2012, para. 15 [ref. REP].

request, as with UNESCO,[117] or are not met at all. This extends also to peacekeeping operations. OIOS reported, for example, that despite a value limit that triggered an obligation for the competent official to prepare a report on the individual procurement operation to be presented to the higher level office, this obligation was systematically disregarded in various peacekeeping missions.[118]

The inefficiency of monitoring, evaluating and reporting mechanisms is also due to the vagueness of the data provided. Even when these mechanisms are present, information on procurement relates to only very general aspects, such as the volume of purchases and categories of goods, services and works purchased, but does not go into more detail by noting, for example, the vendor selection procedures, whether or not they are competitive or the average duration of the selection procedures.[119] This, however, often compromises a proper analysis and monitoring of procurement:

> [t]he lack of relevant, reliable and timely information compromises analysis and monitoring, thus weakening internal controls and increasing the likelihood of efficiency loss, fraud and mismanagement.[120]

And this is even more so the case for decentralized procurement.[121]

7.4.2.2 Controls by Independent Administrative Bodies

Non-hierarchical internal controls that are nevertheless integrated into the decision-making process are conducted in many organizations by the so-called Committes on contracts. As seen above, the contract approval system requires control by these committees when the value of contracts exceeds a certain threshold.[122] The committees are established at the central and local levels in several organizations and primarily perform a control on legitimacy of the procedures. This involves an examination of the correctness of the selection procedures used to identify the

---

[117] JIU, *Procurement Reforms in the United Nations System*, para. 203 [ref. REP].

[118] OIOS, *Horizontal Audit of the Procurement of Core Requirements in Peacekeeping Missions*, para. 12–13 [ref. REP].

[119] The difficulty the JIU itself experienced in obtaining this data is emblematic, see JIU, *Procurement Reforms in the United Nations System*, para. 204–205 [ref. REP]. In reality, the reason for the failure to provide these data seems to be more a pretext aimed at concealing non-competitive practices rather than an actual inability to obtain the information (see also Chapter 4).

[120] *Ibid.*, para. 202.

[121] Some reports from OIOS have highlighted this aspect. See, *inter alia*, OIOS, *Audit of the Procurement Process in UNIFIL* [ref. REP].

[122] See Chapter 3.

contractor and the relative financing, if it is a contract entailing expenditure for the administration. The committees express themselves through recommendations, which, while not formally binding, are nevertheless difficult to ignore. When problems arise regarding the legitimacy of the decisions, the entire procedure may even be repeated (even though this option is rare). The final decision and signing of the contract fall to the administrative body, which, on the basis of delegation, has the authority to bind the organization.

Independent bodies also operate outside the decision-making process and, as previously discussed, their competence extends to the conduct of individual officials: for the procurement activity of the United Nations, the funds and programmes that fall within the authority of the Secretary-General and UN peacekeeping missions, OIOS is the independent internal body with competence to perform controls *ex officio* or at the request of an individual; for the other organizations there are oversight bodies such as the previously mentioned OAI, OSD, OIG and others.

OIOS, for example, has played an important role in UN procurement. Since 1994, it started a systematic review of all phases of the procurement processes as well as of the organizational aspects of this function, on the grounds of alleged widespread irregularities in the procedures.[123] Within this sphere, a particularly significant initiative was the creation within OIOS of a section specifically dedicated to procurement, the so-called Procurement Task Force. Established in January 2006 in response to problems raised by the Independent Inquiry Committee in the Oil-for-Food scandal, the Task Force functioned for about two years, with a specific mandate: to '[i]nvestigate all procurement-related cases involving procurement bidding exercises, procurement staff and vendors doing business with the United Nations'.[124] During the first year of investigations, more than 82 per cent of the cases handled regarded procurement in peacekeeping missions, while the remaining 18 per cent were cases involving UN headquarters and the various agencies.[125] During the two-year period, the Task Force investigated

---

[123] UN General Assembly, *Report of the Secretary-General on the Activities of the Office of Internal Oversight Services*, A/50/459, paras. 14, 17 [ref. REP].

[124] UN Under-Secretary-General for Internal Oversight Services, *Report of the Office of Internal Oversight Services on the Activities of the Procurement Task Force*, para. 1 [ref. REP].

[125] *Ibid.*, para. 6.

a total of 437 cases, with a special focus on supplier companies[126] and individual persons.[127] This last aspect is quite significant: most cases handled by OIOS involved not UN officials, but the economic operators who participated in the tender procedures. When found guilty of corruption, fraud, collusion or alteration of bids, the recommendation was to suspend them from the registers of qualified suppliers and, in certain cases, there was a recommendation to refer the case to the criminal courts of the home state or to civil courts to obtain compensation for damages, as OIOS has neither criminal nor civil jurisdiction.[128]

Thus, first, control by OIOS was aimed not so much to ensure the rights of both parties in the case – the administration and private contractors – but rather was principally to protect the administration from actions filed against it by private parties. The OIOS Investigations Manual indeed states: '[i]nvestigations serve the overall interests of the Organization'.[129]

Second, although it performs internal oversight, OIOS has conducted (and conducts) investigations also on private subjects by virtue of their participation in an administrative procedure. Due process obligations in relation to private subjects nevertheless only arise at the end of the investigation and principally regard protecting the confidentiality of the information collected. In addition, the decision to use the information is always at the organization's discretion:

> it is the prerogative of the Organization to decide how to use the investigation report once issued, taking into account all due process interests of individuals implicated by that report.[130]

Third, OIOS prepares recommendations which can impact the legal positions of the private subjects involved, once accepted and implemented by the competent administrations. However, due precisely to the fact that these recommendations are addressed to the procuring entity, they cannot be appealed by the private subjects before a third impartial body.

---

[126] It is significant that about 60 per cent of suppliers had headquarters in Europe or the United States. See OIOS, *Report of the Office of Internal Oversight Services on the Activities of the Procurement Task Force*, A/63/329, para. 5 [ref. REP].

[127] *Ibid.*, para. 5.

[128] *Ibid.*, para. 43; UN General Assembly, *Report of the Office of Internal Oversight Services on the Activities of the Procurement Task Force*, A/62/272, para. 9 [ref. REP].

[129] OIOS, *Investigations Manual*, para. 3.2.4 [ref. AP&R].   [130] *Ibid.*

Finally, the experience of the Procurement Task Force has shown the limits of oversight, the effectiveness of which still depends on the will of the states: of the sixty-eight recommendations issued between 2007 and 2008, most of which regarded companies incorporated in the member states, thirty-four were not followed up and one was rejected.[131] Furthermore, the duration of the Task Force was temporary – about two and a half years – at the express desire of certain member states. In particular, Russia and Singapore conducted a stubborn campaign against renewing the mandate and funding. The non-explicit reason was that various Russian and Singaporean companies had been the subject of investigations, recommendations and exclusion from the registers of companies authorized to submit bids, with accusations of corruption and fraud.[132]

7.4.2.3   Deficiencies of Internal Control Mechanisms on Procurement Activity

The system of internal controls on procurement activity is, thus, deficient in various ways. First, hierarchical controls are based on a distribution of delegation of authority that is often not clearly regulated. In particular, increased duties and functions and a consequent decentralization have accentuated this phenomenon, creating a misalignment between authority and responsibility. In this same context, even when the lines of authority are clear, field offices often do not adhere to them in practice and make decisions that avoid hierarchical control. Moreover, internal reporting procedures often prove to be ineffective due to a failure to meeting the relative requirements and the vagueness of the information transmitted.

The controls performed by independent bodies show weaknesses at both the regulatory level and in terms of implementation. In the first regard, the impact of the decisions of these bodies is limited: in no case are they binding; instead, they are recommendations that can be disregarded. In practice, in fact, effective implementation is one of the problems: the experience of the Procurement Task Force established within OIOS demonstrates that recommendations may be followed by no

---

[131] See UN Under Secretary-General for Internal Oversight Services, *Report of the Office of Internal Oversight Services on the Activities of the Procurement Task Force*, para. 42 [ref. REP].

[132] See *inter alia* Lynch, 'Russia Seeks to Thwart UN Task Force That Led Bribery Probes'; Stecklow, 'UN Allows Its Antifraud Task Force to Dissolve'; Schaefer, 'The Demise of the UN Procurement Task Force Threatens Oversight at the UN'.

action. Furthermore, the will of the states is decisive and may obstruct implementation of oversight results and in some cases block oversight itself. Finally, although these are internal controls, they can have a direct impact on private subjects, in particular undertakings identified as factors that alter the proper carrying out of procurement procedures. Nevertheless, these private subjects are not guaranteed the right to object and neither are they ensured due process.

7.5 Inter-Institutional Controls on Indirect Procurement

The monitoring by international financing organizations of national administrations that receive and manage financing is aimed, at least formally, at guaranteeing that the funds disbursed are spent to achieve the social, humanitarian and development objectives agreed to by the organization and the state in the individual project. Following the organization's procedures and principles that delineate the procurement activity of states is fundamental to the most efficient achievement of these goals.

The relevant controls are pervasive and are both specific and general. The first type is controls on the individual decisions that are taken during the procurement procedure, which are, thus, always ongoing. The second type comprise financial and overall management controls on segments of the implementation activity. These are usually performed at scheduled intervals during the course of the project. There is a substantial difference between the type of controls by organizations that are financial in nature (development banks such as WB, ADB, AfDB, IDB, EBRD, IFAD and EDF) and EU institutions on the one hand, and controls by other organizations, such as UNDP, on the other. For the former, controls are both specific and general, while for the latter they are mostly general. The UNDP guidelines on national execution, for example, state that the guiding principles of accountability include the

> [o]bligation to disclose performance through regular reporting on results and financial matters.[133]

Specific controls, instead, may be conducted before or after the award decision.[134] The *ex ante* controls are carried out during the entire course

---

[133] In UNDP, *National Implementation by the Government of UNDP Supported Projects*, p. 8 [ref. AP&R].

[134] On *ex-ante* review and *ex-post* review procedures, see WB, *The World Bank Procurement Regulations for IPF Borrowers*, paras. 3.5–3.9; *id.*, *Procurement Post Review, Independent*

of the vendor selection process, while *ex post* controls are activated when the contract is concluded. In both cases, states usually prepare a procurement plan that lists all the contracts to be concluded in the first months of project implementation, the types of goods, services and works intended to be purchased, the procedures for selecting the contractor they intend to use, and the thresholds beyond which prior or *ex post* review by the organization is necessary, based on an evaluation of the risk. The organization must formally approve the procurement plan during negotiations for the loan, if it is a financial organization, and subsequent updates and changes must also receive its approval through an explicit or no-objection procedure.[135]

For procurements that exceed the value thresholds for which the procurement plan requires prior review,[136] these controls are performed during the tender preparation phase: the invitation to bid, instructions to participants, conditions of contract and specifications, and the description of methods of publicity must be submitted to the organization; the organization sends its comments; and changes must be made in accordance with them.

During the vendor selection phase, before taking the award decision, the competent national authority must submit a report to the organization comparing the bids received and indicating the supplier to whom it intends to award the contract. If, after its evaluation, the organization feels that the procedure was conducted in a manner that did not comply with the loan agreement and/or procurement plan, it must advise the national authority, giving reasons for its determination. In any event, the contract may not be definitively awarded until after the organization's approval through no objection. The national authority must also retain

Procurement Review, and Integrated Fiduciary Reviews; ADB, *Procurement Guidelines*, App. 1; AfDB, *Rules and Procedures for the Procurement of Goods and Works*, App. 1; IFAD, *Project Procurement Guidelines*, paras. 63–83; European Union, *PRAG*, para. 2.2 [all documents in ref. AP&R].

[135] WB, *The World Bank Procurement Regulations for IPF Borrowers*, paras. 5.73, 5.76; ADB, *Procurement Guidelines*, App. 1, para. 2(c), (f); AfDB, *Rules and Procedures for the Procurement of Goods and Works*, App. 1, para. 2(c) [all documents in ref. AP&R].

[136] In the case of contracts funded by the European Union and the EDF, the adoption of prior review and post review procedures is not based on threshold values, but on the management method selected. In particular, management of operations may be centralized and indirect, in which case procedures will be post review; or decentralized, in which case procedures will be prior review or *ex post* review depending on how they are defined in the implementation agreement between the Commission and the beneficiary state (See European Union, *PRAG*, para. 2 [ref. AP&R]).

all documentation regarding each contract, usually for at least two years, and must make it available to the organization at its request.[137]

The organization's decisions are binding and an indispensable condition for the national administration to be able to legitimately proceed in implementing the project financed. The organization reserves the right to declare misprocurement and withdraw the portion of financing dedicated to the purchase of goods, services or works in violation of the loan agreement, the procurement plan, the award decisions approved by the organization, or the rules on fraud and corruption included in the procurement guidelines of the international organization.[138]

Ex post review is performed on contracts below the threshold identified in the procurement plan. While prior review requires a proactive approach by the national administration, which must progressively submit its decisions for approval, the frequency of post review is based on the loan agreements and on the procurement plan. For these purposes, national administrations must retain the documentation regarding each contract at least until the end of the project and for some years thereafter (usually two). The documents must regard all phases of the procurement: from preparation of tender documents to implementation of the contract. Guidelines on procurement by financial institutions provide that oversight in these cases can be carried out by the organization or by independent bodies, such as a supreme audit institution, acceptable to the organization.[139] Nevertheless, to be able to use this latter form of control there must be the agreement of the organization, which still reserves the right to directly view the reports provided by the national administration and to conduct additional controls.

Financial and management controls over segments of the activity of implementing operations are instead performed at intervals that vary from organization to organization and are based on the provisions of the procurement plan. In some organizations, mostly those of a non-

---

[137] WB, *The World Bank Procurement Regulations for IPF Borrowers*, Annex II, paras. 8–9; ADB, *Procurement Guidelines*, App. 1, para. 5; AfDB, *Rules and Procedures for the Procurement of Goods and Works*, App. 1, para. 5 [all documents in ref. AP&R].

[138] WB, *The World Bank Procurement Regulations for IPF Borrowers*, para. 3.24; ADB, *Procurement Guidelines*, para. 1.12; AfDB, *Rules and Procedures for the Procurement of Goods and Works*, para. 1.12; IFAD, *Project Procurement Guidelines*, part III, i); EBRD, *Procurement Policies and Rules*, para. 3.41 [all documents in ref. AP&R].

[139] WB, *The World Bank Procurement Regulations for IPF Borrowers*, Annex II, para. 4; ADB, *Procurement Guidelines*, App. 1, para. 5; AfDB, *Rules and Procedures for the Procurement of Goods and Works*, App. 1, para. 8; EBRD, *Procurement Policies and Rules*, paras. 3.35–3.39 [all documents in ref. AP&R].

financial character,[140] they can be conducted not only by the organization itself but also by other entities. In fact, while in the United Nations, UNOPS, ILO and WHO audits are mostly performed by offices within the organization, in UNESCO they are performed by the national administration, which then reports the results to the organization. In FAO and ILO they are performed jointly by the organization and the beneficiary state. In UNHCR, UNFPA and other organizations there are auditors external to both the organization and the state. In one case, the ILO, donor states perform the audits. Finally, mixed bodies can be established that include representatives of donor countries and the recipient state, as in the case of the United Nations Office on Drugs and Crime (UNODC).[141] In addition, in organizations that are part of the UN system, the Board of Auditors controls both the internal activity of each organization and the funds and programmes that fall within its competence, within which operations are provided that national states are responsible for implementing.[142]

Therefore, unlike internal controls of direct procurement activity, which as we have seen are often deficient and ineffective in practice, inter-institutional controls aimed at verifying that procurement procedures are followed and that management adequately meets set objectives are much more stringent. Nevertheless, here too there may be differences in procedures: while financial institutions and the European Commission control the micro-management of procurement activity (so that control becomes a true co-decision system), non-financial organizations function through a control mechanism that gives the national administration greater decision-making autonomy and at the same time general reporting on and evaluation of the activities carried out.

7.6   Private Subjects' Rights vis-à-vis International Organizations

The third component of accountability regards the relationship between the international organizations and private subjects who are not officials within it. As noted at the start of this chapter, this is a component that over recent years has become increasingly significant with the growth of administrative activities of organizations with direct effects on individuals and companies. The result has been that, under pressure from

---

[140] Organizations that, although not being financial institutions, carry out some form of national executed procurement.

[141] See JIU, *National Execution of Technical Cooperation Projects*, para. 67 [ref. REP].

[142] On the contrary, OIOS does not conduct controls of these operations.

states and certain oversight bodies, there have been attempts at reform in order to improve this component of accountability.

Nevertheless, it should be added that, at least with regard to the vendor selection phase in direct procurement, the mechanisms currently provided do not fully guarantee impartial and effective protection of the legal position of the private subjects involved. Accountability to private parties is still the weakest component of the system. Contributing to this is the organization's functional immunity, the inadequate formalization of appeal procedures, the absence of judicial review (in most organizations) and the lack of adequate means of compensation.

Things partially change when the contract is concluded and when the protection of private party rights arises from the contract. As we shall see, all contracts permit disputes related to execution of the contract to be referred to neutral and impartial bodies. Here too, however, the possibility for international organizations to invoke immunity plays an important role in deterring litigation and providing less protection, especially for small economic operators.

In indirect procurement, the mechanisms that organizations provide to ensure the protection of private subjects' rights vis-à-vis national administrations are more numerous and effective. The private subject's interest in protecting its legal position acts synergically with the international organization's interest in proper and efficient management of resources.[143] At the same time, there is no immunity from jurisdiction and execution that prevent the private party from fully asserting its claims against the national administration.

7.6.1 Immunity of International Organizations: Issues in Procurement

The immunity of international organizations from jurisdiction and execution in litigation is traditionally conceived as an instrument to protect organizations from possible host government interference in the pursuit of their institutional purposes.[144] Historically immunity

---

[143] See Chapter 8.

[144] In general, on immunities and privileges of international organizations, see Lalive, 'L'immunité de juridiction'; Jenks, *International Immunities*; Ahluwalia, *The Legal Status, Privileges and Immunities*; Michaels, *International Privileges and Immunities*; Glenn, Kearney and Padilla, 'The Immunities of International Organizations'; Cassese, 'L'immunité de juridiction civile des organisations internationales dans la jurisprudence italienne'; Dominicé, 'L'immunité de juridiction et d'exécution des organisations internationales'; Seidl-Hohenveldern, 'L'immunité de juridiction des Communautés européennes'; Bekker, *The Legal Position of Intergovernmental Organizations*;

originates from the transition, beginning after World War II, from a concept that interpreted organizations as operating instruments of states and not distinct from them,[145] to one that gave organizations a distinct legal status at the international level. So immunity was the attribute necessary to guarantee the autonomy of international bodies distinct from states.

Nevertheless, the concept of immunity has evolved over time: from initially being an application of principles developed for states (and for their diplomatic corps) and, thus, meaning primarily the immunity of officials,[146] it then acquired an independent significance reflected in case law and legal theory, which has highlighted the limits of this construction and the institutional and functional differences between states and organizations.[147] For states, immunity is a function of sovereignty: it guarantees that a state, endowed with its own territory, is not influenced or obstructed in the exercise of its sovereign prerogatives by another sovereign state. It thus has a political objective that consists of 'avoiding the creation of imbalances which are dangerous to the peaceful management of international relations'.[148] In international organizations, on the other hand, immunity is linked to the effective and autonomous pursuit of their institutional functions, which must be ensured despite the absence of a territory over which sovereignty is exercised and without interference from the states in which the organization has headquarters and operates:

> being unable to enjoy the protection conferred by territorial sovereignty, as States can, international organizations have as their sole protection the immunities granted to them.[149]

Wenckstern, *Die Immunität internationaler Organisationen*; Reinisch, *International Organizations before National Courts*; Dorigo, *L'immunità delle organizzazioni internazionali*; Sands and Klein, *Bowett's Law of International Institutions*; Reinisch, 'Privileges and Immunities'; Klabbers, *An Introduction to International Institutional Law*; Schermers and Blokker, *International Institutional Law*.

[145] See Singer, 'Jurisdictional Immunity of International Organizations'.

[146] See Kunz, 'Privileges and Immunities of International Organisations'. This interpretation is, for example, argued by Schröer, 'De l'application de l'immunité jurisdictionnelle'.

[147] See, *inter alia*, Glenn, Kearney and Padilla, 'The Immunities of International Organizations', p. 266 *et seq.*; Reinisch, *International Organizations before National Courts*, p. 348 *et seq.*

[148] In Dorigo, *L'immunità delle organizzazioni internazionali*, p. 10.

[149] In Dìaz Gonzàlez, 'Fourth Report on Relations between States and International Organizations', p. 153 *et seq.* Along the same lines, Bekker, *The Legal Position of Intergovernmental Organizations*, p. 99 *et seq.* and Dominicé, 'L'immunité de juridiction et d'exécution des organisations internationales', which further specifies the concept of the body's political and functional independence.

In this sense, immunity is deemed to protect the organizations against two main forms of interference. The first and least incisive is that which may be exercised through the courts. According to some scholars, review by a national court can negatively affect the resources of the organizations, their political legitimation, and eventually their functioning. In fact, a legal controversy would oblige an organization to use resources and personnel to defend itself in court. It could undermine the organization's credibility and legitimacy. For example, in situations of international tension or when the organization has taken an unpopular decision. It could hamper the functioning of the organization. For example, an adverse reaction to the organizations' decisions may induce the organization to opt for a prudential approach in subsequent similar occasions, and to take actions that are possibly safer in terms of possible lawsuits but less effective in terms of achieving its purposes.[150]

The second form of interference may consist of the direct impact that the enforcement of a judicial decision or the adoption of *interim* measures has on assets or resources of an organization. In these situations, there is a risk to the organization's unhampered functioning, as a national court has an impact on the resources the organization uses to operate.[151]

The possibility of asserting immunity has been codified in many international agreements that dictate criteria and limits, both general ones and those related to specific organizations. The organizations within the UN system have adopted substantially uniform rules and regulations in this regard that have inspired various other organizations. Art. 105, para. 1 of the Charter of the United Nations provides that

> [t]he Organization shall enjoy in the territory of each of its Members such privileges and immunities as are necessary for the fulfilment of its purposes.[152]

The immunity sanctioned by the Charter is, thus, linked to the exercise of functions. According to some interpretations, this would prevent a privilege from being considered legitimate when it is invoked for other than institutional purposes:

> [i]t should be a principle that no immunities and privileges which are not really necessary should be asked for.[153]

---

[150] In Dorigo, *L'immunità delle organizzazioni internazionali*, p. 13.
[151] See Dominicé, 'L'immunité de juridiction et d'exécution des organisations internationales', p. 206 *et seq.*
[152] United Nations
[153] In Preparatory Commission of the United Nations, *Report of the Preparatory Commission of the United Nations*, p. 45 [ref. REP].

On this same basis, other observers have argued that this immunity is in fact absolute, given the broad purposes of organizations. The first interpretation seems to be the most common and accepted, and subsequent conventions on privileges and immunities should be read in the light of this interpretation. Art. 2, section 2 of the 1946 Convention on the Privileges and Immunities of the United Nations states:

> [t]he United Nations, its property and assets wherever located and by whomsoever held, shall enjoy immunity from every form of legal process except insofar as in any particular case it has expressly waived its immunity. It is, however, understood that no waiver of immunity shall extend to any measure of execution.[154]

Exactly the same provision is contained in the 1947 Convention on the Privileges and Immunities of Specialized Agencies.[155] A literal interpretation of the provisions in these conventions would favour the interpretation of absolute immunity that could be invoked regardless of functions: organizations can waive immunity from jurisdiction only through a voluntary and non-compulsory act, while immunity from execution cannot be waived. Nevertheless, as the conventions cited are subsequent to the Charter, they should be interpreted in the light of it and based on the principle of functional necessity:

> [t]he Convention defines the privileges and immunities enjoyed by the Organization and its personnel. It follows the bedrock principle of functionality established in Article 105 of the Charter.[156]

In reality, a joint reading of the provisions cited and case law produces a composite picture that requires a distinction to be drawn between immunity from jurisdiction and immunity from execution, and between the legal position that organizations may assert and the content of the rulings given by national courts.

Immunity from jurisdiction is governed by a system of rules and exceptions: the rule is immunity, the exception is the waiving of immunity. Waiving is a voluntary and autonomous act by the organization, which must in fact determine whether it is appropriate to maintain and assert immunity or to waive it according to functional necessity.

---

[154] Convention on the Privileges and Immunities of the United Nations [ref. T&C].

[155] Convention on the Privileges and Immunities of the *Specialized Agencies, Art.* 3, sec. 4 [ref. T&C].

[156] In UN General Assembly, *Comprehensive Review of the Whole Question of Peacekeeping Operations in All Their Aspects,* para. 85 [ref. REP].

In traditional legal practice, the decisions of national courts called to decide on disputes between organizations and private subjects showed a tendency to accept that organizations might invoke absolute immunity from their jurisdiction.[157] However, the method most frequently used was to apply a narrow concept of immunity that sometimes overlapped with that of functional immunity, albeit with wide variations in the interpretation of what is intended by functional immunity.[158] Moreover, especially in the last decade, the case law of European and national courts has moved even further.[159] The interpretation of immunity provided by the European Court of Human Rights (ECHR) has been emblematic in this evolution. Early ECHR case law interpreted immunity from jurisdiction as not being a violation of the right to a fair trial enshrined in Art. 6 of the European Convention for the Protection of Human Rights and Fundamental Freedoms.[160] In the *Waite and Kennedy* judgment, however, the Court allowed immunity only subject to the fact that the plaintiff could offer other reasonable guarantees of legal protection. In this specific case, there was a dispute resolution mechanism within the organization.[161] This ECHR jurisprudence has paved the way for national courts, which have followed suit by showing a similar restrictive approach to immunity from jurisdiction.[162]

---

[157] Reinisch, *International Organizations before National Courts*, p. 391 and *passim*.

[158] See *ibid.*, *passim*.

[159] On this point also see Gaillard and Pingel-Lenuzza, 'International Organisations and Immunity from Jurisdiction'. In general on judicial review of the acts of international organizations see Lauterpacht, 'Judicial Review of the Acts of International Organisations'.

[160] For earlier case law see ECHR, *Ashingdane* v. *United Kingdom*, Application No. 8225/78, 28 May 1985 [1985] 7 EHRR 528; ECHR, *Ary Spaans* v. *The Netherlands*, Application No. 12516/86, 12 December 1988 [1988] 58 *Decisions and Reports* 119 [1988] 107 ILR 1. For an analysis of early ECHR case law regarding immunity from jurisdiction see Sudre, 'La jurisprudence de la Cour européenne des droits de l'homme', pp. 19–31; Reinisch, *International Organisations before National Courts*, p. 283 *et seq.*, p. 300 *et seq.*

[161] ECHR, *Waite and Kennedy*, Application No. 26083/94, 18 February 1999 [1999] ECHR 13. On *Waite and Kennedy* and its implications see *inter alia* Reinisch and Weber, 'In the Shadow of Waite and Kennedy'.

[162] See, for instance, Cour d'Appel de Bruxelles, *Mme L.* v. *Secrétariat général du Groupe des Etats d'Afrique des Caraïbes et du Pacifique*, 4 March 2003 [2003] *Journal des tribunaux* 684; Cour d'Appel de Paris, *Banque africaine de développement* v. *Degboe*, 7 October 2003 [2004] *Revue critique de droit international privé* 409; Cour de Cassation, Chambre sociale, *Banque africaine de développement* v. *Degboe*, 25 January 2005 [2005] *Journal du droit international* 1142. For a critical comment on this case law see Malmendier, 'The Liability of International Development Banks', pp. 152–153.

On the contrary, as a result of agreements, conventions and, according to some, customary rules and standards that have developed in this area, immunity from execution is absolute: it cannot be waived by the organizations and cannot be interpreted otherwise by courts.[163] An analysis of the problem of immunity, however, requires specific considerations when related to direct procurement, understood in the broad sense as including both the vendor selection phase and the contract itself. As we shall see in the following section, the problem of immunity from jurisdiction and execution does not even arise with regard to the former. Except for procurement by European institutions and a few organizations such as the ESA, the illegitimacy of an administrative decision, such as a tender award decision, can only be asserted through a (formal or informal) internal administrative appeal, but not by a judicial body. Thus, the issue of immunity does not arise because there are no competent fora that judge on procurement undertaken by international organizations.

Conversely, contracts of the organizations resulting from tender procedures usually contain both clauses that make the conventions on privileges and immunities applicable to the contract and arbitration clauses that establish the obligation to settle contractual disputes through arbitration. Thus, while there is immunity from jurisdiction, the organization must nevertheless open up to a form of impartial evaluation of the rights arising from the contract. Therefore, with reference to contract execution, the critical point is not so much that the organization's conduct within the contract is not subject to judicial scrutiny, but rather that there are few solutions designed to compensate any violations suffered by the private party. Indeed, immunity from execution, which as we have seen is generally interpreted as absolute, may prevent the implementation of a final ruling, whether by a national court or by an arbitrator, or the adoption of *interim* measures to temporarily correct violations and later ensure the enforcement of a decision. This circumstance has led some scholars and case law to affirm, rightly in my view, that it is a codified form of denial of justice.[164]

---

[163] Even though, for example, in the case *Quartiere Generale Forze Alleate Sud Europa* v. *Bonifacio e Soc. Fratelli di Benedetto*, the Italian Court of Cassation held that immunity from execution is not absolute but limited to the assets used to achieve the body's institutional purposes. Corte di Cassazione, 8 February 1991, no. 1303, published in [1991] I *Foro italiano* 752.

[164] See, *inter alia*, General Claims Commission (Mexico–United States), *H.G. Venable (U. S.A.)* v. *United Mexican States*, 8 July 1927 [1927] 4 *Reports of International Arbitral Awards* 219 and ECHR, *Immobiliare Saffi* v. *Italy*, no. 22774/93, 28 July 1999 [1999] ECHR 65.

Financial organizations are a partial exception to this system. While other organizations that are not part of the UN system have signed agreements that substantially duplicate the mechanism of functional immunity from jurisdiction and absolute immunity from execution, financial organizations have set up a system that excludes immunity from jurisdiction and sets certain limits to immunity from execution.[165] Art. VII, section 3, of IBRD's Articles of Agreement, for example, states that

> [a]ctions may be brought against the Bank only in a court of competent jurisdiction in the territories of a member in which the Bank has an office, has appointed an agent for the purpose of accepting service or notice of process, or has issued or guaranteed securities.[166]

Even in these cases, there are still limits to the ability to take action against the organization's resources and assets. The first limit is embodied within the provisions just mentioned: immunity can be invoked if the conditions just described are not met. In addition, *interim* measures are not possible:

> [t]he property and assets of the Bank shall, wheresoever located and by whomsoever held, be immune from all forms of seizure, attachment or execution *before* the delivery of final judgment against the Bank.[167]

This also leads to the assumption that, after the decision, the organization's property and resources have no immunity. Nevertheless, even this possibility is circumscribed. The organization's property and resources cannot in fact be subject to any form of search, seizure, confiscation, expropriation or any other form of attachment or forced possession ordered by executive or legislative power.[168] Finally, to the extent necessary to pursue their institutional purposes, all property and activities of organizations must be free from restrictions, regulations, controls and moratoria of any kind.[169]

---

[165] In this case, the reference is to financial institutions as parties to a contract with the private party.

[166] With similar wording, *Agreement Establishing the European Bank for Reconstruction and Development (EBRD)*, Art. 46 [ref. A&C].

[167] Emphasis added. In *International Bank for Reconstruction and Development (IBRD) Articles of Agreement*, Art. VII, sec. 3. Along the same lines, *Agreement Establishing the EBRD*, Art. 46 [all documents in ref. A&C].

[168] *IBRD Articles of Agreement*, Art. VII, sec. 4. Along the same lines, *Agreement Establishing the EBRD*, Art. 47 [all documents in ref. A&C].

[169] *IBRD Articles of Agreement*, Art. VII, sec. 6. Along the same lines, *Agreement Establishing the EBRD*, Art. 49 [all documents in ref. A&C].

The result is a graduated system of immunity from execution based on the type of execution, the functions performed by the organization and the powers to order executive measures: immunity from execution protects the organization's property and resources from interference by executive and legislative powers without affecting the execution of orders handed down by a court, although within certain limits. Indeed these orders may not include the issuing of *interim* measures, or entail the seizure of property and resources that the organization requires in order to function.

Thus, in the case of procurement by financial institutions, accountability to private subjects is based, on the one hand, on the possibility of subjecting (under certain conditions) the organization's activities to judicial review. On the other hand, it is jeopardized by immunity from execution to the extent necessary for the organization to engage in its institutional activity. This contrasts with non-financial organizations, which have functional immunity for the organization's activities and absolute immunity from execution. The rationale for the different approach adopted by financial organizations lies in their need for market credibility. As engaging in and financing public and private activities is their institutional function, it is necessary to encourage the trust of private parties by assuring that any violations of contractual terms will be subject to judicial review.[170]

The exception that these organizations represent, however, has little value from the standpoint of procurement activity for internal purposes carried out using formalized vendor selection procedures. As we have seen, the volume of corporate procurement for financial organizations is minimal when compared to that of organizations of a non-financial nature,[171] and the lesser scope of immunity is not related to procurement needs but to needs linked to their financial nature. This also means the approach of financial organizations is not extendible to other organizations.[172]

---

[170] See Dominicé, 'L'immunité de juridiction et d'exécution des organisations internationales', p. 196.

[171] See Chapter 2.

[172] The opinion of certain scholars that these rules and regulations cannot be extended to non-financial organizations is, for example, set out in Dorigo, *L'immunità delle organizzazioni internazionali*, p. 34.

7.6.2   Remedies in the Vendor Selection Phase

There are different possible mechanisms for protecting private subjects in the phase prior to concluding the contract, depending on whether it involves direct or indirect procurement. In the first case, the instruments of protection question the organizations' administrative action. In the second case, it is the national administrations' activity that is potentially illegitimate and could constitute grounds for a challenge. In terms of the effectiveness of this protection, this difference is fundamental.

7.6.2.1   Administrative Appeals and Judicial Review in Direct Procurement

Supranational rules and regulations on national public procurement usually require states to provide the private subjects with instruments for claiming possible violations by the procuring entity. For example, while the GPA has not established an international body with jurisdiction over procurement claims, it requires national administrations to guarantee a review of their decisions if the private party so requests.[173] In addition, it requires states to provide appropriate procedures before neutral and impartial bodies to claim violations of the provisions set out in the agreement itself and in national public procurement legislation.[174] According to the GPA, the powers that national legislation must grant these bodies are of three types: powers to immediately adopt *interim* measures – including the ability to suspend the procedure – for purposes of temporarily correcting violations and safeguarding commercial opportunities; powers to annul administrative decisions; and powers to order compensation for damages, which nevertheless can be limited to the costs of preparing the tender and court fees.[175]

In the direct procurement of international organizations, accountability vis-à-vis private subjects' rights during the vendor selection phase varies from organization to organization: going from no provision of accountability mechanisms at all to proper review by court. Assuming the nature of the body petitioned to be a distinctive criterion, these mechanisms, when present, can be classified into four models: informal appeals

---

[173] GPA, Art. XVIII, para. 2.
[174] The second case describes controls of the administrative decisions of neutral and impartial judicial review bodies or, in the alternative, of neutral and impartial non-judicial bodies that are similar to judicial bodies and adopt comparable procedures, see GPA, Art. XVIII, paras. 2–6.
[175] GPA, Art. XVIII, para. 7.

to the representatives of the member states within the organizations; hierarchical administrative appeals; administrative appeals to independent bodies; and judicial review. In some organizations, more than one remedy is available and can be activated. For example, an informal appeal to state representatives sometimes intertwines with an appeal filed with independent bodies or with the same administration that made the decision. In addition, the current structure of remedies is the result of relatively recent reforms. In most organizations within the UN system, there are still no formal appeal mechanisms, while in others discussions regarding the ability to petition administrative bodies began in 2006–2007, but this ability did not come into effect until 2009–2010. Examples of the no accountability mechanisms approach and of the four main accountability mechanisms currently available are illustrated below through reference to the main organizations that adopt them.

Of the organizations that have greater volumes of procurement, UNICEF,[176] WFP, FAO and WHO are examples of the *first model* of accountability, i.e. informal appeals to the representative of the member states. These organizations do not give private subjects any formal appeal mechanism against the denial of a registration request, exclusion from the tender procedure due to failure to meet the necessary qualifications or the award decision. Private subjects thus only have informal recourse to the administrative authority that took the decision or to a higher level one, or they may hand the matter over to the representative offices of their home country within the organizations.[177] This second possibility may actually be quite effective, creating synergy between the individual undertaking's interest in being awarded the contract and the state's interest in the financing granted being returned to a national undertaking in the form of a contract award. Nevertheless, this very consideration ties the positive result of the appeal to the economic weight of the individual undertaking, and to the value of the contract. One of the principle consequences is that interests that are already strong end up being protected more, while the mechanism is inefficient for smaller economic operators. This is counterproductive in terms of the objectives of the organizations, which, including through domestic preference policies,

---

[176] The JIU includes UNICEF among the organizations that give private parties formal appeal procedures (see JIU, *Procurement Reforms in the United Nations System*, para. 195 [ref. REP]). Nevertheless, it should be noted that the relative Procurement Manual is not available online, and so private parties may not have advance knowledge of the procedures for filing appeals.

[177] See *ibid.*, para. 195.

may aim to promote local business and small domestic undertakings.[178] In addition, there are risks to the organization's image as a reliable and impartial economic operator. In this regard, the JIU has observed that

[i]n the absence of such a formal mechanism, the organizations are exposed to the risk of being perceived as partial, and of handling complaints depending on who the complainant was.[179]

Partial exceptions to this tendency, and examples of the *second model*, i.e. (hierarchical) administrative appeals, are the United Nations,[180] UNDP,[181] UNOPS,[182] UNHCR,[183] UNIDO,[184] UNFPA[185] and UNRWA.[186] All these organizations have set up formal mechanisms that allow private parties to appeal a decision regarding the contractor selection phase.[187] The degree of proceduralization varies from organization to organization, running from a high level of detail, as in the case of UNDP, to being more general and approximate, as in the case of UNOPS. Moreover, with the exception of the UN, the body petitioned is either the same administration that made the decision or a higher level administration. Since 2009, instead, the UN has had an independent administrative body, i.e. the ARB, entrusted with the task of dealing with this type of appeal. As explained by the UN Procurement Manual, 'the Award Review Board is a UN administrative board which reviews complaints by unsuccessful Bidders who challenge contracts awards made by the UN'.[188] Finally, while for most of these organizations the only decisions

[178] But see Chapter 8.   [179] *Ibid.*
[180] In reality, the UN Procurement Manual of 2013 still does not describe a formal mechanism for appealing award decisions, while it provides for a duty to inform and to debrief unsuccessful vendors (United Nations, *Procurement Manual*, paras. 11.39–11.40 [ref. AP&R]). It, however, makes reference to the Award Review Board (ARB) and it defines its tasks. Furthermore, outside the Procurement Manual, the organization has adopted the *Guidelines to File a Procurement Challenge* in front of the ARB. The possibility of challenging an award decision was first provided in 2009 with the ARB pilot programme, and was later confirmed in 2010. See United Nations, 'Guidelines to File a Procurement Challenge', 2009, available at www.un.org/Depts/ptd/complaints/complaints-guideline (last access: 30 August 2017).
[181] UNDP, *Programme and Operations Policies and Procedures*, sec. 'Handling of Procurement Complaints' [ref. AP&R].
[182] UNOPS, *Procurement Manual*, para. 10.2.2 [ref. AP&R].
[183] UNHCR, *UNHCR Manual. Chapter 8* [ref. AP&R], which is however not publicly available. Instructions on bid protest are however available on the UNHCR website at www.unhcr.org/pages/49f6d3a76.html (last access: 30 August 2017).
[184] UNIDO, *Procurement Manual*, ch. II, sec. II [ref. AP&R].
[185] UNFPA, *Policy and Procedures for Regular Procurement*, paras. 8.9.2 and 10.2.3 [ref. AP&R].
[186] UNRWA, *Procurement Manual*, para. 10.5 [ref. AP&R].   [187] *Ibid.*
[188] United Nations, *Procurement Manual*, para. 1.4 [ref. AP&R].

likely to be challenged are award decisions, the United Nations, UNDP and UNOPS also make it possible to protest against decisions made prior to the award.

UNDP undoubtedly provides the most articulated procedure for hierarchical administrative complaints.[189] The procurement rules establish that both in the vendor selection phase and after the award of the contract the private party may file a protest with the Business Unit of the procurement division. In order to be considered valid, the protest must contain certain information that the manual specifically sets out: in addition to the details needed to identify the protestor and the tender, this includes a detailed description of all factual and legal grounds for the protest and how this has affected the protestor; a copy of all relevant documents supporting these elements; an indication of the form of relief being sought; all relevant documents establishing that the protestor is the interested party; and all information necessary to evaluate the timeliness of the protest. These elements are required to file the action and their absence makes the protest inadmissible. The protest must be directed to the Head of the Business Unit of the procurement division that announced the tender, or in the case of field offices, to the Resident Representative.

The decision of the Head of the Business Unit and the Resident Representative may in turn be appealed before the Procurement Support Office (PSO), which at the central level is part of the Bureau of Management and is a higher level than the individual procurement division. The decision of this body is final. Nevertheless, if the Director of PSO finds evidence of misconduct, she or he may refer the case to the OAI for further investigation.

Once the protest is received, the Business Unit has the duty to take action, notifying the private party of receipt within a very short period of time,[190] initiating the necessary investigations into the merits and preparing a report on the investigations and possible remedies. Based on this, the Head of the Business Unit or the Resident Representative may make two types of decisions. If the award has not yet been made, she must suspend the selection procedure until the decision on the protest. The obligation to suspend may be set aside in several situations: if the investigation conducted in the field office has revealed that there is no solid grounds for the protest; if there is a genuine exigency of service (real

---

[189] UNDP, *Procurement Programme and Operations Policies and Procedures*, sec. 'Handling of Procurement Complaints' [ref. AP&R].

[190] Two days.

needs for guaranteeing the service); or if a prompt award would be in the organization's best interest. Clearly exceptions can be widely interpreted, particularly as determining the 'best interest' of the organization is subject to the discretion of the competent authority. If the award has already been made, the Resident Representative or Head of the Business Unit must determine whether there are valid grounds for the protest based on the investigations conducted and must weigh the impact that suspending the contract could have on the functioning of the organization.

Overall, this is an appeal mechanism that provides several guarantees of protection, including the obligation to take action and the ability to appeal the initial decision. These guarantees, however, are much less effective than those of administrative appeals usually provided by national public procurement legislation. Within EU states, for example, administrative appeals are only one of the methods whereby a private party may challenge an administrative decision: as an alternative or in addition to administrative appeals there is always the possibility of judicial review. In the international organizations mentioned above, administrative appeals are instead the only tool that the private subject has available in the vendor selection phase. Furthermore, the fact that it is the administration that judges itself does not give sufficient guarantees of independence and neutrality. The lesser effectiveness is also due to the powers available to the bodies with authority to hear appeals. Beyond the power to suspend the procedure, there is no explicit mention of either powers to annul or amend the act, or, as these are administrative bodies, powers to order compensation for damages. Finally, the fact that reasons of urgency and the organization's interest are justifications for avoiding suspension of the procedure means that *de facto* the private party is not guaranteed the possibility of *interim* measures.

These weaknesses in the system are even more significant in the appeal mechanisms provided by the other organizations mentioned where there is less proceduralization. For example, the rules of UNOPS and UNIDO do not make it possible for the vendor to appeal the decision on the complaint pronounced by the first body that heard the complaint.[191] The rules of UNRWA provide that the complaint must be filed with the same administrative authority that took the decision and only in exceptional situations may a complaint be filed

---

[191] See UNOPS, *Procurement Manual*, para. 10.2.2; UNIDO, *Procurement Manual*, para. 11.5 [all documents in ref. AP&R].

with a higher authority.[192] Neither UNOPS[193] nor UNHCR[194] provide for an obligation to take action once a complaint is filed by a vendor. Moreover, none of these organizations expressly set out in detail the powers vested in the bodies that are competent to hear the complaint. Within the UN system, the procedure for appealing the United Nations's award decisions provides, instead, an example of an administrative complaint to an independent body, thus of the *third model* of accountability.[195] In early 2009 the organization launched a pilot project[196] that established an independent body, the ARB, which is responsible for hearing challenges from vendors whose bids have been unsuccessful. The ARB may consist of a single expert or be a board of three procurement experts selected from outside the United Nations.[197] It is materially supported by the UN Secretariat and was originally competent solely for procurement activity at UN headquarters, while from 2016 it is also competent for procurements undertaken by the United Nations Offices at Geneva (UNOG), Nairobi (UNON) and Vienna (UNOV). The procedure is available, however, only for procurements that fulfil certain conditions. First, they must be over a certain value, that is very high.[198] Second, the complaint may be lodged only after a formal debrief was sought and obtained by the unsuccessful bidder. Furthermore, the whole process is marked by very short time frames: the appeal shall be filed within ten days after the formal debrief meeting took place. The ARB evaluates the grounds for the vendor's claim and sends its opinion to the Under Secretary-General who then takes a final non-appealable decision.

---

[192] See UNRWA, *Procurement Manual*, para. 10.5 [ref. AP&R].

[193] UNOPS, *Procurement Manual*, para. 10.2.2 [ref. AP&R].

[194] The UNHCR website provides instructions on how to file a protest. The first condition is that the unsuccessful bidder has previously asked and obtained a debrief. The second condition is the high value of the contract. Time frames are very tight (fifteen calendar days after the date of the debrief). The burden of proof is completely on the claimant. Compensation can be given, but its material determination is left to the discretion of the organization. Finally, there are no possibilities of appealing the decision (see also in UNHCR, *UNHCR Manual. Chapter 8* [ref. AP&R]). It is, however, also added that '[n]othing in the above procedures or in any procedure or action by or relating to UNHCR with respect to or in connection with a procurement debrief or a procurement protest shall be deemed in any way to constitute a waiver of any of the privileges and immunities of the United Nations or its components, including UNHCR (as a subsidiary organ of the UN)', *ibid.*

[195] See United Nations, *Procurement Manual*, paras. 7.8.3(d) and 7.12 [ref. AP&R].

[196] See Schroeder, 'Procurement Reform at the United Nations', p. 18 *et seq.*

[197] *Ibid.*, sec. 'Establishing a Panel of Experts'.

[198] For 2017, the minimum value to bring a complaint was identified as $200,000.

On the one hand, this mechanism is a significant advance in protecting the legal position of private subjects vis-à-vis the international administration. It is part of the proceduralization process of the procurement activity that international organizations have been pursuing, in particular since the end of the 1990s.[199] It is also good practice and an example for reforming other international organizations.[200]

On the other hand, it may prove to be an instrument that for various reasons still does not give private subjects a guarantee of impartial treatment and an effective remedy. First, there is a lack of institutional neutrality: although the ARB is a formally independent body, from the operational standpoint it remains bound to the Secretariat. Furthermore, the ARB only has the power to make recommendations: the Under Secretary-General has the discretion to adopt the final decision, which can also differ from the ARB's recommendation. It is, thus, the administration itself that decides upon the actions that it should take to address the protest. Second, the remedies the private subject can seek are limited: these include cancellation of the procedure and rebid; modification of a multiple-year contract to one year followed by a rebid; and partial financial compensation, such as reimbursement of the cost of the procedure directly related to the procurement challenge (excluding attorney's fees) within a maximum limit. Other important remedies, such as monetary damages related to commercial losses, are instead excluded.[201] Third, there is no further accountability mechanism: the decision of the Under Secretary-General is final and the administrative hierarchy cannot be further escalated. Fourth, the procedural requirements are very demanding on the private party. As seen, there is a procedural precondition to file a protest: a formal debriefing has taken place and it is the administration itself that decides upon the request for a debriefing. Furthermore, the time frames for filing a challenge, after the debriefing, are very short (one-third of what is usually granted by domestic public procurement laws). Fifth, these decisions remain, on the contrary, within the discretion of the body that must make the final determination, i.e. the Under Secretary-General. Finally, this opportunity is limited in scope for

---

[199] See Chapter 3.

[200] With regard to extending this model to other organizations, the JIU distinguishes between organizations with large volumes of purchases and organizations with smaller volumes: '[l]arge organizations with substantial amounts of procurement can benefit from this system, but for small ones it may not be cost-effective', in JIU, *Procurement Reforms in the United Nations System*, para. 197 [ref. REP].

[201] See Schroeder, 'Procurement Reform at the United Nations', p. 19.

at least two reasons: it is offered solely with regard to procurement by the organization's headquarters and the offices of Vienna, Geneva and Nairobi, while a large portion of the United Nations's procurement activity is carried out in field offices and in peacekeeping and peace-building missions. Furthermore, the minimum value of the contract required to activate the debriefing and bid protest procedure is very high and, as seen, both the practices of fragmenting procurement con-tracts and the circumstance that many contracts are below that threshold shield a significant portion of UN procurement activity from any scrutiny activated at the vendor's request.

A different solution that partially overcomes the deficiencies in the mechanism established by the United Nations, and at the same time an example of the third model of accountability, i.e. appeals to an independent body, is that adopted by ESA. In 2010, the organization set up an inde-pendent and impartial administrative body and a three-level review sys-tem, which in some respects is similar to that of the United Nations and UNDP but is more articulated and protective of private subjects' rights.[202]

The vendor's protest must first be submitted to the head of the procure-ment division. If she or he does not make a decision or if the vendor is not satisfied with the decision, an appeal may be filed with the Industrial Ombudsman.[203] This body is composed of a member and her alternate, who are appointed every three years by the Council upon a proposal from the Director-General and must meet the requirements of independence and competence. In this case too, the Ombudsman has the main function of making recommendations: after completing the necessary consultations and investigations, she forwards the recommendation to the head of the procurement division and notifies the vendor. The head of the procurement division then makes a decision, which can still be challenged before another body i.e. the Procurement Review Board. This is composed of four mem-bers from outside the organization who have proven legal and practical experience in public procurement. They must meet detailed requirements of independence: they cannot be members of the delegations of member states, of associate member states or cooperating states. They must operate with complete autonomy, without accepting instructions from anyone and without taking part in any other activities involving ESA. At the same time, however, they are financially compensated by the Agency for their activities.

---

[202] See ESA, *ESA Procurement Regulations*, Arts. 51–55 [ref. AP&R].

[203] The role of the Ombudsman in ESA contracts and the contracts of Community institu-tions is dealt with later in this section.

The procedure conducted by the Board allows the parties to be heard before a decision is made. The Board must state the basis for its decision, which is final for both parties. The head of the procurement division, the Industrial Ombudsman and the Board can also propose to the Director General *interim* measures to suspend the procedure. Finally, the Board can order compensation for damages, albeit within the limit of €100,000.

Thus, the ESA solution resolves some of the more problematic aspects of the UN bid protest mechanism: decisions can be challenged; there are some requirements of independence of the review bodies, both from the administration and the states; the powers of the body with competence to pronounce the final decision include the possibility of granting *interim* measures and ordering compensation for damages; and economic operators participating in the tender procedure are accorded procedural guarantees. This solution seems to realize a hybridization between administrative bodies and judicial methods: on the one hand, it avoids the international organization having the cost of establishing a court; on the other hand, it provides private subjects with a mechanism that seems more effective in protecting their interests than those provided by other organizations.

The most articulated and effective accountability architecture, and an example of the *fourth model*, i.e. judicial review, is, however, that built for procurement carried out by European institutions. There are four options available to private parties who wish to protest against a procurement decision taken by EU institutions: an informal complaint; a complaint to the responsible department within the EU institution; a complaint filed with the European Ombudsman; and an appeal to the Court of Justice of the European Union.[204] Petitions to the European Parliament regarding allegations of maladministration in procurement by EU institutions are, instead, not allowed. While the right to petition the Parliament is one of the fundamental rights of European citizens,[205] the Committee on Petitions of the European Parliament has clearly stated that petitions concerning cases of maladministration by the EU institutions are inadmissible:

---

[204] For an articulate analysis of some of these instruments see also Kalogeras, 'Remedies in the Field of Public Procurement'.

[205] Art. 44 of the Charter of Fundamental Rights of the European Union provides that '[a]ny citizen of the Union and any natural or legal person residing or having its registered office in a Member State has the right to petition the European Parliament' [ref. A&C].

[i]nadmissibility of a petition ... Please note that questions concerning maladministration within the Institutions or bodies of the EU should be addressed to the European Ombudsman.[206]

The informal complaint consists mostly of lobbying activities that can be addressed to the members of the Commission or their cabinets, as well as to the members of the European Parliament and national bodies. Many companies are inclined to complain through these informal activities to avoid the more costly, cumbersome and uncertain procedures of judicial review.[207] These lobbying activities, however, are often connected (and limited) to firms that are established in Brussels or that, anyway, have the economic standing to effectively produce some kind of pressure on the competent bodies. These mechanisms are, thus, *de facto* out of the reach of SMEs.

The other option available to the tenderers is to protest with the procuring entity that managed the tender. Also in these cases, the review processes are often informal and the circumstance that the body deciding on the protest is the same that has managed the procurement procedure and eventually taken the award decision ensures a low degree of impartiality. Among the EU institutions, only the ECB has a 'robust internal review mechanism to deal with complaints'.[208] Unsuccessful vendors in ECB procurement procedures can appeal the decision to a Procurement Review Body. This is an internal body, made up of senior managers and supported by the bank's legal service, which can either reject the appeal or order to repeat the procedure (or part of it). It does not have, however, powers to award damages. Data show that, in practice, this mechanism is not often used and the decisions taken are often in favour of the procurement entity. In this regard, the European Court of Auditors has reported that

> since 2007, 35 appeals have been received, of which one was pending as at December 2015, six were upheld, 20 were rejected and eight were forwarded to the responsible Procurement Committee and not further pursued by the appellant.[209]

---

[206] The passage is quoted in European Court of Auditors, *The EU Institutions Can Do More to Facilitate Access to Their Public Procurement*, para. 88 [ref. REP].

[207] See, also, Kalogeras, 'Remedies in the Field of Public Procurement', pp. 219–220.

[208] European Court of Auditors, *The EU Institutions Can Do More to Facilitate Access to Their Public Procurement*, para. 80 [ref. REP].

[209] *Ibid.*, Box 11.

Unsuccessful bidders have, however, a third option: to challenge the decision of the procuring entities before the European Ombudsman. This is an independent administrative entity within the institutional structure of the European Union that is competent to judge on complaints of maladministration by European institutions. The Ombudsman's decisions may originate *ex officio*, or from 'complaints from any citizen of the Union or any natural or legal person residing or having its registered office in a Member State concerning instances of maladministration in the activities of the Union institutions, bodies, offices or agencies'.[210] Data show that between 1995 and 2015 the Ombudsman has constantly devoted part of its activity to settle challenges related to procurement of European institutions, especially of the European Commission.

The effectiveness of its activity has been, however, hampered by several factors. First, the function of the Ombudsman is essentially conciliatory. With regard to procurement procedures, in particular, its powers usually consist of 'granting the complainant access to information or giving a satisfactory explanation of the reasons for rejecting his tender'.[211] Its decisions never extend to ordering the cancellation of the procurement decision, or repeating the procurement procedure, or compensation for damages suffered by the loss of chance or profit by the unsuccessful tender. Only once in the period from 2008 to 2015 did the Ombudsman order reimbursement of costs incurred by the complainant because of her participation in the procurement procedure.[212]

Second, a complaint to the Ombudsman can be filed only after 'the appropriate administrative approaches to the institutions and bodies concerned'[213] have been made. In practice this means that the unsuccessful tenderer must first file a protest with the procuring entity or, more generally, with the institution concerned; wait for a reply; and, then, if the reply is not satisfactory, go to the Ombudsman. As noted by the European Court of Auditors, this procedural prerequisite 'lengthens the

---

[210] Art. 228 TFEU [ref. T&C].

[211] European Court of Auditors, *The EU Institutions Can Do More to Facilitate Access to Their Public Procurement*, para. 87 [ref. REP].

[212] *Ibid.*, para. 87. See European Ombudsman, *Decision of the European Ombudsman Closing His Inquiry into Complaint 3000/2009/JF against the European Commission*, 26 July 2012.

[213] Article 2(4) of the European Union, Decision of the European Parliament of 9 March 1994 (and following amendments) [ref. N&RL-EU]. Also quoted in European Court of Auditors, *The EU Institutions Can Do More to Facilitate Access to Their Public Procurement*, para. 86 [ref. REP].

process and virtually rules out a swift intervention of the Ombudsman before a contract is signed'.[214]

Third, the possibility to file a complaint to the Ombudsman is subject to a territorial link:

> [a]ny citizen of the Union or any natural or legal person residing or having his registered office in a Member State of the Union may, directly or through a Member of the European Parliament, refer a complaint to the Ombudsman.[215]

This means that the competence of the Ombudsman follows not only from the fact that EU institutions are involved, but also from the circumstance that the subject affected by the EU institutions' activity shows a formal link to the European territory. Thus, undertakings incorporated in non-EU states are excluded from accessing this accountability mechanism, even if they have participated in a tender procedure of European institutions. This requirement has at least two consequences. The first is to create an uneven accountability system that is available to some tenderers and not to others. The second is to produce a discriminatory situation that can discourage enterprises incorporated outside the European Union from taking part in a tender procedure launched by a European institution. This is especially true for foreign SMEs that do not have the option of opening a registered office in a member state.

Finally, the decision of the Ombudsman is alternative to judicial proceedings and final. Thus, there is no appeal mechanism that grants a review of its decision.

The third option available to unsuccessful bidders is to ask for judicial review. Based on the TFEU, private subjects can challenge the legislative or administrative actions of EU institutions before the Court of First Instance and, as a last resort, before the Court of Justice of the European Union.[216] The Court of Justice has also considered decisions taken during the tender procedure as falling within the category of administrative acts, without however providing a general criterion to identify which of these can be challenged.

Both the Court of First Instance and the Court of Justice have the power to order *interim* measures, including suspension of the tender

---

[214] *Ibid*, para. 86.
[215] Article 2(2) of the European Union, Decision of the European Parliament of 9 March 1994 (and following amendments) [ref. N&RL-EU].
[216] TFEU, Art. 263 [ref. T&C].

procedure, as well as the power to annul unlawful acts and to order compensation for damages.[217] With regard to this latter aspect, the private subject has the right to compensation if some conditions are met, i.e. those identified by EU case law regarding the non-contractual liability of EU institutions.[218]

Although the European Union is the only international organization that has set up judicial review mechanisms similar to those existing for national public procurement, data on judicial review of EU institutions' procurement show some flaws. The European Court of Auditors has reported, for example, that between 2009 and 2014, out of the 106 cases related to public procurement and with reference to a total of 123 decisions on such cases, actions for annulment were successful only in thirteen cases.[219] During the same period there were no successful actions for damages.[220] Similarly, there were no successful applications for *interim* measures and the sixteen appeals brought to the Court of Justice against the negative decisions of the General Court on *interim* measures were unsuccessful.[221] These data suggest that, although there is an articulated accountability framework as well as rules safeguarding the rights of individuals, their effectiveness is in practice hampered by the narrow interpretation provided by the court on the legal grounds for obtaining remedies against the institutions.

As noted, however, the system of accountability tools adopted at the EU level is an exception when compared to other organizations. The reasons for this are to be sought in the institutional objectives of the organizations: as we shall see, those of the European Union are

---

[217] *Ibid.*

[218] Joint cases 6/90–9/90, *Francovich, Bonifaci et al.* v. *Italian Republic* [1991] ECR I-5375; joint cases 46/93–48/93, *Brasserie du Pêcheur* v. *Federal Republic of Germany* [1996] ECR I-1029; case 160/03, *AFCon Management Consultants* v. *Commission of the European Communities* [2005] ECR II-981 (for a comment, see Braun, 'Damages for Irregularities in the Award Process: Case T-160/03').

[219] See European Court of Auditors, *The EU Institutions Can Do More to Facilitate Access to Their Public Procurement*, para. 82 [ref. REP].

[220] In the following period of 2014–2017, only two cases were concluded with an order to pay compensation. See case T-299/11, *European Dynamics* v. *OHIM*, 7 October 2015, not published in the ECR and case T-199/14, *Vanbreda Risk & Benefits* v. *Commission*, 29 October 2015, not published in the ECR. See European Court of Auditors, *The EU Institutions Can Do More to Facilitate Access to Their Public Procurement*, para. 83 [ref. REP].

[221] See European Court of Auditors, *The EU Institutions Can Do More to Facilitate Access to Their Public Procurement*, para. 84 [ref. REP].

different from those, for example, of organizations within the UN system.[222]

Finally, along with these instruments that are closely connected to protecting the legal position of private subjects vis-à-vis the organizations, there are other tools that, even if activated at the request of a private subject, principally serve the needs of the administration and only indirectly those of the private subject. The rules and regulations of some organizations provide that vendors can report cases of fraud and corruption against both the officials that handled the tender and the other vendors participating in the tender. In the United Nations, vendors can file complaints with OIOS. As already noted,[223] the category of subjects with standing to file a complaint with this body has gradually been broadened, and at present this possibility has been codified in the OIOS Investigations Manual:

> [i]nformation that may lead to an investigation can come from a variety of different sources, including: [i]ndividual witnesses to the possible misconduct, whether a staff member or not.[224]

Similarly, within UNDP, vendors have always recourse to the OAI when there are reasons to believe that the procedure has been marred by episodes of fraud or corruption.[225]

From the standpoint of securing tenderers' rights, there are, however, multiple limits to these mechanisms. A vendor's claim does not create an obligation to act: following the complaint, these bodies have discretion to decide whether or not to open an investigation, with no duty to give reason for their decision. Furthermore, the limited ability to demand justification for administrative decisions and the inability to access documents make it difficult to support a complaint. Also, these investigative bodies only have the power to make recommendations, while the head of the administrative structure has discretion to take the final decision.

Finally, and most importantly, even if the complaint has sufficient grounds, results of this type of investigation primarily have relevance for the administration, rather than for the complainant: the administration can take disciplinary action against the official and impose

---

[222] See Chapter 8.   [223] See Chapter 3.
[224] In OIOS, *Investigations Manual*, para. 3.1.1 [ref. AP&R].
[225] See UNDP, *Programme and Operations Policies and Procedures*, sec. 'Procurement Ethics, Fraud and Corrupt Practices', para. 31 [ref. AP&R].

penalties against the other undertakings involved.[226] Potential additional measures – such as cancellation and/or revision of the award procedure – remain within the administration's discretion and in practice these situations occur only rarely. In this sense, the vendor has a right of complaint only because she has a private interest that coincides with a public one. It would, however, be wrong to hold that the effects of the complaint remain solely within the sphere of the administration. This is because, even if they are only potential, there can be consequences that favour the vendor (cancellation and revision of the bidding procedure, although not compensation for damages). Furthermore, the ability to file a complaint of illegitimate administrative activity should produce a deterrent effect in the future, assuring the vendor who wants to participate in another tender from the same organization that procedures will be followed and that evaluation will be impartial.

7.6.2.2 Remedies in Indirect Procurement

In indirect procurement, the trilateral relationship among international organizations, national administrations and private subjects[227] makes it possible to build a system of accountability based on the interaction between the supranational level and the national one that strengthens the legal positions of private subjects vis-à-vis the procuring entity. Depending on the type of loan agreement between the international organization and the borrowing state, there are at least six possible remedies that the private subject can activate, at least in theory, in indirect procurement. The first is to file a complaint with the national procuring entity for violation of the procurement rules set by the organization. The second is to bring an action before a national court alleging a violation of the international organization's procurement regulation by the national procuring authority. The third is to bring a complaint against international organizations before national courts for the violation of the international organizations' procurement rules. The fourth is to file a complaint with the national procuring entity for the violation of the national rules governing procurement. The fifth is to bring an action before national courts invoking a violation of the domestic procurement

---

[226] Suspension of the corrupt undertaking from future tenders should in fact make it less likely that the administration's resources are diverted from the purposes for which they were allocated.

[227] See Chapter 2.

rules by the national procuring authority. The sixth is to bring an action before *ad hoc* administrative bodies competent on fraud and corruption issues within the international organization. As we shall see in the following sections, although the array of available remedies is wide, some of these are not effectively used and none of them ensures a level of protection of vendors' rights comparable to that ensured by the EU public procurement directives and the GPA. At the same time, however, the overall degree of accountability resulting from these options is higher than that resulting from accountability mechanisms set in direct procurement.

a Administrative Appeals for the Violation of Organizations' Procurement Rules All international development banks require borrowing states to provide effective complaint mechanisms, whether procurement is governed by organizations' guidelines or by national rules. When in the loan agreement financial institutions and the borrowing state agree to adopt the procurement rules set by the financial institutions, the complaint mechanisms show several recurring features among organizations. First, the procurement rules regulating the complaint mechanism apply directly to the borrowing states as well as to the vendors. They define their respective roles, responsibilities and duties. Failure to comply with duties by borrowing states may determine cuts in the banks' funding, while failure to comply by vendors can entail the inadmissibility of the complaint.[228]

Second, if the loan agreement includes such arrangement, complaints procedures are subject to very detailed regulation set by the financial institutions, which cover some of the main aspects of the procedure.[229] In this regard, there has been a shift, in the WB in particular, from general requirements to detailed and stringent ones. The WB regulations go as far as to detail the timeline of the process, e.g. the maximum time allowed to the national authority to respond to the complaint as well as the

---

[228] WB, *Procurement-Related Complaints*, Annex I [ref. AP&R].

[229] WB, *The World Bank Procurement Regulations for IPF Borrowers*, Annex III; WB, *Procurement Guidance. Procurement-Related Complaints. How to Complain*, p. 1; EBRD, *Procurement Policies and Rules*, paras. 10, 11, 12; IDB, *Policies for the Procurement of Goods and Works*, App. III, paras. 11–14; AfDB, *Rules and Procedures for the Procurement of Goods and Works*, App. III, paras. 11–14; ADB, *Procurement Guidelines*, App. III, paras. 11–14 [all documents in ref. AP&R]. A comparison between 2011 WB procurement guidelines and the 2016 WB procurement regulations with regard to complaints in particular is provided in Williams-Elegbe, *Public Procurement and Multilateral Development Banks*, p. 284 *et seq.*

standstill period between the notification of the intention to award and the decision of award (to allow bidders an assessment on whether it is appropriate to submit a complaint); the subject of the complaint, i.e. the tender documents (including call for tender, RFI or RFP), the decision denying prequalification, the decision to exclude a vendor from a tender procedure prior to award and the decision to award; the interested parties, i.e. both actual and potential bidders;[230] and the minimum elements that a resolution of complaints shall include.[231] All these requirements have the overall effects of strengthening the vendor's legal positions vis-à-vis borrowing states and, at the same time, limiting national administrations' discretion and arbitrariness. Where a procurement-related complaint is upheld, the national authority will take different actions depending on the subject matter of the complaint. For instance, where the complaint relates to procurement documents, it can amend the procurement documents. Where the complaint concerns the decision to exclude, the national authority can revise the evaluation and change the results of the procurement process. Finally, if the complaint relates to the award decision, the national authority can decide to change it. The outcomes of the complaint do not, however, include the possibility of awarding compensation for damages.

Third, within this framework, organizations have an important role as guardians of the system. They guide and supervise the decisions taken by the national authorities on the complaints filed by private subjects; they can function as formal addressees of the complaints; and within certain limits they can exercise a subsidiarity function by providing a further debriefing to the unsuccessful bidder who is not satisfied by the decision on the complaint taken by the national authority and with the reasons supporting it.

Supervision on and guidance of the decisions taken by the national authorities include duties of exchange of information, review by the bank

---

[230] As clarified by Williams-Elegbe, although it is not clear what the regulations mean by 'potential applicants', these may be interpreted as 'those who have participated, but chose not to (or perhaps were prevented from participating) to submit complaints', *ibid.*, p. 287.

[231] The borrowing state shall specify the issues raised by the complainant that need to be addressed; it shall present the facts and evidence that, in the borrower's view, are relevant to the resolution of the complaint; it shall state the decision that has been made following the review, referring to the specific decision basis, such as the specific procurement rules applied; it shall provide an explanation why the basis for the decision applied to the facts/issues raised by the complaint necessitates this particular decision; and it shall, finally, clearly state the resolution, see WB, *The World Bank Procurement Regulations for IPF Borrowers*, Annex III, paras. 3.6 [ref. AP&R].

of the content of the decisions and veto powers by the bank if the decisions are not deemed sufficient in addressing the complaint. Exchange of information is bi-univocal: from the domestic procuring entity to the bank, and vice versa. As noted earlier, the complaint can be addressed to the national authority or, alternatively, to the bank. In the former case, if the contract is subject to prior review, the borrower shall promptly inform the bank of the complaints received, and shall provide for the bank's review all relevant information and documentation, including a draft response to the complainant once this is available.[232] In the latter case, the bank shall promptly notify and forward the complaint to the national authority for review and resolution, also with comments and advice for action or response.

As for the powers that the banks can exercise during the complaint procedure, the communication sent by the bank to the national authority or from the national authority to the bank is the first step of a procedure that is conducted primarily by the national authority, but in which the banks can have a final decision-making power. Most organizations make a distinction between the hypothesis in which the complaint regards a contract subject to *ex ante* review and that in which the complaint regards a contract subject to *ex post* review.[233] In the former case, the complaint usually has a suspensive effect on the procurement procedure: the national authority shall not proceed with the next stage of the procurement process, including the contract award and contract execution, until it addresses the complaint and the bank gives confirmation that the proposed resolution of the complaint is satisfactory. In the case of contracts subject to *ex post* review, the entire procurement process, including handling the complaints, shall receive final clearance by the bank during subsequent supervision of the project. This means that in contracts subject to *ex post* review mismanagement of procurement complaints can possibly cause the bank to cut financing. This does not positively affect the complainant in any way. However, it might deter borrowing states from handling complaints in the future in an inadequate way.

---

[232] *Ibid.*, Annex III, para. 3.2; and similarly for other banks.
[233] WB, *The World Bank Procurement Regulations for IPF Borrowers*, Annex III, paras. 3.2–3.5; EBRD, *Procurement Policies and Rule*, para. 11; IDB, *Policies for the Procurement of Goods and Works Financed by the Inter-American Development Bank*, App. III, paras. 12–13; AfDB, *Rules and Procedures for the Procurement of Goods and Works*, App. III, paras. 12–13; ADB, *Procurement Guidelines*, App. III, paras. 12–13 [all documents in ref. AP&R].

Furthermore, the bank can function as the addressee of the complaint. This, however, means only that complaints can be brought both to the attention of the borrower as well as to the bank. It does not imply, on the contrary, that the complaint can challenge a decision of the bank, or that the bank can function as a second forum to which appeal can be made against a decision taken by the national administration.

As for the subsidiarity function, the banks usually provide for the possibility of debriefing the unsuccessful bidder, if the bidder is not satisfied with the manner in which the national administration has addressed the complaint.[234] Although an important instrument for ensuring that the national administration's decisions are more transparent, it is not an appeal mechanism that can produce a revision of the national authority's decision. There are substantial and procedural reasons explaining why a second review has not been provided by the relevant rules. These reasons pertain to the institutional objectives of the banks.

As the mission of the banks is not to establish a competitive market, but to provide development aid, then inter-institutional control and far-reaching monitoring by the banks on the procurement carried out by borrowing states is deemed sufficient as long as it ensures that the resources are spent for this objective. The further possibility for private subjects to obtain a second review not only is not strictly functional to this goal, but also goes against the interest of the bank to avoid an overload of work deriving from handling complaints and, at the same time, against the interest of the borrowing states to maintain some room for autonomy vis-à-vis the bank.

From a procedural point of view, the possibility of filing a complaint with the bank has been judged as serving little purpose because, in procurement subject to *ex ante* review, the decision of the national authority on the complaint is scrutinized by the bank and requires the bank's approval. Thus, the appeal to the bank would be against a decision of the national authority that the bank has already approved. This line of reasoning, however, shows some flaws. First, part of the procurement activities carried out by the borrowing states is subject to *ex post* review and, thus, when handling the complaint, the bank has not yet formally expressed its approval on the decision of the national authority. Second, even in *ex ante* review, an appeal to the bank could be useful, or at least better than just a debriefing, if the body identified to handle the complaint were to be independent of the office that approved the decision of the national authority.

---

[234] See Chapter 5 for further analysis on this point.

The recourse to a third impartial body within the bank, however, has been clearly excluded. On one hand, the Inspection Panel in the WB, and bodies with similar functions in other financial institutions such as the AfDB, ADB, EBRD and IDB, have been established to provide people adversely affected by projects financed by these institutions with an independent mechanism to ensure compliance with the international institution's policies and procedures.[235] On the other hand, these have never included policies and procedures governing procurement. For instance, the rules setting the competences and regulating the activities of the WB Inspection Panel state that

> [n]o procurement action is subject to inspection by the Panel, whether taken by the Bank or by a borrower. A separate mechanism is available for addressing procurement-related complaints.[236]

The reasons for this exclusion are to be found in the expected overload of work due to the large number of complaints from bidders and, thus, in efficiency interests:

> [a]s explained during the Board discussion of September 21, 1993, where the matter [i.e. to include or not procurement matters within the competences of the Inspection Panel] became the subject of a lengthy debate, procurement disputes are different in nature from the typical issues that justified the establishment of the Panel. They also often involve suppliers from countries other than the borrowing country. More important, the number and frequency of such complaints could cause a major disorientation of the Panel's work.[237]

Accordingly, the Resolution establishing the Inspection Panel[238] has been read as excluding both complaints against procurement decisions

---

[235] On the establishment of the WB Inspection Panel and its implications for the international legal order see Bradlow and Schlemmer-Schulte, 'The World Bank's New Inspection Panel'.

[236] In WB, *Review of the Resolutions Establishing the Inspection Panel* [ref. RES]. The statement originates from a question raised before the Inspection Panel regarding its competence over direct procurement by the WB. In this regard, the Executive Directors approved a decision (WB Executive Board, *Decision Number 1*, paras. 55–56 [ref. REP]) and then reiterated it in the Clarification of 1996. On this point, also see Caroli Casavola, 'L'appalto pubblico e la globalizzazione', p. 82 *et seq.*; Boisson de Chazournes, 'Compliance with Operational Standards', p. 67 *et seq.*

[237] Shihata, *The World Bank Inspection Panel*, p. 53. This point is discussed also in Malmendier, 'The Liability of International Development Banks'.

[238] The Inspection Panel was officially created by two resolutions of the IBRD and the IDA on 22 September 1993 (IBRD, *Resolution IBRD No. 93–10* and IDA, *Resolution IDA*

by bank borrowers and complaints from losing tenderers, even if those were addressed against the bank.[239]

Moreover, turning from rules to practices, although the provisions regarding procurement complaints include control and monitoring functions of the bank, experience shows that 'the development banks tend to treat violations of procurement rules by the host state diffidently . . . and are quickly prepared to "turn a blind eye" to this'.[240] The apparent reluctance of banks to declare misprocurement is shown also by the related data. The WB, for example, found that, measured against the total number of contracts awarded annually, misprocurement rates represented an average of 3–3.5 cases per thousand.[241] At the same time, complaints are not frequent, at least in relation to the overall procurement carried out within WB projects. Between 2002 and 2011 the number of complaints has varied little, ranging from 300 to 400 complaints a year on all contracts.[242] When standardized by the number of procurement contracts awarded each year, complaints represented about 2 per cent of the prior-review contracts.[243] More generally, complaints are deemed by the same organizations to reduce the efficiency of procurement activities by imposing delays in the procurement process. The data for complaints related to WB projects have shown that the average time for resolution of complaints is about 150 days, though some are resolved sooner than this, and a significant number take much longer.[244]

b Judicial Remedies for the Violation of the International Organizations' Procurement Rules A controversial issue relates to the possibility of invoking breach of banks' procurement rules in national courts through a judicial remedy, rather than before the national procuring authority through an administrative appeal. In fact, as will be shown later, while the possibility of obtaining judicial review based on breach of domestic procurement rules is not in dispute as it is required by the bank as a condition of the loan, the same cannot be said for hypotheses in

---

No. 93–6 [ref. RES]). They are referred to collectively as 'the Resolution' because the content of the two resolutions is identical.

[239] Shihata, *The World Bank Inspection Panel*, p. 53.

[240] Malmendier, 'The Liability of International Development Banks', p. 137.

[241] Data are found in IEG, *The World Bank and Public Procurement*, p. 123 and footnote 121 [ref. REP].

[242] *Ibid.*, p. 123.   [243] *Ibid.*, p. 123.   [244] *Ibid.*, pp. 123–124.

which a vendor seeks judicial remedies for the breach of a bank's procurement rules.[245]

In this regard, it has been argued that procurement regulations are incorporated into the loan agreement, which is a treaty contract, and is subject to adjudication in accordance with its tenor. This circumstance does not create any rights for third parties and, thus, remedies linked to a breach of procurement regulations may be wholly unavailable in a domestic court.[246] This argument, however, is subject to criticism in one major respect. If a state enters into an international treaty, this treaty is binding in respect of its entire territory[247] and binds the state in all its components, these being the legislative, the executive or the judicial branch. Of course, the way in which the international treaty is enacted may vary from country to country: it can be automatic, through a constitutional norm that bridges the international treaty into the national legal system, or it can require an *ad hoc* law that makes the treaty applicable in the territory of the state. In any case, the treaty has direct and indirect effects on the citizens of the state member of the treaty. Thus, an individual can invoke before a national court the breach of the obligations held by the state vis-à-vis its citizens and deriving from the international treaty concluded by the state. Within this line of reasoning, it cannot be excluded that a vendor may bring an action against the national procuring entity, it being a part of the executive branch, for the breach of the procurement regulations set by the bank and agreed by the state in a treaty contract.[248]

c **Complaints against International Organizations** Borrowing states, and namely the national procuring entities, can be, at least in theory, a target of complaints filed by vendors for breach of international organizations' procurement rules. On the contrary, it is a matter of some dispute as to whether international development banks are, or should be,

---

[245] On the question of how a national court should appraise an administrative rule adopted by an external institution even though that rule may have no binding force in international law or any formal status in the law of the forum see Kingsbury, 'Global Administrative Law: Implications for National Courts'.

[246] Williams-Elegbe, *Public Procurement and Multilateral Development Banks*, p. 289.

[247] Art. 29 of the Vienna Convention on the Law of the Treaties [ref. T&C].

[248] This interpretation has also been confirmed by one of the officers interviewed who, wishing to maintain confidentiality on the issue, did not provide references to the cases, but stated that, although few, there have been cases before domestic courts where the breach of banks' procurement rules have been invoked.

liable before domestic courts for the breach of their own procurement rules.

On one hand, it has been argued that international development banks should be held liable in this regard. Malmendier, for instance, bases this argument on several considerations.[249] First, international development banks have far-reaching monitoring and control rights on how resources are spent by the borrowing states and, in particular, on how procurement is carried out by the national procuring entities.

Second, authority is the base for responsibility: banks are entitled to rights but are also under an obligation to exercise their supervisory functions efficiently. This duty exists, in particular, towards vendors who are affected by the supervised procurement activity undertaken by the national administrations. The procurement rules indeed serve not only the banks' interest as creditors, but reflect the functions of banks, i.e. to contribute to development and growth, to promote democracy and the rule of law etc. Thus, there is an extra-contractual legal relationship between the vendors and the development banks, based on an expectation of special trust.[250]

Third, a breach of the rules governing this relationship entitles the vendor to bring a damages claim against the development bank. For instance, if a vendor was discriminated against by the national procuring entity in the selection process and the bank did not prevent discrimination through efficient controls and monitoring, the vendor could bring a complaint against the bank that did not properly perform its monitoring and sanctioning duties.

Fourth, the claim for damages is to be brought in domestic courts and the damage shall be determined by the national liability law applicable to the injurious act. Furthermore, domestic case law supports these conclusions, at least by analogy. For instance, in the United States and in France, the principle of the lender's liability to third parties has been widely implemented in the case law. The control exercised by the lender over its borrower has been identified as a cause of liability for damage originating with the borrower. In other words, banks that have failed to make

---

[249] These are developed by Malmendier, 'The Liability of International Development Banks', *passim*.

[250] In this regard Malmendier recalls that there is a similar concept in German law (*ibid.*, pp. 142–143). S. 311(3) of the *Bürgerliches Gesetzbuch* [ref. N&RL-Germany] reads as follows: '[a]n obligation with duties under section 241(2)57 may also come into existence in relation to persons who are not themselves intended to be parties to the contract. Such an obligation comes into existence in particular if the third party, by laying claim to being given a particularly high degree of trust, substantially influences the pre-contract negotiations or the entering into of the contract'.

use of their monitoring powers to avoid damage to third parties have been recognized as liable for breach of duty (in French *négligence bancaire*).[251] In addition to these arguments, due consideration must also be given to the general trend towards limiting the immunity of international organizations on the part of European and national courts, beginning with the ECHR judgment in *Waite and Kennedy*.[252]

On the other side, the opposite thesis has been also supported. According to Williams-Elegbe, banks will not be liable in a domestic court to a vendor when the borrowing state breaches the bank's procurement regulations for at least three reasons.[253] The first is that the bank and its staff enjoy immunity from domestic jurisdiction. The second is that procurement regulations, once incorporated by reference in the loan agreement, become an international treaty contract, and cannot be overridden by domestic law. The third is that submitting a bid in a tender financed by a development bank does not create any legal relationship between the bank and the bidders for the purpose of instituting a review procedure.

Given these opposing views, some considerations can be taken into account to tackle the issue of international development banks' liability. A distinction must be drawn between a normative level and a positive level of analysis, or in other words between whether the liability of international development banks could, and should, be recognized, and whether such liability is actually recognized in case law. Taking a normative stand, it is not only possible, but also desirable, to provide for liability of international development banks. It is possible, first because financial institutions can waive their immunity and are among the few organizations that have done so on a number of occasions, especially when claims relate to *iure gestionis* activities.[254]

Second, there is strong evidence arising from the case law of many legal systems that acknowledges the existence of an extra-contractual relationship between public bodies entrusted with supervisory and monitoring functions, especially in the financial sector, and third parties affected by the activities of the supervised bodies. This case law has recognized that, based on this relationship, supervisory bodies can be held liable for *culpa*

---

[251] *Ibid.*, p. 141.
[252] For a brief analysis of the case law on the immunity of international organizations see the discussion earlier in this chapter.
[253] Williams-Elegbe, *Public Procurement and Multilateral Development Banks*, p. 290.
[254] For more in general on waiver of immunity connected to *iure gestionis* activities see Reinisch, *International Organizations before National Courts*, p. 258 *et seq.*

in vigilando when the supervised body causes harm to third parties. This could also apply by analogy to international development banks, given that the final beneficiaries of development projects are precisely individuals and companies, either because they enjoy the final result of the project or because they gain commercial opportunities from the tender launched within the project. From a legal point of view their expectations are supported not, or not only, by an expectation of trust, but by the loan agreement between the bank and the borrowing country. In fact, if it is true that the loan agreement is a contract treaty between the organization and the borrowing state, it is also true that the organization is made by member states, and that it enters the agreement and is bound by it based on an implied representation mandate from the citizens to the member states. The tripartite relationship between the organizations, the member states and the citizens, which has been explained in Chapter 2, grounds the accountability of the banks towards the citizens and companies of the member states (among which there are the borrowing states). Moreover, it is precisely this tripartite relationship that makes accountability and liability of the development banks desirable.

Moving from a normative level to a positive one, development banks were never held liable for lack of supervision and monitoring before national courts, with a major exception: indirect procurement funded by the EDF. With regard to EDF-funded procurement, unsuccessful bidders have brought claims before the European Ombudsman and the Court of Justice of the European Union by alleging a failure of the Commission to properly supervise the tender process undertaken by a state within EDF-financed projects. Based on the fact that the Commission has powers and duties to control and supervise,[255] wrongful acts committed by the national administration during the vendor selection procedure have led to the Commission being sanctioned for breach of supervisory duties. For example, in a case before the Ombudsman, it was established that the Commission 'did not take sufficient account of its obligation to monitor the overall procedure and its commitment to ensure proper regard for the principles of transparency and equal opportunities'.[256] This notwithstanding, the Court of First Instance and the Court of Justice have been

---

[255] See the discussion in this chapter.

[256] European Ombudsman, *Decision of the European Ombudsman Closing His Inquiry into Complaint 2400/2006/JF against the European Commission*, 13 January 2009.

hesitant to impose liability on the Commission, and have refused to do so in many cases due to a restrictive interpretation of its duties.[257]

To conclude on this issue, it is worth noting that, although liability of international organizations for lack of supervision and monitoring in indirect procurement is conceivable from a legal point of view, as well as desirable, the only instances in which it has been sought have been cases involving European institutions. One major difference that explains the reason why it has been so for the EDF, and not for other development banks, is that in the case of the EDF claims of this kind could be brought before judicial and quasi-judicial bodies. These bodies ensure a good degree of impartiality and have jurisdiction over the EU Commission. Thus, with regard to indirect procurement funded by the EDF, the problem of subjecting an international institution to review by a domestic court does not arise; nor does the EU Commission have the option of invoking immunity from jurisdiction. This also leads to consideration that, within a more integrated institutional system, where the tripartite relationship is tighter, and where there are reliable and impartial review bodies, the scope of accountability tends to expand and international institutions are also held directly accountable to private subjects when their activity only indirectly affects them.

d Administrative Appeals and Judicial Remedies for the Violation of Domestic Procurement Rules The other options available to private subjects are to file a complaint before the national procuring entity or the national courts for violation of the national rules governing procurement. When the organization and the borrowing state agree in the loan agreement to apply national rules – and not the bank's regulations – to the procurement procedure, the organizations require states to guarantee national channels that give the vendor recourse against the domestic administration for acts or decisions taken during the procurement process. The WB Regulations for IPF Borrowers, for example, state that

> [w]hen approaching the national market ... the country's own procurement procedures may be used ... Requirements for national open

---

[257] See, *inter alia*, case C-267/82, *Développement SA e Clemessy* v. *Commission* [1986] ECR I-1907, paras. 25–27. And a similar approach has been used in cases that involve the EIB. See, for example, case C-370/89, *SGEEM e Etroy* v. *BEI* [1992] ERC I-6211, paras. 29–31.

competitive procurement include the following: . . . g. an effective complaints mechanism.[258]

Even if in this case the beneficiary state has wider discretion in managing the complaints, a supervisory role on the part of the international
organizations still emerges from several aspects. As mentioned earlier,[259]
the possibility of adopting domestic procurement rules is subject to
a previous assessment carried out by the organizations on the consistency
between the national procurement system, including the domestic
accountability mechanisms available to private parties, and the organization's core procurement principles.

Moreover, the national authority has duties of information: if
a complaint is brought against the national procuring entity, the state
must inform the organization. Also, once the complaint is received, the
state must take appropriate measures to address it promptly and fairly.
Thus, there is a duty to take action.

More generally, even if the procurement guidelines do not apply, the
handling of complaints is guided by the rules and procedures agreed by
the organization and the state through the loan agreement and the
procurement plan. For instance, the WB Regulations for IPF Borrowers
provide that

> [c]omplaints, other than those covered under Annex III, Procurement-
> Related Complaints, are to be handled by the Borrower in accordance
> with the applicable complaint review rules and procedures as agreed by
> the Bank.[260]

Furthermore, the way in which the procurement process is carried out,
including the handling of and responses given to complaints, is subject to
the overall monitoring and control exercised by the organizations on
project execution.

This notwithstanding, the private sector has often expressed dissatisfaction with domestic procurement rules. A survey conducted in 2014 by
the WB has, for example, revealed that, in Morocco, companies have
expressed confidence in the Bank's procurement system, emphasizing,
on the contrary, that the Moroccan system lacked an independent complaints procedure. In Peru, the predominant view was that efficiency,
economy and transparency would suffer if Peru's procedures were

---

[258] WB, *The World Bank Procurement Regulations for IPF Borrowers*, paras. 5.3–5.4
[ref. AP&R].
[259] See Chapter 4.
[260] WB, *The World Bank Procurement Regulations for IPF Borrowers*, para. 3.30 [ref. AP&R].

applied. Similarly, in Turkey, private firms emphasized the lack of transparency, the very slow handling of complaints and dispute resolution, and the length of national debarment lists. The private sector in Senegal denounced the lack of transparency and the risk of fraud and corruption because of the lack of an independent and efficient complaint mechanism and court system.[261] More generally, the use of country systems, and reliance on domestic procurement rules and accountability mechanisms, often seem not to provide adequate protection of vendors' rights.

e **Fraud and Corruption** The other accountability tool available to private subjects relates to cases of fraud and corruption. International financial institutions have developed special mechanisms for allowing private subjects to report instances of fraud and corruption to *ad hoc* administrative bodies set up within the organizations.[262] Fraud and corruption can relate to several aspects of the project execution, including the procurement process.

Within procurement, fraud and corruption can be referred both to the undertakings that have participated in the tenders financed by the bank and to domestic administrations and their officials. Thus, a vendor – like any other party – can file an allegation of fraud and corruption involving certain undertakings and/or national administrative officials involved in a procurement procedure. The competent authority within the bank has discretion as to whether or not to follow up on the complaint. Once the procedure is initiated, however, it consists of a detailed sequence of different phases. These include, on one side, the possibility for the organizations to exercise significant powers affecting the private subjects involved, and on the other side, the opportunity for private subjects to exercise due process rights. The administrative body in charge of managing the procedure has investigative powers, which take the form of inspections and involve fact-finding activities undertaken by the organization. In the WB, for example, these activities go as far as

> accessing and examining a firm's or individual's financial records and information, and making copies thereof as relevant; accessing and examining any other documents, data and information (whether in hard copy or electronic format) deemed relevant for the investigation/audit, and

---

[261] IEG, *The World Bank and Public Procurement. An Independent Evaluation*, Box 1.7 [ref. REP].

[262] As explained by Leroy and Fariello, since 2006 the World Bank had begun to work with other multilateral development banks to harmonize approaches to fraud and corruption in projects, see Leroy and Fariello, *The World Bank Group Sanctions Process*, p. 11.

making copies thereof as relevant; interviewing staff and other relevant
individuals; performing physical inspections and site visits; and obtaining
third party verification of information.[263]

These highly intrusive powers are to some extent counterbalanced by
provisions granting private parties the possibility of defending themselves and replying to the accusations in formal hearings. Moreover, the
burden of proof to present evidence is usually on the competent body
within the organization. The outcomes of the procedure may include
sanctions on the undertaking involved in the fraud or corruption, but
also on the national authority that has managed the procurement, or on
both.

With regard to the undertakings, the competent bodies can choose
from an array of different sanctions, which vary in gravity. Sanctions may
consist of a reprimand, i.e. a formal letter sent to the respondent that
reprimands its conduct. They can be more punitive for the undertaking
determining a conditional non-debarment, i.e. the imposition of reme-
dial, preventive or other requirements as a condition to avoid debarment.
They can result in a debarment, i.e. a permanent or temporary ban on the
possibility of participating in procurement procedures financed by the
bank.

If fraud and corruption also (or only) involve the national authority,
the bank authorities responsible for reviewing and controlling the contract may first ask the national administration to promptly take all steps
necessary to cease the wrongful act. If these actions are not sufficient and
the award has not already been made, e.g. in contracts subject to *ex ante*
review, the organization may reject the proposed award and ask for the
bidding procedure to be revised on penalty of cancelling the portion of
the loan allocated to that contract. In the different situation of contracts
subject to *ex post* review, fraud and corruption will be detected during the
assessment of project execution and may eventually have consequences
for future decisions on continuing to finance the project.

It is interesting to note that, similarly to what happens in direct
procurement, in indirect procurement fraud and corruption schemes
and sanctions procedures are set mainly in the interests of the organization. This is clear from the way the system is designed, but also from the
wording used by the applicable rules. For example, the WB rules on
sanctions procedures state that '[t]his regime protects Bank funds and

---

[263] WB, *The World Bank Procurement Regulations for IPF Borrowers*, Annex IV, footnote 1
[ref. AP&R].

serves as a deterrent upon those who might otherwise engage in the misuse of the proceeds of Bank financing'.[264]

However, together with this main objective and as a positive side effect, in specific instances this regime can also benefit the private subject. In fact, considering that there is no corruptor without a corruptee, the vendor may file allegations against both the undertakings, and the national authority and obtain, through the intervention of the international organization, a revision of the bidding procedure by the national authority.

The procedures set out for indirect procurement funded by the EDF provide for an alternative accountability scheme, which is characterized by two major differences compared to the mechanism just discussed. The first relates to the relationship between the European Commission and national authorities. National systems must provide remedies to tenderers who believe they have been adversely affected by an error or irregularity committed during the selection procedure.[265] Thus, if the complaint involves decentralized indirect procurement, remedies are regulated by national laws and there are no provisions for the intervention of European institutions during this phase.[266] This, however, is the last step of a progressive transition from lesser to greater regulatory autonomy recognized by the states implementing EU financed procurement. Until 2008, for example, the appeal procedure provided for the intervention of the Commission. Indeed, there have been cases in which the private party had appealed directly to the Commission or to a representative of the Commission within the state.[267] The subsequent version of the PRAG, adopted in 2008, also imposed time restrictions and duties of inter-institutional information on national administrations along with greater control by the Commission. National administrations had an obligation to address the complaint within a certain period of time. In addition, the national authorities had to inform the European Commission of the appeal. The European Commission could intervene to settle the dispute and, before the national administration could make any decision on the merits, had to state its opinion on the matter. The opinion was not binding but, nevertheless, if the Commission

---

[264] WB, *Procedure. Bank Procedure*, sec. III, para. 1.01(a) [ref. AP&R].

[265] EU, *PRAG*, para. 2.4.15.3 [ref. AP&R].

[266] Here too, see EU, *PRAG*, para. 2.4.12 and *id.*, *General Regulations for Service, Supply and Works Contracts Financed by the EDF*, Art. 8 [ref. AP&R].

[267] See for instance C-182/91, *Forafrique Burkinabe SA* v. *Commission of European Communities* [1993] ECR I-2184.

found a violation of the tender procedures set out in the PRAG, it had the power to refuse to disburse the financing or to suspend, withhold or demand restitution of financing already disbursed for the contracts in question.

7.6.2.3 Developments and Limits of Accountability in the Vendor Selection Phase

The framework of remedies available to private subjects during the vendor selection phase is thus composite, with significant differences in guarantees of protection that are based on whether procurement is direct or indirect. In terms of direct procurement, the first interesting aspect is the emergence and gradual consolidation of appeal procedures, in many cases still in an initial and experimental phase. The history of procurement rules and practices of international organizations[268] shows that, from the time of their establishment to at least around 2005, even though international organizations were heavily involved in direct procurement, they only provided accountability mechanisms vis-à-vis private parties during the contract execution phase, while during the vendor selection phase such mechanisms were non-existent or merely informal, and could be activated at the discretion of the state delegations within the organizations – thus, they were political. From around 2005 onwards, independent review bodies, such as the JIU in the UN system, began to call attention to the issue of organizations' accountability to private subjects not only after the contract was signed but also during the vendor selection phase. Only between 2009 and 2010, however, have the first procedures of this type been activated (with the exception of EU institutions which started well before then). Providing accountability mechanisms to private subjects can be interpreted as the last act, at least to date, of a gradual process of proceduralization of the administrative activity of international organizations. This is, moreover, understandable in the light of the fact that, in the absence of procedural rules and the resulting rights granted to private subjects, these subjects had no parameter they could use to allege improper administrative actions or any standing to do so. Only after the procedure had been delineated and consolidated did instruments emerge to guarantee compliance and, thus, to ensure protection of the private subjects affected by the activity of international organizations.

---

[268] See Chapter 3.

The second aspect that the analysis reveals goes in the opposite direction. While it is true that in the history of international organizations mechanisms of accountability to private subjects are a significant innovation, it is also true that their full effectiveness is jeopardized by certain factors of fact and law. First, there are still many organizations that do not offer any kind of appeal procedures to vendors, even though these organizations make large volumes of purchases. Moreover, when these procedures are codified in procurement manuals, they often involve hierarchical appeals or protests that do not guarantee sufficient independence and impartiality and, except in certain cases, do not permit a review of the first decision upon appeal to higher-level bodies.

The other critical aspect regards the neutrality of independent bodies when they have competence over complaints, and the extent of their powers. Some organizations have established independent bodies, but the effectiveness of the solutions adopted varies. The solution adopted by the UN appears to be less effective as the problem of independence is only partially overcome: the independent body has the power to make recommendations but not to make decisions, which is held by the administrative head. More effective are the solutions adopted by the ESA and the EU institutions, where the members of the bodies that decide on complaints are appointed with a guarantee of independence and also have powers to order compensation for damages, to cancel the award and to order a revision of the procedure.

Stronger proceduralization, reviewing bodies that are not the same as the administrations being reviewed (and are independent from them), powers to cancel and moreover to sanction, instead, characterize the mechanisms of accountability in indirect procurement. The accountability mechanisms in place are based on a principle of control and, to a limited extent, of subsidiarity in the protection of private subjects' rights. Taken together, they allow the organization's intervention to ensure that the handling of complaints by the national administration is in line with the policies and objectives of the organization. Although it presents many flaws, the accountability scheme in indirect procurement is strengthened compared to that ensured in direct procurement: through the rights accorded to private subjects the organization protects its own interests, i.e. the national administration acts in accordance with the aims and the procurement rules set by the international organization itself.[269] The increased level of effectiveness is, thus, the consequence of a synergy of public and private interests.

7.6.3   Accountability to Private Parties in Contract Execution

The Convention on the Privileges and Immunities of the United Nations establishes an obligation for international organizations to include dispute settlement provisions in contracts, which, as we have seen, are mainly drafted unilaterally by the organizations themselves.[270] In reality, as early as 1977 the Valticos Report[271] noted fragmented practice in this respect: the contracts of many organizations, including UNDP, IBRD, ICAO, OECD, European Organization for Nuclear Research (CERN), ESA, European Commission and the Organisation of African Unity (OAU), contained dispute settlement clauses; the contracts of other organizations, such as the United Nations, UNIDO, ILO, FAO, the Parliamentary Assembly of the Mediterranean (PAM), WHO and EIB, 'generally' contained such a clause, albeit with differences in the body named to settle disputes. For yet other organizations the clause was less frequent, occasional or only exceptional, and was limited to certain types of contracts, such as in UNESCO, WIPO, IAEA and the Organization of American States (OAS). Finally, the contracts of the Council of Europe contained no such clause. Moreover, this practice did not include financial institutions such as the IMF, which waived immunity from jurisdiction to give national courts jurisdiction over disputes.[272]

At present, the scenario seems more homogenous, at least with regard to procurement activity carried out through calls for tenders: most of the general terms and conditions of contract attached to the calls for tenders

---

[269] For criticism of the effectiveness of this protection, see Caroli Casavola, *La globalizzazione dei contratti*, p. 123 *et seq.*

[270] See Chapter 5. The Convention on the Privileges and Immunities of the United Nations in fact states: 'The United Nations shall make provisions for appropriate modes of settlement of ... disputes arising out of contracts or other disputes of a private law character to which the United Nations is a party ...', in Convention on the Privileges and Immunities of the United Nations, Art. VIII, sec. 29. The same is provided in the Convention on the Privileges and Immunities of the Specialized Agencies, Art. IX, sec. 31 [all documents in ref. T&C].

[271] Valticos, 'Les contrats conclus par les organisations internationales avec des personnes privées. Rapport provisoire'; *id.*, 'Les contrats conclus par les organisations internationales avec des personnes privées. Rapport définitif'.

[272] *Ibid.*, pp. 70–72.

of organizations include an arbitration clause that designates or provides the elements for designating the body competent to settle contract-related disputes.

The methods used to identify the deciding body and the nature of this body are important to understand how the relationship between the organizations and the private parties is constructed within the contract and whether the organizations' international public law nature not only influences the provisions of the contract,[273] but also affects dispute settlement methods, limiting the protection the private party may enjoy. The methods for identifying the competent body have already been discussed with regard to the law applicable to dispute settlement procedures.[274] Here, suffice it to note that, with some exceptions, these methods are generally neutral, as they are based on rules that private parties also use in order to identify arbitrators in private law disputes, such as the rules that UNCITRAL and the International Chamber of Commerce (ICC) have developed on the issue. However, there is a significant underlying specificity, i.e. that the choice of which body of procedural rules to apply always lies with the organization, as it is the organization that unilaterally drafts the contract.

7.6.3.1   Dispute Settlement Bodies

The bodies responsible for settling disputes may be permanent arbitration institutions, *ad hoc* tribunals, international judicial bodies or national courts.[275] The first category is certainly the most common choice. The contractual disputes of many organizations are referred to the ICC, with occasional exceptions related to specific contracts. For example, in the past, disputes related to contracts between the UN and a private party with US nationality or headquarters in the United States were decided by the American Arbitration Association, while disputes regarding contracts between the UN and private parties with Latin American nationality or headquarters in Latin America were referred to the Inter-American Arbitration Association.[276] In the contracts of UNDP, UNIDO, FAO, WHO and ESA, a distinction can be made between contracts entailing a significant disbursement of money by the

---

[273] See Chapter 5.   [274] See Chapter 6.

[275] This section regards mainly direct procurement. For an analysis of arbitration related to contracts resulting from indirect procurement see Chapter 5, sec. 3.4.

[276] See Valticos, 'Les contrats conclus par les organisations internationales avec des personnes privées. Rapport provisoire'; *id.*, 'Les contrats conclus par les organisations internationales avec des personnes privées. Rapport définitif'.

organization, where there is a tendency to petition the ICC, and other contracts, where *ad hoc* arbitration is provided. The OECD has distinguished between countries that have ratified the 1958 Convention on the Recognition and Enforcement of Foreign Arbitral Awards and those that have not. If they have not ratified it, disputes are referred to either the American Arbitration Association or to arbitration bodies established according to the ICC's Conciliation and Arbitration Rules. Disputes regarding contracts to which the IMF is a party are generally referred to the American Arbitration Association. Once again, for the OAS, which has a clearly regional character, contracts have often been settled before the Comisión Interamericana de Arbitraje Comercial.[277]

A second option is to establish an *ad hoc* tribunal, which may take various forms. It can consist of a single member or be a three-member arbitration board. Contracts with NATO, for example, provide two alternative and graduated solutions. First, the parties must attempt to agree on the name of an arbitrator. If this attempt fails, then, second, they must appoint a three-member board.[278] A three-member board is instead provided from the outset in ILO contracts where the private party has not accepted the jurisdiction of the organization's administrative tribunal as arbitrator.

A third option is recourse to an international judicial body, in particular to the administrative tribunals of the organization itself, if they exist, or the Court of Justice of the European Union in the case of European institutions. The Statute of the Administrative Tribunal of the ILO, for example, establishes that the tribunal will settle disputes arising from contracts to which the ILO is a party that establish the Tribunal's jurisdiction.[279] In the past, the jurisdiction of the Tribunal essentially extended to three types of contract signed by the ILO: insurance policies, contracts with external consultants and procurement contracts.[280] The clause generally provided that decisions would be final and enforceable within ten days of the ruling. If the contractor did not accept the Tribunal's jurisdiction, a classical arbitration clause was included that provided for the establishment of a three-member arbitration board.[281] In an attempt to provide for similar

---

[277] See Valticos, 'Les contrats conclus par les organisations internationales avec des personnes privées. Rapport provisoire', p. 74 *et seq.*
[278] NATO, *NATO International Staff Procurement Manual*, para. 16.9.6.1 [ref. AP&R].
[279] ILO, *Statute of the Administrative Tribunal*, Art. II, para. 4 [ref. AP&R].
[280] See Valticos, 'Les contrats conclus par les organisations internationales avec des personnes privées. Rapport provisoire', p. 84 *et seq.*
[281] *Ibid.*

opportunities in other organizations, it was proposed to extend the Tribunal's jurisdiction to non-employment disputes in which other international organizations were parties. In fact, while the Tribunal's jurisdiction over labour disputes was and is recognized by other UN organizations (i.e. they allow disputes with their own officials to be heard by the Administrative Tribunal of the ILO), an amendment of the Tribunal's Statute would be required in order to extend its purview to non-labour contracts concluded by other international organizations. However, even without a proper amendment of the statute, it could have been possible to systematically refer to the Tribunal as *arbitrator*, instead of as a judicial body. Moreover, this competence had already been accepted in a certain number of cases that did not fall within its statutory purview.[282]

Nevertheless, as noted, the options that organizations chose took another course. The current general terms and conditions of the contracts of the ILO, in particular procurement contracts, provide that

> [u]nless settled amicably . . . any dispute, controversy or claim arising out of the Contract, or the breach, termination or invalidity thereof, will be settled by arbitration in accordance with the UNCITRAL Arbitration Rules then prevailing. In addition: 13.2.1. the place of arbitration will be Geneva; 13.2.2. the decisions of the arbitral tribunal will be based on general principles of international commercial law; 13.2.3. the arbitral tribunal will have no authority to award punitive damages; and 13.2.4. the Parties will be bound by any arbitration award rendered as a result of such arbitration as the final adjudication of any such dispute, controversy, or claim arising out of the Contract, or the breach, termination or invalidity thereof.[283]

Thus, they mention from the outset the possibility of identifying an arbitrator other than the organization's Administrative Tribunal (which would in any event have competence not as an arbitrator but as a judicial body, precisely because it is an organ of the ILO), but this possibility is subject to certain limitations established unilaterally by the international organization, including immunity.

The option of recourse to the Court of Justice of the European Union for contracts concluded by European institutions is provided by the TFEU, Art. 272 (ex Art. 238 TEC):

> [t]he Court of Justice of the European Union shall have jurisdiction to give judgment pursuant to any arbitration clause contained in a contract

---

[282] *Ibid.*   [283] ILO, *TC ILO Contracts*, para. 13.2.

concluded by or on behalf of the Union, whether that contract be governed by public or private law.[284]

In reality, as mentioned in previous chapters, especially for contracts related to the supply of goods, services and works at the headquarters of EU institutions, the general terms and conditions of contracts instead give national courts, and in particular the courts of Belgium, jurisdiction to render judgment. In the case of EU institutions, the choice may thus differ depending on the subject matter of the contract and the place of its execution.

Recourse to national tribunals[285] is in fact another of the options available, although it is only used by certain organizations, particularly those of a financial nature, and only for certain types of contracts. For example, certain commercial contracts of IBRD permit recourse to domestic courts. The settlement of disputes arising from obligations and from loans granted by this institution is usually entrusted to tribunals of the countries that receive the funds or that use the currency in which the transaction was performed. The same can be said for other financial institutions, such as the EIB.[286]

7.6.3.2 Arbitration and Procurement in Practice

In the practice of organizations within the UN system, the actual number of arbitration cases involving organizations is, however, very low, while the monetary expenditure these cases entail for the organizations can be quite significant.[287] Between 1995 and 2007,[288] for example, there were twenty-three arbitration cases related to contracts involving organizations within the UN system. Of these, eighteen involved the United Nations, three UNDP, one UNOPS, one UNICEF and one UNEP.[289] They were decided primarily in favour of the private parties. However, three cases were concluded with no compensation from any of the parties, in two cases the private party abandoned the case, two cases

---

[284] TFUE, Art. 272 [ref. T&C].

[285] On recourse to national tribunals to challenge the actions of international organizations and thus to assert their non-contractual liability in general, see Reinisch, *International Organizations before National Courts; id.* (ed.), *Challenging Acts of International Organizations.*

[286] See Valticos, 'Les contrats conclus par les organisations internationales avec des personnes privées. Rapport provisoire', p. 86 *et seq.*

[287] On this point see also Audit (ed.), *Contrats publics et arbitrage international.*

[288] Very little data on arbitration involving international organizations is accessible to the general public as most of the arbitral awards are subject to privacy restrictions.

[289] UNDP and UNOPS are in fact called as parties in the same arbitration.

were pending (in 2007) and all others were concluded with an order for the organization to pay compensation, for a total of almost $27 million between 1995 and 1999 and about $2 million between 2000 and 2007.[290] The difference can be explained by the intense peacekeeping activity in the early 1990s, as well as because a major arbitration case was concluded in 1997 that required the UN to pay out about €10 million. It should also be noted that, of the $27 million in compensation up to 1999, at least $23 million regarded arbitration cases involving procurement contracts, while $3.75 million was paid in settlements.[291]

Some issues useful to a legal analysis thus emerge. First, the judgment handed down in most of these arbitration cases seems to be impartial: the arbitrators are not arbitrators *of* the administration, and in fact in most cases they order the international organization to pay compensation.

Second, there are relatively few arbitration cases, but the value of the contracts submitted for arbitration, the sums that the private party claims, and the sums that are then awarded as compensation are significant. From this, one may conclude that, while protection from possible contractual violations by organizations is ensured with a certain degree of certainty in the case of large contracting firms that are capable of supplying significant quantities of goods, services or works, the same cannot be said for smaller undertakings that provide supplies with an overall lower value. The numbers reveal that in fact these latter undertakings are discouraged from submitting a case for arbitration and that they instead tend to accept settlements or to refrain from raising issues, for reasons that include their ability to ensure their business reputation within the organizations.

Finally, the effectiveness of arbitration decisions is always dependent on the problem of immunity from execution. According to the organizations' responses to the Valticos Report, this problem rarely arises: within the sphere of international trade law, in the great majority of cases, parties execute arbitration decisions as a matter of course, and failure to execute is the exception. In particular, it would be unlikely that an international organization fails to execute an arbitration decision that

---

[290] The data are the result of an examination of documents made available by various organizations and are not public.

[291] OIOS, *Report of the Office of Internal Oversight Services on the Review of Procurement-Related Arbitration Cases* [ref. REP].

concerns it.[292] In reality, this seems to be one of those cases in which the perception of an eventuality is more important than the actual occurrence of the eventuality: a small private undertaking that is aware of the organization's ability to always and in any event avoid execution of the arbitration will instead tend to stay away from arbitration – as we can see from the figures noted above. Arbitration in fact entails a significant monetary outlay but does not offer a complete guarantee that a violation by an organization will actually lead to compensation.

7.6.3.3 'Special' Protection?

From the above analysis several conclusions can be drawn on the effectiveness of protection of private parties' rights in procurement contracts with international organizations and on the nature of the relative arbitration cases, in particular when we compare international commercial arbitration[293] to arbitration involving national public administrations.[294]

In private law, arbitration between private parties is a remedy based on the parties' agreement to waive jurisdiction. This decision is reached through a meeting of minds. Arbitration replaces judicial process and is aimed at resolving a conflict. It is also executive: the arbitration decision has the force of *res judicata* on the parties.

In the history of administrative law, arbitration between public administrations and private parties has not always met these criteria. At least in civil law countries, it has instead amounted to administrative arbitration, separate from private law, where the possibility of recourse to arbitration was unilaterally determined by the administration itself or was provided by the law. It thus made 'even the use of contractual, non-unilateral

---

[292] Valticos, 'Les contrats conclus par les organisations internationales avec des personnes privées. Rapport provisoire', p. 83.

[293] There is an enormous amount of literature addressing the issue of international commercial arbitration. Without attempting to be exhaustive, some useful works include Strong, *Research and Practice in International Commercial Arbitration*; Moses, *The Principles and Practice of International Commercial Arbitration*; Martinez-Fraga, *The American Influences on International Commercial Arbitration*; Greenberg, Kee and Romesh Weeramantry, *International Commercial Arbitration*; Bantekas, *An Introduction to International Arbitration*; Cordero-Moss (ed.), *International Commercial Arbitration*; Caron, Schill, Smutny and Triantafilou (eds.), *Practising Virtue: Inside International Arbitration*.

[294] On arbitration in administrative law from the perspective of this work, see Valticos, 'Les contrats conclus par les organisations internationales avec des personnes privées. Rapport provisoire', p. 64 *et seq.*; Conseil d'État, *Régler autrement les conflits*; Cassese, 'L'arbitrato nel diritto amministrativo'; Rosa Moreno, *El arbitraje administrativo*.

systems privileged and partisan'.[295] Starting in the second half of the twentieth century, however, this type of arbitration underwent a process of privatization that brought it under the aegis of private law, in this way salvaging its voluntary and contract-based structure.

The arbitration of international organizations is distinct from both private law arbitration and administrative law arbitration, as originally conceived. The significant aspects concern the substance of the arbitration and the execution of the arbitration.

With regard to substance, recourse to arbitration in international organizations' contracts is not a result of a free meeting of minds between two parties. There are two reasons for this assessment. First, arbitration in national administration contracts is a derogation from the jurisdiction exercised by state bodies. In this sense, recourse to arbitration is the result of the parties' agreed choice. Arbitration in international organizations' contracts is not based on the concept of statehood: most international organizations do not have a territorial jurisdiction because they do not exercise sovereignty over a territory. Moreover, they can hold themselves immune from jurisdiction in order to carry out their functions. Thus, arbitration is not a derogation, but the sole instrument to guarantee the settlement of disputes. Even when the contract refers to the competence of national courts, this is arbitration competence, not judicial competence. Private parties are in fact led to accept arbitration because it is the only solution available to protect their contractual position, which would otherwise have no protection.

The second reason is in part a concrete repercussion of this condition and in part self-standing: in contracts concluded after tender procedures, the general terms and conditions are drafted by the international organizations[296] and their acceptance is either a prerequisite to participating in the bidding or, in the case of flexible approaches, a decisive element of evaluation. In particular, the arbitration clause is one of the fixed clauses that usually cannot be changed. The source of arbitration is thus the organization's unilateral determination, but at the same time it cannot be called a privilege of the organization except from the formal standpoint (since the organization itself determines it and identifies its source of regulation), because from the substantive standpoint it is instead the only guarantee of protection offered to private parties in terms of their legal standing based on the contract with the international organization.

---

[295] Cassese, *L'arbitrato nel diritto amministrativo*, p. 353.   [296] See Chapter 5.

The most characteristic aspect of arbitration involving international organizations is, however, immunity from execution. It in fact creates a potential situation of privilege for the international organization that has no equivalent even in other forms of arbitration. The issue is not the 'illegality' of these provisions, which cloak with the colour of a *free* arbitration agreement an obligation that the state forces on those who contract with its administrations: it is both more and less than this. On the one hand, there is the compulsory nature of arbitration as a unilateral imposition but also as the only form of protection. On the other hand, there is the organization's privilege to be able to avoid execution. The objection by some that organizations rarely evade execution is not particularly relevant, not only because it is the very provision of this option that creates disparity in the contractual relationship, but also because the mere possibility is in fact enough to discourage small businesses from entering into a dispute.

In 1977 Valticos wrote:

> on inclinerait à penser que ce type composite d'arbitrage pencherait plutôt du côté du droit privé, mais que, dans chaque cas concret, la coloration dépendra dans une large mesure de la nature et de l'object du contrat envisage.[297]

In reality, an analysis of the salient aspects of the protection of private parties' rights in the procurement contracts of organizations shows that the alteration of private law is much more than a 'colouring' dependent on the nature and subject matter of the contract. Rather, the protective mechanisms within the contract are based on a hybridization of private law and the international public organization's privileges: in its present form, arbitration is a system that has certain aspects of private law, but is surrounded by special rules because it applies to international public organizations. The special rules, moreover, limit the sphere of protection for private parties much more significantly than do the rules of traditional administrative arbitration, because they could potentially nullify the very reason for the system, permitting organizations not to execute the award.

7.7 Conclusions

The system of accountability of international organizations in procurement has three components: external controls, through which the

---

[297] Valticos, 'Les contrats conclus par les organisations internationales avec des personnes privées. Rapport provisoire', p. 84.

international or national administration is responsible to the member states; internal controls, which provide oversight across various levels of the administration; and mechanisms that private subjects may use to appeal against the procuring entities' actions and decisions. These components are meant first to guarantee that states representing taxpaying citizens as well as the undertakings that participate in tender procedures have knowledge of the procurement activity carried out by organizations.[298] Second, they should ensure that the organization's administrative heads are aware of the actions of officials responsible for procurement and of any deviations from the procurement principles and rules, both during the vendor selection phase and during execution of the contract. Finally, they are meant to provide private parties with the opportunity to assert their rights vis-à-vis the international organizations and the states.

Of these three components, accountability to states is the one that, compared to the others, is most fully realized. The methods by which member states can control the administrative activity of organizations are complex. Oversight is performed through different bodies: for the organizations of the UN system, these include Executive Boards, Boards of Auditors and the JIU. For each of these, the states decide the composition, have representatives or institutions within the body, and at the same time receive the information produced by the oversight. In addition, controls cover various aspects of the organizations' procurement activity: the conformity of administrative activity (including procurement) to policy objectives, the financial accuracy of statements of account regarding contracts, the conduct of individual officials and the decisions of the competent administrative bodies that can divert resources from being disbursed according to legally defined principles. Finally, the result of controls is modulated by states: it is the governing bodies of organizations that decide whether or not to implement regulatory reforms to address the problems emerging from controls.

On the contrary, internal controls in direct procurement have substantial shortcomings, both when performed by higher-level bodies and when conducted by independent bodies. In the first case, an increased volume of procurement activity and the consequent decentralization have not resolved but rather amplified problems in the clear delegation of authority and the respective responsibilities. Also, even when the lines

---

[298] Whether this is conducted by international administrations or carried out by national administrations with funding from organizations.

of authority are clear, practices of evading responsibility are not an exception. In the second case, controls by bodies independent from the procuring entity and implementation of the relative recommendations are still subject to the political will of states. The case of the Procurement Task Force is significant in this regard. Moreover, controls by independent bodies can (the final decision still always rests with the contracting administrations) indirectly weaken the legal position of companies, in particular their interest in being registered in the vendors' rosters and participating in tender procedures, without giving them guarantees of due process.

In indirect procurement, a variant of internal controls is inter-institutional controls between the international organization and national administrations. Unlike what happens in direct procurement, here the oversight methods are more effective. Financial institutions, the European Commission and also some organizations that engage in indirect procurement (UNDP, UNHCR etc.), carry out general controls aimed at determining, over longer periods of time, whether project implementation and, thus, also procurement, are being handled according to the organization's objectives and rules. Moreover, financial institutions and the European Commission carry out specific controls on the acts and decisions adopted during the tender procedure, e.g. the call for tenders, the bid evaluation and the award decision, but also on the activity performed in execution of the contract. In this way, as it pursues its own interest in effective management of the resources granted, the international organization also becomes the guarantor of private subjects' rights as defined in the guidelines.

The third component of accountability is what makes international organizations and national administrations responsible to private subjects during the vendor selection phase and execution of the contract. Within this component as well, there is a significant difference between direct and indirect procurement. In the former, although there have been significant developments compared to the past, the degree of accountability and its effectiveness are still decided by the international organizations. Bid protest mechanisms are proceduralized, but they are mostly managed by the administrations, and consist of hierarchical appeals or protests before the same body that adopted the decision. With the exception of ESA, EU institutions and, within certain limits, the UN, the bodies to whom a protest can be presented do not yet provide sufficient guarantees of independence and have the power to cancel the procedure, but not to order compensation for damages.

On the contrary, in indirect procurement, the mechanisms for accountability vis-à-vis private subjects take advantage of the tripartite nature of the relationships among international organizations, national administrations and private subjects. The organization scrutinizes the handling of complaints by the national procuring entity; it may intervene, blocking an award decision or requiring cancellation and revision of the bidding procedure; it may provide a further debriefing if the vendor is not satisfied with the answer provided by the national procuring entity; or it may conduct an investigation based on a private party's allegations of fraud and corruption against national administrative officials or other private parties who participated in the bidding procedure. In all cases, the international organization has the power of financial retaliation against the financed state. Moreover, in the case of EU institutions it is also possible to file a complaint against the supranational administration itself, asserting failure to properly supervise.

Finally, in executing the contract, while private parties are guaranteed the opportunity of appeal to impartial bodies to protect their legal positions through recourse to arbitrators rather than judicial bodies within organizations, the effectiveness of this protection is nevertheless undermined by the inherent international public nature of the organizations, which can always invoke immunity from execution.

An overall analysis of accountability, thus, underscores two aspects. The first relates to the ties between each of the three components, and more particularly the influence that external oversight has on the other two types of oversight and on the limited effectiveness of public procurement principles. The external controls described show that states have a detailed awareness of how resources are managed and procurement activity is carried out. In direct procurement, regulatory limits and application practices that deviate from the principles of competition, transparency and integrity; the shortcomings of the system of internal controls; and the only partial protection of the private parties' legal position during contractor selection and contractual execution are not the result of states' lack of information, but rather their lack of will, or at any rate their tolerance, dictated by a particular dynamic of interests.[299] Proof of this is that when the balance of interests shifts, as occurs in

---

[299] See Chapter 8.

indirect procurement, the two components of internal controls and accountability to private parties function more effectively.

The second aspect regards the contract. Although, in fact, unlike some national legal systems, there is no administrative judge who settles contractual disputes, the neutrality of the judicial body does not guarantee that both parties to the contract are equally accountable to one another. In this sense, the privileged legal position of the international public body does not come from having a special jurisdiction, as in some domestic legal systems, because, except for a few organizations, the system does not offer this component. Rather, the privilege consists of activating immunities that allow the international organization to jeopardize the effectiveness of the accountability mechanisms even when they are entrusted to neutral and impartial bodies.

8

How the Interplay of Interests Shapes Procurement

8.1 Introduction

Analysis of the principles, procedures and practices of direct and indirect procurement has revealed conflicting features. On the one hand, the structure of the procedures adopted by organizations is similar to that of national public procurement. Furthermore, in indirect procurement the standard of transparency and competition required is more similar to that applied in national public procurement. On the other hand, analysis has brought to light specific features of international organizations' procurement, such as a more limited implementation of the principles of competition, transparency and accountability in direct procurement, and certain deviations from the mechanism of pure competition and accountability to private parties in indirect procurement. These results raise two sets of questions.

The first is preliminary and relates to the soundness of the theory that the rules regulating international organizations' procurement have national roots. That is, while it is true that in many ways the rules that govern international organizations' procurement have historically been built on and replicate the law of national public procurement, it is equally clear that this is not a legal transplant of rules in the traditional sense. So what are the specificities of this legal transplant compared to the traditional legal transplant that legal theory identifies? The answer provides a preliminary explanation of why the adoption of procurement rules by international organizations, despite being based on national public procurement regulation, has developed in a partially different direction.

The second set of questions is related to the first and stands at the core of this research: what reasons explain the principles, procedures and practices of international organizations' procurement? Or, to put it differently, what reasons explain the specific balance between the exercise of public power in the procedure and in the contract, and the recognition of procedural and contractual rights of private subjects (businesses and individuals)? Reasons will be identified in the interplay of political and economic interests underlying international organization law with regard to procurement and contracts. The empirical analysis conducted in the preceding chapters shows that international organizations, far from being neutral entities, carry a whole set of interests, which sometimes even conflict with their institutional mission.

Procurement rules and practices cannot be explained only by reference to international organizations, although in practice they are produced by them. Member states acting in their own interest have very strong formal and informal instruments at their disposal to determine the substance of the law, its development and also its limits. The hypothesis suggested is that states not necessarily act or influence the law-making process and the resulting procedures and contract clauses in a direction that would seem to be in line with their national approach to procurement (more competition, transparency etc.). On the contrary, they often are shown to favour partisan considerations over functional ones, where functional is to be interpreted as contributing to the effective fulfilment of the function of the organization of which they are members. However, these considerations interact with those brought about by international organizations themselves, creating a regulatory net that accommodates multiple and conflicting powers and interests.

Furthermore, as the number of private parties affected by the activity of international organizations expands, the strength and influence that these parties can exercise over internal rule-making processes and procurement practices have also gradually increased. Private parties in their different roles as businesses, taxpayers and also the final recipients of procurement activity have a role in shaping procurement rules and practices, indirectly through the states to which they belong.

8.2   National Roots of Procurement Regulation and the Anomalous Legal Transplant

The complex and somewhat ambiguous results of the historical analysis and the comparison between national public procurement regulation and that of international organizations suggest that there has been a legal transplant between the two, but that this transplant differs greatly from those theorized by the legal doctrine so far. Identification of these anomalous aspects is useful in order to understand why the principles that guide national public procurement change in some major ways when transposed into international organizations, and why their reciprocal relationships change.[1]

The concept of legal transplant that comparatists traditionally use can be summarized as follows:

> the movement of legal norms or specific laws from one state to another during the process of law making or legal reform.[2]

As Twining shows, the characteristics of legal transplants as observed by comparatists are the following: the exporter and importer are identifiable parties; the export and receipt of norms is a horizontal process, as it takes place between state entities; transplant is a one-way process, from country A to country B; the object of the transplant is principally legal concepts and rules; the agents are mainly national governments; the transplant takes place through a formal promulgation or adoption of a provision at a particular moment in time; and the object of the transplant retains its identity without significant changes after the date of reception.[3] In addition, other characteristics are often noted in specific cases, but there is no consensus on them. For instance, export is usually from a civil law or common law country to a 'dependent' country, such as a former colony or an adolescent legal system, where institutional entities are in transition. Likewise, many analyses assume that the norms received fill a regulatory gap or usually replace a law that is outdated and considered inappropriate for the political-social context.[4]

The principles and procedural rules governing international organizations' procurement are the outcome of a legal transplant that diverges in several respects from that usually observed by comparatists. First, the levels of governance where the source system and the recipient system are located are different. The transplant is in fact vertical rather than horizontal, and in indirect procurement it is mediated rather than immediate. In direct procurement, legal principles and norms have been transferred from one or more states that are members of the organization

---

[1] On the phenomenon of the influence of national administrative cultures on international organizations, see Beigbeder, 'L'influence des modèles administratifs nationaux'; Jordan, 'The Influence of the British Secretariat Tradition'; Cassese, 'Relations between International Organizations and National Administrations'.

[2] For literature on the subject, see, *inter alia*, Watson, *Legal Transplants*; Mistelis, 'Regulatory Aspects'; Twining, 'Diffusion of Law'.

[3] Twining, 'Diffusion of Law', pp. 4–5. [4] *Ibid.*

to the organization itself, and not from one state to another.[5] This transplant has taken place in at least two ways. For most organizations, the adoption of a body of rules belonging to a particular national legal system is not explicitly stated in the tender documents, in the contract or elsewhere, but in practice the rules that these organizations draw up and follow are the result of a compromise between various 'dominant' legal traditions, often reflected in international and supranational agreements.[6] In other organizations, however, the reference to traditions of certain countries[7] is explicit and given preference. For example, in 1977 an official report on procurement contracts that international organizations concluded with private subjects stated:

> [L]es organizations se réfèrent généralement à leurs règlements, financiers ou autres, à des manuals administratifs, à des Conditions générales d'appels d'offres . . . Il est intéressant de noter qui l'OMS déclare s'être référée à la pratique des institutions gouvernmentales d'Etats Membres, notamment le règlement du gouvernement des Etats-Unis d'Amerique et, dans une certaine mesure, la pratique au Royaume-Uni.[8]

In indirect procurement, it is the international organization that 'transplants' the rules into the state, but only after these rules have been designed on the model of those existing in some member states. Thus, in the case of direct procurement, the relationship is vertical and ascending, and is between one or more states and the international organization. In the case of indirect procurement, the relationship is built around a double passage: it is first vertical and ascending between various states and the organization, and then vertical and descending between the organization and the states financed, which are usually different from those that influenced the genetic phase of the rules. From the perspective of traditional comparative law theory, this last case could be considered a transplant from one state to another mediated by the organization. In reality, it is much more than a mere transfer. Often it is an important re-working of the principles and rules shared by a number of states and

---

[5] In this regard, Twining criticizes the limits of traditional comparatist theory with regard to legal transplants and observes: 'diffusion may take place between many kinds of legal orders at and across different geographical levels, not just horizontally between municipal legal systems'. See Twining, 'Diffusion of Law', p. 21.

[6] As an example, see MacLaren, 'La culture administrative britannique'.

[7] Explicit reference to certain legal traditions came mostly during the early lives of organizations when a regulatory gap needed to be filled.

[8] Valticos, 'Les contrats conclus par les organizations internationales avec des personnes privées. Rapport provisoire'.

supplemented by characteristics justified by the international nature of the organization.

The second specificity relates to identifying the institutional subjects involved. While in traditional legal transplants the exporting and receiving of legal systems can often be identified with certainty, the same cannot be said in the case of procedural rules that govern international organizations' procurement. In both direct and indirect procurement, the source systems cannot always be identified, while the recipients almost always can be (the international organization or the state that receives the organization's financial support or material assistance). The rules are defined within the organization, with a preponderance of certain legal traditions over others, but it is not possible to identify their origin with a degree of precision comparable to what is possible, for example, when examining colonial and post-colonial Indian law and its English roots. The body of norms that the international organization applies to itself and to the states that it finances or supports is often the result of a re-working of rules common to a number of national systems and legal traditions. Moreover, in indirect procurement the rules that organizations must observe in many respects follow the legal norms contained in international agreements on public procurement, for example the GPA, which a number of the organizations' member states have signed.

The third specificity is a consequence of the first two. As noted above, according to a majority of scholars of traditional legal transplants, the law in question essentially retains its identity without significant changes, otherwise it could not be deemed to be a true transplant. This position has been criticized by those who, adopting a hermeneutic approach, have completely denied the very existence of legal transplants as traditionally conceived:

> [t]he law as a social construct cannot remain the same, once it is dislocated. On this account, the 'transplant' cannot survive the change of context. In the new context, the original meaning of what is transplanted is, of necessity, lost.[9]

Thus, even if the norm is 'transplanted' exactly as it originally appeared, it will always have an application and functioning phase influenced by social and cultural factors that are different in every state and that change

---

[9] Graziadei, 'Comparative Law as the Study of Transplants and Receptions', p. 728; and similarly: Legrand, 'The Impossibility of "Legal Transplants"'; *id.*, 'The Same and the Different'.

its substance, despite any similarity of form. For the rules and regulations on international organizations' procurement, both the 'pure' transplant theory (the transplant is a transfer of norms that remain unchanged in form and substance) and this critical revision are only partially valid.

In fact, when norms regulating national public procurement are transposed to international organizations' procurement, they first change in form. As already pointed out in previous chapters, procurement regulation changes: the rules adopted by organizations are often only a selection of those that certain states generally apply, or do not show the same degree of detail. Furthermore, the substance of the norms changes. In direct procurement, rules drawn from one or more national models, and whose adoption was promoted by certain states, are transposed into an institutional context radically different from the state one: a horizontal transplant occurs between institutional contexts that are essentially homogenous, but the same cannot be said of vertical transplants. While to a certain extent one may assert that the institutional structure of an international organization has some analogies with that of a state, the degree of similarity is certainly lower than that which may occur between two entities that are both recognized as states in the international arena (horizontal transplant). The radical change in the institutional context is the key to understanding the reasons for substantial differences when applying the rules. For example, the essence of the rules changes due to the absence of an independent judicial organ entitled to judge the international administration's decisions.[10] Or, as they are determined principally by administrative and not legislative organs, the rules tend to protect the administration more than the interests of suppliers (or potential suppliers) of the international organization.

The fourth specificity lies in the causes of the transplant. Historical and comparative research identifies multiple, more or less institutionalized, causes of legal transplants, from colonial domination to cultural influence. Nevertheless, the various causes all have a common element: they assume that the source legal systems are different and distinct from the recipient legal systems. In the case of international organizations, there is a partial identity between sources and recipients. While the international organization is a subject with its own legal personality distinct from that

---

[10] See Chapter 7.

of states,[11] and administration officials are not bound by representational obligations,[12] the internal rule-making process that is carried out in technical committees and results in the elaboration of procurement rules is often subject in various ways to the informal inputs of state representatives. This also leads to a re-examination of the widespread assumption that the transplant takes place between a dominant legal entity and a 'dominated' or dependent one. There may be influential relationships in international organizations, but not, strictly speaking, ones of dominance.[13]

Finally, the regulation of international organizations' procurement is particular in another respect: the direction of the transplant. Horizontal transplants are usually one-way: from state A to state B. There are variations on this scheme, and cases of reciprocal influences have been noted,[14] yet reciprocity is not always a constant constitutive component of horizontal transplants. Reciprocity is, however, an element in the transplant of rules governing international organizations' procurement, especially when the organization engages in both direct and indirect procurement. In these cases, using their own national models, states on the one hand contribute to defining the rules governing the organization's procurement activity and the procurement activity of the states that receive financial support from the organization. On the other hand, certain international organizations condition their financial and material support on the adoption, by certain states, of the procurement rules defined by the organizations under the influence of and with the

---

[11] See Cox, Jacobson, et al., The Anatomy of Influence.

[12] According to Eric Drummond, the Secretariat of the League of Nations had to be a 'truly international secretariat, whose members ... must divest themselves of national preconceptions and devote themselves wholeheartedly to the service of the League', cited in Reinalda and Verbeek (eds.), Decision Making within International Organizations, p. 13. Hence, civil servants were expected to be loyal to the international organization rather than their country of origin. The Drummond proposal served as a model for international civil servants in the UN system and other international organizations (ibid.).

[13] See Cox, Jacobson et al., The Anatomy of Influence, passim.

[14] In this regard, criticizing traditional theories, Twining observes: '[t]he pathways of diffusion may be complex and indirect. A nice example is the Indian Evidence Act, 1872 ... It was a great simplification, but also an idealization of the English law of evidence. After its enactment in India it was used as a model in many other parts of the British Empire. It also had some influence on evidence in England ... Of course, reciprocal influence is not uncommon even at state level, for example, the mutual interaction between American states, between England and Scotland, and between the United States, the United Kingdom, and Australia. Reciprocal influences between religious, customary, and municipal legal orders are well documented', in Twining, 'Diffusion of Law', pp. 22–23.

agreement of donor states – and often of only a minority of the member states. Reciprocity is not specific and nominal, as often the states that 'make' the rules within the organization are not those that directly benefit from the outcome of the procurement activity, but generally speaking this can be considered a form of reciprocity as there is an exchange between the international organization and states.

These particularities are not such as to exclude the possibility that, in the definition of the rules governing organizations' procurement, there has been a legal transplant. In fact, an analysis of the history of organizations and of organizations' procurement rules clearly shows analogies between these rules and the ones that govern national public procurement, especially in the structure of procedures and in the declared principles.[15] However, at the same time these particularities create significant variations in rules. Even though generally speaking the principles are similar to those that guide national public procurement – best value for money, impartiality competition, and transparency – their meaning, relative weight and application are different, as they are tied to a particular institutional context – an international organization and not a state – and to the different categories of interests at play. Likewise, the contract itself and the clauses it contains are affected by this interaction of interests.

8.3   Interests and Principles: Dynamics in National Public Procurement

In continental legal systems, the public law rules on public procurement are based on three needs (which in this sense may be classified as *interests*):[16] to ensure that the public administration receives the best value for money, to guarantee administrative impartiality, and to promote and safeguard competition. In reality, in functional terms the three needs are not on an equal footing. While the first and last are primary principles and final objectives, impartiality is instrumental to one or the other, and thus is shaped and implemented differently depending on the objective it serves. The three principles have been asserted at different

---

[15] See later in this chapter for a more detailed analysis.

[16] The term 'interest' is used generically in this context to mean the preference and desire of a certain institutional party or member of the general public for a determined practical result and, thus, with regard to the administration, the basis for its action. For example, from the perspective of a public administration, when we speak of an interest in cost-effective procurement, we are saying that best value for money is the basis for the administrative action.

moments in time: best value for money and administrative impartiality first, and only later competition, with European integration and adherence to international trade agreements.

Traditionally, the rules on public procurement serve the administration's financial objectives. The fact that historically procurement rules have been included in state budget laws and financial regulations – at least in continental legal systems – is a manifestation of this. The reason for this can be found within the administration: procurement contracts represent an economic expenditure for the administration. It was to minimize the expenditure of public resources that specific procedures were set up. Indeed, due to the particular nature of public administrations, the absence of special constraints could compromise the goal of saving. Moreover, according to some economists, public administration should be considered an anomalous market player. Unlike private counterparts, public administration does not have an in-depth and detailed view of the market: its relationship with other market actors is characterized by information asymmetry. In addition, due to the nature of its activity and functions, it might have to sustain high planning, contracting and control costs. Public procurement procedures, thus, have the goal of reducing these transaction costs by introducing correctives to normal contractual activities that mitigate the public operator's initial disadvantages in a market context.[17]

Nevertheless, best value for money, in the sense described above, does not explain the adoption of public procurement procedures alone, especially by modern public administrations. Transaction costs are part of the risks of the administration's normal functioning as a market actor. Tenders also have the additional goal of avoiding pathologies of administrative action. Administrative officials may make improper discretionary decisions and engage in conduct for personal gain or that which is unlawful,[18] to the detriment of the administration and taxpayers.[19] Thus, the administration must defend itself from its own officials: procedural

---

[17] In this regard, Cafagno writes: 'tenders lend themselves to being scrutinized as especially suitable remedies for reducing negotiating costs and strategic problems generated by information asymmetry and imperfect commitment capability', in Cafagno, *Lo Stato banditore*, p. 147.

[18] *Ibid.*, p. 171.

[19] The traditional view places more importance on the interest of the public administration than on that of businesses that participate or intend to participate in the tender. For a more in-depth discussion of this phenomenon and how the interpretation of impartiality changes as a result of this, see later in this chapter.

restrictions should force administrative officials to maintain an equal distance from possible contract recipients. In addition, transparency and impartiality rules generate increased influence costs for businesses – which should thus be dissuaded from bearing them – and make administrations more credible contractual partners. In fact, it has been held that these constraints can guarantee the fairness and impartiality of administrative officials in lieu of or as a supplement to monitoring and control, which can be especially costly in the public sector.[20]

Best value for money and impartiality (the latter primarily for purposes of protecting the administration) are the values that inspired the drafting of public procurement laws, at least in countries with codified law. European integration and international agreements on the liberalization of trade[21] have, nevertheless, led to a partial revision of these priorities. The common practice of awarding contracts to national companies and the historic reluctance of national governments to enter into contracts with foreign businesses were some of the factors that hindered the free trade of goods and services and, in the EU context, the creation of a single market without obstacles of nationality. The principle of non-discrimination between national suppliers and suppliers from other countries provides the basis for the reform of public procurement rules.

The evolution of European legislation on public procurement is explanatory in this respect. While none of the original European Coal and Steel Community (ECSC), European Economic Community (EEC) and Euratom treaties included direct references to public procurement

---

[20] McCubbins, Noll and Weingast suggest that administrative procedures are an ideal instrument for aligning the objectives of agents with those of principals, reducing the costs of controls and sanctions. Impartiality should be ensured *ex ante* by creating procedures for the actions of officials. Nevertheless, such an approach can function only in situations where creating procedures for administrative action is combined with a culture of legality and personal honesty. Where these features are missing or are undeveloped for political, economic or cultural reasons, creating only *ex ante* procedures may not be sufficient, if not accompanied by a system of controls and sanctions. Situations of this type are found in many countries where international organizations operate. See McCubbins, Noll and Weingast, 'Le procedure amministrative come strumento di controllo politico'.

[21] The 1947 text of GATT excluded government procurement contracts from the agreement's sphere of application, see GATT, Art. III (4), para. 8 [ref. A&C]. Nevertheless, Art. XVII provided that, for imports that involved government procurement contracts, 'each contracnt', *ibid.*, Art. XVII.

procedures of member states,[22] the Treaty of Rome has been the fundamental premise for subsequent European regulation of national public procurement. The principles of non-discrimination and freedom (freedom of movement for workers, goods and services, freedom of establishment and freedom to provide services) and the authorization granted to the European Council to issue directives instrumental to the implementation of these principles have provided the legislative basis and legal justification for the development of *ad hoc* rules on procurement. In 1961 the Council adopted a general programme for the abolition of restrictions on freedom of establishment, according to which provisions or practices that restricted the right of foreign nationals to submit offers in public tenders were to be eliminated.[23] In 1971, with the first European directives coordinating national public procurement procedures,[24] the traditional objectives of saving and impartiality to obtain the best value for money began to be integrated with those of the European Community. Thus, while European Community legislation had until then related to government regulation of commercial relationships between private parties, by the early 1970s and then with subsequent directives on procurement in the 1990s and early 2000s, legislation was gradually developed to regulate the private law activity of states and, thus, their contractual relationships with businesses. The objective was to ensure an opening up of the public procurement contract market to competition among European businesses.

This change arose from a shift in the way procurement contracts were interpreted: the contract award decision was no longer viewed only from the perspective of the administration and regulated according to the 'internal' effects it produced on the administrative apparatus, but was also, and primarily, viewed from the perspective of the businesses that were directly or indirectly impacted by the decision and were affected by it. The primary interest underlying the award decision changed, as well as the type of decision: it is no longer solely a decision on expenditure, but above all a decision that attributes an economic advantage to a certain subject.

[22] Reich explains the reason for this omission: 'this was not as a result of a simple omission by the drafters of the Treaty, but of a failure to reach agreement on a set of principles, because of the complexity of the subject matter and the highly sensitive nature of preference policies', in Reich, *International Public Procurement Law*, pp. 71–72.

[23] Council of Europe, *General Programme for the Abolition of Restrictions* [ref. N&RL-EU].

[24] Council of Europe, Council Directive 71/304/CE of 26 July 1971; *id.*, Council Directive 71/305/CEE of 26 July 1971 [all documents in ref. N&RL-EU].

In terms of initiatives to liberalize trade, a similar tendency emerged in the international area as well. During the sixties and seventies, the Organisation for European Economic Co-operation (OEEC) (the then OECD) began to discuss the possibility of an international regulation of public procurement.[25] This debate laid the foundations for the negotiations in the Tokyo Round, and on its completion for the 1979 adoption of the GPA. The agreement provided that each member state should ensure the products, services and suppliers of other states treatment no less favourable than that accorded to national equivalents; it established the principle of non-discrimination for the goods, services and suppliers of other member states;[26] and it established administrative requirements and procedures for the qualifications of suppliers, criteria for awarding contracts and mechanisms for settling disputes (with the latter based on the equivalent remedies provided by the General Agreement on Tariffs and Trade (GATT)).[27] Even though the agreement's original sphere of application was limited[28] and its membership is still restricted to a few states,[29] it was the first international wide-ranging experiment in developing common procurement rules that include principles other than solely best value for money and impartiality for the purpose of saving. It is no coincidence that this regulation comes from a supranational level. The internationalization of trade made it necessary to consider needs that went beyond national administrations and were linked to the relationships between states.

Competition as a political end thus supplements the principles that have traditionally guided rules on public procurement. Nevertheless, this

---

[25] McCrudden, *Buying Social Justice*, p. 100.   [26] GPA, Art. IV, para. 1 [ref. A&C].

[27] McCrudden, *Buying Social Justice*, pp. 101–104.

[28] The 1979 version did not cover military procurement, regulated procurement contracts for goods and applied solely to central administrations, while in federal systems, local and state administrations were excluded. Moreover, among central administrations, only the clients that the state expressly indicated in a special annex to the agreement could be considered bound. Finally, developing countries were exempted from compliance with the provisions of the agreement. On the one hand, these countries could be allowed to favour local suppliers as an exception to the principle of non-discrimination, and on the other hand, when the necessary conditions were met, agreements were allowed through which the richest states financed projects in developing countries on condition that the procurement contracts connected to these projects were awarded to suppliers in the financing state. The 1994 version of the GPA expanded the object of procurements: no longer only goods, but also work and services; it expanded the group of administrations required to follow the rules of the agreement to all local and state entities set out in special lists attached to the agreement; and it extended membership.

[29] Fewer states were parties to the GPA than to GATT: thirty-six signed the GPA and 150 signed GATT. Conversely, despite the exceptions provided for developing countries, not many of them signed the agreement.

statement should be further elucidated. The idea of having suppliers compete for the award of public contracts is not new. Late-nineteenth century legislation in the major European countries already provided for competitive procedures, although the purpose was different. Competition was instrumental to the administration's money-saving objectives because it permitted a simultaneous comparison of a number of suppliers and the selection of the lowest or most cost-effective bid. It also encouraged price reductions and/or a qualitative improvement of bids. Competition was included among the procurement principles as long as it was in the public interest[30] and not in the interest of potential contractors. This is also confirmed by the fact that private parties did not have legal standing to challenge an administrative decision that failed to comply with the principle.

Conversely, the integration of the objectives of best value for money and competition – in the interest of potential contractors and not solely the administration – also leads to a different interpretation of the meaning of impartiality. The conduct of administrative officials has a direct effect on the businesses that participate or intend to participate in the tender. In addition to the indirect and mediated link between the administration and citizen-taxpayers, by virtue of which the administration guarantees that its officials will properly manage public resources, there is a closer, more fully protected, relationship between the contracting administration and participants (or potential participants) in the tender, regardless of their nationality. In compliance with EU law or international law, the former must ensure the latter's right to equal access to economic opportunities, to be treated with impartiality, to know the reasons for administrative decisions and to have access to the relative documents. In other words, setting competition as the primary objective leads to recognizing as worthy of legal protection all rights that are instrumental to it. In this sense, competition deepens the administration's accountability to private parties: the category of subjects to whom the administration is accountable is larger because the criteria by which a private party is entitled to legal standing is not citizenship, but simply its interest in concluding a contract with the administration

[30] In this regard, the unified category of 'public interest' has been used in the sense of the public administration's interest, in order to distinguish it from public interests in the sense of interests that are actually held by different categories of individuals within the general public, i.e. suppliers. For an interdisciplinary review – albeit primarily from the political perspective – see Friedrich (ed.), *The Public Interest*; Schubert, *The Public Interest*.

regardless of her or his nationality. Moreover the rights that these subjects can assert against the administration are wider and more complex.

The expansion of private subjects' rights is, therefore, the result of an economic decision. While traditionally the primary purpose of public procurement law was the protection of the administration, by promoting the idea of an integrated and free market European and international legislations protect businesses in their contractual relationships with national administrations. The outcome is legislation on procurement that promotes a high degree of competition, transparency and accountability of public administrations.

8.4 Interests and Principles: Dynamics in International Organizations' Procurement

A radically different interplay of interests underlies international organizations' procurement. This interplay involves three centres of interest: international organizations, states and private parties – these being suppliers, taxpayers or citizens. More in detail, in international organizations' procurement, stakeholders can be broken down into at least six categories: international organizations, as administrations; the member states that finance the organization and its procurement activity; the citizens and businesses of these states in their dual role as the source of resources (taxpayers) and possible contractors; the states that are the end users of the goods, services or works procured by the international organization (direct procurement) or the recipients of its subsidies and financing for procurement (indirect procurement); the citizens of the recipient states who benefit from the international organization's procurement activity; and the businesses and individuals who are potential contractors and are incorporated or have the nationality of the recipient state or other non financing states. As we will see, the interests of some of these categories overlap: for example, the interest of financing states is at least in part the same as that of their citizens and businesses.

8.4.1   International Organizations

The interests of international organizations vary depending on the type of procurement: whether it is direct procurement (for internal or external purposes) on the one hand, or indirect procurement for external purposes on the other. With the exception of EU institutions, in direct procurement the objectives of international administrations are similar to the traditional ones of national administrations during the period before the liberalization of trade in the public procurement sector. The UN Procurement Practitioner's Handbook singles out the common elements of the procurement regulation set up by the organizations of the UN system and states four guiding principles for administrative action: best value for money; accountability, integrity and transparency; fairness and effective competition; and best interest of the organization concerned.[31] With few variations, the procurement manual of each organization repeats this sequence.[32]

It is easy to trace these principles to those traditionally guiding national administrations, i.e. best value for money, impartiality and competition. Furthermore, they tend to replicate their reciprocal relationships. The interest in maintaining a certain level of competition, in this context, is for the purpose of saving money and is not an autonomous economic policy option.

The Handbook sums up the contractual practices common to organizations of the UN system. And, in fact, as seen in the chapter on principles guiding procurement procedure,[33] the particular instrumental significance of competition and its minor importance as an independent objective become especially clear in the actual methods for selecting suppliers – at least compared to current rules on national public procurement, such as the EU public procurement directives and the GPA, in which competition is a primary value.

Thus, the principle of competition is pursued to the extent that it is necessary to achieve savings and economical use of resources. The ability of this principle to determine and influence procurement mechanisms and dynamics also depends on the need and urgency of the cost-saving targets. In this regard, two further considerations are necessary. The first pertains to the particular relationship between revenue and expenditure in the budget of an international organization.[34] As for states, the budgets of organizations follow a basic rule: expenditures determine the income needed for the subsequent year (e.g. the level of taxation to be applied, or

---

[31] United Nations, *United Nations Procurement Practitioner's Handbook*, 2017, para. 1.3 [ref. AP&R].

[32] See Chapter 4.   [33] See Chapter 4.

[34] On international organizations' financing and budget see *inter alia* Amerasinghe, 'Financing'; Katz Cogan, 'Financing and Budgets'; Singer, *Financing International Organization*; Stoessinger *et al.*, *Financing the United Nations System*. With regard to peacekeeping operations see Mills, 'The Financing of UN Peacekeeping Operations'; Dormoy, 'Aspects récents de la question du financement'.

in the case of international organizations, the level of contributions from member states) and not the other way around. Member states each undertake to pay their portion of the planned expenses through their contribution. However, this also means that, while international organizations have virtually unlimited spending capacity, they also have almost no capacity to save and no incentives to do so:

> [a]ny increase of agreed expenditure will be met by an increase of the contributions of the members; any savings will only lead to a decrease in these contributions.[35]

The second consideration relates to the methods that international organizations use to finance themselves. Most of the income of public international organizations comes from member states in the form of mandatory contributions based on membership.[36] More than 90 per cent of organizations' financing can be traced to this source.[37]

The third consideration arises from an analysis of control and accountability mechanisms. Although states can exercise outside control through organs such as the Board of Auditors and the JIU, internal control mechanisms are deficient in various ways.[38]

The interaction of these three circumstances has a negative effect on achieving the goals of saving and economy. The administration to which the resources are allocated and that carries out the procurement has no incentive to engage in virtuous management, because savings on resources allocated mean cuts to resources to be allocated. Due to ineffective controls, officials in general have no incentive to conserve resources and to purchase by creating competitive situations, especially where they consider the management of a number of bids to be time-consuming or excessively costly.[39] In these cases, there is a tendency to choose the most immediate and safest options, such as suppliers they already know or with whom they already have ongoing contacts.

On the other hand, the willingness of states to limit their contributions is more often based on political expediency than on considerations of poor resource management. Even when the declared reason is poor administration, the basis for cuts is a political criticism that often involves decision-making dynamics within the organization or issues of insufficient economic return. Thus, for example, in the mid-1980s, the

---

[35] Schermers and Blokker, *International Institutional Law*, §926.

[36] For an examination of the problems related to allocating state contributions, see *ibid.*, §967 *et seq.*

[37] *Ibid.*, §966.   [38] See Chapter 7.   [39] From an interview with a procurement officer.

reduction of US contributions to various organizations of the UN system, based on sharp criticism of administrative management,[40] finds a more complex explanation in the paralysis of the Security Council and the decision-making organs of other organizations and in the inability to use these organizations to pursue the US Republican administration's economic and political interests.[41] However, this also means the contrary: as long as these or other interests are protected, management of resources on a non-competitive basis does not necessarily result in cuts to contributions. The political nature of the decision to join and finance an organization makes poor administration of resources relatively unrelated to the determination to finance the organization.

The interaction of these two factors – i.e. the relationship between the budget plan and final balance, and the political motivations underlying the decisions to continue or limit contributions – also explains why the need to save has not been sufficient incentive to bring competition into play and why, therefore, in the absence of an outside determination of economic policy that favours competition-based procurement procedures, this principle continues to play a secondary role in the supplier selection procedures of international organizations.

An exception to this general trend is represented by the guiding principles of the vendor selection procedures for procurement by EU institutions. In this case, the administration's own interest in saving money and impartiality is integrated with the principles of the system within which the administration operates. Unlike the organizations of the UN system, the European Union was created with the goal of removing barriers to trade and the free movement of goods, services and workers. Competition is among its institutional goals. In fact, the same activity principles that apply to European states hold for EU institutions. While the European Commission is not directly subject to the EU public procurement directives, it must observe the principles of the Treaty, which require its activity to comply with the principles of non-discrimination, equal treatment and competition. In addition, the Financial Rules and the implementing regulation that applies these rules to procurement shall be in line with the provisions of the directives aimed at states.[42]

---

[40] See Chapter 3.
[41] On the role of the United States in financing the United Nations see Hüfner, 'Financing the United Nations. The Role of the United States'; Taylor, 'The United Nations System under Stress'; Babb, *Behind the Development Banks*.
[42] Kalogeras, 'Remedies in the Field of Public Procurement'.

Hence, with regard to vendor selection procedures in direct procurement, from the international administration's perspective there are at least two different sets of interests and two different types of relationships between the principles governing procurement. The first, found in the majority of organizations, is based on pursuing the internal interest of the administration itself, such as saving and best value for money, and on the application of certain principles – impartiality and competition – to serve this primary interest. The second, illustrated in the example of the European Union, is characteristic of an organization for whom competition is an institutional goal. In this context, the institutional principles of the organization and the internal interests of its administration are integrated. Similar to what we have seen for member states, saving money and best value for money are flanked by the principles of impartiality and competition, which, however, acquire an autonomous value: they grant to European or non-European businesses the opportunity to take part in the procurement procedure, rather than serving only the internal interest of the organization. In concrete terms, the different structure of interests and principles is evident in the rules governing procurement provided by each organization.[43]

In indirect procurement, the international organization has, first and foremost, an interest to secure for itself the financial support of donor states, and, in order to do that, to ensure that these financial resources are not wasted and are used to achieve the objectives of the project or the programme. In this sense, best value for money and efficiency of state management are among the priorities required by international organizations, and transparency is instrumental to them. Transparency means both inter-administrative transparency – i.e. between the national administrations that manage procurement and the international ones that grant resources and supervise the process – and transparency towards private parties. The first is the basis for the detailed system of controls and verifications that this type of procurement involves.[44] A report on the National Execution of Technical Cooperation Projects, drafted in 2008 by the JIU of the United Nations, reveals how control and monitoring of national administrations that benefit from the support of UN organizations is a fundamental condition for the proper functioning of the system of state execution and that, precisely for this reason, it must be strengthened and rendered more incisive and penetrating.[45]

---

[43] See Chapter 4.   [44] See Chapter 7.
[45] JIU, *National Execution of Technical Cooperation Projects* [ref. REP]. On this see also Chapter 7.

Transparency towards private parties leads to the development of regulations that give private parties rights to publicity and reason giving, including for the purposes of their participation under competitive conditions.[46]

It must be added, however, that, as noted in the chapter on types of organizations and procurement,[47] organizations that engage in indirect procurement, in particular financial institutions, have the goal of encouraging and promoting economic and social growth in developing countries. The interest in maintaining a competitive system, protected in a more articulated and incisive way than in direct procurement, co-exists with the possibility of pursuing these institutional purposes and must be reconciled with them. Recipient states must conclude contracts according to the rules of international competitive bidding set by the financing organization to give equal business opportunities to suppliers from developed and developing countries. As discussed earlier in this book, international competition has served the interests of financing states by allowing their undertakings to place bids and get awards in tender procedures carried out by beneficiary states, thus ensuring an economic return on contributions. However, exceptions have been allowed to this method under the pressure of beneficiary states by giving preference to local suppliers or suppliers who are from a disadvantaged regional area. The procurement guidelines of the WB, ADB, AfDB, IDB, IFAD and EBRD contain special annexes with rules on domestic preference for both products and suppliers. Financial institutions permit the use of preferential comparative evaluations, even if such evaluations must always comply with certain procedural restrictions set by the financing institutions.[48] Competition is one of the principles – the one recommended by the financing organization – but it also coexists with other principles.

These considerations permit a preliminary response to the question of identifying the interests of international organizations. The activity of international organizations is guided by principles that to some extent vary depending on the type of procurement. On the one hand, it is in fact possible to identify interests – and, thus, principles of action – that appear in all types of procurement by international organizations, i.e. direct and indirect procurement, and that are also common to traditional national procurement: best value for money and saving public resources and, instrumental to these, administrative impartiality. On the other hand,

---

[46] See Chapters 4 and 7.   [47] See Chapter 2.   [48] See Chapter 4.

the third element, competition, has at least two different meanings in the procurement by most international organizations: competition for internal administrative purposes (which is analogous to national public procurement before the policies of trade liberalization) and competition for social purposes. Competition as an economic policy goal, instead, can only be ascribed to procurement by EU institutions.

As seen, in national procurement, where states act in accordance with internationally and regionally established rules, such as the GPA or the European procurement directives, competition is a principle introduced by a supranational source outside the state, principally with the goal of protecting interests that are not held by the national administration that carries out the procurement, but by the private parties who contract with it. The principle of competition, therefore, has a completely different meaning and scope compared to that in traditional national procurement, where competition is instrumental to internal purposes, namely saving money and the convenience of national administrations. These different purposes also lead to a reinterpretation of the principles of impartiality, transparency and publicity, which apply not only to the extent that the administration protects itself from misconduct by its own officials, but are strengthened as they become obligations that administrations must fulfil to grant the corresponding rights to private contractors or potential contractors.

In direct procurement by most international organizations, competition is still not seen as an independent value or objective of economic policy, but is instead interpreted traditionally as competition among private parties to meet the administration's objectives of best value for money. This use of the principle has consequences for how measures aimed at guaranteeing impartiality and transparency are shaped: these are primarily internal hierarchical controls, rather than mechanisms guaranteeing accountability to private parties. An exception to this general tendency is procurement by EU institutions, where, unlike the organizations of the UN system, competition is part of the institutional mission and is therefore integrated into the rules also applicable to EU institution procurement.

In indirect procurement, in particular that of financial institutions, competition takes on a third completely distinctive meaning in terms of both the traditional interpretation and the interpretation used in systems that have made competition the primary policy objective. Competition is seen not only as a principle that can guarantee best value for money and savings, but also as a principle that can advance financing states' interests.

At the same time, competition dynamics also involve the risk that more open markets crush weaker operators, often those of developing countries. Thus, the principle is combined, at least from a formal point of view, with social objectives and exceptions are provided to adopt alternative contractor selection methods that give preference to local and/or regional products or suppliers. Furthermore, the mechanisms in place to grant transparency of administrative action and accountability to private parties are strengthened if compared to those in direct procurement: when the international organization finances procurement, it also has a strong interest in holding the national administration that received the funds accountable. The rights recognized to private parties are instrumental to this objective, and, not surprisingly, the mechanisms to grant these rights are well developed and also involve international organizations.[49]

The interaction among the interests of international organizations changes and becomes simpler after the contract is signed. In a contract between the organization and a private party, competition is no longer either a primary objective or one that is instrumental to other objectives, and the purpose that remains preponderant is internal best value for money, i.e. the contract should be executed without wasting the resources used and giving the administration the ability to adapt its content and duration to the administration's public law needs. Thus, unlike the vendor selection phase, the goal of best value for money is not limited by the conflicting interests of other players, such as financing states. The absence of interests, which counterbalances the best value for money criteria supported by the administration, explains why forms of privilege based on public interest still linger in the contracts of international organizations – such as unilateral preparation of the contract, extraordinary clauses,[50] applicability of a hybrid system of public law and common law rules,[51] and immunity from jurisdiction and execution.[52]

In contractual relationships between national administrations and private parties (indirect procurement), on the other hand, the interests of the organizations do not change after the contract is signed. While the objective of international organizations is to ensure that resources are managed in accordance with the purposes set out in the financing project, the economy and efficiency of state action are a priority even during the execution phase. The contractual clauses that international organizations

---

[49] See Chapter 7.   [50] See Chapter 6.   [51] See Chapter 6.   [52] See Chapter 7.

require national administrations to include in their contracts meet these needs by limiting the state's freedom of contract, at least to a certain extent. These clauses usually grant a balanced distribution of rights and obligations between the contracting administration and private parties and set up mechanisms designed to assert the private party's rights even during the contract's execution phase. By granting contractual rights to private parties, the international organizations also enhance the national administration's accountability to the organization itself.

8.4.2   Financing States, Their Businesses and Their Citizens

States that contribute to the administrative costs necessary for organizations to function and to their operational costs – for example, costs for peacekeeping missions, economic assistance, etc.[53] – play a fundamental role in the dynamics that shape procurement rules and practices. With regard to procurement, financing states have two main objectives. The first is a 'minimal objective' and consists of the proper management of the resources they have provided. In this capacity, states protect the interests of their taxpayers, whose taxes indirectly subsidize the activities of the organizations of which the state is a member.[54] As organizations have evolved and the political balances within them have shifted, some aspects of the interest in proper management have changed.

Traditionally, in international organizations most expenditure went on financing administrative activity. As Amerasinghe shows, it has been estimated that on average 85 per cent of the United Nation's regular budget and 90 per cent of the budget of specialized agencies in the UN

---

[53] Sometimes the classification into one or the other category is clear, while other times it is more ambiguous. For example, a discussion in the Security Council on whether a peacekeeping operation should be initiated involves a whole series of expenses (interpreters, accommodation for delegates attending the meeting, financing of information-gathering trips to the country involved, etc.) that are not part of the mission itself, but are necessary for it to commence (the example is from Schermers and Blokker, *International Institutional Law*, §938). The distinction is important due to the different role that states play in the expenditure decision (later in this section). Moreover, the organization also has discretion to decide whether certain expenses are considered administrative costs or operating costs. WHO, for example, includes as administrative costs expenses that other organizations consider to be operating costs.

[54] This relationship was used in the 1990s by various states, in particular the United States, as a demagogical-populist strategy for criticizing the management of resources and justifying decisions to cut funding to organizations.

system are used for this purpose.[55] Administrative expenditure requires fewer controls than operational expenditure. While the administration is entitled to make administrative expenditures without a case-by-case authorization (but only after approval of the general budget), the need for and appropriateness of operational expenditure must be demonstrated each time by the administration and approved by the competent bodies, i.e. within the UN system, the General Assembly. As ruled by the International Court of Justice, the criteria for approval is that the costs must relate to the organization's objectives.[56]

In this sense, the increase in expenditure for operational activities[57] has produced a change in what has been considered to be 'proper management': with regard to purely administrative expenditures, proper management has been interpreted primarily as a limit on *how* resources can be spent, and thus as an objective to prevent waste of resources, corrupt or collusive conduct by officials, and misappropriation of resources. In contrast, state decisions on operational expenses relate to *whether* an expenditure should be supported or not. From this point of view 'proper management' means, first and foremost, that resources must be mobilized for objectives shared by the financing state. For operational costs, the nature of the interest is thus primarily political, and for this reason the decision-making procedure is more complicated and uncertain and the subsequent controls more stringent (even though they also have a variety of weaknesses).[58] Therefore, for example, the many refusals to finance peacekeeping and peacebuilding missions[59] by certain states have been due to political reasons.

The second objective of financing states in direct procurement is the economic return deriving from the procurement activity. The financing states' expectations go beyond the minimum requirement of proper management of the resources provided, and aim at directly or indirectly creating economic opportunities for their businesses and citizens. This, often, gets to the point of, and translates into, exerting pressure to ensure

---

[55] See Amerasinghe, *Principles of the Institutional Law*, p. 353; in agreement Schermers and Blokker, *International Institutional Law*, § 941, who state that 'in most international organizations, by far the largest part of the budgets is used for administrative expenditure'.

[56] International Court of Justice, 'Certain Expenses of the United Nations. Advisory Opinion 20 July 1962', 20 July 1962 [1962] *ICJ Recueil des arrêts, avis consultatifs et ordonnances* 151, p. 167.

[57] See Chapter 3. [58] See Chapter 7.

[59] A complete reference to all UN missions that were opposed by certain states can be found in Schermers and Blokker, *International Institutional Law*, § 1010–1012.

that the contracts concluded by organizations are preferentially awarded to businesses that have a certain nationality or at least that those businesses have a good chance of participating in tenders and being awarded contracts. In these cases, states do not so much promote the interests of taxpayers as a whole as promote certain categories of businesses or certain business sectors. Although very few donors disclose information on the economic benefits coming from contract awards, the available data from international organizations show disparities between developed and developing countries in the distribution of economic opportunities deriving from international organizations' procurement: in 2014 the top ten countries supplying UN organizations were, in decreasing order, the United States, India, Afghanistan, Belgium, Switzerland, the United Arab Emirates, the United Kingdom, France, Denmark and the Russian Federation.[60] The exceptional presence of Afghanistan and the United Arab Emirates can be explained by political contingency and their capacity to supply petroleum-related products, such as fuel. On this issue, already in 2003 the General Assembly[61] started encouraging UN organizations to increase opportunities for suppliers from developing countries and countries with economies in transition, and in 2007 it reiterated the request.[62] Consequent to these resolutions, UN statistics show an increase in contracts awarded to developing countries and countries with economies in transition. Between 2009 and 2014 the cumulative increase in orders with suppliers from these countries amounted to 40 per cent, with an annual compound growth rate of 7 per cent.[63] However, these data should be considered in conjunction with those showing the share of developing countries and countries with economies in transition supplying UN operations.[64] India, Afghanistan, the United Arab Emirates and the Russian Federation are the four major suppliers, while most other countries have little share in the market. Moreover, in addition to the headquarters in a developed country, it is common for multinational enterprises also to have registered offices in developing countries and, thus, to formally present a bid as a local supplier.

---

[60] See UNOPS, *2014 Annual Statistical Report* [ref. REP].
[61] UN General Assembly, *Procurement Reform*, A/RES/57/279 [ref. RES].
[62] UN General Assembly, *Procurement Reform*, A/RES/61/246 [ref. RES].
[63] UNOPS, *2014 Annual Statistical Report* [ref. REP].   [64] *Ibid.*

The objective of gaining an economic return from procurement may be pursued by financing states in an express binding fashion, or it may be implicit and non-binding. An example of the first method is the practice of conditional trust funds: financing states decide to grant funds for certain projects upon the condition that the procurement financed through these resources involves their national businesses.[65] From the perspective of organizations, this has acted as an incentive to the voluntary financing of projects and as a way of gaining legitimation vis-à-vis financing states. From the perspective of the financing state it has been a way of promoting certain production sectors, bringing disbursements to foreign countries back within national borders, and sometimes, when faced with negative public opinion, even justifying membership of international organizations to their citizens. The practice of conditional trust funds began to spread in the late 1970s despite repeated calls from the competent authorities to limit it, primarily based on the principles of multilateralism and the thought that it would jeopardize the positive collateral effects of financed contracts, i.e. the promotion of local businesses. In the annual report on development activities presented to the General Assembly in 1983, the Director General for Development and International Economic Co-operation (DIEC) gave recommendations to all the UN organizations to limit tied aid practices:

> ... [he] felt the need to address such issues as the growing trend towards providing contributions tied to the procurement of goods and services in the donor country; in that context, he recommended that contributions made to special purpose funds and programmes be consistent with the principles of multilateralism and remain a proportion of general purpose contributions.[66]

In 1983 alone, agreements on eighteen projects financed by conditional contributions were, in fact, concluded within the organizations of the UN family: four for the United Nations Capital Development Fund (UNCDF), six for the United Nations Sudano-Sahelian Office (UNSO) and eight for the United Nations Financing System in Science and Technology Development (UNFSSTD).[67] In that same year, the UNDP Council asked the Administrator General to provide detailed statistics on the

---

[65] In general, on trust funds, see Schermers and Blokker, *International Institutional Law*, §§ 1028–1031. For a targeted analysis of tied aid see Lachimia, *Tied Aid and Development Aid Procurement*.

[66] United Nations, *Yearbook of the United Nations 1983*, p. 440 [ref. UNCDoc].

[67] *Ibid.*, p. 470.

relationship between general contributions and conditional contributions; the effects of trust funds in the geographical distribution of resources; the costs of goods and services acquired with these funds compared to the costs that would be incurred if normal financing practices were used; and the effects on organizations' sectorial activities. The report came to the conclusion that

> the authority to accept trust funds [conditioned on procurement from donor countries] has not distorted the basic principles of multilateralism of UNDP, but has enabled the three funds to provide additional assistance of significant importance. He proposed that the mandate to accept trust funds conditioned on procurement from a donor country be extended ...[68]

Nevertheless, this positive opinion was tempered by certain quantitative limits:

> [w]ith regard to UNCDF and UNSO, the Administrator could accept such trust funds provided that: the DONOR country had not decreased its contribution in national currency to UNDP general resources; ... and that the contribution did not exceed 10 per cent in the case of UNCDF and 15 per cent in the case of UNSO of the donor's contributions to the general resources of the Programme and the Fund or Office. All Governments were urged to increase their contributions to the Fund's or Office's general resources so that their activities could expand without recourse to contributions conditioned on procurement from the donor country.[69]

In general, this passage reveals the traditional ambiguity of the competent authorities with regard to conditional contributions: on the one hand seeing them as necessary means of obtaining resources and on the other as a limit to the collateral benefits deriving from direct procurement. Essentially, the choice is between two polarized alternatives: the economic benefit of financing states *versus* that of recipient states. The first was, and still is, sometimes a prerequisite for even obtaining the financing, and the second, while not the primary objective of the individual project or programme,[70] could fall within the organization's general goals. Balancing these two needs often depends on factors unrelated to procurements themselves: a state's decision to finance a project may depend on other types of advantage, for example political, that it feels it can obtain from the operation, and on the other hand there are cases of procurement, for example indirect procurement by financial

---

[68] United Nations, *Yearbook of the United Nations 1984*, p. 450 [ref. UNCDoc].   [69] *Ibid.*
[70] There are also programmes or projects with an explicit condition of local procurement.

institutions, where the financed state is allowed to give preferential treatment to local suppliers.

In addition, the economic benefits of local procurement have at times been considered poor and insufficient, thus fuelling the practice of tying financial contributions to the requirement that tenders are awarded to businesses incorporated in the financing state. In a report on the role of local procurement in the food aid sector, Thomas Melito, Director of the International Affairs and Trade Team of the US House of Representatives, wrote:

> [w]hile the primary purpose of LRP [i.e. Local and regional procurement] is to provide food assistance in humanitarian emergencies in a timely and efficient manner, a potential secondary benefit is contributing to the development of the local economies from which food is purchased. The development benefits to local economies from LRP are secondary because in almost all cases WFP and NGO purchases are not large enough or reliable enough to sustain increased demand over time. Only recently has WFP acknowledged that LRP can contribute to local development. In several of the countries we visited, we observed WFP LRP initiatives under way that might support local economies in the long term and connect LRP to other food security initiatives. However, *many of them are new and limited in scale.*[71]

Despite the critical opinion of many states and the heads of organizations themselves, this type of contribution has continued to be a source of income for organizations, albeit not the most important one. Although the first agreements to untie aid were signed at the OECD in 2001 and the international community agreed to a range of commitments to address aid effectiveness in the Paris Declaration of 2005 and the Accra Agenda for Action of 2008, by 2011 still about 20 per cent of bilateral aid was formally tied.[72] In 2009, in one of the most important sectors for international organizations' procurement, such as food aid, the United States, the largest financing state in the sector, declared that its contributions would require the exclusive purchase of American foodstuffs:

---

[71] Emphasis added. In US GAO, *International Food Assistance, Local and Regional Procurement*, pp. 6–7 [ref. REP].

[72] See Ellmers, *How to Spend It*, p. 4. For further data, see also: OECD, *Implementing the 2001 DAC Recommendations on Untying Aid* [ref. REP]; id., *2008 Survey on Monitoring the Paris Declarations* [ref. REP]. The practice of tied aid for development has been analyzed in several works. See *inter alia* Lachimia, *Tied Aid and Development Aid Procurement*; Clay, Geddes and Natali, *Untying Aid: Is It Working?*; Serra, 'The Practice of Tying Development Aid'.

[m]ost funding for U.S. food aid is authorized under the Food for Peace Act[73] and cannot be used to purchase foreign-grown food. Funding under the act, approximately $2 billion per year, is restricted to the purchase of U.S.-grown agricultural commodities.[74]

Conditional contributions currently do not represent the majority of financing methods. Nevertheless, while the link between financing and the interests of the financing state in creating commercial opportunities for national businesses is not always explicit and declared, it often plays a pivotal role in award decisions. For instance, the majority of formally untied aid contracts from bilateral agencies goes to donor country firms. OECD data regarding donors who chose to submit information on their aid show that in 2007 62 per cent of the contracts open to competitive tenders were awarded to firms from the donor country.[75] From these data, OECD analysts have also inferred that if this is the percentage for competitive tenders, an even higher proportion of all contracts, including those that are not reported and that follow restricted procedures, are awarded within the donor country.[76]

Annual reports from the WB from 2000 until 2015 provide data on the share of contracts financed by the WB and awarded to suppliers from OECD countries (fourteen countries, which include all the top financiers to the WB) and from non-OECD countries (the remaining 181 countries). In 2000, suppliers from OECD countries got a total amount of contract awards of $2,236,892,274 (about 27.1 per cent), while non-OECD countries received a total of $5,993,172,770 (about 72.8 per cent). Fifteen years later, in 2015, OECD countries got a total amount of contract awards of $2,242,587,431 (about 27.3 per cent), and non-OECD countries a total of $5,963,278,210 (about 72.6 per cent).[77] Not only do these data show the scarce variation over more than a decade in the distribution of the resources, but more significantly they show an uneven distribution of resources resulting from contract awards: OECD countries, despite only

---

[73] United States, Food for Peace Act [ref. N&RL-US].

[74] US GAO, *International Food Assistance, Local and Regional Procurement*, p. 7 [ref. REP]. On the close oversight that the American Congress exercises on the way in which multilateral development banks spend the resources provided by the United States see Nelson, *Multilateral Banks: Overview and Issues for Congress.* And on the same topic: VV. AA., *Multilateral Development Bank Procurement.*

[75] Clay, Geddes and Natali, *Untying Aid: Is It Working?*   [76] *Ibid.*

[77] Data from WB, 'OECD & Non-OECD Suppliers Totals 2000–2015', available at http://web.worldbank.org/WBSITE/EXTERNAL/PROJECTS/PROCUREMENT/0,,contentMDK:20251613~pagePK:84269~piPK:84286~theSitePK:84266,00.html (last access: January 2018).

representing 7 per cent of all countries, get about one-third of the resources through contracts awarded to their suppliers consequent to the implementation of WB projects. These data should also be read in conjunction with the statistics on the share of contracts awarded to non-OECD countries, where China and India play a dominant role over all other countries (even OECD ones). A share of 72.6–72.8 per cent of contracts was awarded to suppliers from these two countries.[78]

Moreover, these cumulative data are confirmed when analyzing data by country. In 2014, among the first thirteen countries supplying services, goods and works to WB projects, six were OECD countries (the United Kingdom, Turkey, Spain, Germany, Italy and France) and the first three in the list strong growing economies (China, India and Brazil).[79] Indeed, if one looks at the trends over the long run, for instance in the period 2000–2014, it is evident that, while OECD countries (the United Kingdom, Germany, Italy and France) are constantly among the top suppliers – even with some variations in their positions in the list – and the strong growing economies, such as China, India and Brazil, are usually the top suppliers, awards to suppliers from other countries vary depending on the historical contingencies and the cumulative impact of single development projects.[80] On one hand, it appears that the presence of OECD countries in the list of top suppliers is linked to 'permanent reasons', such as the circumstance that they are among the main financiers of the organization. On the other, the variable presence of other non-OECD countries that are not among the financing states seems justified mainly by external and internal policy considerations of the organization, which can also be transitory.

More generally, although very few empirical studies have dealt specifically with the purchase of goods, services and works by international organizations, the literature on official development assistance (ODA) stresses the link between the motivations behind ODA and the pursuit of financing states' interests.[81]

---

[78] Data from WB, 'Supplier Totals by Country 2000–2015', available at http://web.worldbank .org/WBSITE/EXTERNAL/PROJECTS/PROCUREMENT/0,contentMDK:20251613~ pagePK:84269~piPK:84286~theSitePK:84266,00.html (last access: January 2018).
[79] *Ibid.* [80] *Ibid.*
[81] See, for instance, Alesina and Dollar, 'Who Gives Foreign Aid to Whom and Why?'; Charnoz and Severino, *L'aide publique au développement*, pp. 37–51; Degnbol-Martinussen and Engberg-Pedersen, *Aid: Understanding International Development Cooperation*; Morrissey, 'The Mixing of Aid and Trade Policies'; Riddell, *Does Foreign Aid Really Work?*, pp. 91–162.

The prospect of an economic return in terms of contract awards often influences states' decisions on future contributions, and even the quest for administrative reform. It is paradigmatic that, in 1993, during a critical phase in the relationships between the US government and the organizations of the UN system, the USGAO submitted a report to the US Senate in which account was given of the resources the United States donated to the largest development banks, the commercial opportunities for US companies arising from them, and the proposals, to be implemented internally but also within organizations, to improve the ratio between these two elements.[82] The report reveals that between 1989 and 1994 American businesses were the primary source of goods and services in the projects of major financial institutions. US suppliers were in first place (with about 8 per cent or $1.35 billion per year) as preferred contractors for the indirect procurement contracts of the WB; again in first place (at about 20 per cent or $500 billion a year) for procurement in the IDB's projects, compared to an average of 5 per cent for France, Germany, Japan and the United Kingdom; in second place (at 7 per cent or $204 billion per year), after Japanese companies (with about 10 per cent), in awards of contracts sponsored by the ADB; and in third place (with a share of 11 per cent) after German (17 per cent) and Italian (15 per cent) companies, in the EBRD.[83] Moreover, these data reflect US export numbers to developing countries. For example, during the period considered, US companies' share of WB procurements was one and a half times greater than that of Japanese suppliers. Similarly, during the same period, total exports of US businesses to developing countries who were members of the WB were one and a half times greater than Japanese exports to these same countries.[84]

Despite this, the same report notes the disadvantages, from the US perspective, of an increase in the number of contracts awarded to local suppliers and complains of a series of obstacles that prevent US businesses from competing in projects financed by development banks. These include a lack of complete and timely information on business opportunities; the difficulty of marketing in countries where procurement is carried out, and thus of influencing the competent authorities in making their award decision; the unfamiliarity of US businesses with development banks' procurement procedures; and a general perception that the contractor selection process sponsored by

---

[82] US GAO, *Multilateral Development Banks* [ref. REP].   [83] *Ibid.*, p. 7.   [84] *Ibid.*, p. 10.

financial institutions and implemented by recipient states was not truly open and competitive.[85]

Thus, in the interplay among different interests underlying international organization procurement, it is worth noticing that competition (where the alternative is a preference for local suppliers), transparency of administrative action and publicity of business opportunities, more than being the outcome of a policy option, serve the objective of financing states to have an economic return for their businesses. The interest in supporting these principles is different from the, apparently similar, interest that international administrations may have. Financing states do not require impartiality and competition at all costs; instead, they want to avoid the partiality of national administrations acting in favour of other businesses to the detriment of theirs. The United States may not have complained of the deficiency of these features (competition, transparency etc.) if it had not feared a developing tendency to favour local businesses.[86] The difference lies in the positions that international administrations and financing states choose to favour within such dynamics. The former are expected to be impartial and independent entities that do not include nationality among the criteria for evaluating business partners, and if nationality is taken into account it is because it contributes to achieving general institutional objectives. The latter, the financing states, tend to safeguard the interests of their own businesses and often have the express or implied goal of ensuring a profit margin for national suppliers.

Nevertheless, the interests of international administrations and financing states can sometimes coincide, bringing more stringent rules on competition and its instrumental principles. When some states explicitly or implicitly condition their contributions on an economic return in terms of contract awards and/or on the adoption of certain procedural parameters, then the international organization considers it more cost-effective, or even necessary, to adopt rules and procedures that favour these demands. In this sense, principles such as competition, transparency, reason-giving, publicity and access to documents, found in the indirect procurement rules of financial institutions,[87] are protected to a greater extent because they serve the purpose of satisfying the needs of financing states, which also have the approval and support of the international organization. In direct procurement, they are only developed

---

[85] *Ibid.*, p. 15.   [86] *Ibid.*, pp. 11–13. Also see Babb, *Behind the Development Banks.*
[87] See Chapter 4.

and protected when, as US policy has shown in the past, the financing state makes them a condition for its membership of the organization itself or for future contributions. Therefore the requirements on competition, transparency and publicity are generated and reinforced only when (and to the extent that) there is an overlapping of the interests of the international organization with those of the financing states.

The substance and interaction of the interests of financing states change, however, once contracts are signed. Of the two objectives that guide financing states during the contractor selection phase – the proper management of resources and an economic return in the form of a contract award – the second vanishes when the contract is awarded. In the procedural phase, the interest in proper management is limited precisely by the interest in obtaining contracts for national enterprises, while after the award this limitation ceases to exist. The objective of non-wasteful management, and thus of a contract execution that meets the administration's needs as much as possible, becomes paramount, regardless of whether contracts are signed directly by the organization or are only financed by it. Thus, the interests of financing states align with and strengthen those of the international organization. Hence, on the one hand financing states do not have any interest in mitigating the authoritative nature of the contract, nor in opposing its functionalization in the public interest when direct procurement is involved. On the other hand, they support a more balanced distribution of rights and obligations among the parties (national administrations vs. private businesses) and the ability of private parties to defend their contractual rights in the case of indirect procurement.[88]

8.4.3 Recipient States, Their Businesses and Their Citizens

Recipient states bring into the procurement dynamic a third set of interests. First of all, as representatives of the needs of their citizens, they are interested in the final result of the procurement, for example, development aid, aid during emergency situations, the construction of new infrastructure, etc.

Second, by protecting the interests of certain categories of businesses, they seek to turn the business opportunities created by procurement to the advantage of national suppliers. This interest is opposite to that of financing states, but cannot be supported by a 'strategic threat' equivalent

---

[88] See Chapter 5.

to cutting contributions, as financing states can make. Nevertheless, especially in indirect procurement, they support the general values pursued by organizations, and, more importantly, the best value for money that contracts signed with local businesses can guarantee, for example, through lower operating, labour and transport costs.

Setting aside the first of the two objectives, an analysis of which involves political considerations on the expediency of programmes more than the methods used to implement them, it is worthwhile to examine the second objective and its concrete impact, especially in cases of direct procurement for external purposes,[89] and indirect procurement where the state is responsible for execution.

Data collected from 1989 to 1994 on multilateral development banks (when there was still a prevalence of US suppliers as contractors in contracts financed by financial institutions) reveal for the first time a reversal of the trend of previous years:

> [w]hile most foreign procurement has come from suppliers in industrialized countries, suppliers from developing countries have increasingly been effective in winning contracts.[90]

During this period, businesses registered in recipient countries were awarded about 51 per cent of the contracts of the WB, the IDB and the ADB, with most of the contracts for the execution of works. Seven of the countries financed by the WB (India, China, Mexico, Brazil, Indonesia, South Korea and Argentina) received, in the form of contracts, almost one-third of the resources of the WB, while other developing countries were receiving about 19 per cent.[91]

Financial institutions attribute the change to three factors: the development and growth of the production capacity of these countries; the increasing presence of multinational companies registered in these countries; and the preference granted to local businesses in accordance with special regulations. In reality, the final one seems to be the least important justification. In the ADB and IDB only 3 per cent of the total value of contracts was awarded through preferential methods, while the

---

[89] Indeed, in procurement for external purposes the beneficiary states feature in the procurement dynamics more than they do in procurement for internal purpose. This latter type of procurement is often carried out where the organizations have their headquarters (because it mostly serves the headquarters' needs), which is often in developed countries. Thus it involves more companies from financing states.

[90] US GAO, *Multilateral Development Banks* [ref. REP], p. 14.   [91] *Ibid.*, p. 13.

percentage rises to 11 per cent in the WB.[92] Conversely, the presence of multinationals with local headquarters seem to be a prevailing factor, particularly for the supply of goods and services, while increased production capacity seems to explain most of the contracts for the construction of infrastructure, because, as already noted, there is better value for money in these cases.

Moreover, while the state has the option of making preferential choices in indirect procurement through financial institutions, the same is not true for direct procurement by organizations, which tend to consider best value for money in the strict sense, leaving little room for other types of interests. This consideration is supported not only by the general data provided in the previous section, but more specifically by data on food subsidies. The supply of foodstuffs is one of the largest procurement sectors for developing countries, yet this is in large part accomplished through supplies from donor countries. In a 2009 report, the Director of the International Affairs and Trade Team of the US House of Representatives stated not only that the United States was the world's largest supplier of food aid to developing countries, but also that

> [t]he large majority of U.S. food assistance is for U.S.-grown commodities purchased competitively in the United States and shipped to recipient countries on U.S.-flag carriers.[93]

Thus, even with all the different interests at play, considerations of financial opportunity, particularly in the past, have often led international administrations to favour the interests and positions of financing states in procurement rule making and practices, with the result that the principles that govern the contracts of international organizations have been modulated and adapted mainly to these needs. In addition, reasons of economic convenience, and to some extent reference to the institutional mission of certain organizations, have under certain limited circumstances led to preferential provisions for local suppliers and grounded the provisions that allowed exceptions to the principle of competition.

---

[92] *Ibid.*, p. 11.
[93] US GAO, *International Food Assistance, Local and Regional Procurement*, p. 7 [ref. REP].

9

Conclusions

Global Administrative Law for Procurement of International Organizations: Development and Limits

9.1 The Questions

At the beginning of this work two sets of questions were posed. The first regarded the relationship between international organizations and private subjects. Given that the expanding functions of international organizations and the increase in their activities have multiplied the relationships between organizations and private subjects, the questions related to how these relationships were configured in terms of the exercise of public authority and the recognition of rights to individuals and companies. The second set of questions related to the reasons explaining the phenomenon of the expansion of private subjects' rights vis-à-vis international organizations, as well its limits. These questions led us to investigate various aspects of procurement by international organizations. The analysis included the identification of which principles guide international organizations when selecting a vendor; how these principles work in practice; whether and to what extent they entail new rights for private subjects vis-à-vis international organizations; to what extent the procurement law developed by international organizations has an impact on the regulatory autonomy of beneficiary states both in the vendor selection phase and in contract execution; whether international organizations' procurement contracts allocate rights and obligations to the contracting parties in a balanced way; in terms of the interplay of interests, how the specific features of the governance and implementation of the procurement process and procurement contracts of international organizations can be explained; and, finally, if this emerging legal framework helps to enhance the legitimacy of international organizations.

9.2 Between Past and Future: Multipolarity as the Source of Global Administrative Law for Procurement

In 1962, Jenks envisaged the development of an international administrative law that would go beyond governing relationships between the organization and its officials to apply to relationships between international administrations and third parties as well. However, the traditional concept of national administrative law was built on the dualism of systems by virtue of which there is a domestic law, that of the state, and an international law, that among states. The subjects of domestic law were individuals; the subjects of international law were states.[1] Thus, it was felt that, on one hand, international law could not directly affect the legal rights of the citizens of a state and, on the other hand, that administrative law, as such, would govern and define *only* these rights (i.e. the rights emerging from the relationship with domestic public bodies). Based on these premises, two subsequent formulations of the concept of administrative law were developed. As the first international administrative unions arose,[2] the body of laws produced by these organizations was denoted as international administrative law. It was above all organizational in nature, governing primarily structure and the decision-making mechanisms within the unions. It was a law produced by 'an association of states' – in this sense international – and its content was administrative in nature.[3]

With the creation of the League of Nations, this first concept was joined by another. The League of Nations had its own Secretariat, comprised of officials – international civil servants – who according to the Drummond model did not represent states, but at least on a formal level were bound solely to the organization they served. Appearing for the first time was the idea of a direct relationship between international administrations and private subjects, and of an international administrative law that, unlike administrative international law, was a body of laws, produced by the organization and governing an internal relationship between the organization and private parties (its officials).[4] With the establishment of the United Nations, the rights recognized by this law became protectable before an *ad hoc* judge, the UN Administrative

---

[1] Fusinato, *Di una parte alquanto trascurata del diritto internazionale*, also quoted in Battini, 'International Organizations and Private Subjects'.

[2] On international unions see Rapisardi-Mirabelli, 'Théorie générale des unions internationales'.

[3] Jenks, *The Proper Law*.

[4] In general, on the law governing civil service see Villalpando, 'The Law of the International Civil Service'.

Tribunal. This administrative law has at least three characteristics. First of all, it is an internal law, as it refers to a relationship between the organization and its officials.[5] In addition, although the private party is not subject to this law through the ties of citizenship and membership in a state legal system, she/he is subject to it by virtue of internal membership ties. The official is part of the internal system of the organization.[6] Finally, this administrative law governs both the selection of the official and the service relationship.

Achieving what Jenks had predicted decades ago, contemporary organizations have developed a third line of administrative law related to the procurement designed to carry out their institutional mission. Nevertheless, unlike what he anticipated, this type of administrative law is built on a more complex dimension than the simple relationship between an international organization and a private subject. At the beginning of this analysis, two types of procurement carried out by organizations were identified.[7] Based on certain fixed aspects encompassed within the term *procurement* by international organizations – that is nature and functions – and combining five variable aspects – purpose, modalities of execution, regulation, accountability and contract – a distinction was drawn between direct procurement and indirect procurement.

The combination of fixed and variable aspects shows that direct and indirect procurement differ in one fundamental way: the relationship between public power and private subjects. In direct procurement, the relationship is bilateral: international organization–private subject. On the other hand, in indirect procurement the relationship is trilateral: international organization–state–private subject, with the second accountable to the first also by virtue of the initiative of the third.[8] But it should be added that, even when the relationship is formally bilateral, states as members of organizations play a fundamental role in both determining the rules and practices of the vendor selection phase and the contractual phase.

The administrative law that governs international organizations' procurement is thus constructed around a multipolarity of actors and a relative multipolarity of interests.[9] It is a *global* administrative law. It

[5] Battini, 'International Organizations and Private Subjects'.   [6] *Ibid.*   [7] See Chapter 2.
[8] Reference here is to the main variants of indirect procurement, leaving aside indirect procurement carried out by other organizations and indirect procurement carried out by private parties.
[9] In particular, on how the interaction between these interests can be crucial for the evolution of administrative law see Benvenisti, 'The Interplay between Actors as a Determinant of the Evolution of Administrative Law in International Institutions'.

encompasses and governs the interactions of a number of levels of governance and is built around a notion of public interest that not only goes beyond the monolithic concept of unitary public interest – long abandoned with theories of pluralism in administrative law – but has expanded beyond the purely governmental dimension: not a public interest, but many and also conflicting public interests, which contemporaneously belong to a number of domestic spheres and to the international sphere. Moreover, the public nature of these public interests is diverse and the dividing line between public and private becomes blurred: these interests are held by various kinds of institutional public subjects, such as the state and international organizations, but also by private subjects, who as taxpayers or contractual parties find themselves involved in direct or indirect relationships with international administrations and national administrations financed by international organizations.

In this sense, it also changes the traditional concept of administrative discretion as a weighting of a primary interest against secondary ones, according to a hierarchy of objectives defined at the political level. The discretion of international public administrations relies completely on weighing interests, all of which are essential, at least in theory. Within an international organization the competing interests belong to states (or to private subjects who have the chance of being represented and safeguarded by states),[10] thus becoming essential interests like those of the international administration itself. But the result is that the international administrations' discretionary power is essentially guided by the states and by how much weight the states intend to place on representing these interests.

The interplay of these political and economic interests – public and private, national and supranational – is what creates, but also delimits, a body of laws drawn up by the organizations. These laws create procedural obligations for international organizations and national administrations (financed by the international organization) when selecting private contractors and shape the corresponding rights of private parties. It is a body of laws with a significant procedural content. Moreover, the interplay of public interests attributable to the different levels of government affect the contractual

---

[10] Reference here is made to big and influential economic private actors whose interests, as explained in Chapters 5 and 7, have the chance of being supported, especially during the contract selection phase, by the representative of the state they belong to.

relationship with the private party, justifying the adoption of rules designed by the administration for the administration.

9.3 Proceduralization and New Rights: The Functionalization of Conflicting Interests and Its Limits

Direct procurement of international organizations follows a procedural sequence: the phase of identifying procurement needs, which takes place entirely within the administration, is followed by a phase of soliciting bids, evaluating them, and finally awarding and entering into the contract. In its salient features, the structure of the procedure is similar to the procedure used in the public contracts of states.[11] Similarly, the statement of general principles echoes the national guidelines for state contracts: cost-effectiveness, impartiality and competition.[12]

In the history of organizations, there has been a gradual proceduralization of the decision-making process that has a direct impact on private parties (evaluation of bids, award, contract etc.). Previously, there was a non-proceduralized activity based on the criteria of freedom of contract.[13] On one hand, proceduralization stems the power of the international organization, setting the boundaries of its legitimate action, and on the other it gives private parties parallel rights vis-à-vis international organization.

This proceduralization has, however, some specificities. The development of a procedure and the configuration of rights for private parties have historically been achieved not so much, as in national legal systems, by shifting the modalities of exercising administrative power from unilateral and autocratic patterns to consensual ones, but rather through a particular interplay of the economic and political interests held by states who are members of organizations.[14] Democratic proceduralization, if we can define it thus, is not – or is not merely – the goal and the result of a shifting concept of the relationship between the administration and

---

[11] See Chapter 4.   [12] See Chapters 4 and 8.
[13] See Chapter 3. On proceduralization in international organizations see von Bernstorff, 'Procedures of Decision-Making and the Role of Law in International Organizations'; Casini and Kingsbury, 'Global Administrative Law Dimensions of International Organizations'. More generally, on proceduralization in the global context see Cassese, *Oltre lo Stato*, p. 120 *et seq.*; Kingsbury, Krisch and Stewart, 'The Emergence of Global Administrative Law'; von Bogdandy, 'Legitimacy of International Economic Governance'; Della Cananea, 'The EU and the WTO: A "Relational" Analysis'.
[14] See Chapter 3.

private parties, but is primarily the instrument required to assert state interests. In this case, institutions' need for legitimacy, which has often been referred to as one of the reasons for proceduralization, does not fully encompass the deeper reasons for the phenomenon.

Moreover, proceduralization and the recognition of new rights mimic national legal systems. Nevertheless, the adoption of principles similar to those that govern the procurement of states is not a legal transplant with the characteristics that scholars have traditionally observed.[15] Indeed, these principles have a substance, a mutual equilibrium, and a concrete application different from the state sphere, as they are tied to the peculiar institutional context and the various interests at play in the global arena.[16] Apart from general statements, the rules that govern relationships between the international organizations and private subjects, the relative practices and the guarantees of implementation that surround these relationships[17] are the result of different priorities among principles compared to what occurs at the national level.

This option can be explained by considering the interaction between public and private interests. In the European or global system of national procurement contracts (e.g. European Procurement Directive and the GPA), the principles of cost-effectiveness and impartiality serve the primary objective of competition, with the consequent multiplication and strengthening of the rights of individuals before the administration. This does not occur in direct procurement of international organizations. When scrutinized through a comparative analysis, the three principal elements that characterize the relationship between the administration and private parties in this sector in terms of individual rights, that is competition, transparency and accountability to private parties, prove to have limited implementation, although they represent a significant innovation in the history of international organizations. Limited forms of competition, scanty publicity, minimal reason-giving requirements and appeals of a primarily administrative nature demonstrate that, while the relationship between the administration and private parties has been proceduralized, it remains characterized by the predominance of public power's determinations over those of private parties. Thus, the need for cost-effectiveness and impartiality – with the latter intended as the administration's defence against itself, i.e. its officials – prevails over the need for competition and impartiality, intended as equal treatment of private subjects in

---

[15] See Chapter 8. [16] See Chapter 4. [17] See Chapter 8.

their relationships with the administration. That is, the interplay of needs served produces the opposite result from national procurement: competition and impartiality for purposes of economy and cost-effectiveness, and not, as in national procurement, impartiality for purposes of competition. The one exception to this structure is direct procurement of European institutions, which instead follows a more protective approach towards private parties' rights and shows an interaction of the principles more similar to that of national public procurement.

This hierarchy among principles can be explained on the grounds of the different interests are held by international organizations, by financing states and their citizens and, in the case of indirect procurement for external purposes, by recipient states and their citizens.

The interests of international organizations are based on four circumstances. The first is that the very existence of the organizations depends on financing from certain states. The second is that, due to budget constraints, the international administration has no sufficient incentives to engage in virtuous management. The third is that the system of internal controls, while more developed and detailed than accountability to private parties, has certain weaknesses that inhibit its full effectiveness.[18] The fourth is that none of these organizations, except for the European Union, includes competition among its institutional objectives.

The interests of financing states are based on two other needs. One need, which we may consider a minimum, is that the resources granted are not wasted or poorly managed. An additional objective is to use those resources to create business opportunities for companies (private subjects) and therefore to guarantee an internal economic return from the financing disbursed to international organizations (which can also take the express form of conditional financing).[19] Finally, the interests of recipient states include not only the obvious one of being able to enjoy the final result of procurement, but also to see contracts awarded to domestic companies.

The interaction and balancing of these three categories of interests circumscribes the private subjects' legal sphere and the extent of their rights vis-à-vis the international organization, creating a body of administrative rules characterized by the predominance of public international component. The interests of financing states, combined with the

[18] See Chapter 7.   [19] See Chapter 8.

financing needs of international organizations and, to a more limited extent, of financed states, have contributed to a recognition of rights that extends only as far as necessary to achieve these interests, or to achieve certain political objectives. Moreover, this interpretation also explains the gradual process of proceduralization and the shift towards more transparency. Indeed, this began when various political motivations began to arise in financing countries and the interests of recipient countries began to emerge after decolonization.[20]

Some different considerations apply for indirect procurement of international organizations. Here as well, the procedure, carried out by national administrations but based on the guidelines of international organizations, replicates the procedure for domestic public procurement subject to national, European or supranational law. The stated principles are again those of competition, impartiality and cost-effectiveness, but unlike direct procurement, their relative weight is more consistent with the approach of individual rights-based administrative law. Open competition, indicated as the primary manner of selecting contractors, publicity, reason-giving bolstered by the mechanism of subsidiarity among levels of government,[21] the ability to file complaints against the actions of national administrations, and the right to file fraud and corruption charges against national administrations directly before the international organization,[22] is justified by a different framework of interests than what emerges in direct procurement.

The international organization's primary objective is to ensure that the state uses the financing for the purpose for which it was granted – implementation of the project or programme-, that the resources are not wasted through bad management by national administrations. This objective is achieved through competition, transparency and accountability of institutions to each other and to the vendors that participate in the tender procedures. By giving private subjects these tools to hold national administrations accountable, international organizations can not only exercise inter-institutional control over national administrations, but also an indirect control that is multiplied by all private subjects who enter into a relationship with the national administration and can challenge its decisions. Thus, in pursuing its own institutional interest, the international organization achieves another objective: broadening the legal rights of private parties.

---

[20] See Chapter 3. [21] See Chapter 4. [22] See Chapter 7.

Financing states encourage this dynamic through market considerations that in part replicate those involved in direct procurement. The primary interest is to ensure that contracts are awarded to their companies and competition is the best way to achieve this if we consider that the large multinationals incorporated in these states are favoured in market transactions.

On the other hand, recipient states have strong opposing interests. In addition to the goal of obtaining the financing for a project, which is a political aspect of the operation and does not directly relate to procurement, there is the goal of ensuring that contracts are awarded to local companies. In these cases, however, unlike direct procurement, financing states can invoke the institutional objectives of the international organizations and concrete advantages in the market. These consist, in particular, of the territorial proximity of national companies to the recipients of the services, goods and works provided and of the savings that can follow in terms of operating costs, transport and labour. This advantage becomes even greater because it coincides with the international organizations' interest in cost-effectiveness and with their institutional objectives. Under these specific circumstances, this can create a balancing of interests that favours the recipient states and translates into the possibility of allowing domestic preference, notwithstanding the principle of competition.

9.4 Contracts for Organizations: Privileges and Public–Private Regulatory Hybridization

Whether it involves direct or indirect procurement, the contract that concludes the vendor selection process is the result of an administrative procedure in which the relationship between the administration and the private party is determined by a particular configuration of interests. Moreover, this configuration is also crucial to the contract itself, and explains its main clauses and their impact on the freedom of contract of the private parties and the recipient states.

Compared to the common law contracts entered into by private parties, contracts concluded by international organizations in direct procurement shaped as adhesion contracts. International organizations unilaterally set the terms and general conditions that are to govern the relationship. The adhesion nature of these provisions is bolstered by the circumstance that the contract is integrated in the administrative procedure, becoming a part of it: by attaching the contract to the call for tenders, as occurs for most international organizations, acceptance of such becomes either an indispensable condition for participating in the tender or one of the elements used to evaluate the offer.

Moreover, several contractual provisions serve the public and international nature of one of the two contracting parties. Clauses on terminating the contract are characterized by an absence of reciprocity and serve the interests of the organization, with no guarantees of compensation, justification and advance notice for the private party. Subcontracting conditions and procedures that are imposed on private parties are more stringent than those normally found in contracts between national administrations and private parties; while private parties' provisions on liability regard only private parties' liability towards the international organization;[23] encompass both internal and external duties. But, above all, international organizations can invoke immunity from jurisdiction, albeit within the limits of a functional interpretation, and absolute immunity from execution.[24]

Compared to a contract between private parties with equal standing, international organizations' contracts contain extraordinary clauses that alter the contractual balance from the start to functionalize it to the administration's public and international interest. Moreover, from this standpoint there is also a marked difference between these contracts and those of national administrations, where immunity from execution, has been in many respects abandoned. But it remains a legacy in international organizations, still motivated by a lack of territory over which sovereignty may be exercised, the paucity of assets owned and above all by the need for continuity in exercising functions.

In addition to being shaped almost as adhesion contracts, the contracts of international organizations have another specific feature. This relates to the legal context that governs the execution of the contract, that is the law applicable to the relationship. Once again, because of their status as an international public entity, the law applicable to organizations is not a unitary and homogenous body of norms based on a single legal system, but rather the result of a regulatory hybridization that relies on arbitrators for any concrete determination.

The hybridization is caused by the coexistence of different legal sources governing the contractual relationship. Contractual clauses whose essential aspects are formulated by the organization are the primary source of regulation. Through these clauses, and justified by the

[23] See Chapter 5.   [24] See Chapter 7.

international nature of the organization, international treaty law is also applicable to the contract between the international organization and a private party and, hence, although traditionally conceived as an instrument governing relationships between states, it becomes also an instrument governing a public–private relationship, that between the organization and the private contractor. Finally, and residually, the principles of international commercial law apply. These are either independently identified by the arbitrator or, if the contract refers to them, they may be found in the Model Law of international organizations other than the one that entered into the contract, for example UNCITRAL. Thus, the multipolarity of actors (international organizations, states, private subjects) leads to a hybridization of rules.[25]

Furthermore, the unilateral determination of contractual provisions and the hybridization of the applicable law result in another specific feature of the contractual relationship: they undermine the clear separation between public law and private law spheres. The extraordinary clauses included in the contract are conceived principally by and for the administration and are added as a constituent element of an administrative procedure. In addition, they are designed with the public interest in mind: they govern a contractual relationship that has the ultimate goal of allowing the organization to perform a public service mission. From this point of view these clauses have an administrative nature, despite the fact they are found in a contract. Treaty norms on the immunity of international organizations, as well as all the other international treaties' provisions applicable by virtue of the fact that one of the two contracting parties is an international organization, are part of international public law. Finally, the rules of commercial contracts between private parties often referred to as 'general principles of international private (or commercial) law' are in fact common law. The legal regime applicable to the contracts of international organizations is the result of a mixture of public law and private law provisions and in certain ways differs from the solution adopted – at least in principle – in many civil law systems, where administrative law and private law are supposed to govern, respectively, the vendor selection phase and the contract.

---

[25] See Cafaggi, 'New Foundations of Transnational Private Regulation', p. 44 et seq.; Casini, 'Public Law and Private Law beyond the State'; Moellers, 'Transnational Governance without a Public Law'; Börzel and Risse, 'Public-Private Partnerships'; Knill and Lehmkuhl, 'Governance and Globalization: Conceptualizing the Role of Public and Private Actors', p. 92 et seq.; Ruffert (ed.), The Public-Private Law Divide; Dreifuss, 'L'immixtion du droit privé dans les contrats administratifs'.

These characteristics are also consistent with the interplay of interests that underlie the contract. This interplay can be interpreted as a continuation of the dynamics that, as we have seen, determine the scope of private party's rights during the pre-contractual phase. Despite the fact that in direct procurement the contractual relationship is between international organizations and private parties, this relationship must be interpreted in the light of the multipolarity discussed above.

Once the contract is concluded, one of the principal interests of the financing states – that is, to see the contract awarded to their vendors – ceases to exist. By awarding the contract to a certain vendor, this interest may or may not have been met, but regardless of the result, it is no longer relevant during the contract execution phase. What remains is the interest that the resources conferred through that contract are not wasted due to improper contractual execution by the private party. Along with this interest is the international organization's interest in being the recipient of contract performance. The synergy of these interests, when they are not countered by other types of represented interests, ensures that the contractual relationship retains the signs of the traditional privileges of the administration vis-à-vis private parties, creates a corresponding limitation on the freedom of contract of private parties and allows the applicability of those norms that recognize and reinforce the administrative privilege and limit private parties' freedom, such as the international treaty laws on immunity. This explains the particular hybridization of public and private spheres. Furthermore, this configuration of interests, where the financing states' interest in the award ceases to exist, also explains why, unlike in the pre-contractual phase, historically there has been no development towards expanding protections for private parties within the contract.

In indirect procurement, multipolarity does not limit the private party's freedom of contract so much as result in international organizations restricting the freedom of contract of states. In direct procurement, organizations make participation in tenders conditional on acceptance of unilaterally defined clauses. Similarly, in indirect procurement, international organizations make financing to the states conditional on the adoption of various contractual clauses that the organization has unilaterally drafted and included in the contract between the recipient state and a private party. In this sense, an additional form of hybridization occurs, which is different from that described for direct procurement: the source of regulation is an international public administration, the regulation is addressed to a state and a private subject, but the subject of regulation is not an administrative procedure, but a contractual relationship that is typically based on private law.

The clauses required by international organizations generally include a fair distribution of contractual rights and obligations between the national administration and the private party, a request for performance guarantees from the private party, a provision that the private party is liable for compensation and the presence of a neutral arbitrator in the event of disputes. Thus, these are not extraordinary clauses that go beyond normal contractual practice between private parties, but rather, from the international organization's perspective, minimum provisions that ensure that the resources granted are not squandered by national administrations and private parties during contract execution.

This interest of the international organization coincides with that of the financing states and is not limited by the opposing interests of the recipient states. It has been noted that, during the pre-contractual phase, recipient states have the objective of obtaining financing and, at the same time, the goal of ensuring that contracts are awarded to their businesses. Based on this second objective, guidelines allow for the application of the domestic preference principle in tender evaluation. Nevertheless, once the contract has been awarded, the second of these objectives loses significance, while the first remains: the national administration has an interest in ensuring that the international organization does not withdraw the financing granted, and thus in complying with the conditions the international organization imposes even when they affect its freedom of contract.

From the perspective of private parties, making indirect procurement serve these interests has the effect of insuring the private party against the presence of extraordinary clauses imposed by the national administration. In fact, the organization tends to expand the legal sphere of the private party by containing and making accountable the contractual power of the national administration and its conduct during contract execution.

Finally, one last and more general consideration. In indirect procurement, the national administration cedes not only a portion of its administrative sovereignty, intended as the ability to govern its own non-contractual relationships with private parties, but also its contractual sovereignty, that is the autonomy to govern its own contractual relationships with private parties. This observation requires us to expand the concept of globalization of contracts that various scholars have delineated:[26] the rules produced by international organizations for international administrations do not apply solely to the tender procedure, but go beyond this to govern the contract as well.

9.5 Implications for the Legitimacy of International Organizations

Finally, I come to the legitimacy issue to assess whether, how and to what extent the increase in procurement, and the emergence of the regulatory and adjudicatory activity connected to it, has contributed, or can contribute to enhance the legitimacy of international organizations. This assessment requires, first, an acknowledgement that international organizations have a problem of legitimacy.[27] Since the end of the Cold War, the emergence of global problems has progressively made clear the inadequacy of individual state action to solve such problems and the necessity for a form of global governance. Complemented by other factors, this brought fundamental changes to international organizations and their actual functioning. Not only have new international organizations been established, but existing ones have also grown in terms of their administrative structures, functions and activities affecting individuals. These developments have been regarded as an opportunity for both institutional growth and new legal achievements, but also for the first time posed a problem of the legitimacy of international institutions. As several scholars have noted, the issue of the legitimacy of international

---

[26] See Chapter 2.

[27] Historically, the legitimacy of international organizations has received only cursory attention in the literature. However, the growth in the number and functions of organizations, as well as their increasing impact on individuals, have brought many scholars to deal with this issue. On the basic definition of the legitimacy of public powers see Beetham, 'Legitimacy'; id., The Legitimation of Power; and on the Weberian notion of legitimacy, see Bendix, Max Weber; Lipset, The Political Man. For an overview of the issue of legitimacy at the international level and that of international organizations see Franck, The Power of Legitimacy among Nations; Coicaud and Heiskanen (eds.), The Legitimacy of International Organizations; Zaum (ed.), Legitimating International Organizations; id., 'International Organizations, Legitimacy, and Legitimation'; id.,'Legitimacy'; Schneider, 'The Challenged Legitimacy of International Organisations'. On the legitimacy of specific international organizations see Barnett, 'Bringing in the New World Order, Liberalism, Legitimacy and the United Nations'; Schachter, 'Alf Ross Memorial Lecture'; Stahn, 'Accountability and Legitimacy in Practice'; id. 'Governance beyond the State'; von Bogdandy, 'Legitimacy of International Economic Governance'; von Bogdandy and Venzke, 'International Judicial Institutions'. As for legitimacy within the GAL perspective, see inter alia Black, 'Constructing and Contesting'; Boisson de Chazournes, 'Changing Roles of International Organizations'.

organizations has attracted attention only recently, as traditionally this issue was at the centre of modern political and social philosophy, but mainly with regard to the state apparatus and the relationships between the state and civil society or individual citizens. Two main reasons have been identified for this traditional trend. First, international institutions lacked substantive powers, such as legislative powers. In the initial stage of these organizations, the main problem was instead to ensure the effectiveness of their activities. Second, as these organizations are based on treaties, their legitimacy was implied and ensured by the explicit consent of the member states to the very existence of the organization. Once these two reasons progressively lost validity, the problem of legitimacy has emerged. They have lost validity because, as mentioned earlier, international organizations are acquiring a more and more non-fungible role in terms of addressing global problems and their activity is becoming at least as influential and decisive as that of states. Furthermore, as a consequence, they are expanding their activities and, eventually, their activities and decisions start to directly or indirectly affect private persons and companies.

Second, the problem of legitimacy of international organizations shows several specificities compared to that of states. The legitimacy of states has traditionally been framed by political and social philosophy within two theories, i.e. the continental enlightenment approach and the Anglo-American liberal approach.[28] Continental enlightenment philosophy has regarded legitimacy as the set of conditions under which the primacy of popular sovereignty is established and the public state power is exercised according to the 'will of the people'. Thus, only the exercise of political power, which is based on popularly enacted laws and the administrative machinery that rigorously implements such laws, is legitimate. Mechanisms that link the popular will to political and bureaucratic institutions are the primary and sole source of legitimacy. Liberalism is less concerned with the source of authority (the will of the people), than it is with the modes through which this authority is exercised and the consequences that the exercise of public authority has on citizens. Thus, public power that is constrained by a bulk of inalienable individual rights, which are given precedence over the power itself for their intrinsic value, is legitimate. According to this view, the separation of powers, judicial review of state actions and decisions, and procedural rights of individuals vis-à-vis the public administration are some of the concrete

---

[28] For an overview of these approaches see Heiskanen, 'Introduction'.

mechanisms that enhance legitimacy. The rule of law is, hence, the essential premise of the legitimacy of states' powers.

These approaches disregarded international organizations as beyond their scope. However, this debate has had an influence on the debate on legitimacy related to international organizations. Indeed, correlated to the underlying social and political views on states' legitimacy, a similarly bipolar debate developed around the relationship between international organizations and states, and on the role of international organizations in international affairs. A realist/reductionist theory has emerged in conflict with an idealist/institutionalist theory. Theorists of realism (or reductionism) have argued that international organizations do not have a political will independent of that of states, or an autonomous role or function. According to this approach, organizations are mainly fora for cooperation among states and an administrative machinery that supports states in the management of international affairs. Here, legitimacy is not even an issue: international organizations are regarded as being institutionally designed to respond to the inputs of states. Their legitimation comes directly from the fact that the states' determinations guide the activities of the organizations. In this sense, the theory is an expansion at the international level of the continental enlightenment approach as states ultimately respond to the will of the people. Other scholars, however, support a different view. The so-called institutionalist (or idealist) theory holds that international organizations are autonomous subjects in the international arena formally and *de facto*: they not only have an independent legal capacity but also play a role that is independent from that of states, especially by facing global issues that states alone are incapable of coping with. As international organizations are independent of states and exercise a growing number of new functions and tasks, their accountability becomes a central issue strictly connected to legitimacy. An international organization is 'legitimate' if its activity is not only effective, but also accountable. Here, however, a problem arises as to how to interpret accountability (accountability to whom) and the connected concept of legitimacy. Indeed, traditional theories of state legitimacy have been considered not to be applicable and extensible by analogy to international organizations because purportedly there is not a direct relationship between international organizations and individuals or companies, and neither is there a unified global 'demos' that can be the source of legitimation. Hence, the risk is to reduce the accountability of international organizations only to accountability to states and legitimation to a correspondence between the objectives set by states and those achieved by international organizations.

As a third and final point, I believe that none of these normative frameworks alone has the capacity to provide an understanding of the phenomenon of procurement by international organizations as a source of legitimation of international organizations. It is instead a combination of these approaches that allows procurement rules to be thought of in terms of sources of legitimation and, at the same time, helps in identifying the obstacles to greater accountability and legitimation of international organizations. This hybrid thesis can be summarized in three points.

First, in the evolution of global governance, it cannot be denied that international organizations directly or indirectly affect civil society as a whole, as well as individuals or companies. This is done in two ways. The first is in every instance in which individuals become targets of the decisions of international organizations, such as when the United Nations adopts a decision to freeze the funds of a suspected terrorist, but also when a company is awarded a contract by an international organization or, on the contrary, is excluded from a procedure of vendor selection carried out by an international organization. The second way in which international organizations affect individuals and companies is when the international organization conditions the exercise of sovereign functions by states and shapes the rights that individuals or companies hold vis-à-vis domestic administrations. One of the many examples is making the financing of development projects by the WB conditional on the observance of procurement rules established by the international organization. As a consequence, the issues of accountability and legitimacy must also be reframed to include not only accountability towards member states but also accountability towards single members of a global society (individuals and companies). Thus, legitimacy has to be thought of as a composite concept where not only states, but also private actors must be recognized for their fundamental and increasing role as guardians of global governance.

Second, the body of rules that is gradually emerging in international organizations and that governs many of the relationships between international organizations and private subjects should help to enhance the level of transparency and accountability of organizations. In this regard, global administrative law, despite being in its infancy, serves as a new source of legitimation in global governance. Procurement regulation, in particular, stands at the core of this process of legitimation as it affects the very functioning of organizations.

Third, an assessment of procurement rules and contracts, however, reveals that transparency and accountability mechanisms, as well as the equal distribution of rights and duties in the contract, are deeply affected and limited by the interplay of interests, which can be ascribed to international organizations as separate institutional subjects (idealist/institutional theory), but also to states (reductionist/realist thesis). It is precisely the convergence or divergence of these interests that orients the exercise of public authority by international organizations, and often prevents the development of accountability and legitimation mechanisms. The combination of the realist and the institutional approach and the adoption of a hybrid concept of legitimacy are the necessary consequences of the multipolarity of the driving actors and interests that characterize the global space.

The further issue is then to understand if, given that the current regulatory architecture responds to a specific set of interests, it should be changed and, if so, why. There are several elements that can justify the change, given that a change is desirable, but cannot be a simplistic transplant of regulatory models from the national to the international level. A change could be brought about by several factors. The first and most important is a progressive shift in the interplay of interests, either because new interests come into play or because existing interests change, for instance as a result of untying the functioning of the international organizations from considerations of the economic return for the financing states. As seen in Chapter 3, in the past it has been a change in the interplay of interests that led to the emergence of a first body of rules on procurement.

Another element is what could be called the mimetic effect with respect to a changing global and national institutional context. In other words, the widespread change in the way in which the exercise of public power is conceived and interpreted at the global and the national level can also have an influencing effect on how the powers exercised by international organizations are conceptualized and regulated. Specifically with regard to public procurement, the circumstance that there is a commonly accepted international standard of action for domestic public procurement, characterized by greater publicity, transparency and accountability, can have an influence, within the limits set above, on international organizations and will make it increasingly difficult to maintain that international organizations are an exception to this development.

The final element is that of the foreseeable institutional growth of international organizations and the expansion of their tasks. If, consistently with past and current trends, international organizations will keep engaging more and more in the deployment of activities that directly or indirectly affect individuals and companies, this should in turn, slowly but consistently, create an incremental political demand for accountability and trigger a necessary shift in the interplay of interests mentioned above.

BIBLIOGRAPHY

Abraham, E. 'The Sins of the Savior: Holding the United Nations Accountable to International Human Rights Standards for Executive Order Detentions in Its Mission in Kosovo' (2003) 52 *American University Law Review* 1291.

Achterberg, N. 'Der öffentlich-rechtliche Vertrag' (1979) 11 *Juristische Arbeitsblätter* 356.

Adler, E. 'Constructivism', in W. Carlsnaes, B. Simmons and T. Risse (eds.), *Handbook of International Relations* (Thousand Oaks, CA: Sage, 2003).

Ahluwalia, K. *The Legal Status, Privileges and Immunities of Specialized Agencies of the United Nations and Certain Other International Organizations* (The Hague: Martinus Nijhoff, 1964).

Alesina, A. and D. Dollar, 'Who Gives Foreign Aid to Whom and Why?' (2000) 5 *Journal of Economic Growth* 33.

Alvarez, J.E. *International Organizations as Law-Makers* (Oxford: Oxford University Press, 2005).

Aman Jr., A.C. 'Globalization, Democracy and the Need for a New Administrative Law' (2003) 10 *Indiana Journal of Global Legal Studies* 125.

Amerasinghe, C.F. 'Financing', in R.J. Dupuy (ed.), *Manuel sur les organisations internationales*, 2nd edn (The Hague: Martinus Nijhoff, 1998).

  Law of the International Civil Service: International Administrative Tribunals (Oxford: Oxford University Press, 1994).

  Principles of the Institutional Law of International Organizations, 2nd edn (Cambridge: Cambridge University Press, 2005).

Andic, F., R. Huntington and R. Maurer, *National Execution: Promises and Challenges*, Office of Evaluation and Strategic Planning, 'Lesson Learned' Series (New York: UNDP Publications, 1995).

Archer, C. *International Organizations*, 4th edn (Abingdon: Routledge, 2015).

Arfaoui Ben Mouldi, B. 'L'interprétation arbitrale du contrat de commerce international', PhD thesis, Limoges, Université de Limoges, 2008 [unpublished].

Armstrong, D., L. Lloyd and J. Redmond, *From Versailles to Maastricht. International Organizations in the Twentieth Century* (New York: St. Martin's, 1996).

Arnstein, S.R. 'A Ladder of Citizen Participation' (1969) 35 (4) *Journal of American Institute of Planners* 216.

Arrowsmith, S. 'Transparency in Government Procurement: The Objectives of Regulation and the Boundaries of the World Trade Organization' (2003) 37 *Journal of World Trade* 293.

'Towards a Multilateral Agreement on Transparency in Government Procurement' (1998) 47 *International and Comparative Law Quarterly* 793.

Arrowsmith, S. and A.C. Davies, *Public Procurement: Global Revolution* (The Hague: Kluwer Law International, 1998).

Arrowsmith, S., J. Linarelli and D. Wallace, *Regulating Public Procurement: National and International Perspectives* (The Hague: Kluwer Law International, 2000).

Arsanjani, M.H. 'Claims against International Organizations' (1981) 7 *Yale Journal of World Public Order* 131.

Atiyah, P.S. *Rise and Fall of Freedom of Contract* (Oxford: Oxford University Press, 1987).

Auby, J.B. 'L'internationalisation du droit des contrats publics' (2003) 5 *Droit Administratif* 5.

La globalisation, le droit et l'État (Paris: Montchrestien, 2003).

Audit, M. 'Les marchés de travaux, de fournitures et de services passés par les organisations internationales' (2008) 4 *Journal du droit international* 941.

(ed.), *Contrats publics et arbitrage international* (Brussels: Bruylant, 2011).

Audit, M. and S. Schill (eds.), *Transnational Law of Public Contracts* (Brussels: Bruylant, 2016).

Babb, S. *Behind the Development Banks. Washington Politics, World Poverty and the Wealth of Nations* (Chicago: Chicago University Press, 2009).

Bantekas, I. *An Introduction to International Arbitration* (Cambridge: Cambridge University Press, 2015).

Barberis, J. 'Nouvelles questions concernant la personnalité juridique internationale' (1983) I *Recueil des cours de l'Académie de droit international* 145.

Barkin, J.S. *International Organization: Theories and Institutions* (New York: Palgrave, 2006).

Barnett, M. 'Bringing in the New World Order, Liberalism, Legitimacy and the United Nations' (1997) 49 (4) *World Politics* 526.

'Social Constructivism', in J. Baylis, S. Smith and P. Owens (eds.), *The Globalization of World Politics. An Introduction to International Relations*, 4th edn (Oxford: Oxford University Press, 2008).

Barthes, R. *Elements of Semiology* (London: Jonathan Cape, 1967).

Bastid-Basdevant, S. *Les fonctionnaires internationaux* (Paris: Recueil Sirey, 1931).

Batifol, H. *Problèmes des contrats privés internationaux* (Paris: Association des Études Internationales, 1962).

Battini, S. 'Administrative Law Beyond the State', in VV.AA., *Global Administrative Law: An Italian Perspective*, EUI-RSCAS Policy Paper 2012/4.

Amministrazioni senza Stato. Profili di diritto amministrativo internazionale (Milan: Giuffré, 2003).

'International Organizations and Private Subjects: A Move Toward A Global Administrative Law?', IILJ Working Paper 2005/3.

Beetham, D. 'Legitimacy', in B. Badie, D. Berg-Schlosser and L. Morlino (eds.), *International Encyclopedia of Political Science* (Thousand Oaks, CA and London: Sage Publications, 2011).

The Legitimation of Power, 2nd edn (Basingstoke: Palgrave Macmillan, 2013).

Behn, R. *Rethinking Democratic Accountability* (Washington, DC: Brookings Institution, 2001).

Beigbeder, Y. 'L'influence des modèles administratifs nationaux sur le système administratif des institutions des Nations Unies' (1984) 2 *Revue Internationale des Sciences Administratives* 148.

The Internal Management of the United Nations Organisations: The Long Quest for Reform (London: Macmillan, 1997).

Bekker, P.H.F. *The Legal Position of Intergovernmental Organizations: A Functional Necessity Analysis of Their Legal Status and Immunities* (Dordrecht/Boston: Martinus Nijhoff, 1994).

Bendix, R. *Max Weber. An Intellectual Portrait* (Berkeley: University of California Press, 1960).

Bentchikou, F. 'World Bank Procurement: Contributions to the Harmonization of Public Contracts', in M. Audit and S. Schill (eds.), *Transnational Law of Public Contracts* (Brussels: Bruylant, 2016).

Benvenisti, E. 'The Interplay between Actors as a Determinant of the Evolution of Administrative Law in International Institutions' (2005) 68 (3–4) *Law and Contemporary Problems* 319.

The Law of Global Governance (The Hague: Martinus Nijhoff, 2014).

Beraudo, J. 'Faut-il avoir peur du contrat sans loi?', in VV.AA., *Le droit international privé: esprit et méthodes. Mélanges en l'honneur de Paul Lagarde* (Paris: Dalloz, 2005).

Berelson, B. *Content Analysis in Communication Research* (Glencoe: Free Press, 1952).

Bertrand, M. 'The Process of Reform in the United Nations: A Case Study on Planning, Programming, Budgeting and Evaluation', in United Nations, *International Geneva Yearbook* 1988 (Geneva: UN Publications).

'The Historical Development of Efforts to Reform the UN', in A. Roberts and B. Kingsbury (eds.), *United Nations, Divided World. The UN's Roles in International Relations*, 2nd edn (Oxford: Oxford University Press, 1993).

Black, J. 'Constructing and Contesting Legitimacy and Accountability in Polycentric Regulatory Regimes', IILJ Working Paper 2007/12 (Global Administrative Law Series).

Blokker, N. 'The Independence of International Organizations from Their Host States: From Theory to Practice', 2014, available at https://rm.coe.int /16800c093e (last access: January 2018).

Blokker N.M. 'International Organizations and Their Members' (2004) 1 (1) *International Organizations Law Review* 139.

Blokker N.M. and H.G. Schermers, 'Mission Impossible? On the Immunities of Staff Members of International Organizations on Mission', VV.AA., *Liber Amicorum Professor Ignaz Seidl-Hohenveldern* (The Hague: Kluwer, 1998).

Böckstiegel, K.H. 'The Application of the UNIDROIT. Principles to Contracts Involving States or Intergovernmental Organizations' (2002) *International Court of Arbitration Bulletin.* Special Supplement 51.

Boisson de Chazournes, L. 'Changing Roles of International Organizations: Global Administrative Law and the Interplay of Legitimacies' (2009) 6 *International Organizations Law Review* 655.

'Compliance with Operational Standards: The Contribution of the World Bank Inspection Panel', in G. Afredsson and R. Ring (eds.), *The World Bank Inspection Panel* (The Hague: Kluwer Law International, 2001).

'Relations with Other International Organizations', in J. Katz Cogan and I. Hurd (eds.), *The Oxford Handbook of Comparative Law* (Oxford: Oxford University Press, 2007).

'Relationships of International Organizations with Other Actors', in J. Katz Cogan and I. Hurd (eds.), *Oxford Handbook of International Organizations* (Oxford: Oxford University Press, 2016).

Boisson de Chazournes, L., L. Casini and B. Kingsbury (eds.), Symposium on 'Global Administrative Law in the Operations of International Organizations' (2009) 6 (2) *International Organizations Law Review* 1.

Bonell, M.J. 'The UNIDROIT Initiative for the Progressive Codification of International Trade Law' (1978) 27 (2) *The International and Comparative Law Quarterly* 413.

Borsi, U. 'Carattere ed oggetto del diritto amministrativo internazionale' (1992) *Rivista di diritto internazionale* 365.

Börzel, T.A. and T. Risse, 'Public-Private Partnerships: Effective and Legitimate Tools of International Governance?', in E. Grande and L.W. Pauly (eds.), *Complex Sovereignty: Reconstituting Political Authority in the Twenty-First Century* (Toronto: University of Toronto Press, 2005).

Bovens, M. 'Analysing and Assessing Accountability: A Conceptual Framework' (2007) 13 *European Law Journal* 447.

The Quest for Responsibility: Accountability and Citizenship in Complex Organisations (Cambridge: Cambridge University Press, 1998).

Bowett, D. *The Law of International Institutions*, 4th edn (London: Stevens & Sons, 1982).

Bradlow, D. and S. Schlemmer-Schulte, 'The World Bank's New Inspection Panel: A Constructive Step in the Transformation of the International Legal Order' (1994) 54 *Zeitschrift für Ausländisches Öffentliches Recht und Völkerrecht* 392.

Braun, P. 'Damages for Irregularities in the Award Process: Case T-160/03 R' (2005a) (4) *Public Procurement Law Review* 98.

'Interim Measures against Community Institutions: Case T-303/04 R' (2005b) (2) *Public Procurement Law Review* 25.

Brown, A. 'Interim Measures against the Community Institutions in Procurement Cases: A Note on the Esedra Case' (2001) 2 *Public Procurement Law Review* 51.

Bruti Liberati, E. *Consenso e funzione nei contratti di diritto pubblico tra amministrazione e privati* (Milan: Giuffré, 1996).

Burns, D. 'International Administration' (1926) 7 *British Yearbook of International Law* 54.

Cafaggi, F. 'New Foundations of Transnational Private Regulation' (2011) 38 (1) *Journal of Law and Society* 20.

Cafagno, M. *Lo Stato banditore* (Milan: Giuffrè, 2001).

Caffarena, A. *Le organizzazioni internazionali* (Bologna: Il Mulino, 2009).

Cappelletti, M. (ed.), *International Encyclopedia of Comparative Law* (The Hague/Boston/London: Martinus Nijhoff, 1982), vol. VII, ch. 4.

Caranta, R. *I contratti pubblici*, 2nd edn (Torino: Giappichelli, 2012).

EU Public Contract Law: Public Procurement and Beyond (Brussels: Bruylant, 2013).

Carbonnier, G. 'Procurement of Goods and Services by International Organisations in Donor Countries' (2013) 5 *Revue Internationale de Politique de Développement* 2.

Caroli Casavola, H. 'Internationalizing Public Procurement Law: Conflicting Global Standards for Public Procurement' (2006) 6 (3) *Global Jurist* 1535.

'L'appalto pubblico e la globalizzazione', in C. Franchini (ed.), *I contratti di appalto pubblico* (Turin: Utet, 2010).

La globalizzazione dei contratti delle pubbliche amministrazioni (Milan: Giuffrè, 2012).

Caron, D.D., S.W. Schill, A.C. Smutny and E.E. Triantafilou (eds.), *Practising Virtue: Inside International Arbitration* (Oxford: Oxford University Press, 2015).

Casini, L. 'Public Law and Private Law beyond the State: Dangerous "Doubles" or "Mutual Friends"?', paper presented at the conference 'Toward a Multipolar Administrative Law', New York University School of Law, New York, 9–10 September 2012.

Casini, L. and B. Kingsbury, 'Global Administrative Law Dimensions of International Organizations' (2009) 2 *International Organizations Law Review* 319.

Cassese, A. 'L'immunité de juridiction civile des organisations internationales dans la jurisprudence italienne' (1984) 30 *Annuaire Français de Droit International* 556.

Cassese, S. 'Global Administrative Law: The State of the Art' (2015) 13 (2) *International Journal of Constitutional Law* 465.

'Global Standards for National Administrative Procedure' (2005) 68 (3–4) *Law and Contemporary Problems* 109.

'L'arbitrato nel diritto amministrativo' (1996) 2 *Rivista Trimestrale di Diritto Pubblico* 311.

'Relations between International Organizations and National Administrations', in VV.AA. *XIX International Congress of Administrative Science. Actesproceedings* (Brussels: IISA, 1985).

La crisi dello Stato (Bari: Laterza, 2002).

Lo spazio giuridico globale (Bari: Laterza, 2003).

Oltre lo Stato (Bari: Laterza, 2006).

(ed.), *Research Handbook on Global Administrative Law* (Cheltenham, UK/ Northampton, MA: Elgar, 2017).

Cassese, S., A. von Bogdandy and P. Huber, *The Max Planck Handbooks in European Public Law. Volume I: The Administrative State* (Oxford: Oxford University Press, 2017).

Cassese, S. *et al.* (eds.), *Global Administrative Law: The Casebook*, 3rd edn (Rome/ Edinburgh/New York: IRPA-IILJ, 2012).

Chabanol, D., J.P. Jouguelet and F. Bourrachot, *Le régime juridique des marchés publics*, 5th edn (Paris: Editions Le Moniteur, 2007).

Chandler, D. *Semiotics: The Basics*, 3rd edn (Abingdon: Routledge, 2015).

Charnoz, O. and J.M. Severino, *L'aide publique au développement* (Paris: La Découverte, 2007).

Chesterman, S. 'Executive Heads', in J. Katz Cogan and I. Hurd (eds.), *Oxford Handbook of International Organizations* (Oxford: Oxford University Press, 2016).

Chimni, B.S. 'International Organizations, 1945–Present', in J. Katz Cogan and I. Hurd (eds.), *Oxford Handbook of International Organizations* (Oxford: Oxford University Press, 2016).

Chiti, E. 'Where Does GAL Find Its Legal Grounding?' (2015) 13 (2) *International Journal of Constitutional Law* 486.

Clay, E.J., M. Geddes and L. Natali, *Untying Aid: Is It Working? An Evaluation of the Implementation of the Paris Declaration and of the 2001 DAC Recommendation of Untying ODA to the LDCs*, Copenhagen, December 2009.

Clerc, E. 'La mondialisation des marchés publics: bilan et perspectives de l'Accord OMC sur le marchés publics', in VV.AA., *Les marchés publics à l'aube du XXIe siècle* (Brussels: Bruylant, 2000).

Coicaud, J.M. and V. Heiskanen (eds.), *The Legitimacy of International Organizations* (New York: United Nations University Press, 2001).

Colin, J. and M.H. Sinkondo, 'Les relations contractuelles des organisations internationales avec les personnes privées' (1992) 69 *Revue de droit international et de droit comparé* 7.

Conforti, B. *Scritti di diritto internazionale* (Naples: Editoriale Scientifica, 2003).

Conforti, B. and C. Focarelli, *The Law and Practice of the United Nations*, 5th edn (The Hague: Martinus Nijhoff, 1997).

Conseil d'État, *Régler autrement les conflits: conciliation, transaction, arbitrage en matière administrative* (Paris: La documentation française, 1993).

Conyers, D. 'Decentralization and Development: A Review of the Literature' (1984) 4 (2) *Public Administration and Development* 187.

'Decentralization: The Latest Fashion in Development Administration?' (1983) 3 (2) *Public Administration and Development* 97.

Cordero-Moss, G. (ed.), *International Commercial Arbitration. Different Forms and Their Features* (Cambridge: Cambridge University Press, 2013).

Correll, C. 'Problembereiche und Möglichkeiten des öffentlich-rechtlichen Vertrags. Ein deutsch-österreichischer Rechtsvergleich' (1998) 51 *Die Öffentliche Verwaltung* 363.

Cox, R.W. and H.K. Jacobson, *et al. The Anatomy of Influence: Decision Making in International Organizations* (New Haven/London: Yale University Press, 1974).

Craig, P. *Administrative Law*, 8th edn (London: Sweet and Maxwell, 2016).

D'Alberti, M. 'Interesse pubblico e concorrenza nel Codice dei contratti pubblici' (2008) 2 *Diritto amministrativo* 297.

I 'public contracts' nell'esperienza britannica (Napoli: Jovene, 1984).

Dahl, R.A. 'Can International Organisations Be Democratic? A Skeptic's View', in I. Shapiro and C. Hacker-Cordón (eds.), *Democracy's Edges* (Cambridge: Cambridge University Press, 1999).

Damgaard, B. and J.M. Lewis, 'Accountability and Citizen Participation', in M. Bovens, R.E. Goodin and T. Schillemans (eds.), *The Oxford Handbook of Public Accountability* (Oxford: Oxford University Press, 2014).

David, R. *The International Unification of Private Law* (Tübingen: J.C.B. Mohr, 1971).

Davies, A.C. *The Public Law of Government Contracts* (Oxford: Oxford University Press, 2008).

Davies, M.D.V. *The Administration of International Organizations. Top Down and Bottom Up* (Aldershot: Ashgate, 2002).

de Castro Meireles, M. 'The World Bank Procurement Regulations: A Critical Analysis of the Enforcement Mechanism and of the Application of Secondary Policies in Financed Projects', PhD thesis, University of Nottingham, 2006.

De Laubadere, A. *Traité théorique et pratique des contrats administratifs* (Paris: LGDJ, 1956).

De Laubadere, A., F. Moderne and P. Delvolvé, *Traité des contrats administratifs*, 2nd edn (Paris: LGDJ, 1983–1984).

De Wet, E. 'The Direct Administration of Territories by the United Nations and its Member States in the Post Cold War Era: Legal Bases and Implications for National Law' (2004) 8 *Max Planck Yearbook* 8.

de Cooker, C. *Accountability, Investigation and Due Process in International Organizations* (Leiden: Martinus Nijhoff, 2005).

Degnbol-Martinussen, J. and P. Engberg-Pedersen, *Aid: Understanding International Development Cooperation* (London: Zed Books, 2003).

Delaume, G. 'The Proper Law of Contracts Concluded by International Persons: A Restatement and a Forecast' (1962) 56 *American Journal of International Law* 63.

Delaume, G.R. 'Issues of Applicable Law in the Context of the World Bank Operations', in N. Horn and C.M. Schmitthof (eds.), *The Transnational Law of International Commercial Transactions* (Deventer/Boston: Kluwer Law International, 1982).

'The Proper Law of Loans Concluded by International Persons: A Restatement and a Forecast' (1962) 56 (1) *The American Journal of International Law* 63.

Della Cananea, G. 'Beyond the State: The Europeanization and Globalization of Procedural Administrative Law' (2003) 4 *European Public Law* 563.

Al di là dei confini statuali. Principi generali di diritto pubblico globale (Bologna: Il Mulino, 2009).

Due Process of Law beyond the State (Oxford: Oxford University Press, 2016).

'The EU and the WTO: A "Relational" Analysis', paper presented at the conference on 'New Foundations for European and Global Governance', Wien, 29–30 November 2004.

Detter, I. *Law Making by International Organizations* (Norstedt & Söner: Stockholm, 1965).

Devesh, K., J.P. Lewis and R. Webb, *The World Bank. Its First Half Century* (Washington, DC: Brookings Institution Press, 1997).

Dìaz Gonzàlez, L. 'Fourth Report on Relations between States and International Organizations', in ILC, *Yearbook of the International Law Commission 1989 II* (New York: UN Publications: 1989).

Dimitri, N., G. Piga and G. Spagnolo (eds.), *Handbook of Procurement* (Cambridge: Cambridge University Press, 2006).

Dominicé, C. 'L'immunité de juridiction et d'exécution des organisations internationales' (1984) 187 *Recueil des cours de l'Académie de droit international* 145.

'La personnalité juridique dans le système du droit des gens', in VV.AA., *Theory of International Law at the Threshold of the 21st Century. Essays in Honour of K. Skubiszewski* (The Hague: Kluwer Law International, 1996).

Dorigo, S. *L'immunità delle organizzazioni internazionali dalla giurisdizione contenziosa ed esecutiva nel diritto internazionale generale* (Turin: Giappichelli, 2008).

Dormoy, D. 'Aspects récents de la question du financement des operations de maintien de la paix de l'Organisation des Nations Unies' (1993) 39 *Annuaire Français de Droit International* 131.

Drago, R. 'Le contrat administratif aujourd'hui' (1990) 12 *Droits* 117.

Dreifuss, M. 'L'immixtion du droit privé dans les contrats administratifs' (2002) 58 (22) *Actualité Juridique. Droit administrative* 1373.

Duffar, J. *Contribution à l'étude des privilèges et immunités des organisations internationales* (Paris: LGDJ, 1982).

Dunoff, J. 'The Law and Politics of International Organizations', in J. Katz Cogan and I. Hurd (eds.), *Oxford Handbook of International Organizations* (Oxford: Oxford University Press, 2016).

Durch, W.J. *The Evolution of UN Peacekeeping: Case Studies and Comparative Analysis* (New York: Palgrave Macmillan, 1993).

Dyzenhaus, D. 'Accountability and the Concept of (Global) Administrative Law', IILJ Working Paper 2008/7 (Global Administrative Law Series).

Eagleton, C. 'International Organization and the Law of Responsibility' (1950/I) 76 *Recueil des cours de l'Académie de droit international* 319.

Eco, U. *Trattato di Semiotica generale* (Milan: Bompiani, 1984).

Elias, O. (ed.), *The Development and Effectiveness of International Administrative Law* (Boston/Leiden: Martinus Nijhoff, 2012).

Ellmers, B. *How to Spend It. Smart Procurement for More Effective Aid* (Brussels: Eurodad Publications, September 2011).

Emery, C. *Administrative Law: Legal Challenges to Official Action* (London: Sweet and Maxwell, 1999).

Erichsen, H.U. and W. Martens, 'Il contratto di diritto amministrativo', in A. Masucci (ed.), *L'accordo nell'azione amministrativa* (Formez: Rome, 1988).

Esty, D.C. 'Good Governance at the Supranational Scale: Globalizing Administrative Law' (2006) 115 *Yale Law Journal* 1490.

Evenett, S.J. and B.M. Hoekman, 'Government Procurement: Market Access, Transparency and Multilateral Trade Rules' (2005) 21 *European Journal of Political Economy* 163.

Fatouros, A.A. *Government Guarantees to Foreign Investors* (New York: Columbia University Press, 1962).

Fearon, J. and A. Wendt, 'Rationalism vs. Constructivism', in W. Carlsnaes, B. Simmons and T. Risse (eds.), *Handbook of International Relations* (Thousand Oaks, CA: Sage, 2003).

Ferejohn, J. 'Accountability in a Global Context', IILJ Working Paper 2007/5 (Global Administrative Law Series).

Ferrarese, M.R. *Le istituzioni della globalizzazione. Diritto e diritti nella società transnazionale* (Bologna: Il Mulino, 2002).

Finnemore, M. *National Interests in International Society* (Ithaca, NY: Cornell University Press, 1996).

Finnemore, M. and K. Sikkink, 'International Norm Dynamics and Political Change' (1998) 52 (4) *International Organization* 887.

'Taking Stock: The Constructivist Research Program in International Relations and Comparative Politics' (2001) 4 *Annual Review of Political Science* 391.

Flogaïtis, S. *Les contrats administratifs* (London: Esperia, 1998).

Fluck, J. 'Grundprobleme des öffentlich-rechtlichen Vertragsrechts' (1989) 22 *Die Verwaltung* 185.

Foster, M. 'New Approaches to Development Co-operation: What Can We Learn from Experience with Implementing Sector Wide Approaches?', Overseas Development Institute Working Paper No. 140, October 2000.

Franck, T.M. *The Power of Legitimacy among Nations* (Oxford: Oxford University Press, 1990).

Friedrich, C. (ed.), *The Public Interest* (New York: Atherton Press, 1962).

Fusinato, G. *Di una parte alquanto trascurata del diritto internazionale e della sua organizzazione scientifica e sistematica* (Firenze: Barbera, 1892).

Gaillard, E. and I. Pingel-Lenuzza, 'International Organisations and Immunity from Jurisdiction: To Restrict or to Bypass' (2002) 51 *International and Comparative Law Quarterly* 1.

Galgano, F. 'Squilibrio contrattuale e mala fede del contraente forte' (1997) *II Contratto e società* 422.

Galvani, F. and S. Morse, 'Institutional Sustainability: At What Price? UNDP and the New Cost-Sharing Model in Brazil' (2004) 14 (3) *Development in Practice* 311.

Gannagé, L. 'Le contrat sans loi en droit international privé' (2007) 11 (3) *Electronic Journal of Comparative Law* 1.

Georgopulos, A.C., B. Hoekman and P. C. Mavroidis (eds.), *The Internationalization of Government Procurement Regulation* (Oxford: Oxford University Press, 2017).

Giannini, M.S. *Diritto amministrativo*, 2nd edn (Milan: Giuffrè, 1993).

Ginther, K. *Die völkerrechtliche Verantwortlichkeit internationaler Organisationen gegenüber Drittstaaten* (Wien: Verlag Österreich, 1969).

Glavinis, P. *Les litiges relatifs aux contrats passés entre organisations internationales et personnes privées* (Paris: LGDJ, 1992).

Glenn, H., M. Kearney and D. Padilla, 'The Immunities of International Organizations' (1981/82) 22 *Vanderbilt Journal of International Law* 247.

Goodhart, M. 'Accountable International Relations', in M. Bovens, R.E. Goodin and T. Schillemans (eds.), *The Oxford Handbook of Public Accountability* (Oxford: Oxford University Press, 2014).

Gordley, J. (ed.), *The Enforceability of Promises in European Contract Law* (Cambridge: Cambridge University Press, 2001).

Gorski, J. 'The Reform of World Bank's Procurement Rules', The Chinese University of Hong Kong, Faculty of Law, Working Paper No. 20, October 2016.

Grant, R.W. and R.O. Keohane, 'Accountability and Abuses of World Power' (2005) 99 *American Political Science Review* 29.

Graziadei, M. 'Comparative Law as the Study of Transplants and Receptions', in M. Reimann and R. Zimmermann (eds.), *The Oxford Handbook of Comparative Law* (Oxford: Oxford University Press, 2007).
  'Legal Transplants and the Frontiers of Legal Knowledge' (2009) 10 (2) *Theoretical Inquiries in Law* 722.

Greenberg, S., C. Kee and J. Romesh Weeramantry, *International Commercial Arbitration. An Asia-Pacific Perspective* (Cambridge: Cambridge University Press, 2011).

Groshens, J.C. 'Les marchés passés par les organisations internationales' (1956) 4 *Revue du droit public et de la science politique en France et à l'étranger* 741.

Gruber, J.E. *Controlling Bureaucracies: Dilemmas in Bureaucratic Governance* (Berkeley, CA: UC Press, 1987).

Haas, E. and E. Rowe, 'Regional Organizations in the United Nations: Is There Externalization?' (1974) 17 (1) *International Studies Quarterly* 15.

Hariou, M. *Principes de droit public* (Paris: Librairie du Recueil Sirey, 1910).

Harlow, C. 'Global Administrative Law: The Quest for Principles and Values' (2006) 17 *European Journal of International Law* 187.

Hart, D. 'Un caso esemplare: la giurisprudenza sulle condizioni generali di contract', in P. Barcellona, D. Hart and U. Mückenberger (eds.), *L'educazione del giurista: capitalismo dei monopoli e cultura giuridica* (Bari: De Donato, 1973).

Hartwig, M. *Die Haftung der Mitgliedstaaten für internationale Organisationen* (Berlin/Heidelberg: Springer, 1993).

Hauriou, M. *Précis de droit administratif et de droit public* (Paris: Larose, 1926).

Hay, C. 'Constructivist Institutionalism', in R.A.W. Rhodes, S.A. Binder and B.A. Rockman (eds.), *The Oxford Handbook of Political Institutionalism* (Oxford: Oxford University Press, 2006).

Head, J. 'Evolution of the Governing Law for Loan Agreements of the World Bank and Other Multilateral Development Banks' (1996) 90 (2) *American Journal of International Law* 214.

Heiskanen, V. 'Introduction', in J.M. Coicaud and V. Heiskanen (eds.), *The Legitimacy of International Organizations* (New York: United Nations University Press, 2001).

Henke, W. 'Allgemeine Fragen des öffentlichen Vertragsrechts' (1984) 39 *Juristenzeitung* 441.

Herren, M. 'International Organizations, 1865–1945', in J. Katz Cogan and I. Hurd (eds.), *Oxford Handbook of International Organizations* (Oxford: Oxford University Press, 2016).

Hesselink, M.W. *The New European Legal Culture* (Deventer: Kluwer Law International, 2001).

Heuninckx, B. 'Applicable Law to the Procurement of International Organisations in the European Union' (2011) 20 (4) *Public Procurement Law Review* 103.

'The Law of Collaborative Defence Procurement through International Organisations in the EU', PhD thesis, University of Nottingham, 2011.

The Law of Collaborative Defence Procurement in the European Union (Cambridge: Cambridge University Press, 2016).

Hill, M. 'The Administrative Committee on Coordination', in E. Luard (ed.), *The Evolution of International Organizations* (London: Thames and Hudson, 1966).

Hirsch, M. *The Responsibility of International Organizations toward Third Parties: Some Basic Principles* (Dordrecht: Martinus Nijhoff, 1995).

Holsti, O.R. *Content Analysis for the Social Sciences and Humanities* (Reading, MA: Addison-Wesley, 1969).

Hüfner, K. 'Financing the United Nations. The Role of the United States', in D. Dijkzeul and Y. Beigbeder (eds.), *Rethinking International Organizations. Pathology and Promise* (New York/Oxford: Berghahn, 2003).

Hunja, R. 'Recent Revisions to the World Bank's Procurement and Consultants Selection Guidelines' (1997) 6 *Public Procurement Law Review* 216.

Hurd, I. 'Constructivism', in C. Reus and D. Snidal (eds.), *The Oxford Handbook of International Relations* (Oxford: Oxford University Press, 2008).

International Organizations: Politics, Law, Practice, 2nd edn (Cambridge: Cambridge University Press, 2014).

Jackholt, J. 'The Procurement Policies and Rules and the Procurement Activities of the European Bank for Reconstruction and Development' (2016) 4 *Public Procurement Law Review* 172.

Jenks, C.W. *The Proper Law of International Organizations* (New York: Oceana Publications, 1962).

International Immunities (London: Stevens, 1961).

Jessup, C. *Transitional Law* (New Haven, CT: Yale University Press, 1956).

Jordan, R.S. 'The Influence of the British Secretariat Tradition on the Formation of the League of Nations', in R.S. Jordan (ed.), *International Administration* (New York/Oxford: Oxford University Press, 1971).

Junne, G.C.A. 'International Organizations in a Period of Globalization: New (Problems of) Legitimacy', in J.M. Coicaud and V. Heiskanen (eds.),

The Legitimacy of International Organizations (New York: United Nations University Press, 2001).

Kalogeras, D.A. 'Remedies in the Field of Public Procurement against the Institutions of the European Community: Quis Custodiat Ipsos Custodes?' 1999 (5) *Public Procurement Law Review* 211.

Kapur, D., J.P. Lewis and R.C. Webb, *The World Bank: History* (Washington, DC: Brookings Institution Press, 1997).

Kasme, B. *La capacité l'ONU de conclure des traités* (Paris: Pedone, 1960).

Katz Cogan, J. 'Financing and Budgets', in J. Katz Cogan and I. Hurd (eds.), *Oxford Handbook of International Organizations* (Oxford: Oxford University Press, 2016).

Katz Cogan, J. and I. Hurd (eds.), *Oxford Handbook of International Organizations* (Oxford: Oxford University Press, 2016).

Katzenstein, P.J. *The Culture of National Security: Norms and Identity in World Politics* (New York: Columbia University Press, 1996).

Kell, G. 'Relations with the Private Sector', in J. Katz Cogan and I. Hurd (eds.), *Oxford Handbook of International Organizations* (Oxford: Oxford University Press, 2016).

Keohane, S.R.O. 'Global Governance and Democratic Accountability', in D. Held and M. Koenig Archibugi (eds.), *Taming Globalization: Frontiers of Governance* (Cambridge: Polity, 2003).

Keohane, S.R.O. and J.S. Nye (eds.), *Transnational Relations and World Politics* (Cambridge, MA: Harvard University Press, 1972).

Killmann, B.R. 'Procurement Activities of International Organizations. An Attempt of a First Insight in Evolving Legal Principles' (2003) 8 *Austrian Review of International and European Law* 277.

Kingsbury, B. 'Global Administrative Law: Implications for National Courts', in D. Geiringer and C. Knight (eds.), *Seeing the World Whole: Essays in Honor of Kenneth Keith* (Wellington, NZ: Victoria University Press, 2008).

Kingsbury, B. and M. Donaldson, 'Global Administrative Law', in R. Wolfrum (ed.), *Max Planck Encyclopedia of Public International Law* (Oxford: Oxford University Press, 2012), *ad vocem*.

Kingsbury, B. and R.B. Stewart, 'Legitimacy and Accountability in Global Regulatory Governance: The Emerging Global Administrative Law and the Design and Operation of Administrative Tribunals of International Organizations', in S. Flogaitis (ed.), *International Administrative Tribunals in a Changing World* (Esperia: London, 2008).

Kingsbury, B. and S.W. Schill, 'Investor-State Arbitration as Governance: Fair and Equitable Treatment, Proportionality and the Emerging Global Administrative Law', IILJ Working Paper 2009/6 (Global Administrative Law Series).

Kingsbury, B., N. Krisch and R.B. Stewart, 'The Emergence of Global Administrative Law' (2005) 68 (3–4) *Law and Contemporary Problems* 15.

Klabbers, J. 'Formal Inter-Governmental Organizations', in J. Katz Cogan and
I. Hurd (eds.), *Oxford Handbook of International Organizations* (Oxford:
Oxford University Press, 2016).

'International Institutions', in J. Crawford and M. Koskenniemi (eds.),
The Cambridge Companion to International Law (Cambridge: Cambridge
University Press, 2012), 228.

'The Emergence of Functionalism in International Institutional Law: Colonial
Inspirations' (2014) 25 *European Journal of International Law* 645.

'The Transformation of International Organizations Law' (2015) 26 (1)
European Journal of International Law 9.

Advanced Introduction to the Law of International Organizations (Cheltenham,
UK/Northampton, MA: Edward Elgar, 2015).

An Introduction to International Institutional Law, 3rd edn (Cambridge:
Cambridge University Press, 2015).

An Introduction to International Organizations Law, 3rd edn (Cambridge:
Cambridge University Press, 2015).

Klabbers, J. and A. Wallendahl (eds.), *Research Handbook on the Law of
International Organizations* (Cheltenham, UK/Northampton, MA: Edward
Elgar 2011).

Klein, P. 'Responsibility', in J. Katz Cogan and I. Hurd (eds.), *Oxford Handbook of
International Organizations* (Oxford: Oxford University Press, 2016).

*La responsabilité des organisations internationals dans les ordres juridiques
internes et en droit des gens* (Brussels: Bruylant, 1998).

Knapp, B. 'Questions juridiques relatives à la construction d'immeubles par les
organisations internationales' (1977) XXXIII *Annuaire suisse de droit international* 51.

Knill, C. and D. Lehmkuhl, 'Governance and Globalization: Conceptualizing the
Role of Public and Private Actors', in A. Heritier (ed.), *Common Goods:
Reinventing European Integration Governance* (Boulder, CO: Lanham,
2002).

Koenig-Archibugi, M. 'Accountability', in J. Katz Cogan, I. Hurd and I. Johnstone
(eds.), *The Oxford Handbook of International Organizations* (Oxford:
Oxford University Press, 2017).

Koppell, J.G.S. 'Accountable Global Governance Organizations', in M. Bovens,
R.E. Goodin and T. Schillemans (eds.), *The Oxford Handbook of Public
Accountability* (Oxford: Oxford University Press, 2014).

Koskenniemi, M. 'The Fate of Public International Law: Between Technique and
Politics' (2007) 70 *Modern Law Review* 1.

Kötz, H. and A. Flessner, *Europaeisches Vertragsrecht* (Tubinga: Mohr Siebeck,
1996).

Krippendorff, K. *Content Analysis: An Introduction to Its Methodology*, 2nd edn
(Thousand Oaks, CA: Sage, 2004).

Kunz, I.L. 'Privileges and Immunities of International Organisations' (1947) 41 (4) *The American Journal of International Law* 828.

Lachimia, A. *Tied Aid and Development Aid Procurement in the Framework of EU and WTO Law* (Oxford: Hart, 2013).

Lalive, J.F. 'L'immunité de juridiction des états et des organisations internationales' (1953) 84 *Recueil des cours de l'Académie de droit international* 205.

Langrod, G. *La fonction publique internationale* (Leyde: A.W. Sythoff, 1964).

Lauterpacht, E. 'Judicial Review of the Acts of International Organisations', in L. Boisson de Chazournes and P. Sands (eds.), *International Law, the International Court of Justice and Nuclear Weapons* (Cambridge: Cambridge University Press, 1999).

Legrand, P. 'The Same and the Different', in P. Legrand and R. Munday (eds.), *Comparative Legal Studies* (Cambridge: Cambridge Uniniversity Press, 2003).

'The Impossibility of "Legal Transplants"' (1997) 4 *Maastricht Journal of European and Comparative Law* 111.

Lengwiler, Y. and E. Wolfstetter, 'Corruption in Procurement Auctions', in N. Dimitri, G. Piga and G. Spagnolo (eds.), *Handbook of Procurement* (Cambridge: Cambridge University Press, 2006).

LeRoy Bennet, A. and J.K. Oliver, *International Organizations. Principles and Issues*, 7th edn (Upper Saddle River, NJ: Prentice Hall, 2002).

Leroy, A.M. and F. Fariello, *The World Bank Group Sanctions Process and Its Recent Reforms* (Washington: The World Bank, 2012).

Level, P. 'Le contrat dit sans loi', in AA., *Travaux du Comité Français de Droit International Privé: 1964–1966* (Paris: Dalloz, 1967).

Leyland, P. and T. Woods, *Administrative Law* (Oxford: Oxford University Press, 2002).

Lichère, F. *Droit des contrats publics*, 2nd edn (Paris: Dalloz, 2014).

Lipset, S.M. *The Political Man: The Social Bases of Politics*, 3rd exp. edn (Baltimore, MD: The Johns Hopkins University Press, 1981).

Lynch, C. 'Russia Seeks to Thwart UN Task Force That Led Bribery Probes', *Washington Post*, 24 December 2008, available at www.washingtonpost.com /wp-dyn/content/article/2008/12/23/AR2008122301255.html?hpid=topnews (last access: January 2018).

MacLaren, R.I. 'La culture administrative britannique au sein des Nations Unies' (1994) 4 *Revue Internationale des Sciences Administratives* 719.

Malmendier, B. 'The Liability of International Development Banks in Procurement Proceedings: The Example of the International Bank for Reconstruction and Development (IBRD), the European Bank for Reconstruction and Development (EBRD) and the Inter-American Development Bank (IADB)' (2010) 4 *Public Procurement Law Review* 135.

Malone, D.M. and R.P. Medhora, 'Development', in J. Katz Cogan and I. Hurd (eds.), *Oxford Handbook of International Organizations* (Oxford: Oxford University Press, 2016).

Manin, P. 'La Convention de Vienne sur les accords entre Etats et organisations internationales ou entre organisations internationales' (1986) 32 *Annuaire Français de Droit International* 454.

Mann, F.A. 'The Proper Law of Contracts Concluded by International Persons' (1959) 35 *British Yearbook of International Law* 34.

Martinez-Fraga, P.J. *The American Influences on International Commercial Arbitration. Doctrinal Developments and Discovery Methods* (Cambridge: Cambridge University Press, 2009).

Mashaw, J. 'Structuring a "Dense Complexity": Accountability and the Project of Administrative Law' (2005) 5 *Issues in Legal Scholarship* 1.

Masucci, A. *Trasformazione dell'amministrazione e moduli convenzionali: il contract di diritto pubblico* (Naples: Jovene, 1988).

Maurer, H. 'Der Verwaltungsvertrag. Probleme und Möglichkeiten' (1989) 104 *Deutsches Verwaltungsblatt* 798.

Mayer, O. *Deutsches Verwaltungsrecht* (Leipzig: Duncker and Humblot, 1895).
Le droit administrative allemande (Paris: Giard-Briére Editeurs, 1906).
'Zur Lehre vom öffentlich-rechtlichen Vertrage' (1888) 3 *Archiv des Öffentlichen Rechts* 1.

McCrudden, C. *Buying Social Justice. Equality, Government Procurement, and Legal Change* (Oxford: Oxford University Press, 2007).

McCubbins, M., R. Noll and B. Weingast, 'Le procedure amministrative come strumento di controllo politico', in D. Fabbri, G. Fiorentini and L.A. Franzoni (eds.), *L'analisi economica del diritto: un'introduzione* (Rome: Nis, 1997).

McGregor, H. *Contract Code: Drawn up on Behalf of English Law Commission* (Milan/London: Sweet and Maxwell, 1993).

McLean, J. 'Divergent Legal Conceptions of the State: Implications for Global Administrative Law' (2005) 68 (3–4) *Law and Contemporary Problems* 127.

McNair, A. 'The General Principles of Law Recognized by Civilised Nations' (1957) 33 *British Yearbook of International Law* 1.

Meisler, S. *United Nations – The First Fifty Years* (New York: The Atlantic Monthly Press, 1995).

Meyer, D. 'Les contrats de fourniture de biens et de services dans cadre des operations de meintien de la paix' (1996) XLII *Annuaire français de droit international* 79.

Michaels, D.B. *International Privileges and Immunities. A Case for a Universal Statute* (The Hague: Martinus Nijhoff, 1971).

Micklitz, H.W. and F. Cafaggi, *European Private Law after the Common Frame of Reference* (Cheltenham/Northampton: Edward Elgar, 2010).

Mills, S.R. 'The Financing of UN Peacekeeping Operations: The Need for a Sound Financial Basis', in I.J. Rikhye and K. Skjelsbaek (eds.), *The United Nations and Peacekeeping: Results, Limitations and Prospects* (Houndmills: Palgrave Macmillan, 1990).

Mistelis, L. 'Regulatory Aspects: Globalization, Harmonization, Legal Transplants, and Law Reform. Some Fundamental Observations' (2000) 34 *The International Lawyer* 1055.

Moellers, C. 'Ten Years of Global Administrative Law' (2015) 13 (2) *International Journal of Constitutional Law* 469.

'Transnational Governance without a Public Law', in C. Joerges, I.J. Sand and G. Teubner (eds.), *Transnational Governance and Constitutionalism* (Oxford: Hart, 2004).

Monaco, R. 'Osservazioni sui contratti conclusi da enti internazionali', in VV.AA., *Studi in onore di Francesco Santoro Passarelli* (Naples: Jovene, 1972).

'Les principes régissant la structure et le fonctionnement des organisations internationales' (1977/III) 156 *Recueil des cours de l'Académie de droit international* 79.

Monateri, P.G. 'Black Gaius. A Quest for the Multicultural Origins of the "Western Legal Tradition"' (2000) 51 (3) *Hastings Law Journal* 479.

Moore, J.A. and J. Pubantz, *To Create a New World? American Presidents and the United Nations* (New York: Peter Lang Publishing, 2001).

Morgenstern, F. *Legal Problems of International Organizations* (Cambridge: Cambridge University Press, 1986).

Morlino, E. 'Cosmopolitan Democracy or Administrative Rights? International Organizations as Public Contractors' (2014) 3 (3) *Cambridge Journal of International and Comparative Law* 647.

'Development Aid and the Europeanization of Public Procurement in Non-EU States', in M. Audit and S. Schill (eds.), *Transnational Law of Public Contracts* (Brussels: Bruylant, 2016).

'Procurement Regimes of International Organizations', in VV.AA., *Global Administrative Law (GAL): An Italian Perspective* (Firenze: RSCAS Publications, 2012).

'UN Interim Administrations: The Case of Kosovo, East Timor and Iraq', in S. Cassese *et al.* (eds.), *Global Administrative Law: The Casebook*, 3rd edn (Rome/New York: IRPA/IILJ Publications, 2012).

I contratti delle organizzazioni internazionali (Naples: Editoriale Scientifica, 2012).

Morrissey, P. 'The Mixing of Aid and Trade Policies' (1993) 16 (1) *World Economy* 69.

Moses, M.L. *The Principles and Practice of International Commercial Arbitration* (Cambridge: Cambridge University Press, 2017).

Mosler, H. 'Réflexions sur la personnalité juridique en droit international public', in VV.AA., *Mélanges Henri Rolin* (Paris: Pedone, 1964).

Muharremi, R., L. Peci, L. Malazogu, V. Knaus and T. Murati, 'Administration and Governance in Kosovo: Lessons Learned and Lessons to Be Learned', Kosovar Institute for Policy Research and Development Policy Research Series: Occasional Paper, 2005.

Mulgan, R. 'Accountability', in B. Badie, D. Berg-Schlosser and L. Morlino (eds.), *International Encyclopedia of Political Science* (Thousand Oaks, CA and London: Sage Publications, 2011).

"Accountability": An Ever-Expanding Concept?' (2000) 78 *Public Administration* 555.

Holding Power to Account: Accountability in Modern Society (Basingstoke: Palgrave Macmillan, 2003).

Muller, A.S. *International Organizations and Their Host States* (The Hague: Kluwer Law International, 1995).

Müller, J.W. (ed.), *The Reform of the United Nations* (New York/London/Rome: Oceana Publications, 1992), vol. I–II.

Napolitano, G. 'Going Global, Turning Back National: Towards a Cosmopolitan Administrative Law' (2015) 13 (2) *International Journal of Constitutional Law* 482.

Nelson, R.M. *Multilateral Banks: Overview and Issues for Congress*, CRS Report, 2 December 2015.

Nelson, R.W. 'International Law and US Withholding of Payments to International Organizations' (1986) 80 *American Journal of International Law* 973.

Neuendorf, K.A. *The Content Analysis Guidebook* (Thousand Oaks, CA/London: Sage, 2002).

Neumann, H. *Procurement in the United Nations System* (Frankfurt: Peter Lang, 2008).

Nicholas, H.G. *The United Nations as a Political Institution*, 3rd edn (Oxford: Oxford University Press, 1967).

Ogden, C.K. and I.A. Richards, *The Meaning of Meaning: A Study of the Influence of Language Upon Thought and of the Science of Symbolism* (Abingdon: Routledge, 1923).

Padelford, N.J. 'Regional Organizations and the United Nations' (1954) 8 (2) *International Organization* 205.

Pallis, M. 'The Operation of UNHCR's Accountability Mechanisms', IILJ Working Paper 2005/12 (Global Administrative Law Series).

Papadopoulos, Y. 'Accountability and Multi-Level Governance', in M. Bovens, R.E. Goodin and T. Schillemans (eds.), *The Oxford Handbook of Public Accountability* (Oxford: Oxford University Press, 2014).

Park, S. 'Accountability as Justice for Multilateral Development Banks? Borrower Opposition and Bank Avoidance to US Power and Influence' (2017) 24 (5) *Review of International Political Economy* 776.

Peters, A. and A. Bianchi (eds.), *Transparency in International Law* (Cambridge: Cambridge University Press, 2013).

Peters, B.G. 'Accountability in Public Administration', in M. Bovens, R.E. Goodin and T. Schillemans (eds.), *The Oxford Handbook of Public Accountability* (Oxford: Oxford University Press, 2014).

Peyrefitte, L. *Le problème du contrat dit sans loi* (Paris: Dalloz, 1965).

Piiparinen, T. 'Secretariats', in J. Katz Cogan and I. Hurd (eds.), *The Oxford Handbook of Comparative Law* (Oxford: Oxford University Press, 2007).

Pingel, I. (ed.), *Droit des Immunités et Exigences du Procès Équitable* (Paris: Editions Pedone, 2004).

Plantey, A. *Droit et pratique de la fonction publique international* (Paris: CNRS, 1977).

Poillot-Peruzzetto, S. (ed.), *Vers une culture juridique européenne?* (Paris: Montchrestien, 1998).

Pommier, J.C. *Principe d'autonomie et loi du contrat en droit international privé conventionnel* (Paris: Economica, 1992).

Pritchard, S. 'United Nations Involvement in Post-Conflict Reconstruction Efforts: New and Continuing Challenges in the Case of East Timor' (2001) 1 *University of New South Wales Law Journal* 24.

Puissochet, J.P. 'L'affirmation de la personnalité internationale des Communautées Européennes', in VV.AA., *Mélanges offerts à Jean Boulouis* (Paris: Dalloz, 1991).

Püttner, G. 'Wieder den öffentlich-rechtlichen Vertrag zwischen Staat und Bürger' (1982) 97 *Deutsches Verwaltungsblatt* 122.

Rama-Montaldo, M. 'International Legal Personality and Implied Powers of International Organizations' (1970) 44 *British Yearbook of International Law* 111.

Ranieri, F. *Europaeisches Obligationenrecht* (Vienna: Springer, 1999).

Rapisardi-Mirabelli, A. 'Théorie générale des unions internationales' (1925/II) 7 *Recueil des cours de l'Académie de droit international* 345.

Ratner, S.R. *The New UN Peacekeeping: Building Peace in Lands of Conflict after the Cold War* (New York: St. Martin's Press, 1995).

Rege, V. 'Transparency in Government Procurement. Issues on Concern and Interest to Developing Countries' (2001) 35 *Journal of World Trade* 489.

Reich, A. *International Public Procurement Law: The Evolution of International Regimes on Public Purchasing* (The Hague: Kluwer Law International, 1999).

Reinalda, B. and B. Verbeek (eds.), *Decision Making within International Organizations* (Abingdon: Routledge, 2004).

Reinisch, A. 'Sources of International Organizations' Law: Why Custom and General Principles are Crucial', in S. Besson and J. d'Aspremont (eds.), *Oxford Handbook on the Sources of International Law* (Oxford: Oxford University Press, 2017).

'Accountability of International Organizations According to National Law' (2005) 36 (1) *Netherlands Yearbook of International Law* 119.

'Contracts between International Organizations and Private Law Persons', in *Max Planck Encyclopedia of Public International Law* (Oxford: Oxford University Press, 2009).

'Privileges and Immunities', in J. Katz Cogan and I. Hurd (eds.), *Oxford Handbook of International Organizations* (Oxford: Oxford University Press, 2016).

'Securing the Accountability of International Organizations' (2001) 7 (2) *Global Governance* 131.

'The Immunity of International Organizations and the Jurisdiction of Their Administrative Tribunals', IILJ Working Paper 2007/11 (Global Administrative Law Series).

Challenging Acts of International Organizations before National Courts (Oxford: Oxford University Press, 2010).

International Organizations before National Courts (Cambridge: Cambridge University Press, 2000).

The Privileges and Immunities of International Organizations in Domestic Courts (Oxford: Oxford University Press, 2013).

Reinisch A. and U.A. Weber, 'In the Shadow of Waite and Kennedy. The Jurisdictional Immunity of International Organizations, the Individual's Right of Access to the Courts and Administrative Tribunals as Alternative Means of Dispute Settlement' (2004) 2 *International Organizations Law Review* 59.

Renouf, Y. 'When Legal Certainty Matters Less than a Deal: Procurement in International Administrations', IILJ Paper, Geneva, 19 March 2009.

Reynaud, P.M. 'Le recours precontractuel au sein des marches publics des organisations internationales. Le cas de l'Agence Spatiale Europeenne' (2012) 116 (3) *Revue generale de droit international public* 655.

Richer, L. *Droit des contrats administratifs*, X edn (Paris: LGDJ, 2016).

Riddell, R. *Does Foreign Aid Really Work?* (Oxford: Oxford University Press, 2007).

Rigo Sureda, A. 'The Law Applicable to the Activities of International Development Banks' (2004) 308 *Recueil des cours de l'Académie de droit international* 9.

Rittberger, V., B. Zangl and A. Kruck, *International Organization*, 2nd edn (Basingstoke: Palgrave, 2012).

Rivero, J. *Droit administrative* (Paris: Dalloz, 1987).

Rivero, J. and J. Waline, *Droit administratif*, XXVI edn (Paris: Dalloz, 2016).

Rivlin, B. 'UN Reform from the Standpoint of the United States', lecture held at the United Nations University, Tokyo, 25 September 1995.

Roberts, C.W. (ed.), *Text Analysis for the Social Sciences: Methods for Drawing Inferences from Texts and Transcripts* (Mahwah, NJ: Lawrence Erlbaum, 1997).

Rosa Moreno, J. *El arbitraje administrativo* (Madrid: McGraw Hill, 1998).

Rousseau, C. 'L'indépendance de l'État dans l'ordre international' (1948/II) 73 *Recueil des cours de l'Académie de droit international* 248.

Ruffert, M. (ed.), *The Public-Private Law Divide: Potential for Transformation?* (London: British Institute of International and Comparative Law, 2009).

Russel, G. 'UNDP Procurement: Exceptions Are the Rule', UNDP Watch, 18 April 2008.

Sakane, T. 'Public Procurement in the United Nations System', in K.V. Thai (ed.), *International Handbook of Public Procurement* (Boca Raton/Florida: Taylor & Francis, 2009).

'Public Procurement of UNPKO: Focusing on Its Budgetary Significance and Basic Modalities', paper presented at the 5th International Public Procurement Conference, Seattle, 17–19 August 2012.

'Challenges for Humanitarian Food Assistance: The World Food Programme Procurement Administration', paper presented at the 3rd International Public Procurement Conference, Geneva, 28–30 August 2008.

Salazar, A. and M. Lopez, 'The Inter-American Development Bank: Reforms to Built Up and Increase the Use of National Procurement Systems in Latin America and the Caribbean' (2016) 4 *Public Procurement Law Review* 164.

Salmon, J. *Le role des organizations internationals en matière de prêts et d'emprunts* (London: Stevens, 1958).

Salmon, M.J. 'Les contrats de la Banque internationale pour la reconstruction et le développement' (1956) 2 *Annuaire français de droit international* 635.

Salzman, J. 'Decentralized Administrative Law in the Organization for Economic Cooperation and Development', IILJ Working Paper 2005/17 (Global Administrative Law Series).

Sands, P. and P. Klein, *Bowett's Law of International Institutions*, 6th edn (London: Sweet & Maxwell, 2009) (the first edition, by D.W. Bowett, was published in 1963).

Sarooshi, D. 'Legal Capacity and Powers', in J. Katz Cogan and I. Hurd (eds.), *Oxford Handbook of International Organizations* (Oxford: Oxford University Press, 2016).

Sato, T. 'Legitimacy of International Organizations and Their Decisions: Challenges that International Organizations Face in the 21st Century' (2009) 37 *Hitotsubashi Journal of Law and Politics* 11.

Saurer, J. 'Transition to a New Regime of Judicial Review of EU Agencies' (2010) 3 *European Journal of Risk Regulation* 325.

Savino, M. 'What If Global Administrative Law Is a Normative Project?' (2015) 13 (2) *International Journal of Constitutional Law* 492.

Schachter, O. 'Alf Ross Memorial Lecture: The Crisis of Legitimation in the United Nations' (1981) 50 (1) *Nordic Journal of International Law* 3.

Schaefer, B.D. 'The Demise of the UN Procurement Task Force Threatens Oversight at the UN', The Heritage Foundation, WebMemo No. 2272, 5 February 2009, available at www.heritage.org/report/the-demise-the-un-procurement-task-force-threatens-oversight-the-un (last access: January 2018).

Schafer, H. 'Strengthening the Rules of the Game: Bhutan's Alternative Procurement Experience', 16 November 2016, available at http://blogs.world bank.org/developmenttalk/strengthening-rules-game-bhutan-s-alternative-procurement-experience (last access: January 2018)

Schermers, H.G. and N.M. Blokker, 'International Organizations or Institutions, Membership', in R. Wolfrum (ed.), *Max Planck Encyclopedia of Public International Law* (Oxford: Oxford University Press, 2009).

International Institutional Law. Unity within Diversity, 5th edn (Boston/Leiden: Martinus Nijhoff, 2011).

Scherzberg, A. 'Grundfragen des verwaltungsrechtlichen Vertrages' (1992) *Juristische Schulung* 206.

Schill, S.W. 'The Impact of International Investment Law on Public Contracts', in M. Audit and S.W. Schill (eds.), *Transnational Law of Public Contracts* (Brussels: Bruylant, 2016).

'Conceptions of Legitimacy of International Arbitration', in D.D. Caron, S.W. Schill, A.C. Smutny and E.E. Triantafilou (eds.), *Practising Virtue: Inside International Arbitration* (Oxford: Oxford University Press, 2015).

Schneider, C. 'The Challenged Legitimacy of International Organisations: A Conceptual Framework for Empirical Research', paper presented at the 2005 Berlin Conference on the Human Condition of Global Environmental Change, Berlin, 2–3 December 2005.

Schneider, M. 'International Organizations and Private Persons: The Case of Direct Application of International Law', in C. Dominicé, R. Patry and C. Reymond (eds.), *Études de droit international en l'honneur de Pierre Lalive* (Basel: Helbing & Lichtenhahn, 1993).

Schooner, S. 'Mending Fences, Burning Bridges', *Star Ledger*, 30 March 2003.

Schroeder, J. 'Procurement Reform at the United Nations: Launching a Pilot Programme to Promote Fairness, Transparency and Efficiency', in UNOPS, Transparency and Public Procurement. Supplement to the 2011 Annual Statistical Report on United Nations Procurement (Copenhagen: UNOPS Publications, July 2012).

Schröer, F. 'De l'application de l'immunité jurisdictionnelle des états étrangers aux organisations internationales' (1971) 75 *Revue genérale de droit international public* 712.

'Sull'applicazione alle organizzazioni internazionali dell'immunità statale dalle misure esecutive' (1977) XIII *Rivista di diritto internazionale privato e processuale* 575.

Schubert, G. *The Public Interest* (Hong Kong: Greenwood Press, 1960).

Seidl-Hohenveldern, I. 'L'immunité de juridiction des Communautés européennes' (1990) *Revue du Marché Commun et de l'Union Européene* 475.

Serra, G. 'The Practice of Tying Development Aid: A Critical Appraisal from an International, WTO and EU Law Perspective' (2011) 4 *Law and Development* 1.

Seyersted, F. 'Applicable Law in Relations between Intergovernmental Organizations and Private Parties' (1967/III) 122 *Recueil des cours de l'Académie de droit international* 79.

'Objective International Personality of Intergovernmental Organizations' (1964) 34 *Nordisk Tidsskrift for International Ret* 1.

Common Law of International Organizations (Leiden: Martinus Nijhoff, 2008).

Sharma, V. 'An update on procurement reforms at the African Development Bank' (2016) 4 *Public Procurement Law Review* 151.

Shihata, I.F.I. *The World Bank Inspection Panel: In Practice* (Oxford: Oxford University Press, 2000).

Siekmann, R.C.R. *National Contingents in United Nations Peace-Keeping Forces* (Dordrecht: Martinus Nijhoff, 1991).

Singer, J.D. *Financing International Organization: The United Nations Budget Process* (Leiden: Martinus Nijhoff, 1961).

Singer, M. 'Jurisdictional Immunity of International Organizations: Human Rights and Functional Necessity Concerns' (1995) 36 *Virginia Journal of International Law* 53.

Sinkondo, M.H. 'La notion de contrat administratif: acte unilatéral à contenu contractuel ou contrat civil de l'administration?' (1993) 2 *Revue trimestrelle de droit civil* 239.

'Le rôle de la volonté de l'organization internationale dans la détermination du droit applicable aux contrats conclus avec les personnes privées' (1997) 4 *Revue de droit international et de droit compare* 367.

Smouts, M.C. 'United Nations Reform: A Strategy *of* Avoidance', in Michael G. Schechter (ed.), *Innovation in Multilateralism* (Tokyo: Palgrave MacMillan, 2000).

International Organizations: Theoretical Perspectives and Current Trends (Oxford: Blackwell, 1993).

Stahn, C. 'Accountability and Legitimacy in Practice: Lawmaking by Transitional Administrations', paper presented at the Geneva Research Forum, European Society of International Law, Geneva, 26–28 May 2005.

'Governance beyond the State: Issues of Legitimacy in International Territorial Administration' (2005) 2 *International Organization Law Review* 11.

Stecklow, S. 'UN Allows Its Antifraud Task Force to Dissolve', *Wall Street Journal*, 8 January 2009, available at http://online.wsj.com/article/ SB123138018217563187.html?mod=googlenews_wsj (last access: January 2018).

Stelkens, P., H.J. Bonk and M. Sachs, *Verwaltungsverfahrensgesetz - Kommentar* (Munich: Beck, 1998).

Stewart, R.B. 'Accountability and the Discontents of Globalization: US and EU Models for Regulatory Governance', paper presented at the 'Hauser Colloquium on Globalization and Its Discontents', New York University, New York, 20 September 2006.

'Accountability, Participation, and the Problem of Disregard in Global Regulatory Governance', paper presented at the IILJ International Legal Theory Colloquium on Interpretation and Judgement in International Law, New York University School of Law, New York, 7 February 2008.

'The Normative Dimensions and Performance of Global Administrative Law' (2015) 13 (2) *International Journal of Constitutional Law* 499.

'US Administrative Law: A Model for Global Administrative Law?' (2005) 68 (3–4) *Law and Contemporary Problems* 63.

Stoessinger, J. *et al. Financing the United Nations System* (Washington, DC: Brookings Institution, 1964).

Strohmeyer, H. 'Collapse and Reconstruction of a Judicial System: The United Nations Missions in Kosovo and East Timor' (2001) 95 (46) *American Journal of International Law* 95.

Strong, S.I. *Research and Practice in International Commercial Arbitration* (Oxford: Oxford University Press, 2009).

Sudre, F. 'La jurisprudence de la cour européenne des droits de l'homme', in Pingel, I. (ed.), *Droit des Immunités et Exigences du Procès Équitable* (Paris: Editions Pedone, 2004).

Tallberg, J. 'Transparency', in J. Katz Cogan and I. Hurd (eds.), *Oxford Handbook of International Organizations* (Oxford: Oxford University Press, 2016).

Taylor, P. 'The United Nations System under Stress: Financial Pressures and Their Consequences', in P. Taylor (ed.), *International Organization in the Modern World* (London: Pinter, 1993).

Thai, K.V. (ed.), *International Handbook of Public Procurement* (Boca Raton/ Florida: Taylor & Francis, 2008).

Torchia, L. *Il governo delle differenze. Il principio di equivalenza nell'ordinamento europeo* (Bologna: Il Mulino, 2006).

Trebilcock, A. 'Implications of the UN Convention against Corruption for International Organizations: Oversight, Due Process, and Immunity Issues' (2009) 6 (2) *International Organizations Law Review* 513.

Trepte, P. 'All Change at the World Bank? The New Procurement Framework' (2016) 4 *Public Procurement Law Review* 121.

Trionfetti, F. 'Home-Based Government Procurement and International Trade: Descriptive Statistics, Theory and Empirical Evidence', in S. Arrowsmith and M. Trybus (eds.), *Public Procurement. The Continuing Revolution* (The Hague: Kluwer Law International, 2003).

Trybus, M. 'An Overview of the United Kingdom Public Procurement Review and Remedies System with an Emphasis on England and Wales', in S. Treumer and F. Lichère (eds.), *The Enforcement of the EU Public Procurement Rules* (Copenhagen: Djøf Publishing, 2011).

Trybus, M. and P.P. Craig, 'Public Contracts: England and Wales', in R. Nogouellou and U. Stelkens (eds.), *Comparative Law on Public Contracts Treatise* (Brussels: Bruylant, 2010).

Tucker, T. 'A Critical Analysis of the Procurement Procedures of the World Bank', in S. Arrowsmith and A.C. Davies (eds.), *Public Procurement: Global Revolution* (The Hague: Kluwer Law International, 1999).

Tunkin, G.I. 'The Legal Nature of the United Nations' (1996) III *Recueil des cours de l'Académie de droit international* 1.

Turner, F.J. *La frontiera nella storia americana* (Bologna: Il Mulino, 1975).

Turpin, C. *Government Procurement and Contracts* (London: Longman, 1989).

Twining, W. 'Diffusion of Law: A Global Perspective' (2004) 36 (49) *The Journal of Legal Pluralism and Unofficial Law* 1.

Valticos, N. 'Les contrats conclus par les organisations internationales avec des personnes privées. Rapport provisoire' (1977a) 57 (1) *Annuaire de l'Institut de droit international* 6.

'Les contrats conclus par les organisations internationales avec des personnes privées. Rapport définitif' (1977b) 57 (1) *Annuaire de l'Institut de droit international* 151.

van Hecke, G. 'Contracts between International Organizations and Private Law Persons', in R. Bernhardt (ed.), *Encyclopedia of Public and International Law*, 2nd edn (North-Holland: Elsevier, 1992), vol. I, *ad vocem*.

Vaubel, R. 'Principal-Agent Problems in International Organizations' (2006) 1 *Review of International Organizations* 125.

Vedel, G. *Droit administratif*, 6th edn (Paris: PUF, 1976).

Venzke, I. 'International Bureaucracies in a Political Science Perspective. Agency, Authority and International Institutional Law', in A. von Bogdandy, R. Wolfrum, J. von Bernstorff, P. Dann and M. Goldmann (eds.), *The Exercise of Public Authority by International Institutions: Advancing International Institutional Law* (Berlin: Springer, 2009).

Verdeaux, J.J. 'The World Bank and Public Procurement: Improving Aid Effectiveness and Addressing Corruption' (2006) 6 *Public Procurement Law Review* 179.

Verdross, A. 'Die Sicherung von auslandischen Privatrechten aus Abkommen zur wirtschaftlichen Entwicklung' (1958) XVIII *Zeitschrift für ausländisches öffentliches Recht und Völkerrecht* 635.

'Protection of Private Property under Quasi-International Agreements' (1959) 6 *Nederlands Tijdschrift voor Internationaal Recht* 355.

Villalpando, S. 'The Law of the International Civil Service', in J. Katz Cogan and I. Hurd (eds.), *Oxford Handbook of International Organizations* (Oxford: Oxford University Press, 2016).

Vincent-Jones, P. 'Regulating Government by Contract: Towards a Public Law Framework?' (2002) *Modern Law Review* 611.

Virally, M. 'Définition et classification: Approche juridique' (1977) 29 *Revue internationale des sciences sociales* 65.

'La notion de fonction dans la théorie de l'organisation internationale', in VV. AA., *Mélanges offerts à Charles Rousseau. La communauté internationale* (Paris: Pedone, 1974).

von Bar, C. *The Common European Law of Torts* (Oxford: Oxford University Press, 2000), vol. I–II.

von Bernstorff, J. 'Procedures of Decision-Making and the Role of Law in International Organizations' (2008) 9 *German Law Journal* 1939.

von Bogdandy, A. 'Demokratie, Globalisierung, Zukunft des Völkerrechts – Eine Bestandsaufnahme' (2003) 63 *Zeitschrift für ausländisches öffentliches Recht und Völkerrecht* 853.

'General Principles of International Public Authority: Sketching a Research Field' (2008) 9 *German Law Journal* 1909.

'Legitimacy of International Economic Governance: Interpretative Approaches to WTO Law and the Prospects of Its Proceduralization', in S. Griller (ed.), *International Economic Governance and Non-Economic Concerns: New Challenges for the International Legal Order* (Wien/New York: Springer, 2003).

von Bogdandy, A. and I. Venzke, 'International Judicial Institutions in International Relations: Functions, Authority and Legitimacy', in B. Reinalda (ed.), *Routledge Handbook of International Organization* (Abingdon: Routledge, 2013).

von Bogdandy, A. and M. Goldmann, 'The Exercise of International Public Authority through National Policy Assessment', IILJ Working Paper 2009/2 (Global Administrative Law Series).

von Bogdandy, A., R. Wolfrum, J. von Bernstorff, P. Dann and M. Goldmann (eds.), *The Exercise of Public Authority by International Institutions* (Berlin: Springer, 2009).

VV.AA., *Multilateral Development Bank Procurement: Hearing before the Subcommittee on International Development, Finance, Trade and Monetary Policy of the Committee on Banking, Finance, and Urban Affairs, House of Representatives, One Hundred and Third Congress* (Ann Arbor, MI: Palala Press, 2015).

Waline, J. *Droit administratif*, XXVI edn (Paris: Dalloz, 2016).

Walters, F.P. *A History of the League of Nations* (Oxford: Oxford University Press, 1969).

Watson, A. *Comparative Law: Law, Reality and Society* (Lake Mary/Florida: Vandeplas Publishing, 2007).

Legal Origins and Legal Change (London: Hambledon Continuum, 1991).

Legal Transplants: An Approach to Comparative Law (Athens, GA: The University of Georgia Press, 1974).

WB, 'Bhutan Agency Approved for Alternative Procurement Arrangements by the World Bank', Press release, 16 November 2016 available at www.worldbank .org/en/news/pressrelease/ 2016/11/16/bhutan-agency-approved-for-alter native-procurementarrangements (last access: January 2018).

WB, 'India's PowerGrid Endorsed for Alternative Procurement Arrangements by the World Bank', Press release, 19 June 2017, available at (last access: January 2018) www.worldbank.org/en/news/feature/2017/06/19/india-powergrid-endorsed-for-alternative-procurement-arrangements (last access: January 2018).

Weber, R.P. *Basic Content Analysis*, 2nd edn (Newbury Park, CA: Sage, 1990).

Weil, P. 'Problèmes relatifs aux contrats passés entre un Etat et un particulier' (1969) III *Recueil des cours de l'Académie de droit international* 189.

Weiler, J. H. H. 'The Geology of International Law – Governance, Democracy and Legitimacy' (2003) 64 German Yearbook of International Law 547.

'GAL at a Crossroads: Preface to the Symposium' (2015) 13 (2) *International Journal of Constitutional Law* 463.

Weiss, F. and D.A. Kalogeras, 'Revision of the Financial Rules Applicable to the General Budget of the European Communities' (2007) 4 *Public Procurement Law Review* 97.

'The Principle of Non-Discrimination in Procurement for Development Assistance' (2005) 1 *Public Procurement Law Review* 1.

Wellens, K. *Remedies against International Organizations* (Cambridge: Cambridge University Press, 2002).

Wenckstern, M. *Die Immunität internationaler Organisationen. Handbuch des Internationalen Zivilverfahrensrechts* (Tubingen: Mohr Siebeck, 1994, vol. II/1).

Wessel, R.A. 'Executive Boards and Councils', in J. Katz Cogan and I. Hurd (eds.), *Oxford Handbook of International Organizations* (Oxford: Oxford University Press, 2016).

Westbrook, D.A. 'Theorizing the Diffusion of Law in an Age of Globalization: Conceptual Difficulties, Unstable Imaginations and the Effort to Think Gracefully Nonetheless' (2006) 47 *Harvard International Law Journal* 489.

White, N.D. *The Law of International Organisations*, 3rd edn (Manchester: Manchester University Press, 2016).

Wilenski, P. 'The Structure of the UN in the Post-Cold War Period', in A. Roberts and B. Kingsbury (eds.), *United Nations, Divided World. The UN's Roles in International Relations*, 2nd edn (Oxford: Oxford University Press, 1993).

Williams-Elegbe, S. 'The Evolution of the World Bank's Procurement Framework: Reform and Coherence of the 21st Century' (2016) 16 (1) *Journal of Public Procurement* 22.

  Public Procurement and Multilateral Development Banks. Law, Practice and Problems (Oxford: Hart, 2017).

Wise, E.M. 'The Transplant of Legal Patterns' (1990) 37 *American Journal of Comparative Law* 1.

Woods, N. *The Globalizers: The IMF, the World Banks, and Their Borrowers* (Ithaca, NY: Cornell University Press, 2006).

Zaring, D. 'Informal Procedure, Hard and Soft, in International Administration', IILJ Working Paper 2004/6 (Global Administrative Law Series).

Zaum, D. (ed.), *Legitimating International Organizations* (Oxford: Oxford University Press, 2013).

  'International Organizations, Legitimacy, and Legitimation', in D. Zaum (ed.), *Legitimating International Organizations* (Oxford: Oxford University Press, 2013).

  'Legitimacy', in J. Katz Cogan and I. Hurd (eds.), *Oxford Handbook of International Organizations* (Oxford: Oxford University Press, 2016).

Zimmermann, R. and S. Whittaker (eds.), *Good Faith in European Contract Law* (Cambridge: Cambridge University Press, 2000).

Zwart, T., G. Anthony, J.B. Auby and J. Morison (eds.), *Values in Global Administrative Law* (Oxford: Hart Publishing, 2011).

INDEX